PERSONAL GROWTH AND EFFECTIVE BEHAVIOR

JOSEPH W. CRITELLI

North Texas State University

HOLT, RINEHART and WINSTON

NEW YORK   CHICAGO   SAN FRANCISCO   PHILADELPHIA

MONTREAL   TORONTO   LONDON   SYDNEY   TOKYO

MEXICO CITY   RIO DE JANEIRO   MADRID

PERSONAL GROWTH and EFFECTIVE BEHAVIOR

The Challenge of Everyday Life

Editor-in-Chief Susan Katz
Publisher Robert Woodbury
Associate Editor Stephen Helba
Senior Project Manager Françoise Bartlett
Art Director Robert Kopelman
Designer Celine A. Brandes, Photo Plus Art
Production Managers Annette Mayeski, Stefania Taflinska
Photo Research Nicolette Harlan

Library of Congress Cataloging-in-Publication Data

Critelli, Joseph W.
   Personal growth and effective behavior.

   Bibliography: p.
   Includes index.
   1. Self-actualization (Psychology).   I. Title.
BF637.S4C75   1987   158'.1   86–19402

ISBN 0-03-071052-9

7 8 9 0   039   9 8 7 6 5 4 3 2 1

CBS COLLEGE PUBLISHING
Holt, Rinehart and Winston
The Dryden Press
Saunders College Publishing

PHOTO CREDITS

Cover: Silhouette, "Woman in Motion" — Bill Longcore/Photo Researchers.

(continued on p. 442)

Dedication

To Sandy, Paul, and Amy

PREFACE

This book springs from a premise that many might regard as hopelessly naïve—that real learning is exciting. We want to find out about ourselves; we want to extend ourselves, explore our potentials, and become effective individuals. To these ends, this text tackles the everyday problems of modern living in a way that is personal, practical, rigorous, and engaging. It strips psychological jargon to the bone, emphasizing ideas instead of terminology. And it eschews the simplistic platitudes of most self-help books, relying instead on the basic principles of psychology and on scientific research. We are truly fortunate that psychology has amassed a body of knowledge grounded on systematic observation. This knowledge allows us to begin a journey of self-discovery and personal effectiveness.

Learning Aids

Several innovative features enhance the personal impact of this text. Clinical case studies illustrate major points, so that abstract principles can become meaningful, engage student interest, and "come to life." The text also includes thought questions, application exercises, and questionnaires in each chapter, immediately after relevant material. These provide the student with immediate feedback, creating an informal "dialogue" between student and author.

In-text applications have been specially chosen for their ability to capture student interest by probing controversial issues and real-life concerns. These applications can be used in a variety of ways: They can simply be left "as is" for students to read, helping them digest and gain closure on text contents. They can also be used as written assignments, with students keeping a running journal of their reactions to key points and attempts to apply these ideas in their lives. Finally, they can be used as springboards for class discussion and group projects.

The text also, of course, includes standard pedagogic aids such as color and bold-faced type, a glossary, suggested readings, focus highlights, summaries, photos, diagrams, tables, and cartoons. The *Instructor's Manual/Test Bank* contains chapter objectives, teaching commentaries, film recommendations, detachable crossword puzzle reviews, and a test bank that I have scrutinized for fairness and clarity. The *Study Guide* provides chapter objectives, detachable pages for the in-text applications, and a structured review using a variety of item formats, including a comprehensive crossword puzzle review for each chapter. There is also a *Computerized Test Bank*.

Theoretical Orientation

I believe that humanistic, social learning, and psychoanalytic models all make significant contributions to applied psychology. Each is treated with respect and relied on for organization and insight within its own areas of strength. At the same time, the text repeatedly points out where these orientations clash. Where conflicts arise, arguments on both sides are examined and taken to either a suggested resolution or a choice between opposing assumptions. Clearly, it is more important to develop students' conceptual, problem-solving skills than to ignore these issues and pacify them with pat advice. In the long run, developing a sense for how to approach complex personal problems is one of the most adaptive skills we can offer.

Organization

The text is organized in four sections: The Person, Personal Adjustment, Relationships, and Personal Growth. This framework provides a contrast between the personal and the interpersonal and between adjustment and growth. Part One examines how psychologists view the individual. It deals with students' concerns about "finding themselves" and establishing a sense of identity. Part One also presents the major models of personality and explores various ways of understanding human consciousness.

Part Two describes our modern technological age, in which rapid change is placing tremendous demands on our coping abilities. It examines the current widespread shift in gender roles and shows how our coping abilities depend on the reciprocal interaction between cognitions and emotions. Finally, it presents a systematic treatment of competency skills, including a complete self-modification project which students may carry out on their own.

Part Three develops communication skills and then examines romantic, sexual, and family relationships. In particular, it analyzes scripted dialogues to illustrate the many levels of meaning operating even in ordinary conversations.

Part Four examines the emerging concern with personal growth, health psychology, and body-mind integration. It considers the various ways of thinking about maladjusted and healthy functioning, and it explores the problems and pitfalls of those who seek optimal development. The section concludes with guidelines that individuals can use to find their own path of growth.

In sum, I believe that instructors will find this book theoretically sound, well-researched, and structured to integrate home readings with classroom discussions. I believe that students will find it lively, easy to read, and in touch with to their most pressing concerns.

Acknowledgments

In particular, I wish to thank the many undergraduates who have worked closely with me, especially Jeri Caldwell, Richard Hall, Sue Harrison, Gordon Leeman, Sze Lai Leung, Walt Mercer, Liz Penland, Lori Rohloff, Eileen Spotts, Jerry Summers, Catherine Tang, and Amie Thompson.

I also thank the following reviewers for their many helpful suggestions: Marsha Beauchamp, Mt. San Antonio Community College; Edwin de F. Bennett, Orange County Community College; James J. Berry, Oakland Community College; George A. Cicala, University of Delaware; John Dill, Lorain County Community College; Fred S. Fehr, Arizona State University; Thomas Flanders, Florida International University; Jeff Goodpaster, Gateway Technical Institute; Peter Clark Gram, Pensacola Junior College; John P. Hall, University of Houston-Downtown; Margaret Hewitt, Tyler Junior College; Charles W. Johnson, University of Evansville; Arnold LeUnes, Texas A & M University; Harold List, Massachusetts Bay Community College; Virginia Marshall, University of Texas, El Paso; Carol A. Nowak, University of Buffalo; Sonia Ochroch, Community College of Philadelphia; John Orlosky, Jackson Community College; Nancy Pasko, Oakland Community College; Kathy Petrowsky, Southwestern Oklahoma State University; Robert M. Petty, University of Santa Clara; E. Lakin Phillips, George Washington University; James B. Riley, Southeastern Massachusetts University; Janet A. Simons, Des Moines Area Community College; Sharon Thomas, Miami-Dade Community College; Kenneth Thompson, Central Missouri State University; Thomas L. Weaver, Central Florida Community College; Deborah Weber, University of Akron; Bernard E. Whitley, Ball State University.

Finally, I thank the professional team at Holt, Rinehart and Winston, especially Françoise Bartlett, Nicolette Harlan, Stephen Helba, Robert Kopelman, Alison Podel, and Stefania Taflinska.

                                                            J.W.C.

CONTENTS IN BRIEF

CONTENTS

PART TWO   PERSONAL ADJUSTMENT *87*

4   STRESS and CHANGE   *89*

The Price of Progress

5   GENDER ROLES   *117*

The Social Revolution of Our Times

6   COGNITION and EMOTION   *148*

Interactions and Applications in Therapy

10   SEXUAL FULFILLMENT

Technique and Sensuality

13 MALADJUSTMENT, NORMALITY, and BEYOND   *356*

What Is Healthy Personality?

PERSONAL GROWTH AND EFFECTIVE BEHAVIOR

PART ONE

THE PERSON

PART ONE develops the personal context for understanding adjustment and growth. It begins by discussing personal identity and the ways that our sense of identity can be called into question. The first chapter shows that in many ways, everything we do in life is a search for identity, a quest to find out who we really are.

Chapter 2 carries forward this focus on personal identity by presenting the major theoretical positions for understanding the whole person. These positions, including psychoanalytic, social learning, and humanistic theories of personality, provide an invaluable framework for dealing with problems of everyday life.

Chapter 3 expands our understanding of the person by examining the attribute that most clearly sets us apart from other animals — consciousness. The interplay between what is and is not conscious presents both a fascinating puzzle and a key to understanding human existence.

PERSONAL IDENTITY

1

Who Am I? Where Am I Going?

A CRISIS IN IDENTITY

MARY

Mary trembled. It couldn't have been her, but she knew that it was. Everyone had always told her how practical and normal she was, and Mary kept telling herself, "But I have a steady boy friend!"

It happened at Patty's house. Phil, Mary's boy friend, was visiting his mother, and so Mary

3

spent the weekend with Patty. Mary and Patty had been hiking on Craggy Bend, and both were exhausted by the time dinner was finished. They started talking, reminiscing, recounting childhood experiences, drinking wine, and feeling relaxed. Patty offered to rub Mary's sore shoulder. It was aching, and Mary was grateful for the relief. Mary noticed Patty's breath above her shoulder. With utter simplicity, Patty turned Mary's head around and kissed her on the mouth. For a moment Mary was lost in the sensation. Just as suddenly, Mary spoke as if she were not totally surprised. "Let's not go any further . . . we'll act as if this never happened."

Although Patty agreed, there was no way Mary could put it out of her mind. She had been part of a homosexual act, or at least the beginning of one. And she did not resist it. Did this make her a lesbian? A "latent homosexual"? Maybe it was the wine—but she had only one glass. Anyway, even if it were the wine, what would that prove?

Most of all there was confusion. Mary had Phil. They had a sexual relationship, and she had never been attracted to other women. Mary thought she knew who she was; she had a firm grasp on her life. But Mary couldn't help thinking, "How could this happen to me?" "If I can be so wrong about myself, if I can act in ways that are so 'out of character,' who am I, really?" "What else might I do?"

RON

Ever since Ron could remember, he wanted to become a doctor. Probably a brain surgeon, maybe a pediatrician. Ron's father was a doctor, and that was the problem. Ron would be entering college in the fall, and the time had come to choose a major. Should he sign up for pre-med? Ron had read several psychology books, and the thought kept recurring—maybe the only reason he wanted medicine was to imitate his father, to follow in his father's footsteps. But most of all, Ron wanted to "be his own man."

Ron looked up to his dad. His father was a success, and he was also a great athlete. He had even played minor league ball one year and had been scouted by the majors. Ron, on the other hand, didn't even make first string on his high school team.

At any rate, Ron's preregistration forms had just come in the mail, and he was supposed to pick a major. Ron wanted to please his father, but, on the other hand, his father had never pushed him toward being a doctor. In fact, his father had never discussed a career with him at all. Mostly they talked about sports and the collection of beer cans that they had been saving since Ron was in junior high—that, and their hatred for the Yankees. So Ron thought that he wanted to be a doctor, but he was tormented: Did he want it because he, himself, wanted it or because it would satisfy his father? And if being a doctor wasn't what he really wanted, then what was?

CHARLES

At forty-one, Charles had it made. Right out of college he had started an advertising business with his roommate. But success didn't come easily—it took a lot of hard work, late nights, and self-control. For example, Charles had to develop a knack for dealing with clients. He learned how to tell them what they wanted to hear and how to avoid "ruffling their feathers." Charles realized that he had become a sort of "yes man," but this is what worked for him. At any rate, Charles succeeded where many others had failed. He was financially independent and secure.

Charles also had a beautiful wife and three exceptional children. He was proud that his wife made such a good impression, and she had proved to be a real asset in his business. Charles was often tempted to "fool around," and he did seem to have a way with women, but he had remained faithful "for the most part." Curiously, Charles often experienced the vague apprehension that something was missing in his personal life.

The time had come for Charles to relax, spend some time with his family, and enjoy the fruits of his labor. But whenever he got away from the office for more than a day, he was unable to enjoy himself. Often he would become irritable with his family and be overcome with nagging worries that a job would be fouled up and he might lose a big client. At about this time he also started noticing a voice within, intruding into everything he did. "If I smoke a cigarette, if I tell a woman I like her, if I make a gesture, if I listen to music, if I try to read a book—this third voice is at me all the time—'You're doing this for effect; you're a phoney'" (Erikson, 1968, p. 173).

OVERVIEW

This chapter explores the premise that in large measure, human lives are a journey of self-discovery. As creatures with self-awareness and a need to make sense out of our world, we inevitably form an image of who we are. And this image, this conception of personal identity, is closely linked with the process of growth and adjustment. A central assumption of modern psychology is that this image of identity affects nearly every aspect of our lives—whether we take on new challenges or give up without trying, whether we enter satisfying relationships or neurotic entrapments, whether we learn from our mistakes or push on blindly in a repetition of errors, and, finally, whether we grow or stagnate.

The preceding three case studies illustrate some of the ways that our sense of identity can be called into question. As conscious beings, we all have wondered about our identities. Perhaps during periods of rejection, frustration, stress, or even triumph, we may have questioned our pat answers to the issues of identity: "What kind of person am I?" "What makes me different from my friends?" "How well do I know myself?" "How well do I want to know myself?"

Though Socrates' dictum to "know thyself" is revered as the wisest of counsel, who among us can claim that knowledge? How does one even begin?

IDENTITY CONFUSION

ERIKSON'S CRITERIA FOR IDENTITY CONFUSION

Erik Erikson, a leading psychotherapist, observed that late adolescence and early adulthood are periods often marked by **identity confusion**, feeling unsure of who we are or where we are going in life. The experience of this confusion is captured in a line from Arthur Miller's *Death of a Salesman*, "I just can't take hold, Mom, I can't take hold of some kind of life."

Erikson (1968) named several features of identity confusion:

1. *Lack of inner continuity.* The term identity implies a oneness, an internally consistent whole, that continues over time. Being unpredictable to oneself or seeming to be a different person from one situation to the next can be highly disturbing, as was seen in the case of Mary.

2. *Role confusion.* In a complex society such as ours, we are called upon to mas-

Erik H. Erikson.

ter many roles. It is only natural to have doubts about which roles to adopt and how adequately we can carry them out. In the preceding examples, Mary expressed doubts about her sexual orientation; Ron struggled to make a more conscious choice of occupational roles; and Charles confronted the sincerity of his professional and family relationships.

3. *Self-consciousness and preoccupation with how others view us.* Identity confusion often involves a feeling that we are somehow inadequate and that others are observing our faults. Charles, for example, internalized these ob-

servers in the form of a voice that passed judgment on his social behavior.

4. *Uncertainty about one's point of view.* Part of dealing with identity confusion is finding out where one stands. Which parental values will we consciously select, as opposed to either blindly accepting them out of subservience or rejecting them out of hand in rebellion? To what extent will peer pressure and the fads of the moment dictate our beliefs and attitudes? Ron is a good example here.

5. *Passive experience of life.* In identity confusion, life often seems to be happening *to* the individual rather than being lived through one's own initiative. This passivity often involves feelings of helplessness and depression. Mary's en-

counter with Patty showed some of this passivity.

IDENTITY CONFUSION AND THE LIFE CYCLE

Erikson noted that we are most aware of our identity in times of confusion, especially when our behavior surprises us. But these can also be opportunities for gaining a clearer sense of who we are. Thus periods of identity confusion can play a positive role, precipitating personal growth.

Other times, when our sense of identity is not called into question, may be experienced as moments of well-being, feeling at home in one's body, knowing where one is going, and expect-

Forming a strong identification with a rock star is one way of attempting identity clarification.

ing consistent recognition from those important to us.

According to Erikson, young adults need a transition period during which adult commitments to work and family can be postponed. This moratorium gives individuals the freedom to experiment with different roles and find their niche in society. For Plains Indian males, this moratorium was a time of intertribal horse-stealing exploits and the quest for a vision dream defining one's future role in the tribe. In pioneer days, it was a chance for work "out West." Now it is often a time for college or military service. Too often, it is also the occasion for extended delinquency or psychological disturbance.

Early adulthood is a time to clarify one's identity. For example, we may form a strong identification with a leader or a group and become a disciple, follower, or "true believer." The tendency to join a cohesive social or religious group and become intolerant of those who are "different" is one means of taking a stand, making it clear who one is.

Carl Rogers.

In a culture that values youth, midlife is also a time when one's identity as an attractive individual may come into question.

A number of factors contribute to adolescent identity confusion. First, hormonal changes affect body proportions and strengthen sexual impulses; that is, one's physical identity changes. Second, new demands are made on the individual for physical and emotional intimacy with the opposite sex. Third is the necessity to adopt adult roles, particularly to choose an occupation, and individuals are often overwhelmed by the number of conflicting possibilities that this entails.

Identity confusion, however, does not occur only in adolescence and young adulthood. Rather, our identities are continually being formed and redefined.

Midlife is also a time when questions of identity may surface. Careers are usually firmly established at this point, and evaluations can be

I COME TO A DOOR. I FEEL JUMPY.

I GO THROUGH. I FEEL BRAVE.

I COME TO ANOTHER DOOR. I FEEL FRIGHTENED.

I GO THROUGH. I FEEL STRONG.

I COME TO ANOTHER DOOR. I FEEL LOST.

I GO THROUGH. I FEEL MATURE.

I COME TO ANOTHER DOOR. I FEEL HYSTERICAL.

I GO THROUGH. I FEEL IN CONTROL.

I COME TO ANOTHER DOOR. I FEEL CRAZY.

I REFUSE TO GO THROUGH.

THESE DOORS ARE KILLING ME.

made as to whether one has become a success or a failure, or whether sacrifices made for a career were really worth it. Midlife is also a time when children leave home, putting family routines and commitments in flux. Both homemakers and breadwinners may begin new careers and face the occupational and other role choices that disrupt identity in many young adults. Finally, in a culture that values youth and vitality, midlife is also a time when one's identity as an attractive individual can come into question, especially if one has identified strongly with the cultural ideal of youthful beauty.

Old age has its unique contributions to identity confusion, for in approaching one's death, it is only natural to wonder about this sense of continuity that has held together a lifetime of widely varying self-experiences. After all, over the course of our lives, our physical appearance, moods, competencies, and preferences change drastically, yet the feeling remains that we are the same person, the same identity.

Think of two ways in which your own sense of identity has changed in the past few years. When was the last time you remember experiencing identity confusion?

THE SEARCH FOR IDENTITY

Carl Rogers, a leading humanistic psychologist, views the search for one's true identity as the thread that ties together the elements of our lives. Behind the diverse array of problems that bring people in for therapy — whether these are anxiety, depression, sexual inadequacies, or faltering relationships — lies the search for identity. "At bottom, each person is asking: 'Who am I, *really*? How can I get in touch with this real self, underlying all my surface behavior? How can I become myself?'" (Rogers, 1961, p. 108). Rogers believes that as individuals try to discover their own selves, they find that much of the feeling they experience is not "real." Rather, it is a facade or mask, behind which they have been hiding. In other words, people often believe that they are feeling what they think they should be feeling, not what they are actually experiencing:

> Often the individual discovers that he exists only in response to the demands of others, that he seems to have no self of his own, that he is only trying to think, and feel, and behave in the way that others believe he *ought* to think, and feel, and behave. . . . Gradually,

---

FOCUS

YOUR NAME AND YOUR SELF

Your name is one of the two most important symbols of who you are (the other is your face). Research has shown that men with common names are rated as better, stronger, and more active than are those with uncommon names (Marcus, 1976). Also, children with common names are generally more popular (McDavid & Harari, 1966). Even supposedly objective judgments are influenced by one's name. Essays allegedly written by children with desirable names (e.g., David, Karen) receive higher grades from teachers than do those written by children with uncommon names (e.g., Elmer, Bertha) (Harari & McDavid, 1973).

Highly successful individuals, such as those in *Who's Who*, however, appear to have more than their share of unusual names. For example, Generals Omar Bradley and Dwight Eisenhower. One study (Zweigenhaft, 1977) also found that high school students with unusual names have more than their share of academic achievements.

Taken as a whole, research seems to indicate that our preconceptions of individuals with uncommon names are negative but that many of these people are motivated to compensate for their unpopular names through unusual levels of achievement.

One study (Ellington, Marsh, & Critelli, 1980) found that women with a masculine name who went by that name were less anxious and had greater leadership potential than were women with a masculine name who used a feminine nickname. This suggests that those who accept their names (and presumably themselves) are healthier than those who do not.

---

painfully, the individual explores what is behind the masks he presents to the world, and even behind the masks with which he has been deceiving himself. Deeply and often vividly he experiences the various elements of himself which have been hidden within. Thus to an increasing degree he becomes himself — not a facade of conformity to others, nor a cynical denial of all feeling, nor a front of intellectual rationality, but a living, breathing, feeling, fluctuating process — in short, he becomes a person. (Rogers, 1961, pp. 110, 114)

Sometimes the quest for identity is carried out in desperation, as circumstances combine to loosen one's grasp on reality. At other times, the quest may spring from moods of curiosity, wonder, and a desire to understand oneself more completely. During a lifetime, most of us will make this quest at both levels.

CRISIS REVISITED: TOWARD A HEALTHIER SENSE OF IDENTITY

Let us return to Mary, Ron, and Charles to see how they dealt with their identity confusion.

The text states that Mary did not resist the brief contact with Patty, nor, apparently, did she find it repugnant. Does this indicate that Mary is or should become a lesbian? How is your perception of Mary's sexuality altered by whether or not she had been drinking heavily that evening? If she asked you, what advice would you give Mary?

MARY

Mary decided to follow her own advice, that is, the advice she had given to Patty "to act as if this never happened." She resolved just to put it out of her mind and not talk about it with any-one, least of all Patty or Phil. This gave Mary an immediate feeling of relief; a burden had been lifted from her shoulders. But her relationships with Patty and Phil were no longer the same. Now whenever she saw Patty, she couldn't help but notice Patty's "masculine features" or wonder whether Patty's smile conveyed more than just friendliness. They began spending less time together, even though previously they were the best of friends. With Phil, Mary felt guilty, almost "tainted." She wanted to tell him, but she was sure that if she did, it would destroy their relationship. Somehow it seemed that they now had little to say to each other; their conversations were marked with awkward silences. Phil wanted to know what was wrong, but Mary said she just had been under a lot of stress lately.

After two weeks, Mary became desperate and decided to confront Patty. To her surprise, she found that Patty did not have sexual intentions toward her. They talked it over and concluded that a momentary feeling of intimacy did not make them lesbians. Since neither of them wanted a homosexual relationship, they decided that there was no real problem to resolve. It would be a problem only if they chose to view it as such, which they did not.

Mary told Phil what had happened, knowing that she was risking their relationship. It turned out that Phil was not upset at all. In fact, he made a joke about the three of them "getting together sometime." Mary did not appreciate the joke, and she made a point of avoiding situations in which the three of them would be alone together.

Mary came to view herself as a heterosexual person who could also have occasional feelings of intimacy for females. Mary felt, however, that she would be most comfortable if those feelings were expressed in nonsexual ways. Patty remained her best friend, but her relationship with Phil was soon ended.

How serious do you think Ron's problem was? How serious do you think Ron thought his problem was? How could Ron deal with his problem and still "be his own man?" What if Ron simply resolved to not be a doctor so that he could be sure to avoid any influence from his father?

RON

Ron was getting more and more perplexed about his vocational decision. His college forms were due in two weeks, and they required him to select a major field. Fortunately, Ron was scheduled to meet with his guidance counselor. The counselor pointed out that this was merely a preliminary choice of major and could be changed any time during the next several years. Ron had been "catastrophizing," that is, interpreting his problem in a way that blew it out of proportion.

Still, Ron was worried about whether he really wanted to be a doctor or whether he was choosing pre-med because of his father. The counselor explained that most of our preferences and decisions are affected by past experiences — by people we've known, even by television shows and movies. There is no way to completely divorce ourselves from the past.

Thus it was possible that being a doctor was what both Ron *and* his father wanted. The choice between being a doctor because he, himself, wanted it, rather than because it would please his father, could, in this case, represent a false dichotomy. It is true that individuals are sometimes influenced by their parents into choosing careers that they think they want but later find out were never right for them. But just because this happens in some cases doesn't mean it was happening to Ron. At any rate, it was really too early to tell. After a year or two in the pre-med program, he would have a much clearer idea of whether he wanted to become a physician. The counselor suggested, however, that Ron and his father talk it over.

Ron's father explained that he had hoped Ron would follow in his footsteps but that he hadn't discussed this with Ron out of fear of pressuring him. Thus Ron decided to make a tentative selection of pre-med, which he might or might not change later. Then Ron and his father returned to complaining about how the Yankees were run by a "braintrust of morons."

However, Ron's sense of identity, his image of himself, had changed subtly. He no longer saw himself as different or separate from the person who wanted to become like his father. Ron had broadened his self-image so that he could now consciously choose to identify with certain aspects of his father without the fear that his own identity would be compromised.

CHARLES

Charles's anxiety about taking time from work and his nagging feelings of being a phoney continued to worsen. Eventually he sought the aid of a psychologist. After extensive discussions about his family and business relationships, several things became clear. Charles thought he wanted to spend more time with his family because this is what he had been telling himself for many years. In his mind, the belief that he would eventually "make it all up" to them had justified the long hours at work and the relative neglect of his family. But Charles came to realize that when he did spend time at home, he quickly became bored and restless. The kids were noisy, and although he enjoyed playing with them for a while, after that he looked for excuses to get away.

Charles and his wife rarely argued; their conversations were pleasant, brief, and predictable. In a way, this is just what Charles wanted, or at least what he thought he wanted. He liked the risk and challenge of the business world, perhaps because he knew how to be successful there. At home, he just wanted a peaceful environment with "no hassles" and no emotional scenes.

The psychologist suggested that Charles find an activity that he could share with his family. In addition, he might try being more assertive in bringing forward his own ideas at work.

Charles bought a camper and took the family on occasional weekend outings at a nearby state park. He also started speaking up more at work, and he found that although it didn't make him any more effective, he wasn't any less effective either. However, he did feel more satisfied with himself.

From the psychologist's perspective, Charles's case was rather typical. It wasn't a dramatic success, but there were some positive changes and Charles's original symptoms decreased noticeably. However, Charles was not an ideal family man, and his emotional relationships were still superficial. His actions in business were often calculated responses to control or manipulate others, but he was occasionally spontaneous, relaxed, and sincere. In terms of his self-image, Charles no longer saw himself as the man who was or should be "doing it all for his family." Consequently, he no longer felt so guilty when he was ready to leave them and get back to work. He worked hard because of his own needs, and Charles believed that he could accept himself at that level.

In what ways could Charles have made a better adjustment? Do you know anyone who reminds you of Charles? Suppose you accidentally stumbled into a time warp and fell into the future, finding that, in fact, you are Charles (Charlene). How might you feel? If you then unwarped back to the present, what would you try to do differently in the hopes of changing your fate?

AM I NORMAL?

Perhaps it would be truly abnormal never to have wondered about one's own level of normality. But what characterizes a normal individual? Several senses of "normality" can be distinguished:

THE STATISTICAL VIEW

Most physical and psychological characteristics can be represented by the so-called nor-

---

FOCUS

THE FEAR OF SELF-OBSERVATION

True, whoever looks into the mirror of the water will see first of all his own face. Whoever goes to himself risks a confrontation with himself. The mirror does not flatter, it faithfully shows whatever looks into it; namely, the face we never show to the world because we cover it with the *persona*, the mask of the actor.

But the mirror lies behind the mask and shows the true face. (Jung, 1936/1959, p. 20)

It is often said that in regard to self-understanding, we all have two motives: to know and not to know. We want to see the "true face," but we are often afraid of what we may find. Even those with an optimistic philosophy often seem able to maintain their view only as long as they don't probe too deeply, as long as "appropriate" limits are placed on the exploration.

One reason for this hesitation in looking at oneself derives from the difference between the way that we know ourselves and the way that we know others. In our social world, we view others as they present themselves to us. Often, we can only make vague guesses as to what lies behind these social portraits, for most people naturally try to present themselves in a favorable light.

Our knowledge of ourselves, however, is based on content that is "less filtered," that is, closer to the raw material of experience. Thus we continually view a filtered presentation of others and compare that with the raw material of our own desires and pecadillos. Using a religious metaphor, we know many of our own sins, but those of others are confessed only in private. Thus it is common to wonder whether our own lives represent a deviation from the way things are "supposed to be." This apprehension, which derives from an artifact of perception, contributes to the fear of looking inward.

This text follows the orientation of Rollo May, a leading existential theorist. May claims that we are both better and worse than we think we are. Although a close observation of our thoughts, feelings, behaviors, wishes, and impulses will inevitably uncover areas of pettiness, greed, lust, and spite that were previously hidden, it will also inevitably reveal unexpected capacities for creativity, strength, love, and compassion.

If we can foster a more tolerant, accepting attitude toward ourselves, we can control the fear of looking inward and release the inherent excitement of this exploration.

---

mal curve. Some people fall at the negative extreme of a trait, some at the positive extreme, and most in the middle. Thus the normal curve is said to be bell-shaped, that is, in the form of an inverted "U" with the "tails" trailing off on either side (see Figure 1–1).

On a dimension of mental health, "nor-

mals," constituting the bulk of the population, would fall in the middle of the scale, under the peak of the curve. Correspondingly, abnormals would fall toward the undesirable extreme of this dimension. Abraham Maslow, the founder of humanistic psychology, applied the bell-shaped curve to the concept of mental health

FIGURE 1 – 1
ADJUSTMENT, GROWTH, AND THE NORMAL CURVE

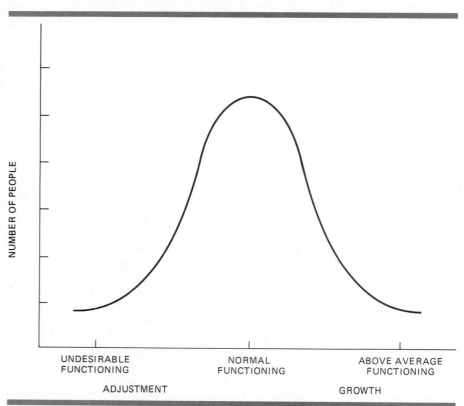

and raised the question, "Who are the people that fall at the desirable end of this scale?" In other words, are some people healthier or "more normal" than average? Maslow believed that the answer to this question is yes, that true mental health is not just the absence of disease or dysfunction, but the attainment of a level of functioning that goes beyond the ordinary. Maslow's notion that there can be positive change beyond normality has taken hold in our culture, as evidenced in the widespread pursuit of self-improvement.

THE MEDICAL VIEW

Another sense of normality derives from medicine, in which normal essentially means "without disease." Here abnormality is the focus of interest, so if you are found not to have a "mental illness," then you must be normal.

Note that authors such as Thomas Szasz have questioned the whole notion of "mental illness," suggesting that this term is merely a metaphor, since mental illness involves no identifiable disease. Rather, "mental illnesses" are really problems of living, problems of finding an adaptive system of values. Thus Szasz places these problems within religion and ethics rather than medicine.

Although the medical model is currently out of favor with most psychologists, it must be acknowledged that certain disturbances such as schizophrenia and cyclical depression do appear to have genetic and physiological underpinnings. This indicates that the medical view may have some validity for these more severe forms of abnormality.

THE SOCIAL VIEW

The social view considers "abnormal" a label that people receive when their behavior is deviant or troubling enough to be called to the attention of mental health professionals. In this view, it is not only the extent of deviance that matters but also the willingness of those around us to tolerate that deviance. This view is especially salient for the aged. In earlier times when extended families were commonplace, people often considered it their duty to put up with a grandparent's eccentricities. Nowadays, with the prevalence of nuclear families and a self- rather than a duty-oriented ethic, the same eccentricities might well lead to a psychiatric diagnosis and institutional commitment.

These three ways of viewing normality maintain a relatively peaceful coexistence. No one of them is more "correct" than another. Rather, each contributes to complex personal and social decisions about normality. The statistical view is perhaps the most widely used criterion, but the medical view is quite useful whenever an identifiable disease or physiological disturbance is involved. The social view operates at a somewhat different level, addressing the process whereby diagnoses are actually given, rather than how they should be given.

In an age of nuclear, rather than extended, families, eccentricities of the aged are more likely to come to the attention of mental health authorities.

ADJUSTMENT AND GROWTH

THE CONTINUUM OF THERAPEUTIC CHANGE

Developing a healthy sense of identity must be understood within the broader framework of adjustment and growth, the two most common terms for describing therapeutic change.

To illustrate, we can represent adjustment and growth as a continuous line with a negative side, a zero point, and a positive side. Each of us is continually adjusting to the stresses and frustrations of everyday life. Adjustment can be viewed as a change in one part of a person's life from a negative state to the zero point, that is, from a condition such as anxiety, depression, or skill deficiency to a middle ground of normal functioning. Growth, on the other hand, might represent changes from the zero point to the positive side, that is, from average to above-average social skills, self-knowledge, or emotional expressiveness. These concepts are shown in Figure 1–1.

But why bother distinguishing between these two kinds of desired change? Although this distinction is not always useful or necessary, it helps clarify the change process by picturing each change against the backdrop of normal functioning. Moreover, changes in different parts of this line may be qualitatively different. For example, people who are self-critical, with feelings of low self-worth, may raise their level of adjustment by developing a sense of pride, even if this is carried to extremes and they become egotistical and "stuck on themselves." Further movement in the positive, growth direction, however, may require a different kind of change, one in which they become less self-centered. Thus, techniques that aid adjustment do not always facilitate growth. Differences between adjustment and growth are elaborated in the next section.

THE WELL-ADJUSTED INDIVIDUAL

The metaphor of "adjustment" conjures up images of a system making mechanical adjustments, reacting adaptively to changes in its environment. Thus adjustment is always evaluated with respect to the physical or social environment. In addition, the changes usually serve to maintain the status quo, so that the system continually returns to a previous state of normal or average functioning.

Well-adjusted people:

1. *Cope with their environment.* The environment is always changing; new demands are always being placed on individuals to adapt. Coping with these changing demands requires the ability to plan ahead, set goals, devise strategies for meeting these goals, monitor progress, and alter plans, if necessary.
2. *Are relatively satisfied with life*, free from psychological problems such as excessive depression or anxiety, and they feel good about themselves.
3. *Show appropriate feelings and perceptions*, that is, accurate reality contact and emotions that fit the situation. For example, both those who break into tears from everyday frustrations and those who cannot cry no matter how deep the hurt display inappropriate emotions.
4. *Can love and work.* Well-adjusted people form stable, intimate relationships and find productive outlets for their energies.

GROWTH VERSUS ADJUSTMENT

The metaphor of "growth" suggests that just as life forms mature physically, individuals can also develop or mature psychologically. Growth implies a movement that is in some sense "onward and upward," not merely one that returns the organism to its original position.

Adjustment emphasizes *reacting* to the changes in the environment, whereas growth points toward the more active ways in which people seem to initiate change in their lives.

In adjustment, desired change usually occurs through a process of goal-directed action. Maslow suggests that in contrast, growth often involves behavior that is carried out spontaneously, for its own sake, because of the pleasure or satisfaction that it generates, not because it leads to a particular outcome.

Life satisfaction can be viewed as a precondition for growth. It is difficult to direct one's energies toward growth while in a state of fear, anxiety, or depression. Albert Bandura, a leading proponent of social learning theory, suggests that dissatisfaction with oneself is a major motivator for improving performance and adjustment. Humanistic theorists, on the other hand, argue that it is doubtful whether growth can derive from self-dissatisfaction.

Although adjustment is linked to the appropriateness of one's emotions, growth emphasizes the expressiveness, range, and depth of emotion. And instead of focusing on the reality contact of perception, that is, whether one's views match the perceptions of others, growth theorists suggest that some people are less defensive, and therefore more accurate perceivers than others. Thus the perceptions of these people should occasionally disagree with those of the majority.

With regard to love, growth theorists claim that the love relationships of most people are somewhat neurotic, centering on dependency, insecurity, and possessiveness. These theorists (Fromm, 1956; Maslow, 1971) suggest that a more healthy form of love is possible but that it is not common.

The ability to engage in productive work is essential to adjustment. For growth, however, the reasons for engaging in the work and the experience of doing it are more relevant than are the work's productivity or social value.

In conclusion, the work of modern psychologists suggests that both adjustment and

growth are important, for they signify change in a therapeutic direction. At the same time, adjustment and growth may represent qualitatively different forms of desired change.

Try to think of ways in which your current functioning is more well adjusted and ways in which it is more growth oriented.

WHO AM I? IMPLICIT THEORIES OF PERSONALITY

Each of us functions in a complex social reality. In a world of continually changing experiences and observations, we make assumptions, draw conclusions, and retain a storehouse of facts, figures, confabulations, and folk wisdoms—all in an effort to make sense out of our worlds, out of ourselves.

Personality is the study of the whole person. It includes both what we have in common with others (human nature) and what makes each of us different and unique. The system of beliefs, assumptions, hypotheses, and speculations that each of us devises for dealing with our complex social reality constitutes an **implicit theory of personality**. It is implicit or unstated because it includes countless rules and expectancies that we follow automatically, without having to think about them. These implicit theories may include beliefs, for example, that people who wear glasses are intelligent, that most people are kindhearted, that people who are nice to you want something in return, or that you have an accurate awareness of the reasons for your behavior.

One way of approaching your own implicit theory of personality is to consider the dimensions of human nature listed below. Where do you feel that most people fall on these dimensions? Where would you place yourself?

good	1	2	3	4	5	6	7	evil
rational	1	2	3	4	5	6	7	irrational
free	1	2	3	4	5	6	7	determined
affected by heredity	1	2	3	4	5	6	7	affected by environment

CORELL

If possible, compare your responses with those of your classmates to get a rough idea of how your implicit theory of personality differs from theirs. In the next chapter, we shall consider several of the most important explicit, formal theories of personality, and you can see how your own implicit theory compares with these models.

Questions that implicit theories of personality address include: What are the most important traits or dimensions for describing people? What are the main factors that have determined the kind of person one is? What is the process through which behaviors are emitted or decisions made? How do internal events such as thoughts, feelings, memories, and images relate to one another and to behavior? How much of one's functioning is conscious? Which are more important, past influences or present situations? What kind of freedom do we have, if any?

Even though you may not have consciously considered your position on any of these questions, your behavior is predicated on assumptions about each of them. Try coming up with a quick reaction to these questions so that you can compare your position with the explicit theories in the next chapter. If you feel bold enough, try using this information to make an explicit model or diagram of how you believe personality functions.

WHERE AM I GOING? IMPLICIT THEORIES OF THE GOOD LIFE

Just as each of us has an implicit theory of who we are, we also have some notion of where we're going, or at least of where we don't want to go. One way of approaching this implicit theory is to imagine yourself ten years from now. If all goes as you hope, what type of person will you be then? In what ways will you be different from the way you are now? What will your life be like?

To aid in making this image more concrete, complete the following profile of your own personal "good life."

Good Life Profile

1. **Work**
   a. **Unimportant 1 2 3 4 5 6 7 Important**
   b. **Hours per week** _____
   c. **Money earned per year** _____
   d. **Primarily dealing with:**

   people _____   machines _____

   ideas _____
   e. **Work stress: Low 1 2 3 4 5 6 7 High**
   f. **Rank importance of reasons for working:**

   money _____   respect _____

   social contact _____   power _____

   self-expression _____
2. **Recreation**
   a. **Unimportant 1 2 3 4 5 6 7 Important**
   b. **Activities:** _____
   c. **What I get out of these activities** _____
3. **Family**
   a. **Unimportant 1 2 3 4 5 6 7 Important**
   b. **Spouse**
      1. **Physical appearance** _____
      2. **Personality** _____
      3. **Treats me** _____
   c. **Kids**
      1. **Number/gender** _____
      2. **Characteristics** _____
   d. **Extramarital Relationships**
      1. yes _____   no _____   if _____
4. **Lovers (for singles and if item 3d is yes)**
   a. **Unimportant 1 2 3 4 5 6 7 Important**
   b. **Number of relationships in a given**

   year _____
   c. **Typical duration of relationships:**

   years _____ months _____ weeks _____

   nights _____   minutes _____

d. Level of emotional involvement:
   Shallow 1 2 3 4 5 6 7 Deep
5. Friends
   a. Unimportant 1 2 3 4 5 6 7 Important

   b. Number of close friends _____

   c. Relationships are based on _____

   d. Number of acquaintances _____
6. Sex Life
   a. Unimportant 1 2 3 4 5 6 7 Important

   b. Distinguishing features _____
7. Health
   a. Unimportant 1 2 3 4 5 6 7 Important
   b. Exercise:
      Sedentary life 1 2 3 4 5 6 7 Olympic ath-
                                            lete
   c. Eating:
      Too much/too rich 1 2 3 4 5 6 7 Health
                                            food
                                            only

d. Alcohol: Check one

   none _____   moderate _____

   social drinker _____

   social problem _____   skid row _____
e. Cigarettes: Number per day _____
8. Sentence Completions
   a. I want to get up in the morning feel-
      ing _____

   b. I want to be the kind of person _____
      _____

   c. I want my friends _____

   d. I want to be able to look back on my life
      and say _____
      _____

Note: If you have the courage, save this profile. Put it into your personal time capsule and dig it up ten years from now. *Guaranteed*: This will be interesting reading.

FOCUS
PSYCHOLOGISTS ATTACK THE AMERICAN DREAM

What is the American dream? If we believe media such as television, movies and magazines, it can be summarized in one simple formula:

Success + Love = Happiness

For much of our population, the goal is to be happy, which means acquiring success and love.

But what is success? According to the media, success ("making it" in the business world) is (1) having enough money to enjoy the "finer things" in life; (2) having a certain amount of power, authority, or status; and (3) commanding the respect of those who count, that is, other successful people.

How about love? Love ("making it" with the opposite sex) is portrayed as (1) having an attractive, desirable partner who is (2) crazy about you.

Given the desirability of love, success, and happiness, why have psychologists attacked our dream? The main assault has come from humanistic and existential psychologists. But what is perhaps more surprising than the attack is the scarcity of supporters.

Sigmund Freud, the founder of psychoanalysis, probably came closest with his views on the importance of love and work. Even here, however, most modern interpreters of Freud would be unwilling to equate his concept of work with our idea of success. "Work" emphasizes the satisfaction in performing an activity with social value, whereas success focuses on the benefits of the work's completion. B. F. Skinner, the leading behaviorist of our time, initially favored the goals of productivity and happiness but was later persuaded that these were inadequate as ultimate values for society (Rogers & Skinner, 1956).

Success has been criticized by Abraham Maslow and others as important only to those who do not feel good about themselves. Maslow believes that if people respected themselves, they would not be so desperate for the approval of others. Rogers suggests that this desire for success and approval results from deficiencies in the type and amount of parental love that one has received. Erich Fromm, a therapist who bridges psychoanalytic and humanistic traditions, goes even further, contending that our fascination with success and its monetary benefits represents a case study in uncontrolled greed. He argues that modern people are largely living a secondhand existence through their objects, that having has become a substitute for being.

But what could be wrong with love? In our culture, love often means finding a socially desirable partner to possess, one who can enhance the lover's sense of worth: in short, another object among one's store of valued possessions. Moreover, the concern is to provide the security of being loved rather than the risk of loving. The result is a dependent and possessive attachment.

Typically, happiness has not been criticized for itself, but what many call happiness has been questioned. First, happiness can derive from cognitive distortions. The clinical literature is full of cases in which people believe themselves to be happy for a number of years and then suddenly reevaluate these experiences as lies to themselves. For example, people often have strong beliefs about what would make them happy. When these conditions are met, they convince themselves that they must, therefore, be happy. In addition, popular novels, such as Aldous Huxley's *Brave New World*, have dramatized the deceptive nature of happiness by showing the absurdity of a society in which happiness is everything and everyone is always happy.

Finally, the existential therapist Victor Frankl argues that the pursuit of happiness is inherently self-defeating. He claims that happiness follows from a commitment to projects outside oneself and that the attempt to short-circuit this process by avoiding the effort of commitment is doomed to fail. It is like trying to respond to the command "Be spontaneous!" The harder you try, the less spontaneous you become. Presumably our widespread misunderstanding of happiness has contributed to the currently unhappy "me" generation. Paradoxically, those most obsessed with happiness are the least happy.

Where do you stand on the "American dream?" Do you agree with these psychologists? Have they overstated their case in some places? Whether or not you agree, you may be able to use their ideas to help redefine what the American dream means to you.

SUMMARY

1. Mary, Ron, and Charles each experienced identity confusion. Mary questioned her sexual orientation after an encounter with her friend Patty. Ron had a problem choosing a college major: He couldn't decide whether he wanted pre-med because of his own desires or those of his father. Charles confronted feelings of being a phoney in his business and family relationships.

2. Identity confusion includes the lack of a sense of inner continuity, role confusion, self-consciousness and a preoccupation with how others see us, feeling unsure of one's point of view, and a passive experience of life. Identity confusion sometimes enhances personal growth by bringing about a clearer sense of who we are.

3. Identity confusion often occurs in late adolescence or young adulthood, but it can also occur at midlife and in old age.

4. Rogers views the search for our true identity as the one thread that ties our lives together.

5. Preconceptions of people with uncommon names are negative, but these people may compensate with high levels of achievement.

6. Mary decided that her episode with Patty was a problem only if she chose to view it that way. Ron had blown his problem out of proportion; he realized that he could choose to be like his father without giving up his own identity. Charles gave up the self-deception that he was working long hours for his family's sake.

7. We are probably both better than we think we are and worse than we think we are. Greater tolerance and self-acceptance are needed to overcome our hesitation to look at ourselves.

8. Normality has been defined as not being different from the average, being free of disease or dysfunction, and not coming to the attention of mental health authorities.

9. Adjustment and growth both refer to change in a desired or therapeutic direction, but they sometimes mean qualitatively different types of change. Adjustment refers to change that takes one to a state of normality or average functioning. Growth refers to change that in some way goes beyond average functioning.

10. Well-adjusted individuals cope with their environment, are relatively satisfied with their lives, and are able to love and work.

11. The beliefs and assumptions we devise for dealing with our complex social reality constitute an implicit theory of personality.

12. The popular media suggest that the path to happiness entails acquiring success and love. Many psychologists question this belief.

SUGGESTED READINGS

Erikson, E. H. **Identity and the life cycle**. New York: International Universities Press, 1959. A classic work from one of the top theorists in this area.

Rogers, C. R. **A way of being**. Boston: Houghton Mifflin, 1980. Fascinating and highly readable essays.

Schlenker, B. R. **The self and social life**. New York: McGraw-Hill, 1985. Identity as seen by social psychologists.

MODELS of PERSONALITY 2

The Structure of Identity

If you tried to turn your implicit beliefs about personal identity into an explicit theory, as suggested in Chapter 1, you know that this is not easy. We are complex creatures, and our behavior continually changes with the immediate situation. Moreover, in trying to theorize about who we are and how we function, we are operating at the boundary of our own intelligence, where the thing explained is just as complex as the mind doing the explaining.

Nevertheless, we must make sense out of our own behavior, first, because we are intensely curious about ourselves and second, because our survival as a species depends on it. We have long since reached the point at which our technical knowledge of the physical world dwarfs what we know about ourselves. We have only to look around and see a world perched on the brink of disaster to realize that something is amiss.

Many theories have been devised to account for people's social, behavioral, cognitive, and emotional functioning. Most of these have been so inadequate that they were discarded soon after being formed. Of the theories that have survived, and there are at least fifty, they generally fall into three categories: psychoanalytic, emphasizing the importance of unconscious processes; social learning, focusing on the way that behavior changes; and humanistic, exploring the limits of human potential.

This chapter presents these three personality theories, shows how they are related to one another, and evaluates their respective strengths and weaknesses. The language from each of these positions will be used throughout the book to better understand the content areas relevant to growth and adjustment.

PERSONALITY

A **theory** is a system of terms used to represent some part of reality. It is like a map that helps you get from one place to another. Even the best map, however, is not the same as the territory that it represents. And since the map and the territory are not the same thing, there will always be a difference, a gap, between them. Thus no theory can be "true," only more or less accurate.

Personality is that part of psychology concerned with studying the whole person. Much of psychology deals with tiny pieces of behavior, for example, isolated actions, thoughts, memories, feelings, perceptions, images, reflexes, and physiological responses. The emphasis in personality, however, is on going beyond these pieces to understand how they come together and form a picture of the whole person. Thus personality is concerned with the interrelationships and organization of the separate pieces and with the structure of the resulting organism.

Each theory of personality is a language for illuminating who people are, both as a species and as individuals. With regard to the differences among people, personality seeks more than a mere description; it tries to explain how these differences come about. Most theories view the development of personality as a complex interaction between genetic inheritance and environmental influence. But in itself, this tells us very little.

A good explanation must be much more specific. Which inherited predispositions are important for understanding a given individual: Intelligence? Body type? Physical attractiveness? Which aspects of the environment have shaped this personality: Maternal love? Sibling rivalry? Inadequate role models? Ideally, a good theory should give a detailed account of the important environmental variables and genetic predispositions that will be needed to explain why, for example, Liz is so "together" and socially poised, why Jerry always plays the fool, or why Albert will never be satisfied with himself.

Psychoanalytic theories evolved from the observations of therapists, who needed to develop conceptual systems to understand their clients and guide the process of cure. Other theories originated from human and animal research on the mechanisms of behavior change.

Findings from this research that had the greatest application to everyday life have been incorporated into the learning-based personality theories. Still another group of theories emanated from studies of people who had found a sense of meaning or completeness in their lives that went beyond ordinary adjustment. These humanistic theories seek to extend the known limits of human potential and point the way toward their realization.

Thus, conceptual systems within personality have evolved from diverse observations and experiences, yet they all carry the promise of direct applicability to the immediate concerns of everyday life. This is the value of these models, not that they are always true for all people, but that they represent our civilization's best attempt at understanding the whole person and guiding its development in healthier, more satisfying directions.

PSYCHOANALYTIC THEORY

ORIGIN OF THE BASIC MODEL

Sigmund Freud pioneered the psychoanalytic model in the late 1800s and thereby ushered in the modern era of personality theory. Freud, a medical doctor, was struck by the enigma of patients with severe physical symptoms for which no known physical cause could be discerned. In fact, many of these symptoms defied medical knowledge, as in glove anesthesia. In this condition, patients report no feeling in the hand, even when pricked with a pin. Yet it was well known in Freud's time that the nervous tissue ran along the arm in a way that made anesthesia to the hand alone physically impossible.

The medical wisdom of that time regarded such patients as fakers and attributed no significance to the symptoms manifested. Freud found that these symptoms could be removed by allowing hypnotized patients to relive the emotions present when the symptoms began. Freud believed that his patients were reacting as

Sigmund Freud.

if these emotions had been "bottled up" and retained in an active state somewhere outside their conscious awareness.

Thus Freud's clinical observations led him to the conviction that wishes and memories that were unconscious, but nevertheless active in the mind, were at the heart of his patients' bizarre symptoms. Later, as a result of his research into dreams, slips of the tongue, memory lapses, and his own self-analysis, Freud concluded that all behavior is strongly affected by unconscious motivations.

Although Freud was not the first to posit an unconscious mind — it had been discussed for centuries by philosophers — Freud's unique hypothesis was that the unconscious mind affects ordinary, normal functioning, even at times when we think our behavior is totally conscious and rational.

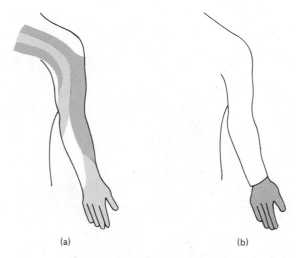

(a)   (b)

Glove anesthesia. The skin areas served by nerves in the arm are shown in (a). The glove anesthesia (numbness) shown in (b) could not result from damage to these nerves.

Psychoanalysts observe that any great discovery jars established thought and therefore creates intense opposition. Copernicus destroyed our sacred conviction that the earth was the center of the universe. Darwin shook belief in our being specially created by God. And Freud's theory meant that we are not even in control of our own minds. Needless to say, his views created much controversy.

THE UNCONSCIOUS

Consistent with his background as a physiologist, Freud was dedicated to a scientific model of personality. His brilliant insight was to apply observational methods from the natural sciences to the study of mind. In effect, the microscope had been turned on itself. Just as physical events did not occur chaotically, Freud reasoned that each and every thought must be determined by previous events. Thus he assumed that the entire stream of mental contents must occur in an orderly sequence of causes and effects. For Freud, the notion that a thought, mood, or impulse could just "pop into the mind" for no reason at all was simply incomprehensible.

Of course, it is natural for us to equate mental functioning with consciousness. Whatever we're aware of is conscious, and so by definition, we cannot become directly aware of something that is not conscious. (If we did become aware of it, it would no longer be unconscious.) Thus the only mental functioning of which we are aware is what is conscious. As a result, thoughts often seem to come to us from "out of nowhere," appearing not to be connected to what went before them. According to Freud, if the unconscious causes could be discovered, these apparent discontinuities would vanish.

Because unconscious events cannot be observed directly, they must be inferred. Freud was convinced that when all of the available evidence is considered, it will usually make more sense to explain behavior by inferring unconscious causes than by couching one's explanations only in terms of conscious contents.

The inference of an unconscious process is not as unusual as it may seem. Consider the case of a bridegroom who is half an hour late for his wedding because he "lost track of the time." Even though he may sincerely desire the marriage, protest that his love is true, and claim that he was trying to be punctual, it would be hard not to wonder whether some part of him wished not to marry. This "part" may be outside awareness and therefore unconscious *for him,* even though other participants in the ceremony may have inferred its presence and be acutely aware of it.

Although there is no way of directly observing unconscious processes, Freud developed observational techniques to approach that observation as closely as possible. First, he studied patients' dreams. Since dreams are conscious products formed with little or no conscious control, it was thought that they closely approximated unconscious mental functioning and would provide a "royal road" to the unconscious. Second, Freud developed the technique of **free association**. Patients were asked to lie down, relax, and simply verbalize whatever came to mind, no matter how trivial, personal, or embarrassing the material might be. Again, the strategy was to examine what is produced when conscious control is relinquished.

Within Freud's assumption of complete determinism, free associations to a dream symbol, for example, could not help but provide valuable clues to its unconscious sources. Since all associational linkages are thought to be lawful, whatever comes to mind should be meaningfully connected to the original symbol.

For example, one man dreamed about shooting his secretary with a gun. His associations to "gun" were "bullet, bullet-in-your-head, sperm, bang." The dreamer's further elaborations revealed that bullet-in-your-head is a phrase an English teacher had once taught him many years before as a way of remembering that "bulletin" is spelled with two ls. He also mentioned that he and his friends used to joke that the English teacher's bald head resembled the "head" of a penis. Based on the evidence of the dream and these associations, how would you explain this dream?

One interpretation might note that sperm are equated with bullets in the head of his penis. Thus bullet-in-your-head and "bang" both refer to shooting with a gun *and* to sexual functioning. Thus the gun in the dream appears to represent a penis, and the dream involves the aggressive wish to have sex with the secretary and perhaps to impregnate her. For Freud, the accuracy of this interpretation could be judged by how consistently it accounted for the evidence, that is, the details of the dream and its associations, and by whether the interpretation produced an emotional "aha" in the client.

LEVELS OF CONSCIOUSNESS

Freud identified three levels of the mind. The **conscious** refers to whatever we are aware

of at the moment. Contents of the conscious are continually in flux, forming the so-called stream of consciousness. Within momentary awareness, there is one object or perception of which we are acutely aware, and this figure stands out against a background of rather dimly perceived sights, sounds, impressions, feelings, thoughts, and images. Both figure and ground change from moment to moment. The **preconscious** merges gradually with this dim background, forming the area of unawareness over which we have partial conscious control. The preconscious includes mental contents that can be called into consciousness with relative ease, such as what you did last night, your phone number, and whether you like your roommate.

Psychoanalysts compare the mind to an iceberg in assuming that the great mass of mental contents lie below the surface of relative awareness. The **unconscious** represents the massive layer of unawareness over which we have little control. Freud believed that either the contents of the unconscious could not be brought to consciousness, as with the biological instincts, or that these contents were actively prevented from coming to awareness, as with antisocial wishes or traumatic memories.

THE STRUCTURE OF THE MIND

Freud observed that his patients often stubbornly resisted free association. They would try to involve him in a normal conversation, complain that nothing would spontaneously come to mind, or do anything rather than forgo conscious control of their verbalization. Yet they were not consciously trying to avoid this task. Freud interpreted their **resistance** as an unconscious attempt to protect consciousness from the emergence of threatening unconscious contents. Freud reasoned that this would make sense if the resistance were consciously initiated, but it was not. Why should the unconscious try to protect the conscious from unconscious meanings? Freud saw this as an internal contradiction of his model, and he sought to correct it by positing entities that ranged across levels of consciousness. In his revised theory, unconscious parts of the ego were thought to initiate defenses that protected the conscious ego from threatening unconscious wishes.

The id. The psychoanalytic model assumes a biological continuity of life; as mammals, we are more similar to the other animals than we are different from them. The **id** is the mental representative of our inherited animal drives. It contains our instinctual cravings to eat, drink, eliminate, maintain comfort, gain sexual release, aggress, dominate, seek revenge, destroy, and, finally, to die.

Freud grouped these drives into two general categories: the life instinct and the death instinct (also referred to as the sex and destructive instincts). The aim of the life instinct "is to establish ever greater unities and to preserve them thus — in short to bind together" (Freud, 1940, p. 5). Freud drew a parallel between this drive and similar processes in the natural sciences, such as attraction in chemistry and physical growth in biology. The death or destructive instinct (when directed outward) corresponded to chemical repulsion and the process by which living systems break down.

Freud introduced the death instinct in his later work because of his conviction that instincts operated through a compulsion to repeat, or return the organism to a state of prior quiescence. In effect, just as hunger leads to behavior patterns that return us to a prior state of satiation, the death instinct takes us back to the quiet repose of inorganic existence. Freud interpreted phenomena such as war, violence, drug abuse, and suicide as movements of the death instinct. For example, consider World War I. Despite world leaders' claims of rationality, Freud saw the wanton destructiveness around him as proof of a biological predisposition.

For Freud, the id is savage, greedy, envious, inherently selfish, illogical, inconsistent, and noncompromising. Since each of us inherits the same basic desires, full instinctual gratification for one person must conflict with that for others. Each of us thus is necessarily in conflict with society. Yet, we must live in groups in order to obtain many of these desired gratifications. As a result, social reality forces us to accept substitute gratifications that do not entirely satisfy our true biological natures. Thus we postpone the purchase of that sports car until we have earned the money; we settle for a legal contract with only one sexual partner; and we restrict ourselves to verbal insult or innuendo when our bodies crave a physical release. But although society restricts the expression of our desires, it cannot eliminate them. At best, these desires are partially restrained below the level of conscious awareness.

What led Freud to such a pessimistic view of the id? One factor was the primitive nature of our fantasies. For example, the amount of sex and violence in our dreams exists in stark contrast with the normal decorum of our conscious lives. Moreover, because we presumably are born as pure id, Freud considered the behavior of young children to provide a clue to our biological inheritance. Every parent can attest to the selfishness, greed, inconsistency, and impulsive violence of the normal two-year-old. The difference for Freud is that whereas other theories assume a qualitative change in two-year-olds as they mature, Freud believed that we remain essentially the same. Through socialization, the irrational and antisocial impulses are suppressed, but they do not go away.

The id seeks pleasure — immediate instinctual gratification — without regard for the consequences. Its thought process allows no words, no conceptions of time, and no qualifiers. It deals in images, analogies, metaphors, and symbols; in short, the stuff of dreams.

The ego. As a result of maturation and experience with the outside world, the infant begins to distinguish between self and external reality. For example, some desired stimuli are often absent, whereas others (e.g., the thumb) are always present. The body feels and is felt; the outside world is only felt. As the distinction between self and environment becomes clearer, part of the id becomes organized for obtaining instinctual gratification from the environment. The **ego** refers to learned reaction patterns for obtaining id gratification. It operates through appropriate actions, self-imposed delay of gratification, and the suppression of impulses. The ego includes capacities for motor control, sensory perception, memory, affect, thought, and planning. Obtaining drive gratification usually requires impulse control, accurate perception of reality, access to memories of past gratification attempts, a plan of action, and a coordination of body movements and speech to put the plan into effect.

Gradually, the ego becomes capable of looking at itself; that is, it develops self-awareness. Presumably, awareness of the difference between one's desire and the object of one's desire leads to a corresponding awareness that "I" have to act in order to fulfill this wish. The ego's awareness of itself makes it the center of conscious identity: It is what we think we are. As a manifestation of identity, the ego has the character of oneness; it is internally consistent. The traits, desires, needs, memories, and attitudes of the ego must combine to form a sensible whole. The loss of this wholeness is tantamount to going insane. Thus we experience ourselves as a continuing identity: To ourselves, we are the same person, even though both our behavior and our physical appearance may change drastically.

Typically, self-awareness occurs gradually, but some people experience it all at once. Carl Jung, a prominent psychoanalyst and colleague of Freud, had such an experience as a young boy:

> I was taking the long road to school from Klein-Huningen, where we lived, to Basel, when suddenly for a single moment I had the overwhelming impression of having just emerged from a dense cloud. I knew all at once: now I am *myself!* It was as if a wall of mist were at my back, and behind that wall

there was not yet an "I." . . . Previously, I had existed, too, but everything had merely happened to me. Now I happened to myself. Now I knew: I am myself now, now I exist. Previously I had been willed to do this and that; now *I* willed. . . . There was "authority" in me. (Jung, 1965, pp. 32–33)

The ego, too, seeks drive gratification, but in a way that minimizes negative repercussions from external reality. The ego delays the impulsive and immediate discharge of energy, and its objects of desire are firmly fixed, so that the mature ego is said to have "will." The ego's thought processes are the ordinary conscious, rational thinking with which we all are familiar. But it must be remembered that in the psychoanalytic model, this form of thinking is not typical, that the bulk of mental functioning follows the thought processes of the id.

The superego. The **superego** accounts for the moral functions of the personality. It is responsible for critical self-observation and the approval or disapproval of actions and wishes because they are right or wrong. It corresponds to the "voice of conscience," the internalized code of right and wrong that we have learned from our parents and other authority figures. The superego emerges from the developing ego, but it goes beyond the ego in representing an image of what we should be. Thus it is an image of perfection, a code of parental prohibitions, a ruling of dos and don'ts, shoulds and should nots.

Superego development can be observed as early as the end of the first year, as children behave appropriately to please their parents. These values, however, are not yet internalized. They do not operate independently — even when there is no possibility of actual punishment — until a later age, perhaps five or six.

The superego initiates and enforces the ego's defenses against impulses of the id. Throughout one's life, the ego fears the super-

ego, as the child fears the parent. Disapproval of the superego can lead to anxiety, guilt, feelings of inferiority, the demand of reparation for wrongdoing, and the unconscious need for self-punishment. For example, Freud maintained that people with low self-esteem often unconsciously accuse themselves of a real or imagined misdeed. Out of an unconscious need for self-punishment, criminals often inadvertently provide the clues leading to their arrest. They might, for example, return to the scene of the crime and begin asking questions, drawing attention to themselves. At such times, they are behaving as if "possessed" by a demon that momentarily takes control of their being for purposes of atonement. Other ways that people unconsciously punish themselves include failing in a career, having an "accidental" injury, and succumbing to illness. Thus the superego can become a real threat to the ego. On the other hand, it can also approve of the ego, leading to joy, self-satisfaction, and the virtuous glow of the righteous.

In one sense, the superego aids the ego by using internalized parental images to contain unacceptable id wishes. But the superego also masters the ego in its restriction of the ego's independence and freedom to enjoy instinctual gratification.

It is a common misconception that the superego represents the reasonable demands of society. Rather, Freud saw the superego as the blind dos and don'ts of a child's mentality, the absolute imperative of parental rules, and the unrealistic image of perfection itself. Thus he viewed the superego as largely unconscious and essentially irrational. It is formed at a time when the child's cognitive abilities are primitive and unsophisticated, leading to black-and-white, all-or-none thinking.

The superego's sense of justice is primitive, often based on revenge ("an eye for an eye"). And as young children do not distinguish clearly between fantasy and reality, the superego threatens punishment for the wish as well as the deed. Thus Freud did not maintain that optimal adjustment was the result of simply following the dictates of conscience. It was equally important, especially during Freud's own sexually repressive Victorian era, for the overly severe strictures of the superego to become more flexible and relaxed.

PSYCHOSEXUAL STAGES OF DEVELOPMENT

One of the most controversial parts of Freud's theory is his hypothesis of childhood sexuality. Freud believed that children progress through distinct biological stages, each centering on a particular body region or focus of erotic gratification. The first year of life encompasses the **oral stage**, in which infants interact with the world largely through sucking, oral exploration, and biting. Next, the **anal stage** corresponds to society's interference with uncontrolled gratification through attempts at toilet training. Here, pleasure comes from the release or retention of feces, especially when timed to thwart parental desires.

The **phallic stage**, occurring roughly between three and six, is crucial to superego development. This stage includes the child's vague, but intense, fantasies of sexual gratification with the opposite-sex parent, along with hostile wishes toward the parent of the same sex. For males, anticipations of retaliation from the father threaten the offending organ, resulting in the so-called castration anxiety. This is eventually resolved through a massive **repression** (automatic forcing into unconsciousness) of the offending wishes. What remains are feelings of desexualized love for the mother and identification with the father. This identification then provides the basis for internalizing parental values, forming much of the superego. For females, the desire for the father's penis gives way to the desire for a substitute—having a baby. (*Note*: Many psychologists do not grant Freud's theory of female sexuality a great deal of credibility.)

The phallic stage is followed by a sexually quiescent period, **latency**. The **genital stage** begins shortly after puberty and lasts throughout adulthood. Its goal is the achievement of sexual maturity, as evidenced in the capacities for love and orgasm.

COMPROMISE FORMATION

Psychoanalytic theory views the mind as a submerged battleground. Beneath the calm waters of conscious experience lies a dangerous and unexpected turbulence, as conflicting forces struggle for control.

Freud's strategy of theorizing was to personify the various components of the mind: id, ego, superego, conscious, preconscious, and unconscious. Freud endowed each component with an awareness and a capacity to seek desired outcomes, as if each were a person in its own right. In this way, the psychoanalytic model has an almost poetic quality in its free use of language to convey emotional meanings. This "as if" quality of the theory should be kept in mind at all times.

Within the battleground of the mind, each behavior or conscious experience results from a compromise among many competing influences, including conscious perception, unconscious perception, superego demands, repressed memories, id wishes, and ego counterwishes. The dynamic process of compromise formation is pictured in Figure 2–1.

APPLYING THE MODEL

The psychoanalytic model can be best understood by considering an everyday example, "boy meets girl." At the level of conscious perception, the boy may be thinking, "She's pretty, I'd like to go out with her." At the level of unconscious perception (for simplicity, preconscious and unconscious perception will be combined), he may be attending to any of a multitude of background features in his perceptual field. For example, he may be unconsciously registering her female smell, the note of discomfort in her laughter, the little bump on her nose, the momentarily disapproving flick of her eyebrow, her pupil dilation, changes in her breathing, and literally thousands of other details of the encounter.

Consciousness, because of its more focused quality, simply cannot accommodate this number of stimuli, and so the psychoanalytic assumption is that the bulk of perceptual information enters outside of awareness. In addition, aspects of the situation that might threaten the

FIGURE **2 – 1**
THE PSYCHOANALYTIC MODEL

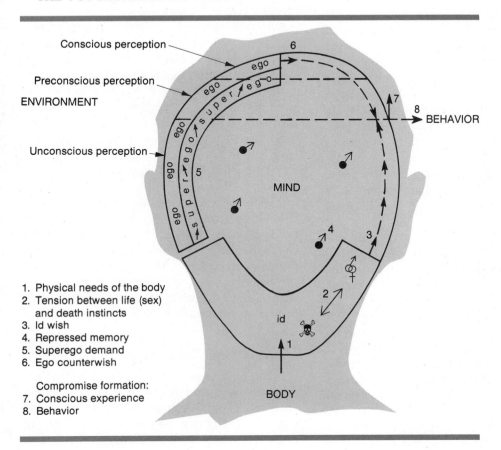

1. Physical needs of the body
2. Tension between life (sex) and death instincts
3. Id wish
4. Repressed memory
5. Superego demand
6. Ego counterwish

   Compromise formation:
7. Conscious experience
8. Behavior

boy's self-esteem or arouse anxiety are often distorted. The psychoanalytic model assumes that all of these stimuli, whether perceived consciously or unconsciously, contribute to the boy's behavior and to the overall feeling tone and attraction of the encounter.

Each perception, whether conscious or unconscious, triggers memories and related, unresolved wishes from the past. For example, the girl may in some way remind the boy of his mother, a favorite teacher from grade school, or

a feared neighbor from down the street. It might even be a television personality to whom he has lingering emotional attachments, such as one of "Charley's Angels." Remember, for Freud, the unconscious is timeless; childhood wishes persist unabated in the adult.

Unconscious id wishes that the girl might stimulate typically combine erotic and destructive desires. For example, the boy might wish to touch her breasts, take her by force, make her his slave, or keep her only for himself. Perhaps, because of her freckles, she reminds him of a teacher from grade school who tactlessly ridiculed his school-boy crush. Because of this, id wishes might center on themes of revenge.

Note that all these id wishes would violate the boy's internalized standards of behavior and therefore generate counterwishes initiated by the superego and conveyed through the ego. The ego cannot allow these raw impulses to find expression either in consciousness or in behavior. The ego's task is to reduce the tension of these instinctual drives, that is, to provide pleasure while minimizing repercussions, both from the superego (e.g., guilt) and from external reality (e.g., punishment).

The boy might begin by complimenting the girl, but even with this tactic, the ego must be careful, for the form and content of the compliment must conform to narrow boundaries of propriety, yet still be effective in winning the girl's favor. For example, saying "I think your shoes are wonderful!" might be perceived as effeminate and therefore be counterproductive. On the other hand, saying "I like your breasts" would be too overtly lustful. Compliments on her smile or eyes are particularly effective, as these features are thought to reflect one's "inner self." After presenting himself as a charming and socially desirable prospect, the boy might then ask the girl for a date, which will at least provide the opportunity for partial gratification.

But love does not always run a smooth course. Romantic relationships often provide a context for bizarre and irrational outcomes. If the girl likes the boy a lot, this may stir his unconscious fears of being smothered by a female (his mother). Or perhaps it might set the stage for avenging the rejection by his grade-school teacher, in which case he might abruptly terminate the relationship and "dump her." On the other hand, if the girl has an unconscious need for punishment, to atone for real or imagined sins from the past, she may reject him if he seems to be a "nice guy," only to fall for someone who will treat her badly. According to the psychoanalytic model, we never simply react to

a stimulus "as it is." Instead, we always respond to symbols that are tied to both past experiences and present needs.

VARIATIONS OF THE PSYCHOANALYTIC MODEL

Psychoanalytic theory is currently fragmented. One overriding problem is that psychoanalysts have yet to agree on a method for resolving theoretical disputes. Each tends to use his or her own clinical experience, thus relying on small, nonrepresentative samples and uncontrolled observations. Nevertheless, psychoanalytic variations clearly share more in common with one another than they do with either learning or humanistic theories. Popular alternatives to a strictly Freudian theory involve: decreasing the emphasis on sex and death, placing more importance on the human need for meaning and spiritual fulfillment, and increasing the power and independence of the ego.

Try going back over the "boy meets girl" scenario, giving a new example for each of the following: conscious perception, unconscious perception, id impulse, repressed memory, superego demand, and ego counterwish. Find each of these in Figure 2–1.

SOCIAL LEARNING THEORY

Social learning theory, sometimes known as cognitive behaviorism, is fast becoming one of the most influential positions in psychology. Its leaders, Albert Bandura, Walter Mischel, and Julian Rotter, among others, developed a theory that emphasizes the relationships among conscious thought processes, overt behavior, and environmental events.

This theory has its origins in **behaviorism**, the study of relationships between behavior and environmental stimuli. Thus to understand the language and development of social learning theory, we must first examine the behavioral

Albert Bandura.

approach to psychology, which is primarily associated with two men, Pavlov and Skinner.

PAVLOV'S CLASSICAL OR RESPONDENT CONDITIONING

A **stimulus** refers to an environmental event such as a light coming on, the clang of a bell, or another person entering a room. A **response** is a behavior that occurs in reaction to a stimulus. For example, touch a hot plate and you respond by jerking your hand back; a friend says hello and you return the greeting. Within the behaviorist framework, every behavior that occurs is also a response, since all behavior is presumed to be caused by earlier events.

The Russian physiologist Ivan Pavlov observed that some stimuli have automatic, un-

learned effects on behavior. For example, the taste of certain foods leads to the response of salivation, or a puff of air directed at the eye results in blinking, or a loud noise produces startle and fear reactions. Pavlov called these **unconditioned stimuli**, and he referred to their natural effects as **unconditioned responses**.

Pavlov's great discovery, which in many ways marked the beginning of modern psychology, was that if another, neutral stimulus regularly occurs close in time to the unconditioned stimulus, the appearance of this neutral stimulus alone will come to elicit a close approximation to the original, unconditioned response. The originally neutral stimulus is known as a **conditioned stimulus**, and the behavior that occurs in response to it is called a **conditioned response**. **Learning** is a relatively enduring change in behavior, and **classical** or **respondent conditioning** is learning to respond to a previously neutral stimulus with a conditioned response.

The classic example of respondent conditioning derives from Pavlov's work with dogs. Meat powder placed on dogs' tongues automatically produced salivation. Eventually, however, the dogs salivated at the mere sight of the powder, even if it were not placed in their mouths. The meat powder placed on the tongue was the unconditioned stimulus for the unconditioned response of salivation. The sight of meat powder became a conditioned stimulus for the conditioned response of salivation.

Pavlov's model applies mainly to physiological reactions, reflexes, and emotional responses. For example, yesterday afternoon Kathy accidentally ran into John and a female companion having lunch. That night, she asked John about it. He became violent and accused her of spying, making Kathy feel agitated and upset. Today Kathy sees John approaching and again becomes agitated and upset. In this example, John's accusations are the unconditioned stimuli for Kathy's unconditioned response of agitation (contractions of stomach muscles, release of gastric juices, sweating, heart pound-

Pavlov's pioneering animal research led to the disovery of classical conditioning.

ing). The next day, the mere sight of John functioned as a conditioned stimulus for a similar, conditioned response of agitation. If John's behavior over the next few meetings is pleasant, however, Kathy's conditioned reaction will disappear or *extinguish*.

SKINNER'S OPERANT CONDITIONING

B. F. Skinner's radical behaviorism differs primarily from social learning theory in its treatment of cognitions. Unlike some behaviorists, Skinner did not question the existence of private events, such as thoughts, feelings, and images, just because they could not be publicly observed. However, he maintained that these private events could not be the causes of behavior, and thus they were of little interest to behavioral science.

The main strategy. Skinner's strategy of analysis was to break down all behavioral occur-

rences into instances of the following sequence:

$$S^D \rightarrow R \rightarrow S^{+/-}$$

S^D refers to the **discriminative stimulus**, or stimulus conditions that have led to reinforcement or punishment in the past. R refers to a specific, publicly observable behavior, and $S^{+/-}$ refers to a reinforcing stimulus (S^+) or to an aversive stimulus (S^-). A **reinforcing stimulus** is one that increases the frequency of the behavior it follows, and an **aversive stimulus** is one that decreases that frequency. A classic Skinnerian example is the following: a light comes on (S^D) $\rightarrow$ the rat presses the bar (R) $\rightarrow$ a food pellet appears (S^+). With humans, a similar sequence might be the following: the phone rings (S^D) $\rightarrow$ you pick up the receiver (R) $\rightarrow$ a friend's voice says "hello" (S^+).

Thus the strategy in a Skinnerian analysis is to understand a concrete piece of behavior by determining what environmental events immediately precede and follow that behavior. The

B. F. Skinner.

A pigeon being operantly conditioned in a "Skinner box."

"person" in this analysis can be regarded as one's entire repertoire of possible responses, along with each of their probabilities of occurrence in various stimulus situations.

Contingencies of reinforcement. Skinner maintained that behavior is situation specific and controlled by its consequences. The relationships between behaviors and their consequent stimuli are called **contingencies of reinforcement**. Behaviors that lead to the presentation of a reinforcing stimulus (**positive reinforcement**) or to the removal of an aversive stimulus (**negative reinforcement**) increase in probability of occurrence. On the other hand, behaviors that lead to the presentation of an aversive stimulus or the removal of a reinforcing stimulus (**punishment**) are less likely to recur. Withholding a reinforcer, that is, not presenting an expected reinforcer, also decreases the probability of response (**extinction**).

Let's apply a Skinnerian analysis to a simple human interaction. Note that in a social situation, one person's behavior is a stimulus for the other. Thus it is important to clarify whose behavior is being examined in a given exchange. Consider the following example: Johnny is playing the drums. His father yells, "Stop that noise!" Johnny stops playing. (You may want to go ahead and try the analysis before reading further.)

The presence of drums (S^D) $\rightarrow$ Johnny drumming (R) $\rightarrow$ the sound produced by the drums (S^+). Johnny's drumming was positively reinforced by the sound produced. The continued presence of the drums (S^D) $\rightarrow$ continued drumming (R) $\rightarrow$ father yelling "Stop that noise!" (S^-). Johnny's drumming was punished by his father's yelling at him to stop. This reduced to zero the frequency of the drum beats. For the father, the drum sound (S^D) $\rightarrow$ yelling at Johnny to stop (R) $\rightarrow$ a removal of the drum "noise" (S^-). Thus the father's behavior of yelling was negatively reinforced by the removal of noise. Note that punishment and negative reinforcement are *not* the same. In fact, they have opposite effects. Presumably, the next time that Johnny starts drumming or otherwise makes noise, the father's response of yelling at him to stop will be even more probable.

Here we also see the operation of **stimulus generalization** in which the father's yelling response, which occurs with one discriminative stimulus (drum noise), may be extended to other similar S^Ds (other noises that Johnny might make, like banging toys around or playing a different musical instrument). At the same time, Johnny's behavior is being shaped to show **response discrimination**, for he is learning to play the drums only when his father is absent.

Special applications. The use of operant techniques will be described in more detail in Chapter 7, but there are two particularly interesting applications of this method that should be explained right away. First, note that the Skin-

nerian approach does not tell us with certainty whether a given stimulus will be reinforcing or aversive. To be certain, we must wait until it occurs and observe its effect on later behavior. Moreover, the same stimulus may be reinforcing on one occasion and aversive on another. A favorite food, for example, will be reinforcing up to the point of **satiation**, after which more of this food can become aversive.

Many reinforcers have consistent effects for most people most of the time. For example, money and social approval are quite reliable as positive reinforcers. Sometimes, however, what appears to be an aversive stimulus may in fact function as a reinforcing one. A common example is spanking a child. If the child has been deprived of parental attention long enough,

Can you explain Charley Brown's shy behavior using the language of reinforcement contingencies?

spanking can function as a reinforcing stimulus, increasing rather than decreasing the child's undesirable behavior. In effect, the attention that comes with spanking can outweigh its pain.

Another potentially confusing situation involves negative reinforcement or **avoidance conditioning**. For example, Len is shy and lonely. He stays in his room studying most nights, even on weekends. Len is obviously unhappy, but what is maintaining his avoidance of situations in which he might make new friends and expand his life? In fact, Len has tried going to parties or joining clubs, but he gets so anxious in social situations that others feel uncomfortable around him. Consequently, he feels that going to these places will bring him only further pain and rejection. The behavior of staying in his room is maintained by negative reinforcement: It reduces the anxiety Len experiences when approaching a social situation.

Social learning theory employs the language of behaviorism, but extends this language to private events. In particular, it posits a causal role for cognitions.

MODELING

The social learning view began as a theory of **modeling**, that is, the process of imitating the behavior of others. Bandura's early research determined that people could learn a new response merely by observing a model perform the desired behavior. It was not necessary for the individual to first emit the response and then be reinforced for it. In other words, learning could occur from observation alone. Bandura emphasized, however, that even though people have *learned* a response in the sense of knowing what to do, the behavior will not be *performed* until they expect it to be rewarded.

Bandura suggested that observing a model receive a reward for performing a behavior resulted in a **vicarious reinforcement** for the observer. This process is vicarious because the observer is not reinforced directly, and it is a

reinforcement because the observer's probability of emitting the response increases. Similarly, observing a model being punished results in vicarious punishment. Note that under vicarious punishment, a new response can be learned, even though its probability of being performed will be low until the subject is convinced that the response will now lead to reward. For example, by observing an older brother say a forbidden word and then have his mouth washed out with soap, a younger sibling may learn the new word but not say it out loud until grown-ups are absent.

Modeling can have three effects on the observer: It can teach new behaviors (**acquisition**), make already learned responses less likely (**inhibition**), or make already learned responses more likely (**disinhibition**). For example, a child may acquire the response of petting a dog by watching another child. But seeing a dog growl at that child would inhibit dog petting. Finally, a child who fears dogs can have the petting response disinhibited by watching other children play with dogs.

According to Bandura, modeling occurs in four steps: attention, retention, motor reproduction, and motivation.

Attention. In order for modeling to occur we must first observe the modeled behavior, encoding it symbolically in words and images. For example, people often attend to a new dance by describing to themselves the foot movements in numbers (one, two, three, one, two, three).

Retention. In order to perform a modeled response at a later time, we must have some way of keeping a representation of that behavior in our long-term memory. Often, using verbal descriptions or special images aids retention. For example, to help us remember a certain route we may remind ourselves, "Turn right at the light."

Motor reproduction. A complex response cannot be performed unless we have the physical skill and coordination to carry it out, even if we have attended to the model and re-

---

FOCUS
MODELING AND THE BIG DAN'S RAPE TRIAL

March 6, 1983. Big Dan's Tavern, New Bedford, Massachusetts. A woman was restrained on a pool table and raped by four men while bar customers looked on.

Much of the trial was carried live on cable television. The same day that the sentences in the trial were handed down, a twelve-year-old Rhode Island boy sexually assaulted a ten-year-old girl on a pool table while other children looked on. An official from the attorney general's office described the boy as a nonviolent, pint-sized, "good kid" who had "unfortunately watched too much stuff on TV." (*Dallas Times Herald*, April 18, 1984, p. A3)

---

member what to do. For example, individuals rarely learn how to drive a stick shift just by watching another driver. It is necessary to practice repeatedly while getting feedback on their behavior.

Motivation. Even if we have learned a response and have the physical skill to perform it, we will not emit the behavior unless we expect the performance to lead to a desired outcome. In other words, there must be a reason to perform it.

Modeling and social learning. For Bandura, modeling is the prototype for all social learning. The basic learning process is assumed to be the same, whether the information learned is conveyed through visual inspection of a live model, through pictures, or even through a verbal description of the desired response. Thus all learning requires attention to discriminative stimuli, the retention of a symbolic representation of those stimuli, the physical ability to reproduce the desired behaviors, and the motivation to emit the behavior in a given situation.

Novel behavior. But how do people come to perform behaviors that they have never observed before? What accounts for creativity? For social learning theory, novel behavior results from active cognitive processing. People code observed behavior symbolically, not literally. In modeling, we do not simply mimic specific acts. We abstract and code the observed

performance using our own idiosyncratic categories for making sense out of the world. These categories, or **personal constructs**, are determined by our own unique genetic and experiential histories. Thus one hundred people may view a ballet, producing one hundred different descriptions of what it depicts.

In other words, learning is an abstract, cognitive process by which the rules and principles underlying a specific performance are coded and can be used at a later date to generate new behaviors. Stimuli are not passively encoded; they are selected, reflected on, and transformed, depending on the individual's personal constructs and current needs. For example, children, after observing discriminative stimuli such as "one boy, many boys; one girl, many girls" learn the rule of adding "s" to form a plural. They then can apply this rule to guide the production of behaviors that were never previously performed or observed. Thus, when the plural of man is desired, they may produce "mans." This deviation from ordinary usage, although incorrect in this context, is the kind of process that leads to new, original responses that will sometimes represent useful and highly creative ideas.

EXPECTANCIES
Social learning theory distinguishes among three types of expectancy. **Stimulus expectan-**

cies refer to the expectancy of a future stimulus based on the presence of a current stimulus. For example, to a baby, the appearance of its mother creates the expectancy that food is on the way. Through years of socialization, each of us learns thousands of these stimulus expectancies. Often these expectancies are used to tell us which stimuli to approach and which to avoid. For example, when coming upon another person, we scan their features for mood-related cues. Facial expressions of disgust or hostility give us important information about what other stimuli we can expect in the forthcoming interaction.

Outcome expectancies refer to the expectancy of a future stimulus (the outcome) based on what behaviors we emit in the current situation. For example, the presence of one's boss while at work generally leads to the outcome expectancy that "goofing off will lead to trouble." Outcomes can be described in terms of their reinforcement value, a subjective judgment of how much the outcome is desired.

Expectancies of self-efficacy refer to the conviction that one can perform a desired response. Bandura noted that even if one has the physical skill and the desire to perform an act, it will probably not even be attempted unless the person believes he or she can do it. Self-efficacy controls the initiation, effort, and persistence of coping responses and thus is important to psychotherapy, especially for fears and phobias. Expectancies of self-efficacy can be produced by four kinds of experience: (1) actually performing the desired response, (2) watching someone else perform it successfully, (3) having someone persuade you that you can do it, and (4) observing your own bodily reactions (e.g., noticing an absence of fear in a situation in which you had anticipated being frightened). Note that these experiences are listed in decreasing order of imparted self-efficacy.

According to the social learning model, then, behaviors are emitted when there is physical skill, positive self-efficacy, and a favorable outcome expectancy.

COGNITIVE COMPETENCIES

Social learning theory makes very few assumptions about human nature or genetic inheritance. The closest it comes is to assume an inborn tendency to construe the events of experience and thereby give them meaning (Maddi, 1980). But people are assumed to differ in their ability to construe the world. For example, they differ in memory ability, in the capacity to find similarities and differences in events, and in the extent to which they can formulate abstract rules combining diverse phenomena into meaningful patterns. Because of this, some people will formulate more accurate expectancies than will others and therefore behave more adaptively.

The greater our cognitive abilities, the more actively we can construe the environment, accept or resist reinforcements, and use self-control to override the automatic effects of the immediate environment. The message of social learning theory is that through inborn abilities, maturation, and effective learning, we can increase the control we have over our lives.

REINFORCEMENT

Social learning theory has expanded the concept of reinforcement to include cognitive processes. In humans, reinforcement occurs through cognitive mediation. Bandura views reinforcement as occurring primarily through its informational and motivational effects. It gives the person information as to what behaviors lead to what outcomes in this situation; that is, it provides the basis for forming outcome expectancies. In addition, by receiving a favorable outcome when reinforcement occurs, a person becomes motivated to obtain additional rewards through appropriate performance. Thus reinforcement increases the probability of a response because it indicates what behaviors lead to reward and because receiving a reward incites us to seek more.

Three types of reinforcement can be distinguished. Direct external reinforcement occurs when others give us a reward such as money or praise. **Vicarious reinforcement**, as described, refers to observing another receive a direct reward. **Self-reinforcement** refers to rewarding yourself with either a tangible stimulus, such as an ice-cream cone, or an intangible one, such as "feeling satisfied" or telling yourself, "I did a good job."

THE SELF-SYSTEM

Social learning theory does not view people as passive reactors to external influences. Rather, people are thought to be actively judgmental and constructive in their thought processes. They not only perceive and interpret what is going on in the environment, but they also are aware of their behavior and can react to that behavior. Their capacities for self-control operate through their **self-systems**. People observe their behavior, describe it to themselves, and compare it with learned, self-selected standards. If their behavior meets these standards, they feel satisfied and maintain their performance until the task is completed. If, on the other hand, their behavior falls short of expectation, they alter it to eliminate the aversive outcome of self-dissatisfaction. In other words, people learn to reward and punish themselves, and because of this, they gain some control over their behavior.

Be clear, however, that the self-system is not an agent or internal identity directing behavior from the inside, as does the ego. The cognitive processes that make up the self-system result from environmental influences. Although the self-system cannot override one's history of environmental inputs, it can at times override the effects of the immediate environment. For example, to avoid later discomfort, one may reluctantly refuse a rich dessert.

Thus social learning theory gives no special importance to one's sense of identity or feeling of continuity as a person. The cognitions that control behavior refer to this identity (e.g., "I want the dessert"; "In the past, overeating has made *me* feel uncomfortable"; "If *I* eat the dessert now, I will probably feel uncomfortable later"; "*I* won't eat it"). However, social learning theory assumes that it is *not* this identity that leads to self-control. Rather, self-control results from the logical flow of cognitions leading to a negative outcome expectancy.

RECIPROCAL DETERMINISM

Although people have some capacity for self-control, social learning theory recognizes no potential for free will or freedom of choice. Like psychoanalytic theory, it represents a complete determinism. Unique to social learning theory, however, is **reciprocal determinism**, a model in which personal (P), behavioral (B), and environmental (E) sources of influence mutually determine one another. "P" includes personal cognitions and observable characteristics such as physique, attractiveness, gender, and race. "B" refers to publicly observable behaviors such as hand gestures, talking, and eating. "E" refers to the external environment. Each component of this triad exists in a reciprocal (two-way) interaction with each of the other two components.

APPLYING THE MODEL

Figure 2–2 presents a diagram of the social learning model. We can see how this model works by returning to a "boy meets girl" scenario.

As Rodney looks at Rebecca, her striking appearance and worldly smile attract his interest. Rodney thinks to himself, "Good looking!" and walks over to introduce himself. In his zeal, Rodney does not see the curb and stumbles over it, nearly bumping into Rebecca. In addition, Rodney's green hair momentarily puts her off, and she pretends not to notice him. But then his friendly manner catches her interest and she starts talking. Rodney can feel his heart beating, and this increases his certainty of wanting her to be his girl friend. At the same time, his awareness of being excited and jittery around her warns him that he may not be able to attract a

FIGURE 2–2
THE SOCIAL LEARNING MODEL

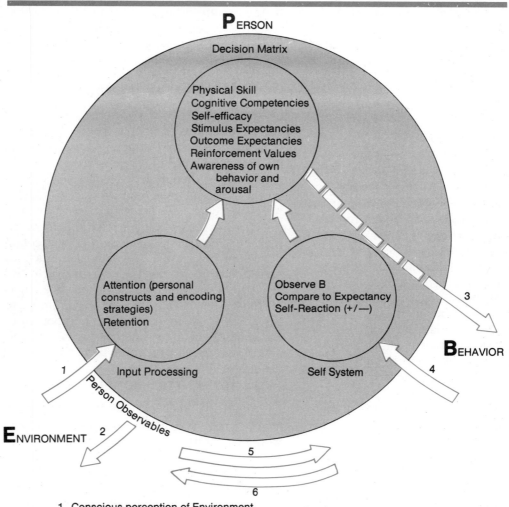

1. Conscious perception of Environment
2. Observable aspects of the Person affect E directly
3. Output Behavior
4. Feedback perception of own B
5. Direct effect of E on B (independent of cognitive processing)
6. B operates on E

woman with her level of class. Rodney can't help thinking, "She must meet hundreds of guys — What would she see in me?" Rodney concludes that he will have to say something impressive to win her over, and so he mentions that he is on his way to football practice. Then he relates a story about how he and his buddies got wild and drunk after the last game. But Rodney was so nervous that he left out some of the key details. He realized he had flubbed the story, and he thought to himself, "You idiot, you're blowing it." He then noticed that although Rebecca hadn't laughed at his story, she was still attentive. Rodney decided to end the awkwardness and see whether she was interested in seeing him again. She accepted, and this marked the beginning of his most memorable high school romance.

Before reading further, you may want to try your hand at analyzing this story from a social learning point of view.

1. For Rodney, Rebecca's appearance and smile are environmental events that enter through his conscious perception and are processed and encoded in terms of his personal construct, "good looking versus nothing special." Placing her in the "good looking" category immediately generates favorable stimulus and outcome expectancies, and so he decides to "make his move" (behavior).

2. The unseen curb is a part of the environment that affects Rodney's behavior directly, without being input through conscious perception.

3. Rodney's green hair is an observable person variable that affects the environment by causing Rebecca to be "put off" and pretend not to notice him.

4. Rodney's friendly behavior affects the environment (Rebecca's behavior) by putting her at ease.

5. Rodney notices his state of arousal and attributes it to Rebecca. This increases the projected reinforcement value of her being his girl friend (stimulus expectancy).

6. But this same awareness of high arousal lowers Rodney's self-efficacy for getting Rebecca to fall for him. Consistent with low self-efficacy, Rodney also begins negative self-talk, "What would she see in me?"

7. From his repertoire of possible responses, Rodney calculates a favorable outcome expectancy: If he can present himself as being in a high-status stereotype (football player), then she will want to go out with him.

8. But Rodney's high arousal interferes with his usual verbal skill. In accordance with the self-system, Rodney observes his behavior of telling the story, compares it with other times when he has tried to impress others, and realizes it is inadequate. Consequently he becomes dissatisfied with himself and changes his behavior, giving up the strategy of "impressive storytelling."

9. Rebecca's continued interest enters as consciously perceived input stimuli, raising the positive outcome expectancy of asking her out directly. The prospect of decreasing the aversive stimulus of a continuing encounter in which Rodney is unsure of her attraction to him also supports this decision (through negative reinforcement).

10. Rebecca's acceptance is an environmental event input through conscious perception.

Describe the "boy meets girl" interaction of the psychoanalytic model using social learning theory. In what ways does it increase your understanding to see the same interaction analyzed from several perspectives?

HUMANISTIC THEORY

ORIGIN OF THE BASIC MODEL

Humanistic psychology, as formulated by Abraham Maslow and developed by Carl Rogers, started as a reaction against the more traditional models of personality. Maslow maintained that the behavioristic tendency to view people only as objects, that is, as complex machines, was inappropriate, for it ignored the reality that people are also conscious, experiencing

Abraham H. Maslow.

subjects. He thought that the scientific, deterministic approach to psychology had forsaken the whole person. Somehow, the uniqueness of the individual had been lost in the search for general laws.

Maslow also disagreed with psychoanalytic emphases on animal impulses, unconscious motivations, irrational thought, and the reduction of all behavior to the drives of sex and aggression. Whereas psychoanalytic theory begins with the observation that we are, after all, mammals, humanistic theory focuses on the qualities that set us apart from animals.

In Maslow's view, the traditional models were based on a paradox: Although most people were assumed normal, traditional theorists often studied abnormals, using them as the prototypes for a general psychology. Maslow, on the other hand, was intrigued by the question of what lay beyond normal adjustment. Could it be said that some people are healthier, more evolutionarily advanced, or in some way better biological "specimens" than others? Is there a path of psychological growth that each of us can follow in our own way, a path that goes beyond the limits of ordinary adjustment?

Humanistic psychology was thus established on the following principles (Tageson, 1982):

1. The experiencing person is of primary interest. The data of psychology should center on the conscious experience of the healthy individual.
2. Meaningfulness should precede objectivity in the choice of research topics. Maslow believed that the behaviorists' fascination with methodology resulted in the precise investigation of inconsequential events—a psychology of rat running, eye blink responses, and nonsense syllables.
3. Topics such as choice, self-actualization, love, and creativity should replace the exclusive focus on the abnormal, maladaptive, and problematic.
4. Value should be placed on the dignity and worth of the individual. The attempts to reduce people to biological drives or environmental influences have wrongly denigrated the way we view ourselves.

VALUES AND ASSUMPTIONS

Maslow argued against a "value-free" or morally neutral philosophy of science, maintaining that this was not possible in psychology. For example, he called into question the goals of prediction and control, asking, "What good is it to give more effective control to evil people?" In this regard, Maslow took a dramatic and controversial step by naming his concept of psychological health, **self-actualization**, as the defining characteristic of the "good person." Moreover, he named the task of science as discovering how to produce these individuals. Maslow reasoned that just as biologists select the best plant or animal specimens for research, psychologists should study the most healthy individuals. In this way, we can find out what we are capable of becoming. (The specific characteristics of self-actualizers are examined in Chapter 13.)

Several controversial assumptions underlie Maslow's theory. First, he assumes that the characteristics of self-actualization are universal. However, if self-actualizing traits such as altruism, democratic values, or nonhostile humor were found to be culture specific, it would be difficult to argue that they reflect essential features of human nature. As a result, the importance of self-actualization would be greatly diminished. Second, Maslow assumes that self-actualizing traits go together, that some people show many of these desirable characteristics. At first glance, this seems to violate cherished democratic ideals. Instead of assuming that each of us has our own good and bad points but that these balance out, making us more or less "equal," Maslow's value orientation is essentially elitist. It suggests that some people are better examples of what it means to be a human being than are others. In Maslow's defense, there is no privilege that goes with self-actualization, only responsibility. And his goal is the use of scientific methods to enhance the possibility that each of us could become more actualized.

THE EXPERIENTIAL FIELD

Carl Rogers, the founder of person-centered therapy, maintains that our perception of "reality" is highly subjective and individualistic. Each of us operates within our own subjective reality; we react to the world as perceived, not to the world as it "is." Rather than portraying the person as something that interacts with an objective external environment, in accordance with social learning theory, Rogers deals directly with reality as experienced. The **experiential field** includes the events going on around us of which we are aware; our memories; the awareness of our own cognitions, feelings, and behaviors; and events that are **subceived**, that is, perceived by the organism but only vaguely represented in consciousness. One way of interpreting Rogers's theory is that what we are in our totality is the entire experiential field, not just the

small part of it with which we consciously identify.

THE ACTUALIZING TENDENCY

Rogers explains the full range of human behavior as stemming from one major innate tendency: the drive to actualize, maintain, and enhance the experiencing organism. Rogers described this **actualizing tendency** as the "forward thrust of life," the tendency to grow at both physiological and psychological levels. An illustration he cited is that of a young child learning to walk. Despite the punishment of repeated falls and stumbling movements, children inevitably persist in their clumsy attempts until locomotion is mastered, until they fulfill their biological potential as moving creatures. Actualization is a reflection within the individual of the evolutionary tendency of life forms to move toward greater complexity, sophistication, and consciousness. In counseling, the actualizing tendency finds expression in the assumption that given a supportive environment, we can cure ourselves; we automatically move in a growth-enhancing direction.

THE HIERARCHY OF NEEDS

Maslow views the actualizing tendency as a set of motives arranged in a hierarchy from the most basic, which are concerned with maintenance and survival, to the most elevated, which involve the enhancement and fulfillment of the organism. In general, once a more basic motive is relatively satisfied, the person naturally pursues the motive at the next highest level.

The most basic level includes physiological needs such as food, water, warmth, and sex. Next come the needs of safety, security, and the avoidance of pain and anxiety. Then are the needs for belonging, love, and affection, followed by those for esteem, respect, and competence. Maslow considered these four levels of motivation to be basic or deficiency based. For example, if we don't feel good about ourselves, we will seek accomplishments that can be used to bolster our self-esteem. In this way, the lack of self-esteem becomes a motivator of behavior.

In contrast, Maslow's highest level, self-actualization, involves self-expression, that is, behavior performed for its own sake, not as a means for obtaining something else such as money, approval, love, respect, or other external rewards. At the self-actualizing level, behavior occurs in the service of values such as truth, beauty, understanding, wholeness, goodness, justice, simplicity, order, perfection, and aliveness. Note that because of its motivational emphasis, the humanistic model is more concerned with why you do something than with what you do. The same behavior could be an expression of any level of motivation, depending on its reason for being performed.

Perhaps the inherent optimism of the humanistic model is best seen in the assumption that, at the level of self-actualization, what is desired by the individual is also best for society. For self-actualizers, there is no conflict between the desires of the individual and the needs of the group. Recall that the presence of antisocial instincts was the primary determinant of the Freudian model's pessimism. Maslow's claim is that although some degree of selfishness, for example, may be present in deficiency-motivated people, this type of functioning is not characteristic of self-actualizers. Moreover, this is not because actualizers hide their antisocial impulses or hold them more strongly in check but because these impulses have been transcended.

In other words, humanistic theorists maintain that both self-preservative and prosocial motives are instinctual but that because the self-preservative motives have already been gratified, the prosocial motives are the ones predominantly active in self-actualizers. Moreover, tendencies to manifest antisocial emotions, such as hostility and jealousy, are not basic drives. Rather, they result from the frustration of positive drives such as those for love, security, and belonging. So, whereas Freud would say that antisocial motives must be either expressed or repressed, humanists would argue that they are triggered only when environmental conditions have hindered basic need gratification.

THE NEED FOR LOVE AND ACCEPTANCE

Rogers maintains that everyone has a need for love and acceptance. (This corresponds to the two highest levels of deficiency motivation in Maslow's hierarchy.) According to Rogers, if this need is not met, one's energies will become directed toward gaining love and acceptance rather than toward actual growth. Attempts to gain love and acceptance then take precedence over activities that would contribute more directly to personal fulfillment. In other words, the individual becomes geared toward security and defense rather than toward growth.

Rogers claims that the way in which love and acceptance are administered, particularly in childhood, strongly affects future development. If we receive a conditional love, that is, if we are loved and accepted when being "good," but not when being "naughty," we will form a rule of what conditions we must satisfy to be worthy of love and acceptance. Typically, this rule encompasses behavior that is polite, respectful, nonsexual, and nonaggressive. Moreover, as children, we internalize the values and attitudes of our parents. We adopt the same attitude toward ourselves that our parents adopted toward us. Thus we form a conception of what we must be like in order to love, accept, and feel good about ourselves.

Since we desperately need love and acceptance and since we feel that we deserve it only when we're "being good," we tend to deny and distort experience so that we can believe that we are deserving of love. In this way, we can still feel good about ourselves. Thus we selectively attend to our acceptable experiences or distort unacceptable experiences so that they seem positive. When this is done, we are not open to all of our experiencing, to all that we actually are, and so the actualization tendency is inhib-

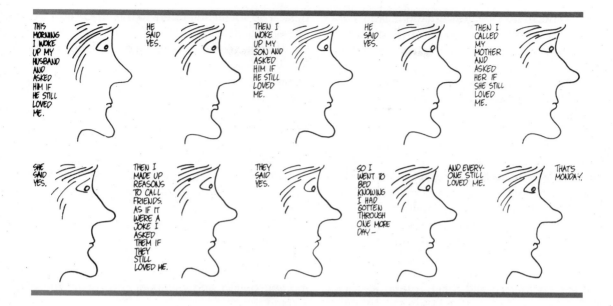

ited. On the other hand, if we receive unconditional love, if we can feel loved and accepted regardless of our behavior, there is no need to distort or deny experience, and actualization is optimized. Unfortunately, very few of us grow up experiencing unconditional love. Thus a major theme in humanistic psychology is learning how to accept yourself.

TWO TYPES OF VALUES

Rogers offered the following scenario of childhood development: Initially, the child is loved by its parents and experiences itself as good and lovable. The child finds many behaviors to be pleasurable, such as excreting, breaking toys, and perhaps hitting baby brother. At first, the pleasurable expression of these behaviors is presumably accompanied by positive feelings of self-worth. As these behaviors are not yet experienced as "bad," there is no conflict between the pleasure of these behaviors and the experience of oneself as lovable. However, parents inevitably try to control behaviors they disapprove of. The child often experiences the parents' reaction as carrying the message "only a

bad boy would hit his baby brother" or "I don't love you when you hit your brother." At such times, the child experiences the temporary withdrawal of love.

When this happens, the child reacts to the threatened loss of parental love by in some way denying responsibility for the troubling behavior. For example, the child may justify his behavior by altering his perception of what happened. He may come to believe, for example, that "He started it." Another way of denying responsibility (and thus symbolically winning back parental love) is to deny the desire or intent of the behavior. For example, "I didn't mean to" or "I was just playing."

From Rogers's experiential viewpoint, the crucial factor in determining how the parents' behavior affects the child is not what the parents meant to convey by their reaction, nor even what unbiased observers would agree had been said; rather, the only issue is what the child experiences.

Rogers reminds us how dependent children are on their parents. In identifying with the parents to ensure parental love, children adopt the same attitudes toward their own behavior that their parents manifested toward them. If the parents cannot love them when they hit baby brother, they cannot love themselves either. Moreover, children often do not distinguish between the *desire* and the deed, and so they may withhold self-love even when their overt behavior is acceptable.

Rogers distinguished between two fundamentally different types of values. We begin life with a direct, unlearned, natural experiencing. Our bodies automatically know what "they" like and do not like. Through normal socialization, we also acquire learned values from our parents, other authority figures, and peer groups. If these **learned values** can be distinguished in experience from **natural values**, so that we know what we want, compare it with what society wants, and make a rational decision from there, these learned values will merely aid our adjustment. *The problem with learned values is that once established, they tend to be experienced as natural; that is, we often can no longer distinguish between what we really want and what we have been led to believe that we want because of our fear that love and acceptance will be taken away.*

Because of this, we may feel out of touch with what we really are. We distort and falsify natural experiences so that we can continue to believe that we are having experiences consistent with our learned values. The child comes to believe "I don't like hitting baby brother; I didn't mean to do it."

The paradox, according to Rogers, is that at an even deeper level, we really are this good person that we want to believe we are.

CONGRUENCE

The humanistic model views the person as composed of three related selves. The **real self** refers to all that you actually are as a biological organism. The real self includes subceptions as well as conscious perceptions, thus it must be partly inferred. The **conscious self** refers to all self-experiences available to conscious aware-

ness. The **social self** refers to the image that we present to others.

Rogers defined **congruence** as the degree of overlap among these three selves. Thus we can distinguish between two types of congruence: that between real self and conscious self and that between conscious self and social self. Rogers considers both essential to psychological health and sees the self-actualizing person as one who is in a state of overall congruence.

Interestingly, congruence not only defines the goal of psychological health but its process as well. Congruent people induce congruence in others. Thus Rogers views congruence as an essential attribute of the good therapist. It also forms the basis for a Rogerian vision of utopia: a society of congruent individuals, each enhancing the health and personal growth of those around them.

Given the desirability of congruence, it is worth wondering, "Why is it so rare?" What are your speculations? Perhaps this question is easier to answer when rephrased, "Why is incongruence so popular?"

First, the incongruence between real self and conscious self allows us to avoid unpleasant truths about ourselves. Also, it keeps us from having to change a rigid self-image. One reason for the incongruence between conscious self and social self is that by pretending to have certain beliefs and values, we can often qualify for others' approval, money, or other external rewards. Also, incongruence can buffer the hurt we feel from another's rejection or disapproval, since we can believe, "They didn't reject me, just my act." Finally, incongruence may play an important social role in allowing us to be tactful, protecting other people's feelings. Those who are uncompromisingly blunt inevitably hurt the feelings of those who do not seek the complete truth.

On the other hand, Rogers sees definite drawbacks to a life of incongruence. To the extent that the real and conscious selves are incongruent, we never know who we really are. We never understand ourselves, and our potential for growth and health becomes limited. (Note, however, it is quite possible for incongruent people to view themselves as "happy and successful.")

To the extent that our conscious and social selves are incongruent, another's approval will not be as satisfying, since part of us experiences the truth that others are not approving of what we are, only of what we have pretended to be. In addition, projecting a false image of ourselves is stressful. The constant calculation and self-monitoring that this entails makes it difficult just to relax and enjoy ourselves. Because of this, incongruence prevents spontaneity and makes creativity difficult. The fear of "slipping up" and contradicting our social image restrains all of our behavior.

FREE WILL AND DETERMINISM

Humanists go beyond psychoanalytic and learning theorists in espousing some area of freedom for the individual. Rogers suggested that from the perspective of a third person, the behaviors of others do appear to be determined by earlier genetic and environmental events. But for Rogers, this description is incomplete, since it ignores a person's experiential field. Subjectively, we feel ourselves to have some free will, some ability to override past influences and change the course of our lives. Though this experiential freedom is certainly acknowledged by psychoanalytic and learning theorists, they dismiss it as an illusion. But for Rogers's experiential model, the third-person perspective cannot be viewed as more real than that of the first-person. Thus he would argue that subjective freedom is an essential component of human life that cannot be dismissed or explained away.

EXISTENTIAL PSYCHOLOGY

Existentialists extend the humanistic interest in free will by exploring what makes us different from other creatures. What does it mean to live a human existence? Because of our ca-

pacity for conscious awareness, we are the creators of meaning. We are continually trying to make sense of the world around us. Thus our nature is always to be "in process." As meanings unfold to form the fabric of our existence, we are continually emerging, becoming something new each instant.

As conscious creatures, we inevitably form an image of who we are. We see ourselves as different from others and separate from the environment. But with this awareness of self comes a feeling of being cut off from physical reality and from the creatures around us. Many modern people see themselves as separate objects in a dead, mechanical, and uncaring universe. This is the ultimate source of what existentialists consider the central problem of modern life. This is the problem of **alienation**, experiencing ourselves as cut off from our inner vitality, cut off from the world around us.

Much of this alienation can be linked to the inherent duality of our language. For example, when we say, "Jack hit the ball," it is assumed that the person and the environment are different. Although they may affect each other, they are separated by an impenetrable boundary. Similarly, the statement "I feel my toe" implies a duality between mind and body.

Existential theorists oppose the dualities of person and environment, mind and body, subject and object. They maintain that in the realm of direct experience, there is no duality, just a continuous flow of experiences. Moreover, they claim that the life-sapping effects of alienation can be remedied only by finding a way to experience our world nondualistically.

To this end, existentialists have taken great pains to manipulate language into forms that might help us experience a nondualistic reality. For example, human existence is described as **being-in-the-world**. "Being" is used here as a verb, not as a noun. Since we are always in process, we are "being" or "becoming." This is different from thinking of ourselves as "beings," or fixed objects that exist in the world. Note the connecting hyphens in being-in-the-world.

These draw our attention to the perception that even though "being" and "world" are written as two separate words, they do not have to be experienced as two separate entities.

Quite naturally, most of us find these ideas tremendously confusing. Presumably this is because we have been taught to identify with the being that is an object in the world, not with the process of being-in-the-world.

Existentialists tend to go even further than humanists in espousing free will. They maintain that since we are not constrained to view ourselves as objects, we can bring to bear a radical free choice at every moment that we are truly conscious. Because of consciousness, we do not have to react in accordance with habitual patterns.

In other words, from the viewpoint of direct experience, causality is not part of external reality. Rather, it is a construct, something made up, a fabrication of the conceptualizing mind trying to make sense out of the flow of experience. Thus causality is an ordering of objects. As such, it applies to us only to the extent that we choose to experience ourselves as objects. This is not to say that we are without limitations. But within certain physical and social limits, we have the freedom and the responsibility to choose the meanings that we will place on the events of experience. Similarly, we have some freedom to select the behaviors that will express those meanings.

Despite its strong emphasis on free will, existentialism is less optimistic than humanistic theory. The exercise of our freedom to choose is seen as a fearsome responsibility. Since there is no God-given meaning "out there" to be discovered, we must create our own, we must decide upon our own values. We cannot look to authority figures to tell us what to do, what to believe in, for this would deny our own free will. There is no authority beyond our own consciousness. Thus existentialists view life as a constant struggle to avoid the tempting but cowardly retreat to authority, conformity, prepackaged belief systems, and self-righteous ideologies. The alterna-

tive is to exercise the "courage to be," the courage to face anxiety, uncertainty, and death. The challenge is to affirm our own personal meaning of life, despite the possibility of its total meaninglessness in any absolute sense.

APPLYING THE MODEL

Figure 2–3 presents the humanistic model. It is assumed that we cannot be aware of everything that our physical organism experiences, and so the conscious self is smaller than the real self. Similarly, the social self cannot represent everything about ourselves of which we are aware, simply because we think faster than we can act. When congruent, the conscious self is an accurate representation of the real self, and the social self accurately represents the conscious self. The driving or motivating force in personality is the gratification of inherent needs.

The workings of the humanistic model can be illustrated by again returning to the theme of boy meets girl. Connie is a high school senior living at home with her parents. They have provided her with the material comforts of middle-

FIGURE **2–3**
THE HUMANISTIC MODEL

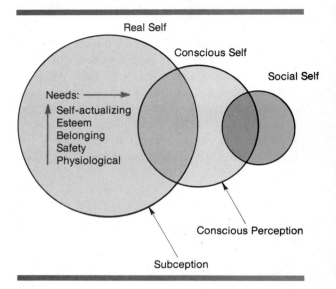

class life, so that her physiological and safety needs are satisfied. Her needs for love and esteem, however, have not been met. She often feels like a stranger in her own home. Her parents seem to be so busy with their own social lives that they just don't have the time to listen to or even to care about what she does. What little attention she does get occurs only when she "goofs up," when she is incompetent, or when she makes jokes at her own expense. Consequently, she has internalized the rule, "I am lovable only when being inept or inferior."

Connie has just met Carl at a party. She perceives Carl as an attractive, intelligent guy who holds a lot of potential as a future dating partner. At a less-conscious level, however, she is vaguely aware that he is not really so bright and that what he says is rather boring and predictable. In terms of her natural reactions, she is both enjoying the attention of his somewhat self-centered conversation and, at a less-conscious level, feeling bored and uneasy. Part of their conversation follows:

Connie: *I hear that you're interested in cars.*
Carl: *Oh yeah, I mean you should see it. I've got this original '57 Chevy. I got a real steal on it. It's so out of sight that I can't describe it enough.*
Connie: *Sounds like a terrific car. I don't even have one—I still have to ask my parents to drive me places. . . . What color is it?*
Carl: *It's funny you ask, really, 'cause I just had it painted two months ago. Actually, I helped paint it myself. It's pure midnight metallic blue. You won't believe it, it's so out of sight, totally. Really, I'll have to take you for a ride in it sometime.*
Connie: *That would be great! I know I'd just love it. You seem to know a lot about cars.*

At the level of her conscious self, Connie is aware that she is interested in Carl and wants him to ask her out. The boredom and dissatisfaction with Carl, which are also part of her natural reaction (real self), however, are not being symbolized in consciousness, perhaps because of her pressing need to find a loving relationship (real self). Although she doesn't really have any interest in cars, she feigns enthusiasm as a way of getting Carl interested in her (social self). Thus Connie is showing incongruence between her real and conscious selves and between her conscious and social selves.

In what way is Connie showing both forms of incongruence? How do you think this dialogue might go if Connie were still attracted to Carl but functioning congruently?

INTEGRATING THE MODELS
KELLY'S METATHEORY

Given the diversity of personality theories, we are left with a number of questions. Which theory is true? If none is actually true or right, which is the best? How do the theories relate to one another? Can they be combined into a

George A. Kelly.

supertheory? These issues can be clarified by considering the work of George Kelly.

Kelly developed a **metatheory**, a theory about theories, that can be applied to personality. Kelly maintains that each theory was originally invented to make sense out of a particular part of the world. For example, Freud developed his notions to explain hysterical conversion symptoms such as glove anesthesia; Skinner's theory was originally applied to animal training; and Bandura's theory started with observational learning. If a theory does well in its original area, it will be extended to other phenomena. This process continues until the theory is extended so far from its original focus that it comes up against phenomena for which its description is no longer useful. The theory may simply be unable to make predictions in this area, or the predictions it does make may be inaccurate.

Perhaps you are wondering, "But why must a theory run out of utility? Why can't there be a theory that is a 'true' representation and thus always accurate?" Recall that a theory is like a map and that a map is never the same thing as the territory it represents. Many different maps can be made to represent the same territory, with each map useful for a different purpose. For example, if you are driving, you will want a map of roads and highways. If hiking, you will want a map of trails and waterways. As you add details to the map, it becomes a closer approximation of the territory. But adding too many details will make the map confusing and cumbersome and therefore less useful for its intended purpose.

Kelly's metatheory suggests that models differ in what phenomena they explain best. In other words, they have differing areas of strength and weakness, but no one model is likely to give an optimal explanation for all human behavior and experience. Thus, many models must be considered to get a comprehensive view of human behavior, even though these models will sometimes contradict one another. The degree to which these contradictions cannot be resolved indicates the extent of our current ignorance. Until such resolutions are formulated, however, we have no alternative than

FIGURE 2—4

PERSONALITY THEORIES AND HUMAN NATURE

			Social Learning				
	Humanistic			Psychoanalytic			
good	1	2	4	5	6	7	evil

	Social Learning						
	Humanistic			Psychoanalytic			
rational	1	2	3	4	5	6	7	irrational

					Social Learning		
		Humanistic			Psychoanalytic		
free	1	2	3	4	5	6	7	determined

				Humanistic			
	Psychoanalytic			Social Learning			
affected by heredity	1	2	3	4	5	6	7	affected by environment

to live with the diversity of these models. Though imperfect, they represent the current fruit of our eternal quest for self-understanding.

KEY ASSUMPTIONS ABOUT HUMAN NATURE

Each personality theory makes certain assumptions about what kind of creatures we are. We shall now consider the four dimensions of human nature used in Chapter 1. Psychoanalytic, social learning, and humanistic theories are rated on these dimensions in Figure 2–4. By comparing these ratings with the responses you gave in Chapter 1, you should get a good idea of how your own, implicit, theory of personality compares with the major, explicit, theories. Which theory seems the most compatible with your views? Which seems the least compatible? Although each of us will naturally gravitate toward some models and away from others, don't ignore a model that initially seems incompatible. The perspective of that model may be precisely what you need to balance your own point of view.

EVALUATING THE MODELS

PSYCHOANALYTIC THEORY

Freud's model marked the beginning of the modern era of personality theories, and because of its comprehensiveness and impact, it remains the standard against which all other theories are judged. Psychoanalytic theory has stimulated hundreds of research studies, and although many details of this theory have not been supported, some key features have withstood the test of time and empirical scrutiny. In addition, the scope and genius of Freud's theorizing has elevated our standard of theoretical sophistication, enhancing our ability to think about ourselves. This theory has been more influential than has any other model of personality, both within psychology and throughout society. Its effects can be seen in literature, philosophy, sociology, anthropology, religion, and art.

As Giovacchini (1983) noted, psychoanalytic theory stands or falls on the concept of unconscious motivation. As detailed in Chapter 3, this hypothesis is supported by findings on brain stimulation, posthypnotic suggestion, slips of the tongue, symptom formation, and dream analyses. Recent research (e.g., Silverman, 1982) has used subliminal techniques to alter unconscious conflicts, showing predicted increases or decreases in psychological symptoms. (There is currently an unresolved controversy, however, because of difficulties that some other researchers have had in replicating this effect; see Heilbrun, 1980.)

Reviews of psychoanalytic research (Fisher & Greenberg, 1977; Kline, 1972) conclude that many parts of the theory have been supported, including the existence of "oral" and "anal" personality types, castration anxiety in males, and other aspects of the phallic stage in some males.

Nevertheless, psychoanalytic theory retains a number of problems and limitations. Many of its terms are highly abstract or difficult to measure because they refer to contents outside awareness. Most researchers feel that Freud's emphasis on sexuality, although it may have been accurate for his own, more sexually repressive era, is inappropriate in our culture. Also, Freud's reliance on tension reduction as the only source of motivation was based on an outdated physiology that did not take into account the many ways that we seek increases in stimulation. Finally, Freud's image of human nature assumed that we have the same drives as do lower animals, that we are inherently selfish, greedy, and incapable of true altruism. Most psychologists believe this picture to be unduly pessimistic.

SOCIAL LEARNING THEORY

The social learning model combines the empirical rigor of behaviorism with a focus on human cognition that is currently very popular.

As such, it promises to assume a central position in psychology. Social learning theory rests on a solid base of research support showing the pervasive influence of imitation and the importance of cognitive variables. Its constructs are more clearly defined and open to observation than are those of psychoanalytic theory, making it more amenable to rigorous research. And unlike humanistic theory, it retains determinism while still dealing with self-control.

Social learning theory brings together many different parts of psychology and thus has the potential of representing the mainstream of psychological thought. At the same time, it is a theory that makes few controversial predictions. In many ways, social learning represents a system for organizing common-sense observations. Thus it may have little utility for telling us something new about ourselves. The theory seems particularly strong in dealing with conscious thought processes, decision making, and behavior change. But it has little to say about feelings, mental functioning outside awareness, healthy personality, or instinctual drives. As a full theory of personality, it is clearly deficient, yet it is a vigorous model in the process of being expanded. It will be interesting to see what form it eventually takes.

HUMANISTIC THEORY

The humanistic model is unique in its emphasis on pushing back the limits of human potential and seeking out the methods for encouraging personal growth. Part of its utility is that it speaks to the concerns of most normal people, that is, those who function adequately but seek to function even better. Thus, unlike the psychoanalytic model, which deals mainly with pathology, the humanistic model's concerns are closer to those of most people in our society.

As with the psychoanalytic model, humanistic theory contains many terms that are difficult to measure or test, such as the actualizing tendency. As a result, there is little in the way of systematic research support. Much of humanistic theory is based on informal observations of modern life and the problems encountered in psychotherapy. In addition, some have criticized its image of human nature as unrealistically positive. If we all are essentially good, altruistic, conscious, rational, and free, how do we account for the evil that permeates our nightly news?

Nevertheless, this optimism and resolve to study humans at their best may prove a useful antidote to the negative views of the other models.

SUMMARY

1. Personality theories seek to describe and explain the whole person. They deal with both human nature, what we share with one another, and with individual differences, what sets us apart and makes us unique.
2. Freud's psychoanalytic model is based on the premise that wishes, memories, and impulses outside awareness strongly affect our everyday behavior, even at times when we believe we are conscious and rational. According to Freud, we don't know who we really are, and we are not even in control of our own minds.
3. Freud assumed a complete determinism: All thoughts, behaviors, and symptoms are caused by other events occurring earlier in time.

4. Unconscious processes cannot be observed; they must be inferred, but techniques such as free association and dream analysis aid this inference.

5. The conscious refers to contents of immediate awareness; the preconscious to contents outside awareness over which we have partial control; and the unconscious to contents outside awareness over which we have little or no control.

6. Freud defined three structures of the mind. The id is the mental representative of inherited drives; the ego forms the learned reaction patterns for obtaining instinctual gratification; and the superego is the internalized voice of conscience, our code of right and wrong.

7. Freud viewed personality development as biologically programmed, occurring through oral, anal, phallic, latency, and genital psychosexual stages.

8. According to the psychoanalytic model, the mind is a submerged battleground in which every experience, behavior, or symptom is the result of a compromise among conscious perception, unconscious perception, superego demands, id impulses, repressed wishes and memories, and ego counterwishes.

9. More recent variations on Freud's model involve: decreasing the emphasis on sex and death, viewing the need for spiritual fulfillment as instinctually based, and increasing the power and independence of the ego.

10. Social learning theory's origins stem from behaviorism, the study of relationships between observable behaviors and environmental events.

11. Pavlov's classical conditioning is the pairing of conditioned and unconditioned stimuli so that the occurrence of an unconditioned stimulus alone comes to elicit a conditioned response that approximates the original unconditioned response.

12. Skinner's operant conditioning involves the change in probability of a response after a behavior is followed by reinforcing or aversive stimuli. Relationships between responses and consequent stimuli include positive reinforcement, negative reinforcement, punishment, and extinction.

13. Research on modeling, or imitative learning, has shown that new responses can be learned merely through observation. Modeling occurs in four steps: attention, retention, motor reproduction, and motivation. In Bandura's formulation, modeling is an active, judgmental, symbolic process; humans do not simply mimic whatever they see.

14. Social learning theory distinguishes among stimulus, outcome, and self-efficacy expectancies.

15. According to social learning theory, reinforcement works by giving individuals information about outcome expectancies and by motivating individuals to obtain additional rewards.

16. The self-system controls behavior by observing one's performance,

judging that performance against some criterion, and then having either positive or negative self-reactions to that performance.

17. Reciprocal determinism refers to a mutual causal effect among personal, behavioral, and environmental sources of influence.

18. Humanistic psychology is based on the study of conscious experience, meaningful events, and positive topics, such as love and creativity, and on an affirmation of the individual's dignity.

19. Humanistic psychology emphasizes the study of positive psychological health, or self-actualization.

20. The central motivation for all behavior is assumed to derive from the actualizing tendency, a drive to maintain and enhance the experiencing organism. Maslow conceived this as operating through a hierarchy of needs: physiological, safety, belonging, esteem, and self-actualizing.

21. Rogers maintains that personal growth will be optimized if the individual has received unconditional love and acceptance from significant others.

22. Learned values can cause problems because, once established, it is difficult to differentiate learned from natural values. In other words, we often cannot distinguish between what we really value and what we have been led to believe that we value, because of our fear that love and acceptance will be taken away.

23. Congruence refers to the overlap among the real, conscious, and social selves.

24. Existential psychology notes that because of conscious awareness and our active human mentality, we are always in the process of redefining who we are. This mentality inevitably creates an image of itself. As a result, we tend to split our world of experience into person and environment, mind and body. This dualistic experience has produced a pervading sense of alienation.

25. Kelly's metatheory suggests that models differ in what they explain best. Thus many models must be considered in order to form a comprehensive view of human behavior.

26. Of the three major models, psychoanalytic theory has had the broadest impact on society. Although many of its specific hypotheses have not been supported, the central tenet of unconscious motivation seems to be standing the test of time. Social learning theory is particularly strong in dealing with conscious thought processes, self-control, and behavior change, but it has not yet developed to where it can function as a full theory of personality. Humanistic theory is unique in its emphasis on optimal functioning, although its image of human nature seems unrealistically optimistic.

SUGGESTED READINGS

Bandura, A. **Social learning theory**. Englewood Cliffs, N.J.: Prentice-Hall, 1977. A compact and authoritative statement of the theory.

Freud, S. **Introductory lectures on psychoanalysis**. Standard edition, vols. 15, 16. London: Hogarth Press, 1963/1917. These are Freud's own lecture notes for a class he taught on psychoanalysis. Very readable and charming.

Maslow, A. H. **The farther reaches of human nature**. New York: Viking, 1971. Creative, provocative, and readable.

THE SELF

3

Known and Unknown

This chapter combines elements from the various models of personality to examine consciousness, the attribute that most clearly defines what makes us unique as a species. Yet, what is consciousness, really? It seems to be everywhere, for wherever we look, there it is. But only a little study shows that consciousness is often not as it appears. To see consciousness more clearly, we will contrast it with events outside our awareness. By working back and forth between the conscious self — what is known — and the unconscious self — what is not known — we can piece together a picture of the whole person.

Along the way, we will touch on a number of intriguing questions. How much of our world is seen for what it is, as opposed to being constructed from a fantasy of what we think it should be? Are we biologically programmed to be dishonest? Why do we deceive ourselves? Is it healthy to do this? Is it more important to have a realistic image of ourselves or to have high self-esteem? What is the difference between self-esteem and pride? How can we raise our self-esteem without resorting to deception?

CONSCIOUSNESS: WHAT IT IS AND WHAT IT ISN'T

Consciousness is the act of being aware. Whatever we are aware of in the present moment is the content of consciousness. Thus consciousness is an awareness *of* something, and that something might be an object in the environment, an internal mood, a feeling, a thought, a fantasy image, a memory from the past, or an expectancy for the future.

THE ILLUSION OF CONTINUITY

Julian Jaynes notes that most people see consciousness as

the most self-evident thing imaginable. We feel it is the defining attribute of all our waking states, our moods and affections, our memories, our thoughts, attentions, and volitions. We feel comfortably certain that . . . it records and stores our experiences as they happen, allowing us to introspect on them and learn from them at will. (Jaynes, 1976, p. 21)

Surprisingly, Jaynes contends that all of these assertions are false.

For Jaynes, most of our behavior is a reaction to stimuli of which we are never aware. Moreover, we are unaware of most behavior as it occurs. For example, some people walk in their sleep. They react to events around them and keep from bumping into walls, yet they do not process this information consciously. Similarly, much of our behavior is habitual. There is no need to process consciously each link in a series of oft-repeated behaviors. Driving a car is a common example. A more subtle one is that our eyes shift twenty times a second when seeing an object, yet our awareness contains only the perception of stability. Similarly, our visual system continually makes adjustments based on the size of the retinal image, contrast effects, and perspective, yet we are unaware of this processing.

Jaynes observed, "We cannot be conscious of what we are not conscious of" (1976, p. 23). For him, this truism provides a powerful lever for self-understanding. Consciousness can be compared to a flashlight in a dark room. There is

Julian Jaynes.

no way the flashlight can discover darkness. Everywhere it looks there is light. Thus it is a kind of perceptual bias that leads us to believe that when we are awake, consciousness is continuous. "Certainly this is the feeling. And whatever we're doing, we feel that our very self, our deepest of deep identity, is indeed this continuing flow that only ceases in sleep between remembered dreams" (Jaynes, 1976, p. 24).

Thus, for Jaynes, this continuity is an illusion. This can be illustrated by the so-called blind spot in the perceptual field. At the point where optic nerve fibers leave the retina is a two-millimeter gap. Ordinarily, we do not perceive a gap in our visual fields, but this everpresent blind spot can be demonstrated under special conditions. Jaynes argues that just as this gap in the spatial field is smoothed over to yield a seamless picture of the world, time gaps in consciousness are automatically smoothed over to create an illusion of continuity.

THE INVENTION OF MEMORY

In a similar vein, conscious memory is hardly ever a literal playback of past conscious images. Jaynes maintains that memory is largely an invention, elaboration, and reworking of past images into plausible patterns. For example, think back to the last time you were swimming. What do you see? Most people "recall" an invented image of themselves in the water, viewed as a spectator would have seen them, not the feel and look of the water at eye level.

Finally, Jaynes claims that even the process of thinking is often not conscious. Consider the sequence 2, 4, 6, 8, ——. What is the next number? How did you arrive at the answer? Jaynes believes that what was actually in awareness were the instruction to find the next number, the sequence of numbers, and the answer, which simply "appeared." Typically, the thoughts that produce the answer are not conscious. In trying to describe these thoughts, however, what appears in consciousness is an invention of what you think those thoughts must have been in order for your answer to make sense.

MINDLESSNESS

Langer (1982), coming from an experimental framework, arrived at a similar conclusion, that an unexpectedly large part of our behavior is carried out "mindlessly," without consciousness. Once individuals have learned a response thoroughly or defined the situation as "routine," there is little conscious processing and little recall of detail. For example, Langer found that most people have no concrete sense of the physical appearance of people that they know. Do these acquaintances wear glasses? What is the color of their eyes? Their hair? As long as the acquaintances look "normal," they are perceived mindlessly. One implication of Langer's work is that individuals differ in how mindfully they approach everyday life, and her research indicates that mindful people actually live longer.

PROCESSING OUTSIDE AWARENESS

Everything about us not in awareness is, by definition, unconscious. It is important to recognize the special character of unconscious functioning. We cannot become directly aware of an unconscious content. Once something enters awareness it is conscious, and whatever form it had before entering awareness can never be known with certainty. This "slippery" nature of unconscious functioning is one of the main reasons for its controversial status in psychology. As you can imagine, the problems in measuring something that can never be directly observed are formidable.

EVIDENCE FOR UNCONSCIOUS FUNCTIONING

Unconscious contents can be approached only by an inference from conscious experiences. And although there are measurement strategies based on such patterns of inference,

Because of a processing delay in the brain, sprinters respond to the starting gun before they consciously hear it.

FOCUS

HYPNOSIS AND UNCONSCIOUS MOTIVATION

Hypnosis is characterized by a narrowing of attention, a passivity in which actions are not initiated by the subject, high suggestibility to the hypnotist's directives, and selective amnesia for what transpires, especially if given suggestions for posthypnotic amnesia.

Hypnosis provides one of the strongest demonstrations of unconscious motivation. Under hypnosis, individuals can be told to complete an activity without recalling the directive to complete it. The carrying out of the directive in the waking state shows how behavior can be caused by factors of which the subject is completely unaware.

Milton Erickson (1939), a master hypnotherapist, recounted such an example. Under hypnosis the subject was given the conflicting suggestions that (1) smoking is a bad habit that should be stopped and that (2) he nevertheless would find himself compelled to smoke. In addition, he was told he would not remember these suggestions after awakening. How do you think such a conflict might be manifested in actual behavior?

After awakening, the subject began checking his pockets for a cigarette. But instead of checking his customary pocket, he seemed to forget where he kept his cigarettes and exasperatedly checked all his other pockets first. After finally locating his cigarettes, he went through a similar routine trying to find his matches. Again, he finally found them in his usual pocket. But by now his cigarettes were again misplaced, and so the procedure of checking each pocket had to be repeated yet another time. When the cigarettes were located, the matches somehow disappeared once more. When he finally placed the cigarette in his mouth and lit a match, the subject became so engrossed in his conversation with the therapist that he burned his fingers!

---

they have generally not fared well in terms of traditional test construction criteria. However, even though it is difficult to describe the precise nature of unconscious contents and processes, their existence seems undeniable.

Mckean (1985) described some fascinating nonpsychoanalytic evidence for unconscious functioning. For example, if a word is presented too briefly to be recognized consciously, people can still guess at it, suggesting words with related meanings. If the word *queen* is presented, you may guess *king*. This suggests that the word is already being processed and analyzed before it reaches consciousness. In addition, evidence indicates that the brain has a processing

delay of about half a second between receiving a stimulus and its entering consciousness. A corrective mechanism adjusts for this time lag so that we don't feel as though we're living a half second in the past. For example, if asked to flick your fingers, brain activity associated with the flick occurs half a second before the conscious decision to flick. Similarly, sprinters respond to the starting gun within one-tenth of a second, but they do not become aware of the gun sound for five-tenths of a second. Thus they begin running unconsciously and only later become aware that the gun has fired. Their experience, however, is backtracked so that it feels as if they heard the gun before starting.

THE INFERENCE TO UNCONSCIOUS PROCESSES

The most common strategy for identifying unconscious contents involves examining experiences produced when conscious control is relaxed. These experiences often reveal a side of ourselves quite different from what our conscious functioning reveals. Because of this, relatively unconscious products have the potential to complete and balance our self-image. Dreams, for example, are often violent, heroic, and sexual in ways that our waking lives are not. Yet, it cannot be denied that they are parts of ourselves. Impulsive actions may be later regretted, yet their occurrence tells us something about who we are (that they are regretted tells us something about who we would like to be). The same is true for slips of the tongue, free associations, and fantasy productions.

How do we know when to invoke unconscious motivations to explain behavior? Because unconscious factors are always inferential, and therefore somewhat speculative, they should be invoked only when explanations in terms of relatively conscious events seem inadequate. For example, when a person's behavior leads to unintended consequences that cannot be explained by other causes, then a hypothesis of unconscious motivation should be entertained.

KNOWING MORE THAN YOU "KNOW": A CASE HISTORY

This case (adapted from Erickson & Kubie, 1938) is a fascinating illustration of how unconscious processes appear to have intentions that operate independently of consciousness.

THE CLIENT

Ann, a twenty-four-year-old female, had become increasingly worried, unhappy, and depressed during the past month, despite being unaware of any particular problem. She was an only child from a happy family, and her adjustment to college had been excellent until the preceding month. Recently she had become interested in symbolism and developed a habit of scribbling or doodling while occupied in various activities. She viewed this as a jittery habit that was objectionable because it "dirtied the walls of telephone booths, tablecloths, and clean paper in her notebooks."

The only personal problem she could name was a gradual separation from her girlhood friend Jane. This separation had taken place over the past few years, beginning when Ann started college. However, the girls did see each other on weekend visits at the home of Ann's parents. During the preceding few weeks Ann felt increasingly lonely, resentful, and angry over the loss of this friendship.

THE INTERVENTION

In the first session, Ann was placed in a light hypnotic trance and given the suggestion that in the next session she would continue her doodles but that they would form an intelligible communication of the underlying problem.

At the next visit Ann remarked that she had lost conscious interest in her problem and had returned only to keep the appointment. She was asked to continue talking and was given pencil and paper for doodling. At one point she relaxed but tightened her grip on the pencil, as if she wanted to lay it down but was unable to do so. The therapist quietly suggested that she keep on writing, and she immediately remarked, "Oh yes, I know where I am, I just lost the thread of the story for a moment," and continued the narrative. At the same time, her hand took a fresh grip on the pencil and she started a new drawing, one that seemed more orderly and systematic than the others. (This picture is reproduced in Figure 3–1.)

Upon completing the picture she tore it from the pad and gave it to the therapist, leaving her hand in a writing position as if waiting for something. The therapist inferred an unconscious desire to make a secret comment and suggested:

FIGURE **3-1**

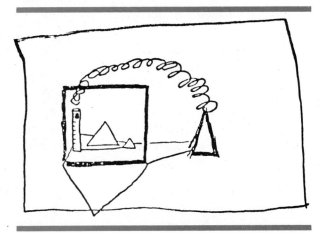

"A short, vertical line means 'yes,' a short horizontal line means 'no.' " Ann seemed confused, saying that she saw no such lines.

The therapist asked, "Is it all there?" She replied, "Well, I suppose if anything is there, everything is," and without awareness, she signaled yes with a short vertical stroke. She asked, "Do you mean to say you can make any sense out of the scratching?" Apparently in answer to her own question, her hand signaled yes again.

Ann mentioned having an urge to give the therapist something. Pointing at the shaded triangle, she threw down a packet of matches from a local hotel. She then said she had to leave but was persuaded to make a few comments on the drawing first.

> "Two pictures in frames; a large one,"— pointing to the rectangle—"and a small one,"—pointing to the square—"with the corner broken." Pointing to the figures in the square, she said, "These are all connected and the connections between the little one"— pointing to the small triangle—"and that"— indicating the cylinder—"is a cigarette with smoke. We all smoke in our family, maybe those are father's matches I gave you. But the whole thing makes no sense at all."

INCREASING TENSION

Three weeks later Ann returned "to report progress," commenting, "I have a feeling that I am getting ready to know something I already know, but don't *know* I know." Two weeks later she appeared, looked at the drawing, and said,

> Really, it still looks like a mess of nothing. I just know it's the whole story, too; but why I say that, I don't know. Yet I am sure that my subconscious knows a lot that it [doesn't] tell me. I have a feeling that it is just waiting for my conscious mind to prepare itself for a shock and it's just making me darned curious so I won't mind the shock.

A week later she came in and said that she was upset about seeing Jane that night for dinner at the hotel. She explained:

> I hate to see our friendship broken up just by drifting apart the way we have. And I don't like my attitude toward Jane. You see, Jane's a year younger than I, and she has a boyfriend and is pretty much in love with him. She says she thinks I know him but she won't tell me his name or anything about him. . . . I'm so jealous that I just hate her intensely; I'd like to pull her hair out. I hate her because I feel as if

she had taken my boyfriend away from me, but that's silly, because I haven't got a boyfriend. I know I'm going to quarrel with her. . . . I don't want to, but it's going to happen and I can't avoid it. And another thing: after I quarrel with her, I'm going to have a fight with my father. I've been working up to this for a week. I've only had two fights with my father and they were both about my college plans; I don't know what this fight's going to be about. Probably some little thing like his carelessness in smoking and dropping ashes on the rug at home.

The next day she reported that she had been cruel and mocking with Jane at dinner and that she had enjoyed making Jane cry. In addition, after going home she picked a fight with her father. She began smoking and pacing the floor, and when her father told her to sit down, she screamed that she "could run around if she wanted to and that she had just as much right to run around as he did."

THE INTERPRETATION

The next day she came to the office, determined to understand the drawing. When nothing came, she asked for a "starting word" to trigger the understanding. The therapist remarked, "Sometime ago, you told me you were terribly interested in symbolism." As he said this, he dropped the hotel matches on the desk. Ann then burst into a torrent of emotion. (Note: Before reading further, see how much of the story you can piece together on your own.)

The damned nasty filthy little cheater. And she calls herself my friend. She's having an affair with Father. Damn him. Poor Mother. She visits Mother, damn her, and Father acts like a saint around the house, damn him. They go to the hotel, the same hotel Father took us to. I hated her because she took my father away from me—and mother. That's why I always stole his cigarettes. Even when I had some, I'd sneak into the hall and get some out of his coat pocket. Sometimes I'd take the whole package, sometimes only one or two. If she thinks she's going to break up my home, she's got another thought coming, plenty too. The first time she told me about her boyfriend—her boyfriend, huh—she lit her cigarette with those matches. I knew then, but I couldn't believe it. And I used to take Father's matches away from him and I'd get so goddamn mad when he'd tell me to use my own. I didn't want Mother to see those matches, and it didn't make sense then. . . .

Pointing to the various elements of the picture, Ann explained rapidly,

This cigarette is Father, and that big triangle is Mother—she's short and fat and blonde—and the little triangle is me. I'm blonde too. I'm really taller than Mother, but I just feel little to her. You see, those lines all connect us in a family group and the square is the family frame. And that line from Father breaks through the family frame and goes down below the social frame, that's the big square, and then it tries to go back to the family and can't, and so it just goes over to Jane. You see, she is a tall, slender brunette. That smoke from Father's penis curls around Jane. That line between me and Jane is broken where it comes to the family frame. . . . See where I blackened Father's face. It should be. When I gave you those matches, I told you they were connected with Jane, even though I didn't know that was Jane then.

Jane later independently confirmed Ann's suspicions. Also, Ann no longer felt the need to doodle. From the psychoanalytic viewpoint, note that Ann's reaction is one of jealousy, as if Jane had taken her lover from her. This, of course, illustrates Freud's theory of sexual fantasies between children and their opposite-sex parents. Note also that Ann's compulsion to steal her father's cigarettes appears to represent both a punishment for "cheating" and a symbolic castration.

Go back through the case and identify places where Ann's words or behavior revealed an unconscious knowledge of what was going on.

SELF-DECEPTION

Many species employ deception. For example, some fish can inflate themselves, increasing their apparent size and threat, and similarly, some harmless snakes mimic the markings of fearsome, poisonous snakes. Because of our capacity for consciousness, however, we are presumably the only animals that can intentionally deceive, and we are the only animals that can deceive ourselves. As we shall see, self-deception provides a perfect context for observing interactions between the known and unknown selves.

SELF-DECEPTION AND CONSCIOUS ATTENTION

Self-deception involves two manipulations of consciousness: one for evading truth and the other for avoiding the awareness that the truth has been evaded.

Self-deception can be understood within the assumption that we cannot be conscious of all that we are doing and all that is happening around us. The sheer number of external and internal stimuli is such that at any moment, we can be consciously aware of only a small fraction of what we are responding to. As Fingarette (1969, p. 42) noted, "Rather than taking explicit consciousness for granted, we must come to take its absence for granted." Fingarette pointed out that it takes many years of childhood practice to acquire the skill of selectively turning our attention to culturally important stimuli and away from stimuli that are inappropriate or irrelevant. Thus turning one's attention away from an unpleasant truth is quite consistent with other uses of attention.

Fingarette (1969, p. 47) described the self-deceiver as one who is

"unable" to admit the truth to himself (even though he knows in his heart it's so). There is a kind of genuineness to his "ignoring"; it is not simple hypocrisy, or lying, or duping of others. Yet we also feel that in some sense, he *could* admit the truth if only he *would*.

THE CONTENTS OF SELF-DECEPTION

What are these "unpleasant truths" hidden in the dark alleys of potential awareness? An obvious starting place is anything that violates our conscious image of ourselves. Such material, even if positive, can be threatening. For example, those prone to depression often overestimate their failures, avoid new projects, or perform at a level below their actual abilities. But what is the payoff for overestimating failure? Once we believe that we have little chance of success, perhaps the best we can do is avoid new failure. Perceiving ourselves as successful, although pleasant, carries the implication that we should act the way that successful people do. We might then be expected to seek out new challenges. The social learning view suggests that for those with strong expectations of failure, a continued lack of success may be preferred to the prospect of new failure.

Research (Alloy & Abramson, 1979) also indicates that nondepressives may have their own forms of self-deception. These people often overestimate their degree of success and the extent of their personal control over events. This may, however, be a deceptive bias with adaptive rather than debilitating consequences. For example, it may motivate individuals to take on new projects and otherwise put themselves into situations in which they can learn new skills. In the long run, this sort of behavior is adaptive.

In an innovative study of self-deception (Sackeim & Gur, 1978), subjects were given either an easy or a difficult vocabulary test. They were then presented with scrambled audiotapes of people's voices and asked to identify which was their own. Those with the easy items, who therefore experienced success, recognized their own voice more quickly or else erred by identifying another's voice as their own. In other words, after their success, subjects increased their willingness to identify other parts of the world with themselves. After failing on the more difficult items, however, the reverse occurred. Subjects were more likely to err by failing to identify their own voice. This study demonstrates the prevalence of self-deception in normal subjects and shows how sensitive deception is to situational changes. It also shows how readily the sense of self fluctuates with success and failure.

SELF-DECEPTION AND HEALTHY PERSONALITY

What attitude should we take toward self-deception? Is self-deception a learned adaptive skill, or is it only a distortive mechanism that undermines our ability to make sound decisions? Are some types of self-deception adaptive?

The psychoanalytic position is that self-deceptive defenses are necessary for normal functioning, but defenses that minimize distortion are preferred. The humanistic position agrees that "normal functioning," that is, the adjustment level of the hypothetical "average person," contains a good deal of self-deception.

Humanistic theorists suggest, however, that most people have not learned to accept themselves independently of their performance. Although it may be possible for some to function more effectively with self-deceptions (e.g., overestimating their degree of control over events), deception may not be necessary for those who can fully accept themselves.

Given the pervasiveness of self-deception, it is sometimes said that others know us better than we do ourselves. One writer even joked that perhaps we should revise our customary greetings. Thus, when approaching a friend, perhaps we should say, "Hello! You're fine, how am I?"

EGO DEFENSES

One form of self-deception involves the so-called ego defenses. In psychoanalytic theory, the ego is thought to use many different methods to protect itself from excessive stress, threats to self-esteem, and other dangers. Some of these methods occur with such regularity that they have been formally identified as the **ego defense mechanisms**. These mechanisms are defensive because they merely keep the threat from consciousness rather than actively dealing with problems in the environment. And although they operate in the service of consciousness, these methods are not consciously initiated. Instead, they are triggered by unconscious parts of the ego. Thus one does not "try" to invoke ego defenses; they operate automatically, outside the bounds of conscious intent.

The consequences of ego defense include a distortion of internal or external reality and a degree of self-deception. Most psychologists consider the ego defenses among the most useful of the psychoanalytic constructs. By becoming more aware of your own use of defenses, you create opportunities for substituting more adaptive strategies of adjustment.

COMMON DEFENSES

Repression is the most basic defense. In it, threatening impulses, wishes, and feelings are automatically kept from consciousness. Thus, by definition, we have little awareness of either the nature or amount of what is repressed. These contents cannot be made conscious by a mere act of will. They are presumed, however, to gain some access to consciousness when the ego is impaired or relaxed, as when dreaming, extremely fatigued, or intoxicated. Repression, as with all of the other defenses, keeps the individual from experiencing anxiety. Thus, when anxiety does appear, it indicates that the defensive system is faltering.

Do not assume that because repressed material has been banned from consciousness, it has been somehow neutralized or made impotent. Indeed, repressed contents are thought to affect all aspects of behavior, including feelings, social behaviors, dreams, and bodily symptoms. Amnesia is a type of repression in which the blocked content is so massive that it creates a noticeable gap in memory. Signs of excessive repression include rigid, inflexible behavior, a lack of spontaneity, a diminishing zest for life, and low stress tolerance.

Denial is often confused with repression. It refers to blocking out part of external rather than internal reality. An example is a mother who continues feeding her dead baby, refusing to acknowledge that the baby is no longer alive. Denial impairs reality contact and is thus considered one of the most primitive defenses. And since denial implies an unconscious refusal to face many of our real problems, it often hinders adaptive responding. In traumatic situations, denial is often manifested in the thought that "This is not really happening to me." It is, however, considered to have some adaptive role in giving people time to adjust to sudden trauma. For example, it is often used to cope with threats of cancer or heart disease (Levine & Zigler, 1975).

Displacement refers to using a substitute person or object to gratify an impulse. Displacement is commonly seen with impulses of hostility, which are often redirected from a more threatening primary object, like one's boss, to a less-threatening individual (who may be completely innocent or perhaps only guilty by association). Finding a scapegoat for one's frustrations and hostilities is an example of displacement. This defense can be carried on at a societal as well as an individual level, as in Nazi Germany when Jews and homosexuals were the identified scapegoats for an entire nation.

Regression is going back to a reaction pattern characteristic of a less-mature mode of adjustment. For example, after parents divorce, children sometimes regress to bedwetting, pouting, or temper tantrums.

Conversion refers to the transformation of an impulse (usually sexual) into a physical symptom. The symptom symbolically represents and expresses the initial impulse. An example is the paralysis of an arm resulting from an impulse to masturbate. Note that the impulse here is thought to receive partial gratification because of the extra attention directed at the arm. Conversion is rare in modern times, perhaps because of the decrease in sexual repression over the last century.

In **reaction formation** a forbidden impulse is replaced with its opposite. Typically the opposite reaction is carried to excess. Thus repressed hostility may be replaced with suffocating expressions of love and overprotection. Often those who are the most enthusiastic crusaders against pornography, alcohol, smoking, or gambling are those who have been most susceptible to these vices in the past.

In **isolation** a threatening impulse is rendered harmless by allowing it to enter consciousness stripped of its feeling tone and emotional impact. Thus violent thoughts may be coolly entertained without anxiety. Out of a

An adult showing the defense of regression by pouting.

fear of being hurt, we may enter relationships but keep ourselves from ever falling in love. Or on a more adaptive note, isolation may be used in traumatic situations to act decisively, without emotional disruption.

Undoing is acting out an unacceptable impulse followed by a ritual of atonement. Examples are the use of a bathing ritual after sex to banish feelings of uncleanliness, or an unscrupulous businessman's compulsion to contribute large sums of money to charity.

In **introjection** some part of the external world is internalized and kept intact in the psyche. For example, the loss of a child, especially if the parent and child were estranged, might be defended against by preserving the memory of the child, perhaps by keeping the child's room intact and untouched for years. As part of their normal development, children introject the values of their parents. At a later stage, adolescents are expected to reexamine these values and make a more conscious choice for themselves.

Identification, which can be viewed as a milder form of introjection, refers to adopting the traits, behaviors, or other characteristics of another. This can allow us to bask in the reflected glory of a hero with which we identify or to protect ourselves by "joining forces" with a feared aggressor.

Projection is the opposite of introjection. Here something unacceptable about the self is attributed unknowingly to someone else. Dishonest individuals may be blinded to their own transgressions yet be highly sensitive to those of others. One of the most common projective patterns is the tendency to deal with your own problems by blaming them on others. This pattern gets you off the hook in the short run, but it inhibits effective action by placing the responsibility, and hence the control, of the problem outside oneself.

Compensation refers to unconsciously balancing a perceived weakness by developing or emphasizing a perceived strength. Compensation has adjustive value when the new

Identification is often used to enhance self-esteem.

trait serves a desirable function, as when someone with a speech defect becomes an accomplished orator. However, compensation often takes maladaptive forms, as in showing off to overcome feelings of insecurity or eating to pacify feelings of loneliness.

Rationalization involves justifying one's behavior with socially acceptable reasons. For example, it is more acceptable to say that you failed because you partied too much than to say that you lack intellectual ability or self-control. Of course, it is quite conceivable that all three reasons combined to determine the final outcome. Thus rationalization is often a clever blend of truth and falsehood so that the balance of causation is subtly tipped in a more acceptable direction. Signs of rationalization include frequently giving reasons for one's behavior and becoming upset when others question those reasons.

Suppression differs from the other mechanisms in being consciously initiated. Because of this, it is sometimes described as an adjustment rather than a defense mechanism. Suppression refers to a deliberate turning of one's attention away from threatening impulses, as in the use of distracting activities.

Another adjustment mechanism is **sublimation**, wherein an unacceptable impulse is transformed and expressed in a more socially acceptable way. For example, hostile impulses are often expressed in organized sports rather than in outright war. For Freud, the entire structure of the civilized world, including business, sports, art, science, and education, was erected through sublimation.

THE ORDERING OF DEFENSES

The defense mechanisms can be aligned on a continuum, depending on how much they interfere with adaptive functioning and reality contact. Sublimation, suppression, compensation, rationalization, and repression all are characteristic of a relatively healthy ego. Introjection, projection, and denial involve greater distortions of reality and thus constitute less healthy functioning. Note that the psychoanalytic assumption is that we cannot function without defenses. What separates healthy from unhealthy functioning is the amount of energy that must be invested in defensive operations and the amount of reality distortion involved.

It is assumed that healthy individuals use all of the defenses from time to time, but some defenses are closely associated with certain personality characteristics. For example, isolation, reaction formation, and undoing often characterize obsessive-compulsive types. Projection and denial are linked to paranoid states (see Chapter 13 for a description of these disorders).

DEFENDING AGAINST THE THREAT OF CANCER

Some researchers have investigated the use of defense mechanisms in natural environments. For example, Katz and associates (1970) studied the defenses used by women hospitalized to determine whether their breast lumps were cancerous. One observed defense was displacing concern for their own health onto their loved ones. For example, one woman when asked, "What brought you into the hospital?" replied,

> I don't know whether you noticed my husband in the room, but if you had, you would have noticed that he's a very sick man. He has cancer of the stomach . . . I have had a lump on my breast for the past two months. I had noticed it but it didn't bother me . . . and besides, I just couldn't leave him alone. Everything went through my mind: What if I had to go into the hospital? What if I had to leave him alone? (p. 136)

One woman projected the belief that she was seriously ill onto the doctors and accused them of holding back information from her and using her as a guinea pig. Because of this she refused to sign release forms for breast surgery. At one point she confronted the physician,

> I don't like the expression on your face . . . I think there's something you want to tell me but are withholding. . . . I think you know and don't want to come out with it. . . . Why are you asking me all these questions. . . . You want to make me nervous. . . . You're trying to find out something. . . . You're trying to tell me there is something wrong with me—worse than what I think it is . . . I think you know. (Katz et al., 1970, p. 136)

The most common pattern observed was a denial of the possibility of cancer based on the rationalization, "Since I'm healthy, there's probably nothing wrong" (even though "feeling healthy" is typical of those in the early stages of

cancer). Although denial was found useful for controlling anxiety, it increased patients' actual risk because they delayed seeking treatment.

Since ego defenses operate outside consciousness, how can you find out which defenses you use most frequently? If you have an open, nondefensive relationship, you might describe the defenses to this friend and find out which ones he or she has observed you using.

THE CONSCIOUS SELF AND THE SELF-CONCEPT

A great deal of our defensive functioning serves to protect and maintain our conscious self and self-concept. Recall that the conscious self includes all those relatively conscious experiences that we believe have something to do with who we are. It includes memories of our successes and failures, our appearance, our fantasies, our beliefs and values, our behaviors, and our feelings about those behaviors. It also refers to all those things in the world we identify with,

to which we affix the possessive *my*. Our continuing sense of personal identity is one of the mental contents comprising the conscious self. Another is the **self-concept**, our beliefs about who we are.

A good example of a self-concept can be found by simply asking, "How would I describe myself?" To do this, you might list traits showing your typical behaviors, feelings, moods, and other characteristics. People often emphasize what is most unusual about themselves, since these characteristics provide the most information. For example, a blond American is more likely to include hair color in the self-concept than would an American with brown hair.

SELF-CONCEPT AND BEHAVIOR

Because the self-concept pertains to our identity, its many contents tend to hang together, forming an internally consistent whole. Whether or not we are consistent in reality, we view ourselves as being essentially the same person from day to day, even though our behavior may change with each situation. Breaking

One's self-concept emphasizes relatively unique characteristics, such as an unusual hair style.

our nature were frozen, when in fact it can be flexible and spontaneous. Most of the time, our cognitive capacities allow us considerable choice in how to behave. But the self-concept, as a definition of ourselves (especially when it becomes public), can restrict our behavioral options and make us more mechanical and one-dimensional than we would otherwise have been.

Why is this? Because the self-concept is a description of experience rather than the experience itself, it will always represent a simplification of who we are. More precisely, it is a simplification of who we *were,* since it derives from past experience. In general, it is too restrictive to let this simplification control our spontaneous inclinations, unless these would violate personal or moral values that we are choosing.

THE FORMATION OF A SELF-CONCEPT

Those who influence our self-concept automatically assume great power in our lives. Much of the self-concept is formed from simply observing ourselves, and this is straightforward, except for the extent to which we may distort the evidence of our senses. Much of the self-concept is also formed, however, from other people's definitions of us. We are continually overhearing these definitions, and it is difficult to avoid being influenced by them. For example, in moments of irritation, a mother may exclaim, "You're a slob, just like your father." Such definitions act like hypnotic suggestions, gradually inducing long-term changes in self-concept and behavior.

Let's consider other examples. "Sammy, put on your hat, you know you catch cold easily." Here Sammy is being informed that he is frail and sickly. "Sue, you're such a sweet person, you could never say anything to hurt another person's feelings." In effect, Sue is being told that she must not become angry or stick up for her own rights. Also note how Sue is being manipulated. She must now be prepared to

this sense of consistency is tantamount to losing our personality, and perhaps our sanity. Thus experiences that conflict with our image of who we are threaten us, and these experiences are often distorted or reinterpreted to reduce the apparent discrepancy. Moreover, we tend to behave consistently with our self-concept. In this way, the self-concept influences both our actual and perceived behavior.

Psychologist Sidney Jourard (1981) observed that although forming a self-concept is unavoidable, it may have unfortunate side effects. By forming beliefs about who we are, we essentially commit ourselves to behave in ways consistent with those beliefs. Thus we act as if meet the speaker's demands, no matter how unreasonable, or be defined as "the person who hurt my feelings."

CHANGING THE SELF-CONCEPT

Psychologist Don Hamachek (1978) pointed out that the self-concept resists change. Since it restricts what behaviors will be permitted, the individual may not attempt new behaviors that would allow the self-concept to be modified. For example, shy people may not want to see their social strengths, for fear that they would then have to enact the behaviors they fear most. Thinking of themselves as shy protects them from the risk of new situations. Thus shy people have a vested interest in retaining the view of themselves as shy, even as they may curse their shyness and desperately wish to change.

Slight inaccuracies in the way that shy people form their self-concepts often help maintain their shyness. For example, they may tell themselves, "I am shy" rather than "In the past I have acted shyly." One description makes change seem impossible, and the other leaves the door open for new behaviors.

This would be a good time to consider your own self-concept. What comes to mind when you try to describe what kind of person you are? Would you say that you have a relatively healthy or unhealthy self-concept? What was your basis for answering this question?

THE SHADOW

EVIL BELOW

As noted above, experiences that contradict our self-concept are threatening. Carl Jung theorized that such experiences are repressed, coming together in the unconscious to form a complex of thoughts, feelings, images, sensations, and perceptions known as the **shadow**.

Shadow contents center on the notion of evil. Although aware that we're not perfect, we still like to think of ourselves as being basically good, fair, considerate, and the like. Thus, because the shadow stands in opposition to the conscious self, it takes on the characteristics of evil. Shadow contents often contain experiences such as cowardliness, callous self-interest, and petty revenge. One exception to its negative theme occurs when we consciously identify with some aspect of evil, as when adopting a criminal role. In this case the shadow contains elements of good.

The shadow also includes nondeveloped potentials. If we have consciously refined our sense of thinking, for example, our ability to discern and express feeling will tend to be simplistic. For Jung, growth is initiated through consciously developing our capabilities along certain dimensions. But, as the opposites of those dimensions receive less attention, they remain crude and undeveloped. For the growth process to be complete, these capabilities must be refined and integrated with the rest of the personality.

Each of us, however, is aware of negative things about ourselves. Why were these not repressed into the shadow? Presumably, only those experiences that are the most threatening, most irreconcilable with our self-concepts, require repression. For example, those parts of ourselves that are held rigidly or self-righteously lead to the greatest repression. Thus, it is often the things we are most proud of that determine the contents of the shadow.

In addition, we must not forget that events are multifaceted. Because we can acknowledge some aspects of an event, that does not mean other aspects have not been repressed. For example, suppose your best friend, Arnold, just landed a job making ten thousand dollars a year more than you do. Perhaps your feelings are ambivalent. Naturally, you are happy for him, but you cannot escape a twinge of jealousy. If you have a strong relationship, perhaps you can even confide this jealousy to him. Nevertheless,

According to Jung, the conflict between conscious ego and unconscious shadow is symbolized in the story of Dr. Jekyll and Mr. Hyde.

this is no guarantee that repression to the shadow has not occurred. You may not be consciously processing the specific impulses that accompanied the jealousy or the full implications of your behavior toward Arnold. Perhaps, in addition to the twinge of jealousy, you also had fleeting wishes that he would fail in his new job. Maybe, without thinking about it, you dropped the name of a desirable romantic partner you are seeing as a reminder of your continuing dominance in *that* domain. Such petty reactions are far more threatening than the acknowledgement of a "twinge of jealousy," and thus more likely to be repressed.

Jung's assumption is that with a little self-observation, you will see that such reactions are not rare. They are part of everyday reality, part of human nature, and part of the shadow.

WHEN "TOO GOOD" ISN'T GOOD ENOUGH

The shadow clarifies an observation that all of us have probably made. Even though we desire and appreciate goodness, we often feel uneasy and distrustful of someone who seems "too good." Those who disguise their shady sides are less revered than regarded with suspicion. The suspicion, of course, is that they are hiding something from us, and perhaps from themselves as well.

FACING THE SNAKE

Jung viewed it as essential to confront our shadows and integrate more of this material into our conscious selves. For Jung, keeping this material out of awareness in no way reduces its impact on behavior. In fact, it gives our conscious selves even less control over our selfish, impulsive, and petty ways. Jung saw the universal recognition of this truth in many forms.

One type of religious worship, for example, involves the ritualistic kissing of a snake's head. The snake, of course, is a symbol of disgust and loathing. This ritual enacts the truth that we must face those things about ourselves that we despise. Similarly, many religions preach that we are sinners. We must acknowledge our sins and seek forgiveness, for God prefers a repentent sinner to a sanctimonious hypocrite. For Jung, these are alternative ways of symbolizing contact with the shadow.

Jung foresaw great danger in not coming to terms with the shadow:

> It is often tragic to see how blatantly a man bungles his own life and the lives of others yet remains totally incapable of seeing how much the whole tragedy originates in himself, and how he continually feeds it and keeps it going. Not *consciously,* of course — for consciously he is engaged in bewailing and cursing a faithless world that recedes further and further

---

FOCUS

THE JOURNAL: A PATH TO THE UNKNOWN YOU

Keeping a personal journal is one way of getting in touch with unconscious processes. Psychologist Ira Progoff (1980) conducts journal workshops in which individuals record their thoughts, feelings, and images in response to selected topics or questions. However, individuals do not consciously *try* to form any particular kind of response. Instead they merely record the flow of images as it occurs, without judgment or evaluation. In essence, the journal is free association on paper.

Progoff claims that with very little practice individuals gain a sense of the independent functioning of unconscious contents. He sees an "underground stream of images and recollections within each of us. The stream is nothing more or less than our interior life. When we enter it, we ride it to a place where *it* wants to go" (Kaiser, 1981, p. 67).

Some of the prompts that Progoff uses to stimulate the flow of images and associations are "Where are you now in your life?" and "Describe brief, significant scenes from your life."

Progoff believes that the images that emerge in the writing disclose what our life's goals and meanings are. He maintains that as a people, we do not know ourselves very well; we are not on intimate terms with much of what we actually are. We do not feel comfortable with ourselves, and this makes it difficult for us to share intimacy with others. Progoff takes the sobering view that we are the loneliest and most alienated people in history.

In Freud's time, sex was the awful secret that people did not want to talk about. According to Progoff, our secret is spirituality. People go to great lengths to avoid their inner lives, which is the source of the God experience. Today, many people, especially those with education, feel that spirituality is something pious, impractical, and dependent on unrealistic dogmas. For Progoff, the importance of spirituality is not in one's religious beliefs but in the experience of a vast knowing from within. And for him, that knowing is not the same as the tiny portion of ourselves that we hold in ordinary awareness.

into the distance. Rather, it is an unconscious factor which spins the illusions that veil his world. And what is being spun is a cocoon, which in the end will completely envelop him. (Jung, in Campbell, 1971, p. 147)

Those who show little acknowledgement of their own flaws and weaknesses are said to cast a large shadow. Presumably, there is an uneasiness that accompanies the faint perception that something powerful and frightening lurks just out of range of our conscious perceptions. As Daniels and Horowitz (1984) pointed out, this phenomenon is nicely illustrated by a simple, yet haunting, piece by Robert Hall:

My popcorn is gone
The seats are half-empty (the cartoon is over)
I've seen the feature several times before
I'm afraid of the dark
And it's time to go home. (Hall, 1975, p. 219)

Have you ever experienced the feeling that Hall described? How did you explain it to yourself at the time?
One way of glimpsing the kinds of experiences that would be found in your own shadow is to list the things you are most proud of. Experiences incompatible with these attributes would presumably find their way into your shadow.

THE CONSCIOUS SELF AND SELF-ESTEEM

THE VALUE OF SELF-ESTEEM

Self-esteem, which is part of the conscious self, refers to how we feel about ourselves, whether we are satisfied or dissatisfied with who we are. A great deal of research indicates that it is better to have high than low self-esteem. Those with low self-esteem report feelings of gloominess and disappointment. They are more prone to depression and are more likely to have psychosomatic symptoms and difficulty making friends. Low self-esteem individuals are

more shy, insecure, easily hurt by criticism, less active in extracurricular affairs, and less likely to show leadership abilities. Children low in self-esteem are more socially isolated, fearful around others, physically weak, and less able to defend themselves (see Maw & Maw, 1970; Rosenberg, 1965, 1979).

On the other hand, children high in self-esteem are more active; more expressive; more confident; more accurate in describing themselves and others; more successful in school, social, and athletic activities; more creative; more curious; and less influenced by pressure from authorities. As should be clear, the merits of self-esteem are quite impressive.

THE DEVELOPMENT OF SELF-ESTEEM

Self-esteem is not something you are born with. As a result of numerous interactions with significant others, each of us learns what value to place on ourselves. For example, children are more likely to have high self-esteem if they come from smaller families, if they are born earlier in the sequence of siblings, and if the family relates to one another with warmth. In addition, boys' self-esteem is related to having a father who is not domineering (Sears, 1970).

Boys with high self-esteem often come from homes with strict parents who are highly involved in their sons' activities but who avoid harsh discipline (Sears, 1970). Boys with low self-esteem, on the other hand, come from families that are permissive but discipline harshly. The use of harsh discipline recalls Rogers's theory of the need for unconditional love and acceptance. Harsh discipline may be viewed as a withdrawal of love and therefore may lead to feelings of being accepted only conditionally. In addition, the permissiveness between punishments may be interpreted as lack of interest.

This suggests that the low self-esteem pattern involves parents who pay little attention to what the kids do until they really get out of line, at which point the parents explode in a rage of hostility. The hostility seems justified because by this time the child's behavior has deteriorated badly, and the parents may not realize their own role in its formation.

HOW LOW SELF-ESTEEM IS MAINTAINED

Despite the debilitating effects of low self-esteem, people often pursue cognitive strategies that keep their low esteem from changing. Those with low self-esteem often find ways to dismiss both their actual successes and the compliments of others. For example, they may think, "I was just lucky." Or they may tell themselves, "She was just being polite; she didn't really mean it." Many people feel awkward when they receive a compliment. Instead of simply saying "Thank you," they feel compelled to explain that their performance was nothing special. This not only dismisses the performance, but it also punishes the person giving the compliment.

Another low esteem pattern involves constantly belittling others. The underlying assumption is, "If I keep them on the defensive, then they won't be able to see how worthless I am." But this strategy often begets rejection, which further reduces the initially low self-esteem. And although this strategy may keep the partner on the defensive, it never rectifies the initial insecurity.

SELF-EFFICACY AND SELF-ESTEEM

Social learning theorists prefer to study self-esteem not as a global trait but as a specific expectancy that one can perform a given response. When there is an expectancy of self-efficacy for a response, we are more likely to attempt it in the first place, to put more effort into it, and to persist until the response is completed. Social learning theorists also emphasize that high self-efficacy for academic or athletic tasks, for example, aids success in those areas. Suc-

cess is followed by feelings of self-satisfaction and, ultimately, by enhanced self-esteem.

It is crucial, however, that the goals we set be realistic. Otherwise, our efforts will only set the stage for failure. Researchers (Bandura & Schunk, 1981) found, for example, that children who selected short-term, realistic goals worked harder, learned more, and felt better about themselves than those selecting long-term, more difficult goals. It is clear that goal seeking should be organized as a series of short-range, manageable goals, rather than relying on the motivating power of a single long-term outcome.

ENHANCING SELF-ESTEEM

Many factors influence self-esteem: genetic endowment, feedback from others, pursued values, models, and social comparisons. Nevertheless, each of these factors is something that you have already chosen to some extent and therefore something that you partly control. Thus it is self-defeating and unrealistic to feel that self-esteem cannot be changed. In fact, it can be altered without changing any of the external circumstances of one's life. Many times, all that is required is a change in attitude. Let's consider each of these factors separately.

Genes. Genetic endowment is probably the least controllable factor. Just by virtue of being born with one set of genes rather than another, we have certain strengths, weaknesses, talents, and predispositions. One thing that we can do, however, is to understand what our strengths and weaknesses are. For example, we could then choose endeavors that rely on our strengths. Alternatively, we may find that the activities we most enjoy require attributes on which we are weak. In this case we can compensate for those weaknesses through greater effort and persistence. In many cases, weaknesses have been turned into strengths because they motivated the extra effort and determination to produce excellence. President Theodore Roosevelt is a well-known case in point. Frail and sickly as a youngster, he resolved to change his condition. Through determination and hard work, he transformed himself into a "rough rider" and famous adventurer.

Parental influences. It is an unfortunate truism that we cannot do much about the way our parents treated us in the past. But *once we are aware* that their behavior may have inadvertently lowered our self-esteem, then we can do something about it in the present. Instead of continuing passively, as if we were creatures without awareness, we can counteract those early influences. Each time we catch ourselves in negative self-talk, we can actively challenge the evidence, assumptions, and conclusions that maintain low self-esteem. We can ask ourselves, "Where did I get the idea that I don't have what it takes?" "Where is the evidence that I will come out second best?" "What makes me think that no one will love me?" We have the capacity to realize that just because one person wasn't able to love us fully (perhaps because of his or her own personal deficiencies), this provides no basis for drawing broad conclusions about our overall worth.

If your parents' attitude toward you was cold, rejecting, and disparaging, or if they accepted you only when you were incompetent, chances are they are still treating you that way today. What can you do about it? First, it does no good to blame your parents. In a real sense, you are an extension of them. They probably treat themselves just as harshly as they treat you. At any rate, they are doing the best they can, given the people that they are. If they are influencing you toward low self-esteem, the chances are that this is the way that they too were raised.

Often, the best that you can do is to realize what they are doing, acknowledge that it is not their "fault," and decide to love them without being a victim. When they tell you that you're not as successful as the neighbor's son or imply that you don't measure up to your sister, you can accept this as a valid description of how

they have come to see the world, not as an objective truth about you.

Values. Performance on activities that we value has a strong influence on our self-esteem. As indicated in the previous chapter, however, many values often seem like "our own," although we have never consciously chosen them. We have passively assumed that what was important to those around us must be important to us. As Rogers explained, these learned values often fool us. Many people have had the experience of striving for something over a long period of time, only to find that it meant nothing when finally attained. This is largely because they merely *thought* that the goal was important to them; its value was not directly experienced "in their hearts"; it was only assumed "in their heads."

Unfortunately, low self-esteem can often be traced to poor performance on activities whose values were never consciously chosen. Conflicting feelings about these activities, of course, are one reason for the poor performance. In our culture, this is a particular problem with job success. Parents and teachers often have a dream for their wards to succeed in a particular field. Over time, in countless ways and with the best of intentions, they are often able to convince youngsters to overrule the evidence of their deepest feelings in favor of these alien values. Thus it is important to understand not only what we value but also why we value it.

Social comparison. A final influence on self-esteem involves the comparison between performance and expectation. Expectations largely derive from the models that we observe, and individuals can decide with whom they will compare themselves. No matter what you are doing, there will always be someone doing it better and someone doing it worse. In this way, self-esteem is fairly independent of actual performance. Some look to the lowest denominator and end up feeling successful no matter how poorly they perform. Others compare themselves only with the best and always fall short.

Thus, many high achievers have low self-esteem.

Those with unrealistically high standards often fear relinquishing these standards, because they believe they will no longer be motivated to strive for excellence. In other words, they think that self-dissatisfaction is the only motive they can depend on to produce their best behavior. Humanistic psychologists argue that this assumption is totally unfounded. High-quality performance can also derive from a desire to express ourselves completely, without regard for how our performance compares with that of others.

Self-acceptance. Self-acceptance is perhaps the most pivotal consideration in the pursuit of self-esteem. In our culture, self-esteem tends to be based on achievement. This is commonly interpreted as meaning that we must perform better than others to feel good about ourselves.

It is worth asking, "What do I have to do before I can feel good about myself?" An external criterion, such as achievement, takes no account of your biological endowment, how hard you have tried, how long you have persisted, and how you have experienced the endeavor. Only the final outcome: win or lose. This attitude is part of our culture. The final product is all that counts, and the process on the way to that product is irrelevant. (Football fans will recognize this as the Vince Lombardi philosophy of winning.)

If taken literally, however, this philosophy dooms 99 percent of us to despair. After all, there can only be one "number one," and even that doesn't last very long. Everyone else is technically a loser. Certainly, this attitude is praiseworthy in some respects. It sometimes generates extraordinary performance, and it refuses to tolerate excuses and self-deception. Overall, however, it lowers self-esteem and blinds us to the costs of winning. Thus it seems healthier to base esteem on self-acceptance rather than achievement. As long as you are

doing your best, without self-deception, then there is no reason to withhold self-esteem.

Respond to each of the following sentences by indicating strongly agree, agree, disagree, or strongly disagree:

1. On the whole, I am satisfied with myself. SA A D SD
2. At times I think I am no good at all. SA A D SD
3. I feel that I have a number of good qualities. SA A D SD
4. I am able to do things as well as most other people. SA A D SD
5. I feel I do not have much to be proud of. SA A D SD
6. I certainly feel useless at times. SA A D SD
7. I feel that I'm a person of worth, at least on an equal plane with others. SA A D SD
8. I wish I could have more respect for myself. SA A D SD
9. All in all, I am inclined to feel that I am a failure. SA A D SD
10. I take a positive attitude toward myself. SA A D SD

For items 1, 3, 4, 7, and 10, give yourself four points for SA, three for A, two for D, and one for SD. For items 2, 5, 6, 8, and 9, the scoring is reversed; give yourself four points for SD, three for D, two for A, and one for SA. Now total up your score. These items form a popular measure of self-esteem, the New York State Self-Esteem Scale (Rosenberg, 1979, p. 291). In college samples, the average score is

21, with about two-thirds of the population falling between 16 and 26 (Perlman, 1985, personal communication).

For those scoring above the mean, it may be useful to think about whether your score reflects a view of yourself as possessing many desirable characteristics or whether it comes from an acceptance of yourself that is independent of accomplishments. For those scoring below the mean, consider whether your score reflects a view of yourself as possessing negative traits. If it does, are these trait ascriptions accurate? Do they reflect dimensions that can be changed with some effort? Note that a low score may also reflect unrealistic ideals and the rigid belief that these ideals *must* be attained.

SINFUL PRIDE: THE DARK SIDE OF SELF-ESTEEM?

Self-esteem is obviously important. But is it possible to have too much self-esteem? What about those people who might be described as "stuck on themselves"? These **narcissistic** individuals are often conceited, self-centered, egotistical, and self-indulgent. Is their self-esteem too high?

SELF-ESTEEM VERSUS CONCEIT

Sometimes individuals who appear to have high self-esteem don't actually feel that good about themselves. Because of the artful creatures that we are, it is quite possible to cover up feelings of inadequacy by acting conceited and superior. Moreover, it is also possible to become gradually less and less aware of how much our behavior is a pretense. Thus it is misleading to equate conceit with high self-esteem.

A similar issue arises with pride. Our culture is divided as to whether pride is good or bad. On the one hand, pride is thought to reflect healthy, effective functioning. On the other hand, there is a long religious tradition that views pride as one of the seven deadly sins, as something that

"goeth before a fall." So which is it? Is pride good or bad? When used in the positive sense, pride essentially means self-esteem. However, when pride takes the form of feeling good because you think you're superior to others or deserving of special privileges, then it crosses over into the realm of conceit.

Certainly, for those who dislike themselves, who take no pride in their work, and who feel they have nothing to be proud of, conceit may well be a step up. But it can never represent a long-term solution to the problem of insecurity.

Perhaps you're wondering, "What, exactly, is so bad about conceit?" Carl Jung made some of the most incisive observations about those who are "puffed up," inflated with a sense of their own importance. Jung described this state as coming about when the conscious self identifies with the social self, that is, when we start believing that we are the person we pretend to be. Since the social self is only a small part of what we know ourselves to be, adopting an attitude of inflation means that a great deal of our actual experiencing becomes threatening. A pressure develops to distort, reinterpret, or simply block out experiences that would contradict this restricted social self. This stresses our adaptive systems, making us vulnerable to fits of temper and other breakdowns in functioning, and it impedes psychological growth. In addition, conceit alienates you from others. The only people you're likely to attract are those whose own self-esteem is so low that the only way they can feel good about themselves is to associate with someone who acts superior. Thus conceit is an indulgence with considerable personal cost.

THE PARADOX OF GROWTH

The human potential movement of the 1970s and 1980s emphasized the importance of self-esteem, yet at the same time it promoted a selfish and narrow concern with one's own happiness, often phrased as "doing your own thing." At what point does a concern with one's own growth and happiness become self-centered, egotistical, and narcissistic? Abraham Maslow and the existential therapist Victor Frankl confirm the importance of growth and happiness but maintain that they are achieved through a devotion to one's work and to helping others, not through self-absorption, self-indulgence, and "me-firstism."

In other words, happiness and self-actualization are paradoxical entities. If pursued directly, with an attitude of narrow self-interest, they slip away. On the other hand, through dedicating oneself to an endeavor outside ourselves, to a relationship, a cause, or an activity that we decide to invest with meaning, then happiness and self-actualization become possible. As Frankl noted, happiness must *ensue;* it cannot be *pursued.*

Yankelovich (1981) argued that the emphasis on "me" is often merely a rationalization for selfishness and the avoidance of responsibility. After interviewing many seekers of "self-fulfillment" he concluded that they

> focus so sharply on their own needs that instead of achieving the more intimate relationships they desire, they grow farther apart from others. In dwelling on their own needs, they discover that the inner journey brings loneliness and depression. They are caught in a debilitating contradiction — their goal is to expand their lives by reaching beyond the self, but the strategy they employ constricts them, drawing them inward toward an ever-narrowing, closed-off "I." People want to enlarge their choices but, seeking to "keep all options open," they diminish them. (Yankelovich, 1981, p. 40)

What is the alternative to an ethic of "me-first?" Yankelovich speculated that the ethic of me-first will be replaced by one of commitment to families, friends, and community. For example, many individuals report a lack of close personal friendships, and the number of those with a need to reach out to others has increased in recent years.

Given the importance of self-esteem, growth, and happiness, it seems likely that each of us has some implicit or explicit strategies for bringing these values to fruition. What strategies have you been using? In light of the preceding discussion, how viable do you think they are?

THE SOCIAL SELF

The social self, how we present ourselves to others, is often a distorted picture of our conscious self, for we usually try to present ourselves in socially acceptable ways. Thus we do not display all aspects of ourselves to others, even to intimates. There is usually some degree of filtering, so that even when we think we know someone very well, there are still hidden facets that would surprise us.

Recall that for humanistic theorists, authentic functioning means that the social self should not differ greatly from the conscious self. Humanists view our efforts to enhance the perception that we are intelligent, successful, popular, and the like as working against us in the long run. Such strategies are manipulative, mechanical, and one-dimensional. Moreover, they restrict individuality. It is as if we all were in the same play, trying out for the same part.

Moreover, by continually monitoring our behavior to avoid seeming "uncool," we lose much of our vitality. In addition, others realize that we are playing a role, and so they cannot trust what we say; they know that we are tampering with the evidence.

Two areas in which the social self might legitimately deviate from the conscious self are business contacts and interactions that require tact. For business contacts, the goal is not intimacy, and so the disclosure of feelings unrelated to the business at hand would be inappropriate. With regard to tact, we must decide when complete honesty would serve only to hurt another person's feelings needlessly. The danger here is that we may deceive ourselves about whose feelings are being saved. It often happens that by avoiding a disclosure we think we're being tactful when we're actually protecting ourselves from negative repercussions of the truth.

For example, a wife may ask her mate, "How do I look tonight?" Depending on the tone of voice, the context, and the unspoken agreements that guide their relationship, this question could mean either "I'm nervous, give me some reassurance" or "I need to know whether my appearance is correct." If the husband interprets the question as a request for reassurance, there would be no point in critiquing her appearance. On the other hand, he may perceive her question as a request for truthfulness yet know that any negative feedback could change her mood and make his evening less enjoyable. After all, there is a long, all-too-human history of punishing the bearer of bad news. Nevertheless, avoiding the truth would be cowardly.

Issues of tact and the possibility of total honesty are debated in the following FOCUS:

FOCUS

IS DISHONESTY NECESSARY?

A hypothetical debate between Carl Rogers and Carl Jung.

Dr. J.: *Well, Dr. R., as I understand it, you believe that total honesty between people is not only possible but also desirable and health inducing. Is that right?*

Dr. R.: *Yes, mm, hmm. I hear you saying that honesty fosters a growth process. Actually, I view honesty with others as part of a total congruence among the real, conscious, and social selves. I would refer you to Chapter 2 of Critelli's* Personal Growth and Effective Behavior *for a discussion of these views.*

Dr. J.: *Yes, I've read it. . . . Pardon my bluntness, but what makes you think that people can stomach total honesty? We're both aware of bitter family disputes and broken friendships — just because one person decided to be totally honest with another.*

Dr. R.: *This does happen on occasion, especially when honesty is sprung on a partner with no preparation or agreement that this will be the mode of communication. After all, total honesty is quite different from what we're used to in most relationships.*

Dr. J.: *But how far do you think people can go with honesty? What if you think that your partner is a bore? Do you just blurt it out? Don't you care whether you hurt the person's feelings?*

Dr. R.: *Well, no, I wouldn't describe it as blurting anything out. But if I were feeling bored in a conversation, I would say so. I might simply say, "I'm feeling bored right now. Why don't we talk about something else?" However, this is not the same as saying "I think you are a bore." The second statement constitutes blaming and name calling, and the partner would understandably be hurt by such rudeness. In the first statement, however, I am taking responsibility for the feeling of boredom. I am not saying it is anyone's fault; I am just reporting my subjective experience.*

Dr. J.: *That seems like an important distinction. But what if your subjective experience involved the thought, "This person is crude and conceited." In other words, suppose your experience involved a specific thought about the other person rather than a vague feeling? Would you express that evaluation of your partner and risk offending him? And even if you did say it, what good would it do? Do you seriously believe this would further either person's growth? Isn't it true that honesty sounds good in theory but is disastrous in practice?*

Dr. R.: *Please, one question at a time. Let's see . . . first of all, I don't usually take an evaluative attitude toward people. I want to understand what they are feeling; I don't particularly want to judge them. But if I did find myself with evaluative thoughts about another, I guess I might or might not express them, depending on the situation.*

Dr. J.: *Again, pardon my bluntness, but aren't you evading my questions? How about getting more specific?*

Dr. R.: *Well, for example, if this were an important relationship and there were an agreement between us to aim for total honesty, I would describe my reaction to the person, but I would be sure to make it clear that it was my perception at that moment and not a statement of fact. If the relationship were more casual or there were no such agreement, then, of course, I wouldn't try to foist this perception onto an unwilling partner.*

Dr. J.: *Very good. But what if your partner had agreed to total honesty, but you felt that this was a sensitive area for the person. So that even though she says she wants honesty, in your opinion, she would likely become hurt, upset, and resentful toward you for saying it?*

Dr. R.: *I'm wondering where this question is coming from.*

Dr. J.: *Fair enough. Through the study of many different cultures, it has become clear to me that in every social system, people deal with one another through their social selves. They have roles, rituals, and rules about what constitutes appropriate social behavior. I conclude that the human species has evolved this style of behavior as a way of keeping social friction to a minimum. We are social beings and we must live in groups. Social niceties, which include a taboo on total honesty, apparently have helped us survive. They make us tolerable to one another, and they promote social bonding. Thus I conclude that we are not the kind of creatures that can handle total honesty and that any attempt to do away with the social self grates against our very nature.*

Dr. R.: *I see. That is a persuasive argument. But perhaps people differ in how much honesty they can accept. For example, those who are insecure, defensive, and not very self-aware might be easily threatened by negative feedback. Total honesty might not work well for them. I'll grant that. On the other hand, those who are open and nondefensive could make a pretty good attempt at honesty.*

Dr. J.: *Yes, I think we are making some progress. Perhaps as people become less defensive, their growth is aided by greater honesty, and*

*they have less need for the social self to differ from the conscious self.
Because there is less to surprise them and jar against their self-concepts, they are not easily offended. Around such people, you don't have
to feel like you are "walking on eggs," always afraid to say something
that will offend them.*

Dr. R.: *I can agree with most of that. I guess I would phrase it a little more
positively, though. Let's say that many people could benefit from total
or near-total honesty and that everyone else could at least benefit from
increased honesty.*

Dr. J.: *Well, our disagreement now is a matter of degree. I would assume
that some people could function at near-total honesty, and many would
benefit from a slight increase in honesty. But I would be wary of
advocating a large increase for most people. You see, I believe most
people are already operating near the level they require to keep their social relationships stable. To handle much more honesty than that, they
would first have to reach a higher level of maturity.*

Dr. R.: *I think we've reached the point at which we can agree to disagree.*

SUMMARY

1. Consciousness may be quite different from what we usually take it to
   be. In the normal waking state, it seems likely that gaps in consciousness
   are smoothed over to create the illusion of being continuously aware.
   Moreover, much of our cognitive processing appears to take place
   outside our immediate awareness.

2. Unconscious processes can be approached only by drawing inferences
   from conscious experience. The most common strategy for drawing
   these inferences is the observation of behavior produced when conscious
   control is relaxed, as in dreams, fantasies, and free associations.

3. The case history of Ann demonstrates the autonomous functioning of
   unconscious processes and the way in which symbols can express
   unconscious knowledge.

4. Self-deception is a common constituent of normal functioning, and
   some evidence indicates that depressed and nondepressed individuals
   differ in their self-deceptions.

5. The ego defense mechanisms represent common ways that consciousness is protected from internal and external threats. Normal functioning
   is thought to include all the defenses, but some are more adaptive than
   others. In general, it is preferable to employ defenses that minimize
   reality distortion.

6. Much of our self-concept is initially defined for us by others, and once
   formed, it tends to resist change.

7. Experiences that threaten us by violating our self-concepts are thought to be repressed into the shadow. Jung believed that psychological growth depended on confronting and reintegrating this material into our conscious selves.

8. When the social self and the conscious self differ widely, behavior tends to be manipulative and nonspontaneous, and the individual is placed under stress.

9. Self-esteem is important to adaptive functioning. High self-esteem has been linked to small family size, warm parents who are involved in their children's activities, strict but nonabusive parental discipline, and realistic short-term goals.

10. Self-esteem is influenced by many variables such as genes, parental behavior, values, and social comparisons. To a large extent, we have the ability to affect each of these variables, if we choose to. In addition, it seems healthier to base our esteem on self-acceptance rather than on external accomplishments.

11. Self-esteem should be distinguished from conceit and narcissism. It seems that psychological growth and happiness are best pursued through a dedication to activities outside oneself, as too narrow a focus on growth leads to self-absorption.

SUGGESTED READINGS

Hamacheck, D. E. **Encounters with the self**. New York: Holt, Rinehart and Winston, 1978. Comprehensive treatment of the self-concept.

Jung, C. G. **Man and his symbols**. New York: Dell Pub. Co., Inc., 1964. Fascinating depiction of the known and unknown selves. Exemplary use of visual art to illustrate concepts, especially in hardcover edition.

Maul, G., & Maul, T. **Beyond limit: Ways to growth and freedom**. Glenview, Ill.: Scott, Foresman, 1983. Good explanations of how repression kills spontaneity and aliveness.

PART TWO

PERSONAL ADJUSTMENT

PART TWO deals with the problems of everyday life. It provides a broad social context for understanding where these problems come from and how they have changed in recent years. It also presents a number of practical strategies for resolving these problems and enhancing adjustment.

Chapter 4 depicts the current upheaval in modern culture and explains why this is creating unique problems for us. It also explores the adaptive and not-so-adaptive ways that people cope with stress. Finally, it presents our culture's response to the stress of modern life — the emergence of health psychology.

Chapter 5 explores one of the most profound social changes of our time, the revolution in male and female roles. It contrasts traditional gender roles and shows how they interact with physical and psychological sex differences. It then examines gender inequality in political and economic power and outlines how this problem might be resolved. The chapter concludes by considering our options for adaptive role enactment.

Chapter 6 takes a more personal approach to the problems of everyday life by examining how thoughts and feelings affect each other. In particular, it considers how negative emotions result from irrational and perfectionistic beliefs. Finally, it provides cognitive strategies for minimizing feelings of depression and enhancing our ability to experience life with a vibrant sense of aliveness.

Chapter 7 carries forward the emphasis on practical application by presenting techniques that can be used to enhance self-control and other competency skills. It encourages students to carry out a self-modification project of their own and offers step-by-step instructions.

STRESS and CHANGE

4

The Price of Progress

OUR CHANGING WORLD

We live in a world that will not stand still, where the only certainty may be change itself. It is a world with a quickening pace, a world on an upward spiral of technology, information, and complexity. Like it or not, life in the fast lane is rapidly becoming the norm. What may not be so apparent is the fundamental nature of this change and the psychological effects of coping with a world in flux. By its very nature, change forces us to deal with new situations, in which accustomed habits and strategies may no longer work. Inevitably, this taxes our ability to adapt and forces us to confront the unknown.

ARRIVAL OF THE INFORMATION SOCIETY

According to historian and futurist Alvin Toffler,

> Humanity faces a quantum leap forward. It faces the deepest social upheaval and creative restructuring of all time. Without clearly recognizing it, we are engaged in building a remarkable new civilization from the ground up. (1980, p. 26)

Toffler views history as taking place across three great waves of change. Each one has created a new civilization with ways of life inconceivable to the old order. Before the first wave, humans lived in small migratory hunter-gatherer societies. The first wave of change brought the agricultural revolution (about 8000 B.C.). The second wave introduced the Industrial Revolution (about A.D. 1700). The third wave, dubbed the "information revolution" by social analyst John Naisbitt (1982), began in the mid-1950s. This is the period when white-collar workers first outnumbered blue-collar workers and when the launch of Sputnik signaled a new era in global communications.

Before the 1950s, a shared image of industrial reality defined our options and gave us a clear sense of who we were and what we were likely to become. With this came a stable sense of self, even in the midst of social change. Toffler believes that much of the current anguish and disorientation results from our being both the last generation of the old age and the first generation of the new. He theorizes that the struggle between the dying second wave and the emerging third wave has fragmented our shared image of reality and undermined a stable sense of self.

THE BURDEN OF OVERSTIMULATION

Toffler (1972) coined the phrase **future shock** for the distress of overloading the individual's systems for adapting to the world. The debilitating effects of trying to cope with rapid change can be seen in such diverse groups as battlefield soldiers, disaster victims, and "culture-shocked" travelers. All three groups show signs of disorientation, anxiety, fatigue, and apathetic withdrawal. Moreover, each group shows decisional breakdowns, in which their ability to act rationally, that is, in their own best interests, is severely compromised. Toffler speculates that our culture is fast approaching a time when the demands on the average individual to cope with change and novelty will approach levels previously associated with those in trauma.

Toffler argues that no matter what the task, informational overload leads to performance breakdown. Moreover, researchers (e.g., Usdansky & Chapman, 1960) have linked overstimulation to disturbed thought patterns. Thus long-term cognitive overstimulation may have serious consequences for mental health.

ACCELERATING KNOWLEDGE AND INFORMATION

In dramatizing the magnitude of change and the unprecedented demands made on the modern individual, Toffler (1972) emphasizes that society is not just changing, it is changing *at an increasing rate*. In other words, the world is not only changing a little bit every day, but it is also changing more today than it did yesterday, and more tomorrow than today. Some examples of this process highlight the staggering implications of accelerative change.

One index of human knowledge is the publication of books. By 1500, Europe was producing one thousand books per year. By 1950 it was producing 120 times that amount. By 1960 the rate of book publication had increased yet another 33 percent over the 1950 figure (Escarpit, 1966; Glaister, 1960). But let's look at these figures more closely to get the full implications of change on an upward spiral. Even though the increase in book production between 1500 and 1950 was truly impressive, if that rate of increase had been maintained throughout the decade of the 1950s, we would have expected the 1960 rate to have increased by only 2 percent over the 1950 figure. But in fact, it increased by 33 percent, or over 15 times what would have been expected by the previous rate of change.

Another index of knowledge acquisition, the discovery of chemical elements, also follows an accelerative curve. By 1450, new elements were being discovered at a rate of one every two centuries. During the next 450 years, new elements were discovered at the rate of one every 7 years. And since 1900 they have been discovered at a rate of one every 3 years (Fuller & McHale, 1963).

Nearly seven thousand scientific articles are written each day, and this rate is rising so fast that Naisbitt (1982) predicted that the *total amount of scientific information ever collected will soon double every twenty months!*

INCREASING DIVERSITY AND FRAGMENTATION

While knowledge and information are increasing geometrically, society as a whole is undergoing an unprecedented decentralization. The large factories of the industrial society required an assembled work force to perform manual labor, but the information society has no such physical requirements. Moreover, breakthroughs in communication and computer technologies are leading a movement toward shifting the decisional load onto the individual. Clearly, this promises increased freedom of personal choice, yet it also adds to the individual's mounting adaptive burden.

INCREASING THREAT

Naisbitt (1982) argues that the change to an information society constitutes a threat to many workers. Computer technology in the information age is doing what mechanization did in the industrial age: taking over functions previously performed by workers. For example, by the end of the century up to 75 percent of U.S. factory workers could be displaced by computerized robots.

Computerized robots are displacing many unskilled workers on automobile assembly lines.

FOCUS

SENSATION SEEKERS AND THE PURSUIT OF CHANGE

Each of us has an optimal level of stimulation, with both overstimulation and understimulation experienced as unpleasant. Chronic overstimulation results in the future shock syndrome described by Alvin Toffler. Understimulation is often experienced as boredom, a negative feeling produced by too little change in the environment. Research by Marvin Zuckerman showed that many forms of sensation seeking go together, forming a general trait on which individuals differ. Some people have a high demand for stimulation and varied experience; they get bored easily and are likely to engage in risky adventures, artistic creation, adulterous sex, alcohol, drugs, and aggression (Zuckerman, 1978). Other individuals characteristically act to limit or reduce environmental stimulation.

One implication of Zuckerman's work is that high sensation seekers will favor a society undergoing radical change, as ours is. On the other hand, low sensation seekers may be somewhat at risk in our fast-paced information society.

Zuckerman suggests that the sensation-seeking motive should be considered when selecting a job or a mate. For example, high and low sensation seekers often have difficulty understanding each other. The high's behavior will seem crazy and foolish to the low. But to the high sensation seeker, the low's behavior will seem timid and inhibited.

Sensation seekers.

Across successive waves of change, the typical worker was first a farmer, then a laborer, and then a clerk. The next emerging position is likely to be technician, a position requiring a quantum jump in skill and intelligence.

The paradox is that precisely when the demands for an educated, technically skilled labor force are greatest, we are facing a crisis in education. Naisbitt (1982) claims that the generation graduating from high school today is the first in American history to be less skilled than its parents were. A 1980 government report described most Americans as moving toward ''virtual scientific and technological illiteracy'' (U.S. report, 1981). Experts estimate that one-third of our youth are ill equipped to make their way in American society (Naisbitt, 1982, p. 31).

It is increasingly clear that without a dramatic turnaround in public education, the skilled labor needed to maintain the information society will not be available. In addition, a sizable portion of the population may be unemployable. For those who will not fit into an information society, the threat is obvious. Even if their material needs are provided, what will maintain their self-esteem? For those who will be required to support them, frustration and resentment seem inevitable.

NUCLEAR THREAT

For over a generation we have lived in a world of precarious nuclear brinkmanship. It would be difficult to overestimate the long-term psychological effects of this chronic threat. Even though we avoid dwelling on such an unpleasant topic, and the horror of nuclear war seems totally unreal, its psychological impact cannot be ignored. John Mack, a specialist on adolescent suicide, found that young people are deeply disturbed by the threat of nuclear war. He claims that we are raising a generation without hope, in whom helplessness has become a dominant emotion (see Gittleson, 1982).

Jerome Frank, author of *Sanity and Survival* (1967), claims that the ineffectiveness of current political strategies stems from an inability to deal with change. Frank argues that most leaders believe nuclear war to be catastrophic, yet they continue stockpiling nuclear weapons, making war all the more likely. He maintains that in fact, piling up nuclear weapons decreases everyone's security. The more weapons there are, the more people who will handle these weapons. Thus, the greater the chance that one will be fired, either by accident or through the actions of a deviant individual.

Frank explained that the major irrationality here is the need to handle an unprecedented threat by making it seem familiar. Thus the strategy of conventional weapons is applied to a nuclear arsenal. President Ronald Reagan, for example, remarked, ''Could we survive a nuclear war? It would be a survival of some of your people and some of your facilities, but you could start again'' (Scheer, 1982, p. 300). According to Eugene V. Rostow, arms-control chief under President Reagan, ''We are living in a prewar and not a postwar world'' (Scheer, 1982, p. 300).

Do you feel that the future shock phenomenon has affected your life? What do you think is the best way of dealing with it?

THE ENIGMA OF STRESS

Although psychologists agree that stress is a monumental health concern, there is curiously little agreement as to what stress is. Some define it as the environmental changes to which we must constantly adjust; some, as the experience of threat to well-being; and some, as the debilitating physiological effects of threat. To develop a consistent language for describing this phenomenon, we shall view the person as an integrated system.

As Maddi and Propst (1971) pointed out, each of us seeks to maintain our own cycles of rest and activity. Needs such as those for food, safety, sex, social contact, and exploration arise, impel action, and dissolve into relaxed satiation. These separate need-satisfaction cycles together form an overall cycle of rising and falling arousal. Both over- and under-stimulation create unpleasant states that we are motivated to alter or avoid.

Whatever upsets one's desired level of arousal poses a threat, and the organism adapts by changing either the external environment or the internal reality (thoughts, feelings, perceptions) so that a desired level of arousal can be regained. **Stress** is the strain or wear and tear on the system from coping with deviations from optimal arousal. Environmental events that place an adjustive demand on the organism are called **stressors**.

The human body, as did that of all animals, evolved through the selection of innate survival mechanisms. We respond to threat with innate physiological reactions that mobilize us for immediate action. The release of key hormones such as adrenaline leads to immediate arousal and heightened muscular tension. Presumably, the survival dangers for which our reactions evolved were those that required immediate muscular action, "fight or flight."

Our problem is that over the past ten thousand years the body has changed little, but society is radically different. Dangers of the modern world are typically psychological rather than physical; disruptions to optimal arousal are nearly continuous rather than sporadic; and there is often no appropriate physical response to dissipate the tension of a body mobilized for action. As noted by Wallis (1983, p. 218), "The saber-toothed tiger is long gone, but the modern jungle is no less perilous. The sense of panic over a deadline, a tight plane connection, a reckless driver on one's tail are the new beasts that . . . set the heart racing."

It is now apparent that the heavy adjustive demand that modern life places on the individual — the steady succession of decisions, frustrations, conflicts, evaluations, pressures,

competition, crowding, noise, and so forth — has become the major health risk of our times. Two-thirds of the visits to family physicians are for stress-related symptoms (Wallis, 1983), and three-fourths of modern diseases are stress related (Pew, 1979). The cost to industry through absenteeism and medical expenses is a staggering $75 billion a year.

Stress is a major contributor to the six leading causes of death: heart disease, cancer, lung ailments, injuries, cirrhosis of the liver, and suicide. As Joel Elkes, a leader in the behavioral medicine movement, noted, "Our mode of life itself, the way we live, is emerging as today's principal cause of illness" (cited in Wallis, 1983, p. 218). Moreover, stress researchers (Cohen, Miller, & Ross, 1982, p. 100) warn that "most of us can expect to suffer, sooner or later, from some form of chronic, stress-related disease."

ENVIRONMENTAL STRESSORS

Environmental events that create an adjustive demand on the individual include major life crises, such as the death of a spouse, as well as the annoying little hassles of everyday life. Factors that affect the severity of stress include the number of simultaneous demands being made on the person, the importance of the needs being frustrated, and the length of time that the demand endures.

It should not be assumed that only unpleasant events lead to stress. Many desired events, such as a new job or love relationship, force the individual to act in new ways which thus create their own adjustive demands. Recall that the goal of health is not to reduce the adjustive demand to zero. This would be tantamount to death. Rather, all individuals have their own optimal levels of stimulation, and deviations above or below these levels place a demand on the organism.

Eustress refers to the positive or desired events to which we must adjust. As might be expected, the debilitating effects of eustress are far less than those of negative stressors. It might be speculated that eustress contributes to health up to a certain point, after which health is undermined (e.g., Holmes & Rahe, 1967). Hans Selye, the father of stress research, found that often the only difference between a negative stressor and eustress is our attitude toward an event (Selye, 1978). And this attitudinal choice is clearly something that we can control.

STRESS OR EUSTRESS?

In our fast-paced world it appears that many people are already operating at the limits of their healthy adaptive capabilities, and so even the addition of what appears to be a positive challenge may strain the system. How might a positive event result in a negative effect on the body? What can be done about it?

Let's take the case of Jack's new job. After many years as a middle manager in a perfume company, Jack was finally promoted to vice-president. Certainly, he saw the promotion as a positive change, a step up that he had long been anticipating. His friends congratulated him and assured him that this was the right move. Naturally it was difficult at first, but he felt that he was doing a good job of handling the increased responsibilities. A year and a half later, Jack suffered a heart attack, at the age of forty-two.

In retrospect, it seems clear that the overall effect of the new position was counter to health. What had gone wrong? Jack's belief that the job was right for him, his desire to identify with this position of success, his ready acceptance of friends' praise and admiration, and his conviction to "look on the positive side" all created a bias against Jack seeing what the job was doing to him. The simple physical signs that the new position was overtaxing his adaptive reserves were overlooked or explained away. Jack couldn't sleep well at night and occasionally resorted to sleeping pills. But by rationalizing, he was able to tell himself, "I've just got a lot on my mind, that's all." He was drinking more now, but he thought of it as "being sociable, enjoying the fruits of my labors." Frequent

headaches were dealt with by the truism, "Everyone has headaches once in a while." In this way, Jack was able to continue his perception of the new job as a positive challenge in his life, despite the evidence of its debilitating effects. In accordance with Rogers's learned values, Jack's beliefs and expectations concerning what should be the case overrode his perceptions of what was actually happening.

But how can people be so insensitive to what their bodies are telling them? Certainly, it is easier to be objective about someone else's problems than about one's own. Also, once a problem is described and simplified, as in Jack's case, the discrimination between what aids or impairs health seems more obvious than it does in real life. For example, one complicating factor is that when taking a new job, it is common to fear that we may fail, disappoint our parents, or otherwise embarrass ourselves. As existential psychologists point out, it is natural to fear what is novel and therefore unknown. But they also argue that the path of growth requires us to endure those fears, even though the more pleasant option in the short run is to shrink in the face of challenge.

In other words, some physiological signs might validly indicate that the new job is undermining your health. Other physiological signs, however, may indicate only temporary insecurities and would be best handled by plunging into the work. Often it is not easy to discriminate between these two situations. Thus whether an adjustive demand promotes or undermines health cannot simply be decided by whether it "feels right." Pleasant feelings might result from strongly held prior expectancies overriding immediate perceptions. And negative feelings could result from irrational fears that will soon dissipate if we push on, committed to the endeavor.

How can we determine whether to persist or abandon an apparently positive challenge accompanied by signs of disturbance? Obviously, there is no simple answer to this dilemma, but strategies can be devised to deal with it. First, although signs of fear and stress overlap to an extent (especially since fear itself contributes to stress), the entire pattern of signs can be considered to determine whether you are primarily dealing with a temporary and manageable fear reaction or a chronic and debilitating stress. For example, feeling uncomfortable, unsure of yourself, and agitated at supervisory meetings after being on a job for two months suggests a temporary fear reaction that will likely disappear with time and experience. On the other hand, fatigue, insomnia, and irritability with colleagues after a year on the job suggest stress.

Second, practice in self-observation can develop the skill of knowing which of your feelings and behaviors indicate that you are carrying too great an adjustive demand. Individual signs of this may include a soreness in the eyes, a feeling of tightness in the forehead or shoulders, indigestion, cold hands (muscle tension blocking blood flow), high susceptibility to colds (weakening of the immune system), accident proneness, and a need for stimulants such as coffee and cigarettes.

Third, an experimental approach can be taken, in which a new challenge is accepted on a trial basis, and then given up if the signs of stress continue.

One factor that hinders stress control is the belief that stress is simply the price we must pay for success. It is part of our cultural lore that excellence does not come easily, that nothing of value is had for the asking. These aphorisms can be misinterpreted to imply that the avoidance of stress is a cowardly refusal to live life to its fullest. In fact, research has shown that stress interferes with optimal functioning and that those who are the most successful have devised effective strategies for controlling the stress in their lives (Seliger, 1982). Moreover, there is also evidence that when working optimally, that is, when you are totally and un-self-consciously absorbed in an activity that you believe in, a tremendous work load can be taken on without stressful effects (Selye, 1978).

THE STRESS OF CHANGE

One way of measuring stressful life events is the approach taken by two psychiatrists, Thomas Holmes and R. H. Rahe (1967). They reasoned that environmental changes that require some form of coping place an adjustive demand on the organism. Since the ability to deal with adjustive demands is limited, a clustering of such events could deplete the organism's adaptive reserves, impairing the immune system. Thus they believed that events as disparate as taking a vacation and being fired were linked in requiring a change in one's adjustive routine. If enough of these events occurred in a short period of time, the individual might succumb to disease.

Holmes and Rahe compiled lists of life events that had been informally observed to cluster at the time of disease onset. With marriage given an arbitrary score of 50 on a hundred-point scale, they asked individuals to rate the amount of readjustment required for each of the other life events. They found that even people from different cultures showed general agreement in their scores. The resulting Social Readjustment Rating Scale, presented in Table 4–1, contains forty-three life events, rated from 11 to 100. Typically, the scale is completed for the previous year and used to predict illness during the next two years. Thus a period of two years from a clustering of life changes is the time when a person is considered at risk. Results obtained with this scale indicate the following:

150 to 199 readjustment units predict a 33 percent chance of illness.
200 to 299 units predict a 50 percent chance of illness.
300+ units predict an 80 percent chance of illness.

(Note that the scale was developed from a nonstudent sample, and so it may underestimate the readjustment demand for students.)

TABLE **4 − 1**
MEASURING STRESS

Holmes's and Rahe's (1967) Social Readjustment Rating Scale follows. Total up your readjustment score for the life events you experienced in the past year. For events that occurred more than once, count each instance.

LIFE EVENT	READJUSTMENT SCORE
1. Death of spouse	100
2. Divorce	73
3. Marital separation	65
4. Jail term	63
5. Death of close family member	63
6. Personal injury or illness	53
7. Marriage	50
8. Fired at work	47
9. Marital reconciliation	45
10. Retirement	45
11. Change in health of family member	44
12. Pregnancy	40
13. Sex difficulties	39
14. Gain of new family member	39
15. Business readjustment	39
16. Change in financial state	38
17. Death of close friend	37
18. Change to different line of work	36
19. Change in number of arguments with spouse	35
20. Mortgage over $10,000	31
21. Foreclosure of mortgage or loan	30
22. Change in responsibilities at work	29
23. Son or daughter leaving home	29
24. Trouble with in-laws	29
25. Outstanding personal achievement	28
26. Wife (spouse) begins or stops work	26

TABLE **4 − 1**   *(continued)*

LIFE EVENT	READJUSTMENT SCORE
27. Begin or end school	26
28. Change in living conditions	25
29. Revision of personal habits	24
30. Trouble with boss	23
31. Change in work hours or conditions	20
32. Change in residence	20
33. Change in schools	20
34. Change in recreation	19
35. Change in church activities	19
36. Change in social activities	18
37. Mortgage or loan less than $10,000	17
38. Change in sleeping habits	16
39. Change in number of family get-togethers	15
40. Change in eating habits	15
41. Vacation	13
42. Christmas	12
43. Minor violations of the law	11

The severity of the illness that the readjustment score predicts is sometimes unclear, with Holmes and his colleagues generally defining it as a "major health change." Holmes (1970), for example, used the scale with a sample of medical students and found that 52 percent reported at least one major health change during a two-year period. Typically, a major health change is viewed as an illness that would require seeing a physician or missing at least several days of work.

Holmes and Masuda (1974) reported that readjustment scores have been linked to sudden cardiac death, heart attacks, bone fractures, pregnancy, beginnings of prison terms, leukemia in children, academic grade point average, teacher absenteeism, injury to college football players, seriousness of chronic diseases, and a host of minor health changes. In addition, stressful life events have also been related to acute schizophrenia, depression, suicide attempts, and neurosis (Dohrenwend & Dohrenwend, 1974). Recent research suggests that although both desirable and undesirable life changes are related to physical illness, it seems that only the undesirable changes lead to psychological problems such as depression and anxiety (Sarason, Johnson, & Siegel, 1978).

Suppose that your readjustment score is over 300. Of what value is it to know there is a statistical probability of 80 percent that you will have a major health change within the next two years? Should you check into the nearest hospital and await the near-inevitable? Obviously not. If you have developed a stress-resistant personality (see FOCUS: The Stress-resistant Personality), you may well have a high readjustment score *and* excellent health. In fact, you may be your healthiest when under a fairly high readjustment load. On the other hand, if you are stress prone, the readjustment score can be a valuable piece of information, telling you that now is the time to cut back on nonessential adaptive demands and simplify your life. It is also the time to attack those old patterns of thinking that increase your vulnerability to stress. Specific techniques for stress control are described later in this chapter.

INNATE STRESSOR REACTIONS: THE GENERAL ADAPTATION SYNDROME

Hans Selye (1976) discovered that we undergo similar reactions when dealing with stressful situations, regardless of whether the stress is caused by disease, noise, cold, job pressures, overcrowding, or a host of other physical and psychological factors. Selye labeled these reactions the **general adaptation syndrome**, and he described them as occurring in three stages: alarm, resistance, and exhaustion.

Hans Selye.

ALARM

The alarm stage brings into play initial attempts to mobilize one's resources and cope with the stressor. Heart and respiration rates increase, muscles tense, pupils dilate, and the organism becomes emotionally aroused and alert. Other bodily processes not involved with coping, such as digestion, may be suppressed. If one is overwhelmed by a sudden environmental threat, signs of distress such as crying, shaking, stomach upset, and urinary incontinence may also occur.

RESISTANCE

If the threat continues, individuals often find some way of holding themselves together and dealing with it. In a single-minded attempt to handle the stressor, people often become rigid, make excessive use of defense mechanisms, and close themselves to other solutions. Physical symptoms of stress may occur, but they are generally kept from interfering with the coping response, even though they exact a heavy toll in wear and tear on the body.

EXHAUSTION

With prolonged stress, coping reserves may be depleted, and so other, more extreme defenses become necessary. Individuals may become vulnerable to other stressors that otherwise could have been handled with ease. They may also break down in physical illness or undergo a psychological break with reality. Selye found that contrary to popular opinion, even long periods of rest do not completely restore the original level of fitness. He maintained that after extreme stress, an indelible "scar" remains. Reserves of adaptability are used up that can never be replaced, and this is one way in which aging may occur.

STRESS AND DISEASE

CORONARY HEART DISEASE

More Americans die of heart disease than of any other single cause. Heart disease typically involves hardening of the arteries. Cholesterol deposits on arterial walls narrow the channels of blood flow. If sections of cholesterol break free, blood clots are formed that may clog up the already narrowed channels of a coronary artery, resulting in a heart attack.

Stress affects this process in several ways. The natural stress reaction includes an increase in blood cholesterol, an increase in blood pressure (making it more likely that cholesterol deposits will break free), and an increase in the rate of clotting. Thus the body's natural preparations for danger become self-destructive when the perceived threat is chronic.

Even though cholesterol buildup may go on for decades, in 25 percent of the cases the first outward sign of disease is sudden death from a heart attack (Brody, 1982). The danger of heart attack is compounded by a natural tendency to

TABLE 4−2

PREDICTORS OF HEART ATTACK

A number of factors have been identified that place an individual at statistical risk for a heart attack:

1. Previous heart attack.
2. Family history of heart disease.
3. High blood pressure. A reading above 120/80 (arterial pressure when the heart beats/ pressure between beats) may be high for adults.
4. Diabetes.
5. High levels of blood cholesterol (above 200 milligrams percent).
6. Smoking. Compared with nonsmokers, cigarette smokers show a 70 percent greater chance of developing heart disease.
7. Obesity. Keep to within about five pounds of your optimal weight. (Forty percent of Americans are more than twenty pounds overweight.)
8. Lack of aerobic exercise.
9. Stressful environments.
10. Type A (rather than type B) personality (see FOCUS: The Type A Personality) (Adapted from Brody, 1982)

deny the symptoms of a first attack. For first occurrences, there is typically a delay of four or five hours between the onset of symptoms and arrival at the hospital. People deny that anything serious could be wrong and attribute the pain to "heartburn" or indigestion. Often the victim's companions share in the denial and fail to take, action.

The symptoms of a heart attack are acute chest pain, blackouts after exertion, noticeable shortness of breath, and severe indigestion. The pain is usually in the center of the chest, but it may extend into the shoulder and neck. Note that this pain is a heavy crushing or squeezing rather than a sharp or burning sensation.

CANCER

Worldwide, nearly 10 percent of all deaths are attributed to cancer, and although heart disease is the greater killer, cancer is the more feared.

The connection between life stress and cancer is somewhat controversial. Clearly, heredity and contact with particular chemical stressors (carcinogens such as cigarette smoke), play a major role in causing cancer. Several researchers, however, have also linked interpersonal stressors and personality to cancer. For example, cancer patients show similarities in personality to those who have committed suicide. Table 4−3 summarizes interpersonal predictors of cancer.

TABLE 4−3

PERSONAL AND SOCIAL PREDICTORS OF CANCER

1. The perception of one's parents, especially the mother, as neglecting and cold.
2. Loss of an important relationship, such as the death of a spouse, one or two years before the diagnosis of cancer.
3. Tension over the death of a parent.
4. A long-standing, unresolved conflict with the mother.
5. Inhibited feelings of motherhood.
6. Feelings of depression, loneliness, and hopelessness, especially if there are physical signs of depression, such as a change in appearance or sleeping habits.
7. Feeling unwanted and unloved.
8. A defensive, inhibited, overly controlled personality; inhibited sexuality.
9. An inability to express hostile feelings; a denial of one's own aggressiveness.
10. Extreme pleasantness; acting happy while feeling depressed; self-sacrificing or self-pitying behavior.
11. Moralistic religious attitudes.
12. A tendency to hold resentments and withhold forgiveness.

13. Difficulty maintaining meaningful long-term relationships.
14. Poor self-image. (Adapted from Bahnson, 1980, 1981; Scarf, 1980)

To clarify, having one or more of these traits by no means makes cancer inevitable. It is just that in a number of studies those who have had or would eventually get cancer differed on these factors from normals or other control subjects (such as those with heart disease). Note also that the research has been inconsistent on several of these characteristics, with some studies finding a relationship and others not.

Critics have pointed out that some of the research has compared cancer patients with a normal control group. Such data may be suspect, since differences may have been due to the presence of the cancer. For example, having cancer may lead to depression rather than vice versa. Nevertheless, the overall pattern of characteristics has been substantiated by studies measuring personality variables up to ten or twenty years before the diagnosis of cancer, suggesting a definite role for social and personal factors.

O. Carl Simonton, a radiation specialist and pioneer in using mental imagery in cancer treatment, speculates that cancer is the bodily expression of the patient's psychological despair. In this view, no one *gets* cancer; rather, "we reach a point at which our deepest need and wish is to withdraw from life, and we therefore 'choose' to develop cancer" (Scarf, 1980, p. 37). Thus Simonton views the illness as a defective coping strategy. For those unable to meet their adjustive demands, death may become a viable option, at a more or less unconscious level. In other words, Simonton's answer to the cancer patient's perennial question, "Why me?" is that often it is "because some time within the past year or 18 months I simply gave up on my life" (cited in Scarf, 1980, p. 39).

Simonton's theory, though certainly controversial, is powerfully illustrated in a case history reported by Bahnson (1980, p. 977). The patient, a twenty-six-year-old female, entered psychotherapy six months before her death, when it became clear that her breast cancer had spread and was not responding to medical treatment. A year *before* her diagnosis of cancer the patient had been experiencing "intolerable losses and frustrations in her love relationships," and at that time she wrote:

I have recently put suicide in perspective. I no longer think it's a matter of hurting or punishing someone else. It's more a matter of ending my own pain—like a cancer patient who knows she is never going to recover. Sometimes I feel clearly that my pain is a terminal disease—that I have it, and it is here to stay. I love to sleep and many days I envy the dead's ability not to wake up when the alarm rings.

COPING WITH STRESSFUL EVENTS

Methods of coping are limited only by the boundaries of ingenuity. Yet despite this diversity, coping methods can generally be classified as **instrumental** or **defensive**, depending on whether they are designed to remove the stressful event or to protect oneself from its effects. Successful coping often combines both strategies into a program of long-term stress control.

INSTRUMENTAL COPING

Successful instrumental methods often involve a strategy of identifying the stressor, assessing one's coping resources, and formulating a plan of action. This may take place instantaneously or over a period of months, depending on the situation. Once action is initiated, the individual must gauge its success and remain

FOCUS
THE TYPE A PERSONALITY

One of the best predictors of risk for heart attack is one's characteristic style of dealing with stressful events. Researchers have determined that those with the coping style known as "Type A" run over twice the risk of dying from coronary heart disease as do their "Type B" counterparts (Rosenman et al., 1975).

Who are the Type A's among us? They are highly competitive, time-pressured individuals who react to frustration with aggression and hostility. They are often workaholics who set deadlines for themselves, frequently bring work home, and generally push themselves to capacity in a frantic race against time. In contrast, Type B's pace themselves and avoid getting into a dither over work or other responsibilities.

Note, however, that most Type A's are not dissatisfied with their lives. Typically, they are proud of the way they have adapted to a competitive world, crediting their use of willpower to "get the job done." Note that most Type A's will *not* experience a heart attack, even though they are at greater risk than Type B's are. Thus a controversy exists over whether the Type A pattern is a problem that should be treated before the occurrence of a heart attack. Many Type A's are reluctant to give up a coping style that has, in their minds, served them well.

Compared with Type B's, Type A's show higher levels of blood cholesterol, sharper increases in blood pressure when frustrated, and faster clotting times. Glass (1976) reported that on a treadmill stress test, Type A's push themselves to a greater extent of their aerobic capacity than Type B's do, but they admit to less fatigue. Thus Type A's push themselves to succeed and suppress bodily signals such as fatigue that might interfere with performance. Glass described the Type A's as people who rise to master challenges out of a need to control their world. The Type A

> at first rises to any challenge. He tries hard to control a highly stressful situation, but when his best efforts fail, he feels helpless and his attempts to master it suffer. The death of someone close, the loss of a job, or a financial setback are all events that we can do little to remedy. Although life's tragedies are hard for anyone, they are particularly dangerous for the Type A. (1976, p. 134)

IDENTIFYING THE TYPE A

To get a rough idea of whether you fit the Type A pattern, answer the following questions. If you answer yes to more than half of the items, you have leanings in the Type A direction.

1. Do you find it hard to keep from finishing other people's sentences for them?
2. Do you feel guilty spending time doing nothing, even on weekends?
3. Do you often try to do more than one thing at a time, such as eating and reading?
4. Do you get flustered when waiting in line?

5. Do you need to win in order to enjoy games?
6. Are you continually checking your watch?
7. Do you get angry and honk your horn in traffic, even when it won't do any good?
8. Do you agree to take on too many tasks and responsibilities?
9. Do you move, walk, and eat quickly?
10. Do you often race through yellow lights when you drive? (Adapted from Friedman & Rosenman, 1974)

The Type A personality is aggressive, hostile, and time-pressured.

Do you think that Type A's who are happy with their aggressive style and who do not have heart trouble should change their behavior?

flexible so that an ineffective strategy can be quickly corrected. Effective action may involve simply trying harder, employing physical force, acquiring better skills, getting new information, enlisting the help of others, selecting new goals, or simply waiting for a volatile situation to change.

An instrumental response that is often overlooked is changing our perception of an event. People differ in their tendency to perceive threat in their lives. The same objective event may be a mild frustration to one person and a crippling blow to the esteem of another. All of us have observed, for example, that some students are more troubled from receiving a test grade of B+ than others are from getting an F.

Let's examine this example further. Perhaps you are thinking, "Maybe I do overreact to test results, but I would rather be an anxious achiever than a carefree failure." If you believe that this is our only choice, then your instrumental options have already been curtailed. Ob-

Depending on the individual, this situation could either be perceived as a feared threat or an awaited challenge.

jectively, all that the situation requires is an assessment of why you did not receive the desired grade and the formulation of a corrective plan of action. Such a plan would typically be little more than an appropriate change in study habits, without any necessity for negative emotion. Why is it then that so many good students continue to become emotionally upset over an unsatisfactory performance?

One obvious reason is that they fear the punishment of disappointing their parents. A less obvious reason is that many students attribute their previous success to having perfectionistic standards and using self-punishment to alter substandard performance. This is a moti-

vational system that many good students have adopted, identified with, and taken pride in. And no one wants to give up a strategy that "works." What goes unnoticed is that others of similar talent have achieved equivalent success without such a heavy reliance on self-punishment.

DEFENSIVE COPING

The most common defensive methods are the ego defense mechanisms (e.g., repression, projection, rationalization), discussed in Chapter 3, and the use of drugs, particularly alcohol and tranquilizers. These methods may be effective in the short term, but since they do not reduce the incidence of stressful events, they offer little long-term benefit. In addition, each has a number of undesirable side effects. The ego defenses distort internal or external reality and so may generate inaccurate information, leading to poor decisions and greater long-term stress. Alcohol and other drugs can have detrimental effects on the body, and they often interfere with adequate coping. (Even though we may feel more skillful when intoxicated, this is rarely a perception shared by others.)

On the other hand, defensive coping can aid adjustment in certain situations. When there is no adaptive instrumental response that can be made or when defensive coping does not interfere with instrumental behavior, it can be helpful (Lazarus, 1979). For example, suppose your doctor tells you that you have a terminal disease. Initial denial buys you time to face the grim truth in a more gradual and manageable way. Denial may also aid the process of recovery. Lazarus (1979) reported that coronary patients who deny the severity of their heart attacks function better when they return to work, and they are more likely to regain full sexual functioning. Even when there is objectively little chance of recovery, denial allows some measure of hope, and through the **placebo effect**, patients sometimes improve just through the hope and expectation of cure.

FOCUS
THE STRESS-RESISTANT PERSONALITY

The stress literature emphasizes the health dangers of stressful environments. The conclusion typically drawn is that stressful situations should be avoided, that the individual should learn to "take it easy." Although often appropriate, this advice is overly simplified, and recent research on hardiness suggests that it can be misleading. Some individuals expose themselves to highly stressful regimes yet remain healthy and even thrive on the pace of their lives. What sets them apart from the rest?

Hardiness research suggests that seeking a minimally stressful environment is only one strategy of stress control. Another is to change one's attitudes and characteristic ways of approaching stressful events. The study of stress-resistant personalities gives a valuable clue as to what changes may work best.

Hans Selye talked about race horses and turtles (also see FOCUS: Sensation Seekers and the Pursuit of Change). Race horses thrive on a vigorous, fast-paced life-style, whereas turtles seek peace and tranquility. Selye suggested that it is useful to know whether you are a race horse or a turtle. Although one is not better than another, it's a good idea to avoid being either a race horse with no chance to gallop or a turtle without a shell.

What characterizes stress-resistant people?

1. A clear sense of one's values, goals, and capabilities, and a belief in their importance (Kobassa, 1979).
2. Active involvement rather than passive acquiescence. Hardy persons actively restructure and initiate desired changes in their personal worlds (Kobassa, 1979).
3. The ability to find personal meaning in stressful life events and to fit these events into one's overall plans and priorities (Kobassa, 1979).
4. An internal locus of control. This is a feeling of being in control of stressful life events rather than viewing them as a function of fate, luck, or the actions of powerful others (Johnson & Sarason, 1979; Kobassa, 1979).
5. A good social support system, including close ties to friends and family (Nuckolls, Cassel, & Kaplan, 1972).
6. High sensation seeking (Smith, Johnson, & Sarason, 1978). According to Zuckerman (1978), this characteristic may have a sizable genetic component and thus it may be difficult to change.
7. A stable, even disposition (Thomas, cited in Garr, 1981).
8. Type B (rather than Type A) personality, indicating an easygoing manner, low hostility, low competitiveness, and little feeling of time pressure (Glass, 1977).

HEALTH PSYCHOLOGY AND THE WELLNESS REVOLUTION

THE RISE OF HEALTH PSYCHOLOGY

Recent trends in psychology and medicine are now coming together, forming an alternative to traditional notions of health and disease. Traditionally, the body has been viewed as a complex machine. As with all machines, the body occasionally breaks down, requiring service from an expert mechanic.

The alternative approach is not intended to deny advances in surgical and chemical treatments, but it does aim to supplement traditional medicine in certain important ways. This alternative, variously referred to as health psychology, behavioral medicine, wellness, or holistic intervention, stems from certain basic assumptions:

Health is not merely the absence of disease. Health psychologists have followed the lead of humanistic theorists such as Abraham Maslow in identifying a dimension of optimal functioning that can be contrasted with the ordinary functioning of the average individual. Whereas Maslow focused on the psychology of self-actualization, health psychologists are hoping to integrate both psychological and physical functioning into one model. The health psychology counterpart to Maslow's self-actualization is sometimes called **high-level wellness**.

Health is a function of life-style. Ken Pelletier (1977) noted that four diseases have become so common in the West that they are known as the "afflictions of civilization." These ailments are heart disease, cancer, arthritis, and bronchitis. Furthermore, he maintains that their major cause is the individual's choice of lifestyle, that is, the decision to accept a rich diet, pollution, and stress. A recent report from the U.S. surgeon general, for example, attributed half of all deaths to an unhealthy life-style (Grossman, 1981).

Carolyn Chambers Clark (1981, p. 2), a leader in the wellness movement, summarized a number of connections between life-style and health:

1. Smoking has been linked to cancer of the lung, larynx, lip, oral cavity, esophagus, and bladder, as well as to bronchitis, emphysema, heart disease, life span, and the health of infants born to smoking mothers.
2. Alcohol is a factor in half of all automobile deaths, half of all homicides, one-third of all suicides, cirrhosis of the liver, malnutrition, lowered resistance to disease, brain and nervous system damage, and physical problems of infants born to drinking mothers.
3. Chronic stress can lead to migraine headaches, peptic ulcers, heart attacks, hypertension, mental illness, suicide, strokes, bowel disorders, diabetes, and skin disorders.
4. Lack of exercise has been linked to hypertension, chronic fatigue, premature aging, back pain, and heart disease.
5. Diet has been linked to five of the ten leading causes of death. For example, the caffeine in coffee and cola drinks induces the secretion of stomach acid, which may lead to heartburn, bleeding ulcers, and nervousness due to B-vitamin excretion.
6. Overeating contributes to half of all cancers.

Health is a function of life-style.

Body, mind, and spirit are not separate "things"; a person is an integrated whole. Since the Middle Ages, Western philosophers have divided the person into the arbitrary compartments of body, mind, and spirit. We have inherited a language that assumes these divisions, which is why they seem so natural to us. The healing professions have undergone a similar division, so that the physician heals the body, the psychologist cures the mind, and the clergy attend to the spirit. The wellness alternative acknowledges that these divisions have served a purpose but maintains it is now more useful to see the person as a meaningful whole, to see that mind, body, and spirit share a common identity. Moreover, health reflects the harmonious functioning of this entire system.

For example, Shames and Sterin (1978) noted that what on the physical level is illness may on the psychological plane be depression and on the spiritual level be experienced as alienation. Clark (1981) observed that people who start exercising and eating better often report changes in the psychological and spiritual dimensions of their lives. Feelings of depression, lethargy, and self-hate lessen, and people may start to experience themselves as part of a greater reality. This reality may be given various names, such as God, nature, or humanity. The important thing, however, is not the name but the mood of connectedness and belonging that these experiences share.

Shames and Sterin speculate that high-level wellness cannot be attained in a state of alienation. If we feel that we must constantly defend ourselves against a hostile environment "out there," then the harmony among mind, body, and spirit is automatically disrupted. But in the modern world we are literally bombarded by newspaper and television broadcasts of war, crime, and violence. One can only wonder about the long-term effects of this information.

Prevention is at least as important as treatment. Since the major diseases result in large part from life-style decisions that we have unwittingly made against our own self-interest, prevention seems both possible and practical. Medicine has already taken treatment measures to a high degree of sophistication and cost, but it has largely ignored comparatively simple and direct preventives. For example, 96 percent of health-care dollars goes to treatment, leaving only 4 percent for prevention and education (Grossman, 1981).

Once life-style and prevention are taken seriously, a number of social changes come to mind. For example, wellness practitioners maintain that the wise doctor is one who keeps patients healthy, not the one who fixes them when they become sick. It has been suggested somewhat facetiously that perhaps physicians should be rewarded for their ability to keep people well instead of the present system, which ties their profits to illness.

A similar dilemma can be found in the business world. The present system rewards employees for being sick by giving them extra time off. This system is based on the erroneous assumption that people don't contribute to their own state of health or illness. How do you think these contingencies could be revised to accommodate the views of health psychology?

You must take responsibility for your own health. Most of us do not distinguish between health care and medical care. Clark (1981) noted that medical care is only one part of health care, and she reported that at least 75 percent of all health care is, in fact, self-provided. For example, most of the problems diagnosed by physicians are self-limiting without any treatment. Franz Ingelfinger, a medical doctor and former editor of the prestigious *New England Journal of Medicine*, estimated that 80 percent of patients are actually unaffected by treatment, with the rest evenly divided between those who are dramatically improved and those who are made sicker by the cure than by the disease (Rubenstein, 1982a). Also, many physical complaints brought to doctors are actually pleas for sympathy and reassurance (Cordes, 1978). In our eagerness to seek the healer, we often forget that our bodies have powerful self-healing abilities when they are not overloaded with stress.

According to William Hettler, a pioneer in the wellness movement, Americans believe that 90 percent of the time doctors can cure them. But Hettler maintains that in fact, with heart disease, doctors can help only 12 percent of the time; with strokes the figure is only 7 percent; and with cirrhosis of the liver, it is even lower. Often the problem can be diagnosed, and some of the symptoms alleviated, but the actual cure is up to the individual patient's self-healing abilities. Hettler commented that "people are killing themselves for the most part. What we doctors do is keep score, and we charge a lot of money for keeping score" (cited in Grossman, 1982, p. 44).

The following sections describe procedures and techniques often used in health psychology.

NUTRITION

First the bad news. Linde (1977) reported that poor nutrition is linked to heart disease, cancer, schizophrenia, intellectual deficits, arthritis, dental problems, diabetes, alcoholism, allergies, chronic fatigue, ulcers, depression, high blood pressure, and sexual malfunction.

FOCUS

MYTHS ABOUT THE FOODS WE EAT

1. *Meat is high in protein.* Meats average only about 25 percent protein, which puts them in the middle of the food distribution. Soybeans, milk, fish, and eggs, for example, all contain higher proportions of protein. One problem is that people sometimes think they should eat more meat to ensure an adequate supply of protein. But most meats contain more fat than protein, and so in effect, these people end up endangering their health by overloading on fats. For example, the calories from a T-bone steak are 82 percent from fat and only 17 percent from protein; the calories from tuna packed in water are 88 percent from protein and only 6 percent from fat.

2. *Large quantities of protein are required to satisfy the body's needs for growth and tissue repair.* Americans eat about twice the amount of protein that their bodies can use. Most would get enough protein even if they eliminated meat, fish, and poultry from their diets.

3. *All proteins are the same.* Amino acids combine to make protein. Eight of these acids cannot be manufactured by the body, and so they should be consumed daily. Some foods contain all eight and are considered complete. Others are incomplete and must be consumed simultaneously with other foods containing the missing amino acids in order to be of use in making protein. Meat, fish, eggs, milk, soybeans, and some cheeses are complete. Complete proteins can be manufactured by combining complete with incomplete proteins or by making the right combination of incomplete proteins. Two rules of thumb are (a) combine beans, peanuts, or peas with corn, rice, wheat, seeds, barley, or oats, and (b) combine rice or corn with wheat germ or seeds (Brody, 1982).

4. *All sugars are the same.* Naturally occurring sugars in milk, fruits, and vegetables enhance wellness because they are combined with other nutrients. Refined, or table, sugar, which is found in soft drinks, desserts, and many processed foods impairs health. Often, foods labeled "natural" contain refined sugars.

5. *Sugar is a good source of energy.* Eating refined sugar leads to less energy because it is digested too rapidly, leading the body to overcompensate for its effects, with a likely end result of fatigue, irritability, and faintness. Frequent high-protein meals are better for sustained energy production.

6. *Carbohydrates, or starches, are the major cause of overweight.* Complex carbohydrates, such as those found in fruits, vegetables, beans, and whole-grain breads are unlikely to cause overweight unless combined with fats (e.g., butter) or simple carbohydrates (e.g., sugared jams). (Adapted from Clark, 1981)

Now the good news. You don't have to be rich to get a healthful diet. In fact, for Americans, having more money usually increases the difficulty. Those rich gourmet meals are deadly.

More good news. What we eat is something that we can control. Once you know what to eat and what to avoid, the rest is a matter of rational self-interest and the battle between the short-term pleasure of eating the wrong foods and the long-term pleasure of feeling good.

Muscle toning, stretching, and cardiovascular training are essential components of fitness.

FITNESS

The health benefits of exercise are well established. Exercise reduces the risk of heart attack, prolongs the lives of those who already have heart trouble, aids in the treatment of diabetes, helps control weight, reduces the loss of calcium in the bones, reduces depression, improves mental functioning, leads to healthier-looking skin (Brody, 1982), reduces medical bills and sick days (Lang, 1982), and enhances self-assurance and emotional stability (Ismail & Young, 1973). In addition, Rubenstein (1982a) found that those who exercised an hour a day were less likely to overeat and felt more happy and successful than did those who exercised less than an hour a week.

Setting up an exercise program. First, see a physician if you are over thirty-five or have any chest pains, shortness of breath with mild exertion, leg pains when walking, swollen ankles, or heart trouble.

Which exercise is best? There are three main types of fitness: strength (muscle toning), flexibility, and endurance (cardiovascular training). A good exercise program should include a balance among these types of fitness. Muscle toning is facilitated by calisthenics and weight training, but weights alone don't aid flexibility or cardiovascular fitness. Flexibility is enhanced by stretching and yoga, but these do little for strength and endurance. Cardiovascular fitness, probably the most important to general health, is aided by continuous movement that raises the heart rate to between 120 and 160 beats per minute (depending on age and conditioning level) and maintains that rate for about fifteen minutes. Stop-and-go activities such as tennis and baseball are not efficient for cardiovascular training. On the other hand, swimming, running, bicycling, and aerobic dance are excellent. To achieve balance, however, running and bicycling should be augmented with stretching and upper-body toning.

Describe your own overall fitness in terms of the three components: strength, flexibility, and endurance.

A major but often overlooked consideration is choosing an activity you will enjoy. If you must "force yourself" to engage in the activity, it is a good bet that before long you will find an excuse for giving it up. Also, begin gradually. A common pattern is an overenthusiastic beginning, followed by aches and pains and a failure to get instant results. The final phase of this pattern is, of course, a retreat to inactivity. For conditioning purposes, there is no need for the activity to be painful. In addition, when your program is working well, you may be temporarily fatigued at its conclusion, but you should feel yourself bouncing back quickly and facing the rest of the day with increased vigor.

Health attitudes. Rubenstein (1982a) identified three types of people with specific health attitudes: those who believe in diet and exercise, those who believe in positive thinking, and those who believe that their well-being is in the hands of fate. She found that those trusting in diet and exercise were the least likely to have a chronic illness, that they reported the fewest physical and psychological symptoms, and that they took the fewest sick days. Surprisingly, positive thinkers had the most chronic illnesses and took the most sick days. The fatalists were described as the most neurotic, being moody, easily hurt, high-strung, self-critical, and sexually dissatisfied.

RELAXATION AND MEDITATION

As two of the most direct means of combating stress, relaxation and meditation are thought to block anxiety and tension and to induce physiological states that promote recuperation of the body. In addition, relaxation training is also designed to control tensions as they occur in everyday settings.

The method of **progressive muscular relaxation** was developed by Jacobson (1938) on the assumption that relaxation and anxiety are mutually exclusive states. This method involves tensing a particular muscle group for a few seconds followed by a complete relaxation of that tension. Immediately after being tensed, the muscles go to a deeper level of relaxation than would have been possible beforehand. This procedure also allows individuals to contrast the feelings of tension and relaxation and to see how far from total relaxation their ordinary state actually is. The tension-relaxation cycle may be repeated several times and then moved to another muscle group. Typically, practitioners start at the feet and work up to the head.

Autogenic training (Luthe, 1977) combines muscular relaxation with visualization and hypnotic suggestion. Suggestions involve specific areas of the body feeling heavy, relaxed, comfortable, warm, and smooth. These suggestions are repeated a number of times and extended to other parts of the body until you are totally relaxed. Individuals also imagine themselves in settings that make them feel warm, comfortable, and heavy. (Warmth is linked to relaxation, because tension inhibits blood flow, creating cold spots on the skin.)

Meditation refers to methods of relaxation involving a mental device such as repeating a particular sound or concentrating on an object. Transcendental meditation (TM) uses the silent repetition of a particular sound or mantra. Research (Wallace & Benson, 1972) indicates that meditators enter a state of alertness, relaxation, and suppressed emotional arousal, with documented changes on a number of physiological indicators. In addition, after three months of TM, meditators describe themselves as happier, more energetic, and more creative (Otis, 1974). They may also be less prone than are nonmeditators to illness resulting from life stress (Goleman, 1976). Note, however, that Taylor (1978) found the various forms of relaxation training to be equally effective.

Herbert Benson (1975), a Harvard cardiologist and meditation researcher, maintains that four factors are necessary for producing a relaxation response: a quiet environment, a mental device to control the focus of attention, a passive attitude of not becoming upset when your attention inevitably wanders, and a physical position that avoids both discomfort and

falling asleep. Benson's procedure for inducing the relaxation response is as follows: Sit quietly in a comfortable position with your eyes closed. Relax your muscles, starting at the feet and working up to the head. Become aware of breathing through your nose and silently saying the word *one* to yourself with each exhalation. Continue for about fifteen minutes, "awakening" gradually. Benson suggests that this technique be practiced once or twice a day, but not within two hours of eating, as digestion interferes with relaxation.

BIOFEEDBACK

Biofeedback refers to the presentation in observable form of a physiological response not ordinarily available to consciousness. This information is typically presented through auditory or visual signals, and it can be used to learn how to control the physiological response. Responses that have been used for biofeedback include muscle contractions, skin temperature (blood flow), blood pressure, heart rate, sweating, brain waves, stomach acidity, sphincter activity, bowel sounds, and sexual arousal. Note that feedback systems occur naturally and control many of the functions necessary for life, such as maintaining body temperature. What is different about biofeedback is the use of sensing devices to present the feedback at a conscious level.

For many, the eventual hope of biofeedback is the control of the healing process itself. Currently, such control is found only in some yoga experts and a few exceptional individuals. One such person is Jack Schwartz, a Netherlander studied at the Menninger Foundation. Pew (1979) described a film in which Schwartz pushed a large, dull, rusty sailmaker's needle into his upper arm, through the bicep, and out the other side. A full range of physiological recording instruments showed no evidence of pain. When the needle was withdrawn, the hole closed instantly, allowing no more than a drop of blood to emerge. Incredibly, the wound completely healed within an hour, with no bruises or internal bleeding. The hope of many researchers is that eventually all people could be taught to develop this level of control over healing.

Although biofeedback in its present state has not shown this level of healing, it has been used to control physiological arousal, and it is a popular treatment for many stress-related disorders. Biofeedback is particularly recommended when control of a specific physiological response is required. For example, Pew described the treatment of patients with circulatory problems in their legs. By using bio-feedback to raise their leg temperature, they increased the blood flow to the clogged areas. This accelerated the development of collateral blood vessels around the clots, in effect, producing a nonsurgical bypass.

Researchers have found, however, that learning to control a physiological response in the laboratory is no guarantee that this will transfer to stressful settings in the natural environment. Thus most therapists emphasize the importance of practicing biofeedback skills under increasingly stressful conditions, gradually weaning oneself from the need for the feedback signals.

FOCUS

THE LONGEVITY FACTOR

It is estimated that prehistoric humans lived for only 20 years, whereas the early Romans lived to be 30. By the mid-1800s, the average life span had increased to 40 years. Today it is about 74 years, and by the year 2000 some experts speculate that it could be over 130! Thus it is possible that the path of geometric growth may also apply to our own longevity. But this conclusion may be premature.

Between 1900 and 1950 life expectancy increased by twenty years, but this was mostly due to improvements in hygiene and the smaller number of infant deaths. For example, between 1900 and 1969 the gain in life expectancy for those already sixty-five was only three years (Barnard & Illman, 1981). Most longevity experts believe that the human life span is biologically ordained and that under optimal conditions it would average about eighty-five.

On the other hand, researchers around the world are taking up a mythological quest (immortality!) to crack the biological code that decrees we all must die. This research centers on two main hypotheses, both of which may be partially correct. One is that the clock of aging is located in brain areas that control hormonal functioning. The other is that the genetic material of each individual cell controls aging.

One group of researchers, for example, is trying to isolate a so-called death hormone, which is thought to block the immune system. Other research has discovered that human cells are programmed to divide about fifty times and then stop. Curiously, the only human cells not limited in this way are cancer cells, suggesting that an understanding of cancer may hold the key to longevity.

Still another group of researchers is working on a way to stimulate the enzymes that repair damaged genes, and this group has already shown remarkable success in extending the lives of one-celled organisms. Other researchers are concentrating on locating an aging supergene; transplanting bone marrow from young animals to old; the use of special nutrients that control the actions of destructive "free radicals"; and the use of diets that maintain nutrition while gradually lowering body weight by 30 percent, a practice that has worked well with experimental animals.

One intriguing idea, put forward by psychologist Lawrence Casler, is that aging is largely in the mind. Casler believes that we have been brainwashed into thinking that we must become less vigorous as we grow older. His strategy uses hypnotic countersuggestions, and he reports success in extending the lives of nursing home residents by several years (Conniff, 1981). A related viewpoint is that of pollster George Gallup, who studied people over the age of ninety-five and concluded that those who live a long time are those who want to live a long time. They are full of curiosity, alert, and take life as it comes (Conniff, 1981).

Linde (1977) and Barnard and Illman (1981) summarized the practical implications of longevity research and found a number of ways to extend life span. According to statistical averages, you can expect about an eleven-year difference between those who follow these rules and those who do not.

1. Get your blood pressure down to 120/80.
2. Don't smoke.
3. Don't be more than 10 percent overweight.
4. Get your cholesterol level down to 180.
5. Set up a regular exercise program.
6. Don't overreact to stress and tension.
7. Simplify your life; don't constantly try to race against time.
8. Study safety measures; avoid recklessness and showing off.
9. Eliminate from your diet sugar, sugared foods, and other junk foods.
10. Keep alcohol to moderate amounts.
11. Eat whole-grain carbohydrates.
12. Eat breakfast.
13. Don't eat between meals.
14. Take supplementary vitamins, especially C and E.
15. Get seven to eight hours of sleep a day.

SUMMARY

1. Toffler described human history in terms of three great waves of change: the agricultural, industrial, and information revolutions. We are currently in the changeover period between the second and third waves, and this transition makes it difficult for us to get a clear sense of who we are and what we are likely to become.

2. We live in a world of accelerating change and the consequent overstimulation of future shock. Knowledge and information are increasing geometrically while society is decentralizing and imposing a greater decisional load on the individual.

3. These changes are endangering the jobs of many workers and increasing the skill level required for adapting to society. Change may also play a role in increasing the probability of nuclear war.

4. People differ in the extent to which they seek external stimulation. Low sensation seekers may be particularly at risk in a society undergoing radical change.

5. Stress is the wear and tear on the body from trying to cope with deviations from optimal arousal. Our complex and changing society has made stress a major contributor to the six leading causes of death.

6. Environmental stressors include the major changes to which we must adapt as well as the annoying hassles of everyday life. They also include positive events (eustress).

7. Positive events can have several unexpected debilitating effects on health. The desirability of an event such as a job promotion can create a bias against seeing the initial physiological signs that the event is undermining one's health. Moreover, it is sometimes difficult to distinguish the normal and temporary fears of a new situation from the signs of chronic stress.

8. Selye found that a wide range of stressful situations trigger a pattern of reactions called the general adaptation syndrome. This syndrome includes three stages: alarm, in which individuals come to a state of physiological readiness; resistance, in which individuals hold themselves together in a single-minded coping attempt; and exhaustion, in which individuals break down into illness or other more extreme defenses if their coping reserves are depleted.

9. Holmes and Rahe developed a scale for measuring the stress of environmental changes to which we must adapt. Accumulated stress has been linked to physical illness.

10. Heart disease has been strongly tied to stress, particularly for the Type A personality, who is competitive, hostile, and pressured by time.

11. Cancer is also stress related. Research suggests that there may be a cancer-prone personality, characterized by feelings of depression, an inability to express hostile feelings, and a denial of one's own aggressiveness.

12. Instrumental coping is designed to remove stressful events, whereas defensive coping is merely self-protective. Successful coping will often employ both methods.

13. A stress-resistant personality can be identified. These individuals tend to have a clear sense of values, internal locus of control, good social support, stable dispositions, Type B personalities, and be high sensation seekers and actively involved in their personal worlds.

14. Health psychology and wellness are forming an alternative to traditional medicine. Some assumptions of this alternative are that health is not merely the absence of disease, that health is a function of life-style, that

body, mind, and spirit are not separate "things," that prevention is at least as important as treatment, and that you must take responsibility for your own health.

15. Poor nutrition is a factor in many disorders, largely because Americans now have the means to eat foods that undermine health.

16. Fitness is a balance among strength, flexibility, and endurance.

17. The four factors necessary for Benson's relaxation response are a quiet environment, a mental device for controlling attention, a nonworrying attitude, and a comfortable position.

18. Biofeedback, the detection and amplified representation of physiological responses, is widely used for controlling specific physiological reactions and producing general reductions in arousal.

19. Longevity research shows a number of life-style factors that, in terms of statistical averages, may increase life span by eleven years.

SUGGESTED READINGS

Benson, H. **The relaxation response.** New York: Morrow, 1975. Practical advice on one of the most important stress control skills.

Friedman, M., & Rosenman, R. H. **Type A behavior and your heart.** New York: Knopf, 1974. A popular book describing the implications of the Type A syndrome.

Lazarus, R. S., & Folkman, S. **Stress, appraisal, and coping.** New York: Springer, 1984. Excellent multidisciplinary theoretical analysis.

Selye, H. **The stress of life** (Rev. ed.). New York: McGraw-Hill, 1976. A classic by the father of stress research.

GENDER ROLES

5

The Social Revolution of Our Times

THE CHANGE IN GENDER ROLES

Changes in modern society have not been restricted to technology and information. Change is also a reality within our most intimate relationships. Psychiatrist George Serban, for example, found that the greatest reported stressor among American adults is the change in society's attitudes toward sex and the new social roles of the sexes (Wallis, 1983). The current upheaval in these new social roles reflects no less than a basic restructuring in what it means to be a man or a woman.

Gender refers to one's physical sex. **Gender identity** is one's feeling of being male or female, a discrimination firmly established by the age of three and probably the most central factor in defining personal identity. **Gender role** is the pattern of behaviors and attitudes considered appropriate for a male or a female in a given culture. Clearly, one of the most fundamental social changes over the past several decades has been the transformation in gender roles.

The percentage of married women who work outside the home (now over 50 percent) has doubled in one generation, and this increase is even greater for women with young children (Davis, 1984). Women are now approaching men in the attainment of higher education, the main vehicle for entrance into the male-dominated career market. Many women, for example, are entering professions previously reserved for men, such as law, medicine, and finance. And to illustrate how pervasive these changes are, the proportion of female criminals is also on the rise (Wesley & Wesley, 1977).

Although most changes in gender role pertain to female behavior, many also concern what is permissible for males. Certainly, males have become more prominent in traditional female occupations such as elementary school teacher, nurse, telephone operator, and airline flight attendant. Some redefinition of the male personality can be seen in the emergence on television and in movies of a new stereotype, the "sensitive male," as exemplified by Alan Alda and Phil Donahue.

Society is reluctant, however, to sanction displays of vulnerability, dependency, or emotionality in males. Note, for example, that these behaviors are still controlled by pejorative labels such as "sissy," "effeminate," and "homosexual." Thus the masculine ideal is also shifting, but at a slower rate than that for females.

The change in gender roles is one of the most controversial issues our society faces. Some picture this change as a misguided pursuit of equality through the masculinization of women and the feminization of men. Others see these new roles as a liberation from rigid and restrictive codes that have limited the potentials of both sexes.

Because gender is such a core characteristic of each individual, few have remained indifferent to these social changes. These changes have either resulted in (or perhaps merely brought to light) powerful tensions between the sexes, as exemplified in the title of a recent book on gender roles, *The Longest War* (Tavris & Wade, 1984). Strong feelings are also evident in the harsh language used to characterize the factions in this struggle. Consider the tension implicit in

Both men and women are now entering occupations that were previously held only by the opposite sex.

In our culture, John Wayne and Marilyn Monroe represent traditional gender roles. Michael Jackson and Princess Stephanie of Monaco point toward emerging nontraditional alternatives.

the labels "male chauvinist pig" and "man-hating lesbian."

But there is also tension within the genders. Some women feel that the belittling of housework by feminists makes it difficult for homemakers to feel good about themselves. There also is tension between traditional and nontraditional men. Is one group insensitive and backward? Is the other effeminate?

Whether you affirm or resist these new social roles, one thing is clear—they represent a powerful and pervasive social revolution, and something with which we all must cope.

How do you view the change in gender roles? Do you think of yourself as following a more traditional or a more nontraditional role? Have these changes affected your heterosexual relationships? In what way?

GENDER ROLE AND THE SEARCH FOR IDENTITY*

MARLENE

Marlene, the youngest daughter in a lower-middle class family, was regarded as the most intelligent of the girls, excelling in school, the arts, and sports. Her parents were proud of her and expected her to outdo her female friends in whatever she tried.

Although they urged her to be independent, her parents were very protective of Marlene, seldom allowing her to try things on her own. Marlene thus came to think of herself as an independent person who made her own decisions, but these decisions accorded closely with what her parents expected.

Competition was a major factor in Marlene's life. Her mother repeatedly compared her performance with that of her classmates, and Marlene cried often in junior high because she was frightened that she could not match the accomplishments of her best friend, Lynda.

Marlene learned to win her parents' approval by meeting their expectations:

> I was also taught some absolutes. Nice girls don't drink, smoke, take drugs, swear, win when competing with boys, etc. The first four made sense to me and do now; the latter never has.

In high school Marlene's interests turned to boys, and although she was still competitive, she knew it was important not to do better than a male did.

Marlene was preoccupied with dating, and she naturally assumed that her life's meaning would ultimately be found in marriage. She was strongly aware of this assumption but was hesitant to acknowledge it, since in her mind, it conflicted so directly with her own need for achievement. Marlene summed up her dilemma in a poem:

> I was taught to be competitive,
>   Yet I must never win.
> I was taught to go to college and to be intelligent,
>   Yet what would I do with it? Marry?
> I was taught to be aggressive and achieve,
>   Yet I must be submissive.
> I was taught to be independent,
>   Yet I was dependent on everyone and his brother!
> I was taught to make my own decisions,
>   Yet I never knew what I wanted or what to do.
> I was taught that nice girls don't drink or smoke or swear or . . . the latter generally not discussed.
> I was taught to be feminine
>   And I do not know who I am.

EDWARD

Edward's father was a construction worker, and his mother stayed home to raise the children. Edward learned to read at an early age and was fascinated by books. But his parents, particularly his father, were concerned that Edward

* The cases of Marlene and Edward are adapted from Forisha, 1978, pp. 12–16.

was too quiet, and so they continually urged him to become more active. Edward recalled often getting hurt when he tried to please them, but his parents accepted these scrapes calmly, as they thought he was at last becoming a "real boy."

Edward's time at school left mostly the remembrance of a terrifying nun whom he recalls as "a Marine sergeant in a penguin suit." Daily encounters with her reduced him to tears:

> My father was furious! His son was a crybaby. Lecture after lecture on being a man was drilled into my head but it did no good. I was terrified and all my father could think of was to call me a sissy.

Soon afterwards, Edward turned to sports. By the fourth grade he had become a "sports freak."

> I found I liked to play and I was good at it. You should have seen my father eat it up. At last he had that son to play catch with! I don't think anything was so strongly reinforced as my enthusiasm for sports. My coaches and my father worshipped victory. To win was the only acceptable outcome of competition. To lose was to be damned, to be weak, to be less of a man.

> The competitive ethic learned in sports was carried onto the academic and the social spheres in high school. We were taught to thrive on competition and achievement. Failure was not to be tolerated. I was taught the school's conception of what it is to be a man. I was to be intelligent and extremely logical in all circumstances; I was to be a leader who helped those less fortunate. I was to be strong and support the weak. I was to strive continually for mental, physical and spiritual greatness.

Edward was also strongly encouraged to be self-reliant. By the age of fifteen, his father required him to pay his school tuition and other expenses, stating that "a man should be self-

supporting, independent, strong, and self-confident."

Edward is currently reevaluating much of his upbringing:

> I was sucked into this achievement vacuum of my own volition. I could feel its pull, which received extensive positive reinforcement from my family, my girlfriend, her parents, and my peer group. I am now slowly fighting the suction power of this vacuum and beginning to surface with a clearer, more autonomous outlook on life. . . . Right now I feel light, almost high, as if weight has been taken off my mind and body. I don't feel pressured anymore to be "masculine," to be a Rock of Gibraltar, a pillar of strength, aggressive, logical, analytic, argumentative, competitive. . . . I feel like a baby discovering himself for the first time.

What are your thoughts on Marlene and Edward? What are their gender-role problems? What are the similarities and differences in their situations? What signs are there that Marlene and Edward are moving toward psychological growth?

REFLECTIONS

A number of parallels can be drawn between Marlene and Edward. As expected, they were raised in accordance with their respective gender roles. Each was also groomed for competition and achievement. For each, the same-sex parent was particularly influential in gender development. Each is reacting to the rigid and absolute sex-role ideals they were taught. And each is going through a period of confusion and reevaluation as they realize that they never really chose the values they had accepted.

Neither Marlene nor Edward felt a need to rebel by doing the opposite of what their parents wanted. Rather than a move toward independence, this would have merely exchanged one form of dependence for another. Marlene and Edward have taken on the challenge of deciding which aspects of their traditional gender roles they would feel comfortable in consciously adopting. In a sense, both are formulating their own interpretations of what it means to be a woman or a man, realizing that they must still live in a society that subscribes to certain stereotyped notions of masculinity and femininity.

It appears that Marlene is not questioning the value of a competitive, achievement-oriented life so much as the frustrating taboo against women competing with men. She is facing a common dilemma of capable young women. Marlene was urged to excel, yet just when it would be time to go out into the world, test her skills, and reap the benefits of her talent, she is expected to give this all up and center her life on a man. In emphasizing achievement, Marlene's mother apparently presented her with a modified female role in order to accommodate Marlene's inherent abilities and her mother's ambitions for her. However, this compromise left Marlene pulled in seemingly incompatible directions.

One solution often sought by women of accomplishment is to find a man who is so competent and self-assured that he is not threatened by her success. In this way, the need to hide one's talents or play the role of "dumb blonde" can be eliminated. Such a man, however, typically expects his career to take precedence over his wife's. In such situations, the potential for conflict is obvious. Nevertheless, in Marlene's case, it seems clear that she would be dissatisfied with a solution that did not allow her to achieve.

For Edward, there is no such conflict between achievement and romance. His adjustment involves deciding which of his father's values he wants to adopt. Thus the path for Edward may be more straightforward than that for Marlene. For him, the burden of carrying a rigid conception of masculinity was overwhelming. His strategy will likely be to relax his father's unrealistic requirements. Note that many of his father's ideals, such as strength and self-reliance, are quite admirable. But in the process of socialization Edward also learned that he was

not entitled to feel good about himself unless he fulfilled each of these goals at a level of near-perfection. Thus praiseworthy ideals became harsh masters, with the net effect of impeding Edward's adjustment and growth. For example, his sense of relief when these values were suspended is a clue that his rigid conception of masculinity had slowly been robbing him of energy and a sense of aliveness.

It is a healthy sign that Edward described his gender socialization as occurring through his "own volition." He was aware of the efforts to shape him into assuming a rigidly masculine gender role and, to some extent, he allowed himself to be taken in that direction. Edward could have easily described himself as a passive victim, a mere child who could not resist the forces of adult society. Instead, he took the responsibility for his own behavior and acknowledged that he did have some choice, some awareness, some participation in the matter. Edward views himself as an active agent with awareness and decision-making capacities, not as a passive object of others' intentions. As such it will be much easier for him to take charge and formulate a gender role more suited to his own personality.

What do you see as the best solutions for Marlene and Edward? How do you think Marlene and Edward would do as marriage partners?

THE NEED FOR SOCIAL ROLES

In reading about Marlene and Edward, perhaps you wondered why they needed to be brought up according to any gender roles at all. Wouldn't it have been healthier for them to be raised so that they could find out for themselves what attitudes and behaviors suited them best? This view is popular today, with many arguing that there is no longer a need for separate roles for males and females.

On the other hand, all cultures establish gender roles, suggesting that these roles must have some adaptive significance, or at least that they did at one time.

Social roles simplify our lives. They make our worlds more predictable by giving us commonly established expectancies for how others will act. It could be argued that without these socially defined roles, interpersonal relations would be complete chaos. For each new person we meet, the "rules of conduct" would have to be invented anew, vastly complicating the decisions required in everyday life.

We might speculate that eliminating social roles would have two effects: It would increase excitement by forcing you to see each new person as unique. At the same time, without roles to guide our behavior, the flow of social transactions would become awkward, complicated, and stressful.

As long as the sexes differ, it is likely that society will incorporate those differences into its formalized structure of social roles. All societies have gender roles, but there is great variability in the ways that those roles are defined. What varies from culture to culture are the extent to which male and female roles are separate from each other and the extent to which deviations from those roles are tolerated. Presumably, what our own culture seeks in this transition period is a new set of roles that accurately reflects the sex differences relevant to our times. Hopefully, these new roles will provide an optimal balance between individual growth and social expediency.

TRADITIONAL GENDER ROLES: WHEN MEN WERE MEN AND WOMEN WERE GIRLS

Traditional roles are based on the assumption that men and women not only differ, they are psychological opposites. This is what presumably stirs their unique chemistry. Both in their personal characteristics and the roles they play, the sexes have traditionally been thought of as separate and distinct.

DEFINING THE MALE ROLE

In the stereotypical male role, men are supposed to be dominant, assertive, logical, analytical, objective, competent, competitive, and capable. They are the leaders, the protectors, the ones in authority. In relationships with women, men take the initiative and the ensuing risk. They ask for dates, propose marriage, and make the first move in sex. But they are not supposed to show vulnerability; it is unmasculine to cry, express sadness, or otherwise be "overly emotional." The male should neither show fear nor admit inadequacy. The Latino male's strutting stance, the Anglo's stiff upper lip, and the Afro's jive-walk all display fearlessness, regardless of the danger.

DEFINING THE FEMALE ROLE

In the stereotypical female role, women are supposed to be nurturing, tender, receptive, sensitive, empathic, submissive, caring, and loving. Their lives revolve around husband and family. They are interested in others, skillful in relationships, and concerned with serving and pleasing men. Traditional femininity also implies inferiority to men in worldly affairs. Women are not supposed to be achievement oriented, they are not mathematical, they are intuitive rather than rational, and they are too emotional to be counted on in a crisis. Thus the stereotype suggests that women are better suited for domestic life than for the jungle of the "real world."

EVALUATING THE TRADITIONAL ROLES

The male role. In the traditional masculine role, men see themselves as strong, competent, and independent. They have taken power, held status, and defined what is important in this world. The main drawback of the male role is that it is nearly impossible to live up to, and the consequences for being unmasculine include an unforgiving loss of respect. Thus many men carry the burden of continually monitoring themselves. They must be sure their behavior is appropriately masculine. Any lapse must be immediately smoothed over, rationalized, or repressed. Some give up trying to fit the role and acknowledge unmanliness, but these "boys" often become social outcasts.

In addition, the taboo against showing vulnerability means that men cannot be spontaneous in their emotions; they must be careful not to show too much. This often prevents them from having close personal relationships, adding to the stress in their lives. As noted in the previous chapter, it is no accident that men die earlier than women do. As one forty-five-year-old male described it:

> My group of friends gets together to play poker almost every week. There are six guys in the group. We shoot the breeze about politics or taxes or football or our cars, but we hardly ever talk about personal problems, not even when only two of us are riding home in the same car at the end of the evening. George is getting a divorce, but he tries not to talk about the troubles he's having with his wife and his lawyers. Don's got a retarded kid but he never talks about his personal problems either. And none of us knew that Eliot had a heart condition until he ended up in the hospital.
>
> Why can't men share personal information the way that women do? My wife's friends are always sharing their problems and trying to help each other out. That seems like a much friendlier kind of friendship. (Derlega & Janda, 1981, p. 200)

Even when men try to break away from the masculine role, they often find themselves coming back to traditional assumptions:

> I still very much hold on to some of [my father's] ideas about being strong and potent, and these feelings used to scare me when I was younger, because I felt that I could never fill those images of masculinity. In some ways

Many men feel uneasy when traditional gender roles are reversed.

> I still feel that I want to be king of my castle, just like him, and my wife and I joke about that a lot. It's also important to me to earn more money than she does, even though she's a professional, too, and I feel sometimes that I still want to hold on to the stereotypes about women that I got from my father, that basically women are emotional and are nincompoops. . . . You know, I try to filter out these attitudes or make light of them, but they're still buried deep inside. (Bell, 1982, p. 12)

Of course, one of the reasons that traditional masculine attitudes are so hard to change is that they are self-serving. It is desirable to be the top dog, and the glory is more visible than the accompanying restrictions. As a twenty-two-year-old liberal arts major put it, he's in favor of the newer roles, but a girl friend paying her own way on a date makes him feel "a little less macho." And a girl friend driving the car is even worse: "I feel like a little kid being driven around by my mother" (Gelman, 1978, p. 60).

The female role. The benefits of the feminine role are the freedom to admit weakness, and the personal intimacy that comes from a freer expression of emotion. The feminine role is also seductive; all of us sometimes want to be taken care of, if only for a few hours. At such times, the risk and responsibility of the male role may not be appealing.

The drawbacks of the female role have been well articulated by leaders of the feminist movement for a number of years now. Women's desires to achieve, to make a mark on the world, and to attain economic and political power cannot be satisfied within the rigid confines of the traditional female role. For women who have such desires, that role can be a prison. For women without those desires, separate roles

and unequal power have nevertheless saddled them with second-class social status. Moreover, in a world where men's values predominate, it is hard to feel good about yourself when your life has been devoted to the opposite values. However much men profess to appreciate domestic activities, the news media and other channels of cultural influence make it clear which values count. The ambivalent attitudes toward femininity characteristic of many modern women are aptly expressed by a female college student:

> Sometimes I feel that the roles we play are so stifling and inhibiting. I sometimes enjoy being feminine and a bit helpless or submissive, but

FOCUS
FEMININITY AND THE BEAUTY TRAP

Author Susan Brownmiller (1984) maintains that traditional femininity means accepting, perhaps even adoring, the handicap that is the woman's role.

In her own life, Brownmiller has experimented with ending the attempt to please men by living up to the ideals of feminine beauty. For example, she has given up many things that she sees as symbols of women's bondage to male approval, such as nonfunctional clothing (high-heeled shoes, skirts, dresses, hosiery), shaving her legs, having her hair done, and wearing makeup. Brownmiller maintains that these things have nothing to do with making a woman a better person: They merely create the illusion of beauty that men desire. She argues that the hours per day required to maintain this illusion could be better spent in any number of other ways. In other words, it makes more sense for men to change their preferences than for women to submit to an unnatural image of perfection.

What makes Brownmiller's case so intriguing is that she freely admits that her own feelings are in conflict. For example, she acknowledges that her unshaven legs are unattractive, even to herself. She believes, however, that this acquired aversion to leg hair is itself an unhealthy reflection of male idealization. (Leg hair is too-direct a reminder of the animal nature that idealized women are supposed to have transcended.) She claims that "if an esthetic convinces you to dislike our body in its natural state, you have to be in conflict with who you are. It's not what you really look like, and the implied message is that there is something wrong with you in the natural state" (Zimmerman, 1984, p. 12).

Brownmiller concludes, "I hardly presume to tell someone to take off her high heel shoes. Even though they're killing her feet, she will feel more psychologically comfortable with heels, and she will be perceived as more feminine in them. I just wish women would understand what they're doing and laugh at it. And I hope one day we have more choice" (Zimmerman, 1984, p. 12).

According to author Susan Brownmiller, it takes many hours a day for women to create the illusion of beauty that men desire.

the problem is turning it on and off when you feel like it. How many times can somebody open a door for you before you start to wonder what's wrong with you? Ultimately, I would like to let go of being so feminine and try to just be more of myself. I wonder if it's really possible? (Rosen & Hall, 1984, p. 27)

BALANCING ROLES OR BALANCING PEOPLE?

The model of traditional gender roles allows a specialization of skills and attributes so that the male and female complement each other.

Although the two halves of this dyad are themselves one-sided, together they form a balanced whole. Currently, however, gender roles are moving toward a balanced state within each *individual* rather than each couple.

Interpersonally, there are reasons for preferring the newer roles. Since traditional males and females are brought up to exaggerate their differences, they often do not share the same attitudes, values, and preferred activities. Thus they may have little to talk about and feel uncomfortable with each other. Often the female expects the male to take the lead in the conversation, but the male is often less verbal than the female and thus may be silent and withdrawn, resulting in a frustrating interaction for both (Ickes & Barnes, 1978).

Moreover, anthropologists Johnson and Johnson (1975) linked the degree of antagonism between the sexes to a culture's organization of work. When males and females work together on the same tasks, gender antagonism is low and husband–wife friendships tend to be stronger than are same-sex friendships. But when work is segregated by sex, with separate and distinct male and female roles, sexual antagonism is high, with friendships rarely crossing sexual lines.

In sum, traditional gender roles have both advantages and disadvantages. Although the disadvantages of the female role have been more widely popularized in recent years, there also are problems with the masculine role. In addition, the strategy in traditional roles is for the marital couple to form a balanced whole. The development of new gender roles, however, is moving toward a model in which balance is sought within each individual.

THE MAKING OF GENDER ROLES

Most psychologists agree that the biological differences between the sexes are relatively small. These differences, however, are exaggerated through a subtle process of socialization that starts at the moment of birth and continues throughout life. As explained in social learning theory, this socialization operates largely through modeling and differential reinforcement for gender-appropriate behavior.

Table 5–1 shows how pervasive are the social influences that reinforce traditional gender roles. Many of these are things we take for granted; thus they escape our attention on a day-to-day basis. As a result, parents are often unaware that they treat their male and female children differently. Even parents who are committed to avoiding gender stereotypes may in-

TABLE 5–1

FACTORS THAT SHAPE GENDER ROLES

1. Male children are preferred to female children (Coombs, 1977).

2. Parents of newborns describe daughters as softer, smaller, finer featured, and less active than sons, even when there are no objective differences in appearance or activity level (Rubin, Provenzano, & Luria et al., 1974).

3. Infant boys receive more physical contact from their mothers, whereas infant girls are talked to and looked at more than boys are (Lewis, 1972).

4. Parents react more quickly to the cries of a baby girl (Frieze et al., 1978).

5. Parents allow a baby boy to explore and wander away more than they will a baby girl (Long Laws, 1979).

6. Boys' toys are action oriented (trucks and guns), and girls' toys are more "quiet and domestic" (dolls, miniature appliances) (Rheingold & Cook, 1975).

7. Children's books show
   a. eleven males to every female.
   b. most males as active and independent and most females as passive.
   c. women as mothers and wives and men engaged in a variety of professions.
   d. boys as four times more clever and resourceful than girls are (Weitzman et al., 1972; Women on Word and Images, 1975).

8. Nearly all television cartoon heroes are male, whereas females are generally shown as companions or victims.

9. Television commercials portray stereotypes almost exclusively: for example, women as confused housewives trying to make decisions about laundry dirt and men as authority figures and sports enthusiasts.

10. Less than 2 percent of female characters on television solve their own problems (Roberts, 1980).

11. Boys are encouraged to show physical competence, competitive spirit, bravery, and self-reliance and to hide their feelings ("Big boys don't cry"); girls are expected to stay neat and to avoid fighting or other dangerous activities. Girls are more often comforted by adults when they cry and thus may be unwittingly taught to solve their problems by acting helpless.

TABLE 5 — 1   *(continued)*

12. Boys are supposed to be career and achievement oriented; girls are often advised against selecting a career that requires extensive preparation and responsibility. Girls often receive the message that academic achievement will lessen their femininity. Men are often threatened by highly successful women, and these women are less likely to be married than those who are less successful (Frieze et al., 1978; Long Laws, 1979).

13. Adult masculinity is measured by job status and financial success, whereas adult femininity is determined by beauty and financial status of the husband.

advertently fall into traditional patterns of socialization (Scanzoni & Fox, 1980). Thus, in order to make a conscious choice for oneself or one's children, it is essential to become aware of these sources of influence.

SEX DIFFERENCES IN PERSPECTIVE

Physical and psychological differences between the sexes have provided the historical basis for separate gender roles. For example, carrying the unborn child and nursing the infant presumably made it impossible for women to participate in far-ranging hunts for large ani-

---

FOCUS
GENDER ROLES AND ROMANTIC LOVE

How do males and females with traditional and nontraditional gender roles differ in their experience of love?

Researchers (Critelli, Myers, & Loos, 1986) examined a sample of young dating couples who filled out questionnaires and then individually wrote a "love letter" to their partner. Items were grouped into scales, and frequencies of romantic, friendship, and emotional themes in the letters were recorded.

The relationship between gender role and love was thought to have particular theoretical interest. Some humanistic and psychoanalytic psychologists have suggested that love depends on the polarity of the sexes and that as men and women become less different, love should decrease. Feminists, on the other hand, contend that a liberation of gender roles should bring the sexes closer together and thus enhance love.

The results show both hypotheses to be partially correct, depending on which aspect of love is examined. The love experienced by traditionals was characterized by feeling dependent, needing the partner, and believing that the partner fulfills all of one's needs. Nontraditionals, on the other hand, emphasized having a solid, communicative relationship.

As compared with men, women disclosed more emotional, romantic, and friendship statements in their letters, and they were more likely to feel that they had a solid relationship and could communicate with their partners. Feelings of physical and sexual arousal did not differ between males and females.

An interesting cross connection emerged for respect and physical arousal. Traditional males and nontraditional females reported high physical arousal to their partners, whereas nontraditional males and traditional females reported high respect for theirs.

mals. This created a natural division of labor in tribes that required such hunts for survival. Of course, times have changed and few members of modern society still depend on wild game for food. Because of this, it may be helpful to consider what is currently known about sex differences so that this knowledge can be used to formulate gender roles for modern times.

INTERPRETING GENDER DIFFERENCES

Several points must be considered if we are to avoid misinterpreting sex-difference research. First, these studies are based on group differences. A sample of men and women is measured on some attribute, and then the average scores of the two groups are compared. Thus the results apply only to men as a group or to women as a group. In the case of height, for example, most men are taller than most women, but some women exceed the height of most men. Confusion often results from the abbreviated way in which research results are reported. For example, a summary of results might say, "Men scored higher than women on a measure of height." This wording may inadvertently suggest that *all* men scored higher than *all* women. In fact, this would be unlikely. So, remember that the results apply only to groups and that exceptions to the group results should be expected.

Typically, boys choose action-oriented toys, while girls' toys are more domestic. This difference is most likely the result of both socialization and natural preference.

TABLE 5-2
HOW THE SEXES DIFFER

PHYSICAL ATTRIBUTES

Size	Males are taller and heavier.
Strength	Males have more muscle fibers and are more powerful, particularly in the upper body.
Endurance	Males have greater aerobic capacity.
Balance	Females have better balance/lower center of gravity.
Activity level	Preschool boys may be more active, especially in roughhouse activities with other boys (DiPietro, 1981).
Manual dexterity	Women are better on tasks requiring precise, quick finger movement (Maccoby & Jacklin, 1974).
Reaction time	Men are faster (Archer, 1976).
Sensory threshold	Women are more sensitive to touch, pain, hearing, taste, smell, and dark vision; men are more sensitive to day vision (Archer, 1976).
Life span	Women are less vulnerable to illness and disease and live about eight years longer.
Childbearing	Women become pregnant, have babies, and produce milk; men impregnate.
Cyclicity	Women's hormone levels are more cyclical.
Brain structure	Male hormones circulating before birth affect neuron connector densities in some parts of the brain and also affect behavior: Females with inappropriate prenatal male hormone levels later become more "tomboyish" (Konner, 1982).
Brain hemispheres	Males use the right hemisphere for spatial imagery and the left for analytical thinking; females' brains are not so clearly specialized (Goleman, 1978).
Sex hormones	Males and females differ in their amounts of certain hormones: Male hormones are linked to the release of sexual and aggressive behavior, and female hormones appear to have the reverse effect (Konner, 1982).
Maturational rate	Girls mature more rapidly, for example, skeletal development at birth, ages for permanent teeth and puberty.

PSYCHOLOGICAL ATTRIBUTES

Verbal ability	Females acquire language earlier and after the age of eleven do better on measures such as spelling, sentence complexity, vocabulary, reading comprehension, and verbal creativity (Droege, 1967).
Quantitative ability	Males are better at mathematical reasoning from the start of adolescence (Benbow & Stanley, 1980).
Spatial-visual ability	Males are better at visualizing objects in space, starting in the tenth grade (Eccles, 1982; see Caplan, MacPherson, & Tobin, 1985, for an opposing view).
Field independence	Males are better at identifying simple figures embedded in more complex wholes, starting at adolescence (Maccoby & Jacklin, 1974).

(continued)

TABLE 5-2

HOW THE SEXES DIFFER   *(continued)*

PSYCHOLOGICAL ATTRIBUTES

Affiliation	Women fantasize more about love and affiliation (Wagman, 1967); women see safety in attachment, and men see threat (Gilligan, 1982).
Smiling	Women smile more from birth (Wilson, 1980).
Self-disclosure	Women are more likely to disclose personal feelings (Cherulnik, 1979).
Nonverbal sensitivity	Females are better at decoding nonverbal signs of others' feelings (Hall, 1978).
Emotionality	Females are more likely to express fear, sadness, and embarrassment (Cherulnik, 1979); males are more likely to express anger (Averill, 1982).
Obedience	Boys are more likely to resist parental demands (Hetherington et al., 1976).
Susceptibility to influence	Women may be more easily influenced in small groups (Eagly, 1978).
Self-confidence	Males are more confident about future performance (Maccoby & Jacklin, 1974).
Attribution of success	Men take the credit for success and blame failure on external factors; women credit success to external factors and blame failure on themselves (Deaux, 1976).
Nurturance	Females are more likely to aid small children (Edwards & Whiting, 1977).
Interpersonal dominance	Men show dominance in conversations with females by selecting the topic, talking more, interrupting, and touching; females laugh more and offer more agreement, admiration, and support (Critelli, Tang, & Piccard, 1985).
Aggressiveness	Males are more aggressive, beginning at age two, especially in physical aggression without anger. Men are also more violent, publicly aggressive, and likely to commit antisocial acts (Maccoby & Jacklin, 1974).
Sexual frequency	Husbands are nearly twice as likely as wives to want sex more frequently (Levinger, 1966).
Values	Males emphasize abstract standards of justice, fairness, and truth; females emphasize compassion, intimacy, and the protection of others' feelings (Gilligan, 1982).
Interests	Men have more scientific, mechanical, computational, adventurous, economic, and political interests; women have more literary, musical, artistic, sedentary, social, and religious interests (Maccoby & Jacklin, 1974).

A second point is that group differences can be highly reliable even when the magnitude of the difference is small. Most gender differences, aside from the obvious—for example, birthing ability—appear to be quite small. For example, in sports, the fastest men run and swim about 10 percent faster than the fastest women. In general, it is unusual to find sex differences greater than 10 percent.

A final clarification pertains to the distinction between heredity and environment. Behaviors (and sex differences in behavior) are caused by an interaction between one's inherited predispositions and one's history of environmental influences. In actuality these two factors cannot be separated: There is no such thing as an individual without genetic inheritance or an organism without a surrounding environment. For purposes of analysis, however, statistical techniques have been used to estimate the relative contributions of heredity and environment to a given response. For example, these techniques might involve comparisons of identical and fraternal twins reared separately and together. If identical twins reared apart (same genes, different environment) are more similar in behavior than fraternal twins reared together (different genes, "same" environment) this would indicate a strong genetic component for that response.

Note, however, that the issue of what causes a response is separate from how that response can be altered. It is entirely possible for a behavior to be strongly inherited and also responsive to environmental change. In general, this will depend on the particular response selected and on the range of environmental manipulations permitted. Height, for example, has a strong inherited component, but it can be radically altered by diet, disease, and hormonal imbalance, especially if these environmental influences occur early in life.

Table 5–2 summarizes gender differences. Note that this table includes only variables on which measured differences have been found.

SPECULATIONS ON HEREDITY AND ENVIRONMENT

Although heredity and environment play a joint role in all of the differences, some generalizations can be made. Aggressiveness, smiling, and nearly all of the physical attributes appear to have strong inherited components. On the other hand, nearly all of the psychological attributes have strong environmental causes. Most researchers agree that the inherited differences between the sexes are relatively small but that the process of socialization exaggerates them, thus establishing the gender roles in each society.

THE ORIGIN OF GENDER ROLES

Even though there is great diversity across cultures in the way that appropriate male and female roles are defined, some similarities have also been observed. Girls are socialized toward nurturance and obedience, whereas boys are encouraged to be self-reliant and achieving. Women provide the bulk of child care, and men wage war, hunt large animals, trap, and mine. Wilson (1980) argued that the male anatomy, with its broader shoulders and greater muscle mass, is particularly suited for running and throwing, activities crucial to the survival of primitive societies. This, combined with the greater male aggressiveness, meant that men provided services such as protection from one's enemies and the provision of meat in quantity.

Thus men's services aided immediate individual survival, whereas women's services were more removed, supporting the eventual survival of the group as a whole. Because of this and because of males' physical aggressiveness, history records a universal male dominance, with not a single culture in which women have controlled men's political and economic lives (Wilson, 1980).

WHY GENDER ROLES ARE CHANGING

In modern life, information is king. Food is obtained through scientific principles of farming and animal husbandry, and wars are won or lost by strategy and technology, not by physical brawn. Many of the historical reasons for separate and distinct gender roles have gradually dissolved. This can be linked to technological advances in the work place, technological advances in the home, changes in marriage, and the current scarcity of men.

THE WORK PLACE

The robotization of industry and the rise of information and service occupations have virtually nullified the male advantage in physical strength. Society's most desirable jobs require intelligence, talent, and education, not muscle power. As a result, these changes have created opportunities for women to enter the work force in unprecedented numbers.

THE HOME

Technological advances in the home have played an important, though often unrecognized, role in transforming gender roles. Invention of the rubber nipple made it possible for the mother to delegate infant feeding to others. The pasteurization of milk reduced infant mortality, eliminating one of the reasons for having many children. And the invention of the sanitary pad did away with the need to wear numerous long skirts to hide odor and bulky menstrual cloths (Bullough, 1980).

But the single most important factor in changing gender roles was the advent of reliable birth control. Before the availability of effective contraception, families of eight to ten children were common. And with a family of that size, it was virtually impossible for a mother to have a career outside the home. When women are continually pregnant and nursing, traditional gender roles, with the male as the protector and provider and the female as the nurturing mother, are nearly inevitable. But once reproduction could be controlled and planned, alternative role structures became possible.

MARITAL PRACTICES

The rising divorce rate has made work a necessity for many women. Even for those who are not divorced, the knowledge that divorce is common makes many women reluctant to base their security on a husband. Also, women are now marrying later, giving them a chance to finish their education and begin a career before accepting family responsibilities.

GENDER AND THE LAW OF SUPPLY AND DEMAND

Guttentag and Secord (1983) developed an economic law of supply and demand that helps explain recent changes in gender roles. According to them, the sex that is relatively scarce holds the balance of emotional power. When marriageable men outnumber marriageable women, females become a scarce resource. Men place great importance on catching a woman and keeping her, and traditional values predominate. Women are valued as romantic love objects, marital commitments are strong, and gender roles are separate and complementary. On the other hand, when women are in abundance, many unattached women must become self-supporting. Consequently, they seek more education, enter the work force, and organize social movements to improve their economic conditions. Not surprisingly, marriageable women have outnumbered marriageable men during the past several decades.

ARE TRADITIONAL GENDER ROLES BIOLOGICALLY PROGRAMMED?

Many in our society are experimenting with new, nontraditional gender roles. Some even claim that the whole notion of different roles for the sexes is outdated. It has also been argued, however, that inherent biological differences between the sexes support traditional values in a way that makes unlikely any major, long-term changes in these roles.

THE ISRAELI KIBBUTZIM: A NATURALISTIC EXPERIMENT

Tiger and Shepher (1975) noted that no culture has achieved economic and political equality between the sexes, even though several, such as the Soviet Union and China, were founded on ideological commitments to gender equality. The Israeli kibbutzim are cited as a case in point. These farming communes were established on the basis of complete gender equality, with women encouraged to enter traditionally male roles. Over time, however, these women, and especially their daughters, who were reared in a society without traditional roles, chose to spend more time with their children and in traditional female service activities. Moreover, they resisted recruitment into the higher levels of commercial and political leadership (Wilson, 1980).

Tavris and Wade (1984, p. 349) commented:

> The Kibbutz, then, presents us with a puzzle. Kibbutz women are economically independent. They do not get status from their husbands' incomes or jobs. They have total job security no matter how many children they choose to have, and they are guaranteed high-quality care and education for their children. They do not have complicated housework to contend with and they do not have to feed their families or clean up after them. Yet Kibbutz women lack political power, and they don't seem to want it. They do not work in high-prestige occupations, and they don't seem to want to.

Tiger argued that women are biologically programmed to bond with children. Thus women's natural predispositions keep them centered in the home. For example, as an indirect consequence of the reproductive differences between the sexes, a woman often experiences the newborn as an extension of her body; men rarely view infants this way.

Although intriguing, the example of the Israeli kibbutzim may be misleading, since they were set up as farming communities requiring considerable physical labor. Thus the goals of equality through the elimination of gender roles may have been premature in such a setting. In other words, these data may not predict what will eventually take place in an information society.

BIOPROGRAMS AND THE ENVIRONMENT

It is possible that gender roles are "biologically programmed" in one environment but not in another. For example, the more primitive an environment is, the more that gender differences in strength and physical aggressiveness will dictate a separation of roles.

Note that traditional gender roles constitute thousands of specific differential expectancies. It seems obvious that most of these expectancies are not strongly tied to biology. Nevertheless, there may well be some that are, for example, males' strength and physical aggressiveness and females' smiling reflex and capacity to give birth and nurse infants.

In conclusion, it seems clear that most of what we mean by traditional gender roles is not biologically programmed. However, some elements of traditional roles may have a biological component that predisposes the genders to have continuing role differences. If so, these may center largely on the roles of the male as the protector and the female as the care taker of small children. But the control of reproductive functioning and the continuing trend toward smaller families suggest that even if there were a predisposition for females to nurture young children, this would not necessarily interfere with their role as breadwinners.

THE GENDER PROBLEM

UNEQUAL POWER

Tavris and Wade (1984) see the main gender problem as a lack of equal economic and political power for women. The solution, as they see it, requires a change in the structure of occupations, so that income-producing work and domestic work become valued and shared equally. Moreover, they believe that the most desirable occupations should enable work and family roles to be combined. It may be useful to explore this argument, as its implications affect all of our lives.

THE VALUE OF "WOMEN'S WORK"

What are the chances that income-producing work and domestic work will be valued equally? I believe that although this may be possible for child rearing, it seems unlikely for other domestic activities such as cooking and cleaning. There are general guidelines for determining how highly various work activities are valued in society. Some of these are the amount of education or training required for the job, how easily the job can be done by someone else, and how important the products of the activity are to others. From this viewpoint, it may be no surprise that most household tasks are held in low regard. They require little expertise, can be done by almost anyone, and are only moderately valued. (One qualification is the romantic view that what matters is that the work be performed *with love*. When this is the case, it may well be true that the work is highly valued and the "worker" considered irreplaceable. The existing power differential between the sexes, however, suggests that this view does not characterize most relationships.)

What about child care? Certainly, the future of our society depends on how good a job we do in developing our children's full potentials and teaching them to respect one another. I believe that many people agree with this position in the abstract but are apparently unconvinced in the specifics. Consider, for example, the low financial rewards accorded mothers and elementary school teachers. Obviously, poor child care often produces antisocial delinquents who contribute little to society. The evidence, however, does not indicate that exceptional care results in the development of an exceptional child. For example, psychologists generally regard adequate day-care facilities to be just as good

for children as staying home with their mothers (Belsky & Steinberg, 1978; Etaugh, 1980; O'Connell, 1983). It appears that the technical know-how for producing exceptional children is just not yet available. Thus, the low status of child rearing may be consistent with the general criteria used for evaluating other occupations.

In conclusion, the hope of making housework valued equally with income-producing work seems unrealistic. Although this hope could certainly be fulfilled within any given relationship, the existing power differential between the genders suggests that it has not been the norm.

SHARING THE LOAD: MEN IN APRONS?

Tavris and Wade also contend that males and females must share domestic work equally. They maintain that a vicious cycle prevents women from being equally represented in the most prestigious occupations: The better the job is, the more responsibility will be demanded. Women know they will have to take time out for child care and thus do not seek the jobs that will prohibit such interruptions. Once they have lower-status, lower-paying jobs, wives become the logical candidates to give up their work during the child-rearing years.

Even males who espouse gender equality rarely divide the household activities equally. Furthermore, many men publicly advocate gender equality but privately expect women to choose a subordinate, domestic role (Komarovsky, 1973). In general, working women are required to juggle their careers in addition to their traditional household responsibilities. Indeed, only about 7 percent of males say they would modify their careers if they conflicted with their wife's work (Komarovsky, 1973). Thus the typical pattern when both partners work is that the male makes more money and has the higher status occupation. His career comes first, and she is expected to do the domestic work.

Some psychologists maintain that real gender equality will require men and women to share domestic work equally.

Thus it seems unlikely that men soon will share equally in chores around the home. But what is the source of men's aversion to "women's work"? On the one hand, it may be related to a certain disdain for women as the "weaker sex" (Tavris & Wade, 1984). A view still held by many men is that women are less competent than men. Men's aversion to domestic work also relates to their fear of being perceived as effeminate and possibly homosexual. For example, there is obviously no logical contradiction between masculinity and washing dishes. Nevertheless, it is precisely the emotional, irrational nature of these associations that makes them difficult to alter.

Perhaps because of a biological predisposition, women universally care for the children, and the prospects of this changing in the near future seem slim. However, although considered a woman's job, child care is not necessarily provided by the child's mother. Indeed, this seems to be the direction in which our society is moving. When women enter the work place, it is not the husbands who bring up the children but, rather, other females hired to rear children as their means of producing income.

In conclusion, it seems unlikely that domestic work will rise in status or that males will soon participate equally in that work. To a large extent, however, domestic work can be done by other agencies in society, such as preschools, maids, and restaurants.

CAREER FLEXIBILITY

The final point in Tavris's and Wade's solution to the gender-role problem is making high-status occupations flexible, so that they can more easily accommodate both work and family roles. It may help to point out two requirements of high-status careers: They invariably demand high levels of responsibility, and they often demand work hours well beyond the forty per week typical of lower-status jobs.

It appears that the most desirable jobs cannot compromise on responsibility. When other people's jobs, health, money, legal outcomes, and other vital concerns depend on one's best performance, compromises will not be tolerated. High-status jobs usually mean high pay, and people do not knowingly pay highly for inferior work.

At the same time, there is no reason that society couldn't provide more "backup procedures" for professionals with family responsibilities. The entrance of large numbers of women into higher-status occupations could easily provide the workers for such backups. A backup strategy is already being used by many physicians, for example. Through joint practices, client's records are shared among doctors, so that the patient is not dependent on a particular physician's being on duty when help is needed.

Redefining many professional jobs as not necessarily full time would enhance flexibility. Presumably, there is a curve of diminishing returns for most jobs, and so peak performance can be expected for only perhaps four or five hours per day. After that, some inefficiency is likely. Time flexibility seems a promising means for allowing men and women to combine high-status careers and family roles and thus move toward greater equality.

POWER AND OTHER VALUES

Let's reconsider Tavris's and Wade's definition of the gender-role problem. Is it possible that having less power and status may not always *be* a problem? Assume, for the moment, that economic and political power do not encompass all that is desirable. If power isn't everything, then other outcomes may be able to counterbalance an inequality in power. What might these outcomes be? One that immediately comes to mind is greater free time for self-expression. Humanistic psychologists maintain that a concern with power comes from a need to make one's world predictable, controllable, and secure. For those who do not feel insecure, the allure of greater power might be negligible.

Similarly, B. F. Skinner (1948) envisioned Walden Two, a behavioristic utopia in which status and economic power are clearly secondary. Instead, the economic system is designed to maximize free time for creative pursuits such as literature, art, music, and dance. The implication here is that if one has satisfied the need for esteem, there will be little motivation to produce money in order to feel good about oneself. Both humanistic and behavioristic theory suggest that for certain individuals, power, money, and status are less important than are the freedom and opportunity for self-expression.

Thus, theoretically, it may be possible for a self-actualizing individual to form a satisfying relationship with a partner who holds the balance of economic power in the relationship. Economic power could be balanced by time for self-expression, especially if child care were part of one partner's desired expression.

The point here is that economic power does not have to be the only issue in a relationship. It is possible to achieve gender equality by balancing power with some other desired outcome. However, because we live in a culture that so highly values power and status, it is sometimes difficult to see an alternative to these values.

Curiously, what has just been described could well be the traditional marriage of the breadwinner and the homemaker. But for humanistic theory, the way an individual experiences the homemaker's role is crucial. If the homemaker values money, status, and power and is living vicariously through the breadwinner's accomplishments, then the stage is set for dissatisfaction and resentment. If, however, the tangible accompaniments of power are not desired, and especially if work in the home is viewed as desirable in itself — not just because someone else will appreciate it — then a trade-off between power and self-expression becomes viable.

Nevertheless, humanistic theory suggests that few people operate at the self-actualizing level, and the force of the women's movement indicates that most women do perceive the inequality of status and power as a problem. Thus, for certain individuals, the so-called gender problem may require no solution. But for most of us, it is clearly a legitimate and pressing issue.

THE FUTURE OF GENDER EQUALITY

Will gender equality be achieved in the near future? If equality is defined in terms of power and status, it seems that the answer for the next generation as a whole is likely to be no. However, for any given individual or couple, equality is entirely possible. Moreover, those who discount the importance of biological sex differences maintain that equality is inevitable in the long run, and perhaps likely during the next century. The noted anthropologist Marvin Harris (1975), for example, speculated that male supremacy was just a phase in the evolution of culture.

Given the universality of male dominance-aggressiveness and female child-care, however, other forecasters see total equality as unlikely without specialized training regimes to over-

ride these genetic differences. As Wilson (1980) commented, if moderate biological predispositions toward traditional gender roles are assumed, three options arise: socialize to exaggerate the differences, socialize equally, and socialize to eliminate the differences. If genetic differences do exist, however, only the last option will result in gender equality. Although such socialization programs could probably be developed, the question remains as to whether their implementation would be desirable.

How would you define the "gender problem"? What are your reactions to Tavris's and Wade's proposed solution? In what way do you see biologically based sex differences as part of this problem? How do you think you will deal with the gender problem in your own life?

ANDROGYNY AND THE HEALTHY PERSONALITY

THE TRADITIONAL VIEW

Traditionally, mental health practitioners have viewed masculinity and femininity as opposites: Men should be masculine and women feminine. Thus healthy women should differ in personality from healthy men (Broverman et al., 1970; Fabrikant, 1974). In this view, however, mental health workers placed women in a bind. They viewed a "healthy adult man" as having characteristics similar to those of a "healthy adult." A "healthy adult woman," on the other hand, was viewed as being different from a "healthy adult" (Broverman et al., 1970).

In other words, what was considered healthy for an adult woman resembled the description of an "unhealthy adult." Healthy women were expected to be less independent, less objective, less aggressive, more submissive, more excitable in crises, and more conceited about their appearance than were healthy men. Thus a woman who thought of herself as "aggressive" and "taking leadership roles" could be viewed as suffering from "gender-role confusion." Similarly, a man who viewed himself as "nurturant" and "soft-spoken" might also be considered unhealthy. More recent research (Lubinski et al., 1983; Taylor & Hall, 1982) rejects this view.

THE ANDROGYNOUS ALTERNATIVE

In the early 1970s, researchers began to question the proposition that masculinity and femininity must be opposites (Bem, 1974; Constantinople, 1973). They reasoned that it would be possible to combine desirable masculine and feminine characteristics and that such persons might be healthier than sex-typed individuals. For example, they might be more flexible and thus able to act in either a masculine or a feminine way, depending on the requirements of the situation. Such people were called **androgynous,** from the Greek terms for male *(andro-)* and female *(gyn-)*.

Actually, research on androgyny was predated by the work of Carl Jung, a psychoanalytic theorist. Jung maintained that each individual had both male and female elements in his or her makeup. Psychological growth occurred through developing and refining one aspect of the personality and then balancing that trait by developing and integrating its opposite. For example, men might consciously emphasize their capacity for logic and objectivity, but to become a complete individual, they would also have to combine that with a refinement of their intuitive, subjective capacities. Neugarten and Gutmann (1958), for example, found that as they age, women become more tolerant of their aggressive impulses, and men more tolerant of their nurturant feelings.

Bem (1974, 1978) devised a measure of psychological androgyny based on an individual's identification with desirable masculine (e.g., ambitious, competitive) and feminine (e.g., compassionate, gentle) traits. Those as-

cribing to themselves both masculine and feminine characteristics were androgynous. High masculine, low feminine types were masculine, and high feminine, low masculine types were feminine. Those low on both traits were described as "undifferentiated." The concept of androgyny generated a great deal of interest. Unfortunately, however, clear-cut conclusions about the desirability of being androgynous have not been forthcoming.

Critics (e.g., Spence, 1983) have pointed out that it is probably misleading to view the Bem scales as measuring the broad categories of masculinity and femininity. Rather it is more accurate to see them as measures of dominance and nurturance. Furthermore, androgyny does not appear to have an independent status, separate from dominance and nurturance, for these two dimensions do not need to balance each other to produce a healthy personality (Taylor & Hall, 1982).

A review article (Taylor & Hall, 1982) indicated that both dominance and nurturance are related to psychological health but that dominance shows the stronger and more consistent pattern of results. For example, dominance was over five times more strongly related to self-esteem and adjustment. Lubinski and associates (1983) found that dominance was related to well-being, social potency, achievement, and adaptive stress reaction. Nurturance was related to well-being, social closeness, and nonalienation. Again, dominance showed the stronger pattern of relationships, this time by a factor of three.

MASCULINITY AND AMERICAN CULTURE

Taylor and Hall (1982, p. 362) concluded that "it is primarily masculinity, not androgyny, that yields positive outcomes for individuals in American society." In other words, ours is a society dominated by masculine values. Not surprisingly, people identifying with these values describe themselves as better adjusted, and they feel better about themselves than do those who do not identify with these values. It seems unlikely, however, that nurturance is irrelevant to psychological health. There is no apparent psychological reason linking dominance more than nurturance to well-being. Rather, this seems to be a cultural phenomenon, not a general finding about human nature.

In other societies with contrasting, more ''feminine'' value systems, such as traditional

---

FOCUS
WHEN THE WIFE RULES THE ROOST

In couples with both partners working full time, about 10 percent of the wives earn more than their husbands. Research on these families illustrates the consequences of violating rigid social expectations. For example:

1. Wives with higher-status jobs than their husbands had a higher divorce rate than other wives. When both spouses held professional jobs, women in typically male jobs had twice the divorce rate of those in typically female jobs.
2. Couples in which the wife had a higher-status job and more postgraduate education had higher rates of mutual psychological and physical abuse, including violence with a knife or gun.
3. Eighty percent of underachieving men (low job status for level of education) married to overachieving women were victims of psychological abuse by their wives.
4. For underachieving men married to overachieving women, death rate from heart disease was eleven times higher than the norm.
5. For husbands who earned less than their wives, twice as many (one-third) said that they loved their wives more than their wives loved them. Correspondingly, wives who earned more than their husbands said they were more likely not to return their partner's love than were other wives.
6. For couples in which the wife earned more money than the husband, over twice as many couples (17 percent versus 7 percent) reported no intercourse at all during the past few months. (Adapted from Rubenstein, 1982b)

Apparently, money is power, and violations of the gender-based rules for holding power have a way of upsetting relationships. As long as both men and women feel that the man should be the major breadwinner, these disruptions are likely to continue. Moreover, attitude surveys of young people indicate that such views will prevail for at least another generation.

But what are the implications of these findings? Should women restrain their achievement strivings and avoid high-status professional careers? It seems clear that this would be a step in the wrong direction. Should women seek high-status careers but pursue an even higher-status mate? The evidence suggests that this would help, but after all, how many men are there at the top? And will those men be attracted to their high-achieving female colleagues when they have traditionally pursued women on the basis of youth and beauty? It appears that, for couples in which the wife holds the economic power, both partners should be prepared to give more to the relationship.

Asians or some Native American tribes, the reverse might well be the case. Moreover, in particular subgroups of our own population, the findings on masculinity and femininity appear to reverse. For example, research on breast-feeding mothers (Baldwin, Critelli, Stevens, & Russell, 1986) linked self-esteem to femininity.

TRANSCENDING GENDER ROLES

ANDROGYNY AND GENDER-ROLE FLEXIBILITY

As indicated, androgynous people, as identified by current sex-role scales, are not healthier than masculine-typed individuals. As a result, some investigators have begun rethinking androgyny theory by returning to the original formulations of what an androgynous person might be like. It appears that the central idea behind androgyny was one of **gender-role flexibility.** Each traditional gender role comes equipped with restrictions that limit growth. The traditional male role restricts emotional expression and personal intimacy. The traditional female role restricts competence and achievement. It seems apparent that an individual who is not encumbered by either set of restrictions would be healthier than one who is.

THE STRUGGLE FOR ROLE FLEXIBILITY

Forisha (1978) maintains that as with all forms of growth, the change to a more fluid and flexible gender role is often fraught with conflict. In such a process, we must often change longstanding imperatives from our own upbringing and repeatedly come into conflict with others' expectations for us. One person undergoing such conflict is Lorraine:

> Where am I today? Oh, I call myself Ms., refer to the world as he or she, not just he. I buy feminist stickers, bracelets, nonsexist books, read MS. magazine, speak up when I hear

sex-role stereotyping from people, try to assert myself when I feel I am being suppressed because I am a woman. But under all of that I don't think I am really much further ahead or liberated than I was five years ago. I have made strides in many obvious and not so obvious ways, but I still curl my hair, wear makeup sometimes, think about appropriate female behavior, watch myself in front of men, and am generally pretty hung up on sex roles, I think.

> I feel a constant conflict between being aggressive and being passive. I don't want to be argumentative, but feel I have something of worth to contribute to conversations. Speaking up with opposing views creates anxiety for me, but keeping quiet is sometimes worse. I want to treat people as people, but I am conscious that I see them as men and women first. Most of all, this constant berating of myself I have always thought of as part of my personality — could it be that it is sex-role conditioning? What do I feel about things? What do I want to do? I am not sure, I have done a lot for myself on my own, but I have also done a great deal because it was expected of me as a woman. My goal for the future is to sort all of this out. (Forisha, 1978, pp. 391–392)

Lorraine is doing all the things that she thinks a liberated woman is supposed to do. Yet in following these cultural prescriptions so automatically, she may merely be placing herself in bondage to another set of rigid social expectations. Certainly, this is not a "liberation" from rigid and restrictive gender roles. Role content has changed, but the blind dependence on a rigid code of expectations handed down from others remains the same.

Yet Lorraine is aware that this change in roles is not working as she would like. Moreover, this does not seem to threaten her. Instead she takes an approach of persistence, of continuing "to sort all of this out." These are good indications for Lorraine, signs that her struggle will be successful.

Lorraine seems to believe that because she still wears makeup and "watches herself in front of men," she has not yet made the transition to a liberated role. What do you think about this?

Of course, we don't know exactly what Lorraine means by "liberated," but her reference to being "further ahead" suggests that for her, a liberated role reflects psychological health. From an extreme humanistic viewpoint, wearing makeup could be seen as trying to create the illusion of beauty by hiding one's flaws. And watching yourself in front of men implies a restriction of spontaneity so that one can convey a preconceived impression, as in being "cool." As such, humanistic theory might agree with Lorraine that these characteristics imply a nonliberated role.

On the other hand, a more moderate humanistic interpretation, and one compatible with role flexibility, might recognize that Lorraine does want to attract the opposite sex. Thus she can freely choose role behaviors designed to increase her attractiveness, as long as there is minimal self-deception and the restriction on spontaneity is not too high. In other words, it is one thing for Lorraine to select certain traditional behaviors as a way of attracting desired men *if she is aware of what she is doing*. It is quite another, however, for her to engage in these behaviors automatically, without making a choice or, even worse, while identifying only with her social self.

Lorraine is caught in a dichotomy between being passive and aggressive. In her mind, she must either be argumentative or not speak up at all. As with being liberated or not liberated, she is forming a dichotomy of extremes and assuming that she must choose between one or the other. Of course, if this were pointed out to her, she might examine this thought pattern and realize that other options are available. But her spontaneous choice of words suggests that as events

unfold in her life, she automatically sees only the choice between argumentation and silence. In all probability, this limits both her subsequent behavior and her likability.

Lorraine shows good insight in suggesting that the tendency to put herself down may derive from her original sex-role socialization. As indicated in Table 5–2, blaming oneself for failure, yet not taking the credit for success, is a restrictive consequence of traditional female socialization. In addition, Lorraine distinguishes between doing something "because it was expected of me as a woman" and doing it "for myself on my own." This is essentially the difference between being bound to a role that is imposed from without and choosing one's own way to fit into society's role structure. Thus Lorraine is starting to see an alternative to her either-or thinking that will permit a greater sense of choice and flexibility.

What are your reactions to Lorraine? Does she remind you of anyone you know? In what ways do you think Lorraine is "hung up on sex roles"? Think of an example for what Lorraine might mean by wanting to "treat people as people" rather than seeing them as men and women first?

LIMITATIONS OF SOCIAL ROLES

Forisha (1978) suggested that most people use gender roles as a crutch to tell them how to behave. Instead of being in contact with their needs and with the subtleties of the social situation, they rely on customary roles so that they do not have to think, be conscious, or choose their own behavior. Gender roles are often used to avoid accepting the consequences of one's behavior. Thus when relationships turn sour, when we fail to reach our goals, we can always claim that it wasn't our fault, that we acted "appropriately."

According to humanistic psychology, social roles simplify our lives by oversimplifying reality. We are biologically either male or female, but all males are not exactly alike and neither are all females. Moreover, even though gender is constant, one is not the same person all the time. Sometimes it is more natural to be active and aggressive; at other times, our inclinations will seek more subtle strategies.

Social roles, because they are such broad, generalized prescriptions for behavior, cannot possibly deal with this level of individuality. Thus humanistic psychologists urge the recognition that we are always changing, and so is the social situation. To the extent that we would otherwise be overwhelmed by this complexity, social roles are necessary. On the other hand, because roles are oversimplifications, they cannot handle the ebb and flow of actual experience. In addition, they limit choice, awareness, and vitality. Although it is unlikely that we could function without any social roles, we can employ roles in a flexible manner.

When gender roles become rigid, our behavior automatically conforms to external norms and expectations. We distrust our own inner experiences and rely on the judgments of others:

> We confuse what *we* want for ourselves with
> what others want for us; this confusion causes
> us to unconsciously adopt the wishes of
> others as our own. Often we are unaware that
> we have suppressed our own viewpoint and
> used that of others to shape our lives to fit the
> external form. In role-oriented behavior, we
> fear change and seek stability; we look for
> clear-cut divisions and avoid uncertainty.
> Also, we are too fearful and too uncertain to
> admit our mistakes. On the other hand, in
> role-oriented behavior we often find the
> illusion of security and safety. In this security
> lies the appeal of role-orientation. (Adapted
> from Forisha, 1978, pp. 30–31)

In essence, humanistic psychology views the excessive reliance on gender roles as a failure in courage, a failure to handle the complexity, individuality, and fluidity of the world as it is.

HEALTHY GENDER ROLES: FUNCTION OVER CONTENT

Gender-role flexibility is not so much a position on the *content* of masculine and feminine roles as a statement about *how those roles are used*. For example, to insist that someone act in a particular way just because she is a woman or to demand a certain privilege just because he is a man indicates role inflexibility.

Factors such as gender can and often are used to help predict how others will act. Using that information is merely prudent. But continuing to use role information when it leads to poor predictions or getting upset when those predictions go awry are clear signs of an inflexible use of roles.

Thus, in regard to gender-role flexibility, it would be perfectly possible for one spouse to be the sole supporter of a family, while the other stays home, caring for the house and family. The content of the roles could follow a traditional division of labor, yet the way that individuals use those roles could also demonstrate flexibility.

CHOOSING YOURSELF

Role flexibility means consciously choosing to play certain roles because they allow the best opportunity for expressing who we are at that moment. Flexibility implies neither being dependent on a given role nor being unconsciously molded by that role. Those with role flexibility shun the unwitting acceptance of societal definitions of what it means to be a man or a woman. For example, a man who has always been fascinated by ballet but who wouldn't think of taking up dance because it is "unmanly" has let society define who he is. To that extent, he has lost some measure of individuality.

Choosing one's gender roles also means being willing to modify those roles to express one's unique personality. In other words, by choice, we may decide to play the roles traditionally assigned us by society; we may disregard traditional roles; we may combine established roles; and we may fluctuate between roles based on the requirements of the situation.

TRANSCENDING TRADITIONAL DICHOTOMIES

As part of our capacity to transcend rigid gender roles, we can rise above the either-or thinking of traditional dichotomies. Recall that Lorraine was caught in the dichotomies of "liberated versus nonliberated" and "argumentative versus not speaking up at all." In fact, the rigid use of roles depends on simplistic and restrictive dichotomies. Sometimes a dichotomy can be transcended by merely finding a moderate position between extreme poles of choice. In other words, we can realize that there is always a range of choices between the poles of an apparent dichotomy. At other times, we may want to organize our world according to entirely different dimensions of choice.

For example, a dichotomy that has placed tremendous restrictions on many women is that between being aggressive or submissive. Many women feel that being aggressive is unfeminine.

Since they see the opposite of aggressive as submissive, they also conclude that to be feminine, they must be submissive. What has happened in recent years is the rise in popularity of the term *assertiveness*. Assertiveness implies standing up for your own legitimate rights, yet it carries no sense of unfemininity. Thus women can now view their behavior as both assertive *and* feminine. This simple cognitive alteration has proved to be a powerful source of therapeutic change for many women.

We thus conclude that gender-role flexibility is a viable guide to adjustment and growth. Role flexibility places little or no constraints on the content of one's gender role — it may embrace either traditional or nontraditional divisions of labor. Rather, role flexibility requires individuals to choose and alter their roles to fit both their personalities and the immediate situation.

Would you say that your own use of gender roles is flexible or rigid? Think of an example to illustrate what you mean.

SUMMARY

1. Gender, one's physical sex; gender identity, the sense of being a male or a female; and gender role, the attitudes and behaviors expected of each gender are basic terms for understanding this chapter.

2. Marlene was torn between her desire to achieve and her belief that this would interfere with marriage.

3. Edward was reacting against the pressures of an extreme competition- and achievement-oriented masculine role he had been taught by his father.

4. Both Marlene and Edward were in the process of modifying the gender roles that they had accepted and formulating new roles more suited to their adult personalities. It was concluded that Marlene would be dissatisfied with a solution that did not allow her to achieve. Also, the way Edward took responsibility for his own part in selecting a rigidly masculine role was a sign that he would make a successful adjustment.

5. Social roles simplify our lives and make the world more predictable. Without them, we probably could not function as social creatures. Our

culture is presumably seeking a new set of gender roles that will accurately reflect the sex differences relevant to our times and that will provide an optimal balance between individual growth and social order.

6. Traditional roles are based on the notion that men and women are psychological opposites. The male role fosters strength and competence, but it is difficult to live up to, and it inhibits spontaneous emotional expression. The female role promotes emotional expression and the freedom to admit weakness, but it inhibits achievement.

7. The traditional psychiatric position on mental health is that men should be masculine and women should be feminine. Current research rejects this view.

8. Sex-difference research applies to males and females as groups, not as individuals. Most differences are small. Sex differences vary in the degree that they are genetically caused, but even if inherited, they may be highly responsive to environmental interventions.

9. There are a number of physical and psychological differences between the sexes (see Table 5–2).

10. It appears that aggressiveness, smiling, and nearly all of the physical sex differences have strong genetic components; nearly all of the psychological differences have strong environmental components.

11. Across cultures, women specialize in child care, and men wage war, hunt large animals, trap, and mine. Men hold power in all known societies.

12. Many of the historical reasons for separate and distinct gender roles no longer apply because of technological advances, the high divorce rate, and smaller families.

13. Tavris and Wade view the major gender problem as the lack of equal economic and political power for women. They maintain that income-producing work and domestic work must be valued and shared equally and that the most desirable jobs must be altered to accommodate work and family roles. It was suggested that this lack of power may not be a problem for self-actualizing people. Also, it seems unlikely that domestic work will rise in status or soon be done equally by males, but it can largely be done by other agencies in society. And although the level of responsibility demanded cannot be compromised in high-status careers, they can become more flexible through the use of backup personnel and reductions in the typical workweek.

14. The issue of complete gender equality is highly controversial. Some maintain that it is now inevitable; others claim that it would require radical new socialization practices designed to counterbalance genetic differences between the sexes.

15. Androgyny refers to the identification with both traditional masculine and feminine characteristics. For current scales, masculinity is mainly dominance, and femininity is mainly nurturance. Current evidence

shows that in our culture, dominance is more strongly associated with psychological health than is nurturance.

16. Households in which the wife earns more than the husband or holds the higher-status job show greater levels of divorce, abuse, and sexual disruption.

17. Lorraine was struggling to find a workable gender-role position. She tended to see only two alternatives at a time, with both of these extreme and unrealistic. She also blindly accepted role prescriptions handed down from others without actively choosing how she would enact a role.

18. Gender-role flexibility refers to how roles are used, rather than to the specific content of a role. It is possible for a couple to choose a traditional division of labor and still have flexible gender roles. Likewise, it is possible for individuals to assume what they believe are liberated roles in an inflexible manner. In essence, role flexibility means that neither partner is constrained by the restrictions of traditional roles, and that partners actively choose and modify their roles to fit their unique life situation.

SUGGESTED READINGS

Brownmiller, S. **Femininity**. New York: Linden, 1984. Fascinating analysis of how trying to live up to the ideals of femininity can lead to a sense of inadequacy.

Fasteau, M. F. **The male machine**. New York: McGraw-Hill, 1974. Outlines the problems of the traditional male role.

Friedan, B. **The feminine mystique**. New York: Dell Pub. Co., Inc., 1964. A classic treatise on how the traditional female role limits human potential.

Tavris, C., & Wade, C. **The longest war**. New York: Harcourt Brace Jovanovich, 1984. Good overview of sex differences and the conflict between the sexes.

COGNITION and EMOTION 6

Interactions and Applications in Therapy

COGNITIONS, EMOTIONS, AND THE BRAIN

What if a plodding reptile, a screeching rodent, and a cold, reasoning computer were to inhabit one body, become a viable organism, and threaten to take over the planet? Don't run for cover, but according to brain scientist Paul MacLean, this has already happened. And happily so, for this bizarre creature is us.

THREE BRAINS

MacLean hypothesized that the human skull contains three brains, layered one over another. In other words, we view the world through three different mentalities, each with its own intelligence, subjectivity, and sense of space-time. The most ancient part of the brain, the **reptilian complex**, is located at the base of the skull and contains the machinery for self-preservation and reproduction. As its name implies, we, in essence, share this part of the brain with our reptilian ancestors from 250 million years ago. Surrounding the reptilian complex is the **limbic lobe**, which is shared with the early mammals and produces the experience of intense emotion. The most recent part of the brain, the **neocortex**, is responsible for thought, and we share this with advanced mammals such as primates and dolphins.

MacLean's model contends that complex brain structures evolved through a process of accretion. Rather than having a completely different brain appear at each stage of development, evolution occurred by adding a newer brain to the existing neural structure. As Carl Sagan noted in *The Dragons of Eden* (1977), this suggests that in addition to the rational self we consciously identify with, part of us is still in some sense experiencing the world as did the dinosaurs, whereas another part thinks the thoughts of pumas and two-toed sloths.

The reptilian complex produces aggression, dominance, territoriality, ritual, and compulsive, repetitive behavior. As Sagan observed, it is surprising how much our social and political behavior can be seen in reptilian terms.

The limbic lobe, dating back to the emergence of warm-blooded animals, represents a change in survival strategy. Most reptiles have little regard for their young. For them, survival depends on producing large numbers of offspring, only a few of which survive. The mammalian strategy, on the other hand, involves careful nurturing of few offspring, hence the importance of strong emotional bonds keeping parent and child together until the young can fend for themselves.

The neocortex can be pictured as a computer introduced by nature about a quarter of a million years ago to counteract the organism's dominance by reflexes and gut-level emotions. It controls traits, such as initiative and caution, and cognitive functions, such as reason, abstract thinking, planning, problem solving, and curiosity. The continuing sense of self, personal identity, individuality, and free will reside in the neocortex, as evidenced by the loss of this sense after cortical surgery.

COGNITIONS AND EMOTIONS

The study of brain evolution suggests that **cognitions**, that is, thoughts, ideas, beliefs, and perceptions, derive from the most recently evolved part of the brain. **Emotions**, or feelings, moods, and other physiologically aroused states, derive from an older part of the brain.

MacLean speculated that the neocortex originally appeared as a cold, impersonal computer but then evolved circuits linking it to the limbic system. In this way, the capacities for reasoning and caring were brought together, resulting in human compassion, altruism, and empathy. Presumably, the ability to care for one another has been a key ingredient in our survival.

This chapter explores cognitions and emotions and relates them to problems of adjustment. We shall consider a number of thought-provoking questions: How do we know what emotion another person is experiencing? In what way is it true that rejection and failure cannot cause unhappiness? Is it good to be a perfectionist? How is depression linked to gender? Are machines affecting our sense of aliveness? Is it possible to banish all negative emotions from one's life and always be happy? How does material abundance interfere with happiness?

THE INTERPLAY OF COGNITIONS AND EMOTIONS

COGNITIONS AFFECT EMOTIONS

Beliefs can create a logical necessity to experience certain emotions. For example, if we believe it would be terrible, humiliating, and disgraceful for someone to reject our offer of friendship, then we are compelled to become upset by rejection. If, on the other hand, we believe that rejection is merely unfortunate but not terrible, we are likely to experience a completely different emotional reaction. Albert Ellis (1962) developed an influential psychotherapy from this linkage between thoughts and feelings, and his system is explored later in the chapter.

Social learning theory suggests that we regulate our behavior through self-reinforcement and self-punishment. When we praise ourselves for outstanding performance, positive cognitions lead to feelings of satisfaction and to a continuation of praised behaviors. But when we castigate ourselves for not measuring up, this negative self-talk produces unpleasant feelings and a change in behavior. In this model, cognitions directly influence emotional states, leading

behavior to change in desired ways (Bandura, 1986).

ATTRIBUTION THEORY: COGNITIONS DEFINE EMOTIONS

Attribution theory is concerned with how we assign causes to events. Despite the clear experiential difference among various emotions such as fear, anger, and excitement, these emotions do not show specific, idiosyncratic patterns of physiological arousal. What is it that accounts for the experiential differences among emotions?

Attribution theory assumes that the way we describe a situation to ourselves plays a major role in determining what emotion we will experience. When we become aware of self-arousal, our minds immediately try to make sense out of this bodily change. Thus we look to the surrounding environment for an explanation. For example, arousal that occurs while at a funeral is likely to be experienced as grief. Arousal in the presence of a new acquaintance of the opposite sex may be experienced as love. And if we have recently taken a new medication, arousal is likely to be interpreted as a side effect of the drug.

Schachter and Singer (1962) tested this theory in what has become one of psychology's few classic experiments. The subjects were given a drug that increased arousal and were either informed of the drug's likely effects or misinformed that the drug would produce itching and numbness. The subjects were then led to a waiting room containing an experimental confederate posing as another subject. In one condition the confederate was angry and irritable. In another condition, he happily threw paper planes, played with a hula hoop, and invited subjects to a game of paper-wad basketball.

What were the experimenter's hypotheses? (Can you guess?) Theoretically, those who were accurately informed of the drug's effects could attribute the confederate's arousal directly to the drug so that their mood should not be greatly

FOCUS

THE EMOTION WHEEL

Psychologist Robert Plutchik (1980) developed an intriguing model to describe the various emotions and their relationships to one another. Plutchik observed that emotions are typically bipolar; that is, they occur in opposites, such as joy-sadness. He also noted that emotions vary in their similarity to other emotions. For example, shame and guilt are more similar to each other than are joy and disgust.

Along with these observations, Plutchik used a number of scaling techniques to quantify the degree of similarity among the various emotions. What he found was that the basic emotions form a circular order, with similar emotions placed side by side on the circle and those that differ placed farther apart.

FIGURE 6–1

PRIMARY AND MIXED EMOTIONS

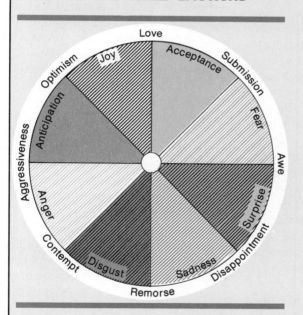

Plutchik's emotion wheel is presented in Figure 6–1. It defines eight basic emotions: joy, acceptance, fear, surprise, sadness, disgust, anger, and anticipation. Each can occur at varying levels of intensity. For example, fear represents a continuum of emotion ranging from apprehension to terror. Opposites are situated across from each other on the wheel, as in joy-sadness.

Plutchik also found that the primary emotions can be combined to form other emotions, just as the primary colors combine to form all other colors. For example, acceptance and fear combine to form submission.

influenced by the confederate's behavior. But those who were misinformed would attribute their arousal to the setting, as defined by the confederate's behavior. As expected, with the happy confederate, misinformed subjects were happier than were the accurately informed subjects. Similar results were found with the angry confederate. In the Schachter and Singer model, arousal awareness (a cognition) leads to a cognitive description of the situation, which then results in the experience of a particular emotion. Thus cognitions help define emotions.

EMOTIONS AFFECT COGNITIONS

It is well known that intense emotional states, such as terror, disrupt cognitive processes and adaptive behavior. In addition, emotions tend to elicit related cognitions. Feelings of depression elicit negative thoughts, just as feelings of joy prompt optimistic perceptions.

Bower (1981) showed that cognitive functions such as memory, perception, learning, and judgment depend on mood. Consider these examples: Subjects learning a list of words in one mood will remember it best when they are in that same mood again. Those in a depressed mood judge both themselves and others more harshly than they will when they are in a happy mood. A sad person looks longer at pictures of sad faces, and a happy person dwells on happy faces. Finally, those in a depressed mood recognize "failure" words more readily, whereas those who are happy find it easier to recognize words of "success."

We can conclude that cognitions and emotions are in continual reciprocal interaction, each playing a causal role in the other's existence. As Gaylin (1979, p. 217) observed,

No one . . . lives in the real world. We occupy a space of our own creation—a collage compounded of bits and pieces of actuality arranged into a design determined by our internal perceptions, our hopes, our fears, our memories, and our anticipations. This "reality" we live in—half fact, half fantasy—

is as much the product of our emotions . . . as our rationality.

Think of an example from your own life of how a thought affected one of your feelings and an example of a feeling or mood affecting what you thought.

EMOTION AND THE FACE
RESEARCHING THE FACE

Emotions are not only experienced, but they are also expressed in bodily movements and communicated to others. And the face is our most sensitive instrument for the nonverbal expression of emotion. Subjectively, it is said that the eyes mirror the soul and a smile has the power to launch a thousand ships. Objectively, the face's soft, plastic features can create hundreds of expressions, many of which carry emotional significance.

Psychologists Paul Ekman and Wallace Friesen have made a fascinating career out of studying people's faces. They maintain that characteristic facial expressions accompany each of the basic emotions (Ekman & Friesen, 1975). Moreover, their research indicates that many facial expressions of emotion are consistent across cultures, suggesting that much emotional responding is biologically rooted. For example, we don't have to be taught how to smile; children blind from birth smile spontaneously, in much the same way as sighted children.

Ekman and Friesen began by identifying three areas of the face: forehead, eyes, and lower face. They used the existing literature on emotion to hypothesize how each of these three facial areas would appear when expressing each of the basic emotions. This theory was then tested by correlating people's subjective feelings with their facial expressions. One technique, for example, was to videotape subjects' faces while they watched movies designed to elicit a particular emotion.

FIGURE 6–2   FIGURE 6–3   FIGURE 6–4

FIGURE 6–5   FIGURE 6–6   FIGURE 6–7

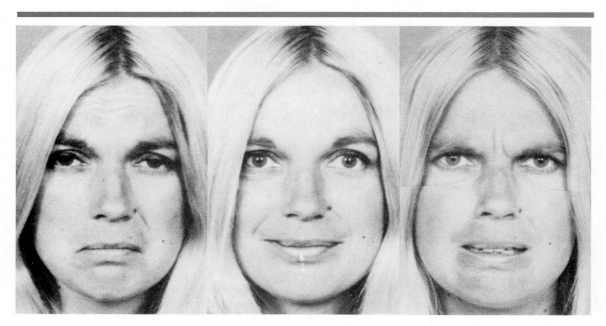

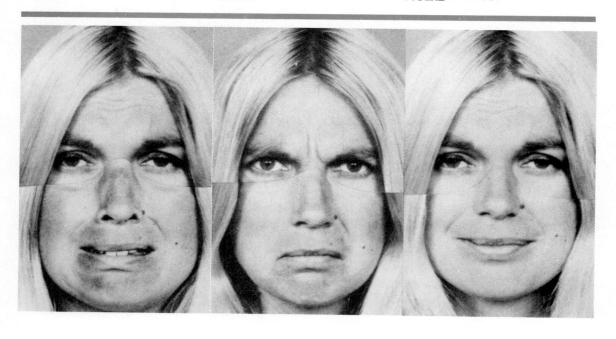

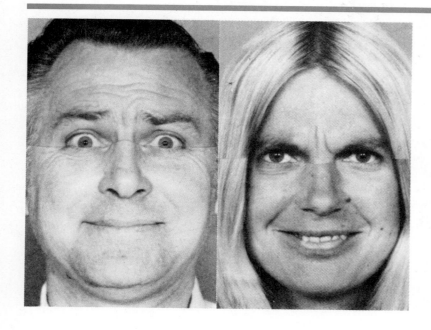

DO YOU KNOW WHAT YOUR FACE IS DOING?

Most of the time we express our emotions and react to those of another without being consciously aware of what either face is doing. What is exciting about Ekman's and Friesen's research is that it opens the possibility of enhancing our awareness of what is being felt and communicated. Ultimately, this knowledge may lead to a new era of social sensitivity and responsiveness.

Facial expressions for some of the basic emotions are described below and illustrated in Figures 6–2 through 6–12. In a manner similar to Plutchik's (1980) model, basic emotions can be combined to form more complex emotions, each with its own blend of facial characteristics. (For each facial description, make the designated changes on your own face and see what feelings are brought out.)

FEAR

The facial expression of fear is shown by

1. Brows that are raised and drawn together, with wrinkles in the center of the forehead.
2. A raised upper eyelid with the white showing above the pupil and the lower eyelid drawn up.
3. The mouth open and the lips drawn back.

Figure 6–2 shows an emotionally neutral face, which can be contrasted with the fear response in Figure 6–3.

ANGER

The anger face (Figure 6–4) shows

1. Brows that are lowered and drawn together, with vertical lines between them.
2. Tension in the eyelids, with a staring or bulging look in the eyes.
3. Lips that are either pressed firmly together or opened, tense, and squared.

The anger face is emotionally ambiguous unless anger is registered in all three facial areas. This makes it relatively easy for anger to be masked.

SADNESS

Sadness (Figure 6–5) is shown by

1. Eyebrows with the inner corners drawn up and the skin below the brow triangulated.
2. Upper eyelids with raised inner corners.
3. Corners of the lips down or the lower lip trembling.

HAPPINESS

Happiness (Figure 6–6) is primarily shown in the lower face and lower eyelids. It is indicated by

1. Wrinkles below the lower eyelid and crow's-feet wrinkles going outward from the outer corners of the eyes.
2. Corners of the lips drawn back and up, with a fold running from the nose to the outer lip, and the cheeks raised.

BLENDED EMOTIONS

The blended emotions are presented in Figures 6–7 through 6–12. Try to determine which blend each one is before reading further.

Figure 6–7 is fear and anger; Figure 6–8 is sadness and fear; Figure 6–9 is sadness and anger. Some of the blends are more difficult to imagine than others. Sadness and happiness are blended in Figure 6–10. This expression might occur in nostalgic, bittersweet moments or when a happy expression is used to hide sadness. Happiness and fear (Figure 6–11) might occur if one were trying to disguise a fear response. Figure 6–12 shows a blend of happiness and anger, sometimes called an "I've gotcha" expression.

Look at the blended faces and see if you can identify which parts of each original face were retained to form the blend.

Albert Ellis.

RATIONAL-EMOTIVE THERAPY: IRRATIONAL BELIEFS AND NEGATIVE EMOTIONS

CROOKED THINKING

Psychologist Albert Ellis constructed a practical approach to personal problems, known as rational-emotive therapy. He assumed that "crooked thinking" was at the heart of most emotional difficulties.

As living creatures with awareness, we all have preferences; we desire some outcomes in life rather than others. But we also have self-centered tendencies to *demand* and *insist* that these preferences become reality. When reality does not bow to our high-minded dictates, we become upset. This irrational pattern can be seen most clearly in children, yet it is a form of immaturity that most adults have not relinquished.

THE ILLUSION OF EXTERNAL CONTROL

Ellis believes that we falsely attribute most of our problems to the external events and cir-

cumstances of our lives. For example, most of us believe we are unhappy because of factors such as failing in school, being rejected by a lover, having someone treat us unkindly, or not having enough money. Ellis maintains that if we observe ourselves more carefully, it will become apparent that in fact, it is not these external events that make our lives miserable. Rather, it is our own beliefs, the things we say to ourselves, that create most of life's unhappiness.

For example, suppose you're at a party and overhear people talking about someone. As you get closer, you realize they are making fun of *you*. They think your clothes are out of place. Most people would feel embarrassed, angry, and humiliated in this situation. For some, this night would stand out in their minds for years to come. If asked why they feel upset, a natural reply might be, "Because those creeps made fun of me!" In this way, upset feelings are attributed to an external activating event.

Ellis, on the other hand, would take a different approach. He would ask, "What must you be telling yourself for their unkind remarks to result in your getting upset?" Ellis notes that although most of us would get upset in this situation, not everyone would. In other words, there is no causal necessity for others' unkind behavior to ruin our evening. Ellis inferred that for this emotional upset to occur, we must believe, whether or not we realize it, that "It's terribly important that everyone, even those whom I hardly know, approve of everything about me (including my clothes)."

But what is the alternative? How might someone who has been purged of irrational beliefs respond in such a situation? According to Ellis, such a person might think, "It would be nicer if people didn't make rude comments" and "It is unfortunate that on this occasion I have been made the object of others' rudeness." Such beliefs wouldn't make the unpleasant episode go away, but they would lead to a different emotional reaction. While irrational beliefs lead to feelings of humiliation and intense anger, rational beliefs result in feelings of mild annoyance

Becoming terribly upset when our preferences don't come true is a behavior pattern that many adults carry over from childhood.

and irritation. For Ellis, the difference between these two reactions is not just a matter of words. When multiplied over the thousands of events that can trigger emotional upset, it is the difference between a life that is essentially peaceful and one that is always at the mercy of turbulent and aversive emotions.

THE ABC'S OF EMOTIONAL DISTRESS

Ellis is fond of analyzing personal problems in terms of an **ABC model**:

A is the external activating event.
B is the irrational belief.
C is the consequent negative emotional re-action.

According to Ellis, we falsely think that C is caused by A, whereas C is actually caused by B. Thus rational-emotive therapy identifies the irrational beliefs that lead to negative emotional reactions and, (D), disputes these beliefs, that is, argues against them, until their irrationality and

destructiveness become clear. They are then replaced with more rational beliefs, and the client is encouraged to act on these more adaptive cognitions.

IRRATIONAL BELIEFS

Several irrational beliefs occur with such regularity that they deserve special attention.

It is necessary to be loved or approved of by virtually every person you meet. Some people may argue that they do not really believe in this irrational idea, yet an apparent rejection, even one by a casual acquaintance, may leave them anxious and upset for days. This is one of the most prevalent irrational ideas in our culture. Ellis pointed out that although it is *desirable* to be loved and approved of, that is quite different from *demanding* that everyone always approve of us. In fact, it is quite likely that some of the people we respect *will* disapprove of us, perhaps for reasons related to their own idiosyncratic histories rather than to any fault of our own. Since it is not within our conceivable

power to control everyone's reaction to everything that we do, it is clearly self-defeating to insist that they react to us only in ways that *we* specify. Even though we might like to believe otherwise, the world does not always dance to our tune.

Ellis suggested that when disapproved of by someone that we respect, the best strategy is to fully admit the annoyance and frustration. At the same time, however, we can refrain from convincing ourselves that the situation is catastrophic or that the other person is objectively right rather than merely presenting an opinion.

To be a worthwhile person, you should be competent and successful in everything you do. Ellis commented that none of us can be perfectly competent in everything we do. Baldly stated, the truth is that most of us cannot and will not be truly outstanding even in a single major respect. But this is no cause for alarm or depression, unless we choose to make it such. It is merely a description of the real-world limitations that each human being faces. It is our choice: Accept the world as it is or curse it for not being the way we want.

It is awful and catastrophic when things are not the way one wants them to be. Ellis pointed out that there is no reason that things *should* be different from the way that they are. What is, is. When things turn out to be different from what we had expected, it simply means that our ideas about the world were wrong. Again, Ellis is saying that a certain amount of frustration is inevitable, yet there is a qualitative difference between being frustrated and being upset. In addition, although we are often loath to admit it, this frustration helps us fully enjoy the other parts of our lives, as a world without any frustration quickly becomes bland and boring.

We need someone stronger than ourselves to rely on. Rather than finding someone "stronger" and then being at that person's mercy, it is more adaptive to develop our own inherent strength.

> Moreover, if you depend on others in order to feel safe—for then you cannot make mistakes yourself or be blamed if you do make them—you essentially lose rather than gain basic security: since the only real security that you can have in life is that of knowing that, no matter how many mistakes you make, you are still not worthless, but merely a fallible human being. (Ellis, 1962, p. 81)

Analyze the problem described at the beginning of this section—being laughed at because of one's clothes—in terms of Ellis's ABC model.

A RATIONAL-EMOTIVE CASE STUDY

Rhoda S., a thirty-five-year-old physician, has a problem forming lasting relationships with males, even though she is eager to be married. Since a last-minute rejection by her then-fiancé ten years earlier, she has had a number of sexual friendships but no deep emotional involvements. Excerpts from one of her sessions with Ellis (1973, pp. 47–50) are presented next. (Note that Ellis is known for his direct, confrontive style of interaction. Many psychologists use Ellis' ideas in a less abrasive manner.)

(T)herapist: *What are you really afraid of in regard to marrying?*

(C)lient: *Of rejection, it would seem. Of being left alone once again, after I had built up high hopes of remaining together with a man forever, as I did with my ex-fiancé.*

T: *That's a surface explanation that really doesn't explain anything. First of all, you are constantly getting rejected, the way you are going on now, because you pick men who aren't marriageable or whom you refuse to wed. Therefore, your hopes of a prolonged, intense involvement are perpetually being dashed—rejected. Secondly, you are really rejecting yourself, all the time. For you are assuming that if you did get refused by some man, just as you once did, you couldn't possibly stand it— weakling that you are! This is a complete vote of nonconfidence in yourself. You are therefore truly refusing to accept yourself as you are. You are demanding that you be perfectly safe.*

C: *But isn't it better to be safe than hurt?*

T: *You mean, isn't it better to have never loved and never lost?*

C: *O.K. But if losing is so dreadful, isn't that better?*

T: *But why should losing be so dreadful?*

C: *Oh, loneliness. Not ever getting what you want.*

T: *But aren't you lonely this way? And do you now get what you want?*

C: *No, I don't. But I also don't get what I very much don't want.*

T: *Partly. But not as much as you think.*

C: *What do you mean?*

T: *I first of all mean what you mean: that you do not like to get rejected — and who the hell does? — and that you are avoiding this dislikable event by not trying to get accepted. But I mean, secondly, that what you really dislike most about being rejected is not the refusal itself — since that merely gets you what you have when you do not try for acceptance: namely, being alone — but the belief that this kind of loneliness makes you a slob, a worthless person.*

C: *Oh, but I do dislike, and dislike very much, the refusal itself. I hate to be refused and then have to be by myself.*

T: *Partly. But suppose you won one of the males you desired and he died, and you lost him that way. Would that make you feel as badly as if you won him, he were still alive, and he then rejected you?*

C: *No, I guess it wouldn't.*

T: *Ah! You see what I'm getting at?*

C: *That it's not really the loss of the man that I'm concerned about, but his rejection of me.*

T: *Exactly! It's not the loss of him — but the loss of you. That's what you're really worried about. If you lose a man by his dying or going away or something like that, you don't like it: for then you're not getting what you want and you feel frustrated. But even if you lose a man by his being available, but his still rejecting you, then you're not only frustrated, but you wrongly conclude that if he rejects you, you must reject yourself. That is to say — you lose yourself as well as him. At least, that's the way you set things up in your mind — that's your conclusion, your hangup. And what you call "loneliness" is not merely your being alone (which I will grant is annoying and bothersome) but your being alone plus your falsely believing that you're no good for being in that state.*

You may now want to try applying an RET analysis to a problem of your own. Identify the A, B, and C of the problem and then dispute the irrational beliefs. Identify beliefs and self-statements that would be more rational and adaptive.

Before reading further, respond to the following items. Decide how much you agree with each statement. There are no "right" or "wrong" answers, so try to respond according to the way you usually feel and behave.

+2 I agree very much.
+1 I agree somewhat.
 0 I feel neutral about this.
−1 I disagree slightly.
−2 I disagree strongly.

_____ 1. **If I don't set the highest standards for myself, I am likely to end up a second-rate person.**

_____ 2. **People will probably think less of me if I make a mistake.**

_____ 3. **If I cannot do something really well, there is little point in doing it at all.**

_____ 4. **I should be upset if I make a mistake.**

_____ 5. **If I try hard enough, I should be able to excel at anything I attempt.**

_____ 6. **It is shameful for me to display weaknesses or foolish behavior.**

_____ 7. **I shouldn't have to repeat the same mistake many times.**

_____ 8. **An average performance is bound to be unsatisfying to me.**

_____ 9. **Failing at something important means I'm less of a person.**

_____ 10. **If I scold myself for failing to live up to my expectations, it will help me to do better in the future. (Burns, 1980, p. 44)**

The next section examines a topic of particular relevance to college students — perfectionism and the ways that perfectionistic beliefs affect emotions. Interpretations of the preceding scale are provided at the end of the section.

COGNITIONS OF THE PERFECTIONIST

WHEN IS IT HEALTHY TO SEEK PERFECTION?

The pursuit of excellence is one of our highest and most respected values. Without a concern for quality, little would be accomplished, and life would seem meaningless. But is there a point at which the pursuit of excellence can take over our lives, making us slaves to idealistic, unattainable goals? What about Mary Ann? She entered law school resolved to strive for the best. After two months, it became apparent that she would be in the bottom half of her class. She ended her life rather than face the humiliation of "failure." How are we to determine when the ideal of excellence enriches our lives and when it becomes an obstacle to living?

One clue is how we experience an activity, independent of its successful or unsuccessful outcome. If we look forward to what we do, experience it as a challenge, and end it with a sense of satisfaction, then chances are it is contributing to our personal growth.

THE HIDDEN COSTS OF PERFECTION

Unfortunately, many people have been seduced by the glorification of perfection and blinded to its hidden costs. Psychologist David Burns (1980) claims that these costs are not only exorbitant but also surprising. Paradoxically, perfectionists often experience a decrease in productivity and quality of work. In addition, they may suffer impaired health, poor self-control, troubled personal relationships, low self-esteem, depression, and performance anxiety (e.g., writer's block).

Burns found that among insurance agents, perfectionists whose sense of self-worth was based on their accomplishments actually made less money than did nonperfectionists. Studies of Olympic gymnasts and other athletes have found that the top competitors tend to *not* be perfectionists. Perfectionists find the memory of past "failures" difficult to forget, and this often raises their anxiety to disruptive levels. In addition, perfectionists tend to apply their unrealistic standards to others. When they show annoyance with others' lack of perfection, resentment and rejection are likely outcomes.

THE ORIGINS OF PERFECTIONISM

Perfectionism appears to have its roots in childhood, in the needs to be loved and accepted. Burns (1980, p. 41) presented a typical pattern:

> The perfectionistic parent often feels frustrated and threatened when a child is having difficulties in schoolwork or in relationships with peers. Because the parent is unrealistically self-critical, he or she personalizes the child's difficulties by thinking, "This shows what a bad mother (or father) I am." Because the parent's self-esteem is contingent on the child's success, the parent puts great pressure on the child to avoid failure. Consequently, when the troubled child turns to the parent for reassurance or guidance, the parent reacts with irritation, not love, and the child is flooded with shame.

Through this process, children may eventually develop an excessive fear of failure. They avoid tasks in which success is not guaranteed at the outset. They distort reality by allowing themselves to believe that their successful performances were "flawless," blinding themselves to how much "perfection" is only an ideal, a guide rather than a goal. The problem often worsens as the child grows older. For example, as one progresses from grade school to college, it becomes more and more difficult to be the best in one's class. At some point, the goal of being "number one" takes on impossible proportions, and the perfectionist's life becomes a study in disillusionment, perceived failure, and self-punishment.

Simply becoming aware that one's goals are unrealistic or realizing how perfectionism is rooted in parental behavior is generally not enough to foster constructive change. The reason is that perfectionists almost inevitably attribute what success they do attain to their drive for perfection. They take pride in their "high standards" and falsely believe that they would be less successful if this drive were compromised.

CHARACTERISTICS OF A PERFECTIONIST

Either-or thinking. Perfectionists often think in black-or-white, all-or-nothing categories. If they are not a perfect success, then they must be a total failure. This leaves little margin for error and sets up the perfectionist to fear any activity in which success is not assured. This thinking makes them subject to the "saint-or-sinner" syndrome. For example, when on a diet, they must see themselves as being either completely on the diet or completely off it. With the first lapse, sainthood ends and sin begins. Sin begets guilt and self-deprecation, yet the perception of oneself as a sinner is also an implicit permission to eat. The result: binge eating and further self-hatred.

Overgeneralization. On the basis of a single mistake, perfectionists often conclude that failure is inevitable. They are quick to say, "I'll *never* get this right!"

Should statements. Perfectionists rely on "should" statements to control their behavior. As Burns explained, when falling short of a goal, several attitudes can be taken. An adaptive one would be asking oneself, "How can I learn from this?" Instead, perfectionists remind themselves, "I shouldn't have goofed up!" Rather than understanding what actually happened, they turn their attention to hypothetical rules about what was supposed to happen. It often turns out that these hypothetical "shoulds" are values that they never consciously chose. In addition, should statements are often unrealistic and impractical. They can be viewed as the internalized, scolding voices of our parents. After telling yourself that you "shouldn't have done it," a natural progression is to think, "I am a bad person. I should be punished for what I've done." Thus, should statements often lead to the next category.

Self-punishment. Perfectionists prefer the stick to the carrot. They motivate themselves through negative self-talk rather than praise. When going off their diet once, they tell themselves, "I am a pig!" and ignore the many times they successfully refused fattening foods. This self-punitive attitude leads to guilt and frustration, not to effective self-control. For example, self-criticism leads to depression, and this can become habitual, occurring even after experiences of relative success. After all, even an outstanding performance is rarely "flawless." But when even success brings self-criticism, what is there to look forward to? What is left to release perfectionists from their prison of self-abuse?

Not knowing when to stop. Perfectionists often have difficulty discerning when a task should be considered complete. Burns noted that every task reaches a point of diminishing returns, after which further effort makes only negligible improvements. If unaware of when this point has been passed, individuals can enter a dead end, wasting time and energy. By persisting too long, they can sacrifice their overall productivity. Thus, inexplicably to them, perfectionists are often underachievers.

THE COGNITIVE TREATMENT OF PERFECTIONISM

Burns (1980) described some of the techniques he uses when dealing with perfectionists. One goal is to make the client aware of the disadvantages of always trying to be perfect. Without this awareness, change is unlikely. Burns simply has the client list the advantages and disadvantages of perfectionism. For example, one of his clients, Jennifer, listed the ad-

FOCUS
PREJUDICE

Prejudice, the judgment of another without adequate evidence, combines false beliefs with negative emotions. We all know that prejudice is wrong, but why is it so difficult to eradicate?

In the popular view, prejudice develops simply because of our limited experience with certain cultural or racial groups. It is presumed that with greater experience, the diversity within these groups would become apparent and prejudice would be ended. But Snyder (1982) suggested that such optimism is unfounded. He contended that we must first appreciate the mechanisms that maintain prejudice, despite sincere efforts to evaluate the truth of our beliefs.

In other words, even though we feel we are being open-minded, judging each person on his or her own merits, we often go about testing our beliefs in ways that do not yield reliable conclusions. For example, one study had men talk on the phone to a female that they had been randomly led to believe was either attractive or unattractive. Those who were shown a photo of an attractive girl said that they expected to talk to someone who was sociable, poised, and humorous. Those shown an unattractive photo expected to meet someone who was awkward, serious, and socially inept. What these men didn't realize was how their behavior when talking on the phone was affected by their prior beliefs. Those shown the attractive photo were warm, friendly, humorous, and animated when speaking with their new acquaintance. Those shown the unattractive photo were cold, dull, and reserved. As might be expected, the difference in male behaviors elicited a comparable difference in female behaviors, even though the women knew nothing about the male's expectations. Thus both groups of males experienced the "validation" of their false beliefs.

Similar processes have been discovered for gender and race. For example, one study simulated a job interview, with white interviewers and either white or black interviewees. The applicants were actually experimental confederates trained to behave consistently, regardless of how the interviewer acted. Videotapes revealed that the white interviewers were less friendly and spent less time with the blacks. A second study had interviewers trained to behave in either a friendly or a more reserved manner. Applicants subjected to the reserved interviewers were more nervous, and they performed less well than did those given the friendly interviewers. Together, these studies show how racial stereotypes create self-fulfilling, prejudicial effects in job interviews.

Stereotypes not only bring about confirmatory behavior, but even when behavior is not affected, history can be rewritten in memory to provide apparent confirmation. For example, Snyder (1982) reported on one study in which subjects read a fictitious biography of Betty K. The biography was purposely made ambiguous as to Betty's sexual orientation. It stated that she never had a steady boy friend in high school but did go out on dates. In college, she had a steady boy friend, but he was more of a close friend than anything else. A week later, subjects were given new information. They were told either that she was now living with another woman in a lesbian relationship or that she was now living with her husband. Subjects were then asked questions about her life history. Without being aware of it, they reconstructed her biography to fit their stereotyped beliefs about her sexual orientation. Those who were told she was a lesbian remembered that she never had a steady boy friend in high school but ignored her active dating in college. Those who believed she was a heterosexual remembered that she had a steady boy friend in college but forgot that this was more of a friendship.

vantage that perfectionism often produces fine work. On the other hand, she found six disadvantages: Perfectionism made her so nervous it sometimes hindered the quality of her work; the fear of mistakes often blocked creativity; perfectionism kept her from trying new activities; being self-critical took much of the joy out of her life; she had trouble relaxing because there was always something that wasn't perfect and thus required her further attention; and it led her to adopt the same fault-finding role with others that she used with herself.

Burns's cognitive therapy also tries to fight the client's assumption that an activity can't be satisfying unless done to perfection. For this he asks clients to identify a number of activities with a potential for some satisfaction and make a rough prediction of how satisfying each one will be on a hundred-point scale. After each activity is completed, they rate the actual satisfaction experienced as well as the flawlessness of their performance. Clients are shocked to find out that actual satisfaction and level of performance are often independent. For example, one professor found that he felt more satisfied after doing a mediocre job of fixing a leaky pipe than he did from giving a lecture at which he received a standing ovation.

To attack all-or-none thinking, Burns has perfectionists spend a day observing whether the world can be accurately described using all-or-none categories. They are instructed to ask themselves, for example, "Are these walls completely clean, or do they have at least some dirt?" "Is this person totally handsome?" Once clients become aware of a dichotomous cognition, they are to substitute a more realistic description. Instead of thinking, "The party was a total flop because the sound system wouldn't work," they might substitute, "Although I didn't get to dance, I did talk to some interesting people."

Another technique is simply to keep a written log of self-critical thoughts. After entering each negative thought, a more realistic and adaptive response is entered next to it. Instead

of "You idiot, how could you have missed that easy question?" the client might have said, "I must have let my attention wander."

As heretical as it may sound, for perfectionists, it often helps to lower one's immediate goals. Consider those who write for a living. One of the most paralyzing things they can do while composing is to think, "This has to be outstanding." It is much more adaptive to describe the project as "getting a quick draft on paper just to see how it looks." That first draft can later be reorganized and polished fairly quickly, and with much less stress than trying to write a finished product from the outset.

Add up your score on the items at the beginning of this section. A higher positive score indicates a greater degree of perfectionism. About half of the population is likely to score from +2 to +16, indicating varying degrees of perfectionism. For those with nonperfectionist or mild perfectionist tendencies, the ideal of "pursuing excellence" is likely to be adaptive. For those with strongly perfectionist beliefs (>16), however, this ideal may be causing problems.

The remainder of the chapter explores two emotions that span the gamut of negative-to-positive feelings, depression and happiness. In addition, we shall try to define what constitutes healthy emotional expression.

DEPRESSION

By any index, depression is a major health problem. Fifteen percent of the population suffers from depression, with 70 percent of college freshmen showing depressive symptoms. In addition, suicide, which is often a result of depression, is the second leading cause of death among young people (Beck & Kovacs, 1977).

Depressives suffer extreme sadness, loss of appetite, impaired sleep, lessened sexual interest, and fatigue. They have lost their motivation and interest in life and thus find it difficult to carry out routine responsibilities. For them, the world is cold and inhospitable. In addition, depressives often cannot avoid thinking negative thoughts about themselves. For example, Hammen and Mayol (1982) found depression linked to the occurrence of negative events that were at least partly within the individual's control, thus allowing the reaction of self-blame.

LIVING THE "BLUES"

What is the experience of depression? One twenty-two-year-old female compared herself to litter on the streets. She was a drifting newspaper, "floating around, being blown around the sidewalk, underfoot, you know, being kicked aside" (Scarf, 1979, p. 47). For another female, the onset of a depressive episode occurred when returning home after successfully playing in a tennis tournament. She suddenly felt

> as if the bottom were dropping out of my life, and that I was a nothing. That I'd promised to do too many things I didn't care about for too many people I didn't give a damn about. I was on all these committees, and running like crazy; but it was stupid and meaningless. And I wanted out — to quit trying — to be dead. (Scarf, 1979, p. 47)

A middle-aged professional man recalled that

> it was a cold, rainy, gray Saturday afternoon but the gloom of the day could not possibly mirror the despondency which filled my whole being. There I sat, a fifty-three-year-old man, happily married, professionally successful, financially affluent, crying like a lost child as I clenched and unclenched my fists. The psychiatrist, whom I had met only ten minutes earlier, had just said, bluntly and finally, "I could prescribe more medicine for you, but I don't think that would help you get better. You need to get in another environment for a few days. There is a bed available this afternoon in the hospital. . . ."

> Here was the verdict I had been secretly dreading for months: hospitalization. Willpower, vacations, tranquilizers, antidepressants, sporadic therapy — none had been able to stop my descent into uncontrollable depression. I had begun to dread what loomed ever larger as the only alternatives — a complete breakdown and hospitalization, or suicide. (Killian & Bloomberg, 1975, p. 42)

DEPRESSION AND GENDER

As might be expected from a knowledge of gender roles, the experience of depression seems to differ for males and females. For women, depression centers on experiences of loneliness, helplessness, dependency, and the need for external sources of security. For males, depression often involves self-criticism and the failure to live up to one's expectations (Scarf, 1979).

Depression is found two to five times as frequently among women as men. This is partly because going to a doctor and adopting the "sick role" fits more consistently with female than male socialization. Males are expected to be strong, to "grin and bear it," whatever the problem. Beyond that, dependency is tolerated more readily in women than in men. As a result, many women do not develop a strong, independent sense of self-sufficiency. Their esteem is more closely tied to how much other people need and value them. Thus the loss of a love relationship often affects women more severely than it does men.

THE ORIGIN OF DEPRESSION

Psychiatrist Silvano Arieti (1979) termed modern times the "Age of Melancholy." He believes that depression originates in childhood and that the depressed individual often comes from a stable family in which love was freely given in the early years. Because of the birth of another child or the family's belief that a child should be treated like an adult, this early bliss is curtailed, and the child experiences a sort of

''Paradise Lost.'' The child then becomes obsessed with trying to please the **dominant other**, usually the mother or father. (Later on, this person may be a mother substitute such as a spouse or companion.)

> Striving to regain paradise, he thus lives not for himself but for others. He believes that love is not available now, but that if he can live up to the expectations of adults, it will be. He becomes a compliant person, a person with a strong sense of duty. When he does not succeed in obtaining what he wants, he tends to blame himself. (Arieti, 1979, p. 57)

When frustrations in work or love occur in later life, this cognitive pattern sets up an overreaction, resulting in a depressive episode. In other words, life's frustrations seem overwhelming because of their implications for the all-consuming fantasy of regaining lost love.

THE COGNITIVE TREATMENT OF DEPRESSION

It seems likely that the fast pace of modern society is at the heart of the recent increase in depression. Emotional bonds are being broken as couples divorce and individuals change their jobs, homes, and friends at ever-increasing rates. For those with depressive thought patterns, such changes can be perilous.

Depressed people show characteristic patterns of cognition. For example, they dream about frustration, humiliation, rejection, deprivation, and punishment, even after they recover (Beck & Kovacs, 1977). In her dreams, one de-

FOCUS
PREDICTORS OF SUICIDE

With an incidence rate higher than murder, suicide is one of the top ten causes of death in the United States. In particular, the number of suicides among teens and young adults has more than doubled in recent years. One reason for this increase is that American parents spend less time with their children than do parents in almost every other nation in the world. In an effort to give their family the good life and to find that life for themselves, many Americans have inadvertently sacrificed close family ties. Without those ties, many young adults find it difficult to weather life's failures and disappointments.

Suicide is often an enigma. Many wonder, "Why would anyone even consider such an extreme measure?" The reason may seem obvious, but actually it is not. Researchers (Farberow & Litman, 1970) estimate that about two-thirds of those who attempt suicide do not really want to die. Rather, they are looking for a dramatic means of telling others that they hurt. About 30 percent are undecided about whether they want to live or die, and they typically choose a means that allows some possibility of being saved. About 4 percent are actually intent on dying. They give little warning and choose a means that offers little chance of rescue. Over half of suicide attempts involve pills. One-third involve cutting. Other common methods include hanging, drowning, shooting, and jumping. One in eight attempts ends in death.

As summarized below, a number of factors have been related to suicide (Farberow, 1974; Lester & Lester, 1971; Schneidman, Farberow, & Litman, 1970).

SUICIDE POTENTIAL IS GREATER

1. If there is disruption in a young person's family, such as divorce, death of a parent, or parental rejection of an intended spouse.
2. If there are no family or friends to turn to for support or if the family denies that help is needed.
3. If a young person comes from an upper-middle-class family rather than one that is poor. One reason is that well-to-do children are given all the so-called advantages, but there is usually a string attached: They are expected to excel in almost everything that they attempt. This places tremendous pressure on them to succeed (even if these expectations have never been verbalized). Also, many apparently successful teenagers live on a delicate balance. As long as things go well, they seem fine, but they don't have the experience and coping skills to deal with frustration. Many come to believe that their lives are "blessed," that things will always go their way. The first setback collapses that fantasy and takes them to the edge of desperation.
4. If the individual is male. Although three times as many females as males attempt suicide, males are more likely to make an attempt that is fatal.
5. If the individual is over fifty. Although there has been a recent rise in young suicides, older people are still more likely to take their own lives.
6. If the individual is divorced or single.

7. If a young person is in college. Suicide occurs twice as often among college students as among those of similar age not in college. This is presumably a result of leaving home to attend college, which disrupts one's network of friendships and emotional ties. Also, college can entail tremendous pressure to succeed. (Suicidal students are not necessarily doing badly in school. Most are good students who set unrealistically high standards for themselves.) Also, the precipitating stressor is more likely to be a relationship failure than an academic problem. Suicides usually occur at the beginning or end of a semester. The beginning is often a lonely time, and the semester's end brings final exams and the heightened probability of a special relationship breaking up.

8. If the individual is under high negative stress and has poor interpersonal problem-solving skills (Schotte & Clum, 1982). Under these conditions there is sometimes a rigidity in thinking that interferes with finding alternative solutions to one's problems.

9. If the individual has high depression, high anger, and *low* anxiety. Apparently, the combination of depression and anger creates a suicidal impulse, which can be inhibited if anxiety is high (Plutchik, 1980). About 80 percent of those who attempt suicide are depressed, withdrawn, and show a decrease in self-esteem.

10. If there is a deterioration in personal hygiene or signs of decreased motivation, such as missing class or sleeping most of the day.

11. If there is a sudden onset of symptoms, such as depression or alcoholism.

12. If the person begins giving away precious possessions.

13. If there is a sudden euphoria for no apparent reason. (This may mean that the person has decided to end the misery.)

14. If there is a verbal warning of suicide. Although most warnings are not followed soon after by actual attempts, about 75 percent of suicide attempts are preceded by warnings. Warnings are sometimes indirect, such as "I can't take it anymore," "People would be better off without me," and "This has got to end."

15. If there is a detailed suicide plan involving a means that allows little possibility of intervention.

16. If the person talks about suicide.

17. If the person has a prior history of attempts or threats of suicide.

18. If there is a history of self-destructive habits, such as drug abuse or reckless driving.

19. If the person has a debilitating illness.

20. If the person is a lawyer, dentist, pharmacist, physician, or psychiatrist(!).

WHAT TO DO IF SUICIDE IS SUSPECTED

Most suicidal college students do not seek professional help. Thus it is imperative for friends and relatives to recognize early signs of suicidal intent and intervene effectively. The American Association of Suicidology offers the following approach:

1. Start with low-key questions, such as "You don't seem like yourself lately. Has something been bothering you?"
2. Don't brush off the individual by merely reassuring them that things will get better. If the person admits to being depressed, try to communicate your understanding of what they may be feeling. For example, you might say, "I guess sometimes it seems like it's not worth it to keep on struggling when things keep going against you."
3. If the individual agrees with this statement, you might inquire, "Do you ever wake up in the morning and wish you didn't have to go on living?"
4. If the answer is affirmative, then you may want to ask directly, "Have you been thinking of hurting yourself?" Often friends and family ignore obvious signs of suicide or fear bringing up the topic, thinking that by ignoring the problem it will go away. This bit of magical thinking can be dangerous. Contrary to popular opinion, suicidal persons are generally willing, and sometimes eager, to talk about their problem once it has been brought into the open. When this discussion starts, the individual then has a chance to see that others do care and that there are other solutions to their problem.
5. In discussing an individual's suicidal intent, do not be judgmental. Avoid saying things like "I think you're making a mountain out of a molehill." Even though this observation is probably true, it is simply not helpful. Trying to understand what the other person is feeling is often more effective than giving advice.
6. If there appears to be genuine suicidal intent, professional help should be sought.

pressive saw herself as inept, ugly, or diseased, and she had recurring dreams of being deserted by her parents. In addition, depressives are self-critical. They distort reality and impose unrealistic standards on themselves. In their minds, they are losers, no matter how well they do according to objective criteria.

Psychologist Aron Beck developed a cognitive therapy for treating depressives. He assumed that if people change the way they see themselves and what they tell themselves, they will feel better. "As a person learns to think more realistically, to approach his problems with more perspective, and to look at his future more objectively his mood improves, while other symptoms such as loss of appetite and insomnia diminish" (Beck & Kovacs, 1977, p. 100). Beck's cognitive therapy often involves having the therapist review the client's recent experiences, suggesting other, more objective

interpretations of them. This is similar to Ellis's rational-emotive therapy in its emphasis on correcting the client's distorted and irrational ideas.

Cognitive therapists try to determine whether the client's cognitions are based on facts or on distortion. The client often keeps a diary, noting times of particular sadness, identifying self-critical thoughts that accompany the sadness, and challenging these self-criticisms. Clients may also keep a log of their accomplishments and pleasurable times, as a way of counterbalancing their selective negative recall. Finally, cognitive therapists treat general attitudes and assumptions, such as the tendency to structure the world in either-or categories, as described in the section on perfectionism.

What symptoms of depression have you experienced? Can you link your times of sadness to the causes described above, such as

disappointments in love or work, the relationship with a dominant other, or rigid and unrealistic cognitions? What have you found to be the best way of getting yourself out of a depressive mood?

After examining depression and suicide, we shall now turn to positive emotions. How does emotional expression enhance our sense of aliveness? What can we do to increase our level of happiness?

EMOTIONS AND ALIVENESS

ROMANCING THE MACHINE

Recently our culture has become fascinated with a highly intelligent but totally emotionless creature, the personal computer. Computers control our means of national defense, our factories, our offices, and even some of our homes. Whether they prove to be loyal servants or Frankenstein monsters, there is certainly no lack of enthusiasm for these paragons of efficiency. For Gestalt therapist Fritz Perls, however, this fascination is just the latest fling in a long-running romance between people and machines.

According to Perls, the machine has entranced us. We not only value it, we idealize and even emulate it. We are both awed and threatened, for we simply cannot match its power, speed, and cognitive capacity. We envy its efficiency, reliability, and predictability. It does not seem to be fallible in the way that humans so often are. But Perls claims that in emulating the machine, we have become more machinelike ourselves. It is often considered appropriate to deny and inhibit emotional expression. Many even pride themselves on their lack of emotion (à la Mr. Spock). Perls concluded that without realizing it, we have become a culture of zombies. Although this may have made us more efficient, he claims that it has also taken away our sense of aliveness and emotional spontaneity.

Similar to Mr. Spock, many in our culture take pride in their lack of emotion.

STAYING ALIVE

When do you feel most alive? Is it when you are repeating a routine activity over and over again? Probably not. People feel most alive when they are experiencing something strongly, when their attention is fully engaged, when they are physiologically aroused, when what they are perceiving seems new, and when they feel free to move and think without constraint or prior expectation. Although machinelike precision, repetition, and predictability are important to our economic survival, they do not contribute to human aliveness.

Psychotherapists often find that their clients have "lost touch with their emotions." This is a common phrase, but what does it mean? Many people deny their feelings, keeping them bottled up somewhere deep inside. Their knowledge of what they are feeling, or in what part of their body they are feeling it, is vague, indefinite. At the same time, they may be unaware that something is missing. In their view, they are simply "in control of themselves." In this way, many modern people have identified with the computer part of themselves, the internal wiring of the neocortex, and somehow defined their emotionality as "not me." For them, experiencing strong emotion has become threatening. It is perceived as a loss of control and a loss of respectability.

Of course, when it comes to efficiency, emotions do get in the way. They are messy. They make people hard to handle and difficult to predict. For a world in which efficiency and success are revered, emotionality becomes a problem. For example, we are continually being told, even as children, "Don't cry," "You shouldn't feel that," "You don't hate me, you're just upset." As Elliot (1976, p. 11) found,

> Pretty soon we learned that we'd better not express what we really felt. Then we learned that the best way to do that was not to feel it. We learned to twist ourselves into the shapes our parents wanted. Feelingless. No bother. No problem. Then we forgot we'd done it.

This forgetting is what makes the path back to emotional expression so difficult. There's no reason to begin the journey toward greater aliveness if you're not aware of having died. Thus, one of the most practical things we can do is become aware of how much our own natural aliveness has been suppressed. This often requires honest self-observation and the courage to seek feedback from others.

TRAUMA AND EMOTIONAL DEADNESS

Sometimes the deadening of our emotional lives comes from a single overwhelming incident rather than a gradual process of social influ-

ence. Coleman (1980, p. 385) described such an event in the life of a young mother who left her two young children at home for a few minutes while visiting a neighbor. She returned to find her home in flames and her children trapped inside. Firemen restrained her from entering the burning house, and the children perished. A year later in therapy she acknowledged,

> I know I must put it in the past, that life must go on . . . that somehow I must think of the present and future. But I can't seem to forget. I shouldn't have left my children alone. . . . I can never really forgive myself. The memory of that awful night will haunt me as long as I live . . . and I can't bear the thought of having more children for fear something awful will happen to them too . . . maybe I will do something irresponsible and crazy again.

Such experiences may leave wounds that never completely heal. This woman, for example, understands that she must go on with her life and not withdraw from emotional involvements. Yet getting over this incident is not just a simple cognitive decision. Her fears cannot easily be swept away, and they are not entirely under rational control. The job of working through the grief, the guilt, and the emotional hurt takes time, and even then, she may always have difficulty with situations that remind her of this traumatic loss. Troubled individuals often find it helpful to discuss their feelings with those who can listen and try to understand, without judging or evaluating them.

HEALTHY EMOTIONAL EXPRESSION

When an emotion runs its natural course, the physiological arousal of the emotion is quickly dissipated in physical activities such as laughter, crying, or talking. However, the most direct expression of each emotion is often not socially acceptable, and without some form of physical expression, arousal is prolonged. Continually bottling up one's feelings is disastrous to health, as it may lead to elevated blood pressure, ulcers, headaches, and other dysfunctions. Continual suppression also affects one's personal relationships. Chronic suppressors come across as emotional "icebergs." Most of us prefer to form a close relationship with someone who can provide a more warm and satisfying experience.

Thus healthy functioning requires a balance between suppression and expression. Suppression and the ability to find suitable alternatives for releasing emotional tension are required for the smooth functioning of society. Expression is required for individual health and for providing the aliveness and warmth that make life worth living.

At what times do you feel most alive? For example, does just being with certain people typically raise your level of arousal and spontaneity?

Do you take pride in being "in control" of your emotions? If so, your emotional expression may be more suppressed than you realize. On a scale from one to ten, how emotionally expressive are you? Get a second opinion by checking your rating with a friend.

What feelings would you say this woman is experiencing?

HAPPINESS

"Happiness is getting what you want in life." Although this is a popular belief, it is false, according to psychologists Shaver and Freedman (1976). (Their sample was younger, more affluent, better educated, and more liberal than the general population, and so the results must be interpreted cautiously.) Their conclusion is that happiness is in the head, not in the objective conditions of one's life. It has more to do with one's expectations than with actual accomplishments. Because of this, we may have much more control over our happiness than many of us realize.

How many people really are happy? About 70 percent say they have been happy over the past six months. On the other hand, one-third report constant worry and anxiety, and 40 percent often feel lonely. Those who spend the least time thinking about happiness are the happiest.

Marital status. Shaver and Freedman found that the components of happiness differed widely depending on marital status. Single men and women listed happiness with friends, job, love life, and success as the most important determinants of their overall happiness. As compared with single men, married men rated personal growth and marriage as more important and friends and success as less important. As compared with single women, married women emphasized marriage, their partner's happiness, and their own sex life and deemphasized friends, job, and success. Physical attractiveness was much more important to singles than to marrieds. Overall, married people reported greater happiness and less loneliness than did singles (Freedman, 1978). Having children had no net effect on happiness, suggesting that for most people, the joys and frustrations of parenthood balance out.

Work. For those working outside the home, job satisfaction is an important component of overall happiness. Freedman (1978) found that those with higher-status jobs tend to be happier, with several noteworthy exceptions. For example, lawyers and physicians described themselves as relatively unhappy, perhaps because of the stress and time commitment required in these jobs. Although the relationship was not strong, those in occupations that serve others and allow creativity (e.g., architects, entertainers, and clergy) were happier than those in more routine occupations.

The relationship among education, income, and happiness was studied by Campbell and colleagues (1976). They found that the happiest individuals are those with little education and high earnings. Presumably, their success far exceeded their expectations. At lower levels of income, those with a college education are happier than those without one. Here, having an education may have helped maintain individuals' self-esteem. Campbell reported that college graduates place less value on money and financial security than do nongraduates. College graduates value a life that is important or exciting more than one that is rich or secure.

Money. Lack of money is a factor only for the very poor. Once past the poverty level, people with more money are no happier than those with less. But how can happiness be so independent of money? Each of us has had the experience of elevating our mood with an occasional splurge. Wouldn't we be that much happier if we could splurge every day? Apparently not. Spending, like any other activity, loses its emotional impact when overdone or made routine.

Health. Health operates in a way similar to that of money. Poor health makes happiness difficult, but beyond that it seems to have no effect.

Residence. Those who live in cities are no less happy than are those in the country.

Religion. Atheists are just as happy as those who believe in God.

Age. Age is unrelated to happiness, with the exception that senior citizens are more likely to be either very happy or very unhappy.

Sex. Sex is related to happiness only if one is not participating. Otherwise, sexual frequency, number of partners, presence of extramarital relations, and sexual orientation (hetero- or homo-) all are unrelated to happiness.

Interestingly, most people overestimate the number of partners and the sexual satisfactions of others. About half the men and one-third of the women were dissatisfied with their sex lives, but subjects estimated that a much lower percentage of their peers was sexually dissatisfied. Women with orgasmic difficulty were less happy than those without sexual problems, and for women, feelings of depression following intercourse were related to suicide attempts.

Love. Love is the one thing most mentioned by unhappy people as needed to make them happy. The happiest situation is being in love with a partner who loves you equally, but women are more likely than men to give more love than they receive.

Childhood. Two-thirds described their childhoods as happy, and these subjects were less likely to have irrational fears than were those recalling unhappy childhoods. In particular, guilt feelings during childhood were related to psychological disturbances as adults. As no surprise to Freudians, males felt closer to their mothers, and females felt closer to their fathers. However, it was closeness to the same-sex parent that predicted happiness in adulthood.

Attitude. True or false:

Good things can't last.
There's a sucker born every minute.
Life has meaning.
I have control over the good things that happen to me.

Shavers and Freedman found that four attitudes

predict happiness. As represented in the items above, these are emotional security, lack of cynicism, meaningfulness of life, and personal control. If you replied F, F, T, T to the above items, chances are you're happy.

Concluding thoughts. Most people want to know how they can make themselves happy. In many ways, this is the one central question that underlies all of the topics in this book. As reviewed above, the evidence links several controllable factors to happiness. One of these is finding some sort of work or daily activity that is satisfying *to you*. Current evidence suggests it is more important to find work that is satisfying in itself than work that leads to money and status.

Another factor is love. We each need to embed ourselves in a network of loving relationships, and many people also desire a particular romantic love interest. Seeking love is largely a matter of opening oneself to others and acquiring the social and communication skills that make love relationships more probable. Many of these skills are directly addressed in the chapters on relationships.

The third predictor of happiness is attitude. We have some control over how we view the

---

FOCUS

HAPPINESS AND THE AMERICAN WAY: THE CURSE OF ABUNDANCE

"How is it that we can be surrounded by plenty and yet remain dissatisfied and unhappy?" Experimental psychologist John Houston (1981) argued that by giving us a wealth of material benefits, modern society has not created utopian bliss. Instead, it has spawned a new sense of loss and a dulled experience of life.

According to Houston, theories of motivation agree that pleasure and gratification occur during the *reduction* of a desire. The greater the desire is, the greater the pleasure will be. But desire is a function of deprivation, and that is the problem.

If everything we want is readily available, there is little chance for deprivation to develop. Consequently, our desires are weak, and their satisfaction yields little pleasure or excitement. For example, we must experience the relatively unpleasant state of hunger before food really tastes good. The sexual response is that much more powerful after a dry spell. And falling asleep is exquisite after a physically exhausting day. Houston noted, however, that in the modern world, biological drives have been abundantly provided for. We eat at the sight, suggestion, or mere thought of food. For many, hunger has become a vague and diluted abstraction, not a powerful drive. For many married couples, sex has become a duty. They fear that if they aren't having sex as often as they think everyone else is, it will mean that something is wrong with them. The result: no deprivation and little excitement.

Houston's remedy is obvious but not easy. He suggests that for Americans, unhappiness derives largely from a self-indulgent mentality. If we are losing the "lean and hungry edge," we must systematically deprive ourselves of what we have in abundance.

Thus Houston's prescription for happiness is to deprive and *then* to indulge. This formula can be applied to any activity that is readily available but has become boring or routine.

events in our lives and what we choose to tell ourselves about those events. Often happiness may require no change in objective conditions, only changes in our attitude toward those conditions.

Nevertheless, people often find themselves satisfying many of the conditions for happiness, yet they are still not happy. For these people, "How can I make myself happy?" may be the wrong question. Recall that the happiest people are those who spend the *least* time thinking about happiness. A good deal of evidence suggests that a direct, goal-oriented approach to happiness often does not work. For example, "making yourself happy" may be similar to forcing yourself to fall in love. What results is not real love. Chapter 14 examines this aspect of happiness in considerable detail.

Shaver and Freedman concluded that happiness is more closely related to what we make of our lives than to what objectively happens to us. Similar to the philosophy of rational-emotive therapist Albert Ellis, happiness is more a function of what we tell ourselves than of external events. In particular, it has a lot to do with simply deciding to enjoy life and accept who we are.

Often we are not good judges of how happy other people are. They may be putting on a false front, and we may be falsely assuming that they are happy because they have acquired all the things we believe would make *us* happy. Of the people you know well, who would you say is the happiest? Why do you think this person is happy?

SUMMARY

1. The brain can be viewed as composed of three structures, each appearing at a different point in our evolution. The reptilian complex controls self-preservation, aggression, and territoriality; the limbic lobe controls emotion; and the neocortex controls thought.

2. Cognitions and emotions exist in complex, reciprocal interaction with each other. Certain beliefs can create a logical necessity for specified emotions to occur. Positive or negative self-talk can lead to feelings of satisfaction or dissatisfaction. Our cognitive descriptions of a situation help define what emotion we will experience. Strong emotions can disrupt cognitive processes, and functions such as memory and judgment are mood-related.

3. Facial expressions are our most dominant nonverbal means of communicating emotion.

4. Rational-emotive therapy maintains that most misery is self-inflicted. It is caused by our own irrational assumptions about reality and by what we tell ourselves about events, not by the events themselves. Interventions include identifying and disputing irrational beliefs and replacing them with more adaptive cognitions.

5. Perfectionism is healthy up to a point, but many people fail to recognize its hidden costs. Perfectionists often show low productivity, high anxiety, depression, and troubled personal relationships.

6. Cognitive patterns characteristic of perfectionists include either-or thinking, overgeneralization, "should" statements, self-punishment, and not knowing when to end a project.

7. The cognitive treatment of perfectionism includes making the client aware of its disadvantages, testing the client's assumption that a task must be done flawlessly to be enjoyed, attacking all-or-none thinking, recording and revising self-critical thoughts, and encouraging clients to lower their immediate goals.

8. Prejudice is often resistant to change because the very procedures we use to see if it is true may contaminate our observations, yielding self-fulfilling pseudovalidations.

9. Depression is a major health problem, particularly among women. Some theorists link depression to childhood experiences and the desperate need to gain the love and approval of a "dominant other." The cognitive treatment of depression assumes that if people change the way that they see themselves and what they tell themselves, they can feel better.

10. Suicide has been related to family disruption, economic status, college attendance, disappointments in love or work, depression, a sudden change in habits, suicide warnings, self-destructive habits, gender, age, and occupation. Most people do not seek professional help before attempting suicide, and so it is important for friends and relatives to notice early warning signs and get the individual to talk about his or her problems openly.

11. Some humanistic psychologists believe that our fascination with technology has led us to deny our emotions and become more machinelike. As a result, many people have lost their sense of spontaneity and aliveness. This denial may make us more efficient for some tasks, but it endangers both our physical health and our personal relationships.

12. Happiness is more closely related to self-expectations than to actual accomplishments. Predictors of happiness include being married, being in love, job satisfaction, emotional security, lack of cynicism, a belief that life is meaningful, and a belief in personal control over one's life. One strategy for increasing happiness is to deprive yourself of what you have in abundance (in order to increase desire) and then indulge.

SUGGESTED READINGS

Brown, G. W., & Harris, T. **Social origins of depression: A study of psychiatric disorder in women.** New York: Free Press, 1978. Insightful discussion of how depressive symptoms are produced.

Ekman, P., & Friesen, W. V. **Unmasking the face.** Englewood Cliffs, N.J.: Prentice-Hall, 1975. This book can be used to increase your ability to perceive accurately what others are feeling.

Ellis, A., & Harper, R. A. **A new guide to rational living**. Englewood Cliffs, N.J.: Prentice-Hall, 1975. A practical and lively approach to cognitive techniques from the grandfather of cognitive therapies.

Gaylin, W. **The rage within: Anger in modern life**. New York: Simon & Schuster, 1984. Good discussion of how anger can be channeled in a positive direction.

Sagan, C. **The dragons of Eden: Speculations on the evolution of human intelligence**. New York: Random House, 1977. Fascinating cognitive journey.

THE COMPETENT PERSONALITY

7

Self-Modification and Other Skills

Americans are the ultimate pragmatists. We seek practical "know-how." We want to know "what works," what techniques will bring about behavior change. How do we increase self-control and learn the skills essential to survival in modern times? The study of self-modification provides just this, a systematic approach for dealing with a wide variety of adjustment problems.

This chapter discusses practical applications of the social learning position described in Chapter 2. This chapter fosters personal competence, both as a general skill for attaining self-control and as an assortment of essential specific skills.

Some of the questions we shall examine are: What is willpower? How can we resist immediate temptations in order to attain desired future outcomes? If behavior is largely a function of the environment, how can we alter environmental events to control behavior? For example, what can we do to use study time more effectively? What are the pitfalls that students encounter when making career decisions? What are some of the common errors that interfere with achieving intellectual competence? And what sets creative people apart from others?

We shall follow a self-modification project from its inception through the stages of problem definition, self-observation, intervention, and evaluation. This is a chance for you to test principles of behavior change in your own life. You will become a scientist — with the subject matter your own behavior. You will become a detective, observing what you do, searching for clues, speculating on the causes of problem behavior, and then testing these hypotheses through your strategy of intervention.

For this material to make an enduring change in your adaptive repertoire, it is a good idea to conduct a self-modification project of your own. Don't just read the material; apply it. This means identifying a single, specific piece of behavior that you would like to change. As you will see, the beauty of self-modification is that the same principles can be used with a wide variety of personal or interpersonal problems.

DEFINING A SELF-MODIFICATION PROBLEM

SELF-CONTROL

The ability to control and modify our own behavior is at the heart of adjustment. Moreover, it forms the foundation for true personal freedom. Without the capacity to set goals and then modify our behavior to attain those goals, we would be pawns, both of circumstance and of our own fleeting desires.

Unfortunately, it is common to think of self-control as something that, magically, you either have or you don't. Certainly, some people can decide to lose a few pounds and then do so without difficulty. Others, regardless of how much they struggle and suffer, are unable to make even modest reductions. What may not be so apparent is that people are not born with self-control; it is learned. And as with most skills, self-control improves with practice.

APPLYING THE PRINCIPLES OF BEHAVIOR CHANGE

Psychologists have made impressive gains in understanding how behavior changes. Moreover, this knowledge can often be applied by individuals to change their own behavior. Of course, in cases of severe disturbance or crisis, it is wise to consult a professional. Nevertheless, research indicates that self-modification does work (Hamilton & Waldman, 1983; Prochaska, 1983; Schachter, 1982).

The principles of behavior emphasized in this chapter derive from theories of learning. What kinds of problems are candidates for self-modification? The answer is any problem that can be defined in terms of the increase or decrease of concrete, observable behaviors in specified stimulus situations. In this context, **behavior** indicates anything you do that is observable to yourself or others. This includes, for example, overt movements, speech, thoughts, feelings, and images. **Stimulus situations** include the physical and social environment, particularly the behaviors of other people.

SHORT-TERM GAINS AND LONG-TERM CONSEQUENCES

A major problem in gaining control over one's behavior centers on the trade-off between short- and long-term outcomes. For example, Bill wants to get good grades so that he can attend law school, but on any given night, he would rather socialize than study. Although he believes that good grades are more important

than a few extra evenings of fun, the grades seem far off in the future and the party is now. As a result, his grades suffer, and he is forced to seek a job in another field. In a nutshell, small, immediate rewards can have a more powerful motivating effect than large rewards that are delayed. This is the central problem behind most forms of self-control.

The solution to this problem involves realizing that we are not simply passive responders. We become victims of circumstance only when we pretend to have no other options. In fact, we can alter our environment directly, we can alter the ways that we interpret that environment, and we can alter what we say to ourselves. For example, Mischel (1981) found that children could resist the immediate temptation of eating a marshmallow by altering their cognitions. Instead of thinking about how good it would taste to eat a marshmallow right now, they distracted themselves by concentrating on other goal objects or by picturing marshmallows in ways unrelated to consumption, such as thinking of them as "puffy clouds."

IDENTIFYING PROBLEM BEHAVIORS

List some of the things that you might want to change about yourself. From this list select a problem behavior, one that you would like either to increase or decrease in frequency. Select a behavior that you have a definite interest in changing and one that you believe you could change.

To initiate a self-modification project, define the problem concretely, in terms of behavior and situation. For example, "being grouchy" is too general a definition. It does not tell us what kinds of grouchy behaviors are involved, and it fails to specify the situations that set off these behaviors or to whom they are directed. It is much clearer to say, "When my wife asks me to do something around the house, I raise my voice or find something about her to criticize." This description provides important clues for how to go about making an intervention.

Sometimes we know what our goal is but have difficulty formulating that goal into concrete behaviors that we would like to increase or decrease in frequency. For example, the goal of losing weight is not, in itself, behaviorally stated. Relevant behaviors here might be eating less of certain foods, eating only at particular times, and exercising more.

Another problem might be wanting to feel more at ease in social situations. Here you can identify what thoughts lead to social tension. For example, negative thoughts such as "These people won't like me" or "There's another stupid thing I said!" would make it difficult for anyone to relax. On the other hand, you may decide that the feelings of tension result from an actual deficit in social skills, not just from overly harsh self-evaluations. Here the task involves breaking down a general skill into one of its behavioral components. For example, listening more attentively, asking questions that show an interest in others, and not talking excessively about yourself are skills that lead to favorable social responses. Because of this, they may reduce feelings of tension.

INFORMAL OBSERVATION

Make informal written observations of your problem behavior. Where does it typically occur? Does it occur at certain times rather than others? What are the specific behaviors involved? Describe those behaviors as concretely as possible. What situational or cognitive events

occur immediately before the behavior? Which of these antecedents makes the problem more likely? What situational or cognitive events immediately follow the behavior? Which of these is responsible for maintaining the behavior?

The informal observation should be recorded. Keep a diary for at least several days, until you have observed a number of instances of the problem behavior and have developed a notion of what situations bring on the behavior and what consequences follow it. The more detailed your observation is, the more likely the modification will be successful (Nezu & D'Zurilla, 1981).

DEFINING THE PROBLEM

As in all problem-solving tasks, the way you define the problem is crucial. From your informal observations you should now be in a good position to define the problem as a concrete behavior in a specified situation. The definition should be stated so that the behavior is one that you want either to increase in frequency (e.g., asking out members of the opposite sex) or to decrease in frequency (e.g., watching television on weeknights).

Obviously, we are always behaving; we are always doing *something*. Furthermore, many behaviors are more or less incompatible with one another—it is difficult or impossible to do both at the same time. For example, chewing gum and eating. Because of these incompatibilities, it's a good idea to deal with behaviors two at a time. If your problem behavior is one that you want to do more often, then also identify what you are currently doing instead of the desirable behavior. This may give you a clue to why the more desirable response occurs so infrequently. For example, to increase the proportion of study time in which you are actively concentrating on the material at hand, it helps to identify what else you are doing while "studying," such as daydreaming or listening to the radio.

If you have identified your problem behavior as one that you want to decrease in frequency, then also specify a corresponding, incompatible positive behavior that you want to occur more often. One reason is that reducing the frequency of one behavior does not guarantee that a desirable response will take its place. Moreover, in an intervention centered on self-punishment, one is likely to become discouraged and give up the project before the behavior has changed. Thus it's more effective to decrease the frequency of an undesired behavior by increasing the frequency of an incompatible positive response. Some examples of incompatible behaviors are smiling and frowning, studying and watching television, eating and exercising, smoking a cigarette and holding an unlit pipe in your mouth, and talking about yourself versus listening to another.

Research indicates that many responses are incompatible with fear and anxiety. For example, kung fu movements have been used to reduce fear in closed places (Gershman & Stedman, 1971); physical exercise is incompatible with the tension of desiring alcohol or cigarettes (Marlatt & Parks, 1982); meditation is incompatible with stress arousal (Throll, 1981); and muscular relaxation is incompatible with feelings of anxiety (Goldfried, 1977).

In sum, you will identify two behaviors: either an undesirable behavior that you want to decrease and an incompatible desirable response that you want to increase, or a desirable behavior that you want to increase and a less desirable response that you are currently emitting instead.

For example, one problem might be described as "eating ice cream before going to bed." The desirable alternative might be defined as "eating nothing before bed or eating only something nonfattening, such as an apple or a carrot."

Once the problem has been defined concretely, then you are ready for the formal, quantitative observation.

Define your problem in terms of behaviors in situations.

FORMAL OBSERVATION

Before you can make a serious attempt at self-modification, you must make a quantitative assessment of exactly how often your desirable and undesirable behaviors occur. Without this formal observation, you have no way of knowing precisely how severe the problem is, and you won't know how successful your intervention has been.

To be accurate, your observation should be recorded in writing immediately after each occurrence of the desirable or undesirable behavior. Waiting until the end of the day to record it introduces errors due to memory limitations or inadvertent distortions. One popular way is to carry a three-by-five-inch card in your pocket so that it is always handy. Wrist counters can also be useful, especially for high-frequency behaviors such as tics or obsessive thoughts (e.g., self-criticism).

Some behaviors, such as studying, should be recorded in terms of duration rather than frequency. Also be sure to record the antecedents and consequences of each behavior. These will provide valuable clues for how to intervene. There is no single answer for how long the formal observation should be maintained before beginning an intervention. In general, continue until there is a stable description of the problem behavior. This will usually take at least a week.

Note that merely observing an undesirable behavior automatically leads to feelings of self-dissatisfaction that may punish that behavior. Thus individuals are often pleasantly surprised to find their goal partially realized through self-observation alone.

STATING THE GOAL

After making the formal observation, you can now specify quantitatively the extent of your problem. This is important because most of us are not entirely rational when it comes to problem behaviors. These responses have become aversive for us; we do not want to think about them. We often have conflicting feelings about problem behaviors. Part of us may not want to know the full extent of the problem. Another part may want to do nothing except hope that the problem will go away. Attend to these varying intentions toward the problem; they are fascinating in their own right and are one reason that this behavior has remained a problem.

Consider this quantitative specification, "When at work, I am now thinking self-critical thoughts at an average of seventy-five a day, whereas my positive self-thoughts average only three a day." From these data you are now in a position to set a quantitative goal, that is, a concrete statement of what changes you would like to see in order to consider your self-modification successful.

Specify your problem quantitatively, and set a quantitative goal for your self-modification project.

REINFORCEMENT ANALYSIS

List the advantages and disadvantages of changing your problem behavior, including both short- and long-term factors. To be maintained, undesirable behaviors must provide some kind of payoff to the individual, and taking this payoff into account aids successful intervention (Brehm & Smith, 1982). As indicated earlier, undesirable behaviors typically have strong short-term payoffs, and this is what makes them so difficult to change. For example, giving in to others' unreasonable requests is a problem for many people. In the short run, it allows an individual to avoid others' anticipated disapproval. In the long run, however, it leads to being used and taken advantage of, and consequently to losing others' respect.

Formulate a preliminary explanation of what is causing and maintaining your problem behavior. This hypothesis will form the basis for your initial intervention. If this intervention does not work, your explanation should be revised, and a new intervention attempted.

Although self-modification is systematic and scientific, there is no foolproof way to set up the optimal intervention on the first attempt. It is more adaptive to see self-modification as an experimental procedure in which you collect data, come up with an initial understanding of the problem, use this to make a fairly straightforward intervention, and note its effectiveness. If the intervention doesn't work completely or if it introduces unanticipated problems, modify it accordingly.

This type of persistence is essential for developing generalized skills in self-control. Although inborn talent and the knowledge of what to do are valuable, just as often it is persistence that determines final success.

PRINCIPLES OF SELF-MODIFICATION

As you will see, many different principles of behavior change have been discovered. Each principle can be used singly, but combining several to form an overall modification package is often more effective. For learning purposes, it may be best to devise a plan that incorporates as many principles as possible.

As noted in Chapter 2, the social learning approach analyzes problems by considering what occurs immediately before problem behaviors and immediately after them. Thus the principles of self-modification similarly divide into techniques dealing with antecedents, problem behaviors, and consequents.

DEALING WITH ANTECEDENTS

Avoid antecedents for problem behavior. It requires less willpower

to avoid buying sweets in the store than to refrain from eating them when they are in the house.

to avoid spending time with people who are drinking heavily than to refuse alcohol when everyone around you is drinking.

Many settings are not conducive to active studying.

to avoid studying in a location with social distractions than to study successfully in a place where your friends are tempting you to join in.

Disrupt the chain of antecedents to a problem behavior. Antecedents often occur in an identifiable sequence, and it is easier to break that chain early rather than late in the sequence (Bergin, 1969). This can be done by avoiding a link in the chain, changing the order of links, or adding new, more adaptive linkages. For example, simply taking a brief pause in the middle of a meal aids weight control (Sandifer & Buchanan, 1983). This pause allows dieters to perceive that they are no longer hungry but were merely continuing to eat out of habit.

Restrict the range of antecedents. To

gain more control over problem behaviors, restrict their occurrence to a specified situation. For example, a couple that argues continually may agree to restrict their disputes to a particular time and place. Thus they may have a standing "date" once a week for hashing out their disagreements. Problems that come up during the week, unless they are emergencies, are simply postponed until the prearranged time. This gives the couple a chance to enjoy each other's company and break the flow of hostilities. Also, by date time their disagreements will have lost some of their emotion and be easier to discuss in a problem-solving manner.

The same strategy can be used to increase desirable behaviors. By restricting the situations in which studying occurs and not allowing other behaviors to occur in those situations, you can

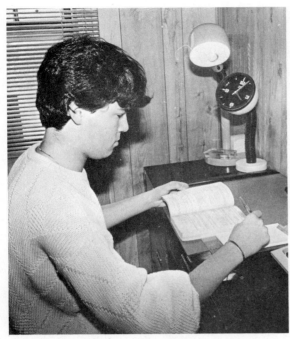

Design a study environment that enhances the likelihood of active studying.

the environment to ourselves, and the language we use strongly affects our willpower. For example, thinking, "Time for a ciggy break," presents cigarettes as friendly little treats, making them seem innocuous and hard to resist. Notice the change in connotation when thinking, "I often inhaled one of those foul weeds at this time of the day."

Use self-instructions. Verbalize instructions to yourself as a way of increasing the likelihood of adaptive behavior (Dush, Hirt, & Schroeder, 1983). These self-instructions may include encouragement ("I can do it") or instructions on how to behave ("If she doesn't accept my invitation for lunch, I'll smile and say something like, 'maybe another time'; then I'll pay attention to how enthusiastically she reacts").

Take advantage of stimulus generalization. A desirable response that can be performed in one situation can be transported more easily to a similar than to a dissimilar new situation. For example, a person may be relaxed, self-assured, and able to talk easily with unattractive members of the opposite sex but be unable to carry on a conversation with those who are perceived as attractive. In this case, it may help to realize that individuals differ in degree of attractiveness and then begin practicing social approach behaviors with those who are mildly, rather than highly, attractive.

Use models for learning complex skills. If you would like to be more assertive, for example, but are not sure exactly what to say or how to handle yourself, identify a person whom you consider to have the desired skills and carefully observe what that person does.

increase the situation's power to elicit studying rather than other competing responses. Thus it is often a good idea to have one place where you study and do nothing else. If you find yourself daydreaming or unable to study on a given occasion, leave the place immediately and return only when you are ready to work (Spurr & Stevens, 1980). In this way, your study place gains control over study behavior and not undesirable, competing responses. Of course, select a place that is pleasant and conducive to studying, so that you will enjoy spending time there.

Revise maladaptive, irrational self-statements or beliefs that precede the problem behavior. Identify maladaptive cognitions, refute them, and replace them with more adaptive beliefs and self-statements. Follow the procedures of rational-emotive therapy as outlined in Chapter 6.

Use cognitions that neutralize tempting antecedents. We are continually describing

DEALING WITH BEHAVIOR

Practice desired behaviors. Especially for complex behaviors that require a physical or verbal skill, practice is essential. Begin practicing the skill in a nonthreatening situation and gradually extend it to naturalistic settings of in-

It is often helpful to practice desired behaviors in a nonthreatening environment.

terest. Practice in imagination has also been shown effective (Suinn, 1985), and this can be used when the feared situation is either too threatening or not easily available. If you have difficulty imagining yourself making the desired response, start by picturing someone else doing it (Kazdin, 1982). Practice will not usually be complete, however, until the desired response is actually practiced in the real-world situation of interest.

Desensitize yourself to feared stimuli. Desensitization is the imagined rehearsal of an adaptive response to a feared stimulus, while in a state of deep relaxation. Typically, the feared stimuli are presented in a hierarchy, starting with the least and ending with the most threat-

ening. If a stimulus proves so threatening that it disturbs relaxation, go back and work with stimuli that are less threatening. For example, someone with a fear of driving a car might first imagine just looking at a car from a distance, then walking up to a car, then sitting behind the wheel, then starting the engine with a friend in the passenger seat, then driving slowly in a deserted parking lot, and so on.

DEALING WITH CONSEQUENTS

Positively reinforce desirable behaviors. Arrange to have reinforcing stimuli immediately *follow* a desirable response. Reinforcing stimuli include food, money, praise, pleasurable activities, and activities that have a high probability of occurrence, such as brushing one's teeth. Make a list of things that are reinforcing *for you*, and then decide which you want to make contingent on the desirable behavior. Every project should make some use of positive reinforcement.

Note that those competent at self-control are three times more likely to use self-reward than are those with self-control deficiencies (Heffernan & Richards, 1981). The only caution in using self-reward is that it should be avoided for behaviors that are already enjoyed for their own sakes. Here, self-reward may actually decrease a behavior's frequency (Heatherington & Kirsch, 1984).

When a reinforcer is made contingent on a desirable behavior, it is necessary that the reinforcer be withheld if the criterion response is not met. (Be sure to set the criterion at a level so that success is probable.) If you have difficulty occasionally withholding a reinforcer, select one that is less potent or arrange to have a friend dispense it to you. For example, you could tell others of your behavior-change program and encourage them to praise you for occurrences of the desirable response. Matson (1977) reported an interesting variation of this procedure. A wife's weight loss program was aided by the husband's dispensing compliments (e.g., "You look lovely this evening") or verbal abuse (e.g., "You sometimes remind me of a fat hog"), depending on whether she had been successful in losing weight. (Although it worked in this particular case, I recommend skipping the verbal abuse, as it undermines the relationship.)

Determine what reinforcers are currently maintaining your problem behavior and arrange to make these same reinforcers contingent on desirable rather than undesirable behaviors. For example, if your goal is to exercise more, your informal observation may have revealed that lying around the house is only enjoyable as long as you can watch television or listen to music. In this case, it would be a simple matter to rearrange these contingencies so that television and music are made available only after your workout.

Sometimes, however, it may not be easy to determine what reinforcers are maintaining undesirable behavior. For example, an undesirable behavior may lead to a reinforcer only occasionally. Also, the undesirable behavior may be an example of **avoidance learning**; that is, the desired behavior may at some time in the past have been followed by an aversive event, such as public ridicule. Afterwards, whenever stimuli similar to those in that original situation appear, they are immediately avoided. In other words, avoidance behavior is negatively reinforced by the reduction of anxiety associated with feared stimuli (see Chapter 2). This behavior resists extinction because the individual never gets a chance to experience the feared stimulus and see that it is no longer as dangerous as it was in the original situation.

Avoidance learning represents an overgeneralization from a past negative event. For example, Brad gave his first oral report to his high school class. He had no idea he would become so nervous speaking in front of his classmates, but he stumbled, stuttered, and, in his eyes, made a fool of himself. After that, he avoided speaking in front of groups of any size. He managed to stay home sick or make other excuses so that he never again had to make an oral presentation. Because of his assumption that all public-speaking situations would lead to aversive consequences, Brad never got the chance to see that public speaking could be enjoyable, and he never developed the skills to ensure that he would be good at it.

To overcome avoidance learning, gradually approach the feared stimulus, first in imagination, as in desensitization, and then in actual behavior. Start with less threatening situations and gradually increase the task's difficulty as your fears lessen. As in all instances in which you want a behavior to occur more frequently, reinforce these approach behaviors.

Immediate positive reinforcement is particularly important for controlling avoidance behaviors and consummatory responses, such as overeating. In each case, there is already an immediate reinforcement for the undesirable response (the relief of avoiding a feared object and the pleasure of eating). And for each, it would be difficult or impossible to separate the undesirable response from its existing reinforcer. Because of this, it is important to introduce an immediate positive reinforcer for desired behavior.

Use a "point system" to increase the immediacy of reinforcers that can't be made available on demand. Some reinforcers, such as going to a movie, can't be available continuously. However, a system can be set up so that you receive points that are recorded immediately after the desirable response, and these points can be exchanged at a later date for desired activities. To do this you will need to write out a formal contract specifying how many points will be required for each reinforcer. It is a good idea to include several reinforcers, as in a "menu." The overuse of one reinforcer runs the risk of **satiation**, the temporary loss of a reinforcer's motivating effects.

Consider imagined reinforcers. Although not as powerful as tangible reinforcers, imagining the presence of tangible reinforcers has been found effective, especially if they can be imagined vividly (Marshall, Boutilier, & Minnes, 1974). The advantage of imagined reinforcers is that they are readily and immediately available at all times. For example, you can develop an image of yourself as you would look after losing weight and getting in shape. Picture this image immediately after avoiding a snack or dessert.

Praise yourself for desirable behavior. Don't be stingy with self-praise. Tell yourself, "Good job!" "I did it!" "Terrific!" Self-praise helps you attend to desirable behavior (Shelton & Levy, 1981), and it is particularly important for depressed individuals, who tend to punish rather than praise themselves (Heiby, 1982; Rehm, 1982).

Shape desired behaviors. After identifying a desirable response, reinforce approximations to it, rather than waiting for the final criterion response to occur on its own. In other words, begin with a behavioral goal that is easy to attain and then raise that goal slowly. Your aim is to reinforce successful responses. Setting your initial goals too high or incrementing them too quickly only leads to discouragement and failure. Watson and Tharp (1985) found that people often resist shaping because they believe that they *should* be performing at a given level and don't deserve to be rewarded for anything less. This harsh attitude toward oneself is a major obstacle to self-modification.

Extinguish undesirable behaviors. Make an assessment of what is currently maintaining undesirable behaviors and intervene so that those reinforcers are removed. For example, perhaps you occasionally pout in order to get your way with particular friends. Although this may seem to work, you realize that it is not a mature strategy, it is unlikely to work with others, and you dislike yourself afterwards. One way of dealing with this problem is to explain these things to your friends and ask that they aid you by refusing to let your pouting manipulate their behavior.

The main limitation of extinction is that there is no guarantee that a desirable response will replace the one that was extinguished. Thus extinction should be combined with a reinforcement program.

Avoid punishment. Punishment is unlikely to work in self-modification, for individuals will often give up an intervention that has become aversive. But with unwanted behaviors that are reinforced by powerful, immediate reinforcers, such as smoking and overeating, punishment may help remind you of the negative consequences of problem behavior. This can strengthen your determination to carry out the project to completion. For example, Youdin and Hemmes (1978) had dieters stare at their naked bodies in a mirror every day while thinking about overeating. Similarly, Rosen (1981) had dieters agree to overeat only while in front of a mirror, wearing as little as possible.

Gradually reduce the frequency of positive reinforcement. Having the desired response reinforced intermittently, rather than every time it occurs, increases its resistance to extinction. Thus start by reinforcing the desired response every time it occurs. After its frequency has reached the final criterion, reinforce intermittently.

A successful self-modification project is usually not static; it should change, slowly becoming invisible over time. Your eventual goal is to maintain the desired behavior through contingencies in the natural environment. To do this, reinforcers may need to be changed and their frequencies "thinned," gradually approaching those in the environment. In this way, the goal, for example, is to generate an enthusiasm for studying, so that the intrinsic benefits of learning and the natural extrinsic rewards of getting good grades come to maintain study behavior on their own.

For easy reference, Table 7–1 summarizes the principles of self-modification.

PUTTING YOUR SELF-MODIFICATION PROGRAM INTO OPERATION

Don't expect your intervention to work perfectly from the start. Changing established behaviors is a tricky business, and relationships between stimuli and behaviors are often more subtle than we realize. Most successful plans will need one or more alterations. As long as you record your desirable and undesirable responses, you will know whether or not your plan is working. If it is not working, your self-observation will usually provide the clues for what changes to make. These changes may be adding other principles of behavior change, identifying more powerful or more immediate reinforcers, reinforcing behaviors that avoid antecedents to problem behavior, or lowering your criteria for what must be done to receive reinforcement.

TABLE 7–1

SELF-MODIFICATION PRINCIPLES AT A GLANCE

ANTECEDENT INTERVENTIONS	CONSEQUENT INTERVENTIONS
Avoid antecedents.	Positively reinforce desired behaviors.
Disrupt the chain of antecedents.	Use a point system to increase reinforcement immediacy.
Restrict the range of antecedents.	
Revise maladaptive beliefs or self-statements.	Use imagined reinforcers.
Neutralize tempting antecedents through relabeling.	Praise yourself for emitting desired behaviors.
Use self-instructions.	Shape desired behaviors.
Take advantage of stimulus generalization.	Extinguish undesirable behaviors.
Use models.	Avoid self-punishment.
	Gradually approach naturalistic contingencies.

DIRECT INTERVENTIONS ON THE BEHAVIOR OF INTEREST

Practice desired behaviors.
Desensitize yourself to feared stimuli.

Make a formal, written contract with yourself. Define the behavior you want to change and the situations in which it occurs. State the interventions that you have decided to try and the consequences to be used. Identify your eventual and your more immediate goals, quantitatively if possible. Sign the contract, post it in a place where others can see it, and then tell your friends about it. These measures help ensure that the plan is clear, and they build commitment.

Write out your contract for self-modification and revise it as necessary. Keep an ongoing observational record of the desirable and undesirable behaviors. When completed, describe the outcomes of your project.

THE LIMITS OF SELF-MODIFICATION

Self-modification represents a highly structured and systematic approach to adjustment. It specifies concrete, detailed strategies for how to intervene and actively deal with your own problems. Because of this, many people like it. Nevertheless, as with all systems, it has certain limitations.

Some adjustment problems may be so severe, traumatic, or crisis oriented that an individual simply cannot cope without professional help. After the crisis is over, however, self-modification may be useful for handling whatever problems remain.

Recall that self-modification is based on being able to define the problem in terms of a specific behavior that you want to increase or decrease in frequency. Humanistic and existential theorists maintain that some problems, such as feelings that one's life is meaningless and there is nothing to live for, do not lend themselves easily to concrete specification.

Similarly, psychoanalytic theorists argue that changing a problem behavior without regard for its underlying cause may simply result in that still-active cause generating a different symptom. For example, one symptom of depression is lethargy. For a depression that derives from an overwhelming and irrational need to regain the love of a parent, reinforcing nonlethargic behaviors may make the individual more active, yet still not remove the depression. Lethargic symptoms may be replaced with other manifestations of depression, such as overeating. Nevertheless, self-modification has proved effective with a wide variety of problems (Watson & Tharp, 1985), suggesting that this limitation is fairly rare.

SHY BOB: A CASE STUDY IN SELF-MODIFICATION

Bob, an eighteen-year-old freshman from a rural southwestern community, received a scholarship to attend a major state university. In high school, Bob was a good student, and he had some friends, though he never dated. Bob had no idea what a change college life would be. Here he was, far from home, living in a place where he knew no one. Although Bob figured that it would take a little time to get used to this new setting, he was now approaching the end of his first semester, and he still felt totally out of place. He had no friends, no one he could really talk to. Gradually, he became more withdrawn, shy, and lonely.

Bob was taking a psychology class in which everyone had to do a self-modification project. It was obvious to Bob that his project should deal with his failure in social relationships. If he didn't find a friend in the next few weeks, Bob felt that there would be no point in coming back next semester. The thought of indefinitely living as a "social outcast" made him shudder. Bob was also interested in finding a girl to date, but he felt that this was almost out of the question, given his past failures with the opposite sex.

Thus, Bob's goal was to find one or two

friends—guys he could talk to and go places with. For self-modification, however, he needed more than a general goal.

INFORMAL OBSERVATION

Bob started with an informal observation of his social conversations. He kept a diary describing each social interaction, including what happened immediately before each of his conversations, what happened during the conversation, and what happened immediately afterwards. In particular, he wanted to find out where the interactions occurred, who they were with, and how the conversations ended.

Bob's informal observation lasted one week. From his diary, Bob found that most of his social contacts were either before class or in the cafeteria. Usually, he talked to Tom, who lived down the hall, and to Sam, who sat next to him in calculus. The conversations all were brief interactions concerning school assignments. It seemed that these conversations were friendly but impersonal, and they didn't seem to "go anywhere." After an exchange of greetings and course information, the conversations just seemed to "die out," and the other person would leave or maybe class would start. Bob liked talking to Tom and Sam but felt anxious and awkward. He just didn't know what to talk about to get these guys interested in being friends with him.

DEFINING THE PROBLEM

Bob thought that Tom and Sam were the two most likely guys for him to be friends with, and so he wanted to pursue those relationships. He also wanted to make more social contacts with other people, including women. In addition, he wanted to get rid of his anxiety and awkwardness around other people. These feelings made the interactions unpleasant for him, and other people probably noticed his anxiety, which may have been putting them off.

The situations in which desired social contacts might occur were anywhere that other people could be found. This meant just about anywhere on campus—except in his room.

From his informal observation, Bob realized that most of the time when he saw someone he wanted to meet or talk to, he did nothing. In fact, many of those times, rather than trying to make eye contact or otherwise attract these people's attention, he would look away or pretend that he was busy reading a book or something. He didn't want to appear desperate.

Bob realized that without intending to, he had formed a hierarchy of behavioral goals for himself, ranging from simple to increasingly difficult social behaviors. This hierarchy started with spending more time in social situations and then progressed to making eye contact and smiling at people he wanted to talk to, initiating minimal conversations with selected individuals, carrying on more extended conversations with these people while feeling comfortable and relaxed, and, finally, inviting people to do various activities with him, such as studying, eating, or going to a movie. Bob decided to start at the beginning of his hierarchy. He defined his problem as "increasing the amount of free time spent in social situations, that is, in places where other people congregate or walk by." He defined his alternative response as "during free time, staying in my room, in a vacated part of the library, or in other locations where I am unlikely to meet people."

FORMAL OBSERVATION

Bob started carrying a three-by-five-inch card and a wristwatch wherever he went. He recorded how much free time he had each day and how much of that free time he spent in social and nonsocial situations. Bob found that he averaged nine hours of free time on weekdays and fourteen on weekends. Of these, he averaged three hours a weekday in social situations and five hours a day on weekends. Note that Bob decided to count study time in the library as social time. He reasoned that since he could meet people at the library and since his grades were good, there was no reason not to study in the library.

STATING THE GOAL

Bob's goal, quantitatively stated, was to double his free time in social situations to average six hours a day on weekdays and ten hours a day on weekends.

REINFORCEMENT ANALYSIS

The advantage of spending more time in social situations was the possibility of meeting people and making friends. The disadvantages were that these were situations in which he could show an interest in someone and then be rejected; he could get into a conversation with someone and start feeling anxious; and although unlikely, he might become a "social butterfly," let his grades slip, and lose his scholarship.

Bob reasoned that spending time in his room was negatively reinforced by anxiety reduction. The prospect of getting rejected or finding himself in the middle of an awkward social interaction made him uneasy, while in his room, he felt "safe." Nevertheless, Bob realized that his continued avoidance of other people would lead only to greater loneliness.

INTERVENTION

Bob decided to try several principles of self-modification. One of the antecedents for spending time alone in his room was having the television on, and so he decided to restrict this antecedent to one hour a day. If he wanted to watch more than that, he would go to the dorm lounge.

Bob also decided to use positive self-instructions to help counteract his fear of spending time in social situations. Upon leaving his room or approaching other people, he would say to himself, "I think I'll hang out, relax, have

some fun, and maybe meet some interesting people."

To reduce further his fear of social situations, Bob decided to practice relaxation through deep breathing, and then when he was feeling relaxed, he would form an image of himself laughing and talking with other people. This desensitization procedure was to be practiced every day for ten minutes.

Finally, Bob decided that his strongest reinforcers were watching television, listening to music, and going to movies. He set up a contingency so that he would watch his television or listen to his stereo only after completing the desensitization exercise and spending the required time in social situations for that day. Bob felt that this wouldn't create a hardship, since he usually didn't do these things until the end of the day anyway. For each day that he successfully met this criterion, he would also give himself one point, and after accumulating three points he could treat himself to a movie.

Bob decided gradually to shape his time in social situations by making the initial criterion one-half hour per day over his current average and increasing the criterion only one half-hour per week.

RESULTS

Bob found it easy to increase the amount of time he spent in social situations. For the most part, he ended up studying in the library rather than in his room. But he made very few social contacts in the library. Because of this, he redefined "social situations" to exclude the library, and he successfully increased his time in these situations also.

Bob had some difficulty with his desensitization procedure. He was able to become relaxed, but he had trouble imagining himself laughing and having fun with other people. He decided to start with images that were easier to form. He began with images of himself having fun with his family, then with friends from high school, and then he imagined himself smiling and saying hello to various people he wanted to meet.

After Bob experienced some success increasing his time in social situations, he started working on smiling, saying hello, and initiating conversations with various people, many of whom were complete strangers. Thus Bob was able to follow his plan of moving toward a mastery of more and more complex social behaviors. As a result, he met a number of new people, some of whom he liked quite a bit. Although Bob didn't have time to form any lasting friendships that semester, he did return to school, and he found several good friends during the next semester.

What do you think of Bob's self-modification program? What might you have done differently if you had been in Bob's position?

One of the most practical applications of self-modification for college students is developing effective study skills. Such skills are valuable for two reasons: they increase learning (and hence raise grades), and they can reduce the amount of time spent studying.

STUDY SKILLS

A number of specific considerations should be kept in mind when attempting a self-modification of study skills.

THE STUDY ENVIRONMENT

Arrange a physical environment for studying that reduces distractions and competing responses. Effective learning requires an active mind and total concentration. Choose a location that is quiet, away from other people who are not also studying, and, if possible, a location where the only thing you do there is study. If you don't have a desk or table devoted solely to studying, modify an existing space. For example, study at the kitchen table, but sit in a position different from the one you use for eating. In other words, somehow modify the environment

so that it becomes a clear reminder of its intended function.

PRETEND STUDYING

Avoid places where people go to pretend that they are studying. Pretend studying is a popular activity on every campus. The general procedure is to have a book with you and to keep it open. Then, when nothing interesting is happening around you, glance down at the page and fit in a little study time. Pretend studying is disguised socializing, and as such, it can be pleasurable. However, it has at least two pitfalls. First, it is not an effective way to learn. The second pitfall is guilt. When people pretend to study but have not faced this pretense directly, the pleasure of pretend studying becomes sullied with feelings of guilt and fears of future repercussions. In other words, pretend studying is inadequate, whether your intention is to learn or to socialize. It is best simply to decide when you want to study and when you want to socialize and then to keep the two activities separate.

As you gain skill at studying effectively, you will find your concentration increasing, so that you lose track of time and perhaps of yourself as well. Then there is only the flow of ideas. During periods of complete absorption, studying is pleasurable and reinforcing in its own right, not merely because it promises an eventual career payoff. B. F. Skinner, the behavioristic theorist, criticized modern educational practices, which, for many students, have made learning aversive. We must "force ourselves" to learn in order to avoid the punishment of failure. Even though society uses aversive controls to enforce the need for education, it is in our own best interests to cultivate the positive reinforcement of satisfying our inherent needs to know and understand (Maslow, 1971; see Chapter 2).

MAKING EFFECTIVE USE OF TIME

Studying in a college setting is characterized by an expanse of unstructured time punctuated by examinations that may be months apart. The result: Students are often overwhelmed by the lack of structure and end up in a cycle of procrastination, guilt, and cramming. Unless you have exceptional learning aptitudes or have chosen an easy course of study, this cycle will lead to poor grades and little satisfaction.

One effect of this unstructured environment is that students constantly feel that they should be studying. Even when all they're doing is procrastinating, those unfinished assignments are an accumulating mental burden. An obvious strategy for overcoming this problem is to treat college like a job. Work out a time schedule that includes time spent going to class, being in class, and studying. If you structure your time as a forty- or forty-five-hour week, as in a nine-to-five job, you can probably increase your actual study time, while still leaving every evening and most of the weekend free for socializing.

Even though many students have the perception that school occupies every minute of their time, once they monitor their actual studying, they often find that a structured forty-hour week gives them both more time for studying and more time for socializing. What has been reduced is pretend studying and the time spent "getting ready to study."

Psychologically, it is interesting how much suffering the guilt from procrastination and pretend studying can cause. In effect, many students have unwittingly elected to "pay their dues" in units of suffering rather than units of learning. It seems more adaptive to use the principles of self-modification to shape study habits that make learning enjoyable.

SPECIFIC LEARNING SKILLS

Reading is the most basic of the learning skills. We all know how to read, yet how effective are we at it? All of us have experienced "reading" for a while, putting the book down, and having no idea what was on those pages. What is required is the skill to make reading a more active endeavor.

Robinson (1970) created an active approach to learning, which he calls the **SQ3R method:**

1. *Survey* the entire reading assignment to get a feel for what it entails.
2. *Question* yourself about some of the major headings and figures that you notice while surveying. Raise questions for which you will seek the answers when you read the material in depth. This automatically gets you into an active, searching mode. It also gets you interested in the material, and it gives you a cognitive structure that will help you retain what you do learn (Anderson & Bower, 1973).
3. *Read* the material carefully, pausing to underline, highlight, or otherwise note important points. Write down your observations and reactions to the material.
4. *Recite* the answers to your questions. This fixes them in memory.
5. *Review* the main points after you finish reading.

Although somewhat more time-consuming than simply reading the material once, the additional time is actually quite minimal, and recall and understanding are likely to be much improved.

Writing is not only a means of expressing your thoughts; it is also a way of becoming aware of what your thoughts are. By making them tangible and permanent, fleeting ideas that may have been barely perceived and immediately forgotten have been captured, so that they can be analyzed, developed, and reacted to.

Many people fear moments of uncertainty while writing, that is, moments when they are waiting for words to come to mind. Some fear that nothing will emerge. In fact, this is never the case. What is meant by "nothing coming to mind" is that nothing is making it past their own devastating censorship. (This censorship violates one of the cardinal rules of creativity: the separation of production and evaluation.) At any rate, many people find that these moments of uncertainty produce anxiety and thus define all writing as aversive. Once this happens, they will likely avoid writing and never develop this important skill.

One approach to writing is to sketch out a brief outline for the whole paper and then one for each paragraph before you attempt the first draft. Write the first draft quickly, with little or no evaluation. Then rewrite. If you can take a nonjudgmental attitude during the outline and first draft, you will probably discover that writing is fun.

Listening during lectures and class discussions is also a valuable skill. Here, the same strategy applies as with reading. Instead of thinking of yourself as a tape recorder and passively recording what you hear, think of yourself as a computer and actively process it. Translate what you hear into your own words, compare it with what you remember from the reading assignment, and ask questions whenever you're not following the professor's line of thought.

Many students feel intimidated by asking questions during class, afraid of asking a "stupid question" and being ridiculed. In fact, what often appears to be a stupid question to some people merely reflects the workings of a highly creative mind, one that can entertain possibilities that have never occurred to others.

If you have a heart-pounding, palm-sweating fear of speaking in class, then this would be a

Attentive students showing a willingness to interact with the instructor.

FOCUS

STUDENT SURVIVAL: THE ART AND SCIENCE OF TAKING TESTS

Psychologists have established what every undergraduate already knows: Independent of content knowledge, some people are better at taking tests than are others (Rowley, 1974). Moreover, test taking is a skill that can be learned. Here are some tips:

1. Use time wisely. Check the time regularly to make sure you will have a chance to respond to all items. Scan the test quickly so that you know what types of items and content areas are covered in different parts of the test. If you get stuck on an item, mark it and come back later if there is time. Also, if there is time, go back over all the items and be sure that you actually recorded the answer you had intended. Many errors occur through carelessness or lapses of attention rather than lack of knowledge.

2. Be sure to read the instructions and the item content carefully so that you know what the examiner is looking for.

3. Don't be afraid to go back and change an answer (Stoffer, Davis, & Brown, 1977).

4. Find out if there is a penalty for guessing. If not, go ahead and guess. Even apparently blind guesses are correct more often than would be expected by chance (Ebel, 1968). If there is a penalty, guess whenever you can eliminate one or more alternatives.

5. Read all options of a test question before responding. Even if you think you have found the correct solution, remember — this may be a trick question with answers that look good but are false.

6. If two options are equivalent, note that they both must be false unless one of the other options includes more than one answer.

7. Sometimes "free information" given in one item can provide a clue to the correct answer on another question.

8. For a question that includes "all of the above" as an option, remember that if one of the other options is false, "all of the above" must be ruled out. In general, however, "all of the above" is correct more often than would be expected by chance.

9. Response options that are longer or more detailed than the others are right more often than would be expected by chance.

10. Response options that form an ungrammatical sentence when combined with the question stem are unlikely to be correct.

11. Sentences with categorical words like *always* and *never* tend to be incorrect. Sentences with qualifiers, such as *sometimes*, *may*, and *generally*, are often correct.

12. On essay exams, take the time to make a rough outline. Be sure the major ideas follow a logical sequence and that your essay has an introduction, supporting arguments, and a conclusion. Clarity is more important than length.

perfect topic for self-modification. Initially, write out questions on paper to make the task easier. Start speaking in small classes, or even after class to the professor alone, and then gradually allow the size of your audience to increase. Practice deep breathing and tension-release exercises to control your state of relaxation. Imagine yourself asking a question in a confident and relaxed manner. Identify possible irrational cognitions that may be inhibiting your class behavior. For example, you may be thinking, "I know that if I open my mouth in class I'll make a fool of myself." Ask yourself, "Is this really true?" Isn't it actually an exaggeration? Furthermore, what if some people in the class do not like your question? After all, the purpose of asking a question is not to win admirers but to clarify a point. If you can get that clarification, then the question has succeeded. My experience has been that whenever one student has a question, it is something that many others were also wondering about. Usually, they are relieved and thankful that someone else had the courage to speak up.

Another self-modification area of particular relevance to college students is making a vocational choice that serves their long-term best interests.

VOCATIONAL CHOICE

The career we choose will affect our standard of living, whether we work on our own or with others, whether we do routine or challenging tasks, whether we succeed or fail, and whether or not we will enjoy the majority of our waking hours. Satisfaction in work is one of the strongest predictors of overall happiness in life (Freedman, 1978).

But selecting a career is not just one decision. It is a sequence of many choices that each of us has already begun. Selecting a college, choosing courses of study, deciding on a major, setting academic goals — whether to seek A's or settle for C's — all are career choices that you make every day.

MAKING A RATIONAL CHOICE

Most career counselors see choosing a career as a process of matching one's interests and aptitudes with the special features of various careers. In this, there seem to be two strategies to choose between. One is to seek a job that offers the money and hours that will accommodate your desired life-style. The other is to find an activity that you enjoy and then to find a job that pays for doing that activity. Which strategy appeals to you more?

INTERESTS

One of the most popular systems for categorizing career-related interests is that of Holland (1962), which identifies six personal styles that can be used to clarify what type of career best suits your personality:

1. *Realistic.* These people are practical and aggressive; they enjoy working outdoors and with their hands.
2. *Investigative.* These people are scientifically oriented.
3. *Artistic.* These people are self-expressive and creative.
4. *Social.* These people are humanistic, often religious, and they wish to help others.
5. *Enterprising.* These people like to sell, dominate, and lead.
6. *Conventional.* These people prefer highly ordered verbal or numerical work.

Rank these six categories to help clarify your own pattern of interests. Surprisingly, Scarr and Weinberg (1978) found that these interests are partly inherited. In biologically intact families, there was considerable overlap between the interests of the parents and the children; in adoptive families, however, parents' and children's interests were essentially unrelated. This suggests that your particular interests should be taken seriously. They are not just an accident of socialization, they are an important reflection of who you are as an indi-

Realistic.

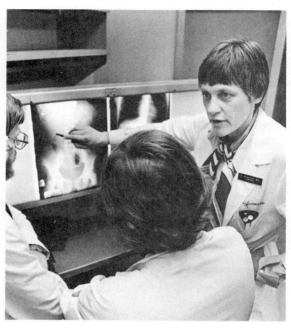

Investigative.

Artistic.

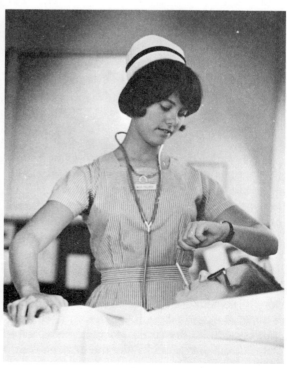

Social.

Enterprising.   *Conventional.*

Knowledge of Holland's (1962) preferred personal styles can help clarify career choice.

vidual. It is unlikely that you will be fully satisfied with a career that does not reflect your major interests.

APTITUDES

Aptitudes refer to particular abilities. Gardner (1984), for example, described seven aptitudes that relate to career success:

1. *Linguistic.* This includes vocabulary and word usage.
2. *Logical-mathematical.* This includes abstract thinking and reasoning.
3. *Spatial.* This includes the ability to visualize objects in space and picture how they would look if viewed from different perspectives.
4. *Musical.*
5. *Bodily-kinesthetic.* This refers to phys-

ical coordination, balance, and awareness of body movement.

6. *Interpersonal.* This refers to knowing how to deal with others, work well in groups, and arrive at joint decisions.
7. *Intrapersonal.* This includes knowledge of self and awareness of one's behavioral patterns and motivations.

Which of these aptitudes best characterize your abilities?

OCCUPATIONAL CHARACTERISTICS

What aspects of a career are most important to you? Money, helping others, social contact, flexible hours, being your own boss, opportunities for being creative? Our society offers diverse career possibilities, each with its own benefits. Making a rational career decision means taking the time to learn what types of careers are available. Talk to people about their jobs. Find out what they like and don't like about them. Most colleges have specialists in vocational counseling who can provide job information, through either personal experiences or suggested readings. A good source of information is a government publication called the *Occupational Outlook Handbook for College Graduates*. This periodical describes most jobs and offers an informed "guesstimate" of which are likely to be in demand. Your professors are also a valuable resource. Chances are they know individuals in careers that you are considering and can either give you advice themselves or put you in contact with those who can.

The important point here is taking the initiative. And if you are old enough to be reading this book, then you should have already begun gathering the information you need. One thing to keep in mind is that many students, even ones who pride themselves on being rational, put off activities related to career choice. Career decisions and the responsibilities of adult life in the "cold, hard (postgraduate) world" can be frightening. For this, the most adaptive strategy is to acknowledge the fear, remembering that fear and growth often go together.

One of the most important general skills in modern society is intelligence, that is, thinking and problem-solving ability. Research clearly shows that intelligence is one of the strongest predictors of success. And as our society becomes more technologically oriented, intellectual competence will increase in value.

INTELLECTUAL COMPETENCE

Current research suggests that raising intellectual competence is not easy, given existing methods of teaching thinking skills (Herrnstein, 1982). However, because intelligence enters into so many tasks that are valued, psycholo-

gists are investigating new ways of developing our thinking and problem-solving skills.

THE PROCESS OF PERFORMING POORLY

One approach that researchers (Feuerstein, 1980; Whimbey & Whimbey, 1975) have tried is closely observing the problem-solving behavior of those who do poorly on intellectual tasks.

Low-aptitude students often react impulsively, picking the first answer that seems likely. If they do not immediately see a plausible answer, they panic and guess. In addition, they may begin looking for an answer before they have a clear idea of what the question is asking. As these tests are constructed, however, the first credible answer is often a trick option designed to catch those who do not thoroughly understand the problem.

Underlying all the basic differences between those who do well on intellectual tasks and those who do not is passivity. Poor performers see themselves as passive receptacles of knowledge. If the answer is not immediately apparent, they automatically assume that the cause is lost. They do not realize that by actively examining problem constituents, reasoning through their relationships, and using deliberate strategies for breaking down the problem into simpler questions, a solution may be in sight.

ENHANCING INTELLECTUAL COMPETENCE

In addition to avoiding the pitfalls of those who do poorly on intellectual tasks, two specific approaches to enhancing performance can be considered.

Whimbey and Whimbey (1975) suggest making thought processes visible to an instructor. To do this, they have students think out loud while analyzing a problem so that they can receive immediate feedback as to whether they are reasoning in ways demanded by the question. To enhance reading comprehension, for example, students might read a few sentences

---

FOCUS

SOLVING THOSE BRAIN TWISTERS

"If you have brown and black socks in your drawer, mixed in the ratio of four to five, how many socks will you need to take out to be sure of having a pair of the same color?" Insight problems such as this, commonly known as "brain-twisters," provide a good index of intelligence (Sternberg & Davidson, 1982, p. 42). This particular problem relies on the ability to sift relevant from irrelevant information, as the ratio of colors is irrelevant to the task of matching socks of two possible hues.

Another insight skill is combining apparently unrelated elements, as in the question, "With a seven-minute hourglass and an 11-minute hourglass, what is the simplest way to time the boiling of an egg for 15 minutes?" (Sternberg & Davidson, 1982, p. 42).

---

out loud and then interpret them out loud, so that the instructor can ask probing questions and lead the student to a clearer understanding of the material.

Feuerstein (1980) maintains that many cognitive deficiencies are not due to a lack of experience with the problem area but to a lack of instruction that would help the student organize problem stimuli. For example, a child may have the repeated experience of stopping at traffic lights while riding in a car. Feuerstein argues that problem-solving skills in this situation are enhanced if someone mediates to help order and clarify the experience for the child, by saying, for example, "The red light means stop and the green light means go. This way, cars can avoid running into one another" (Chance, 1981). With a mediating statement such as this, the child learns the function of traffic lights much more readily. According to Feuerstein, intellectual competence is largely the result of providing such mediating instructions in the thousands of learning situations encountered in everyday life.

With regard to self-modification, we can certainly become aware of which intellectual errors we are currently making, and we can arrange suitable stimulus materials for practicing

deficient skills. On intellectual tasks, however, it is easy to get stuck on a problem so that you can't figure out what to do next. Note, self-modification does not mean that you must do it all "on your own," just that you take responsibility for creating contingencies to handle the problem. Here it would be quite appropriate to have a tutor or fellow student provide learning experiences such as mediated instructions and immediate feedback to vocalized thinking.

CREATIVITY

They are . . . *creators,* living out their ordinary lives in extraordinary ways. They are the innocents who, like young children, are perpetually wonder-ful. They cry out in the crowd that the emperor's new clothes don't exist, and with their insight and courage they rebuke the rest of society for its cowardice in accepting death before experiencing life. (Whiteside, 1981, p. 189)

Creative thinking is bringing into existence something that is new and of value (MacKinnon, 1962). A creative response must be novel or at least unusual, and it must be adaptive in solving a problem.

INTELLIGENCE AND CREATIVITY

Intellectual competence doesn't necessarily imply response novelty. Furthermore, intelligence is restricted to cognitive skills, whereas creativity can extend to more emotive endeavors such as art, dance, and music. Researchers agree that intelligence and creativity correlate moderately over the entire population. But once a person is above average in IQ, creativity and intelligence are relatively independent (MacKinnon, 1962; Prentky, 1980; Stein, 1968). In other words, you need some level of intelligence to be creative, but after that further intelligence is unlikely to help.

It may be easier to enhance one's creativity than one's intellectual competence. Creativity appears to be less genetically linked than intelligence and more closely related to attitudes of self-acceptance and nondefensiveness. Moreover, several theories of creativity suggest that each of us has a great creative potential that can be tapped if we can rise above the social pressures toward conformity.

THEORIES OF CREATIVITY

A number of theories have been developed to explain creative behavior. For psychoanalytic theorists, creative inspiration occurs when the ego loosens its control over thought, allowing a temporary regression to a less structured, preconscious style of thinking. This more spontaneous style approximates the mental processes of little children before they have been socialized to "make sense." In other words, the rigor, logic, and precision of rational, adult thought, although valuable in its own right, may interfere with the production of ideas that in some way "break the mold."

Sterling and Taylor (1980) supported this view in a study relating creativity to brain-hemisphere dominance. For right-handed persons, the left hemisphere is thought to control sequential, logical thinking, and the right hemisphere specializes in pattern recognition. Those with left-hemisphere dominance were found to be less creative than those with right or mixed dominance. The implication here may be that individuals should deliberately encourage functions associated with the right brain, such as daydreams, fantasies, and free associations. This allows ideas to be freely assembled, compared, and restructured. After a number of possibly creative formulations have surfaced, then rational thought can evaluate these ideas and refine their form.

Carl Rogers, the humanistic theorist, explained creativity as coming from an openness to experience. Seeing the problem in front of us without feeling threatened or fearful enhances the likelihood of an innovative solution.

THE CREATIVE PROCESS

One of the most popular descriptions of the creative process (Hadamard, 1945) identifies four phases of creativity:

1. *Preparation* involves a conscious, systematic, logical approach to a problem. Note, how a problem is defined often determines whether a solution will be found. Psychologist Gardner Murphy emphasized the importance of immersing oneself in the problem, advocating a single-minded commitment, even a love, for the problem itself.

2. *Incubation* refers to the period when rational approaches appear to be at an impasse and preconscious thought processes are presumably at work, generating associations and restructuring the problem.

3. *Illumination* refers to the moment of insight, when a creative solution appears from out of nowhere, usually while one's conscious attention is otherwise engaged. Brainstorming, that is, generating many ideas without evaluation, is a popular technique for stimulating insight.

4. *Verification* is a return to the conscious and rational mode of controlled thought.

This phase includes evaluating the discovery, stating it precisely, and determining its implications.

THE CREATIVE PERSONALITY

Research indicates that creative individuals show a definite pattern of traits and characteristics (Amos, 1981; Barron, 1963; Dellas & Gaier, 1970; Gough, 1979; MacKinnon, 1970; Prentky, 1980; Stein, 1974). Creative people tend to be intelligent, confident, persistent, curious, independent, nondefensive, uninhibited, emotional, and intuitive. In contrast, noncreative people tend to be cautious, conservative, conventional, narrow, sincere, and responsible.

ENHANCING CREATIVITY

Creativity is the key to human progress. The accumulated inventions and art forms of creative individuals throughout history constitute what we now call civilization. And the problems of our civilization clearly require creative solutions. Thus we all have a vested interest in enhancing creativity. Consider these suggestions:

Open yourself to change. The uncreative person is happy doing things in customary ways. Anything out of the ordinary makes this person uncomfortable.

Seeking a creative solution means admitting that you do not have all the answers. This admission can be regarded either as a threat or a challenge, and one's attitudinal choice will largely determine the creative result.

Learn to tolerate, and even to enjoy, uncertainty. Creativity often involves throwing oneself into a project without assurance that a solution will emerge. Thus one must cultivate tolerance for uncertainty and faith that a solution will eventually emerge (or at least, that the pursuit of that solution will prove worthwhile in itself). Those with little tolerance for uncertainty are unlikely to persist and sustain the work that creativity often requires.

Practice. Creativity can be aided by practice in problem solving. Stratton and Brown (1972), for example, found that students given such practice were better able to discover innovative solutions, rule out irrelevant information, and eliminate inferior solutions.

Allow adequate time for preparation. Safan-Gerard (1978) observed that a main cause of creative blocks is trying to force illumination before we are ready. Creativity is not something that can be forced. Moreover, expecting instant creativity is self-defeating. When insight does not occur on demand, many people automatically conclude, "I'm just not a creative person." Once they lose faith in themselves, it becomes difficult to risk spontaneous self-expression.

Avoid trying to control the process. The attitude of trying to control or impose your will on the creative process automatically blocks inspiration. It is more effective to adopt an attitude of "letting the problem lead you." Picasso, for example, talked about an attitude of unplanned exploring, looking without trying to reach any specific goal. He observed, "When I paint, my objective is to show what I found, not what I was looking for" (Safan-Gerard, 1978, p. 78).

The problem with having a specific goal in mind is that it prevents you from responding to the problem at hand and from reacting to what you have just written or painted. Goal orientation works well for tasks in which both the goal and the means of achieving it can be clearly specified. For creativity, however, the means to a solution are precisely what must be discovered. (Otherwise, creative solutions would be mass-produced and no longer novel.) Many artists, for example, view the creative process as having a life of its own; one must do what the problem, or the painting, or the composition requires, not what you want to do.

Eliminate preconceptions. It helps to drop our preconceptions of the ultimate solution, for each of these limits the options we will consider. Often, ideas that are totally unworkable in themselves can be modified or combined with other ideas to yield a creative solution.

Thus apparently "stupid" ideas often become keys to creative breakthroughs.

Alternate between periods of wild imagination and ruthless criticism. The full creative process requires periods of both idea generation and critical evaluation. But a common mistake, even among those who "know better," is to mix these periods. In fact, each poisons the other.

In most areas of life, moderation is highly adaptive. For creativity, however, certain forms of excess are preferred. During periods of idea generation, it helps to let one's associations run wild and produce numerous ideas. Often, the more offbeat the idea, the better. During critical evaluation, it helps to be utterly ruthless in tearing ideas apart and seeking their vulnerabilities. Alternating between these opposite moods appears to be one of the best strategies for stimulating creativity.

Entering into the flow of wild imagination may be fun, but for many it is not easy. Many of us unknowingly believe that we can create something worthwhile only while trying to do the "right thing" (Safan-Gerard, 1978). Doing what feels good or seems interesting somehow appears wrong. But for spurring creativity, they are exactly right. Another reason that people find it hard to let go and freely spout out ideas is an attitude of "safety first." It is easier to sit back and criticize than to step forward and risk rejection. Thus one must adopt an attitude of fearlessness, throwing out many apparently simple-minded and absurd ideas. From such rubble spring the green shoots of creativity.

Do you see yourself as a creative person? How do you get yourself into a creative mood? What has been your most creative work?

SUMMARY

1. Self-control is a skill that improves with knowledge and practice.

2. Any problem that can be defined in terms of the increase or decrease of concrete, observable behaviors in specified situations qualifies as a candidate for self-modification. Many self-modification problems involve behaviors with strong, pleasurable, short-run outcomes, but whose long-term consequences are undesirable.

3. After a systematic self-observation, define your problem quantitatively. Be sure to specify the events or situations that both precede and succeed problem behaviors. In addition, identify what you are currently doing instead of the problem behavior or what you would like to be doing instead of the problem behavior.

4. Make a preliminary explanation of what is causing or maintaining the problem behavior. This will guide your initial intervention. As you continue your self-observation, you can clearly evaluate whether the intervention is working. Modify your explanation of the problem and your intervention strategy as more information becomes available.

5. Antecedent interventions include avoiding, disrupting, and restricting antecedents, revising self-statements, using neutral descriptions of tempting stimuli, employing self-instructions, trying desirable responses in similar new situations, and observing models.

6. Behavioral interventions include practice and desensitization.

7. Consequent interventions include positive reinforcement, using current reinforcers to strengthen desirable rather than undesirable responses, using a point system to make reinforcement more immediate, using imagined reinforcers, praising yourself, shaping desired behaviors gradually, and extinguishing undesirable behaviors while avoiding punishment.

8. To increase commitment to the project make a written, public contract with yourself.

9. Keep the intervention flexible, making changes so that the natural contingencies of everyday life can eventually maintain the desired behavior.

10. Study skills can be enhanced by creating an optimal physical environment for studying, identifying and avoiding pretend studying, and structuring your time systematically. In addition, the basic skills of reading, writing, and listening can be developed.

11. Selecting a career is a series of choices in which one's interests and aptitudes are matched with the options available in the world of work. Making a rational choice implies seeking relevant job information and knowing what is reinforcing for you.

12. Intellectual competence is one of the best general predictors of success. Those who do poorly on intellectual tasks react impulsively instead of using systematic strategies, do not break complex problems into a series of simpler steps, and often adopt a passive attitude, assuming that if they don't know the answer immediately, there is no way that they can figure it out.

13. Intellectual performance may be aided by verbalizing thought processes to someone who can provide immediate feedback, asking probing questions and clarifying the relationships among problem elements.

14. Although they are related, creativity is not the same as intelligence. Creativity is bringing something new and valuable into existence. The creative process can be described in stages of preparation, incubation, illumination, and verification. There seems to be a clear linkage between creativity and personality. Strategies for enhancing creativity include opening yourself to change, learning to enjoy uncertainty, practice at being creative, allowing enough time for preparation, not trying to control the creative process, eliminating preconceptions about the solution, and alternating between wild imagination and ruthless criticism.

SUGGESTED READINGS

Michelozzi, N. **Coming alive from nine to five: The career search handbook.** New York: Mayfield, 1980. Uses many types of self-analysis to facilitate career choice.

Pivar, W. H. **The whole earth textbook: A survival manual for students.** Philadelphia: Saunders, 1978. Sound advice on achieving competence in a college environment.

Stuart, R. B., & Davis, B. **Slim chance in a fat world.** New York: Research Press, 1972. Combines overeating, nutrition, and exercise in a self-modification approach.

Watson, D. L., & Tharp, R. G. **Self-directed behavior.** Monterey, California: Brooks/Cole, 1985. A detailed and clearly structured approach to self-modification, including many examples of self-modification projects.

PART THREE

RELATIONSHIPS

PART THREE examines our most important social relationships. Chapter 8 begins this section by discussing essential skills in accurate, nondefensive communication. These skills, dealing with personal disclosure, active listening, open questions, verbal dominance, conflict resolution, and nonverbal signals, largely determine the success or failure of most relationships. The remaining chapters in Part Three apply and refine these skills within specific types of relationships.

Chapter 9 considers love and attraction, from the moment of initial contact through the cycles of romantic and companionate love. In particular, it examines the dilemma of modern love relationships. These relationships are based on love and designed to endure, yet the type of love that spawns them appears to be short-lived. The chapter concludes by exploring possible solutions to this problem.

Chapter 10 examines sexual functioning, with an eye toward reconciling emphases on technique and sensuality. It explores our culture's obsession with orgasmic technique and concludes that although technique is important, for many couples it has become the problem rather than the solution. In accord with most sex therapists, it advocates a more relaxed, sensual approach to intimate relationships.

Chapter 11 considers marriage and family relationships. It analyzes the current crisis in marriage and studies the implications of the rising divorce rate: Can traditional, lifetime marriage be saved, or is it an inappropriate ideal for modern times? The remainder of this chapter examines the family system. It shows how the roles of all family members interconnect to resist change and maintain stable patterns of communication, even when these patterns cause emotional turmoil.

COMMUNICATION 8

The Lifeblood of Relationships

THE FAILURE TO COMMUNICATE

Effective communication unlocks the possibility of developing full, satisfying relationships. It is the key to making contact with others. And when it comes to communication, we all are seasoned veterans. In fact, we cannot *not* communicate. When with others, we are always communicating—either with words and gestures or with the absence of expected words and gestures. Moreover, we are continually trying to make sense out of others' behavior, asking ourselves, "What are they doing and what does it *mean*? How will their behavior affect me?" Thus after years of practice in both **encoding** (sending) and **decoding** (receiving) interpersonal messages, one might expect us to be experts. Nevertheless, this expectation is far from accurate. Consider Al and Dot:

Al: *"There's a costume party at Brian's tonight. People are supposed to go as either 'the person you most admire or the one who makes you want to barf.' Want to go?"*

Dot: *[Thinks: Might be fun. Better than what we've been doing lately. No point in sounding too excited, though. I want to make sure he doesn't chicken out of taking me to the ballet.] "OK."*

Al: *"Are you sure you want to go?" [Sounds like she doesn't want to. I'd like to see Brian and the guys, and I've got my Halloween masks, so we could go as Ron and Nancy Reagan. But I don't want her to go on my account. If she thinks I owe her, she'll pull something on me, like that dumb ballet.]*

Dot: *"OK, let's not go. I wouldn't know what to wear, anyway." [Sounds like he doesn't really want to. If I try to force him to go, he'll pout and ruin the whole evening. We never do anything fun.]*

Al: *"Whatever you say." [I knew she would find some excuse.]*

Even though both Al and Dot want to attend the party, their conversation yields a solution that neither desires. Note that this outcome, which is not rare by any means, didn't come about through a lack of interest or effort. In fact, both Al and Dot were seriously engaged in decoding the other's actions and presenting themselves in a way that might further their own desires. Nevertheless, their communication attempts backfired. Both were more interested in setting up an advantage for the upcoming conflict over going to the ballet than in honestly stating their preferences about this evening's party.

What clues could Al and Dot have used to improve their interpretations of the other's behavior?

Although this is speculative without observing nonverbal behavior and tone of voice, it seems that Dot was too quick to dismiss Al's desire to attend the party, especially since he brought it up. In addition, Dot didn't give Al credit for discerning that her unenthusiastic "OK" suggested that *she* didn't want to go. Instead, she wrongly viewed his reentering the topic of whether to go as a sign of hesitation on *his* part. Even when Al's "Whatever you say" made it clear that he was trying to place the blame for not going on her, Dot failed to check her interpretation by directly asking for his preference. Al, on the other hand, misinterpreted her statement, "I wouldn't know what to wear, anyway." The qualifier "anyway" suggests that if it weren't for not knowing what to wear, she would want to go. Since he had a costume in mind, he could have mentioned this and asked her to clarify her preference.

Note that the whole conversation is really about going to the ballet, even though the ballet is never mentioned. Subtleties such as this sometimes make even the simplest exchanges extraordinarily complex (and fascinating).

THE SEA OF MISCOMMUNICATION

Surprisingly, much of the practical knowledge on effective communication is straightforward and relatively easy to apply. Nevertheless, most people ignore it. Certain natural perceptual biases make accurate communication an elusive commodity. For example, unless there is an explicit misunderstanding, we invariably assume that what we intended to communicate was received *in its intended form*. Without proof of miscommunication, we assume accuracy. Procedures for checking communicational accuracy are seldom employed in ordinary conversations. For example, accuracy can be checked by simply asking one's partner to state in his or her own words what we have been saying. The use of this simple procedure quickly dispels the notion that miscommunication is rare.

SOURCES OF MISCOMMUNICATION

One story illustrating the difficulty of accurate communication concerns a professor who wanted to dramatize for his students the damaging effects of alcohol. He placed one worm in

water and another in gin. After a brief period, the worm in water was fine, but the one in alcohol had died and partially dissolved. "Now," he asked, "What does that prove to you?" A voice from the back retorted, "If you drink alcohol, you won't have worms!" (Swets, 1983).

It can be argued that the potential for miscommunication is almost limitless. Some of its contributing factors include ambiguities in the language, our own conflicted feelings about what we want our partner to know, the tendency to hear what we want to be true rather than what was actually said, and the refusal to view communication as a skill that can be improved.

Language ambiguities. There are about thirty dictionary meanings for each of the most common words in the English language. Thus even in the simplest of messages, there will often be dozens of possible interpretations. The chances that our intended meaning will be the only one received are often quite low.

The motive to conceal. Clear communication is compromised when our aim is to hide rather than reveal. When holding back part of our thoughts and feelings, we must continually stand guard; we must avoid turning our partner's attention to this sensitive area. Thus, our attention is divided between accurate communication and camouflage. Moreover, part of us may want to share this material with the partner, while another part fears the imagined consequences of disclosure. This internal conflict disrupts message clarity.

Certainly, language can just as easily be used to obfuscate as to reveal. Unfortunately, the skillful use of language is often employed to keep others at a distance rather than to promote intimacy.

Selective perception. Even if we say exactly what is on our minds, communication may still break down, for what we say may not be what our partner hears. Given the ambiguities of language, there is always room for the partner to color what is actually said by what he or she wants to be true. Thus it is important to know our own areas of sensitivity, to know when our

FOCUS

ONE TEENAGER'S STORY

Dear folks,

Thank you for everything, but I am going to Chicago and try to start some kind of new life.

You asked me why I did those things and why I gave you so much trouble, and the answer is easy for me to give you, but I am wondering if you will understand.

Remember when I was about six or seven and I used to want you to just listen to me? I remember all the nice things you gave me for Christmas and my birthday and I was really happy with the things . . . for about a week . . . but the rest of the time I really didn't want presents, I just wanted all the time for you to listen to me like I was somebody who felt things, too, because I remember even when I was young I felt things. But you said you were busy.

Mom, you are a wonderful cook, and you had everything so clean and you were tired so much from doing all those things that made you busy; but, you know something, Mom? I would have liked crackers and peanut butter just as well if you had only sat down with me a while during the day and said to me: "Tell me all about it so I can maybe help you understand!"

If Donna ever has children, I hope you will tell her to just pay some attention to the one who doesn't smile very much because that one will really be crying inside. And when she's about to bake six dozen cookies, to make sure first that the kids don't want to tell her about a dream or a hope or something, because thoughts are important . . . to small kids even though they don't have so many words to use when they tell about what they have inside them.

Love to all,

Your son (Swets, 1983, pp. 40–41)

Given the magnitude of the runaway problem in our society, this letter probably represents the feelings of many young people. It is interesting to look at this letter from the parents' viewpoint. Were they abusive individuals who cared little about their children? Perhaps, but this seems unlikely. Moreover, it is nearly inconceivable that they could have realized what they were doing to their son and not have changed their behavior toward him.

On the other hand, how could the boy feel this way for so many years without their realizing the extent of his pain? The letter conveys this pain graphically; it also communicates his wish to punish them with guilt.

Assuming that the son had in some way communicated his unhappiness to them before leaving, how do you think this situation was able to remain unchanged? Why didn't the parents open up the channels of communication and make contact with this boy? What is your guess as to why this problem was not resolved more adaptively?

Do you know anyone who feels this way toward their parents? How do they explain the absence of communication?

strong and perhaps irrational needs may distort what we hear. For example, Arthur is a successful dentist who married a beautiful and much younger woman. Arthur sees himself as ordinary and nondescript, and so he secretly wonders what his bride sees in him. He wants her to stay home and care for the house, fearing that if she were around other young people, she would be easy prey for some young Romeo. When she tells him that she wants to take a night course at the community college, what he "hears" is that she is bored and wants to cheat.

The skill of communicating effectively. Most of us do not think of communication as a skill that we can practice and improve. How we communicate is taken for granted as simply part of who we are. Perhaps we also fear that trying to alter our communicational style would compromise our individuality. As indicated above, however, there are identifiable communication skills that, when mastered, can increase social effectiveness. And far from reducing one's sense of uniqueness, these skills facilitate its expression.

Conversation consists of "turns" in which participants alternate between talking and listening. We shall break down this process into the skills of talking about ourselves, active listening, and asking appropriate questions.

SELF-DISCLOSURE

Self-disclosure, telling another person about yourself, is the main way in which we get to know one another. Thus it provides the foundation for the growth of friendships. One of the best ways of encouraging others to self-disclose is by modeling disclosure oneself. This shows that you like and trust the partner and that this is an appropriate time for getting better acquainted (Millholland & Avery, 1982). Note that those unwilling to reveal themselves are also more likely to distort the truth of what they do disclose (Gitter & Black, 1976).

Typically, disclosure proceeds gradually

from the impersonal and superficial to topics that are more personal and intimate. It also tends to proceed symmetrically, so that partners take turns disclosing and their disclosures are at relatively equal levels of intimacy. Research suggests that under these conditions, the chances for mutual liking are optimized (Cozby, 1973).

What happens when these rules are violated? When one partner immediately discloses their deepest, most embarrassing secrets, then this counternormative behavior is likely to decrease liking, be viewed with suspicion, and be perceived as a sign of maladjustment (Strassberg et al., 1977; Wortman et al., 1976).

LEVELS OF PERSONAL DISCLOSURE

Clichés are often used to make initial contact. These ritual openers allow participants to acknowledge one another's presence and reassert friendly intentions. Typical cliché greetings are "Hi, how are you?" "Fine, and you?" Such greetings may be the extent of the contact, or they may pave the way for greater disclosure.

Facts describe objective events, the outer happenings in one's life. For example:

I went to Purdue University.
I jog twice a week.
My family lives in New York.

Opinions present one's thoughts and beliefs. They represent a personal point of view rather than an objective frame of reference. For example:

I think that people should get into shape.
I believe that politicians are only as corrupt as those who voted them into office.
I think that I'm a fair person.

Feelings express one's emotional reactions to the events of experience. For example:

I like you.
I was furious when you laughed at me.
Rainy days make me sad.

FEELING-LEVEL DISCLOSURE

Feelings express our unique reactions to life. Others cannot really know us unless we communicate at the level of feelings. In general, our most satisfying interactions consist of mutual, feeling-level disclosures. There are a number of reasons, however, why feeling-level disclosure is often avoided. First, because it is more personal: The expression of feelings makes us vulnerable to others' negative evaluations. It hurts more to be rejected after revealing our private experiences. For the insecure, this may be seen as too great a risk. The cost, however, of not having some relationships with regular, feeling-level disclosure is a narrowed and restricted emotional existence, a deadening of our selves.

Another detractor from feeling-level disclosure is the societal value placed on logic and efficiency. It is commonly believed that feelings should be "controlled," especially in the world of work. Although emotional expression may be inappropriate in some situations, it can aid competency in others. For example, feelings can be the source of creative breakthroughs. Many Nobel Prize winners claim that their greatest ideas came from spontaneous, emotional experiences, not just from cold, logical deduction. Nevertheless, in our society, values from the business world are often transposed to one's personal relationships. Thus, in a misguided attempt to appear invulnerable, friends often avoid feeling-level disclosure.

Not surprisingly, the priority of business-oriented values over intimacy is more closely associated with men than with women. Women generally disclose at a more personal level than do men (Cozby, 1973). Many men are dominated by the image of the "strong, silent type," as portrayed in numerous movies by Clint Eastwood. Certainly, it is sometimes necessary to act quickly and coolly, without emotional disruption. But the ability to deal with crisis does not require a restriction on emotional expressiveness across relationships and life situations.

HIDING THE ONE WHO FEELS

One way of reducing the risk of feeling-level disclosure is literally to hide the subject of one's sentences. Instead of "I get angry when someone laughs at me," the sentence can be neutralized by making the subject impersonal: "You get angry when someone laughs at you." At the surface, this statement sounds like a philosophical description of all people. One must infer that it reveals something about the speaker's emotional life. Essentially, it is a cop-out. Although it reduces risk, it also takes the speaker away from his or her emotional state. Most psychologists believe it healthier to "own" your emotions, to make it clear whose emotion is being expressed.

FEELINGS MAKE YOU MORE INTERESTING

Feeling-level disclosure not only reveals your personality; it is also more interesting. By including the details of how we reacted to events, by using vivid emotion words to paint word-pictures of our experiences, it is easier for the listener to get involved and empathize with us. For example, consider this job description:

I'm a bookkeeper for several small companies. I put all their records in order and make sure they pay their taxes correctly.

Although straightforward, this description is dull and lifeless. Contrast it with a more feeling-level revision written by the same individual:

I'm a bookkeeper for several small companies. Sometimes when I'm casually writing down figures, I'll start thinking about the thousands of dollars they represent and I'll get nervous, afraid I've made a mistake. When I start feeling like that I go over it one more time, just to make sure. Sometimes the books I get are totally confused—numbers all over the place. Though I grumble a lot, I like the challenge of straightening it all out and getting the final figures to match. (Garner, 1981, p. 60)

Try writing two descriptions of your day: one at the factual level and the other at the level of feelings. Which is closer to the way you usually talk with friends and acquaintances?

ACTIVE LISTENING

When we hear the term "communication," we often think of talking rather than listening. Ours is an active culture; we emphasize "going out and getting the job done." We attend to the positive, to what is done rather than to what is not done. And so listening, the apparently more passive side of communication, is often overlooked. But true listening is never really passive. Even though there is little physical action, listening requires a great deal of mental activity. More importantly, listening provides one of the major satisfactions of interpersonal relationships. When someone has truly listened to us and understood what we feel, barriers between people disappear, and the loneliness of our separated existence dissolves. Carl Rogers maintains that the feeling of making contact and being

understood is one of the most healing factors in psychotherapy.

How good are most people's listening skills? Researchers at the Sperry Corporation estimate that we often comprehend only 25 percent of what we hear. With appropriate training, however, comprehension can double in a few months (Swets, 1983, p. 40). Thus the potential for improved listening is substantial. Suggestions for enhancing active listening include the following:

Give prompts. Listening is just being quiet while the other person is talking. Right? Wrong! In addition to concentrating on what your partner is saying and feeling, active listening is prompting your partner to make it clear that you understand what is being said and are ready to hear more. These prompts include making eye contact, nodding your head, and saying, for example, "Mmm, hmm," "That's interesting," "I understand," and "Tell me more." Such prompts show that you are in contact, and they convey the message that the partner is important to you, that his or her thoughts matter.

Give feedback. Ask for clarification or

paraphrase what the partner is saying so that you can be sure you understand exactly what is meant. Sometimes people feel that this slows down a conversation or that it runs the risk of making their lack of understanding public. "What if I tell Jane what I think she is saying and it turns out that I was completely wrong?" This person is assuming that miscommunication is so rare that only an idiot would fail to comprehend "plain English." In fact, such miscomprehensions occur daily for each of us.

Put yourself in the other person's place. Try to understand what the other person is saying from his or her point of view. Don't assume that you and the other are so similar that if something wouldn't bother you, then it wouldn't bother her. To make contact, you must develop **empathic understanding.** See the world through other people's eyes, their assumptions, and their values.

Avoid being judgmental. Unless passing judgment is part of the social roles that you both have chosen for this interaction, evaluating the other person will be inappropriate. For example, if your friend is troubled and tells you that she just had an abortion, your personal beliefs about whether abortion is justified would be out of place. Your role in such a conversation might be simply to listen and make contact with your partner, giving her a chance to explore her feelings. Despite a keen awareness of our own insecurities, somehow we quickly forget that few people are so secure that they welcome others to sit in judgment of them. Invariably, the first hint of a judgmental attitude puts the partner on the defensive, restricts open communication, and creates an uncomfortable tension.

Consider the following interaction in which the parent listens only at the surface of the conversation, immediately taking an evaluative attitude:

Boy: *I'm not going to school!*
Mom: *What do you mean by that? Get your things together and head out the door!*
Boy: *But I don't want to.*

Mom: *Don't talk back to me. I said you're going to school, and that is that.*

From the boy's point of view, the mother heard him but did not listen. The implicit message is that his reasons don't matter, that he cannot be trusted, and so the only issue for the mother is one of authority. This type of interaction damages a child's self-esteem, for it tells him that he is not worth listening to. Here is a more adaptive variation:

Boy: *I'm not going to school!*
Mom: *You don't want to go to school.*
Boy: *I hate school.*
Mom: *You seem pretty upset this morning.*
Boy: *Johnny made fun of my lunchbox.*
Mom: *What did he say?*
Boy: *He said only little kids have a lunch box with E.T. on it.*
Mom: *What's wrong with E.T.?*
Boy: *I don't know. He's got a stupid Superman lunch box. Can I get a new one?*
Mom: *Well, you like E.T., don't you? You picked it out yourself.*
Boy: *Yeah, E.T.'s OK. But I think I need a new one now.*
Mom: *Well, I like E.T. just as much as Superman. And your lunch box is still good. I think Johnny was just saying that to get you mad. Did anything happen so that he would want to hurt your feelings?*
Boy: *I didn't let him play with my Masters of the Universe collection.*
Mom: *OK, why don't you tell him that he can come over after school and play Masters of the Universe with you?*
Boy: *What if he says something about my lunch box?*
Mom: *What do you think?*
Boy: *E.T. is just as cool.*
Mom: *Time for school.*

Notice that "Mom" listened for and commented on her son's emotional state as well as on the explicit content of the communication.

In personal conversations emotional tone will often be more important than verbal content.

Which of these two interactions reminds you of conversations you have had with your own parents? Are they good listeners?

ASKING QUESTIONS

Questions are one of our most powerful tools for influencing conversations. Questions demand attention, force the conversational turn, and specify the content of the partner's response. Because of their strong impact, questions set the mood and tone of a conversation. In general, the more questions, the greater the level of excitement or tension. Leisurely conversations between old friends tend to have few questions. At the other extreme are the often tense and dramatic interrogations of courtroom trials.

OPENING AND CLOSING THE LISTENER'S RESPONSE

Closed-ended questions pull for a brief response, perhaps only a word or phrase. These questions are often used to make initial contact (e.g., "Where are you from?" "What's your major?") or to seek specific pieces of information (e.g., "When did the ship go down?" "How much do I owe you?"). As such, closed-ended questions are useful tools. A common error, however, is to overuse them. When used in series, they quickly take on the unpleasant tone of a cross-examination. Typically, **open-ended questions** will be more appropriate. These questions require more than a few words to answer, and so they encourage the partner to self-disclose or develop a line of thought. Open-ended questions often begin with How? In what way? Why? or What? A common strategy is to start with a closed-ended question and immediately follow up with open-ended questions. For example, "Where did you go in Europe?" "Paris." "What was Paris like?"

Open-ended questions can be so broad, however, that they have a reverse effect. When a question would take a great deal of time to answer honestly, it is often taken, not as a request for disclosure but as a cliché greeting requiring only a cliché response. For example, "How are you doing?" "How'd it go today?" or "What's new?" This last question is particularly interesting. Most of the time "What's new?" elicits a reply something like, "Oh, not much." Thus it puts listeners in the submissive role of denying that anything interesting is happening in their lives. In addition, "What's new?" can be offensive if used as an opening for the questioner to report an exciting experience. For example:

Mary: *What's new?*
Jane: *Oh, not much. I'm supposed to study with Ricky again tonight.*
Mary: *Wait 'til I tell you what I'm doing. Robert is taking me to the Willie Nelson concert. It will be so much fun.*

Although Mary should certainly be able to share her excitement with Jane, in this example she has set up Jane with her initial question and then tried to "rub in" her status advantage by calling attention to the difference in their planned activities.

PERSONAL QUESTIONS

Some questions pull for superficial, nonthreatening information, and others request the listener to reveal very private parts of themselves. For example:

Impersonal questions:
Where do you work?
How long have you lived here?
What kind of food do you like?

Personal questions:
How much money do you make?
Who is your best friend?
How do you get along with your parents?

Highly personal questions:
Have you ever had an abortion?
What is the biggest disappointment of your life?
How do you and Janice get along in bed?

In general, conversations start out with impersonal questions and only gradually move toward more personal ones. Most relationships, however, never involve questions that are highly personal. Personal questions that come up "too early" in a conversation or relationship will be perceived as rude and intrusive. In general, avoid asking a question that is more personal than what you have already disclosed to the partner, or more personal than what the partner has already volunteered. Personal questions can be effective in quickly moving the conversation to a more intimate level (Piccard, Critelli, & Nite,

1984), but they are risky, since they put the partner on the spot. A less risky way of raising the intimacy level is through one's own disclosures (Cozby, 1973).

WHETHER IT IS BETTER TO ASK OR TO VOLUNTEER

Most people lean toward one or the other of two conversational rules. The first, the **norm of asking**, assumes, "If she wants to know something about me, she will ask." This norm shows a reluctance to volunteer information and perhaps a sensitivity to not forcing oneself onto the partner. The **norm of volunteering** assumes just the opposite: "If he wants to talk about something, he will, so questions are unnecessary." This rule shows a sensitivity to the partner's privacy. Both norms are reasonable approaches

Some individuals seem interested in a conversation only when it is their turn to speak.

FOCUS

CONVERSATION KILLERS

Paul Swets's book, *The Art of Talking So That People Will Listen* (1983), contains a number of useful pointers. As Swets noted (p. 13), "You are someone special! Of course, everyone has faults. But when you choose to express your best self — that self that is open, humorous, interested in other people, willing to share thoughts and feelings, eager to learn, able to listen deeply — when *that* person talks, people listen." Many people, however, present themselves in a way that is guaranteed to turn others off. Some common examples are described next.

BEWARE THE COMPLAINER

All people are sometimes down in the dumps and need to be comforted, and hiding these feelings from friends amounts to cheating on the relationship. On the other hand, many people fall into habitual patterns of complaining and seeking sympathy. Tip-offs to such habitual patterns are conversation openers such as "My husband never listens to me." "I talk to my son until I'm blue in the face, but it doesn't do any good." "If I've told you once, I've told you a thousand times. . . ." Such conversations punish the listener and guarantee that eventually this person will avoid the complainer or tune out.

MR. KNOW-IT-ALL

Other conversation killers are put-downs, dogmatic statements, and direct contradictions. For example, "Don't be ridiculous!" "I know exactly what you're thinking!" "That will never work!" "Are you crazy?" and "Everybody should. . . ."

Swets offered a checklist of conversation-killing behaviors:

- Do I yell or talk too loudly?
- Do I complain?
- Does the tone of my voice convey disgust?
- Do I talk longer than a minute without giving someone else a chance to speak?
- Do I talk too much about myself or my interests?
- Do I tend to be dogmatic, condescending, argumentative, or egocentric?
- Do I mumble or talk too softly?
- Do I have only one topic of conversation?
- Do I sound like a drill sergeant — always telling people what to do?
- Do I bore people by "talking shop" at the wrong time?
- Do I ask ineffective, intrusive, or offensive questions? (Questions can often be softened by explaining why you're interested in asking the question.)
- Do I seem to be trying too hard to make conversation? (If *you* are tense, your partner will feel ill at ease.)
- Do I criticize or find fault with others? (If partners feel that you dislike them, they are likely to discount whatever you say.)

to conversation, especially if partners are using the same one. When both are following the norm of asking, the conversation can proceed as a flow of brief, reciprocal interviews. With both using the norm of volunteering, the conversation also moves smoothly, with partners taking turns recounting their experiences.

What happens, however, when participants use different norms? One person hesitates to volunteer information unless requested but feels free to show interest in the partner by asking questions. The partner feels free to volunteer information but not to ask questions. The result is a one-sided conversation, with one partner asking questions and the other doing most of the talking. Although such conversations may be satisfactory at first, they eventually run into problems. The volunteer may begin viewing the partner as secretive and feel uncomfortable with the discrepancy in what each knows about the other. The questioner may perceive the partner as self-centered. As a general rule, social conversations work best when partners spend about equal time listening and talking.

"Interpersonal communication" includes an almost overwhelming diversity of possible responses. In the first part of the chapter we examined several classes of interpersonal response: disclosing, listening, and asking questions. These categories are formed without reference to content, that is, what the response is "about" (e.g., love, anger, dominance). Is it possible to classify interpersonal behaviors based on content? If so, how many types of interpersonal response can be reliably distinguished? Do these types relate to one another in any particular way, and if so, can this ordering be used to gain new insight into social interactions?

DIMENSIONS OF INTERPERSONAL BEHAVIOR

THE INTERPERSONAL CIRCLE

Research (Kiesler, 1983; Wiggins, 1982) indicates that the variety of interpersonal behav-

iors can be described in about sixteen categories. And remarkably, if the distance between behaviors is made proportional to the similarity in their meanings, a circular arrangement emerges. Figure 8–1 shows this ordering of interpersonal behaviors, sequenced as dominant, competitive, mistrusting, cold, hostile, detached, inhibited, unassured, submissive, deferent, trusting, warm, friendly, sociable, exhibitionistic, and assured. These terms form the inner circle in Figure 8–1. Note that similar terms occur close together, with opposites (e.g., assured-unassured) placed directly across from each other. These terms are the general labels for each category, but there is also a range of intensity within the category. The middle circle shows the mild, and the outer circle, the more severe level of intensity. For example, "dominant" ranges from "controlling" to "dictatorial."

DOMINANCE AND AFFECT

Psychologists have also determined that the circular ordering of interpersonal behaviors can be described by two key dimensions, dominance-submission and positive-negative affect. **Dominance** refers to an attitude of self-confidence and authority. In particular, it includes taking the lead, controlling the interaction, choosing the topic, giving suggestions, and generally being one-up in the conversation. On the negative side, dominance may also mean being bossy, making accusations, and forcing one's point of view on the partner. Conversational dominance appears to be the human equivalent of pecking order in animal societies. The difference is that for humans, dominance is typically established and maintained through words, subtle body cues, and the display of status objects rather than through force.

Positive and **negative affect** refer to whether behavior expresses liking, affection, and friendliness toward the partner or whether it conveys hostility, rejection, and distancing.

Four quadrants of interpersonal behavior can be identified: positive dominance, positive

FIGURE 8−1

THE INTERPERSONAL CIRCLE

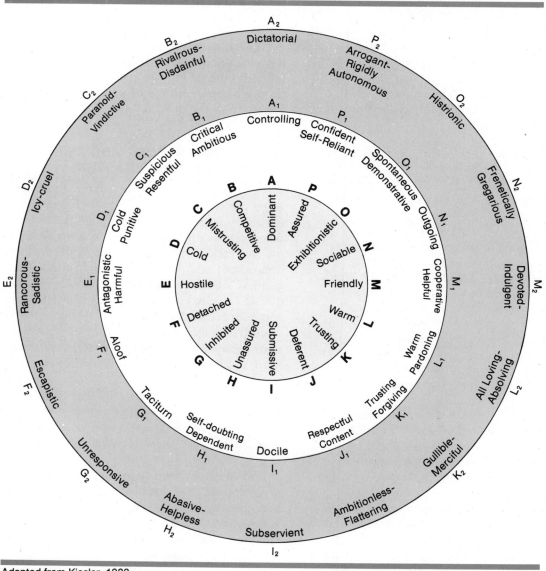

Adapted from Kiesler, 1983

submission, negative dominance, and negative submission. Moreover, these four types often occur in particular sequences. Especially in long-term relationships, in which patterns of dominance and submission are stable and well established, dominance from one partner encourages submission from the other, and sub-mission from one encourages dominance from the other. Positive affect tends to elicit positive affect from the partner, and negative affect encourages negative feelings in return. In initial interactions or conversations of brief duration, however, dominant statements may elicit other dominant statements, as parties wage verbal battles for control of the conversation. When this occurs, the conversation may be terminated early, with no clear victor, or one partner may give in and take the submissive role, thereby stabilizing the interaction. In other words, interpersonal communication can be seen as an attempt to negotiate mutually satisfactory definitions about who will be dominant and what the level of friendliness will be (Kiesler, 1983).

The following conversation illustrates how these quadrants function:

Beth: *Well, don't you look handsome tonight. (positive dominant, pd)*

Bart: *Thank you. I really like your dress. (ps, following Beth's lead in a greeting-compliment ritual)*

Beth: *By the way, why didn't you return my call? I tried to get you all last night. (nd)*

Bart: *I was out — I had to go over to my sister's house. She wanted me to fix her sink. Why do you ask, anyway? (ns, the main purpose being to defend against Beth's implied accusation)*

Beth: *What do you mean, "Why do you ask?" I asked because I needed to talk to you last night and you were nowhere to be found. (nd)*

Bart: *That's a lot of bull, and you know it. You thought maybe I was out bar hopping. Your jealousy really makes me sick sometimes. (nd, making a bid for the dominant role)*

Beth: *Well if that's all you care about me, maybe you'd better just leave right now. You can go spend the night alone and see how you like it. (nd)*

Bart: *Listen Beth, I'm sorry for mouthing off. Let's make up and I'll take you out to someplace special tonight. OK? (ps)*

Beth: *OK, honey, if you say so. I don't know how we get into these little things. (ps)*

At any point in the interaction, each partner is responding either from dominance or submission. Healthy interactions are characterized by the use of positive rather than negative affect and by the effortless transfer of dominance from one partner to the other as the situation or topic

of conversation changes. It also may be desirable for partners to share dominance equally, although partners in many satisfying relationships do not.

To increase awareness of interpersonal behaviors, use the four quadrants to categorize (silently) the responses in your next conversation. What percentage of your responses fell into each of the quadrants?

SEX DIFFERENCES AND THE TOPIC OF CONVERSATION

In male–female relationships, men tend to be conversationally dominant. Topics introduced by men succeed nearly all of the time, whereas those introduced by women succeed (i.e., are picked up and discussed by the partner) only about one-third of the time. In addition, women introduce most of the topics (Parlee, 1979). Thus, women's conversational initiatives are continually being rejected or ignored by men. (Actually, this is typical of all conversations between those of unequal status.) For example:

Jan: *I heard there's a new play downtown.*

Ben: *My mother called this morning. She wants us to come over later.*

Jan: *Just to visit, or for something particular?*

What can women do to equalize this pattern of conversational dominance? First, they can become aware of the flow of dominance and submission. For Jan, instead of allowing Ben to ignore her topic initiative, she could have refused the submissive role by reentering her topic. This would be appropriate as long as there is no reason to assume that the call from Ben's mother indicates an emergency. Thus, the conversation might go like this:

Jan: *I heard there's a new play downtown.*

Ben: *My mother called this morning. She wants us to come over later.*

In conversations with women, men have traditionally assumed a dominant role.

Jan: *Ben, there's a new play downtown. Do you know anything about it?*

Here Jan is presenting herself as someone who expects to be treated with respect. If Ben still doesn't acknowledge her topic, Jan could escalate the exchange to another level of directness by again reentering her topic, but this time emphasizing it with direct eye contact, forward lean, and even by touching Ben's forearm. As Elgin (1983) found, the use of touch to reinforce a message is powerful, but it must be used carefully. Elgin advised touching the forearm. Touching the hand would be treating the partner like a "little boy." Touching the shoulder suggests grabbing and physical threat. However, if the partner is not a personal friend, touching would be inappropriate.

Negative-dominant behaviors present particular difficulties. Because of this, they deserve special attention. In the next section we shall consider several practical strategies for handling verbal attack. Once you have grasped these alternatives, you can make a more conscious choice about how to deal with the insults, threats, innuendos, and accusations that may come your way.

DEALING WITH VERBAL ATTACK

THE THEORY OF UNIVERSAL INNOCENCE

Few people see themselves as initiators of cruelty. Instead, we view ourselves as reactors —we react to the misdeeds of others. After forming the perception that we have been treated badly, then our own unkind behavior seems justified. But it is difficult to believe that we all could be such innocents. If this were the case, who is it that is starting all the trouble in the world? This universal perception of innocence suggests the extent to which our views of the world are personal and subjective. It has often been said that we are locked in our own experiential realities, and with regard to the exchange of hostilities, this is often true.

MOTIVATIONS FOR ABUSE

Verbal attacks have three main outcomes: hurting the partner's feelings, putting oneself in a dominant, accusatory position, and creating an emotional scene. Hurting the partner is presumably satisfying because it repays a perceived wrong. Taking the dominant position is often enjoyable, but more so for some than for others. Psychoanalytic theorists speculate that for those who feel weak, insecure, or in doubt about their own personal powers, dominance holds a special attraction. For others, gaining a position of dominance is not so important. Finally, individuals may initiate a verbal attack out of sheer boredom. After all, having an argument is a way of getting a reaction out of the partner and feeling *something* intensely, even if it is unpleasant.

This analysis suggests a way of evaluating alternative responses to verbal abuse. According to social learning theory, responses that nullify the expected outcomes of abuse should extinguish further abusive behaviors. Thus alternative responses can be compared as to how they affect revenge, dominance, and emotional activation.

What are these alternative responses? They include disputing the truth of the accusation, making counteraccusations, silence, **metacommunication** (i.e., commenting on the form or implied meaning of an accusation), and, strange as it may sound, agreement with the accuser.

DISPUTATION

Jay Haley (1959) devised a number of innovative strategies for the "art of one-upsmanship," that is, controlling the dominant position in a conversation. He maintains that although initiating an attack puts you in the one-up position, defending against an attack is one-down. Essentially, attack and defense interactions take the form:

> You did.
> No I didn't.
> Yes you did.
> No I didn't. . . .

In such an interaction, the person denying an accusation has little hope of regaining the dominant position. There always seems to be an area of doubt as to whether the accusation is at least partially true, and this puts the defender on uneasy ground. In addition, presenting a defense in some way legitimizes the attack. In effect, it says that the attack is at least believable enough to justify a defensive effort. Thus, disputation is defensive and therefore submissive; it is argumentative, thereby creating an opportunity for emotional release for the attacker; and it offers little protection for hurt feelings resulting from malicious accusations. Despite its ineffectiveness, this is the most common strategy for dealing with verbal attack (Elgin, 1983).

COUNTERACCUSATION

Counteraccusation has the advantage of refusing to take the one-down position. It is relatively strong in terms of dominance, especially if you have a good counteraccusation with supporting evidence. Where this strategy fails, however, is in terms of positive affect. Counteraccusations, especially if you win the battle for negative dominance, may irreparably damage the relationship and perhaps earn an enemy for life. Moreover, these negative encounters can create tremendous stress. Thus, counterattack may upset the attacker's bid for dominance but it does not prevent hurting your feelings and creating an unpleasant emotional scene.

SILENCE

Silence can be an effective response. It conveys a complete refusal to enter into an exchange with the verbal attacker. With silence, the nonverbal message becomes particularly important. Silence with a facial display of contempt, for example, is highly effective for dealing with verbal attack, but it constitutes an extreme put-down. As such, it is likely to damage the relationship and create an enemy. Moreover, if the attacker asks a question, the refusal to answer may be perceived as unfair. In selecting a nonverbal response to accompany the silence, one must avoid lowering the head, averting the eyes, and upturning the lip midline. This will be perceived as pouting, which is rarely a viable response. In sum, silence is dominant or submissive depending on body language; it avoids an argument; and it may leave you with hurt feelings, depending on your attitude toward the attack. If you perceive the attack as so ridiculous that it is truly not worth responding to, your feelings are not likely to be damaged. If you are only feigning this attitude, however, that is a different matter.

METACOMMUNICATION

According to Elgin (1983), verbal attacks must be differentiated from blunt and tactless honesty, in which there is no intent to harm. Honest disclosures are usually made directly, without stressing key words. Elgin maintains that verbal attacks always emphasize key words, by increasing their loudness and pitch. For example, "Everyone understands why you're flunking out" may convey a straightforward description of people's perceptions. "Everyone under*stands* why you're flunking out" is a verbal attack.

Verbal attacks typically contain an explicit accusation (the "bait"), to which the listener is expected to respond, and one or more implicit accusations embedded in the structure of the attacking sentence. Usually the bait is so unfair that it cannot be resisted. If you take the bait and try to dispute the explicit accusation, however, you will be accepting the implicit accusations by default. Moreover, since the bait is often outrageously false, the implicit accusations are actually the ones of greater significance. Thus disputation often leads to superficial, pointless, and unresolvable arguments. For example:

Jan: *If you really loved me, you wouldn't desert me by going out tonight.*

Jim: *I'll go out if I want to. Who do you think you are, anyway?*

Jim's response will likely lead to a fruitless and bitter argument, as his response fails to recognize the implied accusation, "you don't really love me." Thus the claim that he doesn't love her has implicitly been accepted! In Jan's mind, she now has a right to feel hurt and to seek revenge if he does go out. Metacommunication involves ignoring what appears to be the obvious content of the attack and responding instead to its implicit message. A possible response might be, "You seem to be assuming that I do not love you. That is not true; I love you very much. I'll see you in a couple of hours."

Another possible response for Jim might be, "When did you start feeling that I don't love you?" This response is a legitimate request for specific evidence. It is almost always easier to deal with a specific instance than with a global accusation.

Let's try another verbal attack. "You *know* I'd never do anything to hurt you, but don't you think you should stop going out with a girl like her?" This question implies that I would hurt you and I am hurting you; I have a right to tell you who to date; your girl friend is not an acceptable person; and I am so nice and polite that you should not get mad at me for saying this. It is amazing how much can be packed into a few words! One possible reply is, "I'm aware that you don't approve of her, but I'll have to make my own decisions about who to go out with." This response is straightforward and to the point. If the attacker continues after that, you can use the so-called broken-record technique and simply repeat your response. After two or three rounds of this, it will become perfectly clear that there is no way to lure you into a pointless argument.

Metacommunication is an effective and often-underused response. Note, however, that it must be delivered without agitation or sarcasm, for otherwise it would constitute a counterattack. In sum, metacommunication allows you to control the dominant position; it avoids arguments on unproductive topics; and it provides some protection for one's feelings by redirecting the discussion away from name calling.

AGREEMENT WITH THE ATTACKER

Haley (1959) made an important contribution to the study of dominance by pointing out that paradoxically, one of the strongest options available is to agree nondefensively with whatever truth there is to the accusation. After all, only a person who is clearly dominant and totally self-confident would feel free to admit error. This is a response that is honest, easy to use, and surprisingly powerful. It defuses the attack, puts you in the dominant position, and reconciles you with the attacker. Moreover, after such a response, the attacker will often imitate your behavior and admit his or her own contributions to the problem.

Some people, however, may feel uncomfortable with agreement. They may feel that it seems submissive or makes them vulnerable to the attacker. In fact, just the opposite is the case. The refusal to admit error is immediately recognized as a sign of insecurity. There is no point in pretending that you're perfect. No one would believe it, even if it were true. That is why the strategy of agreement is so powerful. It is im-

portant, however, that the agreement be made comfortably, and with the clear implication that this admission in no way compromises one's self-acceptance.

The strategy of agreement is inherently self-protective. It is when we feel that others' comments are cruel and unjustified that their remarks hurt us most. Once we see the situation from the other person's point of view, we are less threatened by the attack and we can see that his or her behavior, even if uncalled for, typically results from miscommunication and insecurity. Thus we are more likely to feel sorry for our partner than to feel threatened. In sum, the strategy of agreement controls the dominant position, avoids an argument, protects your own feelings, and reconciles you with your partner.

For the following verbal attack, try using a sample response from each of the categories listed above.

"Why are you completely *indifferent* to what your constant selfishness is doing to your poor mother?"

RESOLVING CONFLICT

Contrary to popular opinion, conflict is not the sign of an unhealthy relationship. Conflict can release pent-up emotions and bring individuals to deeper levels of understanding. The crucial variables are how the conflict is expressed and how it is resolved. Conflict, however, is *not* synonymous with name calling, yelling, insults, accusations, and other forms of verbal attack. Obviously, when conflict is expressed with hostility, nothing productive results. But differences can be aired without hostility and without trying to win an argument. In fact, for friendships, the notion of "winning" is counterproductive. In close relationships, either both win or both lose.

Swets (1983) developed a straightforward model of conflict resolution based on four steps:

Define the problem. There can be no

Which indicators of tension and conflict can you identify?

hope for a mutual solution unless both participants agree on what the problem is. Do not simply assume that you understand the problem because you have heard it with your own ears. After listening to your partner, restate the problem in your own words until your partner is satisfied that you understand it.

Look for agreement. Search for whatever there is in your partner's position that you agree with, and then say, "I agree that. . . . " This defuses the argument and reduces the scope of the problem.

Understand feelings. Say, "I understand that you might feel. . . . " Be sure to describe a feeling, not a thought or a behavior. If that is not what your partner is feeling, restate your interpretation until there is consensus.

State your views calmly. Make it clear that they are *your* views and not something that you assume to be an objective truth. Say "I think . . . " or "The way I see it is. . . . " Do not raise your voice. If you cannot deal with the issue calmly at that moment, arrange to discuss it at another time.

As noted in the section on interpersonal behaviors, when feelings are hurt, it is natural to want to strike out and hurt the person we believe is at fault. This is the cycle that must be broken to enable an effective resolution. First, we may be completely wrong about who initiated the hostilities. Second, any attempt at revenge will only lead to reprisals and an escalation of conflict. It is more important and more adaptive to express the feelings of hurt than to seek revenge. Knowing the existence of this cycle and the importance of finding a way to short-circuit it, we now have the tools for defusing conflicts before they become arguments. The sample dialogues below (adapted from Swets, 1983, pp. 147–148) illustrate how this method works.

Discord Exchange

Pam: *Our life isn't going anywhere. The fun and excitement are gone. Here we are— almost forty-five—and what do we have to show for it?*

Art: *Get off it! You've got a new house. You bought a car last year. What the heck are you complaining about?*

Pam: *Well, Susan . . .*

Art: *Susan! All you talk about is Susan! You think she's got it better than you, right? She doesn't even own her home. You know what your problem is. You're going through your change of life!*

Pam: *(Silent anger treatment.)*

Resolution Exchange

Pam: *Our life isn't going anywhere. The fun and excitement are gone. Here we are— almost forty-five—and what do we have to show for it?*

Art: *I hear you saying that it seems like we're on a treadmill.*

Pam: *Yes, especially when I look at Susan's life.*

Art: *Yes, I agree that Susan seems to be happy. What is it about her life that you like?*

Pam: *Susan has so much confidence in herself. She is growing as a person.*

Art: *I understand how you might feel down when comparing yourself with someone who is so self-assured.*

Pam: *It's not that I'm feeling worthless or inadequate. But she's making progress toward what she really wants in life. I don't even know what I want anymore.*

Art: *Yes, I get those feelings too. I think, though, that we need more information before we can figure out what to do. How*

about inviting Susan and her husband over for dinner? We could ask them what their secret is.

Think back to your last argument. Try to remember as much of the dialogue as you can. Was the conversation geared more to generating discord or to resolving conflict? Can you think of a more adaptive response that you could have made at some point in the discussion?

Interpersonal communication occurs in many situations, and serves many purposes. Thus, healthy conversation styles are context dependent. The next section contrasts two ways of engaging in conversations, each having its own advantages and disadvantages.

CONTROLLED AND SPONTANEOUS INTERACTIONS

Talking and listening differ in rate. We can think about four times as fast as another person can talk, and so there is plenty of time for our minds to wander. Typically, they go to thoughts of what we will say next in the conversation: a rebuttal to the partner's argument, a story to top the one she is telling, or perhaps a well-timed compliment to curry his favor. In addition, there is often a fear that when our turn comes to talk, we won't have anything ready to say. We may be left speechless and socially embarrassed. We all are concerned about how we come across in conversations, and so it seems natural for us to spend much of our listening time planning our next response.

As long as your mind is occupied with your next response, however, you are out of contact with what your partner is doing and saying. An alternative conversational strategy is to use the extra time while your partner is talking to listen "between the words." This entails becoming aware of the underlying meanings that the other is conveying by processing subtle cues such as tone of voice, hesitations, word choice, and nonverbal body signals. But what happens when your turn comes to speak? This strategy involves letting the words come out that directly and spontaneously express yourself without trying to select a response based on its calculated effect on your partner.

These two strategies can be traced to the major models of personality. The **controlled strategy** follows a social learning framework in its emphasis on having a goal in mind for the conversation and then selecting behaviors relevant to that goal. Some common conversational goals are getting the partner to like and approve of us, persuading the partner to do what we want, and moving into a position of dominance over the partner. The means to these goals are planning and rehearsing what we will say next. More specifically, we may consider various behavioral options, calculate the likely outcomes of each one, and then select the response with the best chance of attaining our goal.

The controlled strategy can also be linked to the psychoanalytic model, since it assumes that we cannot simply trust ourselves to say whatever comes to mind. Presumably, if we did this, our behavior would often be antisocial, hurtful, and tactless.

The controlled strategy is particularly useful for filtering out tactless or otherwise inappropriate responses. Thus some amount of controlled processing is essential to avoid being unwittingly offensive or boorish. It also works well in conversations that are essentially business contacts. In such conversations, there is little need for spontaneity, but there often is a need for precise and calculated functioning to ensure the occurrence of a desired outcome.

The **spontaneous strategy** is more compatible with the humanistic model. It involves absorbing oneself in the partner's communication and not worrying about what we will say when our turn comes. The assumption is that we can trust ourselves to respond appropriately, that our spontaneous expression doesn't require extensive filtering, and that making contact and

expressing ourselves honestly are more important than winning the partner's approval or trying to get anything "from" him or her. The advantages include making a more complete contact with the other person and enjoying the experience of unfettered self-expression. After all, there is a certain satisfaction, perhaps even an indulgence, in being able to say exactly what you feel without calculating the effect of each phrase or worrying how the other person will take your response. This is why alcohol is a common ingredient of social functions. It relaxes this controlling, evaluative side of ourselves (while at the same time providing an excuse for whatever social blunders may occur).

Which is better, controlled or spontaneous interactions? Obviously, each of these models represents an extreme position, and some combination of the two is desirable. For example, we all know that it is quite easy to hurt another person's feelings through an ill-considered remark, and so some amount of control and filtering are required for mutual protection. On the other hand, the more secure individuals are, the less likely that their feelings will be hurt by a thoughtless comment.

In general, we are so concerned with social approval that most of our interactions are probably too heavily loaded in the direction of controlled communication, and so some movement toward spontaneity would be desirable.

Think back to each of your conversations during the day, and classify them as being more controlled or more spontaneous. Which goals do you typically work for in your more controlled conversations? Think of situations in which controlled communication would be desired in an intimate relationship and in which spontaneous communication would be desired in a business contact.

It is clear that the way we feel about ourselves affects how we communicate with others. This next section examines the communication styles of those who differ on self-esteem.

It also identifies characteristics of healthy, adaptive forms of communication.

COMMUNICATION AND SELF-ESTEEM

LOW SELF-ESTEEM COMMUNICATION STYLES

Self-esteem is often a precondition for effective communication. Without it, we feel unlovable and our lives become a more or less desperate search for safety, security, and the approval of others. Those with low esteem expect and fear rejection, so they devise communication strategies based on self-protection. Revealing themselves — letting others know what they really feel and think — makes them vulnerable. Thus they use language to disguise rather than to reveal, and what is said verbally may be contradicted nonverbally. Low self-esteem also clouds the ability to listen. Constructive comments may be taken as put-downs and immediately denied, limiting possibilities for growth.

Virginia Satir, a family therapist, described four types of communication manifested by those with low self-esteem: placating, blaming, being superreasonable, and being irrelevant.

Placating conveys the message "I'll do anything to please you." But behind this message is the belief that "I must give in so that they will love me." Nonverbally, placaters are pictured as cringing and whining. Note that placaters do not try to please out of a genuine desire to give, but as a strategy for getting on someone's good side. They subordinate themselves to buy their partner's affection. And they can do this only by suppressing their own feelings of resentment. Outwardly, their behavior seems submissive and helpful, but its effect is to control the partner through feelings of guilt and pity. This, in turn, causes the partner to become confused, suspicious, and defensive. Thus contact is avoided on both sides: The actual thoughts and feelings of one person never meet those of the other.

Blaming conveys the message "You blew it again!" The underlying belief is that "If I don't keep on their tails, nothing will get done. And since nobody cares about me, I don't have to care about them." Thus the blamer seeks security by dominating the partner. Nonverbally, the blamer stands tense and erect, pointing the finger of accusation and using a loud, harsh voice to create fear and helplessness in the partner. Blaming and placating often occur together as complementary roles.

Being superreasonable appeals to intellect, logic, external sources of authority, and lengthy verbal explanations to control the interaction and dominate the partner. The underlying belief is that "Feelings don't count; I am not worth much in myself, and so I must show that I am smarter." The partner is made to feel stupid, inferior, and bored. Nonverbally, the face is often held rigid, as a mask, creating a physical appearance that supports the overall denial of emotion. Superreasonable types may or may not actually be intelligent, but they have learned how to use this role to distance and manipulate others.

Being irrelevant involves using tangential comments, rambling, disconnected thoughts, and inane remarks to distract and confuse. Irrelevant people often have very low opinions of themselves. They give up any semblance of logic or consistency, and so they cannot be pinned down or taken seriously. They try to appease the partner by being nonthreatening, and they often use humor, as in playing the "clown," the "air-head," or the "dumb blond." Nonverbally, the irrelevant may seem scattered, unbalanced, or "schizy."

THE COST OF LOW SELF-ESTEEM

Satir claims that 95 percent of us regularly use low self-esteem communication styles but we may not be aware of doing so. These styles are often learned at an early age. Parents may unwittingly direct us toward these styles by not supporting our sense of esteem, by modeling low self-esteem, or by giving us attention only

Placating.

Blaming.

Superreasonable.

Irrelevant.

Virginia Satir's four communicational body poses.

when we display low esteem. After a while, these styles become habitual, so we simply do not attend to how we sound and what we are saying. Also, what we intend to say is often different from what actually comes out of our mouths, and we are in better contact with the intended than with the actual communication. Thus it is helpful to listen for which communication pattern we tend to use and for whether we use different patterns with different people. Once we get some feeling for our actual communicative behavior, we can start thinking about alternative ways to interact.

Maslow and other humanistic psychologists maintain that those low in self-esteem must satisfy their need for esteem before they can go on to other ways of being. Until they do, they must find some way of maintaining a sense of security, no matter what the cost. As we have seen, Satir suggested that this will often entail social behaviors designed to keep the interaction at a level of minimal contact.

When compared with the potentials and possibilities of human interactions, this cost is exorbitant. It means losing contact with your own thoughts and feelings, and forgoing the possibility of real contact with your partner. Spontaneous interaction becomes a threat because it might reveal new information and force us to change rigid beliefs about who we are or who our partner really is. Thus the risk of being spontaneous, open, and expressive seems too great.

Satir described those with low esteem as looking without seeing, listening without hearing, speaking without meaning, moving without awareness, and touching without feeling. According to her, the price is that they are alive, but not really living.

HIGH SELF-ESTEEM AND CONGRUENT COMMUNICATION

When we have high self-esteem, we are freer to explore our world and let others know who we are. There is little need to make ourselves invisible by confusing our partner, and so it is easier to be clear in what we say. We can also be congruent, so that what we are thinking, feeling, saying, and doing all go together, reinforcing the same message. This way of interacting inspires trust and intimacy.

Congruence implies acting from the heart, without conflict, so that what we feel is right coincides with what we think we should be doing. When cognitive and emotional systems are aligned, we can act directly with one purpose, leading to clear and effective communication.

It is ironic that we often enter a state of incongruence when trying to be "good." Being good often involves following rules that we internalized as children. These rules may have been valid for other times and other places, but they are often inappropriate for adults. For example, Ann's parents taught her "never to show anger" because it is crude and unfeminine. But this rule is impossible to follow. Moreover, it is simplistic in not distinguishing between acceptable and unacceptable expressions of anger. Such a rule may have been appropriate for a child, and it may have allowed her parents to handle their discomfort with Ann's childhood outbursts. But it is clearly too simplistic and repressive for her now. As a result of internalizing this rule, feelings of anger have become threatening for Ann, and rather than feel this part of herself, she has adopted the placater role, going out of her way to please others, while suppressing her own feelings of resentment.

ENHANCING SELF-ESTEEM

Self-esteem clearly derives from life experiences, particularly interactions with our parents. But that is now past history. It can't be changed. What can we do to raise our self-esteem now? The first step is to realize that each of us is unique; we are alive on this earth and this is where we belong. We have a right to be here. We have intrinsic value to ourselves. We want to experience our aliveness, maintain ourselves,

and enjoy being who we are. We may or may not have value for others, but we have value to ourselves just because we exist.

One method for enhancing self-esteem is gradually to open ourselves to new possibilities.

Satir (1976) listed what she called the "Five Freedoms":

The freedom to see and hear what is instead of what should be.

The freedom to say what you feel and think, instead of what you think you should be feeling and thinking.

The freedom to feel what you feel instead of what you think you ought to feel.

The freedom to ask for what you want, instead of waiting for permission.

The freedom to take risks instead of always choosing to be "secure."

According to Satir, self-esteem is not the result of attending only to our good points, our successes and our finest moments. It is more a matter of accepting and respecting all that we are. The natural outcome of this attitude is a communication style that is open, spontaneous, expressive, and congruent.

Note that the five freedoms emphasize the theme "be who you are," not "do what you want." Can you see the difference?

Much of the meaning communicated from one person to another derives not from what we say, but from what we do. Psychologists have only begun a systematic investigation of nonverbal communication, but many fascinating discoveries have already come from this work.

COMMUNICATING WITH OUR BODIES

Nonverbal behavior, or body language, refers to the physical actions of our bodies. It includes gross movements such as touching the face or crossing the legs, as well as subtle actions such as pupil dilation and hand tremors. Nonverbal behavior is described as a "language" because it communicates meaning. Also, body movements occur in combinations, qualifying or changing their individual meanings, much as words convey different meanings, depending on their context in a sentence.

NONVERBAL BEHAVIOR AND CONSCIOUS AWARENESS

Verbal and nonverbal behaviors often retain a figure-and-ground relationship. In our culture the verbal information is almost always figure. We are taught to focus on verbal content when someone is speaking. What they are doing with their bodies becomes a background for what is assumed to be the more important, informational part of the interaction. Thus we often don't attend to the body.

It appears that the verbal and nonverbal aspects of communication also serve different functions. Words carry specific information, whereas the body conveys more general attitudes, such as those of liking, dominance, insecurity, and sexual interest.

Because people are consciously attuned to the verbal channel, when we want to deceive someone, we do it with words. Thus when a discrepancy arises between what is said and what is done, the body is likely to be the more reliable channel. Without thinking about it, we apparently realize the importance of body language, for overall message impact is more than 50 percent nonverbal, with the rest carried by tone of voice and words, in that order (Birdwhistle, 1970; Mehrabian, 1971).

Some nonverbal behaviors appear in all cultures. Examples are nodding the head to say yes, shaking the head sideways to say no, and the facial expressions used to convey basic emotions such as joy, fear, disgust, sadness, and anger. Other nonverbals are culture specific, such as the "OK" hand gesture (making a circle with one's thumb and index finger), which, in some Mediterranean cultures, is an orifice symbol indicating homosexuality. Thus care must be taken to interpret body language in its cultural context. For example, compared with Americans, Mediterranean and Middle Eastern people converse at close quarters. Thus in establishing a distance that is normal for them, they are often perceived by Americans as pushy or overly forward.

TABLE **8—1**

ALMOST EVERYTHING YOU EVER WANTED TO KNOW ABOUT
NONVERBAL BEHAVIOR

ATTITUDE	NONVERBAL SIGNS
Confidence	Corresponding right and left finger tips touching, palms apart.
	Head up, chin out, and one palm gripping the other hand behind the back.
	Both hands behind head.
	Blowing smoke upwards.
Seriousness	Gazing toward other's forehead.
Decision Making	Chin stroking.
Evaluative Thinking	Closed hand on cheek.
Dominance	Palms down.
	Handshake with palm pointed off-vertical, toward the ground.
	Thumbs up with hands in pockets or touching self.
Competitive-Argumentative	Legs crossed, ankle on knee.
Arrogance	Head back.
Ridicule	Pointing at another with thumb.
Aggression	Index finger pointed with palms not exposed.
	"Knuckle-grinder" handshake.
	Straddling a chair, back of chair forward.
	Standing with hands on hips (makes one seem bigger).
	Thumbs tucked into belt or pocket.
	Standing at a close distance, feet evenly spread, body pointing directly at partner.
Anger-Hostility	Collar pull.
	Hand slaps back of neck and then rubs neck (literally, "You are a pain in the neck").
	Clenched fist.
	Pupil contraction.
	Staring.
	Sideways glance with eyebrows and corners of mouth turned down.
Disapproval	Picking imaginary lint off one's clothing, eyes averted from speaker.
	Shaking head side to side.
Negative Thoughts	Hand on cheek, index finger pointing up, thumb supporting chin.
	Head down.
Frustration-Holding Back	Hands tightly clenched.
	Hand gripping the wrist or elbow behind the back.
Negative-Defensive-Threatened	Arms crossed (forming a barrier).
	One arm in front of the body, hand touching other arm or hand, wrist, handbag, and the like.
	Legs crossed (a less reliable sign for women, who are often taught to sit this way).
	Ankles crossed.

(continued)

TABLE 8-1

ALMOST EVERYTHING YOU EVER WANTED TO KNOW ABOUT
NONVERBAL BEHAVIOR   *(continued)*

ATTITUDE	NONVERBAL SIGNS
Negative-Defensive-Threatened *(continued)*	Top of foot pressed against calf of other leg. Blowing smoke downwards.
Lying (speaker)	Hand touching or covering mouth.
Doubt (listener)	Rubbing nose, eye, or ear. Neck scratch. Collar pull. Looking away.
Boredom	Using hand to support head.
Impatience	Drumming fingers on table.
Readiness to End a Conversation	Seated, leaning forward, hands on knees or arm rests.
Weak Character	"Dead fish" handshake.
Submission-Nonthreat	Palms up. Stooping forward slightly.
Humbleness	One foot forward, open coat, palms up and exposed, stooping forward.
Error Acknowledgment	Slapping forehead with palm, closing eyes.
Openness-Honesty	Exposing the palms. Two-handed handshake, if partner is known well.
Agreement	Nodding head. Copying other person's gestures (copying a superior's dominance gestures, however, would be "insubordinate").
Positive Expectation	Rubbing palms together.
Money Expectation	Rubbing thumb and index finger together.
Liking	Two-handed handshake, handshake with left hand on partner's elbow or shoulder. (If liking is not reciprocated, this intimacy may be resented.) Tilting head. One foot forward, pointing at partner. Pupil dilation. Legs crossed toward partner.
Sexual Interest (both sexes)	Increased muscle tone, erect posture, chest out. Preening, that is, straightening tie, rearranging shirt, smoothing hair, adjusting coat. Thumbs in belt or pocket. Tilting head. Pointing body and foot at partner. Extended eye contact, pupil dilation, gazing across body. Hands on hips. Sitting with legs spread (usually by males).
Sexual Interest (females)	Tossing head. Exposing palms and inner wrists. Hips roll when walking. Glancing sideways and looking away, eyebrows up.

TABLE 8−1   *(continued)*

ATTITUDE	NONVERBAL SIGNS
Sexual Interest (females) *(continued)*	Mouth slightly open, wet lips. Sitting with one leg tucked under and pointing at partner. Shoe partially off, toes playing with it. Legs crossed, one leg pressed firmly against the other. Stroking part of own body. (Adapted from Pease, 1984)

THE ART AND SCIENCE OF READING BODY LANGUAGE

The study of body language is, at this point, as much art as it is science. Except perhaps for the head gestures for yes and no, each body movement cannot be assigned a specific meaning. In general, body meanings are confined to global attitudes, and gestures convey more than one meaning, depending on the situation. For example, sitting down with your leg crossed in the direction of your partner is often interpreted as a sign of interest. On the other hand, at times it may indicate only that your leg had become temporarily weary from being held too long in its previous position. Thus one must be careful to understand that gestures are merely *signs* of underlying attitudes.

Each attitude is associated with a number of such signs, and because of our idiosyncratic learning histories, individuals differ on which signs they use to express a given attitude. Thus there is no invariant, simplistic translation that allows us to make rules such as "smiles mean happiness and tears mean sadness." There are times when we smile to hide sadness, and times when we're so happy that we cry.

FIGURE 8−2

Nevertheless, a number of signs are associated with particular emotional or attitudinal states (see Table 8−1). If accepted as *hypotheses* rather than invariant rules, a knowledge of these signs can be most useful.

Which nonverbal signs can you identify in Figure 8−2, and how would you interpret their corresponding attitudes?

SUMMARY

1. Even though accurate communication is not common, we tend to assume accuracy unless presented with explicit proof of miscommunication. Some of the factors leading to miscommunication are language

ambiguities, conflicted feelings about what we want to say, the tendency to hear what we want to be true, and an unwillingness to view communication as a skill.

2. Self-disclosure forms the basis for creating friendships, and disclosure modeling is one of the best ways to encourage disclosure in others. Self-disclosure varies in intimacy from cliché to fact to opinion to feeling-level disclosure. Feeling-level disclosure is sometimes avoided because it increases vulnerability and seems inconsistent with business-oriented values of efficiency and self-control.

3. Listening is an important and often underrated communication skill. Ideally, it involves giving prompts and feedback, putting yourself in the other's place, and being nonjudgmental.

4. Questions demand attention and raise the tension level of a conversation. Open-ended questions are usually more adaptive in social conversations. As with disclosures, questions also differ in degree of intimacy.

5. People have different notions of how conversations should be conducted. When one person employs a norm of asking and the other a norm of volunteering, it can lead to problems in the developing relationship.

6. Interpersonal behaviors form a circular ordering that can be described in terms of two dimensions, dominance-submission and positive-negative affect. Dominance from one partner pulls for submission from the other, and vice versa. Positive affect pulls for positive affect in return, and negative affect yields further negative feelings. In male–female interactions, men tend to be conversationally dominant, especially in terms of topic success. One way to control topic dominance is to reenter one's topic, using nonverbal attention-getters, if necessary.

7. Verbal attacks hurt the partner's feelings, put the attacker in a dominant position, and create an emotional scene. Ways of responding to verbal attack include disputation, counteraccusation, silence, metacommunication, and agreement. Although used infrequently, the latter two responses appear to be the most effective.

8. One model for resolving conflict is arriving at a mutual definition of the problem, establishing points of agreement, communicating your understanding of the partner's feelings, and stating your views calmly in a way that makes it clear that these are your views, not objective truths.

9. Interactions differ as to being more controlled or more spontaneous. Controlled interactions are more appropriate to business contacts, whereas spontaneous interactions are more adaptive for friendships.

10. Low self-esteem leads to communication styles of placating, blaming, being superreasonable, and being irrelevant. These styles impair self-knowledge, limit the closeness of personal relationships, and restrict spontaneity. Those with high self-esteem are freer to engage in congruent communication. Self-esteem can be enhanced by giving yourself

permission to perceive the world as it is, instead of as you think it should be.

11. In most conversations, verbal behavior is attended to more consciously than nonverbal behavior. The verbal channel conveys specific information, and the nonverbal carries global attitudes. Each of these attitudes tends to be associated with a number of nonverbal signs, but there is no simplistic translation that allows each sign always to indicate a particular attitude. Thus, as with words, nonverbal behaviors must be interpreted in context. A list of nonverbal signs appears in Table 8–1.

SUGGESTED READINGS

Garner, A. **Conversationally speaking**. New York: McGraw-Hill, 1981. A clear, concise presentation of conversational skills.

Satir, V. **Making contact**. Berkeley, Calif.: Celestial Arts, 1976. A short collection of communicational pointers by a well-known family therapist.

Swets, P. W. **The art of talking so that people will listen**. Englewood Cliffs, N.J.: Prentice-Hall, 1983. Full of practical advice.

LOVE and ATTRACTION   9

Intrigues of the Heart

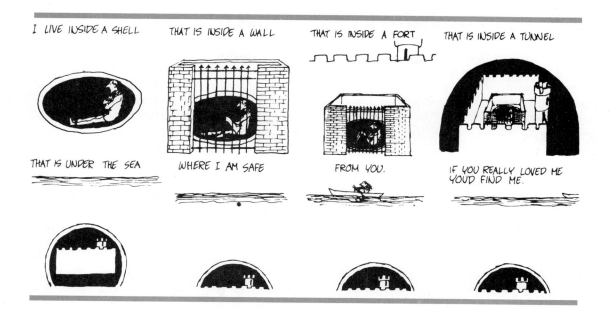

I LIVE INSIDE A SHELL   THAT IS INSIDE A WALL   THAT IS INSIDE A FORT   THAT IS INSIDE A TUNNEL

THAT IS UNDER THE SEA   WHERE I AM SAFE   FROM YOU.   IF YOU REALLY LOVED ME YOU'D FIND ME.

Without a doubt, we are social animals. Friends and lovers form the fabric of our emotional existence. Both the warmth of their acceptance and the chill of their rejection affect us deeply.

Although our need for social contact is great, so are its obstacles. Increasingly, this is becoming an impersonal and efficiency-conscious world. Even though we carefully choose which relationships to invest in, half of all marriages now end in divorce. Every day the news media remind us that ours is a dangerous world, that strangers cannot be trusted. In addition, we are highly mobile, moving, on the average, every six years. Thus our social ties are being continually uprooted. Vance Packard aptly labeled us a nation of strangers. Especially in urban areas, we often feel cut off and alienated from those around us; we lack a sense of community. Many psychologists believe the solution to this problem lies in expanding our ability to love.

This chapter explores the full spectrum of love and attraction, from initial contact to the height of romantic love to the sobering reality of love gone cold. Questions to be explored include, What are the most effective ways to approach and make contact with the opposite sex? What are the different types of love? Does love last? Is romantic love a good basis for marriage? How does love change over time? What constitutes a healthy form of love?

MAKING CONTACT

FIRST MEETINGS AS SCREENING DEVICES

Consider a typical contact attempt. Curt and Joyce, two single parents, have previously been introduced and are now getting a chance to talk after a PTA meeting. Notice the discrepancies between what they are thinking and how they present themselves. Also note that each one's interest in the other is somehow never communicated.

Curt: *"You certainly look great tonight, hair all done up and everything."* [With those clothes, you must get good alimony.]

Joyce: *"Thank you, sir. I had it done for an appointment tomorrow." [I did it myself, and for you.] "I like your jacket."*

Curt: *"Thanks, I bought it to go with my car." [Damn, clothes conscious, too.]*

Joyce: *"Oh? What kind of car?" [Must be a sports car.]*

Curt: *"Little Panther roadster." [That should give me a few points.]*

Joyce: *"I seem to remember riding in one last summer when I was in France." [You don't have to know that my in-laws paid for the trip.]*

Curt: *"Wish I could get away more, but with my job there's always something." [The jet-set type. Out of my league.]*

Joyce: *"Oh? What do you do?" [I don't want you to know I asked around and already know you're a lawyer. Anyway, I'm wasting my time. What would you see in a dull housewife like me?] (Adapted from Bach & Deutsch, 1970, pp. 121–122)*

As can be seen in this dialogue, initial encounters often act as a screening device for "sizing up" the other person. The task in this screening is to compare social assets and see if there is enough in common to justify starting a relationship. As part of this task, Murstein (1980) suggested that the initial encounter involves:

1. Finding an opener to engage the other's attention. (Curt started with a compliment.)
2. Finding a topic of interest to both parties to keep the conversation going. (Curt's car, Curt's job.)
3. Determining whether the other has characteristics that would make a future contact worthwhile. (Curt actively sought clues to whether he earned enough money to be "in her league." In preparing for this meeting, Joyce had already sought out the information she desired by asking about his job.)
4. Determining whether the other person is "taken," or committed to someone else.

(This topic was not broached, but each apparently already knew that the other was unmarried.)

5. Presenting yourself as an interested, rewarding person so that the other will continue the interaction and be receptive to a future encounter if you decide that that is what you want. (Curt began by complimenting Joyce's appearance; Joyce returned the compliment and expressed interest in both of Curt's topic initiatives. However, consistent with the discussion of topic control in Chapter 8, Curt did not follow up on Joyce's sole initiative, her trip to France.)
6. Scheduling a second meeting if the other person passes the screening. (Curt and Joyce both faltered on this point. Because both presented such desirable images of themselves, and because both were actually so insecure—Curt about his lack of wealth and Joyce because of her "dullness"—there appeared to be no basis for setting up a second meeting, despite the presence of mutual attraction.

Note that Murstein's model gives a goal-oriented view of initial encounters. The task is to maximize one's long-term rewards by attempting to influence the other person's behavior. Specifically, both Curt and Joyce tried to present themselves in a way calculated to elevate their social status. Curt steered the conversation toward mentioning his sports car and the importance of his job. Joyce implied that she already had an active social life, plus considerable wealth. In addition, she hid the extent of her interest in him.

In its emphasis on planning a strategy for maximizing anticipated rewards, Murstein's view follows social learning theory. Along these lines, point 5 is intriguing. It suggests that until you decide whether to seek a second encounter, it might be advantageous to lead your partner into believing that you are more interested than you actually are, as a way of keeping your options open. As we shall see, the analysis of couples' "love letters" suggests that this strategy is also used in serious dating relationships.

FIRST MEETINGS AS GENUINE ENCOUNTERS

In addition to the goal-oriented, social learning point of view, it is also possible to see first meetings from a more humanistic perspective. Here, the focus would be on spontaneously expressing whatever thoughts and feelings come to mind during the encounter, as long as these are not grossly inappropriate. Instead of anticipating future rewards, the main point would be to enjoy yourself in the encounter without trying to affect or manipulate the other person's reaction.

Bach and Deutsch (1970) developed an extreme form of this approach designed to create immediate impact and intimacy. They maintain that most of us are afraid to risk revealing who we are, what we want, and how we feel. Instead, we hide behind cute lines, drop the names of impressive people and places, and talk about the past rather than what is happening in the moment. In response, our partner also becomes guarded and defensive. The result is a stale conversation that allows us to learn little about ourselves or the other person. Here is their strategy for high impact:

1. *Express a feeling.* Draw out other people by expressing your feelings rather than by interviewing them or describing the roles that you play in society. A man, for example, might tell a woman what specifically attracts him to her, how he is affected by the way she is behaving at this moment, how he feels about the way she is responding to what he is saying, and what his hopes are for the encounter.
2. *Stick to immediate, here-and-now feelings* rather than describing experiences from the past.
3. *Avoid playing a game,* that is, saying something not because that is what you

have to say at that moment but because you have calculated that it will have a desired effect on the other person. In other words, no manipulation.

4. *Ask for permission* before offering your guesses or impressions of other people.
5. *No unchecked assumptions.* Don't make assumptions about what another person is thinking or feeling without immediately checking out those assumptions with that person.
6. *Interpret their behavior.* With the other's permission, tell them what you think their behavior toward you might mean.
7. *Give reservations.* With the other's permission, introduce a reservation that you have about the other person or the relationship. As noted above, we often suppress reservations for fear of discouraging the other person. This keeps our options open: We keep others interested by allowing them to think that our feelings are only positive. Meanwhile, we have time to decide whether we want to continue the relationship. Bach and Deutsch consider this manipulation.
8. *Request reservations.* Ask others for their reservations about you.

For Bach and Deutsch, the irony of goal-oriented interactions is that the real people we actually are will almost always be more attractive and interesting than the cardboard characters we portray. Thus, they believe that a strategy of high impact will often be both more satisfying and more effective. Note, however, that this approach is not strictly humanistic if immediate feelings are used for a premeditated end — impact. The alternative is to express immediate feelings while experiencing them as an end in themselves, not as a way of getting someone to like you. Admittedly, this is a fine line, but, for humanistic psychologists, an important one.

High impact interactions require a certain level of personal and social awareness. We must be aware of our own feelings, aware of what we want from the other person, aware of what the other is doing in the interaction, and aware of how we react to what the other is doing. Thus this approach both requires and fosters social sensitivity.

The strategy of high impact is illustrated in a second conversation between Curt and Joyce, compiled from fragments of a talk they had during an "impacting" workshop.

Curt: *I guess the strongest feeling that I have right now is that I'm glad of this excuse to talk with you, Joyce, and I'm — a little nervous about it too.*

Joyce: *Why should you be nervous?*

Curt: *I'm attracted to you now, as I was at the PTA, and I'm nervous because I'm afraid I won't really be able to get to you. I think I'm attracted to the way a beautiful woman like you is really a little shy. I like the way you drop your glance when you catch me staring at you. See what I mean? You're starting to do it right now. May I ask you a question about yourself?*

Joyce: *Yes, go ahead.*

Curt: *Are you a little shy because you're curious about me?*

Joyce: *Well, yes. Yes I am, a little. I've noticed you staring at me, and I wonder why. Of course (smiling), you drop your eyes, too, whenever I catch you looking at me.*

Curt: *I'm wondering how you react to that.*

Joyce: *Oh, I think it's kind of cute.*

Curt: *Joyce, may I give you a reservation I have about you, and about us?*

Joyce: *Yes, you may.*

Curt: *Well, I'm afraid you may be out of my league. You're so well dressed, and the places you've been. I'm afraid I'd be dull for you.*

Joyce: *I'm very flattered. You see, the truth is I'm sort of scraping along. I make all my own clothes.*

Curt: *Still, you seem so sophisticated. I just went to a country law school.*

Joyce: *I never finished the country college I went to. I married, instead. My husband was a navy pilot, and I lost him in Vietnam.*

Curt: *Oh, I see. (pause) Joyce, I'm wondering about your reservations about me.*

Joyce: *The truth is, I knew from talking to others that you have an important job, and though I was interested in you, I thought to myself, what could he possibly see in a dull housewife with kids?*

Curt: *I'll be darned.*

What do you think of impacting? Do you think it would work in everyday conversations? Does it seem too risky? Remember, one outcome of impacting is intimacy. When that is not desired, impacting may be inappropriate. Although the immediacy of impacting suggests that it does provide a promising alternative to the more typical, "screening" interactions, some cautions must be considered. First, there is no research evidence showing it to be more effective than screening, and second, one must be careful not to bombard the partner with intimate disclosure too early in a relationship. Research indicates that this can lead to negative partner reactions (Strassberg et al., 1977; Wortman et al., 1976).

We have identified two strategies for thinking about an initial encounter. (Notice that these two strategies correspond to the controlled and spontaneous forms of communication described in Chapter 8.) The humanistic view is that you can trust yourself to be spontaneous and that in fact many people will respond more positively to you when you are spontaneous. The social learning view suggests that you can be more effective if you use your cognitive abilities to plan and control your social behavior.

How would you behave differently under these two strategies? Which more closely corresponds to what you usually do in a first encounter? Which do you think is the more desirable strategy for you? Does it depend on the type of encounter? Is there any way that you could combine these strategies? Try to use each of these two strategies in the next week and experience their different effects.

FOCUS

PICK-HER-UPPERS: THE OPENING LINE

In a short piece entitled "How Not to Pick Up a Woman," Rice (1981) summarized some of the research conducted by psychologist Chris Kleinke. Kleinke polled hundreds of students and then compiled a list of one hundred most popular opening lines. He then had another group of students rate each one on a scale running from "terrible" to "excellent."

Certainly, the opening lines of a dating encounter can be crucial. First, this may be the only chance you get. Second, relationships are being defined right from the moment of first contact. This is your chance to engage the other's interest and define the encounter as potentially romantic. Because of this, many men use lines that are sassy, cute, or flip, such as "Your place or mine?"

Kleinke found that most men underestimate how much women are put off by this approach. In addition to "Your place or mine?" some of the other worst openers were "Is that really your hair?" "You remind me of a woman I used to date." "Let me see your strap marks" (at the beach). "Do you really eat that junk?" (at the supermarket). And "Bet I can outdrink you" (at a bar).

Kleinke found that most men and women preferred a direct or innocuous approach. Some of the top-rated openers were "I feel a little embarrassed, but I'd like to meet you." "The water is beautiful today, isn't it?" (at the beach). "Can you help me decide here? I'm a terrible shopper" (at a supermarket). "What do you think of the band?" (at a bar).

PREDICTORS OF ATTRACTION

In general, current research suggests that we like people who reward us and dislike those who punish us (Berscheid & Walster, 1978). As can be seen below, rewards that others provide can take many forms.

PHYSICAL ATTRACTIVENESS

In first meetings between males and females, physical attractiveness appears to be a better predictor of initial attraction and dating interest than personality, similarity of interests, or intelligence. Moreover, attractive people are often assumed to have better personalities and to be more successful, happier, more sensitive, and sexually warm (Berscheid & Walster, 1978; see Chapter 12 for more on physical attractiveness).

SIMILARITY

A great deal of evidence indicates that we are attracted to those with similar attitudes and values. Meeting someone who agrees with us presumably reinforces our sense of being correct and thus supports a sense of security. Being with someone who shares our interests also reduces friction over incompatible desires. In addition, individuals often select as partners and mates those who are similar to them in physical attractiveness and overall level of mental health (Walster et al., 1978).

COMPLEMENTARITY

Although the evidence for opposites attracting each other isn't nearly as strong as that for similarity, there is reason to believe that complementarity does sometimes play a role in

According to psychologist Chris Kleinke, men underestimate how much women are put off by opening lines that are sassy, cute, or flip.

attraction. For example, relationships between those with traditional gender roles appear to be based on differences between the sexes. The man is traditionally dominant, logical, and competent in dealing with the outside world; the woman is traditionally submissive, emotional, and competent in running the home. Each has characteristics that complement the other's, making the couple-unit more viable than either individual would be alone.

PROXIMITY

Those who are geographically close have greater opportunities for getting to know one another and are more likely to become friends, lovers, and spouses. For example, Festinger and associates (1951) examined patterns of friendship formation in a housing development for married students. Distance between houses was a strong predictor of friendships.

RECIPROCITY OF LIKING

We like those whom we think like us. This suggests that one of the most effective ways of getting others to like us is by showing our liking for them. In addition to simply saying, "I like you," this can be done by offering praise, social approval, and flattery and by choosing to spend time with the other person (Clore & Byrne, 1974). The effects of displayed liking are especially powerful when the other person's self-esteem is low (Walster, 1965).

POSITIVE EMOTIONS AND THE REDUCTION OF NEGATIVE EMOTIONS

We like those who are associated with positive emotions or with easing feelings of loneliness, fear, or stress. For example, Veitch and Griffitt (1976) had students in a waiting room hear a radio news broadcast that was either upbeat or depressing. Those hearing the positive news showed greater liking for a new acquaintance.

We all know that attraction sometimes leads to love. But there is a great diversity in love experiences, and love, itself, seems to have a quality that makes it elusive and hard to define. The next section tries to bring some order to this area by identifying the basic dimensions of the love experience.

THE COMPONENTS OF LOVE

THE NATURAL LANGUAGE OF LOVE

Have you ever wondered whether you were really in love? One of the things that makes love so confusing is the number of terms for describing variations in the love experience. "Is it really love?" Well, maybe it's lust. Perhaps intense liking. On the other hand, it could be (take your pick) infatuation, puppy love, romantic love, platonic love, philia (friendship love), agape (spiritual love), eros (physical love), passionate love, companionate love, head-over-heels in love, or true and everlasting love. The sheer number of descriptors indicates the importance of love to our society. Unfortunately, there are no objective criteria for defining each type of love, and so what might be puppy love for one could be true love for another. As a result, lovers

repeatedly, and often regretfully, assume that each means the same thing when they tell each other, "I love you."

THE MEASUREMENT OF LOVE

Rubin (1970) devised scales for measuring love and liking. He found that couples who scored high on the love scale spent more time gazing into each other's eyes than did those with low love scores. Driscoll and associates (1972) developed a measure of romantic love and used it to demonstrate the so-called Romeo and Juliet effect. The more parents objected to and interfered with the relationship, the stronger the love became.

Critelli et al. (1986) combined the Rubin and Driscoll items with new items dealing with, for example, romantic idealization, relationship quality, and physical arousal. All items were given to a large sample of dating couples and factor analyzed. This procedure uses the correlations among items to identify a small number of underlying dimensions. This analysis found five components of love: dependency, romantic compatibility, physical arousal, communicative intimacy, and respect.

Dependency emphasizes the importance of the relationship, how much the partner is needed, the exclusivity of love, and how much one's happiness depends on a particular partner.

Romantic compatibility combines an idealization of the relationship (putting the partner "on a pedestal") with themes of mood similarity, harmonious interaction, total need satisfaction, and complete contentment.

Physical arousal fits Berscheid's and Walster's (1978) emphasis on feeling romantic, sexually aroused, passionate, and physically attracted to the partner.

Communicative intimacy involves feelings of being understood, having a solid relationship, and being able to really communicate and confide in the partner. It reflects some of the elements that Maslow (1971) and Fromm (1956) viewed as essential to healthy love.

Respect emphasizes viewing the partner as mature, well adjusted, recommendable, and as having good judgment.

THE COMPONENT SCALES

The Critelli and colleagues (1986) love scales are presented below. For each item, indicate your level of agreement or disagreement:

1	2	3	4	5
Disagree	Tend to disagree	Neither agree nor disagree	Tend to agree	Agree

1. My relationship with _____ is more important than anything for me.

2. It would be hard for me to get along without _____.

3. _____ is the only real love for me.

4. I need _____.

5. My friendship with _____ is more important to me than anything else.

6. One of my primary concerns is _____'s welfare.

7. If I could never be with _____, I'd feel miserable.

8. I feel that _____ understands me well.

9. _____ and I have a very solid relationship.

10. _____ is someone I can really communicate with.

11. I feel that I can confide in _____ about virtually everything.

12. _____ is the person I would be most likely to talk to if I had a problem.

13. I find _____ very easy to get along with.

14. _____ and I have very similar values.

15. I feel very romantic about _____.

16. I get very sexually aroused when kissing _____.

17. My feelings for ＿＿ are often highly passionate.

18. I spend a good deal of my time just thinking about ＿＿ .

19. When I see ＿＿ , my first reaction is one of excitement.

20. I often notice my heart beating faster or other physical signs of excitement when I'm around ＿＿ .

21. I am very physically attracted to ＿＿ .

22. In my opinion, ＿＿ is an exceptionally mature person.

23. I think that ＿＿ is unusually well adjusted.

24. I would highly recommend ＿＿ for a responsible job.

25. I have great confidence in ＿＿ 's good judgment.

26. I know I could count on ＿＿ for anything if I needed help.

27. I think that ＿＿ is one of those people who quickly wins respect.

28. Most people would react favorably to ＿＿ after a brief acquaintance.

29. As long as I'm with ＿＿ , happiness will be inevitable.

30. When I'm with ＿＿ , we almost always are in the same mood.

31. ＿＿ fulfills all my needs for love, affection, friendship, and security.

32. ＿＿ and I do not disagree on important matters.

33. I think that ＿＿ and I are quite similar to one another.

34. Because I have ＿＿ , I am not attracted to members of the opposite sex.

35. I could never hate ＿＿ .

Each component scale contains seven items, with the first seven forming the dependency scale, the next seven communicative intimacy, and then physical arousal, respect, and romantic compatibility, in that order. Sum the items for each scale. The average scores for these scales, based on a sample of couples who had been dating for about one year, were, in order: 26, 29, 28, 29, and 24, with two-thirds of the people scoring within five points of the average (Bissett, 1983).

It can readily be seen that these components can combine in various ways to represent many of the types of love described in our natural language. In addition, three types of love have received particular attention in the psychological literature. Romantic love appears to consist of dependency, physical arousal, and romantic compatibility. Companionate love includes communicative intimacy, respect, and dependency. And what humanistic theorists have characterized as a healthy or psychologically optimal love may be represented by communicative intimacy, respect, and physical arousal. (Each of these three types will be considered in detail later.)

Think about the most serious love relationship you have had, and try to characterize your own and your partner's feelings in terms of these five components. Did you each have the same type of love for each other? Does there seem to be any connection between the types of love experienced and what actually happened in the relationship?

In the next few sections we shall examine the two major forms of male–female love that have been identified in our culture. After that,

FOCUS

LOVE LETTERS AND SELECTIVE COMMUNICATION

A central belief for many lovers is, "We tell each other everything." Other sources (Blumberg, 1972; Critelli & Neumann, 1976), however, suggest that evaluative information about another is rarely communicated directly to that person. Critelli (1977) studied this phenomenon by having dating partners write love letters to each other. Half of the couples were told that their partner would read the letter, and half were told that the partner would not.

The letters were surprisingly candid, and they often revealed a great difference between what partners had led each other to believe and what was actually the case. For example, consider the following two letters from the same couple, written under the condition that the partner would not read the letter:

Dear Jane,

I like you and we get along pretty good. . . . Right now, you're the only girl I really like but I don't know if I should have gotten involved with just one person. But, I enjoy being with you and appreciate you cooking for me. . . .

You have sometimes said that I don't care about you or our relationship. This is only partially true as the idea of being completely involved with only one person lingers in my mind so I don't try to give myself up completely to you. Don't get me wrong. I do care, but not to the degree you think I should. . . .

I think you're intelligent, clever, cute, well built, thoughtful, and a good cook. You cry too often, but I understand what you have gone through and also that you are sensitive. I like spending my time with you, probably more than I used to, but not more than when we first went out. . . .

Overall, things have been good, and I enjoy being with you. It's hard to say if we'll ever get married, but it is a possibility. Until then, let's enjoy one another.

Jane's letter is as follows:

Dear Jack,

I really think we have had our share of good times and bad times and that the best way for each of us to go would be in opposite directions. Since you have moved into the same building I live in I feel trapped and it is not a good feeling.

I feel like you are looking for a "mother image" in a girl which probably has come from the fact that you have been spoiled by your mother. . . .

We seem to have a good time when we go out but we always do what you want to do. . . .

I really feel you are a person with many good qualities for the business world but for having a relationship with a girl these are not necessary always. . . . The whole time we have gone out you have never surprised me or done anything "out of your way" for me. When I have gotten upset you don't listen to what I say — you really are rude. . . .

You love to hear me compliment you but you rarely do so to me. . . .

You have been very nice in taking me out but you never have let me forget that you have spent money on me. . . .

For some reason, though, we are still going out together (probably because it's nice knowing you have someone to date and sleep with) and even though I have these feelings I never let you know — so I have no reason to complain. . . .

I really think that by the end of this semester we will have parted. For two months in the beginning I really thought we were meant for each other until we really got to know each other.

An analysis of the sample of letters showed that those in the "will not read" condition were more unfavorable toward the partner, suggesting that negative feelings and reservations about the relationship are often kept from the other person. In effect, this strategy keeps the partner "on the line" while the other is deciding whether he or she wants the relationship to continue.

Females were more emotionally involved in the relationship than were males. At the same time, they underestimated the number of unfavorable statements in their own letters and overestimated the favorableness of their partner's letter to them. Males believed that their partner cared more; females perceived no difference in caring.

One interpretation is that the males accurately perceived the females' greater involvement while females overestimated the males' involvement. Females may have protected themselves by distorting their perceptions of the males' love. Although this strategy may reduce anxiety in the short run, it means losing contact with the partner's actual feelings and intentions, and thus it may increase long-term risk.

we shall discuss their implications for modern relationships. But first, to understand modern romantic love, we must go back to medieval times.

ROMANTIC LOVE

A BRIEF HISTORY

In our own culture, love, sex, and marriage are so closely intertwined that it almost seems that they were made to go together. But in truth, their convergence is relatively recent. Although sex and marriage have always gone together, neither love and marriage, nor love and sex have consistently been linked throughout history. In ancient Greece, for example, love between spouses was almost unthinkable. Women were uneducated and considered inferior to men. Thus men sought emotionally satisfying relationships with their equals, other men, not with their wives.

Courtly love. Most historians trace modern romantic love to the flowering of courtly love in the Middle Ages. In those times, marriage was a social and economic transaction — love had nothing to do with it. Courtly love emerged largely as a masculine invention in the 1100s and flourished outside marriage among the European nobility. It consisted of emotional exultation, adoration, and intense pursuit of the loved one. A gallant knight, love struck at the sight of a fair lady, might court her for years just to win a sign of her favor.

Courtly love flowered among the chivalrous knights of the Middle Ages.

Courtly love was based on the sublimation of carnal desire into worthy causes and service to a lady of nobility. It was often carried out from afar, and the lady might not even be aware of the knight's passions. The chastity and distance between lovers, of course, made courtly love an impossibility for spouses. And although this love was predominantly asexual, the partners were not celibate. Both were often married to other people, and lower-class women were readily available for the knight's sexual release. The knight's lady, however, was reserved for the tender admiration of her gentleness and refinement.

In contrast with marriages, which were arranged, courtly love was freely chosen. Troubadours and minstrels toured the countryside, recounting the delights of a spontaneous and idealistic love. They sang of how esteem for the lady inspired feats of combat and fortitude. In this way, the male was ennobled through self-sacrifice and pure thought: Love raised him from a loutish brute to the heights of gentility.

Eventually, courtly love became stylized (Murstein, 1974). Initially the love-struck knight would worship from afar. If given a sign of favor, he would enter the stage of courtship, during which he wrote songs and poems in the lady's honor, proved his valor in battle, or embarked on a long and difficult crusade. The last stage of courtly love was admittance to the lady's private chambers, though perhaps only for a kiss or an embrace. Apparently the lady's husband permitted the flirtation up to the point of physical contact. But as the husband was often a powerful lord, the last stage of courtship often carried with it great danger, and this is presumably part of what made it so tantalizing.

One of the most famous troubadours was Ulrich von Lichtenstein, who courted a married princess for fifteen years. The magnitude of Ulrich's sacrifice for love was both awesome and bizarre. For example, he let her rip out handfuls of his hair; he cut off his finger and sent it to her in a velvet case; and he went from Venice to Vienna in a series of bloody tournaments, breaking over three hundred lances in battle. Finally, she consented to see him in private, to bestow her favor upon him. And as might be expected, the romance ended soon after.

Courtly love was a triumph of cognition. *Ideas* of the woman as a special being, worthy of sacrifice and devotion, fueled the emotions. Such ideal images could not be sustained in the day-to-day contact of marriage. As a result, love and marriage operated in separate realms.

Love and marriage. The view that love should precede marriage appeared in the 1500s and has slowly increased in popularity. In our own culture, love is now almost universally viewed as *the* precondition for marriage. But some experts suggest that this may have reached its peak in the 1950s. West (1982), for example, claimed that the romanticism of the 1940s and 1950s was fed by war, which raised insecurity and enhanced the value of relationships. She argued that the 1960s diluted love by proclaiming it nonexclusive. "The flower children loved everyone . . . which meant they loved no one in particular" (p. 147). West described the 1970s as the age of "emotional lockjaw" in which the me generation looked inward to find themselves and romantic love went dormant. In contrast, the 1980s are experiencing a return to romantic love and traditional values of monogamy and commitment.

ROMANTIC LOVE—WHAT IS IT?

Romantic love, falling in love, passionate love, and limerence describe the same basic phenomenon. The work of love researchers (Driscoll, Davis, & Lipetz, 1972; Rubin, 1973; Tennov, 1979) can be combined to define **romantic love** as an intense state of positive affect

often characterized by absorption, longing, dependency, sexual attraction, exclusiveness, and idealization of the partner.

A key feature of romantic love is the intensity of its *positive affect*. Romantic love is physically arousing and highly emotional. There is also often a confusion of feelings, rapid mood swings, and alternations of feeling between tenderness and sexual desire, ecstasy and pain.

Absorption refers to the continual intrusive thinking, daydreaming, and talking about the partner that tends to crowd out other relationships and everyday concerns. In extreme cases, this absorption can become a full obsession (see FOCUS: John Hinckley: The Lovesick Assassin).

Longing refers to a persistent desire to be with the partner. Note, however, that romantic love does not necessarily imply actually spending much time with the partner or knowing the partner very well, merely the desire and intent to do so.

Dependency refers to the need for emotional support from the loved one, the desire for the loved one to reciprocate one's love and fulfill one's needs. Because of this dependency, the lover is incomplete and unhappy without the partner. If a cooling of the partner's passions is

FOCUS

JOHN HINCKLEY: THE LOVESICK ASSASSIN

March 30, 1981. John Hinckley, Jr., gunned down a U.S. president to impress a woman. Hinckley fell in love with actress Jodie Foster after seeing *Taxi Driver*, a movie in which she portrayed a twelve-year-old prostitute. Below are excerpts from an unmailed letter to Foster that Hinckley wrote just minutes before he shot down President Reagan in front of the Washington Hilton:

Dear Jodie:
      There is a definite possibility that I will be killed in my attempt to get Reagan. . . . By sacrificing my freedom and possibly my

Jodie Foster as a twelve-year-old prostitute in the movie Taxi Driver.

suspected, misery and depression will often ensue.

Sexual attraction to the loved one presumably provides the physiological basis for romantic love's arousal and emotion. Thus lovers often experience physiological changes on seeing the partner, such as a jumpy stomach, sweaty palms, physical awkwardness, and the heart "missing a beat."

Exclusiveness. Lovers are so absorbed in each other that they often do not want to pursue other love relationships. Also, they tend to be life, I hope to change your mind about me. Please . . . give me the chance with this historical deed to gain your respect and love. (Henry & Shaffer, 1981, p. A8)

What could Hinckley have seen in *Taxi Driver* to evoke such a mad obsession? Hinckley says that he was particularly moved by the scene in which Travis (Robert de Niro) and Jodie were having breakfast in a restaurant. Travis was trying to save her from the sordid characters that were ruining her life, but Jodie didn't understand what he was talking about.

Similarly, Hinckley's quest was to protect the youthful Foster from the harsh realities of upper-class life. He wanted to save her from continuing as a student at Yale, "where sweetness and innocence are not allowed" (Answers, 1981, p. 50).

Hinckley, who in a letter to *Time* magazine refers to himself as the "Lovesick Assassin," used violence to qualify as Jodie's protector and consort. To become worthy of her, he literally had to depose the "man in charge."

Although Hinckley can claim few accomplishments, Jodie is highly intelligent and a movie star. Hinckley wrote to *Newsweek* that her "overflowing brilliance" used to intimidate him. Since the shooting, however, Hinckley considers himself her equal. He pridefully notes that both he and the President wear bulletproof vests and travel with a retinue of bodyguards.

Did Hinckley have anything against President Reagan? Apparently not. He wrote *Newsweek* that he regards Ronald Reagan as the best President of the century, adding "Let's give the man a chance."

While awaiting trial, Hinckley reiterated his feelings for Jodie in a letter to journalist Evan Thomas. But this time, the dark side of his attraction began to surface. Hinckley warned that if he could not have Jodie's love and admiration, then neither could anyone else. He noted that the ultimate expression of his love would be to remove Jodie from Yale and from the world permanently (Is he crazy, 1981).

Hinckley's passion for Jodie is a twisted reflection of romantic love. It is obsessive, exclusive, and extravagant. It is self-sacrificing yet totally selfish. Rather than discounting Hinckley's attraction as that of a madman, it is perhaps more useful to see it as an exaggeration of something that most of us have experienced at one time or another. Romantic love's neurotic, possessive, and insecure overtones have led some psychologists to view it as unhealthy. But often such love is also ecstatic and wonderful. Is it possible to combine the "high" of romantic attraction with a love that is healthy? What do you think?

intensely jealous of rival suitors. Crimes of jealous rage are common, and romantic jealousy has even become an area for psychotherapeutic intervention.

Idealization refers to putting the partner "on a pedestal," exaggerating his or her good points and minimizing the negative. It assumes that the partner and the relationship are in some sense perfect. For example, the Victorian author John Ruskin refused to bed his nineteen-year-old wife, Effie, after discovering that she had pubic hair. (She put up with this for six years and then had the marriage annulled.) Idealization is clearly seen in the customs of courtly love, and many idealistic beliefs have survived to influence modern romantic love. For example: "Lovers intuitively recognize each other at first sight." "True love lasts forever." "Love fulfills all of one's needs."

THEORIES OF ROMANTIC LOVE

Love as psychological growth and fulfillment. Theodore Reik, a psychoanalytic theorist, viewed romantic love as an attempt to become more complete through identifying with a person who has traits that one lacks. For example, one partner may be logical but cold and unfeeling. The other might be warm, emotional, and sensitive but unable to think clearly. Together they form a balanced personality. Thus, for Reik, it is the differences between people that spark romantic love.

Actually, this view goes back to an ancient Greek legend. Originally, there were three sexes: male, female, and hermaphrodite (part male, part female). In a fit of rage, Zeus, king of the gods, punished the humans by severing their bodies in two. Forever afterward, each half-creature wandered the earth in search of its missing part. The original males became homosexuals, the original females became lesbians, and the original hermaphrodites became heterosexuals. In this view, love is the pursuit and desire we feel for the one person who makes us whole again.

Love as disclosure intimacy. Many lovers undergo a period wherein near-total strangers bare their souls and share personal secrets and deepest feelings. The risk is great because they are allowing a desired person to see a side of them ordinarily kept hidden. Moreover, this side is often hidden just because they fear it might be unacceptable to others. Since the other is seeing who they really are, any rejection would be of themselves, not their social masks. Thus the fear is that such rejection would cut to the heart. This risk creates part of the arousal

and excitement of romantic love, and the personal content of the disclosures adds to its intimacy.

Love as a social exchange. Curiously, Erich Fromm (1956) developed the view of love as a social exchange as part of a critique of capitalism. Fromm maintained that in a consumer society each of us becomes keenly aware of our market value to others. The excitement of falling in love is largely the thrill of finding a good bargain in the marketplace of love. This bargain consists of being accepted by someone whose social value equals or exceeds one's own. Since everyone is seeking a bargain, matches are typically made between relative equals in desirability. The social exchange view is illustrated by a study of the "lonely hearts" ads in weekly newspapers (Harrison & Saeed, 1977). Such an ad might read: "Christian woman, 35, 5'5", 120 lbs, very good figure, likes cooking and taking care of a family. Seeks companionship with a sober, established gentleman." "Successful businessman, 55, 6'1", 190 lbs, loves the outdoors. Seeking attractive gal for lasting relationship. Send photo." Women tended to advertise themselves as physically attractive, and men offered financial security. Moreover, attractive women were more likely to demand financial security in an ad, and wealthy men demanded greater attractiveness in a woman.

Love as an attribution for physical arousal. Schachter (1964) observed that emotions involve physiological arousal, yet the various indices of arousal, such as a quickened heart rate, sweating, and heavy breathing, are similar for many different emotions. Schachter theorized that we must be using cues from the social environment to determine what emotion we are in fact experiencing. Walster and Berscheid (1974) extended this theory to the emotion of love. They hypothesized that (1) we are vulnerable to falling in love whenever we are physiologically aroused, for whatever reason, and (2) the social situation and our beliefs about love combine to tell us "This must be love." In our culture, physical attractiveness, age, and power are important social determinants of love. For example, both men and women respond strongly to cultural ideals of physical beauty. Researchers have even found that if one's partner is unattractive, physical arousal in that person's presence may be labeled disgust rather than love (White, Fishbein, & Rutstein, 1981). In addition, men are unlikely to fall in love with a woman much older than themselves, and women often fall for a man with power, wealth, or authority.

The beauty of Berscheid's and Walster's theory is that the lore of romance links love with both agony and ecstasy, with both intense joy and intense suffering. This seeming contradiction is resolved by remembering that both states generate arousal. Positive sources of arousal that contribute to falling in love include sexual attraction, sexual stimulation, and even the erroneous belief that we have been sexually excited. For example, one study had males view seminude *Playboy* pinups while they overheard a supposed amplified recording of their heartbeat (Valins, 1966). The heartbeat feedback, however, was manipulated so that the rate

changed on some slides and remained constant on others. Men were more attracted to the women whom they thought had affected their physiological arousal, and this effect was maintained when the men rerated the women a month later without feedback.

Evidence is accumulating that under certain conditions, unpleasant experiences can also enhance romantic love by creating physical arousal. Researchers have found that the fear of receiving an electric shock, the fear of crossing an elevated, swaying suspension bridge, the punishment of receiving (falsified) negative feedback about one's personality, and the frustration of obstacles to love such as frequent separations from the partner and parental interference in the relationship all increase attraction.

Consider the stereotype of the nice guy who always finishes last with girls. Although reasonably attractive, friendly, and considerate, he always winds up as a platonic friend rather than a lover. (The same stereotype also holds, of course, for nice women.) Attribution theory indicates that this stereotype may contain more

than a grain of truth. It suggests that those who are not associated with arousal are unlikely to become the objects of romantic love. Moreover, individuals who are impulsive, intense, or even somewhat obnoxious may be more likely to inspire passion than will one who is pleasant but bland.

In addition to one's personality, arousal can also be generated by exciting or dangerous activities. Parachuting, skiing, auto racing, and many other sporting events involve an element of danger that gets the heart pounding and the blood moving. In this regard, we may be just catching up with certain natural psychologists from ancient times. For example, the Roman poet Ovid suggested that to inspire passion in their women, men should take them to the arenas of the gladiators.

COMPANIONATE LOVE

Although the volatile nature of romantic love often stirs the greater interest, researchers have also identified another dominant pattern in love relationships. **Companionate love** refers to feelings of caring, trust, respect, friendship, liking, and attachment to another. It is typically an affection for those with whom our lives are deeply intertwined (Berscheid & Walster, 1978). Thus it is the love typically found in good long-term relationships.

In popular terms, romantic love is more like being "in love," and companionate love is more like "loving." Romantic love has been found to decrease over time (Cimbalo, Falling, & Monsaw, 1976), and it is thought to be too intense to last a lifetime. Companionate love, on the other hand, can and often does endure.

In good relationships, romantic love often turns into companionate love over time. If this transition fails, then the relationship will either dissolve or be maintained out of obligation. It is not true, however, that companionate love occurs only after the dissipation of romantic love. Many relationships involve a combination of romantic and companionate love, with the proportion of companionate love gradually increasing after about the first six months of the relationship (Tennov, 1979; Walster & Walster, 1978).

THE CYCLE OF ROMANTIC LOVE

The course of love is often not smooth. It waxes and wanes, changes, regains, and (too often) fizzles and flops. Sex researchers Masters, Johnson, and Kolodny (1985) modeled the transitions of romance, as can be seen in Figure 9–1.

ENTRANCE

Love readiness implies a heightened probability of falling in love. Factors that make falling in love more probable include a desire for love, a belief that love will improve one's life, feelings of loneliness or lowered self-esteem, and sexual deprivation. Individuals differ widely on love readiness: Some are highly susceptible to falling in love; others never do.

Falling in love often occurs early in a relationship, as the couple is just getting to know each other. One stereotype is that love may start with a spark of attraction "at first sight." Another is an initial, arousal-generating conflict or immediate dislike between participants (this is a popular movie theme). Still other relationships begin as friendships and gradually move toward falling in love. These relationships are often more low key and perhaps more stable than are those in which romantic love forms quickly. It seems likely that these would also have a better chance of making a successful transition to companionate love after the romance cools.

Factors that contribute to the excitement of falling in love include the idealization of the partner, being accepted by a desirable other, the risk of intimate disclosure, sexual arousal and release, the satisfaction of one's needs for security and affection, the unpredictability and frustrations of being with someone new, uncertainty

FIGURE 9-1
THE ROMANTIC LOVE CYCLE

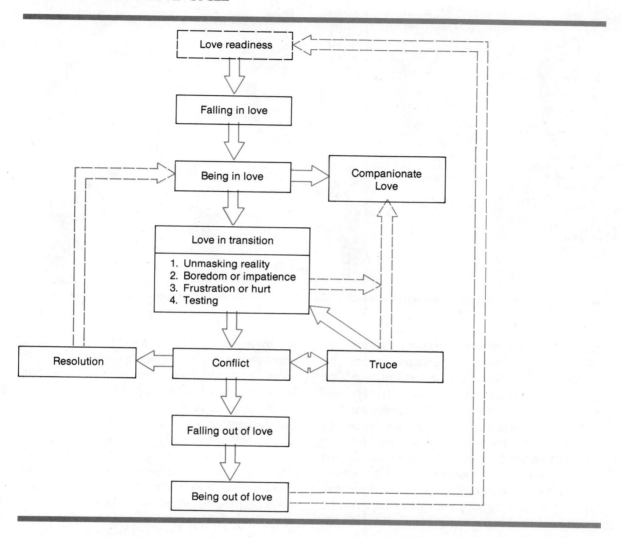

about whether the partner will reject you, and jealousy.

Thus falling in love can occur in an evening or over a period of months, though the characteristics of love will probably differ in these two instances. In addition, the sexes appear to differ, with young women falling in love more frequently (Dion & Dion, 1975) and young men falling more quickly (Hill, Rubin, & Peplau, 1976).

DECREASING EXCITEMENT

Love in transition refers to times when the initial excitement waivers and one begins questioning whether this relationship was "meant

to be." There are many reasons that the excitement does not, or perhaps cannot, be maintained indefinitely. It is well known that physiological reactions decrease with repeated stimulus presentations. The alarm reaction to a gunshot, for example, decreases with repeated firings. It may be unrealistic to expect love's arousal to work differently. A possible exception was suggested by Fromm (1956). He believes that if one can continually see the partner anew, without preconception, then this effect can be held in check. People sometimes adopt this appreciative attitude toward a work of art, for example, but for some reason this is not typical in personal relationships. Instead, over time, we tend to take each other for granted.

Since idealizations are typically built on distortions, they are difficult to maintain over time. In effect, idealization wages a losing battle against the hard evidence of reality.

In addition, we often have conflicting motives with regard to our partner. We want a stable, smooth-running relationship with minimal hassles. Thus, in a long-term relationship

we invariably reinforce each other for being consistent and predictable. However, when successful in this endeavor, we often find ourselves bored with what we have produced.

Also, once we have made a commitment to our partner, either in a marriage contract or a less-formal agreement, we have created an external obligation to remain in the relationship. Thus we begin seeing the partner not as someone we are choosing to be with out of our immediate desires, but as someone who is now seen partially out of duty. Researchers (Seligman, Fazio, & Zanna, 1980) have found that thinking of the relationship in terms of such external reasons decreases the intensity of love.

Another factor that deadens excitement is the potential for pain in an intimate relationship. As a result of minor arguments, oversights, and inconsiderate actions, we often do get our feelings hurt. As a result, we become reluctant to make ourselves vulnerable to the partner. When we do feel love, we may not show those feelings fully and spontaneously, perhaps fearing that the other might show less enthusiasm for us than we did for them. This phenomenon can be seen clearly in small children. The less socialized children are, the more often they respond with a totally loving response, as seen in their facial expression, tone of voice, and all-out enthusiasm. Even though small children are temperamental, inconsistent, and loads of trouble, their vulnerability and nondefensive love evoke powerful, enduring reactions. Over time, however, as children develop a fear of being hurt, their behavior becomes more reserved and defensive. It appears that the same progression occurs in love relationships.

CONFLICT AND LOVE RENEWED

When love is in transition, lovers test each other to determine the meaning and implications of these waiverings in their feelings. Some of the questions that might arise are "Does she still love me?" "In the same way?" "Is he as intelligent as I thought he was?" "Is she as unselfish as I thought she was?" "Is she trying to be the boss?" "Why doesn't he respect me the way he does his friends?" "Where are those romantic little surprises he used to give me?"

This testing process often results in conflict. In itself, conflict may strengthen or weaken the relationship. Partners may find that the other is not losing interest and thus return to being in love. They may risk exploring their problems nondefensively and come to a new appreciation of each other that strengthens their love. Thus conflict may return them to being in love or, by way of truce, lead them toward a more companionate love.

EXIT

Falling out of love. Over time, excitement often wanes, and the failure to find adequate conflict resolutions may prohibit the transition to companionate love. Thus the individual falls out of love. But most relationships do not end by mutual consent. About 85 percent of the time, one partner breaks it off while the other is still in love (Hill et al., 1976), causing disappointment for one and heartbreak for the other. Predictors

of breakups in dating relationships include unequal involvement in the relationship and discrepancies in age, educational aspirations, intelligence, and physical attractiveness (Hill et al., 1976). In addition, men high in the hope of power, that is, those who seek to have a strong impact on others through force, persuasion, or charm, are particularly likely to become dissatisfied and break up (Stewart & Rubin, 1974). Nevertheless, women are more likely than men to perceive problems in the relationship and precipitate a split. For college students, breakups are often conveniently timed to occur before a vacation or at the end of a semester (Hill et al., 1976).

Being out of love. This corresponds to a "mourning period" in which one is not quite ready to pursue a new relationship. The extent of mourning, however, depends on the circumstances for falling out of love. If you initiate a break that has been planned for some time, the mourning period may be negligible. Individuals often experience lowered self-esteem after a breakup, especially if they view the past relationship as a failure. In this case, once love readiness is reentered, they may be particularly susceptible to falling in love again "on the rebound" (Walster, 1965).

Identify the most important love relationship you have had, and trace it through the cycle of love. If the excitement in this relationship has cooled, which factors most contributed to this? How did your styles of handling conflict affect the outcome? If you have reached the out-of-love stage, how long did that last before love readiness returned?

THE DILEMMA OF MODERN RELATIONSHIPS

LOVE AND MARRIAGE

Many researchers believe that our misunderstandings about love often result in marital unhappiness. Marriage is designed and entered into with the expectation of lasting "forever." In our culture, romantic love is the overwhelming precondition for marriage. We want to marry the one who generates that spark of excitement in our hearts, not necessarily the person we get along with best. Romantic love, however, cannot compare with companionate love in endurance. Thus it would seem that we have set the stage for heartache and disillusionment, as marriages founder on the brief life span of romantic love.

We often believe, for example, that "true love" will last. And this belief is often maintained no matter how many counterinstances have been recorded. Relationships that did not endure are simply redefined after the fact as not true love. As Branden (1980, p. 160) commented, it is difficult not to feel sadness when we think about the hurdles of romantic love. "Sadness for every couple who [has] ever fallen in love, and then helplessly watched while love slipped away and they did not know how to stop it."

Certainly, it seems overly pessimistic to anticipate love's demise while in the spell of its powerful delights. Moreover, the strength of romantic love is often no predictor of whether the transition to companionate love will be successful. We often fall in love because of the differences between us and despite the lack of a strong friendship. As noted in Chapter 5, traditional gender roles complicate the transition to companionate love. Males and females are brought up in separate worlds. Their occupations, leisure activities, values, and interests often differ, leaving them with little in common.

Perhaps it would be of use for lovers who are contemplating marriage to consider this question: "If I suddenly fell out of love with this person, how much would I want to continue seeing him or her on a regular basis as a friend?" Note that an answer in the negative would *not* necessarily pose a problem for the couple as romantic lovers. It would, however, bode poorly for them as marriage partners.

IS COMPANIONATE LOVE INFERIOR?

Although intriguing, this question is perhaps unanswerable without considering the personalities of those involved and the purposes for which love is intended. Romantic love offers excitement and joy, but it often brings anxiety and suffering. And it tends to fade. Companionate love is more robust. It provides friendship and caring, but it is not as exciting. As Coleman (1984) observed, companionate love is usually more comfortable and relaxing, but there is always the possibility that it will become dull. With this comes the danger that one partner will meet someone new and fall in love all over again.

POSSIBLE SOLUTIONS

One solution is to find a way of combining the best of both types of love. This has become a popular goal in our society, as evidenced by the flood of articles in "women's magazines" on how to rekindle the excitement and romance in marriage. It is not clear, however, that many couples are successful at sustaining their rekindled excitement. Moreover, some feel that if you have to work at it, you have already lost much of the fascination and spontaneity of a love that is simply "fallen into." It seems clear that the concept of "working at the relationship" fits companionate love better than it does romantic love.

Another solution to this dilemma is to reserve companionate love for a long-term relationship, while allowing short-term romantic involvements "on the side." This strategy has been quite popular in our society, as indicated by the pervasiveness of the double standard and themes of the "other woman" in song lyrics and movies. This strategy typically runs into problems because, again, there is always the possibility that one partner will fall in love and leave the companionate relationship. Also, as is well known, partners are often jealous of each other's outside involvements, even if their passions for each other have cooled. Thus most couples do not openly sanction outside relationships.

Another strategy is to forgo companionate love or relegate it to platonic relationships and to plunge into a series of romantic involvements. Although often appealing, this strategy just about precludes having a family, and it sometimes seems superficial when actually carried out.

Still another strategy is to be technically monogamous while encouraging fantasies of romantic involvements with others. Note that the display of sexually appealing individuals is a mainstay of television and movies. This suggests that romantic and sexual fantasy plays a major role in providing the spice and excitement that companionate relationships lack. Studies have found, for example, that it is common for individuals to have sex with one person while fantasizing they are with another (Hariton & Singer, 1974). Although this is a relatively safe and socially acceptable source of romantic excitement, few would argue that such fantasies are adequate substitutes for the real thing.

The dilemma of combining the most desirable features of romantic and companionate love is by no means trivial. Certainly, if living on the edge of survival, such concerns will seem frivolous. But inevitably, when survival is no longer an issue, we start seeking more out of life, and much of what we seek is in the realm of love.

The tension between romantic and companionate love has generated a number of societal solutions, and it forms the basis for many of the personal tragedies we may experience. Yet it seems clear, at this point, that no one solution is entirely satisfactory for all people. At the very least, we can suggest that partners be honest with themselves and open with each other as to what they want out of a relationship.

How do you evaluate each of the above strategies for combining the best of romantic and companionate love? Note that some strategies combine both in one relationship and others combine them in separate relationships. Which do you prefer? What are the reasons for your preference? Can you think of a solution not mentioned above?

Although the psychological literature has emphasized romantic and companionate love, there is also a question as to what form of love is healthiest. Companionate love appears to be healthier than romantic love, but there may be other, more optimal forms of love that go beyond the companionate.

LOVE AND HEALTHY PERSONALITY

Many psychologists have observed that some love relationships are healthier than others. Some forms of love foster individual growth, whereas others lock people into stagnant and infantile dependencies. Although these dependencies do meet human needs, there is a persistent belief that love relationships can be much more. The following discussion identifies those factors that mediate qualitative differences in the experience of love.

ACTIVE CARING

In healthy love, individuals are more concerned with what they can give to their partner than with what they will get in return. Loving takes precedence over being loved. Abraham Maslow (1968) maintains that the concern with being loved stems from feelings of insecurity and the fear of being left alone. Although love relationships are often used to ease these fears, they are no substitute for dealing with such fears directly. A love based on need, attachment, and security may be far better than loneliness, but it is not in itself a substitute for maturity.

Thus Maslow believes we cannot be free to love unless we first feel secure and worthwhile in ourselves. If we *must have* the reassurance of another's approval in order to feel good about ourselves, then healthy love cannot flourish.

Without an independent sense of security and self-acceptance, love relationships take on a compulsive, sometimes desperate tone. There is quite a difference, for example, between enjoying someone's company and *requiring* their presence to stave off depression. The latter situation is precarious, often leading to restrictive, clinging relationships that stunt growth and smother the partner.

CHOOSING TO BE A LOVING PERSON

Fromm (1956) found that people often say they haven't fallen in love because "the right person hasn't come along yet." He maintained that this attitude is entirely too passive. By implication, it denies responsibility for our emotional lives and is thus inauthentic. We cannot just wait on the sidelines until love sweeps us off our feet. Such a view places all the control in the love object, as if the qualities of the lover were inconsequential. In contrast, Fromm maintained that lovers are those with the ability to love. He claimed that there is an art to loving, an art that must be learned, or at least relearned, before healthy love becomes possible. For example, we must learn how to give ourselves freely to others, how to risk opening ourselves to an intimate relationship, even though we may be rejected.

People often unwittingly shut themselves off from close relationships to avoid the possibility of being hurt. For example, as soon as Fred starts feeling love for an intimate partner, he inevitably begins to notice her annoying little faults. Fred takes great pride in his intellectual abilities and powers of observation. From his point of view, he is just being intelligently observant, protecting himself from falling in love with the wrong person. But everyone has faults. The end result is that Fred's behavior keeps him from having tender feelings for anyone. In the long run such a strategy is a refusal to join the flow of life.

REALITY CONTACT AND THE PARTNER

At the height of romantic love there is often a feeling that the partner is "near perfect." With this may come a fear that he or she might do something to break the spell of this perfection. We may be afraid to examine our partner too closely for fear that some flaw will be revealed. When partners are idealized in this way, we are dealing with a fantasy image of who we want them to be, not with real, flesh-and-blood individuals. In healthy love, on the other hand, there is a continuing desire to know the partner as he or she actually is.

Fromm maintained that we are too quickly satisfied with a superficial understanding of ourselves and our partners. Especially in long-term relationships, we assume that views of our partner that were formed yesterday automatically apply today. Thus, either out of sloth or the fear of discovering that the loved one is not who we thought he or she was, we fail to find out who this person really is today, right now.

In other words, we look but we do not see. We have not adopted an attitude of appreciating our partner's unique being as that being is revealed to us in the moment. Love can be based on a distorted image of our partner or on who that person actually is. Healthy love must operate on the side of truth.

The other side of reality contact is that healthy love implies a continuing willingness to present our own subjective reality to the partner. But lovers often subtly pressure each other to reveal only what has become expected. For example, we may hide feelings of boredom with the partner out of a desire to avoid conflict or not hurt his or her feelings.

In this way, we often fail to let our partner see who we are. Each becomes a cardboard character for the other. As a result, love becomes boring; spontaneous feelings are shut off; and the sense of intensity, discovery, and excitement diminishes. In the early, idealization stages of a relationship, excitement can be maintained without reality contact by our fascination with an image of the partner. As the relationship progresses, however, idealization eventually fails.

ACCEPTING THE PARTNER'S INDIVIDUALITY

In healthy love, individuals have little desire to control their partners or to change them. Such attitudes suggest a lack of respect for the partner as a separate individual. In our culture, possession and ownership seem to be useful ways for thinking about the world. Each of us has a clear notion about what we can claim as our personal property. And if we own something, it is ours to do with as we please.

Unfortunately, these attitudes have been transferred to love relationships, and so we often think of lovers as "belonging" to each other. The feeling of belonging carries with it a sense of security. What belongs to us cannot lawfully be taken away, and the one we belong to is under obligation to care for us. But in healthy love, security is assumed within the individual; it does not have to be generated by the relationship. Thus greater value is placed on growth than on security, and the attitude of possessiveness, which stems from insecurity, becomes inappropriate. The other person is a center of consciousness like ourselves, not an object to be owned, controlled, shown off, and manipulated.

As social learning theorists have pointed out, in a love relationship there is no way for our behaviors not to change or partially control the partner's behaviors. Each becomes such a powerful reinforcing agent to the other that such control is inevitable. *Trying* to change or control the partner, however, is a different matter altogether. As indicated above, trying to change your partner when he or she is aware of what you are doing goes against the grain of healthy love, unless your partner requests this aid. Trying to control your partner without his or her knowledge is simply manipulation, and this violates every notion of healthy love. Even if you believe you are acting in your partner's best interests, manipulative behavior shows a clear disrespect for the partner's rights as a separate individual. It cannot be justified by claims of "love." To this end, the noted psychiatrist R. D. Laing asserted that love is the most violent word in the human language, since the damage done in its name is the hardest to defend against.

Possessiveness often becomes an issue with sexual behavior. Individuals in love typically do not want to share their partner. From the viewpoint of healthy love as developed by Maslow and Fromm, sexual and romantic exclusiveness may well be chosen by partners because they are simply not interested in outside relationships. If, however, exclusivity is demanded from the partner, or offered as a barter for the partner's fidelity, it is clearly coming from insecurity, indicating a love that is less than optimal.

One of the most beautiful expositions on the importance of respect for the partner's individuality can be found in Kahlil Gibran's *The Prophet* (1967, pp. 16–17):

> Love one another but make not a bond of love:
> Let it rather be a moving sea between the
> shores of your souls.
> Fill each other's cup but drink not from one cup.
> Give one another from your bread but eat not
> from the same loaf.
> Sing and dance together and be joyous, but
> let each one of you be alone,
> Even as the strings of a lute are alone though
> they quiver with the same music.
> Give your hearts, but not into each other's
> keeping.
> For only the hand of Life can contain your
> hearts.
> And stand together, yet not too near together:
> For the pillars of the temple stand apart,
> And the oak tree and the cypress grow not in
> each other's shadow.

FOCUS

LEARNING HOW TO LOVE

Leo Buscaglia, a charismatic educator of love, recounted an incident that helps clarify the difference between giving oneself and self-sacrifice:

I go around the country a lot, and when I do, I take my work because it's the only really peaceful time I have. My rule is always, "People first and things second." So when I'm in my office, there is no peace. And when I'm at home there's the telephone ringing and people around — it's what I ask for and what I want and what I love. But when I'm on an airplane — it's like having your own private office.

On this particular day there was an empty seat between me and a very attractive middle-aged lady who was all jeweled and beautifully attired. She watched as I spread out all my things, but I could feel that she *wanted to talk.* I thought, "Oh, my God! I love her but I have exams to grade and papers to read!"

She said, "I bet I can guess what *you* are!"
I said, "What am I?"
She said, "I'll bet you're a lawyer."
I said no, I wasn't a lawyer.
She said, "Then you're a teacher."
I said, "Yes, that's what I am. I'm a teacher."
So she said, "Oh, how nice," and I went back to my work. But she started to talk, and all of a sudden I realized: "Where are you going? You're always talking about people first. If you really mean it, this lady *needs* you. She obviously wants to talk — talk to her awhile, then maybe you can explain you need to get to work."
Well, it didn't work out that way . . . but it was magical because like an *avalanche*, she began to tell me all kinds of things! . . . So she started to tell me she had four children, and that she had just come from the Bahamas. I said, "Did you have a good time?" She said, "No, it was terrible."
I said, "Were you alone?"
She said, "Yes."
I just said, "Oh." I thought that was rather interesting, but I wasn't going to pursue it. But she immediately told me. She was on a holiday by herself: "I'm trying to get myself together."
"Oh, really?"
"Yes!" she said. "Two months ago my husband left me."
"Oh, I'm sorry."
And then she started. And she told me the story of her life!
"Imagine. I gave him," she said, "the best years of my life!" I didn't think people still said that. "I gave him the best years of my life. I gave him three beautiful children, a magnificent house, and I always kept it clean. There was no dust anywhere!"

I was sure of that.

"My children were always on time to school"—she went on and on—"I was a magnificent cook, I always entertained his friends, I was always ready to go every place *he* wanted to." I really felt sorry for this lady! Because all of the things she had considered *essential* were things that he could have paid for.

She had lost her *self!* She had not given her husband what was essential about *her* . . . the magic, the wonder . . . the undiscovered self. She'd given him good food—he could have gone to a restaurant. She cleaned his sheets—he could have gone to a laundromat! That's frightening!

I asked her, "What did you do for *you?*"

She said, "What do you mean, for *me?*"

"I mean what did you do for *yourself?*"

"There wasn't any *time* to do anything for myself!"

There was a pause, then I said, "What would you *like* to have done?"

"Oh, I've always had a dream of making ceramics."

How wonderful, if she had only done that. . . . She didn't know it was essential. I felt sorry for her because what she did was what she *believed* was essential. This is what the culture had *told* her was essential. She was fulfilling a role. And she had lost herself in her role! Then the story unfolds, "Husband Meets Interesting Young Lady in Office," who isn't interested in dust and doesn't care a damn about clean sheets.

We talked for a long time that day about what is essential. She cried a little bit, I cried a little bit. We hugged each other, and she went her way and I went mine. . . .

And if you don't know this yet as a lover, think about it a little. If you are truly a lover, you want to give the best *you* there is. And that means developing all the wonder of you—as a unique human being. . . . How marvelous it would have been if somehow we had taught this woman her uniqueness and taught her the wonder of sharing it. (Adapted from Buscaglia, 1982, pp. 45–46)

SUMMARY

1. Murstein views initial meetings as a screening device to see whether there is a basis for starting a relationship. This social learning approach can be contrasted with a humanistic one that emphasizes faithfully expressing whatever thoughts and feelings come to mind during the encounter.

2. Most people prefer opening lines that are direct or innocuous rather than sassy or flip. The Bach and Deutsch strategy for having high impact in first meetings is to express immediate feelings, ask for permission, introduce reservations, and avoid games and unchecked assumptions.

3. In general, we like those who reward us and dislike those who punish us. Some of the rewards others offer are physical attractiveness, similarity, complementarity, proximity, reciprocity of liking, positive emotions, and the reduction of negative emotions.

4. Love can be described in terms of five components, and these components can be combined to form romantic love, companionate love, and an approximation to the healthy love described by humanistic theorists. These components are dependency, romantic compatibility, physical arousal, communicative intimacy, and respect.

5. Although love partners often believe that they tell each other everything, current research suggests that there are systematic distortions in the way they perceive and present themselves to each other. In particular, females may be more emotionally involved than males are, and they may overestimate their partner's love and underestimate their own unfavorable reactions to the relationship.

6. Historically, the convergence of love, sex, and marriage has been relatively recent. Modern romantic love derives from medieval courtly love, which was predominantly chaste, freely chosen, and idealistic. Courtly love can be described in three stages: worship from afar, courtship proper, and admittance to the lady's chambers.

7. In our culture, romantic love has become the most important precondition for marriage. Romantic love is an intense state of positive affect, often characterized by absorption, longing, dependency, sexual attraction, exclusiveness, and idealization of the partner.

8. There are a number of theories explaining romantic love: (1) Love is an unconscious attempt to become a more complete individual by identifying with a person who has traits that one lacks. (2) Love results from the risk and intimacy of disclosing highly personal information to a relative stranger. (3) Love is the thrill of finding a good bargain in the marketplace of love. (4) Love is an attribution (explanation of cause) that one makes for states of physical arousal.

9. Companionate love refers to feelings of caring, trust, respect, friendship, liking, and attachment to another.

10. The cycle of romantic love is depicted in Figure 9–1. It includes love readiness, falling in love, love in transition, and conflict, followed by love renewed, a transformation to companionate love, or falling out of love.

11. Marriage is typically entered with romantic rather than companionate love, even though the life spans of marriage and romantic love do not match. A number of solutions have been proposed for combining the best features of romantic and companionate love.

12. Some relationships seem to be healthier than others; that is, they do more to foster individual growth. Characteristics of healthy love relationships are active caring, choosing to be a loving person, seeking reality contact with the partner, and accepting the partner's unique individuality.

SUGGESTED READINGS

Fromm, E. **The art of loving**. New York: Harper & Row, 1956. A readable classic.

Tennov, D. **Love and limerence**. Briarcliff Manor, N.Y.: Stein & Day, 1979. Well-written introduction to the romantic and passionate side of love.

Walster, E., & Walster, G. W. **A new look at love**. Reading, Mass.: Addison-Wesley, 1978. A practical treatment of romantic and companionate love.

SEXUAL FULFILLMENT 10

Technique and Sensuality

Too much of a good thing can be wonderful.
Mae West

Human societies show amazing variation in attitudes toward sex. At one extreme, consider Inis Baeg, an isolated island off the coast of Ireland whose inhabitants have been described as the most sexually naive in the world:

Daughters are not taught about menstruation, intercourse, orgasm, or childbirth. Both the onset of menstruation and of menopause are greatly feared. . . . Oral sex, fondling of the penis or breast . . . and even French

kissing are either unknown or considered totally depraved. The men believe that sexual intercourse will destroy their health. The only position for intercourse is the male-above . . . with no foreplay. Female orgasm is considered a sign of possession by the devil.

Nudity is naturally forbidden. Mothers bathe their children in a smock so that they never see them nude. Husbands and wives never see each other naked, and the children and adults only wash hands, feet, lower arms and legs, and faces. In fact, being caught with one's socks off is considered disgusting and scandalous. (Francoeur, 1984, p. 42)

At the other extreme are the Mangaians of the Cook Islands in the South Pacific. They believe that sex should come first — before affection — when beginning an intimate relationship. After an initiation ritual at the age of thirteen, teenage boys have intercourse with an experienced older woman. Both sexes are taught the art of pleasuring, and orgasm is universal. Nearly all forms of sex are encouraged, including intercourse in a variety of positions, masturbation, oral stimulation, and anal sex. Parents encourage their adolescent children to have sex with many partners. While young, Mangaians engage in sex several times a night. They believe that regular sex maintains health and keeps one safe from madness (Francoeur, 1984).

Our own society is at about the middle of this spectrum. We have undergone rapid, complex changes in our sexual mores over the past few decades. In general, we have moved in a liberal direction, although a backlash toward more conservative views may be starting. (This has been attributed to a certain disillusionment with casual sex and to recent concerns about genital herpes and AIDS.)

Nevertheless, it is apparent that we are a sex-conscious society. Still rocking from the aftershocks of a sexual revolution, the media bombard us daily with titillating scenes and whispered promises — using sex to sell every product imaginable. Within this milieu, being sexy has become the ultimate in fashion, and sexual failure the ultimate disgrace.

In our culture, sex has somehow combined with the work ethic, and as a result, sexual *performance* has become an obsession. It now seems almost natural to adopt a critical, evaluative attitude toward our own sexual behavior — and that of our partner. The bed has become a competitive arena, where men and women measure themselves against fictional rivals contrived from media fantasies (Lydon, 1971). One result is a possible increase in "skill" (e.g., intercourse lasts longer now than it did in the 1950s). But this competitive orientation has also raised anxiety over sexual performance and increased sexual dysfunction.

Sex therapists are agreed that as a society, we need to adopt a sensual, playful, non-goal-oriented attitude toward sexuality. According to existential theorist Rollo May (1969), we have anesthetized feeling in order to perform better; we have wielded sex as a tool to prove prowess and identity. As a result, we have robbed sex of its emotional power, leaving it banal and empty.

THE SEXUAL BODY

MALE ANATOMY

We were all bathing in the pool naked. I hated to do it, because my [penis] looked so small—

men's get so small in the cold water. So when I got out, I quickly wrapped a towel around me. (Delora, Warren, & Ellison, 1981, p. 81)

The male sex organ that has received the most attention in sex manuals, popular fiction, graffiti, and locker-room conversations is, of course, the **penis**. This organ consists of a shaft and a glans. The **shaft** is tubular and comprises most of the penis's length. The **glans** is the smooth tip or head of the penis, and it is the primary center of erotic sensitivity.

The glans contains the urethral opening, a small hole through which urine or other fluids may pass. At birth, the glans is covered by the **foreskin**, a continuation of the loose skin cover-

ing the shaft. Most American males have had this foreskin removed shortly after birth in a surgical procedure known as **circumcision**. There is currently somewhat of a controversy over whether to continue this procedure, with some authorities arguing that it aids cleanliness and others suggesting that it diminishes sensitivity by exposing the glans to irritation from clothing. Current evidence (Masters & Johnson, 1966; Terris, Wilson, & Nelson, 1973) supports neither claim.

Internally, the penis is composed of three chambers of spongy tissue which fill with blood to produce an erection, much like a balloon filling with water. Most erect penises measure between five and seven inches in length, with a

FIGURE **10—1**
MALE SEXUAL ANATOMY

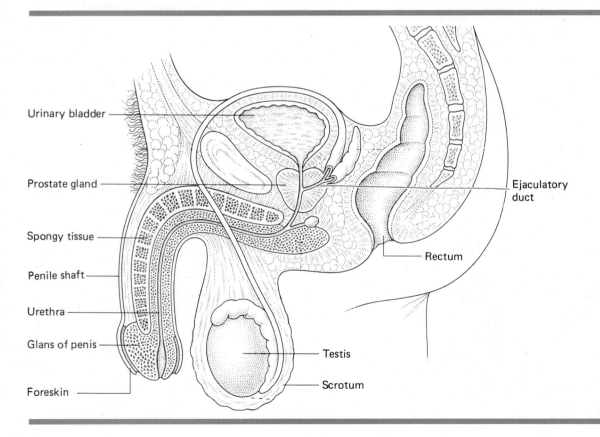

Urinary bladder

Prostate gland

Spongy tissue

Penile shaft

Urethra

Glans of penis

Foreskin

Ejaculatory duct

Rectum

Testis

Scrotum

mean of six inches. Penis length is unrelated to race, body size, or virility. Given the frequency with which penile dimensions are bandied about, you might expect that a large penis provides more physical pleasure for its owner or his partner. Such is not the case. Nevertheless, many men worry about their penises. "Is it big enough?" "Doesn't it have a funny shape?" "Maybe it bends too much to the right." And so on. Although these and other such worries are common, they are almost always unfounded.

The **scrotum** is a sac of loose skin that hangs behind the penis. It houses the **testes,** egg-shaped sex glands that produce sperm and the male hormone testosterone. The scrotum is moderately sensitive to touch, and Hite (1981) reported that many men stroke or pull their scrotums during masturbation. As is well known, however, even a slight pressure on the testes, themselves, can be painful. Figure 10–1 shows the male sexual anatomy.

FEMALE ANATOMY

Somewhere around the age of 10 or 12 I wanted to see what I looked like "DOWN THERE." . . . When the house was empty I got my mother's big ivory hand mirror from her dresser and went into my bedroom, closed the door, and went over by the window with sunlight pouring in. I looked . . . and was instantly horrified! I was obviously deformed. . . . When I saw [my inner lips] hanging out the only association I could make visually was that they looked like those things that hang down from a chicken's neck, a wattle. I thought I had stretched them like that from masturbating. . . . I swore off masturbation on the spot, asking God to get rid of those things that hung down, in exchange for my promise to be a good girl, stop swearing, love my little brothers, and to keep my room clean. (Dodson, 1974, p. 23)

Two folds of hair-covered skin run along either side of the vaginal opening to form the **outer lips.** Within the outer lips are the moist,

hairless, and sexually sensitive folds of the **inner lips.** The inner lips look more delicate than do the outer lips, often resembling the petals of a flower. At the bottom, the inner lips enclose the vaginal opening. At the top, they often meet to form the **clitoral hood,** a sheath of tissue covering the clitoris.

The **clitoris** (klit′-or-iss) derives from the same embryonic tissue as the penis, and it is the most sensitive part of a woman's genitals. Like the penis, it consists of a shaft and a glans. The shaft is covered by the clitoral hood, and the glans may either be exposed or retracted under the hood. When exposed, the glans appears as a pea-sized bump of skin. The clitoris measures about one-half inch in length and is composed of erectile tissue which expands slightly when aroused.

The clitoris is unique in being the only organ with the sole function of sexual pleasure. Although much smaller than the penis, the clitoris has an equal number of sensory nerve endings, making it highly sensitive (Lewis & Lewis, 1980). In fact, most women find it uncomfortable to have the clitoral glans touched directly.

Contrary to popular belief, women do not urinate through the vaginal opening. A separate urinary opening is located roughly midway between the vaginal opening and the clitoris.

The **vaginal opening** is located below the urinary opening, toward the bottom of the inner lips. Although often pictured as an open hole, it is usually not visible because of the outer and inner lips and because the muscles surrounding the vaginal opening keep it partially closed. In virgins, the vaginal opening is often partly covered by the **hymen,** a tissue of unknown function. Many cultures regard the absence of an intact hymen as evidence of nonvirginity. Some girls, however, are born without hymens, and others have theirs ruptured through nonsexual activities.

The **vagina** is the organ entered by the penis during sexual intercourse. When unaroused, it is about four inches long, existing as a potential space with its walls collapsed. Just as penis size

FIGURE 10-2
FEMALE EXTERNAL SEXUAL ANATOMY

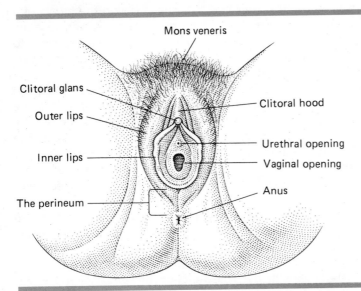

is a topic of much concern, there are also pervasive fears about vaginal dimensions. Young women often worry (needlessly) that they may not be able to accommodate an erect penis. In contrast, older women sometimes worry that their vagina may be too large to stimulate a male. During sexual arousal, however, the walls of the lower third of the vagina (the part closest to the opening) swell so that there is a relatively snug fit around the penis. And although childbirth does stretch the vaginal muscles, much of this can be remedied by appropriate exercises (see below). Figure 10-2 presents the female sexual anatomy.

HOW THE SEX ORGANS FUNCTION

Masters and Johnson (1966) pioneered the observational study of sex by bringing subjects into the laboratory, hooking them up to a com-

William Masters and Virginia Johnson.

plex physiological apparatus, and finding out how their bodies actually functioned during sex. They observed people during masturbation and during sexual intercourse. They even observed females during intercourse with an artificial penis rigged to film the vaginal interior. Masters and Johnson concluded that the sexual response is essentially the same, regardless of the source of stimulation, and they described it in four stages called the **sexual response cycle**.

The first stage, **excitement**, involves the flow of blood to the sexual organs and the increase in muscular tension throughout the body, particularly in the genital area. In men, the first sign of excitement is penile erection, which is a direct result of increased blood retention in the penis. In addition, the scrotum tightens and the testes rise closer to the body. In women, the first sign of arousal is vaginal lubrication. In addition, the clitoris and the inner lips swell, the clitoral glans protrudes from the hood, and the upper vagina expands.

In the second, or **plateau** stage of the re-

sponse cycle, the penis reaches full erection, the testes increase in size, and a few drops of clear fluid may appear at the tip of the glans. In women, the lower vagina engorges with blood so that the vaginal opening narrows. In addition, the clitoris retracts within its hood, presumably as a protection against overstimulation.

The third stage is **orgasm**, a state of high sexual tension followed by a rapid and intensely pleasurable tension release. During orgasm, muscles throughout the body tense up, and muscles in the genital region contract rhythmically for a few seconds. In males, it is typical to use the terms orgasm and ejaculation interchangeably, but these processes do not always occur together (Hyde, 1982). Ejaculation refers to the release of semen, typically caused by the muscular contractions that accompany orgasm. It is possible, however, for ejaculation to occur without orgasm, as in the case of spinal-cord victims whose reflexive ejaculatory nerves are intact but whose nerve pathways to the brain have been severed. Alternatively, prepubescent

FIGURE 10-3

THE SEXUAL RESPONSE CYCLE

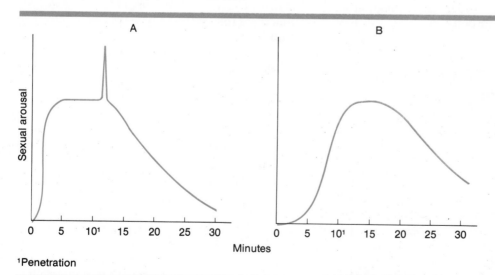

¹Penetration

youths often experience dry orgasms, and Robbins and Jensen (1977) suggest that men can train themselves to orgasm without ejaculation.

The fourth and final stage of the response cycle, **resolution**, returns the body to a sexually quiescent state. Muscular tensions subside and blood moves away from the genitals. The penis becomes semiflaccid and typically undergoes a period of several minutes to several hours during which it does not respond to further stimulation. Females also undergo a resolution stage, but Masters and Johnson report that they do not experience a period of nonresponsiveness. Thus, if sexual stimulation is continued, orgasmic women may return immediately to the plateau stage and experience additional orgasms. Multiple orgasms are less frequent among men, but Pomeroy (1976) found that roughly 20 percent of adolescent males experienced repeated orgasms with ejaculation, suggesting that their periods of nonresponsiveness were negligible.

The sexual response cycle is depicted in Figure 10–3a. Figures 10–3a and 10–3b show the response cycles for a heterosexual couple. Which is likely to be the male? The female? This couple is experiencing somewhat of a problem in their sexual adjustment. Can you tell what it is?

THE PURSUIT OF ORGASM

THEORIES OF ORGASM

How many types of orgasm are there? Researchers agree that there is only one basic male orgasm, although it differs in intensity depending on the man's state of exhaustion, sexual deprivation, and attraction to the partner. The male orgasm occurs in two stages, involving two distinct reflexes. In the **emission** stage, semen is emptied into the duct at the base of the penis. In the **expulsion** stage, muscular contractions push the semen through the urethra.

In contrast to males, there is considerable controversy as to the number and types of female orgasm. Freud held that women can have orgasms that are centered primarily in the clitoris or in the vagina. He further maintained that psychologically mature women should experience and prefer the vaginal type. (Most modern psychologists find no basis for judging one type of orgasm healthier than another.)

Masters' and Johnson's (1966) physiological observations indicated that there is only one type of orgasm. This orgasm is triggered by direct or indirect clitoral stimulation and mainly involves muscular contractions in the lower vagina.

It now appears that the grounds for yet another theory of female orgasm are coming to the fore. Seaman (1972) found that some women experience orgasm in the clitoris, others feel it in the vagina, and a third group experience both simultaneously. Perry and Whipple (1981b) claim that Masters and Johnson found only one type because they used only one electrode to detect muscle tension in the vagina. Perry and Whipple maintain that two electrodes are required to separate contractions in the lower vagina from those in the upper vagina and uterus.

Recent research (Bentler & Peeler, 1979; Butler, 1976; Singer & Singer, 1972) suggests that there may be three types of female orgasm: **Vulval orgasms** are triggered by direct or indirect clitoral stimulation and roughly correspond to the Masters and Johnson orgasm. (**Vulva** refers to the area between the inner lips, thus including both the clitoris and the vaginal opening.) **Uterine orgasms** involve contractions of the upper vagina and uterus, may be triggered by "G" spot stimulation, may be associated with female ejaculation, and may cause an interruption in breathing. Perry and Whipple hypothesize that just as male orgasm involves the separate reflexes of emission and expulsion (each triggered by a different nerve pathway), female orgasm may also involve two reflexes. Furthermore, these reflexes may occur together or separately. When occurring together, they result in the third type, a **blended orgasm**.

FOCUS

THE "G" SPOT AND FEMALE EJACULATION

Several researchers (Addiego et al., 1981; Belzer, 1981; Perry & Whipple, 1981b) claim that the "G" (Grafenberg) **spot** does exist, that it is highly orgasmic, and that it triggers the release of a substance from the urethral opening that resembles male ejaculate without the sperm.

Does every woman have a "G" spot? This question has not yet received a definitive answer. Perry and Whipple studied over two hundred women and claimed to have found the spot in every one of them, but other researchers (Goldberg et al., 1983) reported finding the spot in only about half of their sample.

What are its vital statistics? Although it varies from woman to woman, the Grafenberg spot is generally about the size of a nickel. When ejaculation occurs, between one and three teaspoons of fluid are released. (Males ejaculate about one teaspoon.)

Where is it? The "G" spot lies in a part of the vagina not typically inspected in medical exams, which is one reason it has been overlooked for so long. Another is that few women can easily reach their own Grafenberg spot; a partner's help is often required. The spot is located on the upper surface of the vaginal wall about halfway into the vagina.

How do I find it? Lie down on your back with knees apart and partially elevated. Place one or two fingers in the vagina. About halfway in, on the upper surface, begin pressing with your fingertips, using a gentle but firm pressure. It may help to bend the fingers slightly forward. It may also help to put pressure on the outside of the lower abdomen with the other hand. When the spot is hit, the first sensation will be an impulse to urinate. With continued pressure and friction, this leads to sexual pleasure, and the spot swells.

The "G" spot versus the clitoris. Are the sensations derived from the "G" spot and the clitoris essentially the same? Perry and Whipple (1981a) report that they are distinctly different, though both may lead to orgasm. Moreover, unlike the clitoris, which often becomes too sensitive to touch, the "G" spot thrives on repeated contact. The clitoris and the Grafenberg spot also appear to have different physiological effects. Stimulation of the clitoris leads to contractions in the lower vagina, whereas stimulation of the "G" spot causes contractions in the upper vagina and in the uterus.

Female ejaculation. Perry and Whipple (1981a) found that ejaculation occurs during the "deeper" orgasms involving contractions of the uterus. They estimated, however, that only about 10 percent of women routinely ejaculate with orgasm. It seems likely that many women have the capacity for ejaculation but have learned to inhibit it because they mistakenly believed their ejaculations to represent a loss of urinary control. Perry and Whipple (1981a) speculate that by trying to avoid ejaculation, many women have unknowingly inhibited their orgasmic capacity as well.

FOCUS

SEX AND THE BODY BOUNDARY

Some people report occasional strange or unusual perceptions of themselves during periods of extended sexual intercourse. A thirty-six-year-old janitor, for example, stated "Sometimes after having sex for maybe an hour or more I start to lose track of where my body leaves off and where hers begins. It's like I can't tell if I'm the one with the penis or the one with the vagina."

According to psychoanalysts, we maintain our sense of identity and self-integrity by having clear boundaries between body and environment. Loss of body boundary is one sign of the ego disintegration found in many psychoses. It is also often a characteristic of religious experiences, drug states, and mystical visions. As a temporary, controllable phenomenon, as in sex, there is no danger in this breakdown of the body boundary. It can, however, stir a reexamination of who or what we really are.

From the viewpoint of nineteenth-century science, which assumed a mechanical world composed of separate objects, our being is that of a complex machine. In such a world, these experiences make no sense and must be dismissed as mere hallucinations. Some humanistic psychologists, on the other hand, suggest that these experiences are clues to a larger definition of who we are. The implication is that restricting our sense of identification to the bounds of the physical body may be more arbitrary than we realize. (For more on this point of view, refer to the Asian practice of Tantric sex, a discipline for exploring the spiritual implications of sexuality.)

Although conclusions regarding this and other theories of orgasm must await further evidence, it seems ironic and intriguing that a basis is developing for once again considering some types of orgasm to be healthier than others. After all, if two nerve pathways are involved in female orgasm, it could readily be argued that the blended orgasm is physiologically complete, whereas the others may be only partial.

ORGASM AS A GOAL: THE SEXUAL OVERACHIEVERS

It would not be newsworthy to discover that everyone wants to have orgasms. Because of their obvious desirability, it seems natural for us to view orgasms as goals to be achieved, and their attainment can be a very serious business. Note that the phrase "achieving orgasm" is almost always applied to women rather than men. Why is that? For most men, orgasm arrives all too easily; its occurrence doesn't seem like much of an achievement. But for many women, orgasm is uncertain at best and thus a worthy goal. It is important to remember, however, that this goal-oriented view of female orgasm has become popular only in recent years.

In effect, the attitude that sex is a shared task with the goal of mutual orgasm is an application of the Protestant work ethic to the domain of sexuality. And as such, it makes a great deal of sense to us. If a desired event is not occurring as frequently as we would like it to, why not use our intelligence and effort to solve the problem? Thus orgasm has become a product, and our job is to master the techniques required for its efficient production.

Other times and other cultures, however, have considered orgasm from entirely different metaphors. In turn-of-the-century Victorian times, female orgasm was not desired. Since "good women" weren't supposed to have strong sexual desires, the occurrence of a female orgasm caused more problems than did its absence. A metaphor common in Victorian times was that of "preserving one's vital juices." Having an orgasm was described as "spending oneself." It was thought that the squandering of these juices debilitated one's health and paved the way for a variety of diseases, including pneumonia, rickets, and mental illness. To us, this way of viewing sex seems bizarre and pathological. Nevertheless, we can only wonder whether those a hundred years from now will look back on our own era of goal-oriented technique with the same evaluation.

A change in attitude, away from a work metaphor of sex, has already begun. For example, Hyde (1982), in a human sexuality text, refused to use the phrase "achieving orgasm" because of certain drawbacks of the work metaphor. First, if orgasm is a goal to be attained, then nonorgasm automatically becomes defined as a failure. Second, making orgasm into a goal draws our attention away from the immediate pleasure and sensuality of the moment. Instead, it forces us to think about *eventual* satisfaction, the tension reduction at the act's conclusion. In this sense, the work metaphor is sexual but not sensual. It detracts from the enjoyment of pleasure for its own sake. Slater (1973) suggests that this work orientation is essentially a form of puritanism.

> The term "climax" expresses not only the idea of a peak or a zenith but also the idea of termination or completion. Discussions of the sexual act in our society are thus primarily concerned with how it *ends*. Leisurely pleasure-seeking is brushed aside, as all acts and all thoughts are directed toward the creation of a successful finale. The better the orgasm, the more enjoyable the whole encounter is retrospectively defined as having been. . . . In such a system you can find out

how much you're enjoying yourself only after it's all over, just as many Americans traveling abroad don't know what they've experienced until they've had their films developed. (pp. 19–20)

A number of sex therapists are now formulating an alternative to the "sex-work" mentality; perhaps this alternative can be described as an attitude of "sex-play." The play metaphor emphasizes the process of sex, the leisurely enjoyment of sexual titillation, without preconceived ideas that the encounter must include a certain act (even intercourse) or have a particular ending (including orgasm).

The main advantage of the play metaphor is that it takes the performance pressure out of sex. Sex therapists are finding that the cognitions surrounding the work metaphor — the expectations, goals, ideals, and demands that define adequate performance — are often counterproductive. When the point of sexual contact is pleasure, the inclusion of performance pressures becomes maladaptive.

What do you see as the trade-offs between these two ways of viewing sex (work versus play)? How do you evaluate these trade-offs? Can you find a way to combine the best features of each metaphor?

THE RESPONSIBILITY FOR ORGASM

Our culture has a long tradition in which the male is expected to take the lead in sex. Thus there is often an unspoken agreement that he holds the responsibility for the female's orgasm. The man is supposed to know how to arouse a woman and bring her to orgasm. Traditionally, the female plays a passive role; she is not expected to initiate changes in sexual position or types of stimulation. And the male takes either the credit or the blame for her orgasm.

In contrast, sex therapists generally favor each person taking responsibility for his or her

FOCUS
THE LOVE MUSCLE

First, the love muscle is not the penis. Neither is it the vagina. The love muscle is an organ that you probably have never heard of. It is called the **PC muscle,** and if recent research reports are born out, you will be hearing more about it in the future.

PC and the female. The PC is the muscle that surrounds the vaginal opening, the base of the penis, the urethra, and the rectum. Arnold Kegel (1952) brought it to popular attention by developing a set of PC exercises to prevent the unintended release of urine in women. To his surprise, Kegel found that the PC exercises also enhanced orgasmic functioning. Those women who could not orgasm had the weakest PC muscles, and those who were consistently orgasmic had the strongest. Over half of a large sample of women with orgasmic difficulties became orgasmic after conditioning their PC muscles. Kegel estimated that about one-third of all women have PC muscles so weak that they cannot be voluntarily contracted.

PC and the male. What about the males; what are the effects of exercising the male PC? Powell (1981) suggests that just as PC exercises enhance female orgasmic functioning, they may also increase the intensity of male orgasms. Moreover, increasing the strength of and control over the PC allows men to last longer during intercourse. When ejaculation is imminent, the PC can be tightened until the ejaculatory impulse subsides.

Orgasm without ejaculation. The most amazing claim for PC conditioning, however, comes from Robbins and Jenson (1977). They interviewed a number of men claiming to have trained themselves to hold back ejaculation *while still experiencing orgasm.* Presumably, tightening the PC shuts off fluid ejaculation in the same way that it shuts off urination. As a result, males may be able to experience multiple orgasms. Of course, final conclusions about the benefits or possible side effects of PC conditioning must await further evidence.

PC workout. Now for the good news. You don't have to be an Olympic athlete to do the Kegel exercises. As Dailey (1980) found, learning to contract your PC muscles is as easy as wiggling your nose. Start during urination. Whatever you have to do to stop the flow of urine constitutes a flexing of the PC muscle. So one easy exercise is routinely to stop and start the flow during urination. A second exercise is to consciously tighten the PC when not urinating. Women can check that this is being done correctly by inserting a finger into the vagina during the contraction. You should be able to feel the vaginal opening tighten around the finger. Men can check by noting that the penis should move slightly when the PC is tightened.

own orgasm. The advantage is that the female is no longer kept in the passive role. Since she knows what pleases her or what will trigger her own orgasm better than the man does, it makes sense for her to take an active part. Additional responsibilities for each sex are examined next.

Male responsibilities. Should the man have any responsibility for the woman's orgasm? Even though men have traditionally assumed this responsibility, women usually do not blame their partners when they don't orgasm (Loos, Bridges, & Critelli, 1986). Nevertheless, research shows that the probability of female orgasm is linked to intercourse duration (Gebhard, 1966). If the male ejaculates within one minute of penetration, there is little chance that the woman will have an orgasm during intercourse. If he lasts for more than fifteen minutes, the chances are two out of three. Thus it seems that the man might at least take the responsibility to "be there" longer than a few minutes. But how long is long enough? For some women, two minutes will do, and for others, one hour won't. Hunt (1974) indicated that the average duration of intercourse for married couples is about ten minutes, and so this might provide a rough guideline. Beyond mere duration, however, the male also has a responsibility for paying attention to what the female may be communicating verbally or nonverbally about her sexual preferences and state of excitement.

If the female does not have an orgasm, the male may have some responsibility not to act disappointed, as if she let him down. Many women feel so much pressure to orgasm — often for his sake rather than her own — that they feel obliged to fake it. In other words, the male is responsible for not letting his own ego involvement become a burden on her.

Finally, there appears to be a code of "good manners" for occasions when the female has not been satisfied but the male has. Rather than immediately going to sleep, as if his orgasm automatically signaled the end of the encounter, the male should offer to continue, perhaps by providing manual or oral stimulation.

Female responsibilities. The woman's responsibilities toward the man are roughly comparable to his obligations toward her. One area of special attention, though, involves the male erection rather than the orgasm per se. It has often been said that the male ego is a fragile thing, and there is some truth to this, especially when males feel that they must uphold an image of supermasculinity. But there come occasions in most men's lives, whether because of drinking, fatigue, stress, or old age, when the penis just doesn't work the way "it's supposed to." At these times the female should avoid overdramatizing an absent erection by being either critical or patronizingly understanding. A number of men have developed long-term erectile problems from one such episode. It is more adaptive to view erectile difficulties as normal events that will occur from time to time in most men's lives.

What is the female's responsibility toward her own orgasm? Quite simply, it is to know her own body. Because sexual taboos are stronger for women than for men, and because female sex organs are not out in the open the way a man's are, women often know surprisingly little about what they look like "down there." Furthermore, women often know little about the specific kinds of stimulation required to induce orgasm. If you're female and have never really looked at your genitals, get a hand mirror and see yourself. In addition, the most effective way to find out what types of stimulation you respond to is through masturbation. (*Note:* for both men and women, there is no medical or psychological reason to avoid masturbating.) Once the female can orgasm on her own, then she can more effectively guide her partner.

SEXUAL TECHNIQUE

TECHNIQUES OF AROUSAL

Students in my sexual behavior class talk as if the world were made up of two kinds of people: those who "know how to do it" and those who wish they did. What is this specialized, technical knowledge for inducing ecstasy in a sexual partner?

The fascination with technique. Our culture has placed a great deal of faith in the belief that every problem has a technical solution. Sexual problems, for example, are resolved by simply moving a finger a millimeter to the right, adjusting the angle of the hips, or trying out a new, exotic position. This technical point of view, however, often produces undesirable effects. In other words, we seem to have the makings for a paradox: Even though sexual technique is obviously important, it is possible that an overreliance on technique has now become the problem rather than the solution.

Our culture usually sees to it that we begin our sexual lives in a state of ignorance or misinformation. For example, even those who have discussed the "birds and bees" with their parents have rarely talked in detail about how to arouse a sexual partner. The usual assumption is that sex is "natural" and therefore requires no elaboration.

This initial ignorance often leads to a consuming quest during adolescence for the knowledge of "how to do it." This, coupled with our penchant for technical solutions, leads many of us to form an attachment to the techniques we have gleaned from books, magazines, hearsay, and haphazard experiences. Ultimately, this attachment leads to a mechanical, repetitive plan of how to make love. And it is this plan that makes it difficult to be spontaneous, sensual, and sensitive to the partner's mood.

Another way in which the emphasis on technique can lead us astray involves the tremendous variability in sexual preference. Some people like wet, slurpy kisses; others are repulsed by them. Some like their nipples nibbled; others find this irritating. Moreover, preferences change from day to day, mood to mood. The one thing you can depend on is that if you make love the same way each time, your partner will eventually find your technique unimaginative, predictable, and boring.

I suggest a rule of technique: Learn what you can about sex — then forget it. That is, put this knowledge in the back of your mind. Let it come out when necessary, but avoid entering sexual encounters with a fixed plan in mind.

Mood. One dimension of mood is whether the sexual encounter is approached from a more lighthearted or a more serious frame of mind. Each is appropriate and desirable in its own way. The lighthearted, fun approach is good, but too much of it reduces emotional involvement. When lightheartedness becomes the only mood a couple shares, chances are it is being used to avoid intimacy, to keep the partner from getting too close. On the other hand, seriousness is also good, but when taken too far, it reduces spontaneity. Partners need to find a balance between

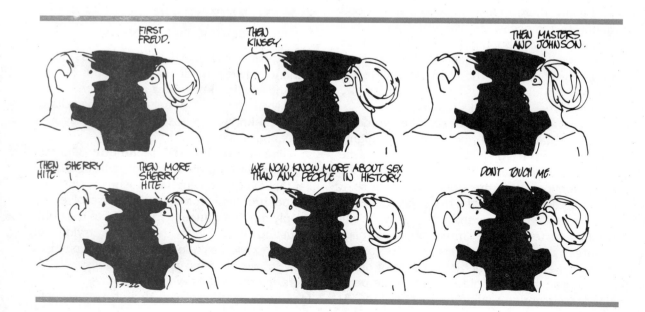

lightheartedness and seriousness to fit whatever is happening between them in the immediate situation.

Fantasy. Thinking about sex can itself be highly stimulating. In fact, Kinsey and associates (1953) reported that 2 percent of women can orgasm from fantasy alone. Most men and women fantasize while masturbating (Kinsey et al., 1953) and while having intercourse (Hariton, 1973; Sue, 1979). Many fantasies involve some sort of forbidden behavior. Men often imagine group sex, impersonal sex with a stranger, and forcing someone to have sex with them. Women often imagine romantic situations or being forced to have sex. It is important to realize that because people find a fantasy exciting doesn't mean that they would actually carry out the fantasy, or even that they would like to. Also, such fantasies do not indicate problems in adjustment or in one's sexual relationship (Hariton, 1973).

Is it healthy to fantasize? There is, however, some controversy as to whether using fantasy during intercourse is healthy. Psychoanalysts maintain that fantasy may be a way of escaping from or punishing a partner who is not loved. In this regard, Hariton found that the most common fantasy of married women was thinking of an imaginary lover while having sex with their husbands. Other psychologists have argued that fantasy is a practical way of bringing variety and excitement to a long-term monogamous relationship without breaking the bonds of fidelity. Thus they might consider the same behavior an adaptive solution to a problem all marriages face.

Whether or not you have had intercourse, how do you view fantasy during coitus: neurotic avoidance of the partner or healthy adaptation to monogamy?

One question you might ask is, "How would I react if my partner revealed that he or she was fantasizing sex with another person as a way of increasing excitement with me?" If you would react negatively, does this indicate

that fantasy is unhealthy or only that your capacity to hear the truth is limited?

Perhaps it is healthier to fantasize about surrounding events, such as where you are, rather than imagining you're with a different partner. Also, it is a better sign for the relationship if partners can share their fantasies, using them to stimulate each other.

Physical contact. We all like to be touched, fondled, hugged, rubbed, stroked, kissed, cuddled, massaged, and held. This is part of our animal nature. For example, Harlow (1959) found that infant monkeys formed maternal bonds with a cuddly terry-cloth mother rather than with a wire-mesh mother that was their source of food. This indicates how basic is the need to touch.

Kissing. Kissing is one of the most frequently used forms of sexual touching. There are two basic kinds of kiss: the drier lip kiss and the wetter tongue kiss. What makes a good kiss? Unfortunately, this question is difficult to answer. For every person put off by kisses that are too wet and loose, there seems to be another who is left cold by kisses that are too dry and tight. Some people like a lot of movement or "mouth action"; others complain that their partners kiss as if "eating a hamburger." In general, most people do not like to feel the other person's teeth during the kiss; they do not like a great deal of lip pressure; and they do not like a passive tongue that never ventures out of its own mouth. Beyond that, the only issue on which I can detect much agreement is that nearly everyone hates bad breath. It is perhaps a sad commentary on our society that we prefer the smell of mouthwash to the natural smells that mouths otherwise generate, but this is one preference that we all seem to share.

Light and heavy touch. Although it may seem obvious, note how the feeling of being touched varies with the pressure applied. More pressure is not necessarily more arousing. Heavy pressure, as in deep muscle massage, can be arousing because it relaxes, dissolving muscle tensions that inhibit a full sexual response. However, heavy pressure almost immediately deadens the sensations from the skin itself. Optimal skin sensation is produced by a very light touch. (Try this on your own skin right now.) Thus it is probably wise to vary the pressure of touch, depending on whether a muscle relaxation or a skin-tingling feeling is sought.

Genital touch. Touching your partner's genitals, is, of course, a direct and immediate arousal technique. Alex Comfort, in *The Joy of Sex* (1972), suggested that the female encircle the penis just below the glans, making a back-and-forth motion along the shaft. It is probably best to avoid touching the head of the penis directly, unless some form of lubrication is used.

Male stimulation of the female genitals involves the outer and inner lips, the vaginal opening, and the area around the clitoris. In general, use a light touch and avoid contact with internal skin tissue until lubrication is present. Most women find direct contact with the clitoris irritating and prefer being touched to the side of the glans or on the clitoral shaft. One variation involves using the palm of the hand above the clitoris while inserting a finger into the vagina, so that a range of genital stimulations can be produced with one motion.

Common male complaints. Two complaints often heard from males are instructive in their contradiction. The first is that their partner doesn't initiate sex or new forms of arousal and therefore seems uninterested and overly passive. The second is that the female does initiate sexual contact and is therefore too aggressive and demanding. Most men, even those who see themselves as liberated from rigid sex roles, have a difficult time dismissing certain myths about "real men." One such myth is the notion that men are always ready for sex and have a much stronger sex drive than women. Thus when the female does initiate sex at a time when he is "not in the mood," this can put him in a bind. If he doesn't respond (or if he cannot), his masculinity will be called into question. At such times it is easier to blame the female (seeing her as "overly demanding") rather than question his rigid notions of masculine identification.

On the other hand, the male also wants to feel that he is desired. An obvious way for the female to show this is by taking an active part in initiating sexual contact. Thus the female is under pressure to walk the fine line of showing interest in initiating sex without placing demands on the male to perform. Often this can be accomplished nonverbally. If she begins touching him and he doesn't respond, then she can simply conclude that he's not in the mood. If, however, she verbally states a desire for sex, then the male is put on the spot. He must explicitly admit to a lapse in masculinity in order to follow an inclination not to have sex.

Common female complaints. Many women complain that their partner is selfish; he's not concerned with whether she is sexually satisfied or not. Even if he makes a point of asking whether she had an orgasm, women are often left with the impression that the man's actual interest was in finding out how *he* did.

One approach that might prove helpful is for the male to avoid asking whether or not the woman had an orgasm. Once this is asked explicitly, it defines the entire encounter as "for the purpose of orgasm." If the male wants to make a direct inquiry, it may be more adaptive for him to ask whether she wants continued stimulation.

If this is a long-term relationship, however, and the female wants to have orgasms more frequently, information about the occurrence of orgasm needs to be communicated. It's probably best for the female to verbalize this information rather than being asked by the male. This is more consistent with the female taking responsibility for her own orgasms. But it is important for her not to convey negative information in a way the male will construe as a complaint that he didn't "give her an orgasm." Thus it might be best to indicate when she does orgasm, leaving the negative information unspoken.

Another complaint often heard from women is being treated "like a sex object." A woman wants to feel that *she* is the one desired, not that any body would do. Some male behaviors that give this impression are reaching for the genitals too soon, going to sleep immediately after intercourse, or not talking to her in a loving or affectionate way during the encounter.

Whether or not you have had intercourse, what complaints can you add to those already given for your sex? How do you respond to the complaints made against your sex? Are they legitimate? Do they apply to you?

SEXUAL INTERCOURSE

Sexual intercourse, or **coitus** (co′-it-us), refers to vaginal penetration by the penis. Sometimes the penis has difficulty finding the vaginal opening on its own, and penetration is facilitated by one or the other partner guiding it in manually. If entrance is difficult, this indicates that the female is not sufficiently aroused.

Sexual movement. Sexual intercourse usually involves movement of the penis within the vagina. Often this is a back-and-forth movement, but it might also be circular or side to side. Although the sensations of intercourse can be modified by using various positions, small changes in the angle of penetration, in whether the penis is above or below the vaginal opening (riding high or low), or in the pressure exerted against the partner's genitals can also alter the sensations produced. One thing to determine is whether the changes that increase pleasure for you have the same effect on your partner. Don't simply assume that this is the case.

Both partners may want to experiment with various ways of controlling their movements during intercourse. For example, thrusting can be done mainly with the buttocks, with the arms and shoulders, or with the feet. Another variation involves whether the hip movements are smooth and well controlled or whether the hips

dangle loosely. Other sensations may result from sucking in the abdominal muscles, arching the back, or contracting the PC muscle.

Often males begin rapid thrusting before the female is anywhere near orgasm. Also, some males, as they approach orgasm, use thrusts that are rapid but shallow. Masters and Johnson found that most women need a continuous, uninterrupted stimulation for orgasm. Hite (1976) suggested that orgasm during intercourse can be facilitated by having a good deal of contact between the base of the penis and the clitoral area, and so a change to rapid, shallow thrusting may not be optimal for the female. One way of providing additional stimulation during intercourse is for either partner to touch the clitoral area.

The basic positions. There are only a small number of body positions that allow the penis to find its way to the vagina, though there are an infinite number of minor modifications.

The first position, and by far the most popular in our culture, is the *face-to-face, male-above position*. (This used to be known as the "male superior" position, indicating that its popularity may be linked to sexual politics.) This position is also commonly known as the missionary position, a derisive label given to it by Polynesians who felt that the European missionaries were sexually inadequate. (The Polynesians preferred a squatting position.)

The advantages of the face-to-face, male-above position are it is optimal for impregnation (if that is desired); it is highly personal, allowing the partners to easily see each other's facial expressions, kiss, and talk; and the female's hands are free to touch the man's body or provide clitoral stimulation to herself. The disadvantages are that the man's body weight may inhibit the woman's movements, especially if he doesn't support himself on his hands and arms; the increased body tension from supporting his own weight makes it difficult for the man to delay orgasm; the man's body weight may create discomfort for a pregnant female; and penetration may be inhibited if either partner is obese. (Note that in all positions, penetration is increased by the female moving her legs apart and up, while clitoral and vaginal friction are increased by the female bringing her legs together.)

The *face-to-face, female-above position* appears to be increasing in popularity (Hunt, 1974). This position can be entered by the female sitting onto the erect penis or by rolling over from the missionary position. The female may sit upright or lie down. The advantages of this position are that the female can control the angle and depth of penetration to optimize clitoral friction; males can usually last longer because of the reduced muscle tension in lying down; and the facing position maintains emotional intimacy. The disadvantages are that the couple may feel uncomfortable with the woman in what would appear to be the more "dominant" position and that the male's movements may be inhibited if the female is heavy.

In the *rear-entry position* the male faces the female's back. Usually, the female is on all fours or lying on her stomach with her hips elevated. The advantage of this position is that the male's hands are free to stimulate the clitoris. The main disadvantage is that some couples feel it is impersonal or "animalistic." This position tends to be used mainly for variety, although Hunt (1974) found that about a fifth of those under twenty-five use it fairly often.

In the *side-to-side position* partners lie on their sides and usually face each other, with one of the female's legs over the male's hip. (This can also be done with the male facing the female's back, in which case the side-to-side and rear-entry positions would be combined.) The advantages of the side-to-side position are that the man can usually delay orgasm and that it works well if the woman is pregnant, if one or both partners are obese or tired, or if the couple must restrict physical exertion for health reasons. The disadvantages are that penetration is shallow and thrusting may be less vigorous than in other positions.

THE ORAL REVOLUTION

One of the most remarkable changes in sexual behavior is the increased incidence of oral sex. Although still illegal in most states and nearly unmentionable just a generation ago, Hunt (1974) found that 90 percent of married couples under the age of twenty-five practiced oral sex at least occasionally.

Stimulating the male. There are two forms of oral sex. **Fellatio** (fell-a′-shio) refers to oral stimulation of the male genitals. It typically involves sucking and licking the head and shaft of the penis, with care taken to avoid contact between penis and teeth. Note that if the penis goes too far into the throat it can trigger a gag reflex. This can be handled by using a hand to control movements of the penis or by relaxing the throat muscles.

Another issue regarding fellatio is what to do about ejaculation. Male ejaculate has little taste except for being salty, and there is no medical reason that it shouldn't be swallowed. Nevertheless, many couples prefer to reserve ejaculation for intercourse. If one is against taking ejaculate into the mouth, these feelings should obviously be discussed before fellatio is attempted.

Stimulating the female. The other form of oral sex is **cunnilingus** (pronounced as spelled, with emphasis on the third syllable). This includes licking and sucking the clitoris, inner lips, and vaginal opening. Tongue movements, for example, might be quick and darting or slow and thrusting.

Simultaneous fellatio and cunnilingus is referred to as the sixty-nine position. This may be done with both partners on their sides or with one on top of the other. If the female is below, however, it may be difficult for her to control the depth of male penetration.

One issue regarding oral sex concerns the smell of the partner's genitals. Although there is no danger to one's health, if the partner has not bathed recently, genital smells can be offensive to some people. Some even find the smell of recently washed female genitals unpleasant (recently washed male genitals have no distinctive odor). This appears to be another instance of the perfume and deodorant manufacturers successfully convincing us to dislike the natural smells of our own bodies. Because of this, recent years have witnessed the rise of a whole industry of feminine douches and deodorants sanitizing the female body for oral sex. These remedies are completely unnecessary for cleanliness, as the vagina has its own system of cleaning. Furthermore, these products contain chemicals that can irritate genital membranes or lead to infection.

SEXUAL PROBLEMS AND THEIR SOLUTIONS

SEX PROBLEMS IN PERSPECTIVE

Masters and Johnson (1970) speculated that half of all marriages will experience a sexual problem of a sort that might lead the couple to seek professional help. This figure, however, is greatly influenced by what a particular couple decides to label as a problem. Presumably, the sex lives of all couples could be improved in some way. On the other hand, it is not unusual for a couple to endure a lifetime of abysmal sex rather than admit failure and seek outside help.

Snyder and Berg (1983), investigating couples in sex therapy, found that having a partner who did not respond to sexual requests was one of the best predictors of dissatisfaction. In addition, having a nonorgasmic partner predicted male dissatisfaction, whereas infrequent sex was a good predictor of female dissatisfaction. Curiously, males were more likely to complain about infrequent sex, but this factor was more strongly related to female than to male dissatisfaction.

Most sexual problems are thought to be of psychological rather than physical origin. Some of the most typical causes are simple ignorance of how to stimulate self or partner, anxieties about not having an erection or an orgasm, disrupted communication between partners, sex guilt, early traumatic or humiliating experiences, and hostility toward the partner.

Helen Singer Kaplan, a noted sex therapist, presented a case illustrating how anxiety from a single unfortunate incident could lead to long-term disturbances in sexual functioning. The subject was a thirty-year-old male who had been married for five years and whose wife had left him for a close friend of the family:

> The husband became insecure and depressed and constantly thought about how inferior he was to his wife's lover. Eight months after the separation he met a woman at a party who wanted to have sex with him. She urged him to go upstairs, and so they went to an unlocked room and attempted to have intercourse on the floor. He became aroused but lost his erection for the first time in his life and could not regain it. After this experience, the problem escalated with other partners. He became engaged to his current fiancée but was unable to get an erection with her. Despite her reassurances, he felt humiliated and fearful that she would reject him. (Adapted from Kaplan, 1974, pp. 128–129)

Offir presented another example of a sexual problem, this time one triggered by resentment toward the partner:

> My husband and I were always arguing over his participation in the care of our home and family. I'd nag, and he'd agree to help more around the house or to take the kids off my hands for a few hours, but then he wouldn't do it. He'd come home, wolf down his dinner, and disappear into his study for three hours, with hardly a word to me. Yet at bedtime he was ready to screw. I was so angry I'd just go limp and passive. There was no way I was going to have an orgasm or even show arousal. It's not that I *couldn't* get aroused; actually, I could. My lack of enthusiasm was a way of hurting him back. (Adapted from Offir, 1982, p. 271)

THE STRATEGY OF SEX THERAPY

Assessment. Sex therapy typically begins with taking a detailed history of the sexual problem. Points of particular interest might be when and under what circumstances the problem began, exactly what happens when the couple has sex, and an assessment of attitudes toward various sex acts.

Accurate information. Simple education is often a component of sex therapy. Unbelievably, some marriages remain unconsummated for years because the partners are unaware that the penis goes inside the vagina. Other couples might have the mistaken impression that the man's penis is too large for intercourse. Many have never heard of the clitoris. Because of the large number of sexual myths and fallacies, providing accurate information will sometimes be all that is required.

Relearning sensuality. Most sex therapists believe it is essential for couples to relearn a natural, sensuous, nonpressured orientation toward sex. The goal-oriented, performance attitude of many couples in our culture is usually thwarted by forbidding the couple to have sex until explicitly instructed by the therapist. This takes the pressure off the participants. The couple is then taught a series of **sensate focus** exercises to enable them to relax and enjoy attending to the pleasure of touch. The exercises start by allowing only nonsexual touching, with the

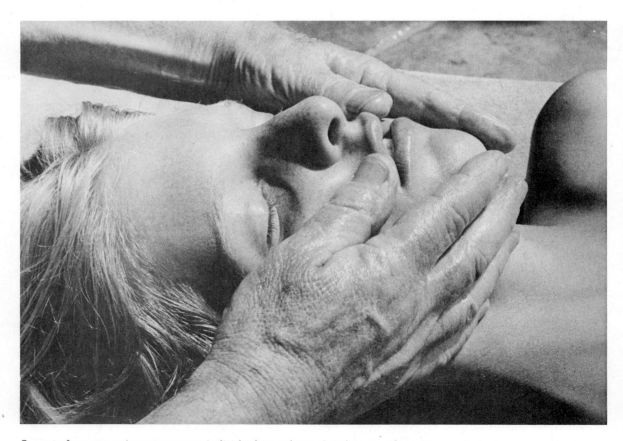

Sensate focus exercises encourage individuals to relearn the pleasure of touching and being touched.

partners taking turns in the giving and receiving roles. Couples are encouraged to communicate verbally, telling the partner what is wanted and what feels good.

The next phase of sensate focus might be genital touching, but without coitus or orgasm. As in the earlier phases, the aim is to experience sexual pleasure without distraction. **Spectatoring** is a common form of distraction in which a person behaves while simultaneously watching and evaluating that behavior. Many of my students report an irrepressible urge when watching a love scene in a sexually explicit movie to rate the characters on a ten-point scale of sexual performance. This attitude, especially when applied to oneself, inhibits a full sexual response.

In the last phase of sensate focus, the couple is allowed to have coitus, but without any expectation that it must or should lead to orgasm. As an involuntary response, orgasm cannot be willed, and any attempt to "force" its occurrence is unlikely to succeed. It can be seen that sensate focus is a gradual, nonpressured relearning of how to become a more sensuous person. Sex therapists find it so basic to the kind of problems found in our culture that it is prescribed for nearly every type of sexual dysfunction.

Practice giving and receiving a massage. When receiving it, describe to your partner what you are feeling and indicate which kinds of touch you like best.

MALE SEXUAL PROBLEMS

Erectile dysfunction refers to an inability to get or maintain an erection. Kaplan (1974) estimated that half of the general male population has occasional erectile difficulties, and Offir (1982) observed that nearly all men will experience erectile problems at some time in their lives. Most erectile problems are due to psychological factors, but they can also be brought on by spinal-cord injuries, diabetes, and vascular problems (recall that an erection is produced by blood flow to the penis). The presence of an erection while sleeping is a good indication that the problem is psychological rather than physical.

Once a physical problem has been ruled out, treatment usually begins with the sensate focus exercises. The primary aim is to reduce the anxiety and the pressure to get an erection. A relaxation response facilitates blood flow to the penis. Fear and anxiety inhibit relaxation. Thus erectile difficulty is the perfect self-fulfilling prophecy: The fear that it will not occur is the major cause of its absence.

Once the man has some erectile capacity, the sexual partner is often told to tease the man by stimulating him to erection and then deliberately allowing the erection to subside. This teasing cycle is repeated a number of times. This reduces his fear that a penis that starts to go soft will not become hard again.

The final stage of therapy might involve extending the teasing technique to coitus. With the woman in the female-above position, she may insert the penis in a nondemanding manner, disengage, and repeat this cycle a number of times. Once coital ejaculation occurs several times, the problem is usually resolved.

Premature ejaculation is a common problem, particularly among young men with strong sex drives who have simply not yet learned how to control ejaculation. At what point does an ejaculation become premature? Of course, any answer will be somewhat arbitrary. In general, if the male is disturbed by the duration of his erection and if he has little voluntary control over when ejaculation occurs, it is considered premature. As a rough index, many individuals perceive a period of less than two minutes to be premature.

Treatment typically includes teaching the male to recognize the sensations preceding ejaculation so that he can control the level of excitement before ejaculation becomes inevitable. Once anxiety over being premature is reduced, it is fairly easy for the male to identify these sensations in time to control ejaculation. One control technique is the **stop-start method** (Semans, 1956), in which the partner stimulates the male until ejaculation is imminent, and then stops, letting the arousal subside. In effect, the male practices his ability to delay ejaculation, and as with most skills, this ability improves with practice. A similar method developed by Masters and Johnson is called the **squeeze technique**. In this the partner stimulates the male until ejaculation is imminent and then firmly squeezes the penis for several seconds with her thumb on the underside of the glans. Although this may sound cruel, it's not painful. It is, however, most effective in eliminating the urge to ejaculate.

FEMALE SEXUAL PROBLEMS

In **orgasmic dysfunction** women become highly aroused, yet have difficulty reaching orgasm. Surveys such as those by Hunt (1974) and Hite (1976) found that about 10 percent of all women have never had an orgasm and another 20 percent seldom have them. Moreover, about 60 percent do not orgasm regularly from coitus alone. One issue is whether a woman who can orgasm from manual and oral stimulation, but not from coitus, can be said to have an orgasmic dysfunction. Curiously, sex therapists suggest that intercourse alone does not provide optimal stimulation for female orgasm. Thus it is probably misleading to view such a woman as having a dysfunction. Instead, she might be said to have an overly rigid notion of how her orgasms must be produced. Nevertheless, many couples prefer female orgasms to occur during intercourse, and so this is a common problem for sex therapists.

In addition to information about the location of the clitoris and the sensate focus exercises, treatment for women who have never had an orgasm often involves training in masturbation. LoPiccolo and Lobitz (1972) found that masturbation is the technique most likely to produce orgasm in women. The rationale here is that

when a woman knows how to trigger her orgasms she can see to it that that stimulation is provided during intercourse. Often, Kegel exercises are also prescribed, and the woman may be instructed to contract her PC muscles during coital thrusting.

When the female can masturbate reliably on her own, she is encouraged to show her partner how to stimulate her manually to orgasm. The next stage might involve coitus, first with manual stimulation and then without it if the partners can position themselves so that enough contact is provided through coitus alone. Most women find it easier to orgasm in the female-above position, as this allows them greater freedom in adjusting their bodies to maximize stimulation.

Bruijn's (1982) survey of Dutch women sheds some light on the occurrence of female orgasm. Most women reported that the feeling of warmth and closeness with the partner was more important to them than orgasm and that they often preferred to experience this intimacy rather than "work for" an orgasm. Many women also had types of stimulation that reliably produced orgasms for them but that they rarely engaged in with their partners. The two most common of these were manual stimulation of the clitoris and actively rubbing against the partner. Bruijn speculated that these activities may have been avoided because they violate the traditional passive female sex role.

Bruijn also found that the variety of petting techniques was less important than was the continuity of stimulation. For example, women who didn't orgasm from manual stimulation typically received about five minutes of touching, whereas those who did, received ten minutes. Similar proportions held for oral sex and coitus (oral sex: three minutes for those who didn't have an orgasm and seven for those who did; coitus: six minutes for those who didn't and ten for those who did).

Sara and Sam have been married for four years. They have sex several times a week, but

Sara has never had an orgasm with Sam. She can, however, orgasm reliably through masturbation, and she typically does this once a week in private. She has never mentioned her masturbation to Sam. One night after discussing her sex life with a close friend, she stimulated herself manually while having sex with her husband. When Sam realized what she was doing, he became upset and accused her of "being a lesbian."

How would you describe Sara and Sam's problem? How would you suggest that they handle it?

SEX TALK

THE TWO LANGUAGES OF SEX

Sexual content can be expressed in two basic ways. The first is the formal language of science and medicine. Its terms are largely derived from Latin. This formal language comprises the socially appropriate terminology of sex in our culture and includes terms such as penis, vagina, and sexual intercourse. The other language of sex is the informal, slang, or colloquial language of the locker room, the streets, and private places. This language is often viewed as socially crude, and a number of these terms carry hostile or abusive connotations.

The formal language. The formal language of science and medicine is a precise vocabulary for making fine discriminations among the various sexual organs and activities. It is emotionally neutral and thus ideal for discussions of intimate topics between people who are themselves not intimate. An obvious example is the interaction between a physician and his or her patient. The purpose in these public discussions of sex is to transfer information without embarrassment or overt titillation.

When, however, the purpose of the encounter is to invite sexual contact, to express humor, or to convey some other informal message, medical terminology may be awkward.

Consider the husband who whispers to his mate, "I'm experiencing genital activation and intruding coital mentations. Prepare vaginal intromission." Although correct, this language somehow doesn't work.

The informal language. In contrast with the formal terminology, the informal language of sex is emotional, sexy, humorous, and sometimes antagonistic. In selecting informal words, one must be careful to avoid unwanted abusive connotations. In general, one-syllable terms with hard, terse sounds (e.g., screw), tend to carry abusive meanings. These terms would be out of place, for example, when the intent is literally to make love.

A special case of informal language includes terms made up by a couple as their own private language of sex. Many couples personify their sex organs by giving them names. This creative use of language aids the expression of sexual feelings.

THE VERBAL APHRODISIAC

Although complete silence during sex may fit the mood on a given occasion, when silence becomes the norm, people forgo one of the most effective of all arousal techniques — the spoken word. In general, silence makes the sex act more impersonal, whereas verbal communication enhances intimacy.

Couples often wonder what to say "at a time like that." Song lyrics refer to those "sweet little nothings," but this language is so personal that we are almost never taught what to say. What most people verbalize during sex are probably expressions of love and pleasure, compliments, and, perhaps, sexual information such as orgasmic updates and requests for different forms of stimulation. Some people enjoy using "dirty words" to increase the sense of excitement. When particular words don't come to mind, amorphous sounds, that is, "moans and groans," can be effective in letting your partner know that you are enjoying the program. As a cautionary note, keep questions to a minimum. Because questions demand an answer, they force the partner to interrupt the flow of experience to think of a reply.

ROMANTIC MISCOMMUNICATION

One of the romantic beliefs ingrained in our culture is that words are unnecessary for those who are truly in love. Instinctively, each should know what the other is thinking. All of us have probably known moments when a seemingly magical rapport between partners made words superfluous. Communication was instanta-

The romantic belief that those in love should know what the other is thinking often leads to communication problems.

neous and complete without words. Unfortunately, few couples sustain these moments throughout the day-to-day routine of an ongoing relationship. Moreover, these magical, intuitive moments are usually unpredictable; they cannot be planned or forced.

Thus, although there probably is some truth to this romantic belief, overall, it causes a great deal of trouble. The rationale runs something like this: Since words would be unnecessary if we were truly in love, and we are truly in love (aren't we?), then words *should* be unnecessary. The sobering truth is that most of the time, partners will not be able to read each other's minds. If your partner is to get the point, you will have to show or describe what you want.

TALKING ABOUT SEX

As Offir (1982, p. 274) commented, "talking with a partner about sex seems more difficult than doing it." Because the topic is so intimate, there is always the risk of hurting the partner's feelings, even if the content of the communication is not rejecting. Even such a peripheral topic as, say, telling your partner that his or her breath is offensive, can cause a great deal of anxiety for many couples.

In addition to its intimacy, there are a number of reasons why communicating about sex is not easy. Although our culture gives us many models of how to act at social events or at work, we are taught very little about how to express sexual feelings. Some people think that stating one's sexual preferences outright may seem selfish or overly forward. Or we may simply be embarrassed to state openly what we want. In addition, men may feel that asking a sex partner what she prefers communicates indecision or an unmanly lack of experience.

Often, nonverbal communication, such as gestures and facial expressions, are used to avoid the awkwardness of words. This is generally a good strategy, since nonverbal behaviors don't call attention to themselves the way that words do. Because of this, however, they are also more vague and easier to ignore or misinterpret than are words. Thus, much of the time nonverbal behaviors will need to be augmented with words.

Research has shown that when compared with happily married couples, unhappily married couples show communication deficits (Markman & Floyd, 1980). Moreover, communication adequacy at one point in time predicts satisfaction with the relationship several years later (Markman, 1979). The following are guides to effective communication suggested by sex and marital therapists:

1. *Be specific.* To make sure that your message gets across, state it explicitly and in detail, with at least one concrete instance of what you're talking about. Remember, there are a number of reasons (listed above) for why we will tend to avoid specific, explicit statements. Merely hinting at the problem will usually not be enough. For example, suppose that Jane is happily married and loves her husband but wants to bring more romance into their relationship. Maybe she wants to go out "parking" as they did when they were teenagers, but she feels silly bringing up such an "immature idea." If Jane says, "Jack, our sex life isn't very exciting anymore," Jack will immediately be put on the defensive, and he will have only the foggiest notion of what she is getting at. There's a good chance he will misinterpret her as saying, "You're a boring and inadequate lover." In this case, his most likely response will be to counterattack.

2. *Disclose your own feelings and reactions; don't blame your partner.* Focus on what you know best, your own feelings and reactions. One way of doing this is to begin sentences with "I." "I want you to touch my clitoris more" is better than "You don't touch my clitoris enough." Starting an uncomplimen-

tary sentence with "you" automatically blames the partner and puts him or her on the defensive.

Distinguish between disclosing your own feelings and disclosing a negative opinion about the partner. Negative opinions quickly degenerate to name calling. If you think that your partner is a total klutz, withhold that negative opinion, even though, in some sense, it may be true, and find another way to handle the situation. Jane could deal with her problem of insufficient clitoral stimulation, for example, by waiting until she and Jack are in sex play and he is touching her genitals. Then she could say something like "I love it when you touch me like that." In this way, rather than complaining to Jack that he is inept, she has created an opportunity to make him feel like an effective lover. If Jack never spontaneously touches her in a pleasurable way, Jane can simply guide his hand, placing it on her body in a way that she enjoys.

3. *Don't mind read.* Don't make assumptions about what your partner is thinking and feeling. If you believe your partner is thinking something that would adversely affect you, then it is your responsibility to bring it into the open. Perhaps Jane rarely touches Jack's genitals on her own because she feels it's unladylike. Jack may interpret her reluctance as a disinterest in his body, perhaps a belief that she finds him unattractive. He is guilty of mind reading if he concludes that she dislikes his body without checking his interpretation with her. What makes mind reading so deceptive is that it's hard to know when it is occurring. We often see no other interpretation for what is happening and so we think we are merely observing the "facts." It is amazing how often those facts will be interpreted differently by our partner.

4. *Listen actively.* When your partner is talking, listen for the words, listen for the feelings, and listen for the nonverbal qualifications provided by tone of voice, gestures, and facial expressions. This is what it means to be a conscious listener. If the topic is important and there is any reason to believe that you may not have understood what your partner meant, then paraphrase what was said to see if you got it right. For example, you might say, "Do you mean . . . ?" or "I hear you saying. . . ."

5. *Emphasize the positive.* Most of the time information to the partner can be phrased in either a positive or a negative way. It will almost always be more effective to avoid negative phrasing. For example, suppose Jack and Jane are having intercourse; Jack is on top and has inadvertently pinned Jane's hair under his elbow, and his vigorous movements are pulling her hair. Jane must say something right away. She could scream, "You're pulling my hair!" This would get Jack off her hair, but it would also break the mood, make him feel clumsy, and generate a note of antagonism between them. The same information could be conveyed by saying "My hair is caught." Here, there is no implication that anyone was at fault.

SUMMARY

1. The major male sex organs are the penis, the scrotum, and the testes. The penis passes urine and spermatic fluid; it stiffens and increases in size when aroused, facilitating sexual penetration. The scrotum houses the testes, which produce sperm and male hormones.

2. The major female external sex organs are the clitoris, which is the focus of erotic sensitivity, and the vagina, the organ entered in sexual intercourse.

3. Masters and Johnson identified four stages in the sexual response cycle: excitement, plateau, orgasm, and resolution.

4. The "G" spot is a small area in the vagina thought to be instrumental in producing orgasm and female ejaculation.

5. There is thought to be one type of male orgasm, which occurs in two stages: emission and expulsion. Recent evidence suggests that there may be three types of female orgasm: vulval, uterine, and blended.

6. Two ways of viewing sexual activity were contrasted. The work metaphor views orgasm as something to be achieved through technical proficiency and adequate performance. The play metaphor emphasizes the leisurely and sensual enjoyment of sex without preset goals.

7. The PC muscle surrounds the base of the penis and the vaginal opening. Its condition is thought to affect both male and female orgasmic functioning.

8. The male's particular responsibility in sex is to give his partner a reasonable chance of having an orgasm, either by prolonging intercourse or

offering other forms of stimulation. The female's responsibilities are to know her own body and to deal appropriately with male erectile problems.

9. Our culture overemphasizes sexual technique. Nevertheless, it is helpful to consider some technique-related issues. Among these are the uses of fantasy, ways of touching the partner's body, the positions for intercourse, and oral sex.

10. Many married couples, perhaps half, will experience some type of sexual dysfunction. Two common components of sex therapy are giving information and teaching a relaxed, sensual orientation toward the partner.

11. Two common male problems are erectile difficulty, which is often treated with sensate focus, and premature ejaculation, which is often treated with the squeeze technique.

12. A common female problem is orgasmic dysfunction, which is often treated with sensate focus and masturbation training.

13. Formal and informal languages for expressing sexual ideas were contrasted. It was suggested that each has its own utility.

14. Some suggestions for sexual communication are: Be specific; disclose your own feelings without blaming the partner; don't mind read; listen actively; and emphasize the positive.

SUGGESTED READINGS

Barbach, L. G. **For yourself: The fulfillment of female sexuality**. Garden City, N.Y.: Doubleday, 1975. Practical advice for women with orgasmic dysfunction.

Comfort, A. **The joy of sex**. New York: Crown, 1972; rev. ed., 1986. A popular, well-written sex manual.

Gottman, J., Votarius, C., Gonso, J., & Markman, H. **A couple's guide to communication**. Champaign, Ill.: Research Press, 1976. A practical guide for enhancing communication skills.

Zilbergeld, B. **Male sexuality**. New York: Bantam, 1978. A thorough yet highly readable treatment of the subject.

THE FAMILY UNIT

11

A Personality of Its Own

This chapter examines each person's most important social environment, the family. Is the family endangered? Or is it merely evolving, adapting to modern times? What effects do children have on a marriage? In what way does the intimate daily contact of family life set up habitual patterns of interaction, so that the family takes on a personality of its own? What forms might destructive family communication take? And how can you protect yourself from

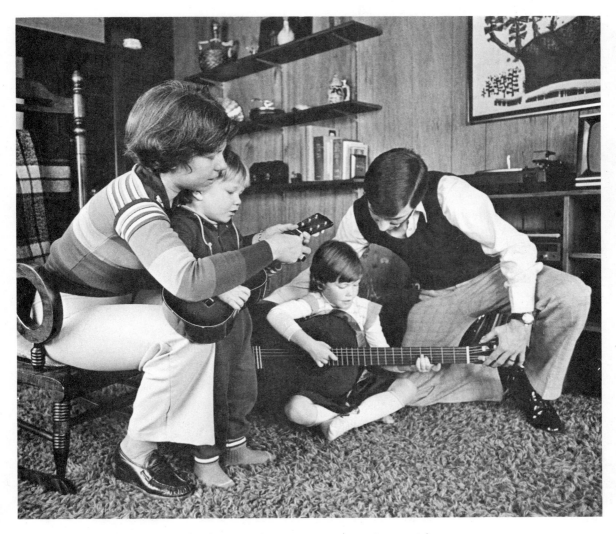

When they are functioning well, families provide a warm, secure environment for personality development.

these influences? After reading this chapter, you should be able to answer these questions and, if you are willing, estimate the chances that your first marriage will be a happy one. In addition, you should have a basis for examining your own family system with greater objectivity and, hopefully, with more compassion.

MARRIAGE

THE MARRIAGE CRISIS

Over 90 percent of Americans marry, yet one-half of these marriages ends in divorce. Nearly all marriages are entered with hopes of their yielding a lifetime of happiness and mutual satisfaction. Nearly all succeed for a while, but many cannot rise above the yearly accumulation of frustrations and disappointments. These either break in divorce or bend by becoming less than they once were. When couples divorce or continue in a state of resigned disharmony, the result is measured in personal anguish. The contrast between the marital fantasy and the experienced reality becomes overwhelming. At such times, it is difficult to escape the belief that someone must bear the guilt for a momentous personal failure.

The U.S. divorce rate is now the highest the world has ever known, nearly doubling in the decade between the mid-1960s and mid-1970s (Albrecht, 1979). And the increase has been particularly dramatic in the middle class.

The reasons for this increase usually center on two aspects of modern society. The first is change. As the number of options, decisions, and demands placed on us increases exponentially, it becomes more and more difficult to maintain a stable, lifetime relationship, even though the need for stability may be greater than ever. For example, most families now move every six years. If both spouses work, it may be impossible for each to live near their place of employment. Moreover, moving disrupts the children, especially those between the ages of six and eleven (Inbar, 1977). And children's adjustment problems increase parental stress. Thus, individual stressors interact and multiply, making it more and more difficult to maintain long-term stability.

It is not just that the environment is changing but that people themselves are changing. Many middle-aged housewives are going back to school and entering the job market. Many men are changing careers at midlife. Under these circumstances the person you are married to at forty may bear little resemblance to the one you married at twenty. Although it is certainly possible, it is not easy for two individuals to change and grow together, maintaining their initial compatibility in interests, values, and life goals.

The second factor in the rising rate of divorce involves the meaning of marriage. In the 1950s, people married for three main reasons: sex, children, and economic security. Typically, males were motivated by the first two reasons and women by the latter two. Today, because of dramatic changes in sexual mores, gender equality, and attitudes toward having children, people are more likely to seek marriage as a way of satisfying the psychological needs for love, companionship, and self-fulfillment (Tavris & Jayaratne, 1976). In other words, people are expecting more out of marriage than they used to. It is no longer unusual for people to end a marriage just because they are not as happy as they believe they should be or because their personal development is not being optimized.

PREDICTING MARITAL SUCCESS

It is estimated that half of the marriages that do last are relatively unhappy, being maintained for the sake of the children, because of religious beliefs, or for lack of a desirable alternative.

Given the proportion of marriages that eventually falter, it seems wise to use both the heart and the head when choosing a mate.

Thus the chances are roughly three out of four that your marital selection will eventually go sour. Given these odds, it seems wise to use both our hearts and our heads when choosing a mate. One way of helping to ensure a happy marriage is becoming aware of those factors that predict marital satisfaction.

1. *Be happy*. Happy people tend to form happy marriages (Greenberg & Nay, 1982). Some people have learned the skill of looking on the bright side and being easy to get along with. Not surprisingly, these people make better marital partners.

2. *Have happily married parents.* (Greenberg & Nay, 1982; Pope & Mueller, 1979). Those with happily married parents have had years to watch their parents model adaptive ways of relating to each other. In addition, they have developed positive expectations; they know that minor conflicts can be handled without hostility and resentment. However, if you were not reared in a happy household (you are probably in the majority, if that is a consolation), you need not be a victim of statistics. Instead, identify what your parents did to sabotage their relationship. Then observe yourself to be sure you don't make the same mistakes.

3. *Avoid brief courtships.* The intense passions of romantic attraction often lead people to believe that they know each other better than they actually do. Although you may not require much time to fall in love, you do need considerable contact with a person to be sure that you both can function together in a marriage (Locke, 1951; Spanier & Glick, 1981).

4. *Consider marrying late.* Those who marry in their teens have twice the divorce rate of those who marry later (Spanier & Glick, 1981). For teens, interests, values, and personality may change dramatically within a few years. Also, teen marriages are often precipitated by pregnancy, which may lead to financial hardships.

5. *Develop a healthy personality.* Well-adjusted individuals are likely to have realistic expectations, communication and problem-solving skills, and a high tolerance for stress. These traits enhance the outlook for marriage. On the other hand, those with immature traits such as selfishness, impulsive hostility, deceitfulness, and irresponsibility would be expected to do poorly in any long-term endeavor (Renne, 1973).

6. *Participate in belief systems that emphasize commitment to marriage.* For example, most religions discourage divorce, and divorce rates for Catholics, Jews, and certain other religious groups are lower than those for people without religious affiliations (Levad, 1982).

7. *Select a partner with whom you share interests and values.* It may be desirable for partners to manifest some differences, as a way of "spicing up" the relationship. However, too many differences or differences on basic values strain the marriage. Similarity on certain personality variables may be of particular importance. For example, couples are known to select each other in terms of similarity in needs for sex, external stimulation, and affiliation (Murstein, 1980).

8. *Start from a secure economic base or be certain that you both favor non-materialistic values.* Divorce is less likely in the middle and upper classes than in the lower and working classes, presumably because of differences in financial burdens and economic stress (Hollingshead, 1968).

9. *Find a partner with whom you can share power more or less equally* (Tavris & Jayaratne, 1976). Marriages

---

FOCUS
THE MYTH OF MR. (MS.) RIGHT

The belief that you can find true love with only one other person in the world is beautifully romantic. As Robert Ringer (1978, p. 287) stated,

> You're absolutely right if you think you'll never find another love like the last one. You won't, but what you will find is a different love, one which can bring you happiness in many new ways. The old and the new can't be compared, so don't try. . . . The plain truth is that there are many people with whom you can fall genuinely in love.

As with all myths, that of Mr. Right has presumably survived because it has some adaptive value. For example, it characterizes a feeling that many lovers have experienced. They meet and feel that they have known each other forever. They speak and it seems that the words had been written for them, as in a play. In other words, it sometimes seems that this other person had been preselected, that their destinies are somehow intertwined. Although this experience can be powerful, it is usually fleeting.

In modern times, the myth of Mr. Right probably does more harm than good. It overdramatizes what is at stake, placing undue fears on the decisions of whom to marry and whether to divorce. Moreover, it leads one to expect perfection in a mate, and this inevitably causes disappointment. It is more adaptive to appreciate and even love your partner's unique, human foibles than to dwell on a fantasy of perfection.

---

in which one partner holds most of the power may lead to various forms of abuse. In addition, power holders are likely to develop little respect for their mates. Both of these factors lower the couple's overall satisfaction.

10. *Marry for love.* Women who marry primarily for love show greater satisfaction than do those marrying for sex, financial security, or to avoid loneliness (Tavris & Jayaratne, 1976).

MARRIAGE AND THE SEXES: IS IT AS GOOD FOR YOU AS IT IS FOR ME?

Although our society depicts men as dreading matrimony, the evidence suggests they are the ones it benefits. As compared with bachelors, married men show better physical and mental health, higher earnings, and a longer life span. Men have traditionally carried the economic burden, but wives have catered to their needs and provided much-needed emotional support (Bernard, 1973).

In contrast, women are less satisfied with marriage than are their husbands. They report more frustration and dissatisfaction, more negative feelings, more marital problems, greater regrets, and more symptoms of psychological disturbance (Bernard, 1973). Moreover, these findings hold for both housewives and working women (Locksley, 1980). Although the traditional role of wife and mother provides security and insulation from the business world, it also leads to restricted opportunities for social and intellectual stimulation. Working women are often expected both to hold down a job and to carry out the domestic duties of a housewife.

Early in the marriage, wives' marital satis-

faction is higher than husbands'. After the birth of their first child, however, wives' satisfaction drops (Waldron & Routh, 1981). Suggested reasons for this include: biological changes after childbirth, feelings of being tied down, fewer opportunities for social interaction, and decreased attention from the husband (Ryder, 1973).

MARITAL HAPPINESS AND CHILDREN

In recent years, married couples have shown less interest in having a family. The average number of children per marriage has dropped from four at the turn of the century to two in the 1980s. Some 20 percent of young people say they do not want to have children. In addition, today's parents report they are less willing than parents in the past to sacrifice for their children (Yankelovich, 1981). Not surprisingly, parents' relative influence has also decreased. In the 1960s, young people viewed their parents as the primary influence in their lives. Today, their beliefs and values are determined more by peers than by parents (Johnson, 1981).

Even though children are desired in most marriages, and many adults enter into marriage for the expressed purpose of raising a family, current evidence indicates that the presence of children in the home is associated with *lowered* marital happiness (Glenn, 1982; Spanier & Lewis, 1980). Glenn (1982) noted that our society prizes individualistic and hedonistic values and that marriage is expected to provide all of one's sexual and romantic needs. Glenn reasoned that in a society such as this, children lower happiness because they interfere with marital companionship and sexual spontaneity.

CHILDREN AND DIVORCE

Minimal friction between parents and frequent visits with the noncustody parent affect children's adjustment after divorce (Wallerstein & Kelly, 1980). Children whose noncustody parent visits less than once a month are often deeply disturbed, showing signs of depression and low self-esteem.

REMARRIAGE

Despite the high divorce rate, marriage has retained its popularity. About 80 percent of divorced individuals remarry, and of these, about half divorce again (Glick, 1980). Those who have remarried are about as satisfied with their remarriage as are people in their first marriage (Glenn & Weaver, 1977).

Remarrieds list the most important reasons for their previous divorce as the spouse's sexual infidelity and no longer loving each other (Glenn & Weaver, 1977). In their current marriage, remarrieds' greatest difficulty is financial, since many have to make alimony or child-support payments to a previous spouse.

What would you say is the probability that your first (or next) marriage will be a happy one? What can you do at this point to increase the likelihood that it will? What have you learned from your own parents, either by example or counterexample, that could help your marriage to succeed?

MARRIAGE AND DIVORCE: A CONFLICT OF VALUES

The impermanence of marriage sets the stage for a pitched battle between value systems: commitment and family stability, on the one hand, versus self-fulfillment, on the other. One of the choices that modern society now offers to a greater extent than ever before is whether to continue with a marriage that is not meeting one's current needs. Rather than being a choice made at the beginning of a relationship and maintained "til death do us part," many individuals are continuously evaluating their relationships and often choosing self-fulfillment over commitment. In effect, we have raised our criteria for how good a marriage has to be in order to endure. Is this a change for the better or the worse?

Certainly, it is growth enhancing for relationships to deemphasize security. Although we all require some sense of security, it is healthier to find it in ourselves rather than through dependence on another. A marriage that endures because its members are afraid to extend themselves and seek new experiences can be satisfying because it shelters one from fear, but this must be considered a minimal adjustment.

On the other hand, individuals who are unable to commit themselves to a long-term project cannot be held up as models of healthy functioning. One way of approaching this dilemma is by considering the amount of frustration that one will endure before seeking a new relationship. As in any endeavor, the person who flits from one activity to another, without developing an abiding interest in any, seems superficial and immature. The same holds true in marriage, especially when the long-term commitment involves children. In addition, traditional marriage is based on the assumption that persisting in a commitment does more for one's personal growth than does seeking out a series of temporarily attractive new partners.

But how much frustration and dissatisfaction should one endure before ending a marriage and breaking up a family? How does one know if the decision to divorce is growth enhancing or simply a sign of immaturity?

Toffler (1980), for example, suggests that with the rapid changes in modern society and with people continuing to change throughout their adult lives, it would be unrealistic and overly restrictive to think that all marriages should last until death.

Nevertheless, many experience tremendous guilt and self-blame when their marriages end in divorce. They believed in their vows of a lifetime commitment and feel that the reality of divorce somehow labels them a failure. Toffler observed that personal blame makes some sense when marital permanence is the norm. In modern times, however, impermanence is becoming the norm. Under such circumstances we cannot hope to understand the changes the family is undergoing in terms of personal blame. Thus guilt and self-blame for marriages that "fail" are often no longer appropriate responses.

The decision to live outside a nuclear family framework should be made easier, not harder. Values change more slowly, as a rule, than social reality. Thus we have not yet developed the ethic of tolerance for diversity that a demassified society will both require and engender. . . . Taught that one kind of family is "normal" and others somehow suspect, if not "deviant," vast numbers remain intolerant of the new variety in family styles. Until that changes, the pain of transition will remain unnecessarily high. (Toffler, 1980, pp. 241–242)

Although there can be no pat answers to the issue of whether to divorce, some guidelines can be suggested. First, it must be acknowledged that there is value in commitment. Long-term commitments should be ended only as a last resort, when it has become clear that the individuals

1. Have unalterable differences in basic values.
2. Have learned how to use communication skills so that they are sure the problem is not due to an unfortunate series of misunderstandings.
3. Have sought advice from an objective third party.
4. Have taken into account long-term consequences as well as short-term gratifications.

After considering such factors, then it may be clear that divorce, especially if it can be accomplished without blame or recrimination, may be a viable and honorable end to a good relationship.

MARITAL MONOTONY AND THE LURE OF EXTRAMARITAL SEX

THE APPARENT FAILURE OF FIDELITY

It would be difficult to overestimate the concern with sexual fidelity in our culture. As noted above, infidelity is one of the major causes

of divorce. Movies, television, and song lyrics often revolve around the love triangle and the dilemma of what to do with sexual desires that don't seem to fit the bonds of matrimony. Television soap operas and country music, in particular, specialize in infidelity. For example, consider one song title from a list of "cheatin" songs that number in the hundreds, "She's acting single and I'm drinking doubles." As is typical with many of these songs, an element of humor softens, but does not negate, the serious implications for the emotional lives of all married couples.

Traditionally, marriage includes a vow of **sexual fidelity**, the promise to have sexual contact only with one's spouse. Not all married couples, however, have actually promised complete fidelity. Thus, **extramarital sex** is a more neutral term for sexual contact with someone other than one's spouse.

Research suggests that about half of all married individuals have had extramarital sex at least once. Given the high expectations of most engaged couples, this "failure rate" seems alarmingly high. Are our expectations too idealistic, given the realities of human nature and the temptations of modern society? Or are we simply allowing ourselves to slip into a state of moral laxity? The next section examines these complex value decisions.

WHY FIDELITY?

Why do lovers promise each other sexual fidelity? Some of the traditional reasons include:

1. As a biological fact, a man cannot be certain that he is the father of a woman's children. Thus, restricting women to sexual fidelity helps assure a man that the children he rears are actually his. Sociobiologists, for example, regard ensuring the survival of one's genes as the most important task in our lives. Even so, the time is not far off when physiological tests will be able to determine paternity with certainty. (At present, they can only disqualify some with certainty.)

2. Fidelity is thought to stabilize the marital union, making it a more secure and effective environment for raising children. For example, extramarital sex may increase the probability that one partner will fall in love with another and dissolve the family unit.

3. A more personal reason is that many lovers experience intense jealousy at the mere thought of their partner having a romantic or sexual interest in another. Most psychologists, however, suggest that jealousy is a function of insecurity and the lack of self-esteem. By implication, healthy individuals are not threatened, or at least are less threatened, by their partner's interest in another. When well-being is based on self-acceptance rather than dependency, the threat of infidelity is reduced.

4. Love may be so consuming that there is no desire for outside relationships. Here, the pledge of fidelity is a show of confidence that love will endure. According to the statistics on extramarital sex and divorce, however, the belief that extramarital sex will be neither missed nor

desired is, for most couples, unrealistic. Even in totally monogamous marriages, fidelity is usually maintained only through exercising considerable resistance to temptation.

THE ARGUMENT FOR EXTRAMARITAL SEX

Psychologists and marriage counselors vary in their attitudes toward extramarital sex. There is no uniformity of opinion as to whether it is psychologically adaptive or destructive. Some experts in the field (Ellis, 1976; Francoeur & Francoeur, 1976; Jourard, 1975) argue that extramarital sex allows a degree of sexual variety that is more in keeping with our actual biological desires. It also allows a more extended network of intimate relationships that, in principle, could enhance personal growth. Theoretically, extramarital sex could enrich the marriage and even prolong its longevity by removing one of the major reasons for divorce. However, such extramarital arrangements are definitely not for every couple. Both partners must feel secure in themselves and in their love; otherwise jealousy will undermine the relationship (Clanton & Smith, 1977).

It is also important that partners be mature enough to know who they are and what they want from an extramarital relationship. Without this maturity, the probability that one partner will fall in love and seek a divorce rises, and the destabilizing effect of extramarital sex may become unacceptably high. Unfortunately, questions of psychological maturity are highly subjective, at least at present. For example, in many couples, each partner feels that he or she has the maturity for occasional affairs, but at the same time, each is convinced that the partner does not.

Nevertheless, the main argument in favor of extramarital sex is that expecting one person to fulfill all of one's needs for physical and sexual intimacy is unnecessarily restrictive. Although this often occurs in the early, high-intensity stages of a relationship, the voluntary desire for exclusivity is usually short-lived. After that, fidelity may no longer function as a pledge freely given, but as a quasi-legal contract. When its character has changed from a free offering proclaiming "I want only you" to a contract that specifies "I won't if you won't," then something very basic in the relationship has been altered.

THE ARGUMENT AGAINST EXTRAMARITAL SEX

Other experts, such as noted sex therapists Masters and Johnson (1975), take a dim view of both extramarital sex and the experts who espouse it. According to Masters and Johnson (1975, p. 183), these experts are acting out their own erotic fantasies. By sanctioning extramarital sex, they are "irresponsibly encouraging people to jump into a deep river with dangerous undercurrents, ignoring the fact that they may not know how to swim."

Masters and Johnson acknowledge that the feeling of aliveness is a powerful value and a good index of the quality of one's life. They contend that people feel most fully alive when they can be stimulated by the challenge of the unknown and yet have the security of the known to give them the confidence for trying new endeavors. For many, monogamy ends this alternation between the new and the old. According to Masters and Johnson, however, these people lack either the imagination or the motivation to revitalize their marriages. For them, the only variety they can think of is having other partners. But "since they find this morally unacceptable, or simply too risky, they settle for security and, no matter how reluctantly, accept as a fact that monogamy inevitably becomes monotony" (Masters & Johnson, 1975, p. 184).

But what alternative can Masters and Johnson offer? They suggest that to override this marital monotony, we must first become more fully alive ourselves. We must discard our stereotyped conceptions of sex and instead see it as a medium for creativity. For Masters and Johnson, those who tire of sex with the same partner are like artists who believe they cannot be creative using the same old colors. Masters and Johnson believe that sex can be a living medium from which the mood of the time, place, and circumstance creates a unique experience, in which sex is "lived" rather than "performed." They are suggesting that sex can be experienced more fully and more consciously and that this experience can then be communicated to one's partner. In this process lies the continuing excitement of monogamous love.

This is the challenge of combining sex, love, and fidelity to form a growth-enhancing marriage. And although Masters and Johnson did not rule out extramarital sex, they fear it may be a cure that is more destructive than the disease.

It should be noted that most psychologists draw an important distinction between extramarital sex and infidelity. Whereas the notion of extramarital sex enhancing a relationship is sometimes entertained, this is rarely the case with infidelity. Its dishonesty almost guarantees destructive effects on the relationship.

Masters and Johnson alluded to a crucial distinction between sex that is lived rather than merely performed. What do you think they mean? If sex is carried out as a "performance," who is the audience?

CASE OF THE SUCCESSFUL BUSINESSMAN AND THE YOUNGER WOMAN

Psychologist Sidney Jourard (1975) found that whether extramarital sex is good or bad in itself, it often springs from a positive motivation. When one's emotional life has stagnated, choosing extramarital sex is often a movement (even if misguided) toward life, toward enhancing one's state of aliveness. Jourard took the controversial position that this movement may be healthier than accepting emotional stagnation. Consider Harry R., an affluent man in his late forties who recently left his wife and three children to live with a woman in her twenties.

Look, you get to be 46, 47 years old. You look at your life. You came out of school with a lot of dreams, and some of the dreams you got, some of them you didn't. Maybe most of them you didn't. You've got a wife you've known for so long it's hard to remember when you didn't know her. My own wife, I met in high school. You've got kids who are almost grown up themselves. The challenge is gone out of your work. If you're lucky, you've reached a position that's good. If you're not lucky, you haven't reached that position and you're never going to make it because the young kids are going to crawl right over you.

You look at your life and it's all going to be downhill. There is nothing for you to look forward to, nothing really new. All you're expected to do is get up in the morning, go to your job, and spend the evening with the wife and kids. . . .

It's such a trap. And you feel everything slipping away from you. You know you're going to do everything you're expected to do until the morning you die. And then you meet a girl.

The girl I now live with knew I was married when we first started going out. She let me know she knew it. Do you know how great that made me feel, that she was accepting me for myself? There were never any demands. She said she liked being with me. . . .

Well . . . all I know is that she made me feel young again. That's not saying it strong enough. Listen, being with her was the difference between life and death. When I was at her place I was living, when I was at home I was dying.

And it became a question of did I want to spend the rest of my life alive or dead? Did I do the right thing and wake up every morning of the rest of my life miserable, or did I do the thing that's supposed to be wrong and start my life over again?

I agonized over it. I looked at my wife at night, and I looked at my children, and I wondered what kind of monster I was. But that was in my head. In my heart, I was aching to make myself happy. I had spent my entire adult life making a life for my wife and my children. Now I wanted to make a life for myself.

The day that decided it, I was playing tennis with my new girl. I looked at her in her tennis dress, and she was so young and full of life. And without even wanting to, I thought what my wife would look like on the tennis court, and it repulsed me. Isn't that a terrible thing to admit? But that's how it happened, and from that day on I knew I was leaving.

I don't know (if anyone would feel sympathetic toward me). Probably not. But I can live without sympathy. I've got love. (Adapted from Greene, 1978)

The social psychology of leaving your wife. Harry's story can be understood from several points of view. According to social psychological theories (social exchange and equity), we would expect people to form relationships based on their values in the social marketplace, with partners of equal "value" forming the more stable pairings. In romantic relationships, men tend to be judged on their wealth and social power, and women on their youth and beauty. Thus, it is not unexpected that an affluent middle-aged man would (and could) leave his aging wife for a younger woman.

As indicated in Chapter 10, the emotional intensity of romantic love often wanes over time. Many married individuals long to reexperience the passion of young love. It could be argued that it is easier to do this with a new partner than through a revitalization of the type that Masters and Johnson described. (On the other hand, it is unlikely that the passion of the new relationship will last any longer than it did in the original marriage.)

Thus it could be argued that Harry is simply doing what comes naturally. Within the rules of his social environment, Harry is seeking a greater state of aliveness by trading on the wealth and social status that he has worked hard to attain. And although moral rules have evolved to protect the stability of the family, his children are grown and there is little reason to continue with an unsatisfying relationship when more desirable alternatives await. Certainly, there will be hard feelings and many of his friends will think less of him. But if he is willing to accept these consequences, then why not make himself happy?

As an aside, note that in real-life situations, rules such as "doing what you want as long as you don't hurt anyone" are so general that they are often useless. In intimate relationships, almost everything you do will have repercussions on those around you. Sometimes others will be hurt because they want more than they have a right to expect. At other times, they may want only what was promised.

The failure to take responsibility. Many psychologists would disagree with Harry, claiming that his characterization of what happened is self-serving, biased, and immature. They might point out, for example, that Harry took little or no responsibility for his boredom. His view was completely externalized. He says that the challenge has "gone out of his work," as if *he* has nothing to do with what he will perceive as challenging. It could as easily be said that Harry stopped challenging himself. He allowed his life to become a boring routine in which he did only what was expected of him. It is no wonder that his life lacked excitement. When one continually does "what is expected," rather than what his own heart and feelings impel, boredom is the inevitable result.

Harry's marital relationship had also succumbed to routine. But Harry describes it as an outsider, as if he weren't one of the participants, as if he neither contributed to the problem nor has any control over its solution. Although he didn't elaborate, it seems that Harry and his wife have fallen into a habit of discussing "appropriate topics" in predictable ways. By saying what is appropriate rather than what one actually

feels, conversations naturally become dull. If one has a low need for excitement, these predictable conversations can be soothing, comfortable rituals. But this was not Harry's case.

Harry wants to characterize his adult life as a sacrifice made for his wife and children. And now it is time to make himself happy. Although we are not given the details, this account sounds suspiciously self-serving. We might wonder, "What motivated this tremendous sacrifice in the first place?" It seems likely that what Harry now describes as a sacrifice is a strategy he originally chose for making himself happy. A common pattern, for example, is doing things for others that in our hearts we don't really want to do. Nevertheless, these things help ensure that our partner will not tire of the relationship. In other words, these sacrifices might be made not out of love but out of a calculated strategy of control.

It is clear that Harry has become disillusioned with his whole life, not just his marriage. In a sense, leaving his family for a younger woman is a symbolic act, a way of trying to turn around his whole life-pattern. As such, he is placing a tremendous burden on the new relationship. It is unrealistic to expect his new love to overturn the deadening habits he has constructed over many years.

Curiously, Harry said very little about his wife, other than suggesting that she has become physically unattractive. Apparently, there has been little real intimacy between them over the years. Although he was reluctant to leave her, it was not because he would miss her or even because he didn't want to hurt her. Instead, Harry has a more impersonal conception of right and wrong, and in terms of those principles, he would be a "monster" to leave his family.

Attraction to the younger woman. What is the basis for Harry's attraction to the younger woman? One reason is that she accepted him for who he is, without trying to change him or pressure him to leave his wife. In addition, this acceptance undoubtedly boosted Harry's ego. It raises one's own sense of worth to be accepted by someone of social value. It might be argued, however, that if Harry already felt good about himself, this acceptance from a younger woman would mean much less.

Harry described the moment when he decided to leave his wife as involving a realization that his new lover was attractive, young, and full of life. In contrast, his wife had become physically repulsive. Harry claims that he feels happy and alive when with his mistress but miserable and dead with his wife. Has Harry merely outgrown a wife who has allowed herself to deaden? If so, perhaps he is responding to the younger woman in a natural and desirable manner.

Some might feel, however, that Harry's emphasis on physical beauty is superficial, revealing his shallowness in relating to others. Moreover, he might be forsaking his "true values" for a mere status symbol. Note also that Harry may well have allowed himself to deaden just as much as his wife has. But now he is able to let his wealth and social position buy him another chance at aliveness.

Concluding thoughts. Did Harry act honorably? Although his behavior was understandable and not uncommon, he violated his own professed values and his word. A healthier course of action would have been for Harry to take the responsibility for turning around his job and marriage. He might have changed jobs, developed other interests, or found job-related activities about which he could get excited. He could have changed the way he interacted with his wife, varying their routine and increasing the spontaneity and genuineness of his time with her. Instead of looking at her with the preconception that there would never be anything new to see, he could have taken the responsibility to see her anew, looking for ways that she has changed, encouraging her to reveal aspects of herself that she usually concealed from him, even confronting and challenging her to move toward a greater sense of aliveness.

If Harry's efforts to turn their marriage around did not work, he might next have negotiated for more freedom to form outside relationships and find alternative ways of bringing a greater sense of aliveness to his life. In a context of negotiation, Harry's family would at least be given some opportunity to control their fate.

It seems clear that Harry acted selfishly and unethically. Although his desire for greater happiness and a sense of renewed aliveness are positive motivations, there are many routes by which these goals might have been pursued. Moreover, the issue of extramarital sex seems in some ways tangential; perhaps the more basic concern is finding a way to live each day so that one's sense of aliveness is enhanced rather than beaten down.

What did you think of Harry? What would you add or change in this analysis? If you found yourself in Harry's position, how would you like to handle it? How do you think you actually would handle it?

It may help to conceptualize a number of marital alternatives, thinking about which you would prefer and why. Rank the following alternatives in terms of your personal preferences:

_____ **Fidelity offered out of a desire for your partner only, without any obligation for fidelity in return.**

_____ **Fidelity willingly offered under the condition that your partner also be faithful.**

_____ **Fidelity (reluctantly) accepted to ensure stability of the family.**

_____ **Extramarital sex for you; fidelity for your partner.**

_____ **Occasional extramarital sex for both partners, with the agreement that these relationships be carried on discreetly and that they not be discussed.**

_____ **Controlled extramarital sex, such as wife swapping or swinging.**

_____ **Extramarital sex for both partners, openly discussed.**

One of the most influential positions in marriage and family counseling approaches the family as a system in which the behaviors of each individual cannot be understood without seeing their effects on the system as a whole. Within this framework, treatment is carried out with the family itself and not with the individual patient. This part of the chapter explores the dynamics of family systems and examines patterns of dysfunctional communication found in many families.

THE FAMILY SYSTEM

THE IDENTIFIED PATIENT

For family therapist Salvadore Minuchin, the behaviors of all family members are intertwined. Typically, one member will be presented as having a problem. But one of the most striking observations of family therapists is that analysis of the verbal and nonverbal interactions in the family often reveals that the problem behavior is caused and maintained by the family itself. Problems of the identified patient often play an essential role in the family's stability. In other words, they come to depend on the patient's pathology in order to function.

THE FAMILY RULE

Minuchin (1974) observed that families function according to unstated rules that all members follow, usually without realizing it. These implicit rules determine how, when, and to whom each of the family members will relate. The rules not only guide behavior, but they also tell family members who they are and how they will perceive one another. For example, one rule, explored in detail below, is that the mother must be protected, that each member must prevent the mother's bizarre behavior from coming to attention.

For Minuchin, the goal in family therapy is making people aware of their rigid and destructive patterns of interaction. His approach has been applied to a wide variety of problems, including child discipline, failure in school, depression, and even psychosomatic complaints such as asthma.

Minuchin pointed out that when a child is the identified patient, he or she plays a role in the parents' conflict with each other. For example, a family composed of a mother, father, and diabetic daughter was observed while monitoring each member's free fatty-acid level (an index of emotional arousal). When the parents were alone together, their acid levels increased. When the child was present, allowing the parents to switch from spouse to parent roles, their acid levels decreased, whereas that of the diabetic child increased.

THE FAMILY'S RESISTANCE TO CHANGE

Family members' roles are often so tightly interlocked that any effort to change one member elicits resistance from the others, even when a family is presenting itself for change in therapy. Strategies that family therapists use to circumvent this problem usually involve finding some way of upsetting the family's equilibrium. This may include, for example, making an open alliance with one member, acting "more crazy" than the identified patient, or using two therapists to gain more control over the interaction.

Umbarger and Hare (1973) described a disordered family composed of the mother, father, and twelve-year-old son, Eddie. Eddie displayed a number of bizarre mannerisms, including incoherent speech, odd posture and walk, and numerous fears and bodily complaints. The family had been seeing various therapists for several years, with no improvement in Eddie's condition. As Umbarger and Hare characterize it, "The family had defeated a variety of therapeutic efforts" (p. 274). This family's uncanny ability to resist change and destroy the efforts of skilled therapists is documented in the following excerpt:

> Harry and Imogene Decker seemed to costume themselves for the role of patients. Their outfits, down to the smallest detail, were comic parodies of a dress style fashionable only for the back wards of state mental hospitals. Theirs was a kind of chronic chic.

Imogene, a small woman, wore pink sweat socks, blowsy skirts of indeterminate age and style, and mismatched blouses. Harry, a heavy man, was less floridly dressed, yet there was an unmistakable air of cultivated defiance about his clothes. His grey work pants, always several sizes too large, were bunched together at his waist by a beaded Indian belt. Like Imogene, he carried at least one paper shopping bag and sometimes two, filled with items that were indispensable only for a person going on the bum in an unfriendly climate: extra socks, woolen scarfs, a foreign language dictionary, and a box of Girl Scout cookies.

In the midst of the shuffle of parental shopping bags was Eddie. He was tall, ungainly, yet delicately made, a marionette whose strings were of the wrong length. He spoke in a rapid voice, sometimes slurring his words so badly that even the most practiced and patient parent would have difficulty understanding him.

Therapy sessions inevitably began with this small family of three dividing themselves into two whirlwind armies who would descend on the therapist from opposite ends of the corridor. With gales of strained laughter they would finally enter the therapy room.

"I might choke to death," said Imogene, "since this room seems filled with chalk dust. Too much erasing, not enough correctness." She settled into one chair, then tried another, looking suspiciously under each chair for some evidence of dust and dirt. Harry was solicitous though uneasy with his wife's behavior. He offered to change seats with her, made a few ineffectual efforts to clean the blackboard, and then returned to his seat.

"There's dust at school, too," volunteered Eddie.

"Tell the doctor what happened there, if he wants to know," Mr. Decker said.

The therapist, feeling that a direction and topic were emerging, readily agreed. "By all means. What happened?" He was unaware that he had fallen in with Harry and Eddie who were effectively diverting attention from Imogene's odd behavior by introducing Eddie's school problems.

Eddie stared intently at his mother, never losing eye contact with her as he told his story. "I fell on the playground and scraped my side. Then when I got to the nurse's office I thought I might faint from the algebra left to do, so naturally I made the nurse call my mother and then I went home. And that's all of that. Aside from the three tongues." So saying, he seemed to consider the matter closed, although Mrs. Decker clearly had more on her mind.

"Thank God I was at home, the streets being what they are. Boy Scouts or no Boy Scouts," she concluded as a kind of mysterious afterthought.

"I think we should get down to an efficient discussion of why we are coming here, not why there are no Boy Scouts on the streets." Mr. Decker was again responding to his wife's meanderings by trying to organize the family.

"I thought we settled that last year," replied Mrs. Decker, "when we were worried about how Eddie was picked on in school. And his dizzy spells, some of which must be due to all the dust that's around."

"Is that what you've been worried about all this time?" asked Harry. "I thought you wondered about the fatigue of your mental processes and why your feet are swelling."

"Mother's feet don't swell," said Eddie, heading off my focus on his mother.

"I'm sorry." Harry grinned weakly.

"Why can't you just be wrong like other men without having to be sorry all the time?" Mrs. Decker said. "Then our social life would improve."

The therapist, losing track of the bewildering school problems, moved quickly in support of Mrs. Decker's new topic. "Are you asking your husband to change something about your social life?" Though well intended, the question supported an implicit criticism of Mr. Decker and ignored his efforts of only a moment ago to "organize" the discussion, a typical fate for Mr. Decker's efforts to be efficient. As the therapist slipped from side to side, first in alliance with efforts to ignore Mrs. Decker's concern with a dusty, poisonous environment and then with *her* efforts to ignore Mr. Decker's attempt at organizing the family, he got a premonition of the trip to come.

Mrs. Decker grew wistful for a second. "We used to go to parties all the time, but the person who invited us died."

"I asked you to go to a meeting of Radicals Over Thirty with me and you refused. You complained that political people don't know how to polka. I mean I tried." Harry seemed genuinely hurt by his wife's attack.

The therapist, trying to hold onto a topic, said, "Each of you seems to really want the same thing, to do something together socially." He skipped over Harry's hurt feeling, inadvertently supporting Mrs. Decker's injunction that her husband should stop feeling "sorry" every time he was criticized. The family "rule" that mother should never be found wanting was being scrupulously, though inadvertently, observed by the therapist. Just to make sure, Imogene flared up, scooting to the edge of her chair. "Are you implying that we are a failure in social ethics?"

"Etiquette," said Harry.

"Ethical societies don't interest us and never will," Imogene continued. "Moreover there is nothing funny about trying to be ethical and I resent your implication that my husband and I aren't ethical."

"I only suggested that the two of you might do something social together . . . that is, not separate. Ah, thinking for the future . . . that is, since the past is over." The therapist was uncomfortable, but still trying to give cogent meanings to the conversation and smooth over ruffled feelings, a response typical of outsiders who tried to get inside this family.

"Mommy and Daddy can't go out," whined Eddie. "I need them at home to help me with my merit badges." He too was sitting on the edge of his chair, eyes fastened on his mother, with a glazed look, as if transported by thoughts of a merit badge in social ethics.

Suddenly, on some secret signal, all three members of the family arose and, crossing impolitely in front of the therapist, switched seats, each person moving over one chair.

"Whenever I stand up in here, the room gets small," said Eddie in his Alice-in-Wonderland voice.

"Then sit down!" replied the harassed therapist. He relaxed, happily unaware that he sounded just like one of the family.

"What is the rationale for peephole therapy?" asked Imogene, apparently referring to the observation mirror along one side of the room.

"Whatever it is," replied Harry in his efficient voice, while pulling a thermos from his shopping bag, "I think it's time for a tea break."

"It's always the same here," sighed Eddie, taking a small wax cup of tepid tea. "Nothing ever changes, week after week."

"Better safe than sorry," commented Mrs. Decker dramatically.

"Precisely how many weeks has it been?" said Mr. Decker, still dreaming of organization.

"Thirteen," said the therapist, holding out his cup. (Umbarger & Hare, 1973, pp. 276–278)

This account vividly portrays the workings of a disturbed family and illustrates the difficulties in trying to change long-established patterns of interaction. Here, the husband and son had formed an unspoken collusion to divert attention away from the mother's disordered thinking. Following the father's cue, the therapist was led to focus on the son's symptoms as if he were the sick one and the mother were perfectly sane.

Eventually, the therapists achieved some success with Eddie by structuring the sessions to gain greater control of the family. One therapist conducted the session while the other observed through a one-way mirror. Sessions were divided into two periods, and during the break between periods the therapists conferred, allowing the participant-therapist to get objective feedback on the patterns of interaction. In the first period, all members were present, and the discussion had to deal with promoting Eddie's autonomy. For example, they might discuss his conduct at school, club activities, or his plans to take swimming lessons. In addition, a demand was placed on Eddie for "clear speech" as a way of preventing his use of bizarre statements to distract attention away from the mother's behavior. In the second period, the therapist met with the parents, who were allowed only to discuss their own relationship and not their son's symptoms.

Go back through the therapy excerpt and identify instances in which the father's and son's behavior functioned to justify or to divert attention from the mother's unusual behavior.

DISORDERED FAMILY COMMUNICATION

DISTURBING MESSAGES

Family systems are ideal for studying patterns of communication. They provide a context of intimate relationships in which the members' strategies for dealing with one another have had a chance to stabilize over a period of years. In addition, the context of intimate living fosters strong, often ambivalent feelings for one another.

Families consist of individuals holding differing levels of power. Because of their extreme dependency, children are vulnerable to their parents' dysfunctional communications. And because of their youth, they often have not developed the sophisticated defenses that might thwart maladaptive parental influences.

Not surprisingly, research indicates a clear link between disturbed family communication and psychopathology of the offspring (Al-Khayyal & Jones, 1981; Jones et al., 1977; Wild, Shapiro, & Goldenberg, 1975; Wynne et al., 1977). We shall next examine several of the most common forms of dysfunctional communication.

Mystification refers to telling other people what *they* are feeling. This leads mystified individuals to doubt and lose touch with who they are and what they are experiencing. Parents, because of their greater power, can exert considerable influence in defining a child's internal life.

Paradoxical communication refers to a message that contradicts itself. For example, two verbal components of a message may form a logical contradiction, as in the command "Try to be more spontaneous!" (trying harder negates spontaneity). Another form of paradox occurs when a verbal message is disqualified by nonverbal behavior, as in saying "I like you" while shaking the head back and forth.

The **double-bind** is a more complex form of communication, often containing one or more paradoxical messages. The double-bind involves a message to respond, with the implication that there is a correct response, when in fact no correct response is possible. In addition, the individual is blocked from escaping the situation or commenting on the impossibility of the task. Examples of several double-binds appear below. Although the double-bind was originally hypothesized to be the cause of schizophrenia, more recent research indicates that many factors, including genetic predispositions, create this disturbance. Nevertheless, double-binds clearly undermine the quality of a relationship and contribute to interpersonal stress and psychopathology (Loos, Critelli, Stevenson, & Tang, 1984).

CASE OF THE AMBIVALENT MOTHER

The preceding three forms of disordered communication are illustrated in the following

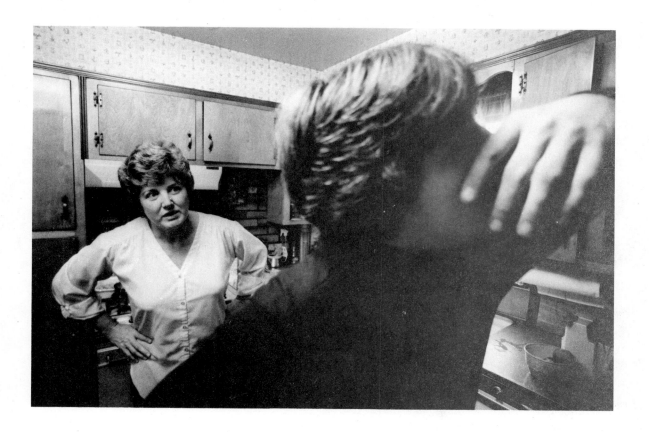

case involving a mother and her eleven-year-old son, Ted. Ted is doing poorly in school and is complaining of headaches and anxiety attacks. The mother became pregnant as a teenager and was coerced by her own mother into a hasty marriage, with the husband leaving shortly after Ted was born. The mother is consumed with ambivalent feelings toward her son. She bitterly resents him for causing her to "lose her youth and her freedom." At the same time, she loves him intensely and depends on him to give her an excuse for withdrawing from the adult world. Note that her conflicts with Ted center on themes of love-rejection and dependence-independence. (This dialogue [Critelli & Loos, 1984] is a composite of actual case studies of disturbed children. Nevertheless, the types of communication it shows can be found in any American household.)

[Ted is coming home from school.]

Mom: *Teddy honey, you know you really hurt my feelings when you raised your voice and just walked off and left me all alone this morning. (Although she is honestly expressing her hurt feelings, she has also managed to interpret his leaving for school as an abandonment.)*

Ted: *I'm sorry Mom, I won't do it again.*

Mom: *Oh, it's OK. I know you didn't really mean it. You just weren't feeling yourself, that's all. . . . When you talk back to me like this morning, I get afraid that you're not well. (By telling him that he didn't really mean it, she is using mystification. She is also implying that he must choose between being "bad" or "sick"; either he is bad for intentionally hurting and abandoning his own mother or he is "not well." Ted's perception of himself as getting genuinely* angry with his mother and intentionally leaving the scene to go to school now becomes threatening.)

Ted: *I feel fine, Mom, really.*

Mom: *I'm glad you're feeling better; I would hate for anything to be wrong with you. (By reasserting her interpretation that Ted has been sick, the mystification continues. In addition, she denies wanting him to be sick. But for a loving mother, this would require no denial. The effect of this out-of-context denial is to introduce the possibility that she may want something to be wrong with Ted. She may be subtly telling him that she would prefer that he be sick rather than "disrespectful," that is, no longer dependent.)*

Ted: *Did anybody call or anything? (Attempting to change the subject.)*

Mom: *Sweetie, I know you didn't really mean to leave me like that, but sometimes I wonder if you love me the way a son should love his mother. (Refusal to let Ted control the topic; manipulating Ted into an expression of love.)*

Ted: *I love you, Mom. (Putting his arms around her and kissing her on the cheek.)*

Mom: *Yes, and you know that I love you too. [Turning her face away and stiffening her body, holding him at a distance.] (Paradoxical communication: verbal statement of love is disqualified by nonverbal behavior. Note also that she chose to verbalize the love indirectly, as "you know that I love you" rather than simply saying "I love you." This indirect usage also acts as a disqualification.)*

[Pause]

Mom: *There, there, you don't need to be embarrassed about loving your mother. (Mystification and perhaps projection, since she was the one who evidenced discomfort during the embrace.)*

Ted: *Mom, I've got to tell you something. We got our report cards today, and Mrs. Andrews flunked me in math. (Trying to blame it on the teacher.)*

Mom: *Oh, my God! Let me see it! (Grabs report card.) I knew it. You're making bad grades on purpose, aren't you? How do you think this makes me feel? (Accusing son of wanting to hurt her.)*

Ted: *I'm sorry, Mom. I don't know what happened. I tried.*

Mom: *Oh, well . . . I know you're doing all that you can. Just try harder, OK? (Double-binding statement. If Ted is doing all that he can, then it would be impossible to "try harder." If he isn't, then he is intentionally getting poor grades in order to hurt his mother.)*

Mom: *Yes, try harder. Homework must be done every night from now on.*

Ted: *OK, I promise.*

Mom: *Oh, by the way, Jackie called. He wants you to come over to his house after supper and do homework with him and his Dad.*

Ted: *Oh boy! Can I?*

Mom: *Sure. You'd better go. It will give you a chance to bring up your grades.*

[Phone rings.]

Ted: *Who was it?*

Mom: *Grandma. She can't come over tonight as she planned. She's going to play bingo with her friends instead. . . . Say, are you hungry?*

Ted: *Yeah, I sure am.*

Mom: *Good. I've been baking cookies for you all afternoon. I hope you like them. Here, but don't spoil your appetite for supper.*

Ted: *(Takes and starts eating chocolate-chip cookie) It's really good, Mom!*

Mom: *(Sad and disappointed) The oatmeal cookies you don't like? (Double-bind. Ted is led into believing that there is a correct response, to take a cookie and show enthusiasm for it. Presumably, if he had taken the oatmeal cookie, she would have been disappointed that he didn't like the chocolate-chip, and if he had taken some of each, he would be in danger of spoiling his appetite.)*

Ted: *I'll eat some.*

Mom: *Please, don't make excuses. I know how you really feel. (Using mystification to nullify Ted's attempt to get out of the bind.)*

(Feeling frustrated and depressed, Ted begins to distract himself by looking down at the floor and playing with his fingers, using this activity as a way of escaping into fantasy.)

Mom: *Listen, Ted. Don't feel like that. You know I love you as if a son. (Paradoxical communication: She appears to be affirming her love, but the "as if" implies he may not even be her son.)*

Mom: *You know I was glad that Jackie called. He's a nice boy and very smart too. Sometimes I wonder, though, if he isn't a bad influence on you. Didn't he run away from home and leave his parents all alone once? My God, a mother could disown her son for something like that. (Implied put-down in mentioning Jackie's smartness after Ted brought home a bad report card. Implied threat of disowning a son who would abandon his mother.)*

Ted: *No, that was Jerry Anderson who ran away from home.*

Mom: *Oh well, Jerry, Jackie, whatever. . . .*

Mom: *Oh, by the way, Ted, before we get ready for dinner, you know you ought to call up Jackie and tell him what you're going to do tonight. What did you decide? (By raising this as a question rather than just a reminder, she has reopened the decision and created a double-binding setup: If he leaves, he will be abandoning his mother [who now would be alone for the evening], but if he stays, he will be neglecting his studies.)*

Ted: *What do you think I should do? (Trying to escape the bind.)*

Mom: *Oh none of that, young man. You are old enough to make such decisions for yourself.*

Ted: *Well, I guess I'll go over and study just for a little while.*

[Pause]

Mom: *I don't know if I can even eat any dinner right now. I just feel a little uneasy to my stomach. But I'll be all right. I just need to lie down for a while. You don't have to worry about me. It's not your fault. (Closing the bind. The out-of-context denial that her illness is not Ted's fault implies, of course, that it is his fault. The illness, which in some sense may be real, can be used to ensure that Ted stays at home. Presumably, if Ted had chosen to stay home, he would be punished with reminders that he must be trying to hurt his mother by neglecting his studies.)*

DEFENDING AGAINST DISORDERED MESSAGES

How would you try to protect yourself from these sorts of disturbing messages? One of the most obvious and reliable protections is simply being able to identify what the other person is doing as it occurs in the conversation. If you can discern these word games and understand that the problem is coming from the other person, you will be a giant step ahead.

Another protection is trying to get outside these games by verbalizing your understanding of the other person's disordered communication. In other words, instead of merely responding as the other person expects, you can comment on his or her style of communication. (Recall that this is called metacommunication.) For example, you might say, "Mom, I did mean to leave for school as I did this morning, because at that time I was feeling angry with you." Metacommunication can be highly effective, especially between individuals of equal power, but it takes considerable practice and immediate awareness of what is going on in the interaction. Often, we realize what was happening only much later, after the optimal moment for commenting has passed. Of course, the power differential within families makes it even more difficult for children to metacommunicate.

Go back over this dialogue and try to formulate metacommunicational responses for

Ted. As a way of seeing what a fix Ted is in, try getting into his mother's frame of mind and formulating her possible counterreplies.

CHILD REARING: LOVE AND DISCIPLINE

Without discipline, children are unlikely to learn the behaviors that will allow them to fit into society. Beyond that, they may not develop self-control and the capacity for self-discipline. Many parents, however, equate discipline with punishment. At the same time, they think of punishment and expressions of love as opposites. Thus, parents often feel that they must choose between loving their children and trying to control them. The following section analyzes this dilemma and suggests a possible solution.

THE NEED FOR LOVE AND ACCEPTANCE

Carl Rogers ascribes to a theory of discipline that revolves around our need to feel loved and accepted by the important people in our lives, particularly our parents. Rogers contends that if our parents selectively reward us for being good and withdraw expressions of their love when we misbehave, we will come to believe we are worthy of love only when experiencing socially appropriate thoughts, feelings, and behaviors.

When this is the case, we become oriented toward establishing security and seeking the approval of others, rather than toward furthering our potential for growth. For example, we may avoid taking risks and extending ourselves into challenging new endeavors. Thus, for Rogers, the lack of unconditional love forms the basis for enduring character deficiencies, causing us to lead lives that are far short of our genetic potential.

THE PUNITIVE PARENT

According to Rogers, parents must find a way to discipline their children without taking

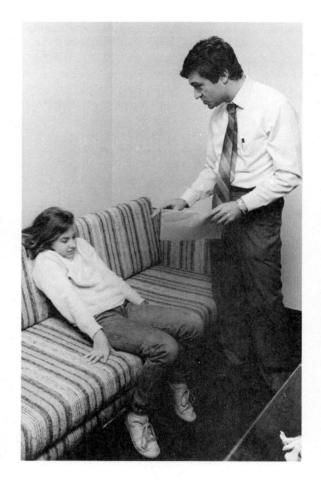

away the experience that they are loved for who they are, not just for what they do. For example, consider the following dilemma: Dad walks in on Sally, who is slapping her baby brother in the face. Sensing that he must act quickly, Dad rushes into the room,

Dad: *You little brat, get your hands off of him (yelling, hostile tone of voice).*
Sally: *But Daddy, he started it. He pulled the eye off my baby doll.*
Dad: *I don't care. You're a bad girl, and don't ever let me catch you hitting him again.*
Sally: *I hate him!*
Dad: *That's not true. Don't say that. You do not*

hate your brother; you're just upset right now and you know it.

From a Rogerian point of view, the above exchange is a disaster. By using a hostile tone of voice and by calling Sally a "brat" and a "bad girl," the father is momentarily rejecting her and damaging her self-concept. Although the situation demands that he get her attention quickly, one might wonder why his voice carried a hostile, cutting tone. The use of this tone and the negative labels suggest that the father was trying not only to control the situation but also to hurt his daughter. In effect, he was seeking revenge in the name of his son. This sort of hurtful behavior is common; according to the psychoanalytic model it is an instinctive response to threat. Nevertheless, Rogers maintains it is personally destructive and unnecessary if the goal is discipline rather than retribution.

In addition, the father included the ambiguous message "Don't ever let me catch you hitting him again." As Wood and Schwartz (1977) pointed out, this is an implicit permission to hit her brother as long as she doesn't get caught. It is much clearer to say, "Don't hit your brother," repeating this command several times if necessary.

When Sally verbalized her hatred in an outburst of anger and frustration, the father resorted to mystification. She was obviously in an agitated state. It is entirely possible that in that moment she did hate her brother. Through his interpretation, the father initiated a split in her experiencing, between what she thought she was feeling and what her father told her she was really feeling. His statement falsely undermined her ability to feel comfortable in knowing who she was.

In effect, Sally was told that she is not worthy of love when she is feeling anger. A repetition of similar experiences would eventually make anger a highly threatening feeling for her. Inevitably, she would lose touch with this vital part of herself. She would find it difficult to ex-

press her anger appropriately, perhaps developing a habit of suppressing anger when it arises in day-to-day interactions but, at the same time, occasionally losing all control and "blowing up." In addition, she may come not to recognize her own feelings of anger. For example, she may be aware only that she feels "uncomfortable" when she is actually experiencing anger. For example, some women cannot clearly distinguish anger from having to go to the bathroom. For them, both are states vaguely located in the lower abdomen. To reiterate, for purposes of discipline, it is important that Sally not hit her brother, but there is no reason to block her genuine feeling of anger.

THE ADAPTIVE PARENT

What might this interaction be like with a more Rogerian father?

Dad: *Stop hitting your brother (raised voice, but not hostile; grabbing and controlling her hands if she doesn't stop immediately).*

Sally: *But Daddy, he started it. He pulled the eye out of my baby doll.*

Dad: *You were hurting your baby brother. That's not acceptable behavior and I can't allow it.*

Sally: *I hate him!*

Dad: *I understand that you may feel that way right now. But it's not OK to hit your brother. Remember, he's a little baby, and he doesn't know yet that he's not supposed to hurt your doll.*

In this exchange, the father is trying to control the situation but not to punish Sally by calling her names or using a harsh tone of voice. He is clearly stating the rules for acceptable behavior, and he is distinguishing between her right to her own feelings and her brother's right not to be hit. In addition, he is helping her interpret her hatred as a natural momentary reaction, rather than as an enduring commitment to have negative feelings toward her brother.

The father's last sentence is an aid to help Sally see this situation from her brother's point of view. This may help soften her feelings and open the way for a reconciliation once her anger has subsided. If she shows signs of feeling genuinely hurt (as opposed to acting hurt as a manipulative ploy), then it would be appropriate for the father to reassure her, using a soothing tone of voice.

If, however, the father has become so upset by this incident that he momentarily hates Sally (just as she hated her brother), it is best to admit his momentary anger rather than pretend to be a "perfect father." From the Rogerian viewpoint, once the father develops his own personality to a more optimal level of functioning, he will be less likely to handle emergencies by becoming personally threatened and vindictive.

Many students feel that Rogers's approach sounds fine in theory, but how many parents actually respond to their children in the way that he suggests? This is precisely Rogers's point. Most parents habitually practice control techniques that sound closer to the first than to the second dialogue. When this is multiplied across millions of parents and thousands of interactions, the implications for society as a whole become staggering. Moreover, once Rogers's approach is carefully thought through and prac-

ticed, it can seem as "natural" as the punitive approach in the first interaction.

THE NECESSITY OF DISCIPLINE

Once parents clearly see how much harm they can do a child over the long run, they sometimes become hesitant about enforcing any form of discipline, for fear of causing permanent injury to the child's psyche. Thus many parents have misinterpreted Rogers as endorsing permissiveness. Rogers, however, is clear in stating that the failure to discipline is not a viable option. Children need and want clear limits on their behavior. The failure to set these limits may result in their feeling that their parents just don't care enough to bother. And without learning self-discipline from their parents, through both example and discipline enforcement, children will be ill-equipped for facing the demands of adult life.

How do you think your own parents would have handled the situation between Sally and her brother? Analyze your parents' hypothetical behavior from a Rogerian point of view. How do you think their behavior in these types of situations has affected your personality?

SUMMARY

1. About one-half of all marriages now end in divorce. This is largely due to the tremendous changes that our society is undergoing and to the fact that people are now expecting more from marriage than they used to.

2. Predictors of marital satisfaction include happiness, happily married parents, extended courtships, marrying later in life, a healthy personality, commitment to marriage, similar interests and values, economic security, sharing power equally, and marrying for love.

3. Men appear to benefit from marriage more than do women.

4. The presence of children in the home is associated with lowered marital happiness.

5. Children fare better after divorce if they are able to maintain a close relationship with both parents.

6. Most divorced individuals remarry, with about half divorcing again.

7. The impermanence of marriage has set the stage for a battle between the values of commitment and self-fulfillment. For an age in which impermanence is becoming the norm, the view that divorce is a personal failure is often inappropriate.

8. Sexual infidelity is a major cause of divorce. Traditional reasons for fidelity are that a man cannot be sure he is the father of a woman's children, that fidelity stabilizes marriage, and that fidelity controls jealousy. Some experts believe that expecting one person to fulfill all of one's sexual-emotional needs is unnecessarily restrictive. Other experts maintain that extramarital sex is a cure more dangerous than the disease. The case of a middle-aged man who left his family for a younger woman was examined.

9. Problems of a family's identified patient often play a key role in maintaining the family system. The family comes to depend on the patient's symptoms for its own functioning, and therefore, it resists therapeutic intervention.

10. In the case history discussed, Eddie and his father had formed an unspoken collusion to divert attention from the mother's bizarre behavior.

11. Three types of disturbing communication are: mystification, paradoxical messages, and double-binds.

12. Ted's mother showed ambivalence in expressing both love and rejection and in encouraging both dependence and autonomy. The main methods Ted could have used to defend against his mother's disturbing communications are simply being aware of what she was doing and metacommunicating.

13. According to Carl Rogers, a parent must find a way to discipline children without taking away their feeling of being loved for who they are, not just for what they do. Discipline with love is not the same as permissiveness.

14. The traditional nuclear family is giving way to many increasingly acceptable options, such as living alone, nonmarital cohabitation, single-parent households, and remarriages.

SUGGESTED READINGS

Berne, E. **Games people play**. New York: Grove Press, 1964. The classic text on identifying the ways that people use "games" to avoid intimacy.

Rogers, C. **Becoming partners: Marriage and its alternatives**. New York: John Wiley, 1972. The humanistic perspective on marriage, with particular attention to extramarital relationships.

Weiss, R. S. **Marital separation**. New York: Basic Books, 1975. Useful for dealing with the trauma of dissolving a marriage.

Zerof, H. G. **Finding intimacy: The art of happiness in living together**. New York: Random House, 1978. Practical suggestions for improving intimate relationships.

FOCUS

FAMILIES OF THE FUTURE

The following are speculations by psychologists, futurists, and assorted visionaries on how social and technological changes may affect the family:

A MULTIPLICITY OF VIABLE FAMILY FORMS

As industrial society moves toward the world of information and as individuals' options and decisions increase almost daily, the traditional family (husband, wife, and their children) is giving way to a new variety of acceptable forms. To a large extent, this change has already occurred, and it continues. Nearly three-fourths of our population now live outside the nuclear family. But the social acceptance of these new forms has yet to catch up with their reality.

Futurist Alvin Toffler (1980) argues that the nostalgic desire to save the traditional family is a futile attempt at rolling back the clock. Not that the traditional family faces extinction, but it will have to share center stage with many diverse and increasingly popular forms of family life. In other words, the traditional nuclear family can no longer function as an ideal for all families to emulate. Other forms of family life include

- Living alone.
- Nonmarital cohabitation.
- Single-parent households.
- Remarried adults and their children.
- Spouses living and working in separate cities.
- Homosexual marriages.

In addition, family arrangements may include any number of individualized combinations, such as mother, children, and grandmother. One neighborhood in Chicago, for example, had at least eighty-six different combinations of adults and children.

MORE INDIVIDUALS WILL WORK AT HOME

There is an increasing trend for individuals to work part or full time at home, largely because of the personal computer. This will put family members in closer and more frequent physical contact. Of necessity, they will take over the social, friendship, and support functions of office relationships. In a way, this will be similar to the family units often found in agricultural communities. The net result will likely bring these families more closely together.

COMPUTERS WILL BE USED TO REVOLUTIONIZE DATING AND MATE SELECTION

Cornish (1979) suggests that computers will be used to increase the range and efficiency of the initial screening procedures for dating. Thus initial dates would at least be based on similarities in interests, values, and personality. Too often, people who are dating rely on physical attraction and chance encounters, with the couple falling in love and marrying before they realize how little they have in common. Date selection through videotaped interviews is already being used in many larger cities, and other systematic ways of using technology to aid the dating process seem inevitable. Note that the net effect of such technology follows Toffler's model, for it increases one's options dramatically. Not long ago, someone growing up in a small town might select a mate from a list of eligibles numbering less than ten. But with this dating technology in place, one could select from a list of thousands.

SCIENCE WILL BE USED TO INCREASE OUR INTERPERSONAL EFFECTIVENESS

It seems likely that psychological research on relationships and communication skills will be applied in university courses or other training settings to increase interpersonal skills and avoid many of the pitfalls in getting along with another person. It seems obvious that the more we know about ourselves and the more we can put ourselves in the other person's place, the better chance we will have to establish sound family relationships. Some of these skills include learning how to relate in a straightforward, nonmanipulative manner, learning how to listen for feelings as well as for content, reducing our defensiveness and insecurity, and learning how to take a problem-solving approach to conflict.

DUAL-WORKER MARRIAGES WILL CONTINUE TO INCREASE

It is estimated that by 1990, 85 percent of all marriages will have both spouses working for money (Masnick & Bane, 1980). As a result, traditional, one-earner families may represent an economic underclass. These statistics also suggest a drop in the birthrate, as dual-worker couples typically have fewer children.

THE DIVORCE RATE WILL CONTINUE TO RISE

In time, divorce may come to be seen as the normal way to end a marriage. Long before the year 2000, marriages between divorced individuals will outnumber those between first-marrieds.

PART FOUR

PERSONAL GROWTH

WE HAVE some idea of what it means to be physically healthy. Part Four explores whether there is a comparable psychological dimension to organismic health.

Chapter 12 emphasizes the healthy integration of mind and body. It analyzes the implications for health of excluding the body from our conscious self-definitions. It then considers physical attractiveness, a powerful social variable. In particular, is attractiveness superficial, and therefore irrelevant to health, or is there a basis in health for the social emphasis on attractiveness? The chapter concludes with a detailed look at the goals and techniques of body therapies.

Chapter 13 examines the full continuum of psychological health from disordered to optimal functioning. It compares psychoanalytic, social learning, humanistic, and existential conceptions of the healthy individual and concludes that these models emphasize different parts of the health continuum. Thus, when considered together, they present a full picture of optimal functioning. Nevertheless, these models disagree on several key points, and these issues are examined in detail.

Chapter 14 addresses a major problem in the human potential movement, that the conscious pursuit of self-fulfillment may be counterproductive. After examining the reasons for this paradox, the chapter identifies more adaptive pathways to personal growth.

THE BODYMIND 12

In Search of the Whole Person

To live in fear of being fully alive is the state of most people.

Alexander Lowen

327

This chapter examines the relationship between the mind and the body. In particular, it explores ways in which we can move toward growth by healing the split between these two fundamental aspects of ourselves. Some of the questions raised are: Why is it a problem to identify with our mind? How does our ordinary language promote the separation of mind and body? Why is physical attractiveness so important in our culture? Is reacting to a person's physical beauty a sign of immaturity? What types of people are attracted to, for example, large chests? What is the relationship between the body and our visualization of it? What techniques are used in body therapies?

The early Greeks idealized the integration of mind and body.

IDENTIFICATION WITH THE BODY

WHAT IS THE BODYMIND?

Answer true or false:

I have a body.
I use my body to accomplish certain tasks.
I sometimes exercise my body.

If you are a part of this culture, these statements probably make sense to you; they seem "normal." When examined more closely, however, we see that they contain certain questionable assumptions about who we are. They assume that what we are is different from our bodies. They reflect the cultural belief that mind and body are separate entities and that what we are is some part of the mind. We are that little person who lives somewhere in the head, directing this big, comparatively lifeless mass of flesh to do our bidding. Many psychologists now realize that this is a restrictive way of experiencing human existence. But before getting ahead of ourselves, let's take a quick look at the history of mind and body.

At least since the time of the ancient Greeks, it has been common to divide the individual into the mind and the body. This distinction was often cast in a religious metaphor — the soul could be saved only through denial of the body. Mind became the divine gift that set us apart from animal and material reality. The body held a lesser position as our animalistic and sinful throwback to the past. Thus the split between mind and body resulted in the overwhelming tendency to identify with the presumably eternal mental and intellectual self. The other, baser self served only as a temporary, fleshly vehicle for the mind.

It is becoming increasingly clear, however, that mental and physical realities are more closely connected than the two separate words, mind and body, would lead us to believe. For example, physical changes in the body are reflected in consciousness, and medicine has repeatedly shown that patients' thought processes are expressed in their physical symp-

FOCUS
THE LANGUAGE OF SELF-ALIENATION

"You're so naive," she told him. "You probably still believe that they are your friends. If only you knew what those parts of speech were doing behind your back."

Perhaps you too have noticed the nefarious activities of nouns and pronouns. Ever since the futurist Buckminster Fuller threw down the gauntlet, proclaiming, "I am a verb," the handiwork of the noun family has become suspect.

George Kelly, a renowned cognitive theorist, views us as living in a world of constant flux. The weather changes; moods vary; people look and act differently each time we see them. In this flux of potentially overwhelming confusion, we search for similarities — apparent repetitions of events, so that we can order our world, making it more predictable and therefore more manageable.

For example, Tommy looks more or less the same from day to day; his corny jokes make us laugh, and we have come to expect a jovial, pleasant time when we see him approaching. But after all, he doesn't look or act *exactly* the same each time, and we are not always in the same mood when we're with him. In other words, out of the flow of experiences, we extract apparent similarities and give them a name, "Tommy." By naming experiences in our lives, we freeze them, temporarily treating them as if they were not really in flux. In this sense, we create the objects or things of the world. They derive from an organizing intellect that simplifies our experience of flowing sensations by treating them as if they were static objects.

For example, experiences of sitting are grouped together, forming the concept of "chair." Once this is done, we can classify our perceptions as chairs or non-chairs. Our construct tells us that chairs have a certain shape and substance and that they can be sat on when we're tired. Consequently, the next time fatigue sets in, we naturally look around, identify a "chair," and rest ourselves upon it, even if we have never been in that room before. As a result, we are saved the frustration and embarrassment of sitting on lamps, flowers, sandwiches, ice-cream cones, and other parts of the world that don't work well for sitting. In this way, we simplify our world by treating processes as objects; nouns and pronouns are the names we give to those objects.

Some of our most important nouns and pronouns are "mind," "body," and "I." At the level of experience, there is no separation between mind and body. But when parts of that experience are extracted, categorized, and labeled with nouns (body) and pronouns (I), the separation between mind and body emerges. And within that separation, we have deadened the body, making it into an object. Presumably, this separation has some utility, but it does have drawbacks. For one, it fosters a restricted experience of ourselves. Strange as it may seem, a way of glimpsing a nondualistic world is simply to banish nouns and pronouns from our vocabularies for a brief time, perhaps just an hour.

You may be wondering what speech would sound like if it didn't include nouns and pronouns. That will largely depend on your own creativity in de-nouning the language. Here is a sample dialogue to get you started. Does it make sense? Not in the way that we are used to making sense. On the other hand, communication is clearly taking place.

Jack: *See studying hard. Enjoying?*
Lori: *Not especially. Reading boring and sitting too long. Get away together?*
Jack: *Yes, very good. But where?*
Lori: *Maybe eating.*
Jack: *How about drinking?*
Lori: *Green spending left?*
Jack: *All gone. Green spending left?*
Lori: *A little.*
Jack: *Great! Get ready and go.*

Try revising the following conversation without using nouns or pronouns:

Alvin: *Hey, Brian, want to come fishing on Saturday?*
Brian: *Oh, are you kidding? Put my hands on some worms and smelly fish? It's simply too awful to imagine. No, I couldn't possibly go. Besides, I'm playing football on Saturday.*
Alvin: *Suit yourself.*

toms. Numerous case histories in medicine also suggest that apparently hopeless diseases can be miraculously reversed without any identifiable physical intervention.

Existential psychologists believe that the dualities we have placed on our world are, in large measure, the source of the problems we face as human beings. And the most central of these dualities is that between mind and body. Accordingly, we need a language that does not hypnotize us into experiencing ourselves dualistically. The term, *bodymind*, is an attempt to facilitate this unified experience.

THE CASE OF MARY JANE: DO YOU LOVE ME FOR MY MIND OR MY BODY?

Mary Jane, a twenty-four-year-old secretary, had been working for an insurance firm ever since graduating from high school. She liked her job, but she didn't want to be a secretary forever. She was convinced that she was "quite a bit smarter" than the other employees and that if she just stayed at the job long enough, she would be promoted to office manager.

Mary Jane also had a steady boy friend, Arthur, who worked as a stockbroker. Arthur was a shrewd businessman, and at times she thought she wanted to marry him, but then at other times she was sure it would never work.

Mary Jane has struggled with a weight problem for almost two years now, fluctuating between five and twenty-five pounds overweight. She wanted to be thin like all the lovely models in the fashion magazines. In addition, Arthur was always nagging her to lose weight. Whenever she stayed on a diet for several weeks, she noticed that it really pleased him. He would become more affectionate with her in public and generally go out of his way to do special little things for her. She could see the pride in his eyes when her figure was looking better, and it also led to an increase in Arthur's sexual desires. Of course she loved this attention, but at the same time she felt an increasing resentment toward him.

"Arthur is so transparent," she said. "It's all just a matter of sex to him. He wants a certain type of body to live out his sexual fantasies. He wants his own little playmate of the month."

Before and after. In what ways is Mary Jane the "same person" when she is overweight? In what ways might she be a "different person"?

Mary Jane felt that Arthur wasn't really interested in *her,* even though he had told her many times that he loved her. His idea of a relationship was purely physical. For example, he didn't try to hold intelligent conversations with her about the business world, the way he did with his male friends. Arthur was just a typical one-track male, and this burned her up.

Each time she lost some weight and Arthur started showing more interest, her resentment would increase and eventually she would go off her diet, for two reasons. First, she wanted to know whether Arthur would remain attentive or lose interest, as he had in the past. Second, she wanted to punish him for treating her like a sex object. Of course she never told him this. She would just say that she had gotten tired of the diet and wanted to eat "regular food."

Mary Jane felt that if Arthur were the person he seemed to be when she was thin, she would definitely want to marry him. On the other hand, since he couldn't accept her just for being herself, his displays of affection must be counterfeit, and she would be a fool to stay with him.

What does Mary Jane identify with in herself? What do you think of Arthur? How might he view this problem? What do you see as the cause of her (their) problem?

MARY JANE: ANALYSIS AND SPECULATION

It seems clear that Mary Jane's identification is with her mind, particularly with her intellectual skills. She thinks of her body as something that she *has* rather than something that she *is*. Still, she would like to have a nice body, perhaps in the same way that she might want a fur coat or an expensive watch. She shows no awareness, however, that it might feel better to be a body that is alert, full of life, and moving effortlessly.

Note that Arthur seems to be rewarding her when she loses weight and punishing her when she gains it. But his actions are having an effect opposite to what one would expect from reinforcement theory. In this case, rewarding a part of her that she doesn't identify with has reversed the effect of his apparently positive response.

Mary Jane's reaction to Arthur depends less on his personality than on the meaning of his affection for her. She wants to be sure that he loves the person that she thinks she is; otherwise his love is meaningless. But the only way she can be sure that his love is true is for him to love her when she is fat. Thus even though she wants to be thin for her own reasons, she has bound herself to obesity.

Thus Mary Jane wants to be loved for herself, not for her "good behavior" (not overeating). She doesn't want to have to earn the love she gets. Instead, she wants a love that is unconditional yet romantic and exclusive. It may be unrealistic of her to expect such a love to be independent of her behavior.

Mary Jane is probably quite a different person when fat. Chances are that she moves differently, feels more uncomfortable, carries guilt because she is fat and doesn't want to be, and, in general, doesn't like herself. Nevertheless, it disturbs her when Arthur takes the same attitude toward her that she takes toward herself. Mary Jane has identified with a legalistic notion of who she is. She is not the moods, feelings, and behaviors that emerge in the moment. Rather, she is the same person, that is, the same social identity, she has always been. She has the same name, the same legal rights, the same memories, and the same ties to the past, even though she is not the same person in the immediate present.

Of course, a solution to Mary Jane's problems would require more information than we currently have. For example, if Arthur's reaction to her weight came from a calculation that being with a fat person would make him "look bad," it could be argued that he was merely using her as a status object. On the other hand, if his reaction stemmed from an immediate perception of her as being simply less attractive when fat, that might be a different matter.

At any rate, Mary Jane has clearly turned her own body into an object. And she may be sacrificing an important love relationship in the process. She has caught herself in a bind that demands that she cut off her nose to spite her face. Although her problem is not unusual, it does carry an element of tragedy. The impression seems inescapable that she is unnecessarily living a diminished version of what her life could be.

PHYSICAL ATTRACTIVENESS

THE SOCIAL IMPORTANCE OF PHYSICAL ATTRACTIVENESS

There seems little doubt that physical attractiveness is a significant determinant of one's "social impact." Although somewhat more salient for female than male attractiveness (Bar-Tal & Saxe, 1976), a large body of research supports the pervasive effects of being beautiful. Originally, it came as quite a surprise to many psychologists that something as superficial as physical attractiveness should play such

FOCUS

PHYSIQUE AND PERSONALITY

According to William Sheldon (1949), when it comes to the human form, structure and function (behavior) fit hand in glove. At least in part, body structure determines behavior.

Sheldon classified front, side, and rear photos of several thousand nude men and women. He theorized that the variety in human bodies can be described by three basic dimensions and that body type is relatively constant throughout life, even though physical appearance may change markedly. Moreover, each body type is linked to a different pattern of personality traits.

The first component of body type, **endomorphy**, is manifested by softness, roundness, and an underdevelopment of bone and muscle. Endomorphs tend to love food, comfort, and sociability. They are often relaxed, slow to react, even-tempered, tolerant, and easy to get along with.

The second component, **mesomorphy**, is indicated by a hard, rectangular body with a predominance of bone and muscle. This body is strong, resistant to injury, and designed for strenuous activity. Mesomorphs tend to like physical adventure, risk taking, and vigorous muscular activity. They may also be aggressive, insensitive to the feelings of others, noisy, courageous, and uneasy in closed places.

The third component, **ectomorphy**, is characterized by a linear, fragile body with a flat chest and an overall delicate appearance. Ectomorphs tend to be restrained, inhibited, secretive, self-conscious, introverted, and comfortable in closed places. They may also react overquickly, sleep poorly, and avoid attracting attention to themselves.

Although Sheldon's original research overestimated the strength of the relationship between body type and personality, later research substantiated his major findings (Lindzey, 1967; Rees, 1973). Thus body type is certainly one of the many factors that influence personality.

In addition, body type is linked to a number of other factors. Endomorphy occurs more often in women, with mesomorphy more common in men. Each body type may be predisposed toward its own brand of abnormality. Sheldon (1949) found that when there are disturbances, endomorphs show extreme mood shifts between elation and depression. Mesomorphs often exhibit paranoid delusions of persecution or self-importance, and ectomorphs show signs of social withdrawal. College students tend to combine the three dimensions in equal proportions, whereas criminals tend to be endomorphic mesomorphs.

According to Sheldon, a good approximation to one's body type can be found by dividing the cube root of one's weight in pounds into one's height in inches. Endomorphs tend to score between 11.2 and 11.8. Endomorphic mesomorphs score between 11.9 and 12.4. Mesomorphs score about 12.5. Ectomorphic mesomorphs score between 12.6 and 13.9. Ectomorphs score about 14.0 or higher. For example, a person 5'5" tall and weighing 125 pounds would score 13 on this scale (5 into 65) and be classified as an ectomorphic mesomorph.

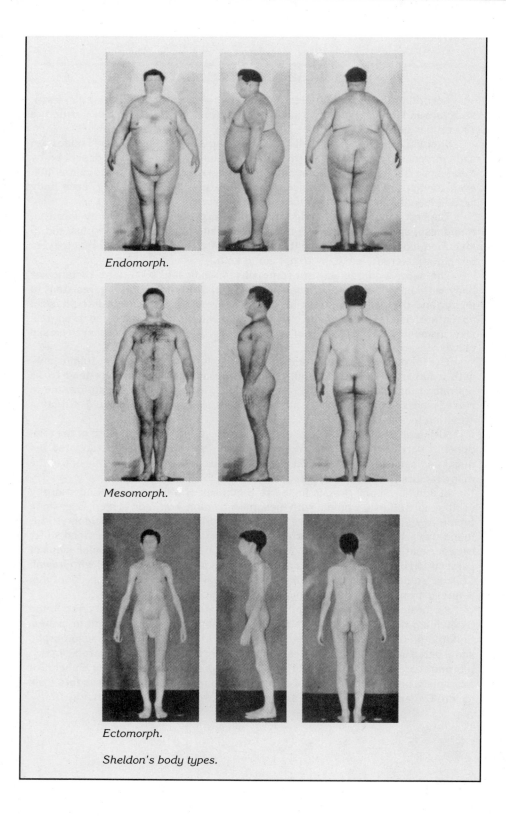

Endomorph.

Mesomorph.

Ectomorph.

Sheldon's body types.

Hollywood celebrities such as Bo Derek and Tom Selleck represent ideals of physical attractiveness in our culture.

an important role in social evaluations. Nevertheless, the importance of beauty can no longer be denied. For a summary of the major findings on attractiveness, refer to Table 12–1, page 354.

DEFINING THE BEAUTIFUL BODY

What features determine body attractiveness and how do they differ for men and women? The shape of the legs, hips, and thighs is more important in judging female beauty, and height and shoulder width are key variables in male attractiveness (Lerner et al., 1973). Feingold (1982), for example, found that taller men were more likely than shorter men to have dating partners more facially attractive than themselves.

Several researchers (Beck, Ward-Hull, & McLear, 1976; Wiggins, Wiggins, & Conger, 1968) have measured body attractiveness using

profile silhouette figures in which size and proportion were systematically varied. Overall, women preferred men with moderately large chests, and men liked women with moderately large breasts (see below). Both men and women were attracted to small buttocks. Preferences for leg size were less clear, but women did show a slight dislike for men with skinny legs. In general, both sexes preferred bodies that were moderate in size.

Horvath (1981) conducted a similar body-preference study with line drawings as stimulus objects. He found that females with large hips and those with a large waist-to-hip curvature were seen as unattractive. Females preferred women with small or moderate-sized breasts, and males showed no preference in breast size. (This finding appears to contradict Wiggins et al., 1968. The discrepancy may be due to differences in the stimulus figures used, or it may

FOCUS

IS IT SHALLOW TO BE ATTRACTED BY PHYSICAL BEAUTY?

Is beauty merely skin deep, or is it something more? One way of answering this question is to set up a model in which beauty results from several related factors. First, beauty may derive from a person's health and vitality. Second, cosmetics and clothing are often used to simulate the appearance of health and vitality, as in clothes that disguise the extent of obesity. A third factor is that some physical features may not reflect health in themselves, but they may be correlated with it. For example, baldness is not necessarily an indication of poor health or physical dysfunction, but those who are bald do tend to be older and therefore probably less robust than those with a full head of hair. A fourth factor is that we are probably genetically programmed to respond positively to certain physical features, such as a symmetrical facial appearance. A fifth factor, which presumably includes all the features that do not apply to the other four categories, is that many physical characteristics simply conform to arbitrary fads and fashions of the time. In this model, overall beauty can derive from one or more of these five factors.

Try to classify each of the following body characteristics as pertaining to (a) health and vitality, (b) simulations of health and vitality, (c) correlates of health and vitality, (d) genetic predisposition, or (e) arbitrary fashion:

1. curly hair _____

2. long hair _____

3. dyed hair _____

4. blond hair _____

5. baldness _____

6. big eyes _____

7. sparkling eyes _____

8. bloodshot eyes _____

9. glassy eyes _____

10. eyes too close together _____

11. long eyelashes _____

12. blue eyes _____

13. acne _____

14. wrinkles _____

15. pasty skin _____

16. overly pale complexion _____

17. makeup _____

18. rouge _____

19. eyebrows that run together _____

20. mustache (men) _____

21. facial hair (women) _____

22. large nose _____

23. hook nose _____

24. upturned nose _____

25. thin lips _____

26. white teeth _____

27. straight teeth _____

28. symmetry (right and left sides of face and body match) _____

29. nice smile _____

30. pouty, downturned mouth _____

31. large ears _____

32. ears that stick out _____

33. weak chin _____

34. double chin _____

35. large breasts (women) _____

36. large chest _____

37. shoulder breadth (men) _____

38. obesity _____

39. small buttocks _____

40. flat buttocks _____

41. long legs (women) _____

42. big feet _____

43. tallness _____

44. posture _____

45. muscle tone _____

46. muscle mass _____

47. slenderizing clothing _____

48. "in" clothing _____

49. jewelry _____

50. heels (women) _____

Note that this model is speculative, and so there is currently no way of objectively classifying each of these body characteristics. For now, you may want to check your ratings with those of others in your class and see how much you agreed. My own judgments, some of which are clearly debatable, are as follows: 1.e, 2.e, 3.b, 4.e, 5.c, 6.d, 7.a, 8.a, 9.a, 10.d, 11.d, 12.e, 13.a, 14.a, 15.a, 16.a, 17.b, 18.b, 19.d, 20.e, 21.d, 22.e, 23.e, 24.e, 25.d, 26.a, 27.a, 28.d, 29.d, 30.a, 31.e, 32.e, 33.d, 34.a, 35.e, 36.a, 37.a, 38.a, 39.e, 40.a, 41.d, 42.d, 43.d, 44.a, 45.a, 46.a, 47.b, 48.e, 49.e, 50.d.

Go back over the list and indicate which body features are important to you. This is a good way of finding out where your identifications with body attractiveness lie. Do this before reading further.

It could be hypothesized that those with healthier personalities would use more of the health-vitality and genetic predisposition items in their attractiveness judgments than would less healthy persons. What do you think?

Even though many of these body parts can't be definitively classified at this time, it is clearly erroneous to think about beauty in black and white terms. Must beauty be either shallow or not? It seems probable that some aspects of beauty are shallow and that others go well beyond conformity and fashion.

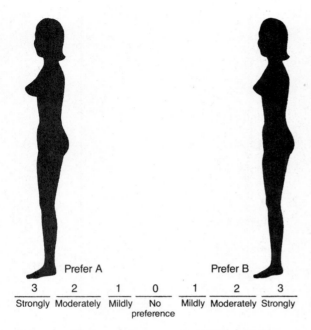

3	2	1	0	1	2	3
Strongly	Moderately	Mildly	No preference	Mildly	Moderately	Strongly

Silhouette figures used to measure body preference.

indicate changes in body preference from the late 1960s to the late 1970s.) Both men and women preferred men with broad shoulders and muscular physiques. Both sexes, but especially women, reacted negatively to the presence of a "spare tire" around the male's middle.

PERSONALITY AND BODY PREFERENCE

The above findings refer to what most people like or dislike about the body, but it is well known that there are large individual differences in what will appeal to any given person. Psychologists (Beck, Ward-Hull, & McLear, 1976; Wiggins et al., 1968) have clarified what types of people are attracted to particular features of the body. These data are summarized in Table 12–2, page 355.

The relationships between body preference and personality outlined in Table 12–2 are fascinating data for theorizing about the meanings of various body parts in our culture.

For example, buttock size is related to the needs for order and neatness, a finding that immediately suggests Freud's theory of the anal type. This theory links events during toilet training to adult preoccupations with cleanliness and neatness. Large buttocks, however, have opposite meanings for males and females. Males who prefer females with large buttocks have a high need for order, but females who prefer males with large buttocks have a low need for order.

Females who prefer males with a large chest want to depend on others to make decisions for them. Thus females who don't want to take responsibility for their actions may seek out males with large chests in the hope that a strong male will take on these responsibilities for them.

What other patterns can you find in Table 12–2?

BEAUTY AND THE ECONOMIC BEAST

In addition to personality, economic conditions also affect body preference. For example, it is generally acknowledged that the feminine ideal in poor countries is heavier than it is in rich countries. There may be a biological reason for this preference, since in a poor country, being heavier is a sign of relative health, whereas in a rich country thinner people are healthier.

Note that the rich-poor distinction also seems to hold in our own country in the preference differences between the upper and middle classes. Fashion models, who appeal to those with money and status aspirations, are almost always slimmer than are the Hollywood sex symbols, who appeal to the masses. This same pattern is apparent in personality, as shown in Table 12–2, in which slimness is associated with upper-class values.

FOCUS

HOLLYWOOD SEX SYMBOLS AND THE CHANGING FEMININE IDEAL

The search for the "ideal feminine body" has haunted artists throughout the ages, and in the twentieth century, it has been a special interest of cinematographers. No single female form, however, has emerged as a universal ideal over time and culture. A brief history of changes in the ideal feminine body may give us a context for understanding our own times.

The desired women of ancient Greece and Rome had full, shapely figures with medium-sized breasts, fairly wide waists, and heavy legs.

This trend was accentuated in the 1600s by the paintings of Rubens, who idealized women with large breasts, protruding stomachs, thick arms, and large buttocks.

In the early 1800s, an ethereal, emaciated ideal became popular in England. The later 1800s idealized the hourglass figure, as personified in actress Lily Langtry's "perfect" 38-18-38 measurements. (For most women, this ideal could only be approximated with the help of whalebone corsets, which often displaced the internal organs.)

The early 1900s brought forth the Gibson Girl, a tall and stately personage, with hair in a pompadour, a very full bust, a tiny waist, and medium-sized buttocks.

This was radically changed in the flapper era of the 1920s, which emphasized short hair, a flat chest, and a medium-sized waist.

The 1950s were dominated by the Marilyn Monroe look, characterized by large breasts, narrow waist, ample hips, and medium-sized buttocks.

The late 1960s underwent a brief fascination with the Twiggy child-woman, featuring short hair and an absence of curves or bulges.

The 1970s belonged to Raquel Welch, who returned the popularity of a shapely body, but one with slimmer hips and legs.

It is not clear yet who will best represent the 1980s, but Bo Derek and Brooke Shields seem to be two of the front-runners. Both have slim, athletic bodies, with small buttocks, small hips, and trim legs, although they differ somewhat in breast proportions.

Time magazine's Richard Corliss contrasted the 1950s and the 1980s by comparing Dolly Parton and Jane Fonda. Dolly is a sentimental throwback to the curvaceous Marilyn Monroe body, and Jane represents the emerging fitness ideal. This contrast is aptly capsulized as a choice between "juiciness" and "angularity" (Corliss, 1982). Corliss suggested that the new female body, with its emphasis on fitness and muscle tone, is one whose natural function is movement, sexual athletics, and competition with men in sports and business. It is a vehicle for meeting the challenge of equality.

But wait, there is a further tangle in this web. Although it may seem clear that the fitness ideal is a move toward greater physical health, research (Hewson, 1979; Vincent, 1981) indicates that about one-third of the women in strenuous fitness programs cease menstruating, presumably as a combined effect of physical stress and reduced body fat. Although reversible, and not an immediate health risk, menstrual stoppage could be interpreted as a sign that the female body "is

Dolly Parton, Jane Fonda, and Cory Everson (Ms. Olympia).

not made" for strenuous activity. Apparently, health increases up to a point, and after that the body refuses to continue and still be reproductively "female."

The most radical departure from previous body ideals can be found in the vanguard of fitness enthusiasts, the female body builders. The past several years have witnessed the emergence of a new feminine prototype, one with rippling muscles, popped-out veins, virtually no body fat, and large muscle mass. Furthermore, the popularity of female body builders in magazines suggests that they are slowly being accepted and could even become the role models for the next generation of women. It will be fascinating to see how far society will go toward making the muscular woman our new ideal.

What are your views on male and female body builders? When, if ever do you feel that muscular development is "too much"?

BODY IMAGE

Body image, the way that we think of or visualize our bodies, is an important factor in personality and one that has generated a good deal of fascinating research. For example, many changes in personality or environment are reflected in perceived body size (Fisher & Cleveland, 1968). When heat or touch accentuates the skin boundary of the head, the head is judged to be smaller. Individuals perceive their arms as longer when they are pointing at an open, unobstructed view than when pointing at a wall. After a failure experience, people see themselves as shorter than they actually are. Schizophrenics, and normals given hallucinatory drugs, exaggerate the size of their bodies.

This also occurs in females with obsessive fears of obesity.

DO YOU LIKE YOUR BODY?

Research (Mahoney, 1974) has shown that how you feel about your body is related to how you feel about yourself. Overall, people are fairly satisfied with their bodies, with women somewhat more dissatisfied than men (Berscheid, Walster, & Borhnstedt, 1973). Men want to be more muscular, and women want to be both slimmer and more muscular (Hankins, McKinney, & Bailey, 1979).

Berscheid and associates (1973) surveyed *Psychology Today* readers about their bodies. In general, the respondents were most concerned with having a trim body. Nearly half the women were dissatisfied with their hips, and a third of the males were dissatisfied with their spare tires. Because of the American preoccupation with sexual performance, the researchers expected a great deal of dissatisfaction with breast and penis size, but this was found for only one-fourth of the females and only 15 percent of the men. Male homosexuals were the one group that did show considerable dissatisfaction with penis size. A positive body image was related to having more sexual partners and to greater sexual enjoyment. Finally, body image showed a good deal of stability across age groups, with older subjects being as satisfied with their bodies as were younger ones.

Franzoi and Shields (1984) found that both males and females respond to their bodies in terms of three major dimensions and that these dimensions are similar but not identical for the sexes.

Use the following five-point scale to rate each of the body items below. Be sure to rate only the items appropriate to your own gender.

5. Have strong negative feelings.
4. Have moderate negative feelings.
3. Have no feelings one way or the other.
2. Have moderate positive feelings.
1. Have strong positive feelings.

FEMALES

BODY ITEM	RATING	BODY ITEM	RATING	BODY ITEM	RATING
Body scent	———	Appetite	———	Physical stamina	———
Nose	———	Waist	———	Reflexes	———
Lips	———	Thighs	———	Muscular strength	———
Ears	———	Body build	———	Energy level	———
Chin	———	Buttocks	———	Biceps	———
Breasts	———	Hips	———	Physical coordination	———
Appearance of eyes	———	Legs	———	Agility	———
Cheeks/cheekbones	———	Figure	———	Health	———
Sex drive	———	Stomach appearance	———	Physical condition	———
Sex organs	———	Weight	———		
Sex activities	———				
Body hair	———				
Face	———				
Totals	———		———		———

		MALES			
BODY ITEM	RATING	BODY ITEM	RATING	BODY ITEM	RATING
Nose	_____	Muscular strength	_____	Appetite	_____
Lips	_____	Biceps	_____	Physical stamina	_____
Ears	_____	Body build	_____	Reflexes	_____
Chin	_____	Shoulder width	_____	Waist	_____
Buttocks	_____	Arms	_____	Energy level	_____
Appearance of eyes	_____	Chest	_____	Thighs	_____
Cheeks/cheekbones	_____	Sex drive	_____	Physical coordination	_____
Hips	_____	Physical coordination	_____	Agility	_____
Feet	_____	Physique	_____	Physique	_____
Sex organs	_____			Stomach appearance	_____
Face	_____			Health	_____
				Physical condition	_____
				Weight	_____
Totals	_____		_____		_____

The three dimensions that females use in evaluating their bodies appear to reflect sexual attractiveness, weight concern, and physical condition, respectively. Total up your scores for each dimension and compare them with the normative data below.

The three dimensions that males use to describe their bodies appear to reflect physical attractiveness, upper body strength, and physical condition, respectively.

The Body Esteem Scale has been given to large samples of college students (Franzoi & Shields, 1984; Franzoi and Herzog, 1986), and the results may be of help in interpreting your own body esteem scores. The means for females on the three body esteem dimensions are 47, 30, and 33, in order of the above presen-

tation. The corresponding male means are 39, 34, and 50. These normative scores can give you a rough idea of how you compare with others in your degree of liking or satisfaction with your own body. For a more detailed comparison, note that the standard deviation for each of the scales was about 7. Thus, roughly two-thirds of the normative sample scored within seven points above or below the mean on each scale.

VISUALIZING THE BODY AND ITS MOVEMENT

Moshe Feldenkrais, a physicist who began studying the body to cure his own knee injury, developed an intriguing theory and set of exercises for exploring the linkage between movement and awareness. Feldenkrais's goal is the development of a complete self-image, that is, a full awareness of all the joints in the skeletal system and of all areas of the body surface. Feldenkrais (1972) believes that the body parts that cannot be clearly visualized represent gaps in our self-image and that filling these gaps is an important avenue to personal growth. In addition, he maintains that completing the self-image aids our actual physical movements. Similarly, Irene Dowd, a noted dance therapist, claimed, "Any movement that can be imagined correctly can be performed" (Pierpont, 1983, p. 20).

Feldenkrais noted that doing does not imply knowing. Consider the simple action of getting up from a chair. How is this done? By contracting the stomach muscles or those of the back? Which is done first, tensing the leg muscles or leaning forward? What role do the eyes play? It could be said that most of the time, we don't really know what we're doing. In other words, much of what we do is habitual, carried on outside awareness and essentially a mystery to us. Feldenkrais maintains that this is what makes most behavior so difficult to change. He believes that behaviors that were originally learned in a conscious, self-observant manner or that are later made conscious can be changed most easily.

Much of the time we rely on willpower to achieve our ends, and the development of a strong will is a highly valued attribute. Although willpower is obviously useful in many situations, Feldenkrais believes that it can also be a problem. People who rely on willpower are often those with relatively poor ability; that is, willpower may cover up an inability to act properly. Muscles occur in pairs that work in opposition to each other, one extending a limb and the other retracting it. Instead of contracting one muscle while its opposite is relaxed, willpower does the job by tensing both muscles and straining so that one overcomes the effects of the other. Feldenkrais prefers to change a habit by relaxing the muscle that inhibits action rather than strengthening the muscle that initiates it. He defined optimal action as that requiring the least effort. Although both strategies get the job done, Feldenkrais argued that the extra force that willpower employs does not simply disappear. Rather, it is dissipated within the system, damaging the joints and muscles used to create effort.

Feldenkrais believes that to become more effective, we must sharpen our powers of **kinesthetic awareness**, that is, our consciousness of movement and tension in the muscles and joints. This awareness can then be used to ensure that our actions are not derived from muscles working at cross-purposes to one another.

For Feldenkrais, completing the self-image and the image of the moving body are essential to growth of the bodymind.

BODY THERAPIES

BASIC ASSUMPTIONS

The various systems of body therapy have evolved around a common set of assumptions. They maintain that the personality is not different from the body. In addition, the stresses, rejections, conflicts, and fears that we all have experienced do not operate solely at a psychological level. They are also etched into our bodies. We carry our history of psychological scars and trauma in the form of chronic muscle tensions that restrict our capacity to express emotion, feel pleasure, move gracefully, breathe fully, and experience the vitality that is our birthright. Moreover, our characteristic patterns of muscle tension have become so habitual that we no longer notice their presence. Consequently, what feels "natural" to us is often merely a matter of habit.

Notice how this complicates the process of growth. Most theorists, whether from psychotherapy or the body disciplines, identify the growth process as a way of becoming more natural or getting in touch with what we really are.

On the other hand, if what feels natural are merely the limitations to which we have become accustomed, we cannot simply use those feelings to guide our growth. Thus popular slogans such as "be yourself" and "follow your gut feelings" may be true in one sense, yet utterly useless in another. For example, to someone accustomed to a life of comfort, overeating, and sloth, it may initially feel strange and unnatural to do stretching and warm-up exercises. After a while, however, the freer movement and greater sense of relaxation that result from these activities may come to be valued. At a still later point, the sensations of stretching may come to be enjoyed for their own sake rather than for their long-term benefits.

A final assumption of body therapies is that because psychological problems are not separate from the body, changes in personal functioning may sometimes require working directly with the body, through touch, deep massage, postural realignment, abdominal breathing, or other exercises. Note, however, that there is as yet no grounding in empirical research for the body therapies. Support for these procedures is still at the case-history level. Nevertheless, they do represent a provocative and potentially important new approach to personal growth.

THE CASE OF THE FORGOTTEN SCREAM

Wilhelm Reich is regarded as the father of the current body therapies, for he pioneered the emphasis on breathing and on the therapist's use of touch. His student, Alexander Lowen, extended Reich's work into what is now called **bioenergetic therapy**. Lowen gives the following fascinating account of his own therapy with Reich.

My first therapeutic session with Reich was an experience I will never forget. I went with the naive assumption that there was nothing wrong with me. It was to be purely a training analysis. I lay down on the bed wearing a pair of bathing trunks. Reich did not use a couch since this was a body-oriented therapy. I was told to bend my knees, relax and breathe with my mouth open and my jaw relaxed. I followed these instructions and waited to see what would happen. After some time Reich said, "Lowen, you're not breathing." I answered, "Of course I'm breathing; otherwise I'd be dead." He then remarked, "Your chest isn't moving. Feel my chest." I placed my hand on his chest and noticed that it was rising and falling with each breath. Mine clearly was not.

I lay back again and resumed breathing, this time with my chest moving outward on inspiration and inward on expiration. Nothing happened. My breathing proceeded easily and deeply. After a while Reich said, "Lowen, drop your head back and open your eyes wide." I did as I was told and . . . a scream burst from my throat.

It was a beautiful day in early spring, and the windows of the room opened onto the street. To avoid any embarrassment with his neighbors, Dr. Reich asked me to straighten my head, which stopped the scream. I resumed my deep breathing. Strangely, the scream had not disturbed me. I was not connected to it emotionally. I did not feel any fear. After I had breathed again for a while, Dr. Reich asked me to repeat the procedure: Put my head back and open my eyes wide. Again the scream came out. I hesitate to say that I screamed because I did not seem to do it. The scream happened to me. Again I was detached from it, but I left the session with the feeling that I was not as all right as I thought. There were "things" (images, emotions) in my personality that were hidden from consciousness, and I knew then that they would have to come out. . . .

It took about nine months of therapy for me to find out what had caused the scream in that first session. (I had not screamed since then.) As time went on, I thought I had the distinct impression that there was an image I was afraid to see. Contemplating the ceiling from my position on the bed, I sensed it would appear one day. Then it did, and it was my mother's face looking down at me with an expression of intense anger in her eyes. I knew immediately that this was the face that had frightened me. I relived the experience as if it were occurring in the present. I was a baby about nine months of age, lying in a carriage outside the door of my home. I had been crying loudly for my mother. She was obviously busy in the house, and my persistent crying had upset her. She came out, furious at me. Lying there on Reich's bed at the age of thirty-three, I looked at her image and, using words I could not have known as a baby, I said, "Why are you so angry with me? I am only crying because I want you." (Lowen, 1975, pp. 17–21)

BIOENERGETICS

Layers of defense. Lowen theorized that a person's defenses occur in layers. The outermost layer includes the ego defense mechanisms, such as denial, rationalization, and projection. Beneath the ego defenses is the layer of chronic muscular contractions. These both support the ego defenses and at the same time protect the person from experiencing threatening feelings such as rage, panic, and pain. Lowen assumed that just as we "tense up" in the dentist's chair in an attempt to block out the pain from drilling, we also contract other muscles to control experiences of psychological threat. At the core of personality Lowen placed the heart, that is, the feelings of love and reaching out to the world. Thus bioenergetic therapy is aimed at relaxing defenses at the ego and muscular layers, releasing and experiencing the repressed feelings, and opening the heart to love.

Healthy personality. For Lowen, a healthy personality is one that functions with minimal defenses. Such individuals put their hearts into everything they do. It's not just that they try hard but that they would love whatever activity they were engaged in, whether it were

something traditionally defined as work or play. In addition, all behavior would have a feeling component, but the feelings involved would be appropriate to the situation and not colored by repressed feelings from the past. For example, suppose Jane has always resented her sister, Ann, because she secretly believes that their parents loved Ann more than her. Then Jane takes a new job and develops an immediate dislike for a coworker because she perceives the coworker as "playing up to the boss." To the extent that impartial observers would agree that Jane's perception of the coworker is unfounded, Lowen would see her current feelings of dislike as signs of poor adjustment.

Lowen also believes it is undesirable to suppress your feelings in order to increase efficiency in doing intellectual or repetitive work. Any attempt to separate the intellectual from the emotional breaks the organic wholeness of the individual and eventually becomes counterproductive.

For bioenergetics, health is a particular balance of energy intake and discharge. The upper body primarily concerns itself with energy intake through breath, food, and sensory stimulation. The lower body primarily conveys energy discharge through locomotion and the elimination of food by-products. According to bioenergetics, insufficient intake leads to lowered energy reserves, and insufficient discharge leads to overexcitation, as in the experience of anxiety.

People tend to remain in a state of relative energy balance, but because of their defensive structures, that balance usually means low levels of both intake and discharge. Consequently, many people complain of chronic fatigue. Therapy involves two processes: raising energy intake through relaxing psychic and somatic defenses, and raising energy discharge through the freer expression of emotion.

The meaning of chronic tensions. Bioenergetics assigns a psychological interpretation to the body's chronic muscular contractions. Tension in the jaw, throat, or diaphragm inhibits breathing and thus restricts oxygen intake. This tension keeps the body in a state of depleted vitality. Tension in the arms and shoulders shows an inhibition of the urge to reach out and express affection. Tension in the waist cuts off sensations from the genital area. Lowen believes that we learn to control our erotic impulses by pulling in the belly and tightening the waist. This also results in a constriction in the diaphragm, so that inhibitions in abdominal breathing are linked to the control of sexual feelings.

Body therapists Kurtz and Prestera (1976) maintain that the meaning of chronic tensions can also be discerned from what emotions arise from the massage of particular body areas. For example, massage of the jaw, neck, and pelvis tends to release feelings of anger. Massage of the chest frees feelings of longing, which are often accompanied by deep sobbing.

Full body orgasm. The bioenergetic approach focuses on the energy discharge resulting from orgasm. Lowen maintains that all orgasms are not created equal. He distinguishes between a regular orgasm, in which the sensa-tion of discharge and release is restricted to the genital apparatus, and a full body orgasm in which the convulsive movements extend to the pelvis, legs, and other parts of the body. Bioenergetic theory maintains that full body orgasms are our birthright but that most people do not experience them because their bodies are blocked at the muscular level and because they are too frightened to give up conscious control and completely give in to their sexual feelings.

A body that is free enough from muscular tension to experience a full body orgasm manifests a particular undulation or wave movement during normal breathing, and much of bioenergetic therapy is directed toward developing this breathing reflex. Moreover, this reflex is thought to occur in every instance of a full orgasm. Lowen maintains that one can test for the presence of this reflex by lying on a bed with the knees bent and the feet making contact with the bed. The head should be back and the arms at the sides. When the breathing is correct, that is, without restriction from muscular block-

---

FOCUS

ELVIS! LET MY PELVIS GO FREE

The following is an exercise used in bioenergetic therapy for freeing the pelvis and promoting fuller body orgasms.

Stand in front of a chair with your feet six inches apart and your knees almost fully bent. The chair is to be used for balance only. Pitch your body forward until your heels are slightly off the floor. Put your body weight on the balls of your feet but not on your toes. Arch your body backward and bring your pelvis forward to form an unbroken arc. Do not strain. Press downward on both heels without letting them touch the floor. Lean forward and keep your knees bent so that your heels don't touch the floor.

Hold this position as long as you can without making it a test of will. Breathe easily into your belly; hold your pelvis loosely. When you can no longer hold the position, fall forward on your knees onto a blanket. The legs will usually begin vibrating before you fall. If your breathing is relaxed and deep and you stay loose, your pelvis will also vibrate. Repeat this exercise several times, as the vibratory movements will increase with each repetition. (Adapted from Lowen, 1975, p. 255)

STOOL OR CHAIR   BLANKET

ages, respiratory waves pass through the body, and the pelvis moves spontaneously with each breath. The pelvis and throat move upward with exhalation and fall backward on inspiration, and the head moves in the opposite manner.

In addition to this breathing reflex, the sensation of energy should extend through the legs and feet. Lowen noted that forward movements of the pelvis can occur in three different ways. It can be pulled forward by contracting the abdominal muscles, or it can be pushed forward by contracting the buttocks. Both of these methods restrict the flow of erotic feeling and thus inhibit full body orgasm. The third method of moving the pelvis is to press down on the ground with one's feet. In this way the stress is on the legs, and the pelvis can swing freely rather than being pushed or pulled.

Although Lowen was not explicit about this, he seemed to be suggesting that certain sexual positions can be used to optimize full body orgasm. Can you think of a position that would facilitate moving the pelvis without tensing the abdomen or the buttocks?

THE ALEXANDER TECHNIQUE

The Alexander technique refers to methods of body work developed by Mathias Alexander in the first part of the twentieth century. The basic premise of this system is that incorrect alignment of the head, neck, and shoulders unbalances the whole body, creating tension, awkwardness, discomfort, and pain.

Alexander practitioners maintain that postural misalignment is almost universal by the age of eleven. But why is modern society so destructive of optimal body usage? In addition to the stimulus overload of our fast-paced world, body therapists have identified several other likely causes. Some believe that the current emphasis on conformity and competition leads us to overvalue the effects of our actions on others, while neglecting the personal and internal sensations that accompany those actions. Other therapists believe that children may be urged to walk too soon, before they have gained sufficient neural and muscular maturation from creeping and crawling.

Body therapists believe that most of us arrive at adulthood with disturbed breathing patterns, restricted joints, inflexible spines, and a self-concept and body usage far short of their potential. Moreover, through habit, we have become unaware of our present condition; we have accepted discomfort and pain as a normal part of life (Myers, 1983).

Unlike **Rolfing**, a popular body therapy that uses a deep and often painful form of massage to break up chronic muscle tensions, Alexander practitioners employ a light, fluid touch. The teacher's hands are used to guide the student toward better alignment by touching key points on the body. For example, touch may be used behind the knees to release the energy of the legs, and behind the ears and up the neck to release the head forward and up. Learning correct use of the head is especially important. The head should be above the torso "like a ball floating in a fountain."

Alexander therapists abhor a mechanistic approach to body movement, noting that it is neither efficient nor enjoyable. Thus, many body therapists oppose traditional calisthenics such as push-ups and sit-ups. "If you treat your body as an object, feeding, dressing, and exercising 'it,' you reduce the potential richness of your body image and thus of your self-image" (Myers, 1983, p. 6). They maintain that you are never working with a bicep or a thigh muscle, but with these parts in the context of the whole body, and that movement with an awareness of the whole body is quite different from movement without this awareness. Similarly, body therapists have found that most people view their bodies as opaque, solid masses that are fixed and static. In contrast, body therapists prefer the metaphor of the body as a fluid, flexible, energy field, filled with life and consciousness (Johnson, 1977).

This section described two ways of thinking about the body. In one, the body is a sophisticated machine, and in the other, it is a conscious energy field. What might be the pros and cons of each metaphor? How would it affect your behavior, your feelings, or your experience of your body to use one metaphor rather than the other? For example, if you were a surgeon, which metaphor would you find more useful? If you were an athlete? If you were making love?

One Alexander practitioner presented a fascinating case illustrating the psychological underpinnings of muscular tension:

> Not long ago I was working on a client's shoulders to broaden her chest and free her breathing. As I guided her shoulders, her arms lengthened. She became frightened and began to cry. When I asked her to fantasize about what would happen if her arms were longer, she answered that she then might be able to touch her genitals. Her voice and appearance had become much younger. When I asked her how old she was feeling at the moment, she said: "Two or three . . . in a crib." Later, she released this fear in a flood of screams and tears. She told me this was the first time since she had grown up that she had remembered her mother tying her hands to the crib with colored ribbons to prevent her from masturbating. (Rubenfeld, cited in Kurtz & Prestera, 1976, pp. 144–145)

THE BELLY MIND AND THE HEAD MIND

Kurtz and Prestera (1976) maintain that chronic muscle tensions result from trying to hold back emotions that others have told us are inappropriate. Thus part of growing up in our culture means learning that it feels safer to suppress these emotions. Kurtz and Prestera argue that the rings of tension formed from withholding emotional expression restrict energy flow from one body segment to another, so that

gross changes in the form, color, size, and development of body parts can occur. Hands and feet, for example, may become cold and small. The head may become congested, increasing in size. Or the belly may expand while the chest collapses.

The belly. In normal breathing, the belly expands with each breath. Free movement of the diaphragm pulls air into the lower abdomen, and the belly wall expands outward to accommodate the increased air intake. In our culture, adults have typically learned to maintain a trim appearance by keeping the belly muscles tightly drawn in. Kurtz and Prestera claim that the more primitive the society, the greater the ease with which the belly wall moves. In our world, normal breathing is found with regularity only in children, who have rounded, protruding bellies, as shown in Figure 12–1.

Kurtz and Prestera raise an interesting point in wondering whether the cultural custom of keeping the belly drawn in is merely a matter of fashion and vanity or whether it has a more psychological meaning. They observed that the belly is soft, tender, and vulnerable. It contains many vital organs, including the intestines, or "guts." In our civilized world, the individual is rarely expected to express "gut" feelings. Instead, our cultural script demands that we "calm down," "stay cool," and "pull ourselves together." Our world is pervaded by the fear of emotional expression. Those who show outrage, panic, or hopelessness may be viewed as "crazy." In this way, society conditions us not to experience our emotional existence.

A number of Eastern disciplines such as Japanese Zen and Chinese Tai Chi make special reference to a point at the center of the belly a few inches below the navel. This point is felt to be a center of vitality related to basic instinctual drives. Some people identify with this point in the same way that most modern people identify with the brain. Thus the belly center can be seen as having a mind of its own or as being a center of consciousness. It might include, for example, the consciousness of one's state of hunger,

FIGURE **12 – 1**
THE BELLY OF A YOUNG CHILD

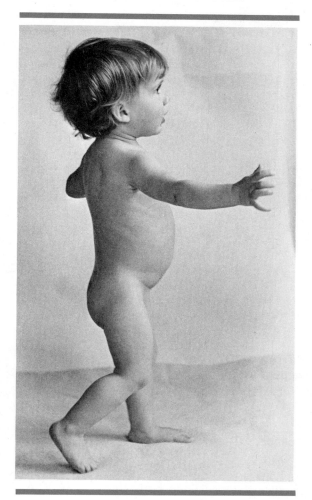

is atypical simply to eat when hungry and to stop eating when hunger is appeased. We believe that too many other factors must be considered to satisfy the social and work-related functions of eating. For example, we must eat at "lunchtime" or when "dinner is ready" in order to coordinate our eating with others' schedules. If someone has prepared food for us, we must eat enough not to offend our host. When not hungry, we often see pictures of food or hear others talking about food, and this reminds us of how good that food tasted in the past. Through the workings of memory, we want to repeat that pleasure even if we are currently full. Thus for many reasons our ideas about eating may interfere with our feelings of hunger. The same pattern presumably operates for all of our instinctual needs.

Kurtz and Prestera speculate that tightening in the throat, for example, occurs when the head center demands that we say something not in tune with our actual feelings. The lower abdomen tightens, cutting off genital feelings, whenever the head dictates sexual behaviors and feelings. Kurtz and Prestera believe that our culture has overvalued the head mind, giving it too much authority. They contend that the pervasive miseries of the modern world, the senses of isolation and cold destructiveness that mark our civilization, are due in large part to the lack of contact with our instinctual existence.

YOUR BODY PROFILE

Kurtz and Prestera (1976) identified five basic body types and developed a theory relating each type to personality. Their body types can be represented visually so that people can determine their own body type by looking in a mirror, being photographed, or having a friend observe them and then comparing their own bodies with the visual profiles.

Four profile illustrations are provided for each type. The first represents a normal or ideal body, and each of the others represents increasing degrees of pathology, that is, more deeply

one's sexual appetite, and the intuitive awareness of others. In contrast with the belly mind, the head mind is thought to calculate when and how to satisfy the basic needs.

The belly versus the head. In contemporary culture, the head mind is highly trained and usually placed in control of the belly mind. Rather than our belly telling us when, what, and how much to eat, this function is often taken over by our head. Thus the two are often in conflict. In a complicated world such as ours, it structured muscular tensions. If you match the first picture in each series, the psychological description for that type will not apply to you. If you match the second picture, the description will apply only as a typical reaction when under stress. If you match the third picture, much of your life is probably colored by the feelings and attitudes described. If you match the fourth picture, the description should fit very well, even though it may seem alien or distasteful to you. (It may be helpful to check these descriptions with the perception of an honest friend.)

Mimic the fourth picture in each series to see which emotions arise with each posture. If you do this before reading the personality description for each type, you can make an inde-

FIGURE 12—3
THE BURDENED TYPE

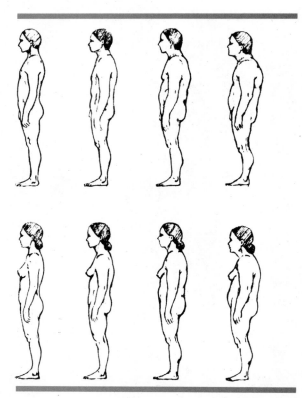

FIGURE 12—2
THE NEEDY TYPE

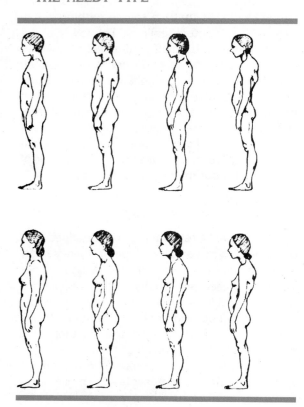

pendent test of how well this theory applies to you.

As a word of caution, these profiles represent a theory linking body to personality. Although there is general agreement among body therapists on these interpretations, no empirical validation is presently available. Also, no matter how deeply structured the contractions, body therapists maintain that all bodies are capable of change.

The needy personality. This type is depicted in Figure 12—2. Note that the body slumps downward and becomes thin, the head shifts forward, the chest sinks, and the knees lock. In general, the body looks tired, weak, and in need of support. This person finds it difficult

FIGURE **12-4**
THE RIGID TYPE

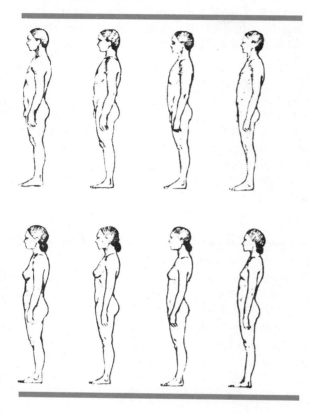

FIGURE **12-5**
THE TOP HEAVY TYPE

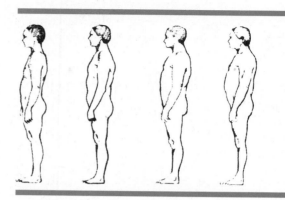

to cope, becomes depressed easily, and has a strong need for attention from others. The voice may be sad and weak.

The burdened personality. Figure 12-3 shows that in this type, the body is squeezed downward and curved forward and thus is shortened and thickened. The body looks as if it is carrying a heavy load. This person feels bogged down, under pressure, and getting nowhere. There is a sense of suffering and inferiority. Emotions are expressed with difficulty, and the person may be stubborn, submissive, and a whiner.

The rigid personality. Figure 12-4 shows this body curving backward, with the neck and shoulders held stiffly and the chest

inflated. The body looks stiff, as if braced against a challenge, with a sense of aggression. This type often feels frustrated, with a strong need to achieve and be admired and difficulty in relaxing. Although active, productive, rational, and matter-of-fact, this person is easily angered and often has difficulty expressing tender feelings.

The top-heavy personality. This type is usually male, and Figure 12-5 shows that it involves an expansion above the waist, with thinning below the waist. The body looks swollen with pride or anger. This type often feels self-important, alienated from others, and reckless, with strong desires for power.

The bottom-heavy personality. This type is usually female, and Figure 12-6 shows that the general appearance is opposite to that of the top-heavy person. The body often seems girlish above the waist and womanly below. This type often centers on love relationships, home, and children and typically is emotionally expressive. This person is often concerned with others' feelings and has feelings that are easily hurt.

For simplicity, the above descriptions are of pure types, but actual bodies often combine characteristics of several types. In these cases

FIGURE **12–6**
THE BOTTOM HEAVY TYPE

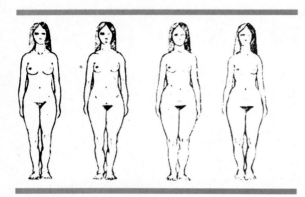

the personality descriptions should also be combined. Younger students may have a little difficulty classifying their bodies. With age and the accumulation of life stress, bodies are more likely to acquire the more extreme postures.

Which body type fits you best? Do the personality characteristics of that type also apply to you?

Recall the quotation from Lowen at the beginning of the chapter: "To live in fear of being fully alive is the state of most people." In what way does this apply to you or to those you know?

SUMMARY

1. The term bodymind is a way of referring to the entire personality without separating it into the duality of mind and body. Many psychologists speculate that this self-alienation or dualistic experience of ourselves is a key problem of modern people. The use of nouns and pronouns in ordinary language encourages this dualistic experience.

2. Mary Jane has a cyclical weight problem that is tied both to her boy friend's conditional acceptance of her and to her own identification with her mind rather than her bodymind.

3. Sheldon identified three body structures that are thought to remain fairly constant throughout life: the rounded endomorph, the rectangular mesomorph, and the linear ectomorph. A number of personality correlates have been found for these structures.

4. Physical attractiveness has emerged as one of the best predictors of one's social impact. For example, it is related to expectations of happiness and intelligence; to likability, dating interest, receiving help, and social skill; to early happiness and later unhappiness (women only); and to relative power and control in a relationship.

5. It was suggested that aspects of beauty that derive from health and vitality or from genetic predispositions are not shallow and that those that stem from simulations or correlates of health or from arbitrary fashion can accurately be considered superficial.

6. In general, men prefer women with small buttocks, relatively small hips and small waist-to-hip curvature, and little body fat. Women prefer taller men with moderately large chests, broad shoulders, muscular physiques, and little body fat. In addition, a number of relationships between personality and preference for specific parts of the body have been discovered.

7. What is considered the ideal feminine body has changed many times in recent history. Currently, a slim, athletic, "fit" body is popular.

8. Body image, and particularly the perception of one's own body size, is a sensitive indicator of both one's psychological state and of changes in the environment. Most people are fairly satisfied with their bodies, with their main concern being trimness.

9. Three dimensions seem to characterize how people feel about their bodies: sexual attractiveness, conditioning, and weight (for women) or strength (for men).

10. Feldenkrais emphasized completing the physical self-image and fostering kinesthetic awareness. He maintains that learning and behavior change are facilitated by the conscious awareness of bodymind activities.

11. The body therapies assume that personality is not separate from the body, that psychological trauma is reflected in chronic muscle tensions, and that verbal therapies will often need to be augmented by physical interventions.

12. Wilhelm Reich is regarded as the father of modern body therapies. He extended psychoanalytic therapy by using deep-breathing exercises and directly touching the patient.

13. Alexander Lowen extended Reich's work to create bioenergetic therapy, a system that aims to relax defenses, release pent-up feelings, and open the heart to love. A balance between energy intake and discharge is attained, in which intake is increased through more natural breathing and discharge is increased through the free expression of feelings and full body orgasms.

14. The Alexander technique emphasizes correct postural alignment of the head, neck, and shoulders.

15. Kurtz and Prestera contrast the belly mind with the head mind and argue that our culture has overidentified with the head. They also describe a system of body types, including the needy, burdened, rigid, top-heavy, and bottom-heavy personalities.

SUGGESTED READINGS

Barlow, W. **The Alexander technique**. Westminster, Md.: Random House, 1973. A definitive presentation of Alexander's system.

Dychtwald, K. **Bodymind**. Westminster, Md.: Random House, 1977. Combines Eastern and Western ways of understanding the relationship between mind and body.

Keleman, S. **Your body speaks its mind.** New York: Simon & Schuster, 1975. A clear and direct presentation of the bioenergetic experience.

Tohei, K. **Aikido in daily life**. Elmsford, N.Y.: Japan Publications Trading Co., 1966. Excellent approach to the body from the viewpoint of the martial arts.

TABLE 12–1

EVERYTHING YOU EVER WANTED TO KNOW ABOUT BEING BEAUTIFUL

1. We expect attractive people to be:
   a. More sensitive and to have more fulfilling lives, happier marriages, and more prestigious occupations (Dion, Berscheid, & Walster, 1972).
   b. More intelligent (Clifford & Walster, 1973).
   c. More pleasant (Adams & Huston, 1975).
   d. More glamorous (Bassili, 1981).
   e. More vain, egotistical, materialistic, snobbish, and unsympathetic and more likely to request a divorce or have an extramarital affair (Dermer & Thiel, 1975).

2. Attractive people are:
   a. Liked better (Byrne, London, & Reeves, 1968).
   b. More sought after as dates (Curran & Lipold, 1975; Walster et al., 1966).
   c. More persuasive (Mills & Aronson, 1965).
   d. Taken more seriously when they give evaluations of others (Sigall & Aronson, 1969).
   e. More likely to receive help from a stranger (Benson, Karabenick, & Lerner, 1976).
   f. Judged to be more socially skilled and likable by observers who have talked to them on the phone but have not seen them (Goldman & Lewis, 1977).
   g. Better liked by jurors and given less punishment as defendants in jury simulations (Efran, 1974).

3. Attractive women:
   a. Expect to be more successful in relationships and on intellectual tasks (Abbott & Sebastian, 1981).
   b. Date more, have more male friends, fall in love more often, and have more sexual experience (Kaats & Davis, 1970).
   c. Are happier as adults until middle age; then they tend to be less happy (Berscheid, Walster, & Bohrnstedt, 1973).
   d. Are judged to do better work, especially by male judges (Kaplan, 1978; Landy & Sigall, 1974).

4. In relationships:
   a. Attractive people end up together (Murstein & Christy, 1976).
   b. The less attractive partner loves more, expends more effort to please the other, has fewer opposite-sex friends, and worries more that the relationship won't last and that the partner might become involved with another (Berscheid et al., 1973; White, 1980).
   c. Attractive males are more likely to desire extrarelationship involvements (White, 1980).
   d. Partners who are similar in attractiveness show a greater increase in love as the relationship progresses (White, 1980).
   e. Those who believe they are more attractive than their partner also perceive themselves as more dominant in the relationship (Critelli & Waid, 1980).
   f. Male marital satisfaction relates to how attractive he thinks his wife is and to how attractive she thinks he is (Murstein & Christy, 1976).
   g. During first meetings, people do not behave in a more friendly way toward attractive people, even though they do prefer the attractive people as potential dates or marriage partners (Crouse & Mehrabian, 1977).
   h. After being exposed to popular "centerfold" erotica featuring highly attractive nudes, people, especially males, tend to rate their mates as less sexually attractive and report less love for them (Kenrick, Gutierres, & Goldberg, 1984).

TABLE 12-2

PERSONALITY CORRELATES OF BODY PREFERENCE

MALES

Female Bodies	Characteristics of Males Who Prefer These Bodies
Overall largeness	High need for achievement
Overall moderateness	High desire to appeal to and please the opposite sex
Overall smallness	Upper-class background; comfortable with those in authority
Large breasts	Socially independent; strong desire to appeal to and please the opposite sex; low desire to care for others; frequent daters
Small breasts	Mild depression; low achievement motivation; indefinite about career; fundamentalist religion; working-class families. (Since attitudes toward female breasts appear to be changing, these findings may no longer apply.)
Large buttocks	High need for order and neatness; dependent in social situations; puts self down
Small buttocks	High self-esteem but does not try to be the center of attention; perseverance
Thick legs	Focuses on own thoughts and feelings; restrained; nonaggressive; puts self down
Thin legs	Exhibitionistic; seeks out others

FEMALES

Male Bodies	Characteristics of Females Who Prefer These Bodies
Overall largeness	Physically active; enjoys sports; not traditionally feminine; not interested in dance or music
Overall moderateness	Desires to appeal to and please the opposite sex; traditionally feminine; home and family oriented; conscientious; neat
Overall smallness	Socially reserved; mothers are college educated
Large chest	Socially outgoing; high need to achieve; depends on others to make decisions for her; physical symptoms when under stress
Small chest	Passive; indecisive; religious
Large buttocks	Little concern for order and neatness; feminine; enjoys sports; not excitable; introverted
Small buttocks	High need for achievement; emotionally mature; competitive; need to be a leader; not religious
Thick legs	Focuses on own thoughts and feelings; not traditionally feminine; not interested in appealing to and pleasing the opposite sex
Thin legs	Low dominance; low self-sufficiency; high need to belong; socially introverted

MALADJUSTMENT, NORMALITY, and BEYOND 13

What Is Healthy Personality?

Models of Healthy Personality: Critique and Synthesis
The Psychoanalytic Model / The Social Learning Model /
Humanistic Models / The Existential Model / Contradic-
tions Among the Models
Summary
Suggested Readings

This chapter examines the ways that psychologists have tried to define personal growth. What does it mean to say that one individual is "healthier" than another? Among the less healthy, what are the various disorders? What about the "average" person? Is this individual positively healthy or only mildly disturbed? Can people change from maladjusted to normal functioning, and if so, can they then progress to a level of functioning that in some way goes beyond normality? This is the process witnessed by countless therapists, and these observations have stimulated the notion that there is a state of positive well-being that is not simply the absence of dysfunction. If this ideal exists, we should be able to describe it or, at least, to identify some of the forms it may take. Note that identifying these forms does not, in itself, tell us how to become healthier. But it does give us new alternatives to consider when planning our own path of future growth.

MALADJUSTMENT

CRITERIA OF DISORDER

To be considered a psychological disorder, an individual's behavior usually manifests one or more of the following:

1. *Psychological pain*, such as depression or anxiety.
2. *Self-destructiveness* or behavior that is otherwise incompatible with adequate functioning, as in alcoholism or compulsive gambling.
3. *Loss of reality contact*. Those whose beliefs or perceptions deviate from what society defines as "real" are considered abnormal. For example, I knew one man who complained that aliens had implanted an antenna in his brain and that he was receiving radio communications from them via an orbiting satellite.

Reality contact is of particular interest, since it appears to follow a curvilinear path. Extreme reality distortions, as in the man above, obviously constitute disordered functioning. Normals, however, may have *less* accurate reality contact than do depressed individuals. In an apparent attempt to bolster self-esteem, normals tend to exaggerate the amount of control they have over desirable outcomes and minimize their control over negative outcomes. Depressives, on the other hand, accurately perceive their control over both positive and negative events (Alloy & Abramson, 1979). Also, depressives describe themselves on trait inventories in ways that more closely match the descriptions of objective observers (Lewisohn et al., 1980). Although it has yet to be proved, it is thought that the healthiest individuals do not require self-concept–enhancing distortions and thus show the accuracy of depressed individuals while maintaining positive emotions (Maslow, 1971).

4. *Social inappropriateness.* Behavior that violates a culture's social rules is often considered disordered, even though the same behavior might be acceptable, even laudatory, in another culture. For example, ambition is a desired trait in the

United States; yet among the Zuni Indians of New Mexico, those who tried to accomplish more than others were apt to be branded as witches and hanged by their thumbs. Also, it would be abnormal for an American male to experience "labor pains" when his wife gives birth; yet, in many primitive societies, this is not unusual.

THE CLASSIFICATION OF DISORDERS

Psychological disorders are more common than most people believe. About one-fifth of the population shows clear signs of a disorder, with another three-fifths showing signs of a mild disturbance (Altrocchi, 1980). For example, there may be over fifty million U.S. citizens with mild to moderate depression (Coleman, Butcher, & Carson, 1980).

The classification of psychological disorders has always been controversial, partly because description implies labeling. To receive the diagnosis of *schizophrenic,* for example, means that even after a full recovery, one would find it difficult to lead a normal life because of the tremendous prejudice against that label. Moreover, once individuals accept a label and start thinking of themselves as "schizophrenic," the label then forms the basis for a self-fulfilling prophecy. For example, we might use the label to hide from the demands of everyday life by escaping into the sick role (Laing, 1967).

It is worth noting that psychological disorders result from many causes over which we have little control, such as genetic predispositions and family background. Thus there is no more reason for a person to feel ashamed about a psychological disorder than about a physical condition such as heart disease. Also, people falsely assume that psychologically disturbed individuals are a threat to society, when they are actually no more violent than the rest of the population.

A second problem is that the classification of psychological disorders is often unreliable, with experts regularly disagreeing on a patient's diagnosis (Spitzer & Wilson, 1980), particularly for milder disorders. In defense of classification, it can only be said that there is no reasonable alternative. To study any phenomenon, we must first describe it. Dividing abnormality into separate disorders provides our best hope for identifying the causes and optimal treatments for the varieties of disorder. It is highly unlikely, for example, that all disorders would have the same cause or be cured by the same intervention. Nevertheless, this area is so complex that existing descriptive systems leave much to be desired.

The standard system for classifying psychological disorders is contained in the *Diag-*

Edvard Munch's The Scream *conveys the pervading sense of anxiety and alienation that often accompanies psychological dysfunction. (Munch Museum, Oslo.)*

TABLE 13-1

PSYCHOLOGICAL DISORDERS

DISORDERS	CHARACTERISTICS
Somatoform	Physical symptoms without an obvious organic basis. Those with hypochondriacal disorders worry constantly about their health and report a wide variety of aches and pains. Conversion disorders involve more specific and serious physical maladies, such as loss of vision or hearing. In general, somatoform disorders allow one to avoid life problems while garnering sympathy for what appears to be a physical problem outside one's control.
Anxiety	Intense, chronic agitation inappropriate to the situation. This includes (1) cases of incessant worrying; (2) phobias, involving fear of a particular object or situation; and (3) obsessive-compulsive disorders, characterized by intruding thoughts and compulsions to act out senseless, repetitive rituals to keep anxiety under control. Anxiety reactions may be predisposed by feelings of insecurity stemming from childhood. They are often learned through contact with an aversive event and then maintained by anxiety reduction (through negative reinforcement), as feared stimuli are avoided.
Affective	Depressive disorders are characterized by intense, persistent, disruptive, and often cyclical feelings of sadness, loss of interest in previously desired activities, low self-concept, and low energy. Bipolar mood disorders involve a mood shift from a manic phase, with total euphoria, excessive self-esteem, high energy, and reckless behavior, to a depressive phase. Pessimistic thinking, self-blame, and feelings of helplessness have been linked to depression.
Dissociative	An uncommon disorder involving loss of contact with memory (amnesia) or conscious identity. Multiple-personality syndrome is the coexistence of several distinct personalities in the same individual, with the original personality often unaware of the others' existence. Secondary personalities are often linked to a history of child abuse and can be triggered by stress.
Schizophrenic	Impaired reality contact, severe disruption of normal functioning, delusions (false beliefs), hallucinations (false perceptions), blunted or otherwise inappropriate affect, and incoherent speech. The paranoid type shows delusions of persecution; the catatonic type shows motor disturbance such as limited body movement; the disorganized type shows incoherence and social withdrawal; the undifferentiated type shows symptoms from each of the other three; and the schizoaffective type blends symptoms from schizophrenic and mood disorders. Schizophrenics show neurological problems in maintaining attention, and their family dynamics often include hostility and conflicting messages.
Personality	Mild disturbances in which adjustment is judged "borderline." This includes eleven types, most of which are mild versions of the disturbances mentioned above. Antisocial personalities show a lack of moral development and are typically exploitative, manipulative, and guiltless. The histrionic personality is overly dra-

TABLE 13-1

PSYCHOLOGICAL DISORDERS   *(continued)*

DISORDERS	CHARACTERISTICS
	matic, with exaggerated emotions and attention seeking. The narcissistic personality shows exaggerated self-importance, expectations of special treatment, and low empathy. The passive-aggressive personality shows indirect resistance to legitimate demands, such as procrastinating or claiming that their destructive behavior is accidental.
Substance Use	Drug dependence, psychological or physiological. Drugs commonly abused in our culture include alcohol, sedatives, cocaine, amphetamines, hallucinogens, marijuana, caffeine, and tobacco. Linkages have been established between alcoholism and depression, opiate addiction and the antisocial personality, and hallucinogens and identity problems.

nostic and Statistical Manual of Mental Disorders (DSM-III). Table 13-1 summarizes the main disorders relevant to personal adjustment. Disorders with a purely physical cause are not discussed, and sexual disorders were considered in Chapter 10. As a note of caution, do not over-identify with the various symptoms. It is common when reading descriptions of pathology to notice that we also have experienced some of these symptoms and to wonder whether we may have the disorder described. Obviously, we all have occasional feelings of depression, moments of anxiety, and instances of confused thinking. But these in themselves do not constitute psychological disorders.

Each disorder results from a complex interaction between genetic vulnerability and learning history. In particular, schizophrenia, depression, and alcoholism show strong genetic components. In addition, most disorders are stress related. Thus, in the context of severe or prolonged stress, individuals who break down will develop a disorder consistent with their genetic predisposition and learning history.

Do you know anyone who fits one of the descriptions in Table 13-1? What is your theory for how this person's disorder came about?

Clearly, most people who can function in society are healthier than those with psychological disorders of the sort listed in Table 13-1. But within the group that can be considered relatively normal, does it still make sense to think of some as healthier than others? And if it does, is there only one type of healthy personality, or are there many, as in the psychological disorders? We shall now consider each of the major theoretical approaches to these issues, and at the end of the chapter, we shall try to tie together the loose ends and draw some conclusions. The value of examining optimal functioning is clear —the journey of growth is likely to be more successful if we have a map of where we are going.

Note that the humanistic and existential models have more or less specialized in defining optimal functioning. In contrast, psychoanalytic models have focused on defining the psychological disorders, and social learning models have concentrated on identifying methods of behavior change, as elaborated in Chapters 6 and 7. Consequently, this chapter reflects the greater interest of humanistic and existential models in conceptualizing optimal functioning. Nevertheless, psychoanalytic and social learning models have made significant contributions in this area, as we shall see.

FOCUS

CASE STUDIES OF DISORDERED PERSONALITY

Try to identify the psychological disorders illustrated by the following case excerpts.

1. Carol R., 34, an attractive, divorced mother of two boys appears to be a warm, outgoing person. However, although men find her appealing, she has no close friends. Other women find her boring and self-centered. She is talkative but never shows an interest in others. She prefers talking about herself and feels hurt and irritated when others do not seem interested in the endless details of her life.

   Her marriage lasted twelve years. During the early years, her husband was deeply in love with her. He appreciated her femininity and felt grateful that such an appealing and sought-after woman would marry him. When his career began to take more of his time, Carol became angry. She had childlike temper tantrums when she wasn't receiving enough of his attention. She did not seem capable of understanding or caring about the pressures he faced.

   Carol had always engaged in "innocent" flirting. Now she began to have occasional affairs, although she derived little pleasure from them. Her husband filed for divorce when he discovered one of these relationships. Carol's reaction was that he should have been more understanding of her needs. (Adapted from Derlega & Janda, 1981, p. 254)

2. "I've always been an organizer . . . so that from the time I get up in the morning until I go to sleep at night I'm thinking about what's going to happen. I worry, but I can take it and it's not too bad . . . but it's when those terrible thoughts come into my head that I become afraid. The thoughts are all different, and they're sickening and terrible. Like when I was outside with my child, I thought of what would happen if my metal rake slipped and flew over and hit my child in the head. I don't know why I would think of this. It made me feel like a crazy person, and then I'm worried sick the rest of the day that I'm going to think that thought again. Here's another example of what I mean. While eating dinner the thought suddenly came to me . . . how would it look if I drove my fork through the eye of my husband . . . I mean my husband's eye. I can see the fork puncture the eye and the liquid squirts out . . . and then I break out in a cold sweat and have to leave the table. Why in God's name would I think such things? I love my child and my husband. I'm a kind person . . . I go to church. . . . It makes me feel crazy and different. Even telling you makes me feel weird about myself." (Duke & Nowicki, 1979, p. 255)

3. "All I can remember is the sense of worthlessness I felt. I couldn't believe that anyone could care about me or try to help me. I just wanted to die. My doctor gave me this note that I wrote then: 'Dear Doctor ————, Please don't waste your time on me. Please help the ones who deserve to live. . . . When they take me to my grave I'll feel relieved. Death will be my punishment for the evil I've done to you and to my fellow man.'

   It scares me to even read such a note and even more to realize that I wrote it. But my most recent episode was an uncontrollable high—I mean, happiness with no bound. It started at a party I was at over New Year's

> Eve — always a tough time for me to get through, anyway. I felt that wave, that uncontrollable surge of feeling, and I was there before I knew it. I couldn't stop myself from moving around, talking, singing, and carrying on. I felt like I could lick the world; I felt that the whole world thought I was something special. I really like that feeling, but again, I've been told by Dr. ——— that I was acting crazy and out of control. He said that I went around making believe that I was a dog looking for a fire hydrant and that I wet my pants." (Duke & Nowicki, 1979, p. 198)
>
> Diagnoses for these excerpts were, respectively, histrionic personality disorder, obsessive-compulsive disorder, and bipolar mood disorder.

PSYCHOANALYSIS AND THE GENITAL TYPE

DEVELOPMENT

For Freud, the healthy individual has passed successfully through the childhood stages of psychosexual development, receiving neither too little nor too much bodily gratification at each of the oral, anal, and phallic stages. If these stages are traversed without significant fixation, the genital type presumably will emerge sometime after puberty. (Note that evidence on the psychosexual stages derives from the interpretation of memories and dreams brought up in therapy rather than from more systematic observations.) The genital personality shows no major character defects that might impede adjustment; the ability to delay gratification and follow the rules of society; and a willingness to live with substitute, rather than direct, instinctual gratifications whenever this aids adjustment.

Development that leaves extensive fixations at the pregenital stages results in immature personalities with heightened chances of breaking down under stress. For example, a breakdown of the oral type may lead to schizophrenic disorders, of the anal type to obsessive-compulsive disorders, and of the phallic type to sexual disorders. In contrast, the genital type has avoided major fixation and so is thought to have considerable ego strength or ability to deal with stress.

THE CONTINUITY OF NORMAL AND ABNORMAL

Freud viewed normal and disordered individuals as having the same types of problems and conflicts, differing only in degree. Freud's model includes disturbed individuals, those of average adjustment (oral, anal, and phallic character types), and the genital type. In this system, disordered individuals have major character flaws that lead to maladjustment; average individuals have minor flaws that occasionally lead to adjustment problems; and the genital type corresponds to the normal personality, one that is without disease or dysfunction.

Genital types are thought to be competent at achieving instinctual satisfaction (largely sex and aggression) while still adjusting to society. What matters is the amount of instinctual satisfaction and the social appropriateness of one's behavior. There is no concept of personal growth beyond these considerations.

THE GENITAL PERSONALITY

As Maddi (1980, p. 304) summarized,

Genital persons are fully potent and capable in whatever they do. They are fully socialized, adjusted, and yet do not suffer greatly from this. They are courageous without the driven recklessness of the phallic character. They are satisfied with self without the overweening pride and vanity of the phallic character. They love heterosexually without the alarming neediness and dependence of the oral character. They work diligently and effectively without the compulsivity and competitiveness of the anal character. They are altruistic and generous without the sickening saintliness of the anal character. In short, they maximize instinctual gratification while minimizing punishment and guilt.

Freud theorized that the mainstays of our entire civilization—art, science, and business—result from the sublimation of animal desires.

The genital personality must still employ defenses in order to function, as the unsavory contents of the unconscious cannot be transcended. But the defenses of genital types would be minimally distortive, consisting largely of sublimation, compensation, and rationalization.

Freud identified the abilities to love and to work as the hallmarks of healthy functioning. By love he meant the ability to maintain a lasting, intimate, heterosexual relationship involving mutual sexual satisfaction. Work implies the ability to channel instinctual energies into labor that contributes to society.

For Freud, human values are equated with whatever is valued by society. Conscience is internalized from these values and has no independent source from within the person. There is no internal basis for ethics, other than the pursuit of individual pleasure and the need for society to devise rules allowing some measure of gratification for all its members.

The genital type has struck a good balance between the needs of the person and the needs of society. Thus the genital type's superego should not be overly severe. In other words, healthy functioning involves the minimum repression required to maintain functioning and fit into society. In this way, the genital type has retained a capacity to enjoy life and experience a sense of energy and aliveness.

Think of one person you know who best fits the genital type. Identifying actual people helps bring the model to life. You will be asked to make a similar identification for each model. After all the models are presented, we shall use this information to make some interesting comparisons.

How might we determine to what extent Freud is right in asserting that all the "higher activities" of culture (e.g., art, science, and business) are merely sublimations of sex and aggression? If he were correct, what would be the implications for optimal functioning?

SOCIAL LEARNING THEORY'S COMPETENT INDIVIDUAL

Social learning theory (Bandura, 1977, 1986) is more concerned with specifying *how* behavior changes than with describing the person whose behavior has changed. Thus, there is as yet little explicit theorizing about healthy personality. The same could also be said of Skinner (1974) and other behaviorists. Nevertheless, these theories are a vital force in understanding human behavior, and with a little literary license, we can draw out the implications of these positions for healthy personality.

Bandura suggests that behavior is emitted when we have the physical skill for performing it, the expectancy that we can emit the behavior (self-efficacy), and the expectation that a desirable consequence will follow its emission. For Bandura, a behavior's desirability is only a function of the amount of reinforcement it brings. Moreover, it doesn't matter whether the behavior is maintained because it leads to a desirable external reinforcer such as money or praise, or because it is intrinsically reinforcing, as are eating, drinking, sex, and play.

Thus a healthy personality is one in which the individual has the physical and cognitive skills for obtaining reinforcers, the expectancy of self-efficacy to ensure that competent behaviors will be attempted, and the self-management skills to ensure that behaviors leading to reinforcing stimuli will be maintained at a high rate, even if reinforcement is delayed. In addition, self-control will be more effective if maintained by positive reinforcers rather than aversive stimuli.

COGNITIVE ABILITIES

Bandura observes that our cognitive abilities allow us to influence both our environment and our behavior. These cognitive competencies include the ability to learn by observing someone else's performance, to code observed behavior into words and images, and to anticipate future consequences of behavior and use these expectancies to motivate ourselves in the present. Most importantly, they include the ability to regulate our own behavior through self-administered rewards and punishments.

PLANS

Healthy individuals operate rationally to maximize their long-term outcomes. They do this by planning how to obtain these goals and by developing an ability to divide long-term plans into a series of smaller, more immediate goals. Since it is assumed that all significant learning is available to consciousness, these consciously experienced plans are essential to effective functioning. Because of this, healthy individuals rely heavily on their preconceived plans.

SELF-CONTROL

The social learning model suggests that healthy individuals are not at the mercy of the immediate situation. Rather, they use their cognitive abilities to control their own behavior and exert some influence on the environment. Again, the purpose of this control is to obtain reinforcing outcomes.

Thus healthy individuals not only control desirable environmental events but also use cognitions to control their own behavior and future experiences. This model pictures healthy people as those who are in control of themselves, in control of their experiences. They show an internal locus of control in two ways: They perceive themselves as controlling the important events in their lives, and they actually do exert considerable control over those events. Research (Kobassa, 1979; Taylor, 1983) indicates that individuals with an internal locus of control and a sense of mastery over their environment are better adjusted and more stress resistant than those without a sense of mastery. For example, cancer patients who believe they

The social learning model of healthy functioning emphasizes skill mastery and self-control.

have some control over their disease show a more positive adjustment to it (Taylor, 1983).

SOCIAL LEARNING AND PSYCHOANALYTIC MODELS

It is interesting, and a little unexpected, that in many ways the psychoanalytic and social learning depictions of healthy personality are quite similar. Both models describe a level of functioning close to that experienced by average adults. They both emphasize competence in obtaining desired outcomes, and both suggest there is no basis for considering some desired outcomes healthier than others.

ROGERS'S FULLY FUNCTIONING PERSON

For Rogers, personal growth comes about as a natural unfolding of our genetic potential. Given a supportive environment in which our need for unconditional love and acceptance is met, the actualizing tendency flowers, yielding a life that

> involves a wider range, a greater richness, than the constricted living in which most of us find ourselves. To be a part of this process means that one is involved in the frequently frightening and frequently satisfying experience of a more sensitive living. . . . It seems to me that clients who have moved significantly in therapy live more intimately with their feelings of pain, but also more vividly with their feelings of ecstasy; that anger is more clearly felt, but so also is love. . . . And the reason they can thus live fully in a wider range is that they have this underlying confidence in themselves as trustworthy instruments for encountering life. (Rogers, 1961, pp. 195–196)

Thus Rogers pictures the fully functioning person not as someone who is always happy but as someone who is more fully alive, more sensitive to experience, and more aware of his or her emotions. Rogers identifies a number of closely related characteristics of the fully functioning person.

OPENNESS TO EXPERIENCE

Openness is the most central feature of the fully functioning person. It refers to a nondefensiveness in which every stimulus, whether originating in the organism or from the environment, is potentially available to consciousness in an undistorted form. Only when the individual is open to all experience can the actualizing tendency function to capacity.

Rogers and his colleagues (e.g., Rogers & Wood, 1974) developed a way in which a client's openness to experience can be judged from recorded therapy sessions. This measure identifies six types of experiencing in which level of openness can be rated:

1. *Owned feelings.* At the closed end, people externalize their feelings, perhaps believing that they are hearing voices telling them to commit improper acts; that is, they do not recognize the voices as part of themselves. In the middle, feelings may be intellectualized or discussed in the past tense. At the open end, feelings are expressed immediately, in the present, without ambiguity as to who is experiencing the emotion.

2. *Feelings as guides for behavior.* This indicates the extent to which clients use their feelings as data for guiding immediate decisions.

3. *Rigid versus flexible construing.* At the closed end, the person's perceptions are rigid and treated as unchanging facts. At the open end, interpretations of events are perceived as such; they are held tentatively and are readily altered as new information comes in.

4. *Self-disclosure.* At the closed end, people feel threatened and self-conscious, refusing to reveal much of themselves to another. At the open end, the individual can identify, discuss, and express emotions to another person.

5. *Taking responsibility.* At the closed end, people either do not recognize their problems, or they see problems as entirely outside themselves. At the open end, they accept personal responsibility and show a willingness to understand and confront their problems.

6. *Social intimacy.* At the closed end, the person shows a marked fear and avoidance of close personal contact. At the open end, warm, intimate contact is encouraged.

Considerable research (Meador, 1971; Tomlinson, 1962) indicates that clients become more open to experience over the course of Rogerian therapy.

CONGRUENCE

Congruence is the degree of overlap or identity among the real self, the conscious self, and the social self (see Chapter 2). It refers to an internal consistency or harmony among the various parts of personality. Note that congruence includes openness to experience and adds the notion that not only should we be potentially conscious of all that we are experiencing but also that we should be genuine in communicating who we are to others. To implement congruent functioning, both self-deception and the deception of others must be eliminated.

THE ATTITUDE OF SELF-DISCOVERY

For Rogers, the real self is something discovered from self-observation. Rogers saw the feeling of certainty that "I know who I am" as a transitional stage in human development. Certainly, this feeling is more adaptive than the sense of identity crisis associated with disturbed functioning. But it is too rigid for the fully functioning person. Rigid certainty in one's sense of identity automatically sets the stage for distortion. It implies an attachment to seeing only things about ourselves that will confirm our preconceived image. In other words, the certainty of self-identity is a defense against seeing other parts of ourselves. In contrast, Rogers believes it healthier to adopt the attitude that we are continually discovering who we really are.

Rogers points out that the effort to resist experiencing our real selves places tremendous stress on the individual, as illustrated in the following client's comments:

> It seems as if all the energy that went into holding the arbitrary pattern together was quite unnecessary—a waste. You think you have to make the pattern yourself; but there are so many pieces, and it's so hard to see where they fit. Sometimes you put them in the wrong place, and the more pieces not fitted, the more effort it takes to hold them in place, until at last you are so tired that even that awful confusion is better than holding on any longer. Then you discover that left to themselves the jumbled pieces fall quite naturally into their own places, and a living pattern emerges without any effort at all on your part. Your job is just to discover it, and in the course of that, you will find yourself. You must even let your . . . experience tell you its own meaning; the minute *you* tell it what it means, you are at war with yourself. (Rogers, 1954, 1985, p. 6)

Rogers found that in therapy, clients become more and more themselves. They enter the process of discovering themselves by dropping the false fronts, pretenses, and roles that they have used for facing life. In this process they discover something more basic, something more truly themselves. At first they lay aside the false faces that they are aware of using. Later, they engage in the frightening task of removing masks that they had thought were parts of their real selves.

WILLING TO BE A PROCESS

Rogers suggests that in the fully functioning person, the experience of self is radically changed, "It is more fluid, and less rigid and static, the 'I' almost lost in the individual's perceptual field." (Rogers & Wood, 1974, p. 220). Rather than thinking of themselves as fixed and identifiable objects, fully functioning persons see themselves as a flow of ideas, images, and feelings.

Rogers notes that in our daily lives we often do not allow ourselves to experience the thoughts and attitudes going through us. It seems too dangerous. If we allowed ourselves to really become these feelings, experiencing them to the limit of what they are, we would, for a moment, lose sight of who we are and what we're supposed to be doing. For that moment, we would actually *be* the fear or the anger or the tenderness. In other words, we would lose the awareness of "ourselves as experiencing something" and have only the awareness of feeling. Rogers maintains that "the individual in such a moment is coming to *be* what he *is*" (Rogers, 1954, p. 5).

As one facet of being in process, Rogers is wary of using preconceived plans as a basis for action. Certainly, one must be able to formulate and follow plans to attain normal functioning. Rogers maintains, however, that for the average person, the problem is not so much the inability to plan as the rigid attachment to whatever plan is formulated.

Plans aid growth when they can be held tentatively as guides for behavior. It is common, however, for individuals to form an attachment to a plan, so that when the situation changes or new information becomes available, they inflexibly pursue plans that no longer work. For example, suppose you have been thinking about eating chocolate cake for dessert after supper. Not that you're obsessed with eating the cake, but you know that it is sitting there waiting for you when you get home. The image of eating that cake has crossed your mind two or three times during the day; it has given you something to look forward to. After supper, however, you are full and not really in the mood for cake. Nevertheless, there is a strong tendency for that plan, once formed, to override one's immediate bodily desires. Rogers would say it is more adaptive to listen to what you feel you really want to do right now rather than to thoughts about what you should want to do based on the person that you were earlier in the day. Individuals who accept themselves as "in process" are

less likely to let preset plans override immediate experience.

TRUSTING ORGANISMIC EXPERIENCE

In deciding on a course of action, fully functioning people identify and attend to their own feelings rather than relying on what others say. Rogers suggests that our bodies, our organisms, our complete personalities usually know what is right for us, but this often comes as a feeling or intuition. In contrast, what others want us to do is more clearly internalized as a thought or rule that we have been taught. Thus we often must choose between an intuitive feeling that we cannot logically defend and a more cognitive belief that seems "more real." Rogers recommends that we attend to this intuitive feeling and trust it as our basis for action.

Thus the fully functioning person doesn't look to others for approval or for standards. "He recognizes that it rests within himself to choose; that the only question which matters is: 'Am I living in a way which is deeply satisfying to me, and which truly expresses me?' This . . . is perhaps *the* most important question for the creative individual" (Rogers, 1954, 1985, p. 7).

Underlying this trust, of course, is Rogers's assumption that at the instinctual level, we are basically good, nondestructive, and growth oriented. Thus, we can have faith that this trust will not be harmful, either to ourselves or to others.

Trust in one's organism is closely linked to openness. For example, in making an important decision, such as whether to marry his high school sweetheart, Ted's openness to experience allows him to use all available information for making this decision. He has knowledge of his own feelings and impulses, which are contradictory. He can sense the desires of his parents and friends. He is aware of the social and legal taboos and of his own internalized beliefs about right and wrong. He can remember what happened in similar past situations, and he has observed what happened to his friends when they

FOCUS
"I BEGAN TO LOSE ME"

The following letter written to Carl Rogers shows how the process of personal growth often follows a circular path. Relative normality may give way to periods of disturbance which are finally resolved in a jump forward toward greater health. In other words, what to others may look like psychological disturbance can often be viewed as the personality's attempt to cure itself.

I think that I began to lose me when I was in high school. I always wanted to go into work that would be of help to people but my family resisted, and I thought they must be right. Things went along smoothly for everyone else for four or five years until about two years ago. I met a guy that I thought was ideal. Then nearly a year ago I took a good look at us, and realized that I was everything that *he* wanted me to be and nothing that *I* was. I have always been emotional and I have had many feelings. I could never sort them out and identify them. My fiancé would tell me that I was just mad or just happy and I would say okay and leave it at that. Then when I took this good look at us I realized that I was angry because I wasn't following my true emotions.

I backed out of the relationship gracefully and tried to find out where all the pieces were that I had lost. . . .

I remember one night in particular. . . . I had come home feeling angry. I was angry because I wanted to talk about something but I couldn't identify what it was. By eight o'clock that night I was so upset I was frightened. I called [my psychologist] and he told me to come to his office as soon as I could. I got there and cried for at least an hour and then the words came. I still don't know all of what I was saying. All I know is that *so much hurt and anger* came out of me that I *never really knew existed*. I went home and it seemed that an *alien* had taken over and I was hallucinating like some of the patients I have seen in a state hospital. I continued to feel this way until one night I was sitting and thinking and I realized that this alien was the *me* that I had been trying to find.

I have noticed since that night that people no longer seem so strange to me. Now it is beginning to seem that life is just starting for me. I am alone right now but I am not frightened and I don't have to be doing something. I like meeting me and making friends with my thoughts and feelings. Because of this I have learned to enjoy other people. One [elderly] man in particular—who is very ill—makes me feel very much alive. He accepts everyone. He told me the other day that I have changed very much. According to him, I have begun to open up and love. (Rogers, 1980, pp. 208–210)

Use ideas from Carl Rogers and other theorists to explain what this woman meant by "I began to lose me." In particular, who or what are the "I" and the "me"?

were deciding on marriage. From this matrix of inputs (in which there is minimal repression or distortion), Ted can permit his total organism, including conscious, rational thought processes, to weigh and balance each factor and arrive at a response that takes into account both long- and short-range considerations.

Contrary to the social learning position, Rogers maintains that wanting to be in control of ourselves is not characteristic of healthy functioning. Just the opposite, it indicates how far we are from being able to trust our organismic experience. For Rogers, the full, bodily organism is assumed to have a wisdom, a relatedness to the growth process, that the conscious self does not have. To be concerned that the conscious self be "in control" puts the cart in front of the horse. For Rogers, wanting to control ourselves is the problem, not the solution. He advocates being an observer and participant in ongoing experience rather than trying to control it.

CREATIVITY

Fully functioning persons are creative, not so much out of inborn talent, but because of an intimate contact with their entire organismic reality. This reality functions as a source of wisdom that the conscious self alone may lack. In addition, fully functioning persons' nondefensive attitude allows them to take chances, and although these chances may often result in ideas that don't work, they sometimes lead to artistic or intellectual breakthroughs.

SUBJECTIVE FREEDOM

Fully functioning people feel that they are free to choose their own course in life, free to make their own decisions, and free to adopt whatever attitude they desire toward the events of their lives. Whether or not their behavior is determined in some objective sense, the attitude of freedom (and the responsibility that comes with it) is essential for living a full, exuberant existence.

A FINAL NOTE

Consistent with his nondirective beliefs, Rogers is adamant in cautioning that his image of ideal personality is not *prescriptive*. In other words, he refuses to play the role of an authority figure, defining healthy personality for others. He is not presenting a *goal* for other people. As a scientist, he believes that healthy personality can be described, but, ultimately, personal growth can occur only by means of individual choices. Blindly following someone else's image of optimal functioning violates organismic trust and thus disrupts actual growth.

Identify someone you know who best fits Rogers's model of the fully functioning person. What are some clues that would tell you that you are *not* being open to experience?

MASLOW'S SELF-ACTUALIZATION

Maslow observed that not all our experiences are equally valuable. Every so often, one stands out from the others. It might be when we are functioning more effectively, when we behave with heightened awareness, when we seem more alive, or when we cut through the social roles and contact another person more intimately, if only for a few moments. Maslow wondered whether it would be possible to increase the frequency of these valued experiences.

Maslow also noted that some people seem more admirable than others. In a moment of insight, he realized that these admired individuals shared certain traits, attitudes, and ways of approaching life. Maslow concluded, using a biological metaphor, that some people were simply better specimens of what it means to be a human being. These people had fulfilled their unique human potential to a greater extent than had most others, and Maslow called them **self-actualizing** individuals.

For Maslow, self-actualization is the most important value in life; thus the task for psychology is finding out how to produce self-actualizing people. The result is a theory that, in many ways, has altered the values and self-images of a whole generation of Americans. As we shall see in Chapter 14, whether its impact has been beneficial or harmful is now being hotly debated.

Before considering the characteristics of self-actualizing people, we must review some key ideas in Maslow's theory.

THE HIERARCHY OF NEEDS

As outlined in Chapter 2, Maslow identified the following five levels of needs:

5. Self-actualizing needs for play, curiosity, truth, goodness, justice, beauty, creativity, aliveness, perfection, and fulfillment.
4. Needs for esteem, competence, independence, recognition, and status.
3. Needs for belongingness, love, physical contact, affection, and group membership.
2. Needs for safety, security, stability, routine, protection, order, and freedom from fear and anxiety.
1. Physiological and survival-related needs, such as those for oxygen, food, water, sex, and sleep.

Maslow hypothesized that needs lower in the hierarchy must be at least partially gratified before higher needs become salient. The lower four needs concern the survival and maintenance of the organism, and the self-actualizing needs develop our uniquely human potentialities.

For Maslow, all of these needs are biologically based. In contrast with psychoanalysis, Maslow believed that the needs at the self-actualizing level could not be reduced to sublimations of animal instincts. He maintained that a failure to satisfy self-actualizing needs, even when lower needs were fully gratified, would result in feelings of depression, anxiety, boredom, and meaninglessness.

The lower needs differ from self-actualizing

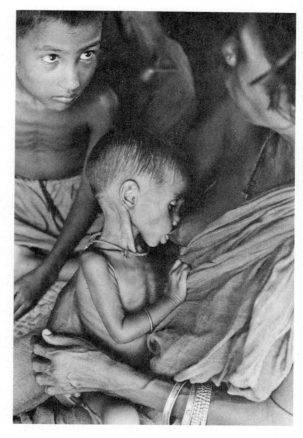

Maslow theorized that survival-related needs must be at least partially gratified before higher needs become salient.

needs in several ways. They are more easily appeased, and they appear to follow a tension-reduction model, as illustrated below:

Need Deprivation → Tension → Behaviors to Satisfy the Need → Return to Quiescence

In contrast, self-actualizing needs are less cyclical. They have no clear end points at which the need is gratified, leading to a state of quiescence.

Not all of the need levels are equally relevant in modern, affluent societies. The waking lives of most adults are spent largely in pursuing the love and approval of others, that is, levels 3 and 4. This is where we have become "fixated." Maslow was not suggesting that individuals could or should operate only in pursuit of self-actualizing needs. Obviously, survival and security needs must be met on a daily basis. But he was suggesting that a life spent largely in pursuit of actualizing needs is a qualitatively more desirable existence.

Observe that activities at the self-actualizing level are intrinsically reinforcing. They are engaged in for themselves, not because of the benefits or payoffs that they will bring. Thus, for Maslow, an artist who paints to earn money is engaging in a qualitatively different endeavor from one who experiences the painting as a way of expressing feelings or pursuing beauty.

THE INCIDENCE OF SELF-ACTUALIZATION

Maslow believed that self-actualization is rare, perhaps characteristic of less than 1 percent of the population, but not because it must be reserved for a gifted few. He stated, "I think of the self-actualizing man not as an ordinary man with something added, but rather as the ordinary man with nothing taken away. The average man is a full human being with dampened and inhibited powers" (Lowery, 1973, p. 91).

Moreover, it would be erroneous to think of self-actualizers as attaining perfection. For example, they may have silly habits or undesirable traits, such as stubbornness. They also possess their share of negative emotions, such as guilt, anxiety, and sadness. Maslow believed that negative emotions cannot and should not be purged from experience. If self-actualizers violated ethical principles that they had accepted, then guilt would follow naturally. The absence of guilt would not show perfection but, rather, pathological development along the lines of the antisocial personality. Similarly, some anxiety cannot be avoided, for growth means venturing into the unknown, taking chances, and trying new activities in which no one can guarantee success.

BEING COGNITION

In our ordinary consciousness, we observe an object by labeling it, classifying it in a way that relates it to our needs and interests. In other words, we seek to know it for our own sake, for a purpose. We may study a work of art, for example, in order to improve ourselves, to make us more knowledgeable, or to impress our friends. Alternatively, we may observe it, lost in its beauty, looking without trying to analyze, categorize, or make mental notes for future reference. Here, the immediate perception is the end in itself. This is **being cognition**. Maslow recognized that we need our ordinary, practical consciousness in order to function in society, but he felt that ready access to being cognition is highly desirable.

Peak experiences refer to extreme states of being cognition, moments of highest happiness and fulfillment that occur when we are able to love something for its own sake. They may involve, for example, a religious or nature experience, an aesthetic perception, a creative moment, an intellectual insight, an orgasmic delight, or an athletic fulfillment. Peak experiences often involve losing one's sense of boundary, so that the experiencer seems to become a part of all people, a part of all nature, temporarily losing the sense of self or personal identity. For example, the exultation of a sports victory in which one thinks "I won!" would not qualify as a peak experience, as it is too closely linked to ego satisfactions (level 4 on the hierarchy).

In peak experiences, the object perceived is seen as complete and unique, without needing to be compared with or related to anything else. The object is perceived with loving care, often accompanied by an emotion of exultation. And the object is seen with "fresh eyes," as if for the first and last time ever.

A peak experience typically is an experience of "unity," as if we were one aspect of a larger design in which everything is connected to everything else. In this state of unity, all apparent dichotomies are reconciled. As the visionary William James commented, "It is as if the opposites of the world, whose contradictoriness and conflict make all our difficulties and troubles, were melted into unity" (James, 1902, p. 388).

When studying peak experiences Maslow was shocked to find that they are not rare. Many individuals report having had at least one or two at some time in their lives, and self-actualizing people were particularly likely to report peak experiences. (Examples of peak experiences are described in Chapter 14.)

MASLOW'S STRATEGY FOR STUDYING SELF-ACTUALIZATION

From informal observations of his acquaintances and from biographies of historical figures, Maslow identified a group of about sixty potential self-actualizers, including Albert Einstein, Eleanor Roosevelt, Eugene Debs, Adlai Stevenson, Sigmund Freud, Henry Thoreau, Abraham Lincoln, and Thomas Jefferson. It is interesting that although Maslow considered many younger individuals, he found that self-actualizers were usually sixty years of age or older.

CHARACTERISTICS OF SELF-ACTUALIZING INDIVIDUALS

For Maslow, self-actualizing individuals are

1. Relatively free of psychological disturbance.
2. Fulfilling their positive genetic potentials; becoming all that they can be; developing their talents and positive capabilities.
3. Relatively gratified in their lower needs.
4. Motivated by values that go beyond personal gain, that is, motivated by self-actualizing needs.
5. Spontaneous, flexible and creative, without being impulsive. As with Rogers's fully functioning people, their creativity doesn't derive so much from special talent as from an uninhibited, childlike way of approaching problems.
6. Accurate in their reality contact. Actualizers perceive the world in unstereotyped ways, seeing people as they are rather than as they used to be or as we would like them to be. Because of this, they maintain realistic expectations for themselves and others.
7. Open and intimate in friendships, but they do not have an overriding need for company. They tend to have a few close relationships rather than many superficial ones.
8. Valuing privacy and solitude; they can enjoy being alone. In contrast, many people in our culture feel anxious if they find themselves alone in a quiet room. They feel that they must immediately turn on the radio, call a friend, or do *something* to occupy themselves.
9. Nonjudgmental and accepting toward self and others.
10. Democratic and ethical in refusing to exploit or take advantage of others.
11. Nonhostile in their sense of humor. They often find humor in puns, coined words, and double meanings, rather than in someone else's misfortune.
12. More likely to have peak experiences.
13. Devoted to some activity or work for its own sake rather than for fame or profit.
14. Appreciative of life, approaching everyday activities with a sense of awe. Note that this conflicts with the oversophisticated attitude that one has tried everything and is therefore "not impressed."
15. Interested in the welfare of others. They show a sense of identification and kinship with all humanity, not just with their own family or social group. They show altruistic, unselfish, and nonpossessive love. They are more motivated by the activity of giving than by the objects of receiving. They aid others for the sake of helping, not for the credit of having helped.

16. Self-reliant, relatively independent of their social environment and culture. They choose their own values rather than simply accept the values of their culture. They often have more in common with actualizers from other cultures than with nonactualizers in their own culture. They are relatively independent of the rewards that others provide, such as affection and respect, and so they are freer to follow their own path. Thus they may often seem "unfashionable." Though able to adapt, if necessary, they may not seem "well adjusted" in societies that value power, wealth, domination, or social injustice.

EMPIRICAL EVALUATION

In contrast with most other models of healthy personality, self-actualization has been fairly well researched. It appears that the actual number of need categories is somewhat arbitrary, but there does seem to be a basic distinction between lower and self-actualizing needs (Betz, 1984; Wahba & Bridwell, 1976). The hierarchical arrangement of needs, with the lower ones requiring gratification before the higher needs become salient, has received mixed support. Note, however, that this part of the theory is difficult to test in contemporary society. Most modern individuals operate largely at the esteem level. Although we often say we are working "to put food on the table," hunger, physical safety, and even belongingness needs are relatively well gratified in our society. For example, most of us do not seek food for survival. Rather, we seek particular types of food to satisfy socially acquired tastes. Similarly, we don't just seek shelter, but a socially desirable dwelling. In fact, most of us spend the bulk of our waking hours in the pursuit of respect, social acceptance, and symbols of status. Thus the hierarchy applies mainly to the distinction between lower and actualizing needs, and actualizers do report

being more motivated than are nonactualizers by these higher needs (Mathes, 1978).

We can conclude that the need hierarchy is a useful way of looking at human motivation, but one that has a number of exceptions and limitations. It applies best under conditions of hardship and deprivation, in which the lower needs have a chance to go ungratified and exert a powerful effect. In this broad context, the model appears to be useful.

Two exceptions, however, should be kept in mind. One is that there are so few actualizers and so many people of achievement who, for some reason, remain at the esteem level. For many individuals, there seems to be no specifiable level of achievement that would gratify their esteem needs and allow them to move on to more actualizing needs. Maslow has no explanation for this, although it may be less common in noncompetitive cultures. Another limitation is the occasional circumstance in which someone violates the lower needs, perhaps even sacrificing his or her own life, for the sake of a higher principle such as justice or freedom. Thus it is certainly possible for some individuals to place their actualizing values above all else.

Shostrum (1976) found attempts to measure self-actualization with a paper-and-pencil test to be encouraging. Measures of self-actualization correlated with therapists' ratings of actualization and distinguished among nominated actualizers, normals, and hospitalized mental patients. They also distinguished between those in beginning and ending stages of therapy. Actualizers appeared to be healthier than nonactualizers; they had lower neuroticism scores, and they were assertive, happy-go-lucky, self-assured, and able to resist social pressure. Moreover, self-actualization scores did not seem to result from merely presenting oneself in a positive light. When the subjects were asked to "fake good," their scores moved in the nonactualizing direction, for example, by espousing traditional desirable values rather than ones they had chosen for themselves.

Identify someone you know who best represents the self-actualizing individual. Do you disagree with any of the characteristics that Maslow attributed to self-actualizers?

EXISTENTIAL AUTHENTICITY

And who is authentic? . . . The individual who is free and who knows it, who knows that every deed and word is a choice and hence an act of value creation, and, finally and perhaps decisively, who knows that he is the author of his own life and must be held personally responsible for the values on behalf of which he has chosen to live it. (Morris, 1966, p. 48)

THE OPEN-ENDED SELF

Whereas Freud started with the assumption that we are essentially animals with a small capacity for awareness, existential theorists take an opposite approach. They emphasize what is unique to human beings, the capacity for conscious awareness, particularly self-awareness. We are creatures who continually seek meaning; we want to understand and make sense of our lives. In agreement with Rogers, existentialists maintain that our identities are thus always in process and that this gives us a type of existence qualitatively different from that of other life forms.

As humans, we can view ourselves objectively, from the outside, as if we were fixed entities. We can experience ourselves in a way that emphasizes "me" or "what I am," as if viewing a tree or a rock or any object in the world. We can think of ourselves as having fixed characteristics, such as color, weight, and hardness. We think of ourselves in this objective way by keeping in mind our name, what we look like, our traits, habits, and other objective characteristics. This way of seeing ourselves is often useful, especially when we want to predict our own behavior.

For authentic existence, however, we must balance this view with an awareness that those characteristics are not nearly so fixed as we might like to believe. We also exist as a flow of thoughts, feelings, and perceptions, and this process is essentially open-ended. We do not know what thoughts or feelings we will experience in the next moment, and we are continually in the process of defining ourselves. As Keen (1970) remarked, our experience can emphasize either "what I am" or "that I am." This awareness that we are always in process, always becoming, creates a feeling of radical freedom and opens the way for change and flexibility. Thus for authentic living, we must be able to contact the experience of "I" as an open-ended process, as a cause rather than an effect.

Existentialists agree with Maslow that for most people, inauthentic being is the norm, authenticity the exception. To illustrate, consider Jean-Paul Sartre's (1953) example of a man who explains his stealing by saying that he is a thief. He defines himself in terms of his past behavior, of what he appears to be in the eyes of others. As a being in process, he would remain a thief only if he continued to choose thievery. To deny this choice by thinking of himself as an object, a result of past history, would be inauthentic. By denying his continuing choice, he fails to take responsibility for his own life.

AWARENESS OF DEATH

For existentialists, the awareness that our own death is inevitable, and perhaps imminent, enriches the experience of life. At these times, we can readily see our life as a gift for which we can be thankful. Thus existential theorists agree with Maslow that feelings of awe and appreciation contribute to healthy personality; yet they add the cautionary note, "Do not dull your sense of aliveness by pretending that death is not real."

If we believe we are an object with set characteristics, we immediately become invested in having others confirm our self-beliefs. Thus we become a performer and others are our audience. We play roles to gain their applause. This is how we confirm our self-concept as being attractive, intelligent, competent, and the like. Existentialists suggest that ultimately, we seek this confirmation as a security against the threat of death. We seek reassurance that the game really matters, for, in the face of death, it is hard to believe that it does.

As Shaffer (1978, p. 29) observed,

> In an authentic existence a person confronts directly the ever-emergent possibility of nonbeing, makes decisions in the face of uncertainty, and takes responsibility for them. When it comes to his human relationships, he is secure enough to respect the autonomy of other people; he appreciates that they have their own purposes to fulfill and do not exist simply for his own pleasure and self-enhancement.

THE WILL TO MEANING

Existential therapist Viktor Frankl centered his view of authentic functioning on the will to meaning. In human beings, instincts obviously function, but consciousness transforms instinctual tendencies to a higher plane of activity. With consciousness, we can conceptualize the available options and choose how to gratify our needs. Moreover, we retain a capacity for self-determination, for consciousness creates the choices that we will consider. Because of self-determination, we are responsible for those choices.

Frankl's harrowing experiences in a Nazi death camp convinced him that meaning is something to be constantly discovered in our daily lives. And no matter how difficult the situation, it is up to us: Use our cognitive powers to invest experiences with meaning, or deny these powers and watch as our "spirit" weakens.

Frankl maintained that there is no general meaning to life. Life confronts each of us with different tasks based on our personalities and life situations. He compared the search for "the"

Viktor Frankl.

meaning of life to the question "What is the best move in chess?" Neither question can be answered in the abstract.

Frankl pointed out that suffering and frustration are inevitable. They cannot be wished away. And although negative in themselves, our attitude toward these events determines our level of authentic existence. Frankl maintained that despite outward circumstances, we remain free to accept suffering with courage and dignity or to give in to self-pity and despair. And this, in large measure, determines the quality of our lives.

For Frankl, authenticity occurs as an effect of creating meaning in our lives. "Only to the extent to which man fulfills a meaning out there in the world, does he fulfill himself. Conversely, if he sets out to actualize himself rather than fulfill a meaning, self-actualization would immediately lose its justification" (1969, p. 116).

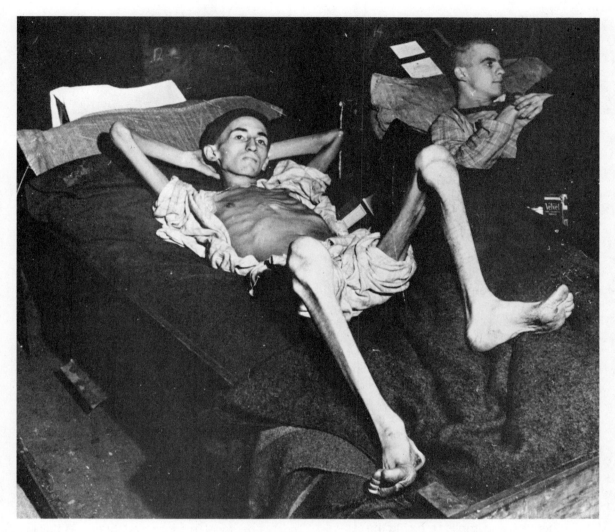

Frankl's identification of a will to meaning originated from his experiences in a Nazi death camp.

When the will to meaning is frustrated, that is, when we fail to accept the challenge to find meaning and pursue activities that fulfill these meanings, the result is existential neurosis. We may become depressed because of the guilt from not living up to our potentials. For example, we may remain in a job that provides financial security but little intrinsic satisfaction. The challenge here is to modify the job so that it can provide meaning, perhaps in the form of cre-

ative involvement or through aiding other people. But, to be authentic, we must find some basis for experiencing the job as meaningful; otherwise, we must give it up. Recalling the importance of death awareness, Frankl observed that we simply cannot afford to fritter away our few precious moments on activities that are not meaningful to us.

Moreover, those who feel they have a definite purpose in life show the least fear of death

(Durlak, 1972). Death fear reflects inauthentic being, for those who put off living, who put off doing the things that are really important to them, are gambling that they can cheat death. They are betting that death will accommodate their intention to begin living sometime in the future. Thus death is the wild card that defeats their plan. These individuals are the ones who feel love but won't express it, who crave challenge but anticipate failure, who could have burned their candle more brightly but feared the heat.

CHOOSING THE FUTURE

Existential theorists view life as a series of choices. In each decision, one alternative propels us into the future, which is unknown and unpredictable. The other alternative represents the past, which is safe and familiar but does not take us forward. Choosing the future provides the possibility for challenge and growth; yet it is uncharted and anxiety provoking. Choosing the past is comfortable and safe, but it sacrifices the possibility for growth and thus carries guilt, for we know that we could have been more. Authentic being requires choosing anxiety over guilt.

ACCEPTING RESPONSIBILITY FOR DECISIONS

Authentic being implies refusing the self-indulgence of blaming other people. Responsibility stems from our freedom to choose one alternative over another and, perhaps more importantly, to use our cognitive abilities to form what we will construe those alternatives to be. And although reality does limit us, authentic persons do not take the easy way out by denying their freedom and perceiving possibilities as necessities.

For example, suppose your friend Robert really wants you to go to a party with him, but you would rather not go. He is so persistent, however, that you decide to go along, partly to

please him and partly because you are now wondering whether or not he may be right. So you go to the party, and it turns out to be very boring. You are beginning to resent Robert. He ruined your evening. How might an existentialist interpret this chain of events?

According to existentialists, a typical response would be to blame Robert. After all, you knew the party would be dull. It would be easy to deny any responsibility for the decision to go and act as if Robert's persistence turned the *possibility* of going to the party into a *necessity*. He made you do it. He seemed so sure it would be a good party that you trusted him. And now your resentment of him is only natural and justified.

In truth, it would require great courage to see that you *decided* to trust Robert's judgment. Although he may have been wrong about the party, you were wrong about his judgment. And in succumbing to his persistence, you ignored your own judgment. Furthermore, by calling the party "boring," you are acting as if you were not part of it. By sitting back, waiting for others to entertain you, you have conveniently defined yourself as only a passive observer. Certainly, your unpleasant evening could not be blamed on *you*. This strategy may succeed in evading self-blame, but what are its costs? To avoid blame, you must see yourself as a victim, a passive respondent to others' initiatives. In other words, blame is avoided at the cost of personal freedom, and for existentialists, this price is not acceptable.

NORMALITY: THE MOST COMMON ALTERNATIVE TO AUTHENTIC BEING

Maddi (1980) presents a sobering picture of how inauthentic a normal life can be. For Maddi, the rejection of authenticity leads to a life of conformity, in which one's sense of identity is limited to playing social roles, and the possibility of choosing to violate what is expected becomes unthinkable, and hence impossible. Inauthentic

persons espouse materialistic values, for they see themselves only as embodiments of biological needs and social roles. Thus there is little of value in the world except the desire for the goods that will satisfy these needs. Inauthentic people's relationships are contractual rather than intimate. If the important parts of our lives are social expectations and material satisfactions, then our relationships will be based on the economics of "Who is getting what from whom." It would be difficult just to let an interaction go in whatever direction. Instead, inauthentic people want their relationships structured in advance so that it will be clear what is in it for them. Thus their relationships "will tend to be rather cold-blooded, even though the absence . . . of intimacy and spontaneity will leave a nagging sense of loneliness and disappointment" (Maddi, 1980, p. 378).

Identify someone you know who best represents authentic functioning. You have now selected people to represent each of the five models of optimal personality. Look at the individuals you have selected. Where you have selected the same person for more than one theory, you are, in effect, perceiving these theories as similar. Based on the people you have selected, would you say that these five theories agree or disagree as to what constitutes healthy personality? Of the people you selected, which one is most similar to you? Which is most similar to the person you would like to be?

MODELS OF HEALTHY PERSONALITY: CRITIQUE AND SYNTHESIS

Perhaps the one thing that stands out in these five models is their general agreement about what constitutes healthy functioning. Despite dramatic differences in their assumptions about human nature, there are only a few issues on which these models directly contradict one another. What is more common are differences in emphasis, with the models together tending to form a complementary whole.

THE PSYCHOANALYTIC MODEL

Although psychoanalysis has received much criticism, as outlined in Chapter 2, its vision of healthy personality has not been particularly controversial. Certainly, the link between healthy personality and the resolution of psychosexual conflicts appears tenuous, at least for many psychologists. But the characteristics of healthy personality, for example, ego strength, minimal distortion and repression, appropriate sublimations, and the abilities to love and work, seem both credible and essential to healthy functioning.

The strongest argument against the psychoanalytic model comes from humanistic theorists, who claim that it doesn't go far enough. According to Rogers and Maslow, we can identify levels of optimal functioning that go beyond the minimal requirements of the genital type. The psychoanalytic model describes a level of normal functioning that is only slightly beyond that of the average, socialized individual. In addition, its emphasis on adjustment to society leaves little room for the possibility that some societies may be less healthy than others. What about a healthy individual living in a relatively sick society? (The traditional example here is Nazi Germany.) Maslow questioned whether adjustment to the status quo could adequately describe healthy functioning in these circumstances.

THE SOCIAL LEARNING MODEL

As with the psychoanalytic model, social learning theory deals with a level of functioning that does not extend much beyond that of the average. In defense of both positions, it may be that (1) this is as far as we can legitimately go within a scientific approach or (2) making distinctions at higher levels of optimal functioning may lead to unintended problems (this possibility is explored in the final chapter).

Although the importance of self-determination is mentioned in several models, it appears most central to social learning theory. But Brewster Smith (1973) contends that self-determination is too one-sided to be used as a basis for optimal functioning. It reflects a "male" bias, a bias of doing rather than not doing, of American rather than Asian values, of *yang* rather than *yin,* of will rather than love (May, 1969), and, probably, of left brain rather than right brain.

Thus Smith was arguing that there are at least two sides to healthy personality: One emphasizes the virtues of autonomy, activity, and self-control; the other, the virtues of relationship, passivity, and "letting be." Note the similarity to Maslow's distinction between ordinary, evaluative thinking and being cognition. Recall from Chapter 2 that this is also central to the distinction between the behavioral and experiential points of view. Thus within this pervasive bipolarity, the social learning emphasis on self-determination may need to be balanced by something like Rogers's trust in organismic experiencing.

HUMANISTIC MODELS

In contrast with the psychoanalytic and social learning models, the humanistic theories were designed with healthy personality specifically in mind. Thus they describe a level of healthy functioning that is "higher" than those of the previous two models. It can be seen that the various theories complement one another, with each being strongest at a different segment of the continuum stretching from maladjusted to optimal functioning.

Because many of the same criticisms apply to both Rogers and Maslow, they will be treated together.

Overemphasis on immediate feelings. Maslow defined the growth process in terms of immediate feelings:

> Growth takes place when the next step forward is subjectively more delightful, more joyous, more intrinsically satisfying than the previous gratification with which we have become familiar and even bored; that the only way we can ever know what is right for us is that it feels better subjectively than any alternative. The new experience validates *itself*. . . . It is self-justifying. . . . This is the way in which we discover the Self and answer the ultimate questions, "Who am I?" "What am I?" (Maslow, 1968, p. 45)

Thus Maslow's model rests on trusting one's feelings and having faith in the wisdom of the organism. But critics (e.g., Smith, 1973) argue that there is no basis for placing feeling above thought. What about the impulsive feelings to harm others, to take what is not ours, to eat foods that undermine health, to distort reality, and to engage in self-destructive habits such as compulsive drinking and gambling? Smith concludes that we should not regard the "'gut feel' as more enduringly valid than the considered thought, the passively eruptive as 'higher' and 'truer' than the actively sought" (Smith, 1973, p. 27).

Here is where Rogers may be in a stronger position than Maslow. Recall that Rogers defines the wisdom of the organism as based on an openness that includes cognitive processes as well as immediate feelings. In practice, however, it may be difficult to distinguish between these organismic evaluations and immediate feelings.

We can conclude that the humanistic position emphasizes feelings more than thoughts,

but it is not restricted to momentary feelings. In a culture (such as ours) that elevates thought and rationality while denigrating feeling and intuition, this overemphasis may be adaptive. Thus the humanistic message would be, "Do not dismiss intuitive feelings too quickly, merely because one does not immediately see their rational justification." With this admonition, one can then try to follow a total, organismic decision that includes thoughts as well as feelings.

The humanistic model's naiveté. Humanistic models have been characterized as naive in their faith in the goodness of human nature and their trust in actualizers' value judgments. In defense, Maslow (1959) maintained that self-actualization is a widely misunderstood concept. In fact, self-actualization is not an end state but a continuous, day-by-day process of living. Although self-actualizing persons are relatively free of immature or neurotic problems, they are likely to experience the "real," unavoidable problems of human suffering to a greater degree than do nonactualizers.

Maslow thus implied that much of the guilt, fear, and anxiety that people experience is irrational and avoidable, such as guilt over normal sexual desires. Actualizers would largely transcend this sort of problem. Other problems, however, remain. For example, actualizers face the consequences of their behavior directly, with little defense or distortion. Thus, when they do transgress and behave in selfish, greedy, or inconsiderate ways, they are less likely to evade guilt by distorting the situation or blaming the other person.

Limits of being cognition. Maslow emphasized being cognition, which reflects an attitude of passive, compassionate noninterference. However, being cognition is incompatible with action. In life, we are often called upon to act decisively in our own best interests or to help others. Such behavior requires a more active, evaluative frame of mind. Thus effective personal growth not only requires engaging the world through being cognition, but also the ability to disengage and relate to the world in terms of ordinary, evaluative consciousness.

The selection of self-actualizers. A number of critics (e.g., Kendler, 1980; Smith, 1973) suggest that the criteria of healthy personality are values and that there is no way that science can determine which values people should live by. Once values have been selected, however, scientific methods can be used to select the best means for their implementation. In other words, science can describe what is valued, but it can never tell us what to value. It can describe the consequences of selecting certain values, but it cannot decide which consequence to prefer. According to Smith, Maslow defined his own personal values in his theory of self-actualization, and as a creative and thoughtful observer, his choices should be studied. But it may have been misleading for Maslow to suggest that there is anything universal about his particular preferences. We can pursue this argument by considering his research strategy.

Maslow's sample of actualizers consisted of people he admired. Individuals that other selectors may have viewed as equally admirable were not included. Thus his research cannot provide an empirical basis for understanding "the fully human individual," only for studying one person's vision of full humanity. In regard to the actualization of one's potentials, Smith pointed out that many other historical figures could have qualified, such as Napoleon or Lenin. Kendler observed that a psychologist who valued practicality more than Maslow did might have selected Henry Kissinger, Neil Simon, and Andrew Carnegie as exemplars. A psychologist fascinated with the irony of life might have chosen Groucho Marx and W. C. Fields.

In the absence of cross-cultural studies showing convergent validation, Maslow would find it hard to defend the universal desirability of self-actualization. On the other hand, among psychologists in our own culture, there is little argument with the characteristics Maslow used for defining healthy personality.

Many psychologists feel that Maslow's

strategy of studying the healthiest individuals is a good idea, even if there is some disagreement as to who should be included in the sample. What this strategy can do is give us clues as to what kind of people we might want to become and ideas about how to set this process in motion.

What Maslow's system lacks and will never have is a moral authority to say that we should strive for a given value. All it can do is describe the life experiences of those motivated by a particular value. After that, we must make our own decisions. For example, we might inquire, "Is it healthier to spend one's time helping others or amassing wealth?" When stated baldly in this way, a life of helping others may seem more desirable, but how can this be proved? If we find, for example, that those with altruistic rather than selfish motives experience more satisfying lives, as many psychotherapists suggest, then this would provide important information about the consequences of pursuing these alternative life goals.

THE EXISTENTIAL MODEL

As should be obvious, the existential model is highly compatible with humanistic notions of healthy personality. One point of difference, however, is that the existential position does not place feelings above cognitions. Another is that it does not picture growth as a natural unfolding of genetic potential. Instead, growth is seen as an act of will in which one decides to accept the risk and anxiety of the unknown. Thus existential theorists place more of an emphasis on conscious, rational, goal-oriented behavior than do humanists.

CONTRADICTIONS AMONG THE MODELS

Effort. Rogers and Maslow described growth as resulting from the natural unfolding of genetic potential. Whether or not we want to, we naturally move toward growth when environmental conditions are supportive. In other words, humanistic theorists present a model of growth that does not emphasize "trying harder" (Maddi, 1980). Moreover, they are suspicious of attempts to force or speed up the growth process, for these efforts often operate in the service of motives such as self-esteem, which are below the self-actualizing level. Thus such efforts may subvert actual growth.

In contrast, existential and social learning models emphasize the role of effort and will in healthy personality. For them, healthy personality does not come about "naturally" as a push from behind through inborn potentials seeking outward expression. Rather, it can be pictured as a "pull" from ahead. We are pulled forward by an image of perfection, of idealized functioning, that we must strive to attain, and this striving often transcends social and biological limitations. For example, someone with a speech deficiency might go to great lengths to compensate for this problem and eventually become a great orator.

Existential theorists stress using our beliefs, cognitions, and will to force ourselves to do what we don't want to do. Maslow and Rogers emphasized following our feelings and doing what we "really" want to do, rather than what our internalized rules and beliefs tell us we should do.

This apparent contradiction can perhaps be reconciled by recognizing that for some types of goals or activities, trying, effort, and willpower make sense. For others, conscious effort only interferes. Whenever growth depends on spontaneous action or natural preference, trying harder is of no avail. You cannot become more spontaneous by trying harder. You cannot force yourself to enjoy life. On the other hand, when the emphasis is on producing a behavior that does not require spontaneity, such as approaching feared objects or practicing a desired skill, then effort, persistence, and willpower are called for. A healthy individual should have both capabilities.

Desire for self-control. Social learning theory posits the importance of being in control

of oneself; thus individuals should desire self-control. Although humanistic theorists are not against self-control per se, they are suspicious of the desire for it. For Rogers, this desire indicates a failure to trust organismic experience. It would be inappropriate for the conscious self either to be in control of the entire organism or to seek such control, as if this were possible. From Maslow's viewpoint, this desire is not a manifestation of self-actualization but of insecurity. Seeking self-control may be appropriate under conditions of high stress, when the personality itself is under attack or in danger of breakdown. But for the normal individual in ordinary circumstances, such an attitude may block actual growth.

Intrinsic motivation. Maslow maintained that at the self-actualizing level of need gratification, behavior is performed for its own sake, not because of any environmental outcomes that it might produce. In other words, Maslow believed that it is better to experience one's behavior as an end in itself rather than as a means to some other end. Thus one index of healthy personality is the proportion of one's behaviors that is intrinsically motivated.

For social learning theorists, the total amount of reinforcement should be maximized, but it makes no difference whether that reinforcement is intrinsic or extrinsic.

Deemphasizing the ego. Psychoanalytic theorists and some humanists (e.g., Branden, 1984) emphasize the importance of ego strength, self-esteem, and a strong sense of identity. For them, healthy individuals have a clear sense of who and what they are; that is, they have a well-defined self-structure. It is only natural, however, that such people would also show a considerable emotional investment in or attachment to that self-structure.

Rogers, Maslow, and existential theorists agree that these are important considerations, up to a point. In moving from maladjusted to above-average functioning, they are indispensable. These theorists maintain, however, that at some point, further growth involves loosening one's sense of identity, relinquishing the attachment to any fixed self-image, and identifying with the process of experiencing. This more fluid sense of identification does not imply a decrease of self-esteem but, rather, a decrease in the importance of esteem needs. This change in identity is thought to be adaptive in requiring less defensiveness and allowing greater flexibility.

It seems reasonable to view both positions as accurate, with each applying to a different segment of the growth continuum.

You have now had a chance to see how each of these models depicts healthy personality. You have some idea of how the various models are similar, complementary, or contradictory. By now you have also had a chance to select features of each model that you find particularly appealing. What are these features? Is there one model that you identify with more than the others? What do you think of Maslow's strategy of studying exemplars of healthy personality? Is there anything in particular that you would like to know about these individuals? Finally, where do you currently see yourself on this dimension of maladjusted-to-average-to-optimal functioning?

Identifying models of healthy personality is important in itself, for it helps make us aware of other ways of being. In addition, however, we also expect these models to provide useful guidelines for personal growth. The next chapter examines how these models can be interpreted and applied in daily life. Equally important, it suggests how misinterpretations of the models can be avoided.

SUMMARY

1. Criteria of psychological disorder include pain, self-destructiveness, loss of reality contact, and socially inappropriate behavior.

2. The classification of psychological disorders creates problems with labeling and diagnostic reliability. Nevertheless, there is no viable alternative to classification. The standard system for classifying psychological disorders, DSM-III, includes somatoform, anxiety, affective, dissociative, schizophrenic, personality, and substance use disorders.

3. The psychoanalytic model's genital personality demonstrates a successful resolution of pregenital conflicts, competence at gratifying instinctual desires within the limits of acceptable social conduct, the abilities to love and work productively, minimal repression and distortion of experience, an ability to delay gratification and sublimate instinctual needs when direct gratifications are not feasible, and a superego that is not overly severe, retaining some sense of vitality.

4. Social learning theory's competent individual has a wide range of physical and cognitive skills; the expectation of being able to enact these skills when desired; control over their behavior through the selective use of rewards and punishments; the ability to behave rationally, maximizing long-term outcomes; the ability to influence the environment, making reinforcing outcomes more probable; and the use of plans and other cognitive mechanisms to aid in performing complex behaviors.

5. Rogers's fully functioning person is open to experience, nondefensive, congruent, experiencing life as a process of self-discovery, willing to see oneself as a process rather than a fixed entity, wary of attachment to preconceived plans, able to trust organismic experiencing, not dependent on others' approval, creative, and subjectively free to choose one's own course in life.

6. Maslow's self-actualizing individual is free of disorder; has unique skills and talents; is gratified in lower, that is, physiological, safety, belonging, and esteem needs; is spontaneous, creative, accurate in perception, and intimate in relationships; values privacy; accepts self and others; is nonexploitative and nonhostile in humor; may have peak experiences; and is devoted to work for its own sake, and appreciative, altruistic, and self-reliant.

7. The existential model's authentic individual experiences the self as an open-ended process, is aware of his or her own death, uses cognitive powers to invest experiences with meaning, chooses to grow and extend himself or herself despite anxiety, accepts complete responsibility for his or her decisions, and refuses to blame others or perceive possibilities as necessities.

8. These five models tend to agree as to what constitutes healthy personality, or they emphasize different, but complementary, aspects of healthy functioning. The psychoanalytic and social learning models emphasize functioning that is slightly beyond society's norms, whereas Rogers, Maslow, and the existential theorists describe a higher level of functioning. The models disagree on the role of effort, the desire for self-control, the value of deemphasizing the ego, and the importance of intrinsic motivation.

SUGGESTED READINGS

Frankl, V. E. **The will to meaning.** New York: NAL, 1969. Interesting perspective on growth.

Maslow, A. **Toward a psychology of being.** Princeton, N.J.: Van Nostrand, 1962. Brief, readable, and motivating.

Mischel, W. **Introduction to personality.** New York: Holt, Rinehart and Winston, 1981. Forceful presentation of the social learning approach.

Rogers, C. R. **On becoming a person: A therapist's view of psychotherapy.** Boston: Houghton Mifflin, 1961. A classic that has deeply touched many readers.

Waelder, R. **Basic theory of psychoanalysis.** New York: International Universities Press, 1960. Excellent presentation of the psychoanalytic position.

OPTIMAL FUNCTIONING

14

The Path of Growth

As noted in the previous chapter, psychologists generally agree as to what constitutes healthy functioning. It might be supposed, then, that the path of personal growth would be, if not easy, then at least straightforward. We need merely select one of these models of optimal functioning (or desired characteristics from each) and, with our goal firmly in mind, set out to become that type of person. Unfortunately, knowing what a healthy person is like and becoming that person are very different endeavors.

It appears that there is no simple formula for attaining healthy personality. First, there is no one path for all to follow. And second, there is no one who can tell you which is the right path for you. Each person must follow his or her own path, and the way is often treacherous. Moreover, the stakes are high—no less than the quality of our lives.

To a large extent, we have become a culture of fulfillment seekers.

This chapter examines the problems and pitfalls of seeking personal growth. What we shall find is that ironically, theories of healthy personality sometimes interfere with actual growth. By examining how these theories have been misinterpreted, we can hopefully avoid these pitfalls and enhance the practical effectiveness of these models. In addition, we shall try to reconcile competing points of view and suggest guidelines for finding your own path of growth.

THE MISGUIDED PURSUIT OF SELF-FULFILLMENT

It is not difficult to understand the wide appeal of [self-fulfillment] at a time when hope is an anachronism, when ethical and religious skepticism is dominant, when disillusionment with social and political institutions is rampant, and when human relationships and personal identity are in deep crisis. (Geller, 1982, p. 57)

THE PURPOSE OF LIFE

Daniel Yankelovich conducts national surveys, and according to him, we are in the midst of a cultural revolution that is transforming our shared meanings on the nature and purpose of human life. The 1950s stressed values of self-denial, hard work, and duty to others. During the 1970s and 1980s these values were largely replaced by an ethic of self-fulfillment and duty to self, a movement inspired by humanistic psychologists such as Carl Rogers and Abraham Maslow.

In the past, self-improvement meant denying one's immediate preferences so as to attain external goals: material goods, family life, and symbols of respectability. Now the object of these efforts has become the self. Many believe that the highest value in anyone's life is personal growth, which is attained by satisfying personal needs.

According to Yankelovich (1981), we are

beginning to realize that as a guide to conduct, self-fulfillment is a failure.

A GENERATION OF SEEKERS

Those who follow the self-fulfillment ethic stand in the mainstream of American values, comprising some 80 percent of our adult population. We are searching, experimenting with our lives and relationships, trying to find out what is really important. Yankelovich comments that "something about our times . . . stimulates Americans to take big risks in pursuit of new conceptions of the good life" (1981, p. 39).

Consistent with Maslow's analysis, fulfillment seeking characterizes middle-class, affluent societies, where the lower needs have largely been met. In addition to traditional material demands, these seekers are looking for meaning and self-expression; they seek intangibles such as creativity, autonomy, stimulation, and joy. For them,

> the meaning of life is not exhausted by earning a living, raising a family, doing one's duty, acting out the roles society assigns, using and being used by others. These chores have their place, but dwelling on them blinds us to the truth that life, in all of its forms, is to be lived and experienced and enjoyed and cherished—for its own sake. Life is self-expression. It is creativity. It is adventure. (Yankelovich, 1981, p. 39)

How would Maslow view these seekers? Are they the self-actualizers he sought to produce? Certainly, Maslow could have little quarrel with the goals being sought—after all, he was largely responsible for popularizing them in our society. These goals are among the reported motives of Maslow's identified self-actualizing individuals. Still, Yankelovich describes us as a culture of "seekers," suggesting that we have yet to find what we are looking for. Maslow's self-actualizers dedicated themselves to these values, but they were not "seekers."

In fact, Yankelovich is describing people who are relatively gratified in the lower needs but who have not yet graduated to the self-actualizing level. Their seeking is motivated by boredom, meaninglessness, loneliness, and despair. These are people who vaguely perceive that they require satisfactions at the actualizing level but who have yet to devote their lives to those values.

STRATEGIES OF A FULFILLMENT SEEKER

For Yankelovich, the strategy of those who seek fulfillment negates any chance of the fulfillment they seek. In particular, he faults the assumption that self-fulfillment is an inner journey to discover and gratify personal needs.

The plight of fulfillment seekers is illustrated by a couple that Yankelovich interviewed:

> Mark and Abby are in their early 30s; Mark works as a lawyer in a public interest firm and Abby as a magazine editor for a large chemical corporation.
>
> Mark and Abby have been married for six years. They delayed having children until each could establish a career. Abby says that she would like to have one child, but at this stage in her career, she is reluctant to leave work for an extended period of time. In addition, marital tensions have also made her reluctant to become pregnant.
>
> Without ever agreeing to an "open marriage," and in fact arguing with Mark that it would be too risky, she has been silently "going along" with a way of life that makes extramarital affairs all too easy. She and Mark both work late several nights a week, and it is understood that no questions will be asked. She believes that Mark is currently sleeping with one of his clients.
>
> Abby admits that she, too, experimented with brief affairs, but she did not pursue them. While seeing nothing morally wrong with affairs, she nonetheless found herself flooded with guilt.

Abby confides that she often finds herself in a conflicted mood, even though she knows she has more freedom to shape her life than her mother had. Abby likes being married, even though her needs for sexual fulfillment and intimacy are not being fully met by her husband. Eventually she wants a child "to fulfill my maternal needs." She also wants to travel more, spend more time with friends, read more, listen to music, and relax and enjoy life more than she has been, "while I still have the vigor to appreciate those other values. . . ."

Abby cherishes her job but worries that, because she is a woman, the corporation may not give her the full editorship when the current editor retires in several years.

At least once a week Abby has "anxiety attacks" in which her optimism is drained and she feels dry-mouthed and empty. A recurring fantasy of growing fat and slovenly frightens her. Abby explains these attacks saying, "I guess it is guilt. My mother always warned me not to be too piggy and self-centered. Sometimes I feel I really am too preoccupied with my own needs and wishes." Later, she adds, "I know you can't have everything. But I'm not sure what to give up and what to hang on to. Sometimes I feel like all the doors in the world are open to me, and yet at other times, I feel as if they are all closing."

Abby implies that while she has many of the things she desires in life, she nonetheless feels up in the air about her life as a whole. Her decisions have a tentative character. Her commitments are qualified. She senses that she could withdraw from any one of them tomorrow. She inquires, bitingly, "What kind of a marriage is it if every day two people ask themselves, 'Should we stay married? Should we each go our own way?'"

Abby's talk is replete with the language of needs: she keeps referring to the requirement that they all be filled as if they were sections of an ice-cube tray and she is under an obligation to fill each section to the brim. For Abby, self-fulfillment means having a career

and marriage and children and sexual freedom and autonomy and being liberal and having money and choosing nonconformity and insisting on social justice and enjoying city life and country living and simplicity and graciousness, and on and on. (Adapted from Yankelovich, 1981, pp. 44–50)

Yankelovich sees Abby as trapped. First, she is confronted by an abundance of choices without knowing how to make the "right" ones. Yet she believes that her choices must be correct in order to consider her life worthwhile. She values her personal freedom so much that each new choice, and the commitment it entails, creates a threat to her other possibilities. Thus each commitment becomes tentative, always open for re-evaluation, making her life unsettled.

Second, her definition of self-fulfillment depends on a precarious network of circumstances that are largely out of her control. For example, it assumes continued economic abundance, career opportunities, flexible work arrangements, low burdens of responsibility, and cooperative social relationships. Any disruption in these factors will drastically upset her plans.

Third, Abby has adopted the language of "needs" for viewing the fulfillment of her life. She sees herself as an assemblage of needs. For Abby, each and every emotional craving is sacred and must be fulfilled.

Yankelovich views Abby as an intelligent, attractive, well-educated woman with a career she values, married to someone she loves. Yet she is unhappy. Abby has set herself up for continual frustration. She believes she has a sacred duty to herself: She must "become all that she can be." She thinks of herself as a collection of needs and pictures her personal growth as resulting from their systematic gratification. What she has defined to herself as "needs," however, are a nearly infinite stream of transitory and conflicting desires.

Albert Ellis, the founder of rational-emotive therapy (see Chapter 6), argued that one of the main ways in which we make ourselves miserable is by redefining our desires as needs. This simple relabeling changes everything. When a desire is not satisfied, we carry on and function much as before. But if a *need* goes ungratified, our life is disrupted. Thinking of something as a "need" means that we must have it to be happy. If something we *need* is not provided, we naturally become upset. Clearly, many of the things Abby has defined as needs are really desires. Moreover, many of these desires either cannot be fulfilled, conflict with one another, or clash with the desires of those around her.

Certainly, most of us can sympathize with Abby's situation. In the best American tradition, she has set her sights high. And what's so bad about wanting it all? On the other hand, by becoming frustrated and upset when one of her desires is not met, Abby demonstrates that she has gone beyond mere "wanting." In fact, she is selfishly and irrationally demanding that she get whatever she wants. By wanting and demanding it all, she has put herself in a no-win situation. She must face the cold reality that desires often conflict, and so the dream of having it all is never a realistic alternative.

Can you identify with Abby? How would you explain her anxiety attacks? What would Rogers say about Abby's guilt over sexual affairs that she finds morally acceptable?

Do you disagree with Yankelovich's analysis? Would you maintain that you *can* have it all?

What fascinates me is that for every valuable piece of advice, it almost seems as if the opposite advice is just as good. In Abby's case, she is merely following the cultural dictum to "go for it." Clearly, this advice is adaptive, for example, in overcoming a restrictive fear of failure. Nevertheless, in Abby's case, it is causing considerable distress. For her, it may be more adaptive to decide what is really important to her and then forget about the rest. How are we to know when "going for it" is adaptive and when it merely constitutes a form of greed? If Abby asked you for advice, what would you tell her?

FOCUS
THE TYRANNY OF DUTY TO SELF

Consider the following anecdote:

A psychotherapy patient in her mid-20s complained to her therapist that she was nervous and fretful because life had grown so hectic: too many big weekends, too many parties, too many late hours, too much talk, too much wine, too much lovemaking, and too many partners.

"Why don't you stop?" the therapist asked mildly. The patient stared blankly, and then her face lit up. "You mean I really don't have to do what I want to do?" (Adapted from Yankelovich, 1981, p. 80)

From the viewpoint of Rogers's theory, we can see that the difference between natural and learned values can occur even when the learned values are dictated by the self. Here is a patient who decided what she liked to do, concluded that if some were good, more would be better, and set off in the pursuit of hedonistic indulgence. Her belief that this was what she ought to like obscured her actual bodily awareness that these activities had become aversive through satiation.

SELF-FULFILLMENT AND THE WELFARE OF OTHERS

Wallach and Wallach (1983, 1984) claim there is a fundamental mistake in the human potential movement, and curiously, it is inherited from Freud. Psychoanalysis contends that the welfare of society dictates restraining the individual. But it assumes that for the individual, what would be best is the direct and total gratification of all instinctual needs. Humanistic psychologists considered Freud's emphasis on restraint too pessimistic. They believed that under positive environmental conditions, people would be motivated to seek others' welfare as well as their own, and thus the full expression or self-actualization of the individual could be wholeheartedly endorsed.

The Wallachs argue, however, that looking toward one's own fulfillment cannot be relied on as the best way of serving others' welfare. For them, it is an absurd and romantic illusion to believe there is no conflict among people's maximum self-developments. Suppose a woman is both a mother and an artist, and she finds child care actualizing, but art even more actualizing. The Wallachs contend that according to the way Maslow and Rogers are popularly interpreted, she should put her work first, even if that compromises her children's welfare.

As another example, consider a married couple in which one partner becomes chronically ill, requiring extensive care from the other. The one who is ill can contribute little to the spouse's actualization. The Wallachs argue it is hardly clear that the marriage vows should therefore be abandoned. Thus they agree with Freud that for the general good, restrictions on immediate gratification are essential.

PERSONAL GROWTH AND NEED GRATIFICATION

The Wallachs maintain that humanistic psychologists erred in retaining Freud's assumption that personal fulfillment is best served by complete need gratification. There is no reason to

assume that all external constraints reduce actualization, as is implicit in the humanistic emphasis on unbridled self-expression. Existentialists, for example, have long argued that growth often comes through facing adversity. We must recognize that some constraints further "our own most deeply held values — so that subjecting ourselves to them is something we ourselves want to do" (Wallach & Wallach, 1984, p. 5). For example, real commitment to another means standing by that commitment even when our immediate desires tell us not to. Caring about justice means following the course of fairness, even when it works against our personal interests.

PROBLEMS WITH TRUSTING ORGANISMIC EXPERIENCE

Geller (1982) contends that because self-deception is so prevalent, we cannot simply trust the organism. How are we to know, with certainty, whether a feeling, impulse, or perception is arising from true organismic promptings or from self-deceptive biases? For those with minimal powers of critical self-reflection, Rogers's advice to trust the organism may reinforce dogmatism, prejudice, and selfishness.

In reality, there are no guarantees or certitudes on the path of growth. In addition to organismic trust, we must use all of our rational abilities to guard against bias and distortion. Thus the struggle forward in the face of self-deception is always open to reevaluation. In other words, self-deception presents a formidable challenge; it complicates the game of life, but perhaps it also makes the game more interesting.

THE DEHUMANIZING EFFECTS OF PURSUING FULFILLMENT

Geller observes that in modern nations, relationships have become instrumental, adversarial, competitive, and casual. Their cohesion and durability are precarious, and their vitality and meaning diminished. Intimate tribal communities have been replaced by an aggregate of isolated individuals. "Despite no paucity of relationships in their lives, they still remain separate, isolated, and alone. They tend to be insecure, anxious, fearful, and distrustful. Their lives fall under the obsessive domination of self-interest and self-concern" (Geller, 1982, p. 70).

Modern society encourages a pragmatic approach to life. When this is combined with the ethic of self-fulfillment, the result is an instrumental approach to relationships. We become concerned about what we will get out of a relationship, with many seeing it as inevitable that relationships will be based on mutual use. Other ways of relating are dismissed as naive or utopian. In this way, a limited cultural phenomenon has been mistaken for a reality of human nature.

Geller maintains that if self-actualization is viewed as the consciously sought goal of life, others will be evaluated on whether or not they further one's personal actualization. Therefore, the only practical way to approach life is, at each choice point, to ask ourselves, "Which alternative will advance my personal development the most?" For many, this appears to be the straightforward way of applying the ideal of self-actualization to everyday life. Within this framework, other people become instrumentalities, that is, means to the higher goal of personal fulfillment. And in this way, popular interpretations of "self-actualization" may have contributed to dehumanization. For Geller, it is a bitter irony that two men as deeply concerned about the human condition as Rogers and Maslow would develop systems that have inadvertently reinforced the problems their theories were designed, in part, to alleviate.

THE FAILURE OF NARROW SELF-INTEREST

Unfortunately, theorists such as Maslow and Rogers have used a language that allows, and sometimes encourages, a misinterpretation of their ideas. In some places, however, Maslow is quite explicit: although self-actualization is highly desirable, it cannot be directly pursued as a goal in itself.

> People who seek self-actualization directly, selfishly, personally, dichotomized away from mission in life, i.e., as a form of private and subjective salvation, don't, in fact, achieve it. (Maslow, 1969, pp. 128–129)

To act for the purpose, and in anticipation, of the growth and happiness that your actions will bring may seem reasonable. Many psychologists, however, Maslow included, consider it unworkable as a pathway to personal growth.

Thus, some forms of personal growth cannot be forced, speeded up, or enhanced by trying harder. These forms of growth must be allowed to happen spontaneously. For example, creativity is inhibited by pressure and fear. Other kinds of self-improvement, however, such as the development of athletic talent through hours of practice, can obviously be aided by a goal-oriented strategy of self-discipline.

Although wanting happiness and not wanting unhappiness are logically the same, they may differ psychologically.

Since that which fosters optimal actualization for one often interferes with the actualization of another, society must enforce restraints on individual behavior. But which should come first, one's own personal welfare or that of others? Do we encourage an ethic of self-denial, sacrificing the individual for the good of others? Or do we encourage personal self-interest on the premise that society is a collection of individuals and they should be allowed to compete when their respective self-interests conflict?

The only approach to this dilemma that seems defensible to me is giving up the notion that one can go through life evaluating situations by "what is in it for me." On the other hand, self-sacrifice appears equally misguided. How can a balance between these positions be struck?

One possible solution is the age-old ethic of treating other people's actualization on a par with one's own. Thus, in the example of the mother who believed that her actualization was fostered more by her work in art than by caring for her children, she might balance the enhancement to her own life that would result from spending more time with her work against the detriment to her children's actualization that might come from spending less time with their mother. The challenge here is arriving at a compromise that doesn't distort the negative effect on her children in order to justify her personal preference. Similarly, it must not commit her to a life of self-sacrifice because of the rigid belief that a mother's duty is only to her children.

Either placing the self first or the interests of others first inevitably leads to problems. Those who reluctantly sacrifice out of a sense of imposed duty will provide a love that is counterfeit. Those who justify choosing their own interests, regardless of the circumstances, find that they have no real linkage to others; their relationships are necessarily superficial.

Are you one of the "seekers" that Yankelovich describes? Since none of us probably wants to view ourselves as "self-centered" or "self-indulgent," how can we know whether we have fallen into the "self-actualization trap"?

If the rational, straightforward, goal-oriented pursuit of actualization often does *not* work, then what does?

To summarize, we have found relative agreement as to our journey's destination (optimal functioning), but it appears that the main road is blocked. Now we must seek a path through the bushes. But which one? And how are we to know if our path is a good one? The remainder of this chapter presents guidelines that can help you find your own path and discover yourself along the way.

OBSERVE YOUR BEHAVIOR

Often we do not know ourselves as well as we think we do. Our behavior is highly complex, and our ability to see the truth is limited by what we want to believe. Because of our proclivity for self-deception, we cannot always trust our informal observations of behavior. If the pervasiveness of self-deception is not immediately apparent to you, then consider watching a game of baseball. It is common in baseball for thousands of fans to watch the same play and disagree violently on its outcome, with individuals' perceptions highly predictable from a knowledge of one simple factor — which team they are "for." Presumably, the same sort of bias operates in our everyday self-perceptions.

One of the best ways of countering self-deception is to observe concrete, specifiable pieces of our behavior. As Chapter 7 explained in detail, the behaviorist methodology for counting behaviors in situations gives us a way of arriving at clear, unbiased estimates of virtually any behavior we may wish to change. It seems undeniable that our efforts at effecting personal growth by increasing desirable behaviors depend on these self-observation skills. Thus, rather than relying on informal and possibly biased self-perceptions, take the time to get accurate data.

UNDERSTAND YOUR MOTIVES
USING THE HIERARCHY OF NEEDS

You can use Maslow's hierarchy of needs to explore the motivations behind your everyday activities. Of the five types of needs — physiological, safety, belonging, esteem, and self-actualizing — how much of your day is spent in pursuit of each? In making this assessment, however, it is important to adopt an attitude of curiosity rather than one of ambition. Find out something interesting about yourself; don't try to "prove" that you are at one need level or another.

One way of beginning this exploration is simply to list the various activities you engage in during a given day. Record your main activity for every half-hour segment throughout the day, starting from the time you get up in the morning.

For each activity, list your reasons for engaging in it, in order of importance. Note that life activities tend to be complex, and so many will require more than one reason. For simplicity, keep your reasons to four or fewer. To help identify reasons for behavior, ask yourself, "What were the pressures influencing me to do this activity?" "What payoffs did I expect to get from it?" "Would I still have engaged in the activity if this payoff were no longer provided?" "How did I experience the activity — was it enjoyable or not?" "How did I feel right after it was over?"

Assign each reason a percentage figure based on how important you feel it was for producing the behavior. The percentages for a given activity should add up to 100 percent. The list of activities and reasons should be made during the day of observation, preferably right after each activity is completed, to be sure the experience is fresh in your mind.

The next step is applying Maslow's hierarchy to the reasons. Remember that for Maslow, the motivation behind an activity is more important than is the activity itself. For each reason, identify the major corresponding need.

It is best to record your activities, reasons, needs, and percentages in a standard form such as that shown below. To illustrate, suppose your activity during one time period consisted of being in class. Perhaps the reasons for going to class, in order of importance to you, were "Avoiding a bad grade because my parents would be disappointed," "Being with friends," "Seeking a good grade to enhance my chances for success," and "Expected interest in the lecture material." Suppose also that the percentages for these reasons are 40 percent, 30 percent, 20 percent, and 10 percent, respectively.

Parental disappointment may relate to several of the needs, depending on its specific form. If the thought of this disappointment creates a feeling of fear or anxiety and going to class controls this fear, then class attendance is being motivated at the level of safety-security. If the disappointment is from not wanting your parents to decrease their feelings of love or affection toward you, then the motivation is at the level of belonging-love. If it relates to not wanting your parents to think less of you, then the motivation is at the esteem level. You will have to decide which aspect of this reason was strongest in this particular instance. As for the other reasons, being with friends relates to the need for belonging. Enhancing success indicates esteem needs. And interest in the material represents self-actualizing needs. Overall, these reasons might translate into something like the following: physiological needs 0 percent, safety-security needs 0 percent, belonging 30 percent, esteem 60 percent, and self-actualizing 10 percent. This example is shown in the chart below.

After completing this chart for an entire day, you would have a percentage index of the importance of each need for each activity. You may want to compare your morning, afternoon, and evening activities and see whether they satisfy different needs. The chances are that they will. You may also want to average the need percentages over the whole day and get some idea of your average position on the hierarchy of needs. A self-observation such as this should give you valuable clues to how you might increase the percentage of activities you engage in at the self-actualizing level, by either choosing different activities or approaching the "same" activities with a different frame of mind.

SELF-ACTUALIZATION AND THE COLLEGE STUDENT

It is rare to find a college student whose time is devoted largely to self-actualizing needs. Recall that Maslow believed most self-actualizers to be over sixty! It seems that college years, in particular, foster the experience of doing something (attending classes and studying) as a means to something else (getting a good job). Perhaps this is inevitable, given the amount of material that must be covered in four short years. Nevertheless, the most authentic way to approach college involves finding a way to experience it positively; dedicate yourself to learning something that is meaningful to you.

DEALING WITH THE NEED FOR ESTEEM

If you find that much of your day is spent maintaining esteem, which is typical of most

TIME	ACTIVITY	REASONS	%	NEEDS
9–9:30	In class	1. Avoid bad grade, disappointed parents.	40	Esteem
		2. Be with friends.	30	Belonging
		3. Enhance chances for success.	20	Esteem
		4. Interest in topic.	10	Self-actualizing

people in our culture, you may want to ask yourself, "What would I have to do to achieve a stable and lasting sense of self-esteem?" If there is some goal or accomplishment that you believe you must meet in order to solidify your esteem, ask yourself if this goal is realistic. If it is, then don't hold back or make excuses. Find a way to attain your goal. Then, after this goal is reached, if you *still* feel your self-esteem is shaky, you may start suspecting that your need for esteem is not entirely rational.

If you feel that no matter what you accomplish today, you will still feel required to spend most of tomorrow buttressing a faulty and precarious self-esteem, then an entirely different strategy is in order. To go beyond the esteem level, you may need to inquire why you are withholding esteem from yourself, which leads us to the next section.

ACCEPT THE IMPERFECT BEING THAT YOU ARE

THE STRATEGY OF WITHHOLDING SELF-ACCEPTANCE

Each of us has the power to give or withhold self-acceptance. If you have feelings of insecurity, unworthiness, and low self-esteem, find out what is preventing you from accepting yourself. Usually the reason will revolve around a significant other, often a parent, whose attitude of nonacceptance you have unwittingly internalized. But why would a well-intentioned parent withhold acceptance? Almost always, it is *not* because the child's behavior was inferior or inadequate. Parents often believe that the best way to spur their child on to greater heights is by setting high standards and applying the motivating power of their disapproval. In fact, this is not a good strategy, for it undermines self-esteem, and the child is likely to give up in despair.

Although this is a poor strategy for changing the behavior of someone you care about, it is even worse to internalize this strategy and apply it to yourself. Nevertheless, individuals often use

In contrast to what research indicates, parents often believe that the best way to spur their child on to greater heights is through setting high standards and applying the motivating power of their disapproval.

it to implement self-improvement. Bandura, for example, in his social learning analysis, notes that self-dissatisfaction is often used for regulating behavior. If behavior does not meet expectations, we feel dissatisfied and become motivated to change the behavior or to try harder in order to reduce our dissatisfaction. This can be an appropriate and adaptive self-regulatory function. In practice, however, it is often coupled with the adoption of perfectionistic goals. The result is an aversive system of self-improvement that undermines esteem.

Psychologists have found that the threat of self-dissatisfaction is effective only with small, easily reached goals, so that the overwhelming experience is one of satisfaction and success (Watson & Tharp, 1985). In other words, one's ultimate goal may be quite lofty, if it is realistically attainable, but the immediate goals should always be small and easily achieved.

Once we have attained an attitude of self-acceptance, we no longer need to fear whatever thoughts or feelings we are experiencing. This allows us to welcome and become excited about our unfolding experience; it gives us the freedom to learn more about who we really are. Once we can accept ourselves, instances of pettiness, greed, revenge, and selfishness, which we all experience, can be recognized, acknowledged, and transcended. Psychologists are in virtual agreement that we do not become better by denying our weak points. Neither must we punish ourselves for them. Often the best strategy is simply to acknowledge their presence without making excuses. In this way, undesirable behaviors will often decrease without our becoming self-punitive and undermining self-esteem.

THE CASE OF THE ILLEGITIMATE DAUGHTER

The importance of self-acceptance is illustrated in a case history recounted by the existentialist Rollo May. Sally, twenty-eight, had entered therapy because of anxiety spells in closed places, severe self-doubts, and uncontrollable rage. An illegitimate child, Sally was raised in a psychologically devastating home environment. In moments of anger, her mother often brought up Sally's illegitimacy and described how she had tried to abort her. Sally could remember her mother shouting at her, "If you hadn't been born, we wouldn't have to go through this!" During family quarrels, relatives had shouted at her, "Why didn't you kill yourself?" and "You should have been choked the day you were born!"

After several months of therapy she had the following dream: "I was in a crowd of people. They had no faces; they were like shadows. It seemed like a wilderness of people. Then I saw there was someone in the crowd who had compassion for me" (May, 1977, p. 66). Soon afterwards, she reported the following experience:

I remember walking that day under the elevated tracks in a slum area, feeling the thought, "I am an illegitimate child." I recall the sweat pouring forth in my anguish in trying to accept that fact. Then I understood what it must feel like to accept, "I am a Negro in the midst of privileged whites" . . . Later on that night I woke up and it came to me this way, "I accept the fact that I am an illegitimate child." But "I am not a child anymore." So it is, "I am illegitimate." That is not so either: "I was born illegitimate." Then what is left? What is left is this, "*I Am*." This *act* of contact and acceptance with "I am," once gotten hold of, gave me (what I think was for me the first time) the experience "Since I am, I have the right to be."

What is this experience like? It is a primary feeling — it feels like receiving the deed to my house. It is the experience of my own aliveness not caring whether it turns out to be an ion or just a wave. It is like when a very young child I once reached the core of a peach and cracked the pit, not knowing what I would find and then feeling the wonder of finding the inner seed. . . . It is like a sailing boat in the harbor being given an anchor so that, being made out of earthly things, it can by means of its anchor get in touch again with the earth, the ground from which its wood grew; it can lift its anchor to sail but . . . at times it can cast its anchor to weather the storm or rest a little. (May, 1977, p. 66)

May believes that personality changes not grounded in this "I-am" experience are often incomplete. Without it, new coping skills may be experienced only as a compensation, as a proof that one is worthy, despite the certainty on a deeper level that lacking the "I-am" experience, one really is not worthy. As May (1977, p. 69) observed, "If your self-esteem must rest in the long run on social validation, you have, not self-esteem, but a more sophisticated form of social conformity."

May argues that this basic experience of being, of I-am, is quite different from the experience of "I" implied in the phrase "I did it." The emphasis is not on the identification with an abstract self-image, that is, an attachment to a particular view of oneself. Instead, the emphasis is on the "am."

Sally came to the following realization: "Since I am, I have the right to be." What do you think about this statement? Does this describe how you feel about yourself? If it doesn't, modify the statement in some way so that it conveys your current feelings.

DEVELOP PERSONAL COMPETENCIES

Self-actualization implies finding out which activities you have a special interest in, talent for, or feeling for, and then systematically developing your abilities in those areas. This is a large part of what it means to "find yourself." Thus, rather than spending your life always dabbling, switching from one activity to another, self-actualization means making a choice and dedicating yourself to excellence in some activity. Note, however, this is not the same as trying to be the "best," for in actualization, the relevant comparison is not against others but with one's own potentials.

Social learning theory creates a context for helping people to develop their personal competencies. As detailed in Chapters 6 and 7, this context employs contingencies of reinforcement to build willpower, self-discipline, and the ability to delay gratification. In this way, the extended chains of behavior required for refining a complex skill can be produced and maintained. Remember that these skills not only provide eventual reinforcement from the social environment, but the experience of mastery, of operating with poise, awareness, and bodymind coordination, is itself intrinsically reinforcing.

CREATE A LESS RIGID SELF-IMAGE

A healthy self-concept is not the same as pride. A healthy self-concept implies self-acceptance, feelings of being worthy of others' love and respect, and feeling good about yourself. It does *not* mean believing that one is better than others.

Pride is dangerous for a number of reasons. First, it implies a conditional approval, an acceptance based on performance, so that a security based on pride is always tenuous, always in need of supporting evidence. Second, pride implies a strong identification with and attachment to the traits of which we are proud. This attachment gives us a vested interest in seeing ourselves a certain way. For example, if we take pride in our intelligence, being "wrong" becomes threatening. We may distort or deny our errors, perhaps blaming them on someone else, so that we don't have to deal with the dissonance between our self-beliefs and actual behavior. In addition, we may become irritated with anyone who "tactlessly" fails to go along with our pretense of being so intelligent.

If we could nondefensively see the error in our behavior, we would have a good chance of being able to correct it and avoid that error in the future. If that error is defended against, however, chances are we will continue making it over and over again. In this way, pride, and its corresponding rigid self-concept, limits optimal functioning. It is more adaptive to "soften" the self-concept, thinking, for example, "I am usually intelligent, but every once in a while I do things that are really stupid."

Think of three statements describing the things you are most proud of. These areas of life probably give you a great deal of satisfaction. Because of this, they may also be areas in which your self-concept is most rigid. Thus they are areas in which further growth will be

FOCUS
THE SPLITTING OF IDENTITY AND EXPERIENCE

Self-awareness — the experience of oneself as a center of intention, a center around which all else revolves — seems to many the most certain of perceptions. This self or ego is what we identify with, and the formation of this self is the shining achievement of human cognition. Many psychologists, however, have argued that this self is not as it appears; despite the certainty of its perception, it exists for us, essentially, as a mystery. In many ways, we are a mystery to ourselves. Hence the age-old fascination with questions such as "Who am I?" "Where am I going?"

One line of thought, reverberating through many theoretical camps, is that because of our special cognitive powers, we have conceptualized ourselves. We have constructed the abstraction of an experiencing agent and then identified with that agent. From a continuous flow of experience, we have split off a part and identified with it. The result is an awareness of our selves as separate from the rest of experience, separate from other people, and separate from nature.

Alan Watts (1951) suggested that our cognitive ability to picture the future creates this split between experience and ego identity. Given this ability and our intense dislike of pain, we try to gain some leverage over events by controlling our behavior to avoid pain. At the same time, we assume that the trying implies a "trier," and this perception is reinforced by our more or less continuous memory of past attempts at self-control. The presumed entity that tries then becomes our ego identity. In this way we identify with the trier rather than with all of our experiences.

If you look at it carefully, you will see that consciousness — the thing you call "I" — is really a stream of experiences, of sensations, thoughts, and feelings in constant motion. But because these experiences include memories, we have the impression that "I" is something solid and still. (Watts, 1951, pp. 42–43)

Many psychologists contend that forming this self and developing a strong sense of identity are necessary to personal growth, *up to a point*. After that point, however, further growth may require deemphasizing the self, withdrawing our attachment to a fixed sense of identity, reexperiencing our connectedness to whatever we define as "not me," and expanding our self-perception to include a larger part of the unfolding mystery.

difficult. Self-acceptance combined with a less rigid self-concept provides a level of satisfaction that is equivalent to that of pride, without the drawbacks. Try restating each of your three statements in a way that is less rigid. Could you accept yourself fully if these less rigid formulations were true?

OPEN YOURSELF TO PEAK EXPERIENCES

One way of enhancing our receptiveness to peak experiences is to examine something that we have seen hundreds of times before, something that we take for granted as "nothing spe-

At zoos, you are allowed to "look" in ways that are not accepted in most other social environments.

cial," such as a pencil or a piece of fruit. Spend some time looking at this thing again, but this time suspend your deadening beliefs. Stop telling yourself that you already know everything you need to know about it. Look at it as if it were a sacred object you are seeing for the first time. Look at it as if this were your last chance to see it again.

In discussing peak experiences, Maslow suggests that our attitude in looking is more important than the object observed. This is one reason art museums and zoos hold such fascination for many people. At these places, you are allowed to look in ways that are not acceptable in most other social environments.

Marion Milner (1977) began her study of peak experiences by systematically observing and recording in a journal what she called "each day's best moments" or "the coming and going of delight." What she found was that these moments never came from a willful attempt, from trying to make herself happy or experience something special. Instead they always had the character of "not trying."

> One day I was idly watching some gulls as they soared high overhead. I was not interested, for I recognized them as "just gulls," and vaguely watched first one and then another. Then all at once something seemed

to have opened. My idle boredom with the familiar became a deep-breathing peace and delight, and my whole attention was gripped by the pattern and rhythm of their flight, their slow sailing which had become a quiet dance. (p. 191)

Milner used the metaphor of a tower to contrast her new and old ways of looking at the world:

My ordinary way of looking at things seemed to be from my head, as if it were a tower in which I kept myself shut up, only looking out of the windows to watch what was going on. Now I seemed to be discovering that I could if I liked go down outside, go down and make myself part of what was happening. (pp. 191–192)

Milner commented, however, that this new way of looking was something that most of the time, she "forgot" to do, adding that she was afraid of this new freedom, afraid to leave the security of her tower. The fear of making these gestures of "feeling out" centered on a feeling of losing herself, of being overtaken by something. She suggested that the attachment to our sense of existing as a separate identity creates a pervading sense of alienation and a fear that full contact with reality would threaten our identity, plunging us into a vast unknown.

I saw a gull alight quite close to me, with wings stretched above its back in that fashion peculiar to great winged birds when they settle on the ground. Without thinking, I felt myself into its movement with a panic ecstasy and then turned quickly round upon my fear, for the first time framing the question: "What is this ogre which tries to prevent me from feeling the reality of things?" (p. 196)

Milner found that for her, thoughts and preconceptions about how one is supposed to react made peak experiences impossible.

I had always been vaguely interested in pictures, but worried because so often I could not say what I liked. . . . But one day I stopped in front of a Cézanne still-life — green apples, a white plate, and a cloth. Being tired, restless, and distracted by the stream of bored Sunday afternoon sight-seers drifting through the galleries, I simply sat and looked, too inert to remember whether I ought to like it or not. Slowly then I became aware that something was pulling me out of my vacant stare and the colors were coming alive, gripping my gaze till I was soaking myself in their vitality. Gradually a great delight filled me, dispelling all boredom and doubts about what I ought to like. . . . Yet it had all happened by just sitting still and waiting. . . . If I had not been too tired to think I would have said: "Here is a Cézanne, here is something one ought to like," and I would have stood there trying to like it but becoming less and less sure of what I felt about it. (p. 195)

Milner puzzled:

If just looking could be so satisfying, why was I always striving to have things or to get things done? Certainly I had never suspected that the key to my private reality might lie in so apparently simple a skill as the ability to let the senses roa unfettered by purposes. I began to wonder whether eyes and ears might not have a wisdom of their own. (p. 197)

In agreement with Maslow, Milner concluded that "to want results for myself, to do things with the expectancy of happiness, was generally fatal, it made the stream of delight dry up at the source" (p. 200).

What would you describe as your own peak experiences? What sorts of moods, actions, or environments seem to make these experiences more likely? Do you agree with Milner that consciously trying to produce peak experiences does not work?

LIVE IN THE MOMENT

SELF-CONTROL AND THE MANIPULATION OF ATTENTION

D. T. Suzuki compared humans and machines on how they do their work:

> The Chinese love life as it is lived, and do not wish to turn it into a means of accomplishing something else. They like work for its own sake. The machine, on the other hand, hurries on to finish the work and reach the objective for which it is made. The work or labor in itself has no value except as means. (Suzuki, 1910)

Gestalt therapist Fritz Perls observed that modern people have unwittingly patterned themselves after the machine. In an attempt to defuse the threat of being replaced by machines, we have emulated their approach to work. Thus it has become natural for us to evaluate work only in terms of cost, efficiency, and the final product. Perls claims that we have lost sight of the experience of the work itself. Just as the machine does not calculate a job's unpleasantness; so too, people have become accustomed to overlooking the experience of an activity and instead directing their attention solely to anticipating the final product and its eventual reward. This attitude prevents living in the moment.

Through anticipating future rewards, we can maintain high productivity under aversive conditions. In other words, to compete with machines, we have become more like them, which means dulling our awareness of the experience of work. For Perls, this amounts to a trick that we have been taught to play on ourselves for the purpose of goal attainment. And indeed, this can be a useful trick, for it allows us to delay gratification and accomplish the complex activities that modern civilization requires.

On the other hand, to know whether the end reward is worth the effort, we must stay in contact with the experience of the work. Otherwise, we can be shaped so that more and more of our lives is controlled by fewer and fewer reinforcing outcomes. For example, the behaviorist B. F. Skinner has been highly successful at shaping pigeons' behavior from a ratio of one peck for one piece of grain to ratios of one thousand pecks for a single piece of grain. From the viewpoint of management, this constitutes a tremendous increase in efficiency.

What does this mean, however, for the individual? What does it mean when the individual is the manager of his or her own behavior? Would such an increase in efficiency constitute a desirable increase in self-control or a gross error in the calculation of actual rewards experienced? In order to decide, we must stay in clear, conscious contact with both the experience of the work and the experience of the eventual reward. Any blocking or distortion of either experience leads to irrational decisions. A common problem in many marriages, for example, is that one spouse, in order to provide financial security for the family, becomes a "workaholic." This person spends less and less time at home, "temporarily," until certain financial goals are attained. The problem is that it usually requires years to achieve such goals, and family relationships may be so badly damaged through neglect that the marriage dissolves before financial security is attained.

CONTROLLING REALITY IN THE MOMENT

The following Zen parable depicts the experience of living in the moment:

> A man was fleeing, pursued by a tiger. He came to the edge of a precipice, the tiger right behind. In desperation he climbed over the edge down a long vine. Above him the tiger roared. Below him lay a thousand-foot drop into raging rapids. Further, two mice, one white and one black, had begun gnawing through the vine. Suddenly, the man noticed a luscious strawberry growing just within reach. Holding onto the vine with one hand, with the

other he plucked the strawberry. How delicious it tasted! (Reps, 1958, pp. 22–23)

This story reveals how powerfully we select and control what we will call "reality." Who would blame this man for spending his last moment in terror, anticipating his imminent plunge to the rapids below? Who would blame him for lamenting a fate that would bring on such a cursed predicament? In the moment, however, he chooses what to focus his attention on, he chooses his reality. As Shapiro (1978) pointed out, among a multitude of competing stimuli, he attends to the strawberry, decides to pick it, and even evaluates its taste. Instead of bemoaning his poor luck, he finds a way to take advantage of his last moment and live it to the fullest.

IN THE MOMENT VERSUS HERE AND NOW

Living in the moment is usually interpreted as giving attention to the "here and now." This popular phrase, however, is somewhat misleading. Optimal functioning implies using our awareness to best advantage. In our culture, people generally run into problems because they cannot forget past failures or they worry about future ones. This sort of thinking is usually unproductive. It is aversive in itself, and it leads to no benefits. Moreover, it serves to avoid dealing with events in the present.

Obviously, however, there are times when living effectively in the moment requires rethinking past events or planning for the future. For example, we can sometimes learn from past mistakes and use this information to change current behavior. Thus optimal functioning involves living in the moment, awakening consciousness from the dulling reveries of habit, self-trickery, and preconception.

A Gestalt technique to coax people into a more immediate state of awareness is to begin each sentence with the phrase "Now I am aware that. . . ." Try having a conversation with someone under the mutual stipulation that each sentence begin with this phrase.

TRANSCEND LIMITING DICHOTOMIES

The noted Swiss psychiatrist Carl Jung saw consciousness coming about through the splitting of a unified but unconscious whole into separate, dichotomous meanings. Initially, this might take the form of an infant's becoming aware of the difference between hunger and fullness, warm and cold, light and dark. As the number of discriminations increases, so does the degree of consciousness. Similarly, in order to become aware of "right," we must separate it from its opposite, "left." These separate, dichotomous meanings are closely connected, since each makes sense only in the context of the other. "Right" gives information only if there is a "left." Thus, Jung felt that the process of fragmenting the world into dichotomous meanings is simply another way of describing the growth of consciousness.

Nevertheless, although a given dichotomy makes us aware of one meaning, it may interfere with our awareness of other meanings. Thus, further growth and enhancement of consciousness often require the ability to form new constructs in which the opposite poles of the old construct have somehow been transcended or combined. This is the case in the two important dichotomies discussed below.

LOVE AND NONATTACHMENT

Is it possible to love deeply, with emotional involvement and full commitment, without becoming attached to the love object? It seems natural to want to possess, control, and keep for ourselves that which we love. This is the type of love that Maslow had in mind at the level of belongingness. But Maslow also felt that there is another, nonpossessive, noncontrolling, altruistic love at the self-actualizing level of functioning. Similarly, Asian models of healthy personality emphasize the importance of nonattachment, suggesting that it is possible to love fully without becoming dependent on the love object.

Love that is manifested as an attachment shows the workings of greed. It is as if we calculated, "This gives me pleasure; instead of just enjoying this pleasure in the moment, I will devise controlling strategies to guarantee its continuation in the future." When the object of pleasure is an inanimate object, this strategy makes some sense (as long as the emphasis is still on enjoying the pleasure rather than ensuring its continuation). But when the object is another person, possessiveness becomes inappro-

priate. It turns the other into a means for our ends. It denies the reality that this other is also a center of consciousness with its own priorities, choosing its own path through life. In other words, possessiveness implies a lack of respect for the freedom and intentionality of the other person.

Moreover, possessiveness defeats itself. Inevitably, the partner comes to resent the feeling of being owned. And even if our machinations succeed in making someone dependent on us, that person's love, since it is now coerced, loses part of its value. Individuals who feel insecure may prefer the greater certainty of a coerced but tainted love to the relative uncertainty of a love

Edvard Munch's The Dance of Life *suggests the possessive, devouring nature of many love relationships. (Munch Museum, Oslo.)*

that is freely given. Maslow felt, however, that those with the security to move beyond the lower needs would make a different choice.

The possibility of reconciling deep love with nonattachment is suggested in the following parable:

The Zen Master Hakuin was praised by his neighbors as one living a pure life.

A beautiful girl whose parents owned a food store lived near him. Suddenly, without any warning, her parents discovered she was with child.

This made her parents angry. She would not confess who the man was but, after much harassment, named Hakuin.

In great anger, the parents went to the Master. "Is that so?" was all he would say.

After the child was born it was brought to Hakuin. By this time, he had lost his reputation, which did not trouble him. But he took very good care of the child. He obtained milk from his neighbors and everything else the little one needed. Although Hakuin had no expectations of raising a child at his age, he found great joy in the little one.

A year later the girl-mother could stand it no longer. She told her parents the truth—that the real father of the child was the young man who worked in the fish market.

The mother and father of the girl at once went to Hakuin to ask his forgiveness, to apologize at length, and to get the child back again.

Hakuin was willing. In yielding the child all he said was, "Is that so?" (Adapted from Reps, 1958, p. 7)

SELF-CONTROL AND SPONTANEITY

Experiential models emphasize spontaneity, while behavioral and social learning models value self-control. (Chapter 7 presents a behavioral program for systematically increasing self-control.) Although these appear to be opposite and contradictory virtues, both are essential to complete functioning.

It seems true that many who are highly spontaneous have poor self-control and that many with strong self-control seem overly rigid. Nevertheless, optimal functioning requires that we find a way to move beyond this apparent dichotomy. One solution is to move between abilities for self-control and spontaneity, depending on which is more appropriate to a given situation. For example, learning to play a musical instrument requires the self-control to spend hour after hour in practice that is often repetitive and frustrating. On the other hand, playing an instrument well also requires relaxing one's conscious control to enable a more spontaneous, fluid, and emotional style of play.

Another solution is to combine the benefits of both self-control and spontaneity at the same time. Shapiro (1978) maintains that the bipolarity between self-control and spontaneity is transcended in meditative breathing. To meditate effectively, we must breathe spontaneously with awareness, but without voluntary control. To do this requires the self-control to relinquish control without diminishing consciousness. "The goal is to breathe effortlessly and to maintain total awareness of the process of breathing. In meditation, the individual is no longer breathing: rather, *breathing is*. Further, the individual *knows* that breathing is" (Shapiro, 1978, p. 192).

What do you feel are the pros and cons of possessive and nonpossessive love? Do you agree with the argument that possessive love is a sign of insecurity? Of course, it is easy to be nonpossessive when caring is weak. In what relationship have you come closest to experiencing a strong, nonpossessive love?

Would you say that you are more self-controlled or more spontaneous? Think of one area of life in which you show self-control and one in which you are spontaneous. Can you think of an area in which you would like to be both more self-controlled *and* more spontaneous?

THE PATH OF HEART

Anthropologist and author Carlos Casteñada recounted advice he purportedly received while in apprenticeship to an Indian sorcerer and man of knowledge:

Anything is one of a million paths. . . .
Therefore you must always keep in mind that a path is only a path; if you feel you should not follow it, you must not stay with it under any conditions. To have such clarity you must lead a disciplined life. Only then will you know that any path is only a path, and there is no affront, to oneself or to others, in dropping it if that is what your heart tells you to do. But your decision to keep on the path or to leave it must be free of fear or ambition. I warn you. Look at every path closely and deliberately. Try it as many times as you think necessary. This question is one that only a very old man asks. My benefactor told me about it once when I was young, and my blood was too vigorous for me to understand it. Now I do understand it. I will tell you what it is: Does this path have a heart? All paths are the same: they lead nowhere. They are paths going through the bush, or into the bush. In my own life I could say I have traversed long, long paths, but I am not anywhere. My benefactor's question has meaning now. Does this path have a heart? If it does, the path is good; if it doesn't it is of no use. Both paths lead nowhere; but one has a heart, the other

doesn't. One makes for a joyful journey; as long as you follow it, you are one with it. The other will make you curse your life. One makes you strong; the other weakens you. (Casteñada, 1968, pp. 152–153)

It is fascinating how this slice of practical wisdom summarizes many of the most important themes in contemporary psychology. For example, "a path is only a path" reminds me of a quotation from C. William Tageson, who was describing the difference between an actualized and a nonactualized approach to life. For Tageson, there might be very little outward difference in the behaviors stemming from these two approaches. As he observed, we cannot avoid living by social conventions, but what we can do is clearly see these conventions for what they are. We can

play the game, the social roles, while seeing through their artificiality and the divisions they impose to the reality beyond. All the world is indeed a stage on which is enacted the play of Being. But the play is *not* the thing. To take it too seriously . . . is to court despair. We must enact [it] playfully. (Tageson, 1982, p. 196)

Note that Casteñada's "if you feel you should not follow it, you must not stay with it" is *not* an encouragement to take the easy way out, to quit a path that has become long, difficult, or inconvenient, for the path that Casteñada chose was all of these. The use of "should" implies that a decision to change paths would be based on one's values and principles as well as on immediate feelings. Thus, in the Rogerian sense, it implies a total organismic decision that takes into account one's moral values and social commitments.

Casteñada observed that choosing a path while seeing that it is only a path requires clarity and discipline. In accord with existential theorists, we must have the discipline to see ourselves with minimal distortion and self-deception, knowing that this is often not easy. And in accord with Asian theorists, we must avoid becoming attached to a chosen path.

Casteñada concurs with the existentialists in maintaining that a path of heart must be selected "free of fear." We often cannot trust our immediate feelings when fear is involved. For most of us, fear incites an impulse to flee, hide, deny, or procrastinate. Existential theorists argue that for authentic being, we must face our fears. If this seems unduly Spartan, it can be tempered with the behavioral strategy of approaching feared stimuli in graduated stages, so that the predominant experience is one of success and mastery. When this is done, we usually find that our fear was out of proportion to the actual danger.

In agreement with Maslow and many contemporary critics, Casteñada argues that the path of heart must also be chosen free of ambition. As we have seen, self-actualization cannot be successfully pursued with self-interest foremost in mind.

In a similar vein, Casteñada claims that all paths are the same, since they all lead nowhere. This can be understood at many levels. All paths lead nowhere, since the immediate experience is more important than any ultimate destination. And as noted above, choosing a path with a destination in mind disrupts actualization. At another level, in the existential sense, the destination of all paths is death, the ultimate equalizer. Our choice is to use our cognitive powers to create meaning, to commit ourselves to a meaningful path, not because of where that path will lead, but because this is the way that fulfills our truest nature. In addition, all paths are objectively the same, for no path is better than another. Where they differ, subjectively, is that some are paths to which we can give our heart and others are not.

Finally, you are one with a path of heart. Casteñada's imagery provides a healing vision, allowing us to break through the dualities that the mind rightfully devises for making the world conscious and predictable. As Maslow and many other theorists, both existential and cognitive-behavioral, have found, personal growth transcends the fracture between one's sense of identity and actual experience. On the path of heart, you are one with your experience, one with your life's activities, one with humanity.

SUMMARY

1. Cultural values from the 1950s revolved around self-denial, duty to others, and hard work in the pursuit of material gain and social status. These values have largely been replaced by the ethic of self-fulfillment and duty to self. Many social critics are suggesting that as a guide to conduct, self-fulfillment is a failure.

2. Yankelovich describes us as a culture of fulfillment seekers. But these seekers are not Maslow's self-actualizers. They are individuals who are relatively gratified in the lower needs but have not yet graduated to the self-actualizing level. In effect, these people are "stuck" either at the esteem level or somewhere in the gray area between esteem and actualization. They vaguely perceive that they require satisfactions at the actualizing level, but they have yet to dedicate their lives to these values.

3. Abby used the language of needs to think about the fulfillment of her life. In this belief system, every desire, whim, or emotional craving

becomes a sacred need that must be fulfilled. In large measure, this was the source of her unhappiness.

4. It seems clear that looking toward one's own fulfillment cannot be relied upon as the best way of serving other people's welfare. Moreover, growth often comes about through constraints on immediate need gratification.

5. Because of the prevalence of self-deception, we cannot simply and unthinkingly trust organismic experience.

6. Partly because of the pragmatic pursuit of self-fulfillment, many relationships have become dehumanized or instrumental: Each person approaches the relationship with an attitude of "What's in it for me?"

7. Unfortunately, Maslow and Rogers used a language that allows misinterpretation. Maslow explicitly stated, however, that those who seek self-actualization directly, as a goal in itself, for their personal benefit, do not achieve it.

8. It is suggested that approaching life with an attitude of either self-sacrifice or "What's in it for me?" is unworkable. Instead, it is more adaptive to value others' welfare on a par with one's own.

9. Because of the pervasiveness of self-deception, we cannot rely on informal self-perceptions. Systematic, quantifiable observations of specific behaviors are more likely to yield an accurate self-image and enhance personal growth.

10. Maslow's need hierarchy can be used to help understand the motivations behind everyday activities. For those operating largely from the esteem level, it may help either to identify the specific goal required to satisfy one's need for esteem or to explore why they are choosing to withhold esteem from themselves.

11. Parents often withhold approval and acceptance as a way of motivating their children to greater achievement. In turn, individuals often adopt this same strategy on themselves. This strategy may aid adjustment if the immediate goals are so small and easily attained that approval and acceptance are highly probable. Otherwise, it undermines self-esteem and inhibits growth.

12. Optimal functioning implies developing personal competencies and pursuing excellence in areas for which we have a particular talent or interest. In addition, it implies developing a healthy self-concept, which is not the same thing as pride.

13. One way of opening the way for peak experiences is to look at something ordinary as if you were seeing it for the first time. Peak experiences typically come from an attitude of "not trying."

14. Self-control often comes about by turning our attention away from the activity of the moment and focusing instead on an eventual reward. We must be sure to evaluate whether the experience of the reward justifies

the effort to attain it and the possible loss of contact with what we are doing in the moment.

15. Growth means finding a way to transcend or combine seemingly opposite meanings. Theorists suggest that it is possible, for instance, to combine deep love with nonattachment and self-control with spontaneity.

16. A promising metaphor for guiding personal growth is that of following a "path of heart."

SUGGESTED READINGS

Casteñada, C. **The teachings of Don Juan**. Berkeley and Los Angeles: University of California Press, 1968. Fascinating presentation of an experiential world view and its image of healthy personality. Also see other books in this series.

Shapiro, D. H., Jr. **Precision nirvana**. Englewood Cliffs, N.J.: Prentice-Hall, 1978. Interesting combination of behaviorism and Zen.

Wallach, M. A., & Wallach, L. **Psychology's sanction for selfishness**. San Francisco: W. H. Freeman, 1983. Solid analysis of the problems associated with "looking out for number one."

Yankelovich, D. **New rules**. New York: Random House, 1981. Penetrating study of the fulfillment seekers.

GLOSSARY

ABC model Term used to describe Ellis's rational-emotive therapy. A is the external activating event, B an irrational belief, and C the consequent negative emotional reaction.

Absorption In love, the continual thinking and talking about the partner.

Acquisition The learning of new behaviors.

Actualizing tendency The drive to maintain and enhance the experiencing organism.

Adjustment The process of coping with environmental change; personal change on the continuum from maladaptive to normal or average functioning.

Affect Feelings or emotions.

Alexander technique A method of body work developed by Mathias Alexander emphasizing postural alignment.

Alienation Experiencing oneself as separate, alone, and cut off from others.

Anal stage According to Freud, the second stage of development, covering roughly ages one through three.

Androgyny The combination of both traditionally masculine and traditionally feminine characteristics in one person of either sex.

Antecedent stimuli Stimuli that precede the behavior of interest.

Aptitude A specific ability.

Attribution theory A theory in social psychology concerned with how causes are assigned to events.

Authenticity Existential model of healthy personality; emphasizes the feeling of complete freedom, taking responsibility for one's actions, and avoiding self-deception.

Autogenic training A technique for treating stress-related disorders; entails muscular relaxation, visualization, and hypnotic suggestion.

Aversive stimulus A stimulus that decreases the frequency of behavior that precedes it.

Avoidance conditioning Behavior that is maintained because it leads to the reduction or avoidance of aversive stimuli.

Behavior Anything one does that can be observed by oneself or others.

Behaviorism The study of causal relationships between overt behavior and environmental stimuli.

Being cognition Immediate perception as an end in itself.

Being-in-the-world Existential phrase for describing human existence nondualistically.

Bioenergetic therapy Body therapy emphasizing breathing and the therapist's use of touch; developed by Alexander Lowen.

412

Biofeedback The presentation in observable form of a physiological response not ordinarily available to consciousness.

Bioprogram The genetic predisposition for certain behaviors to occur.

Blended orgasm Theoretically, a blend of vaginal and uterine orgasms.

Body image The way one thinks of or visualizes one's body.

Bodymind Term referring to the entire person, without the dualism of mind and body.

Burdened personality Body type with torso squeezed downward and curved forward.

Circumcision Surgical procedure for removing the male foreskin.

Classical conditioning Pavlov's observation that by being paired with an unconditioned stimulus, a previously neutral stimulus can come to elicit a response that is similar to the unconditioned response.

Clitoris The most sensitive part of the female genitals; composed of glans and shaft; located at the top of the inner lips.

Closed-ended questions Questions that require only a brief response.

Cognition Thoughts, ideas, beliefs, and perceptions.

Companionate love Feelings of caring, trust, respect, friendship, liking, and attachment to partner.

Compensation Ego defense mechanism of unconsciously balancing a perceived weakness with a developed strength.

Complementarity In attraction, the belief that opposites attract.

Conditioned response A response that occurs as a reaction to a conditioned stimulus.

Conditioned stimulus A previously neutral stimulus that, by being paired with an unconditioned stimulus, has come to elicit a response similar to the unconditioned response.

Congruence The degree of overlap among the real, conscious, and social selves.

Conscious Whatever one is aware of at this moment.

Conscious self Experiences relating to who one is that are available to awareness.

Contingency of reinforcement The relationship between behavior and its consequent stimuli.

Controlled strategy of conversation Having a goal in mind and selecting conversational responses relevant to that goal.

Conversion The transformation of an impulse into a physical symptom.

Courtly love A cognitive, idealized, asexual form of love popular among European nobility of the Middle Ages.

Creativity Bringing into existence something that is new and of value.

Cunnilingus Oral stimulation of the female genitals.

Decoding The process of receiving a message.

Defensive coping Coping efforts designed to protect oneself from the stressor rather than to deal with it directly.

Denial Ego defense mechanism that automatically blocks out a threatening part of external reality.

Depression A state of extreme sadness, characterized by loss of appetite, impaired sleep, lessened sexual interest, and fatigue.

Direct external reinforcement A reinforcing stimulus that is presented by someone or something other than oneself.

Discriminative stimulus A stimulus that has preceded reinforcement or punishment in the past.

Disinhibition Increasing the probability of a learned response, especially if that behavior's probability had been held in check by punishment.

Displacement Ego defense mechanism using a substitute person or object to gratify an impulse.

Dominance An attitude of self-confidence and authority.

Dominant other A person that one is obsessed with pleasing; often a parent or parent substitute.

Double-bind A message to respond, with the implication that there is a correct response, when actually no correct response is possible.

Ectomorphy The predisposition to have a linear, fragile body.

Ego Learned reaction patterns for gratifying the id and defending consciousness from threat.

Ego defense mechanisms Common strategies by which one keeps threatening material from consciousness.

Emission The first stage of male orgasm, in which semen is emptied into the duct at the base of the penis.

Emotion Feelings, moods, and other physiologically aroused states.

Empathic understanding Seeing the world through another's eyes.

Encoding The process of sending a message.

Endomorphy The predisposition to have a body characterized by softness and roundness.

Erectile dysfunction The inability to maintain an erection.

Eustress The positive or desired events to which one must adjust.

Excitement The first stage of the sexual response cycle, marked by male erection and female lubrication.

Experiential field Perceived internal and external reality, including events that are not consciously perceived yet affect behavior.

Expulsion The second stage of male orgasm, in which semen is propelled through the urethra by spasmodic muscular contractions.

Extinguish To reduce response frequency by withholding reinforcement.

Extramarital sex Sexual contact with someone other than one's spouse.

Fellatio Oral stimulation of the male genitals.

Foreskin Skin covering the glans of a nonerect, uncircumcised penis.

Free association Saying whatever comes to mind, no matter how trivial or embarrassing.

Future shock The distress caused by overloading an individual's adaptive system.

Gender One's physical sex, male or female.

Gender identity One's feeling of being male or female.

Gender role The behaviors and attitudes considered appropriate for male or female in a given culture.

Gender-role flexibility The ability to enact either traditional masculine or feminine behaviors, depending on which is more adaptive in a given situation.

General adaptation syndrome The typical pattern of reactions used for dealing with a wide variety of stressful situations, occurring in three stages: alarm, resistance, and exhaustion.

Genital stage Freud's psychosexual stage signifying sexual maturity, that is, the capacities for love and orgasm.

Genital type Psychoanalytic model of healthy personality.

Growth Personal change in a positive or healthy direction, especially when that change can be viewed as going beyond average or typical adjustment.

"G" spot A theoretically sensitive area on the upper vaginal wall of a reclining female.

High-level wellness A term describing optimal functioning in health psychology.

Hymen Tissue of skin partly covering vaginal opening of many virgin females.

Hypnosis A state of consciousness characterized by narrowed attention, passivity, and suggestability.

Id The mental representative of one's inherited animal drives.

Idealization In love, putting the partner "on a pedestal," acting as if the partner were in some sense perfect.

Identification Ego defense mechanism of adopting another's traits, behaviors, or other characteristics.

Identity confusion Feeling unsure of who we are or where we are going in life.

Implicit theory of personality The system of beliefs and assumptions that each person devises for making sense out of people's behavior.

Inhibition Reducing the probability of a learned response.

Inner lips Moist, hairless, sexually sensitive folds of skin within the female outer lips.

Instrumental coping Coping efforts designed to remove a stressor.

Introjection Ego defense mechanism in which a part of the external world is internalized and kept intact in the psyche.

Isolation Ego defense mechanism in which a threatening impulse is rendered harmless by removing its emotional component.

Kinesthetic awareness Consciousness of movement and tension in the muscles and joints.

Latency According to Freud, a sexually quiescent period following the phallic stage.

Learned values Values and preferences that are acquired as a result of others' influence.

Learning A relatively enduring change in behavior.

Limbic lobe The part of the brain surrounding the reptilian complex; controls intense emotion.

Locus of control Whether one believes that the important events in life are under one's own control (internal) or outside one's own control (external).

Meditation Methods of relaxation using a mental device such as repeating a particular sound or concentrating on an object.

Mesomorphy The predisposition to have a hard, rectangular body.

Metacommunication Commenting on the form or implied meaning of another's response.

Metatheory A theory about theories.

Modeling The process of imitating others' behavior.

Mystification Telling other people what they are feeling.

Narcissistic Self-centered, self-indulgent, immature.

Natural values The direct, unlearned preference for some stimuli and behaviors rather than others.

Needy personality Body type with head shifted forward and sunken chest.

Negative reinforcement The increase in the frequency of a response as a result of its being followed by the removal of an aversive stimulus.

Neocortex Evolutionarily, the most recent part of the brain; the part of the brain responsible for thought.

Nonverbal behavior Body language.

Norm of asking The assumption in conversation that if someone wants to know something about me, they will ask.

Norm of volunteering The asssumption in conversation that if someone wants to disclose an item of information, he or she will, so questions are unnecessary.

Open-ended questions Questions that require more than a few words to answer.

Oral stage The earliest of Freud's stages of development, covering roughly the first year of life.

Organismic experience Experience of the total person, including the body and perceptions outside conscious awareness.

Orgasm The third stage in the sexual response cycle, characterized by a state of high sexual tension followed by rapid and intensely pleasurable tension release.

Orgasmic dysfunction Inability to have orgasm.

Outcome expectancy The expectancy of a future stimulus based on the presence of a particular behavior.

Outer lips Two folds of hair-covered skin running on either side of the vaginal-to-clitoral midline.

Overgeneralization Drawing broad, sweeping conclusions on the basis of limited evidence.

Paradoxical communication A message that contradicts itself.

PC muscle The muscle that surrounds the vaginal opening or the base of the penis; thought to affect sexual responsiveness.

Peak experience Extreme state of being cognition; moment of highest happiness and fulfillment.

Penis The male sex organ, consisting of a tubular shaft and a bulbous head or glans.

Persona The mask of the actor; the way we present ourselves to others; the social self.

Personal constructs The categories used to describe and make sense out of the world.

Personality The study of the whole person, emphasizing both human nature and individual differences.

Phallic stage According to Freud, psychosexual stage occurring roughly between ages three and six and involving sexual attraction to the opposite-sex parent.

Placebo effect The improvement that some patients experience from the hope and expectation that they will be cured.

Plateau The second stage of the sexual response cycle, characterized by the testes elevating and enlarging, and the clitoris retracting under its hood.

Positive reinforcement The increase in frequency of response resulting from a behavior's being followed by a reinforcing stimulus.

Preconscious The "area" of unawareness over which we have partial conscious control.

Prejudice Literally, pre-judgment; the judgment

of others based on false beliefs rather than valid evidence.

Premature ejaculation Dissatisfaction with the duration of penile erection or with a lack of voluntary control over ejaculation.

Progressive muscular relaxation A method for inducing relaxation that entails tensing a particular muscle group for a few seconds, followed by a complete relaxation of that tension.

Projection Ego defense mechanism in which something unacceptable about the self is unknowingly attributed to someone else.

Psychoanalysis The method of treatment developed by Freud, emphasizing free association and the interpretation of unconscious determinants of behavior.

Psychoanalytic theory A personality theory developed by Sigmund Freud, emphasizing the role of unconscious factors.

Psychosexual stage of development Freud's view of childhood development as occurring in stages, with each stage centered on erotic gratification associated with a particular body area, such as the mouth, anus, and genitals.

Punishment The decrease in frequency of a response as a result of its being followed by an aversive stimulus or by the removal of a reinforcing stimulus.

Rationalization Ego defense mechanism of justifying one's behavior with socially acceptable reasons.

Reaction formation Ego defense mechanism in which a forbidden impulse is repressed and its opposite is manifested.

Real self The totality of what one actually is.

Reciprocal determinism The social learning view that personal, behavioral, and environmental influences all determine one another.

Regression Ego defense mechanism entailing a retreat to a reaction pattern characteristic of a less mature mode of adjustment.

Reinforcement value A stimulus's desirability.

Reinforcing stimulus A stimulus that increases the frequency of the behavior that precedes it.

Repression Automatic forcing of mental contents into unconsciousness.

Reptilian complex The part of the brain located at the base of the skull, controlling self-preservation and reproduction.

Resistance In psychoanalysis, any behavior that violates the rule of free association; an attempt to protect consciousness from the emergence of threatening unconscious contents.

Resolution The fourth stage of the sexual response cycle, in which the body returns to a sexually quiescent state.

Respondent conditioning See classical conditioning.

Response A behavior occurring in reaction to a stimulus.

Response discrimination The selective reinforcement of a response so that it occurs only in the presence of certain stimuli.

Rigid personality Body type with body curved backward and shoulders held stiffly.

Role confusion Having doubts about which roles to adopt and how adequately one can carry them out.

Rolfing Body therapy using deep and often painful massage.

Romantic love An intense state of positive affect often characterized by absorption, longing, dependency, physical attraction, exclusiveness, and idealization of the partner.

Satiation The temporary reduction in a stimulus's reinforcement power as a result of overuse.

Scrotum Sac of loose skin housing the male testes.

Self-actualization Maslow's model of psychological health; the active fulfillment of one's positive potentials.

Self-concept The way that we describe ourselves.

Self-deception The evasion of some truth about oneself, especially when there is no awareness that the truth has been evaded.

Self-disclosure Telling another about yourself.

Self-efficacy The conviction that one can perform a desired response in a specified situation.

Self-esteem How we feel about ourselves; whether we are satisfied or dissatisfied with who we are.

Self-reinforcement A reinforcing stimulus that is self-administered.

Self-system The self-regulatory process by which we observe our behavior, compare it with learned standards, and react to it positively or negatively.

Sensate focus Exercises used in sex therapy to encourage a relaxed, sensual approach to all forms of touching.

Sexual fidelity The promise of exclusivity in sex.

Sexual response cycle The four stages of sexual arousal: excitement, plateau, orgasm, and resolution.

Shadow A complex of thoughts, feelings, and images that are threatening (and therefore repressed) because they contradict the self-concept.

Should statement Telling yourself that you should behave in a certain way.

Social exchange theory In social psychology, the view that relationships are formed on the basis of comparing prospective partners' assets and liabilities, so that those of equivalent social desirability would tend to group together.

Social self The part of ourselves that we allow others to see.

Spectatoring Engaging in sexual behavior while simultaneously watching and evaluating one's performance.

Spontaneous strategy of conversation Absorbing yourself in a conversation and not planning what you will say next.

SQ3R method An approach to reading skills: survey, question, read, recite, and review.

Squeeze technique Method for delaying male ejaculation involving squeezing the penile glans.

Stereotype Generalized belief about a group of people.

Stimulus A perceptible environmental event.

Stimulus expectancy The expectancy of a future stimulus based on the presence of a current stimulus.

Stimulus generalization The increase in probability of a response as a result of the occurrence of a stimulus that is similar to a previously established discriminative stimulus.

Stimulus situation The physical and social environment.

Stop-start method Technique for delaying

ejaculation that stops coital movement and then restarts it after control is regained.

Stress The strain from coping with deviations from optimal arousal; the debilitating effects of threat.

Stressor Environmental event that places an adjustive demand on the organism.

Subception The reception of stimuli that are not consciously perceived.

Sublimation An unacceptable impulse that is transformed and expressed in a more acceptable manner.

Superego One's internalized voice of conscience and image of perfection.

Suppression A consciously initiated turning of one's attention away from threatening impulses.

Testes The male sex glands.

Theory A system of terms used to represent some part of reality.

Type A personality Highly competitive, hostile, and time-pressured.

Type B personality The opposite of Type A.

Unconditioned response A response occurring automatically in reaction to an unconditioned stimulus.

Unconditioned stimulus A stimulus that has automatic, unlearned effects on behavior, such as a puff of air to the eye that automatically causes blinking.

Unconscious Whatever one is currently unaware of; the "region" of mental contents that are outside awareness and outside conscious control.

Undoing Ego defense mechanism in which an unacceptable impulse is acted out, followed by a ritual of atonement.

Uterine orgasm Theoretically, a female orgasm involving contractions of the upper vagina and uterus, possibly triggered by "G" spot stimulation.

Vagina Female organ entered in coitus; birth canal.

Vicarious reinforcement Observing someone else's behavior being reinforced.

Vulval orgasm Theoretically, a female orgasm triggered by clitoral stimulation, mainly involving the lower vagina.

REFERENCES

Abbott, A. R., & Sebastian, R. J. Physical attractiveness and expectation of success. *Personality and Social Psychology Bulletin,* 1981, *7,* 481–486.

Adams, G., & Huston, T. Social perception of middle-aged persons varying in physical attractiveness. *Developmental Psychology,* 1975, *11,* 657–658.

Addiego, F., Belzer, E. G., Comolli, J., Moger, W., Perry, J. D., & Whipple, B. Female ejaculation: A case study. *Journal of Sex Research,* 1981, *17,* 13–21.

Albrecht, S. L. Correlates of marital happiness among the remarried. *Journal of Marriage and the Family,* November 1979, pp. 857–867.

Al-Khayyal, M., & Jones, J. E. Healthy communication as a predictor of competence in risk families. Paper presented at the annual convention of the American Psychological Association, Los Angeles, 1981.

Alloy, L., & Abramson, L. Judgment of contingency in depressed and nondepressed students: Sadder but wiser? *Journal of Experimental Psychology: General,* 1979, *108,* 441–485.

Altrocchi, J. *Abnormal behavior.* New York: Harcourt Brace Jovanovich, 1980.

Amos, S. P. Personality differences of groups defined on the basis of different criteria of creativity. *Journal of Creative Behavior,* 1981, *15,* 266–267.

Anderson, J. R., & Bower, G. H. *Human associative memory.* New York: Wiley, 1973.

Answers from John Hinckley, *Newsweek,* 1981, *98,* 50–51.

Archer, J. Biological explanations of psychological sex differences. In B. Lloyd & J. Archer (Eds.), *Exploring sex differences.* New York: Academic Press, 1976.

Arieti, S. The power of the dominant other. *Psychology Today,* April 1979, pp. 54–58, 92–93.

Averill, J. R. *Anger and aggression: An essay on emotion.* New York: Springer-Verlag, 1982.

Ayllon, T. Intensive treatment of psychotic behavior by stimulus satiation and food reinforcement. *Behavior Research and Therapy,* 1963, *1,* 53–61.

Bach, G. R., & Deutsch, R. M. *Pairing.* New York: Wyden, 1970.

Bahnson, C. B. Stress and cancer: The state of the art, Pt. 1. *Psychosomatics,* December 1980, pp. 975–980.

Bahnson, C. B. Stress and cancer: The state of the art, Pt. 2. *Psychosomatics,* March 1981, pp. 207–218.

Baldwin, A. C., Critelli, J. W., Stevens, L. C., & Russell, S. A. Psychological androgyny: A personal construct approach. *Journal of Personality and Social Psychology,* in press.

Bandura, A. *Social learning theory.* Englewood Cliffs, N.J.: Prentice-Hall, 1977.

Bandura, A. *Social foundations of thought and action.* Englewood Cliffs, N.J.: Prentice-Hall, 1986.

Bandura, A., & Schunk, D. H. Cultivating competence, self-efficacy, and intrinsic interest through proximal self-motivation. *Journal of Personality and Social Psychology,* 1981, *41,* 586–598.

Barnard, C., & Illman, J. (Eds.). *The body machine.* New York: Crown, 1981.

Barron, F. *Creativity and psychological health.* Princeton, N.J.: D. Van Nostrand, 1963.

Barry, H., Bacon, M. K., & Child, I. L. A cross-cultural survey of some sex differences in socialization. *Journal of Abnormal and Social Psychology,* 1959, *55,* 327–333.

Bar-Tal, D., & Saxe, L. Physical attractiveness and its relationship to sex-role stereotyping. *Sex Roles,* 1976, *2,* 123–133.

Bassili, J. N. The attractiveness stereotype: Goodness or glamour? *Basic & Applied Social Psychology,* 1981, *2,* 235–252.

Baumgartner, A. *My daddy might have loved me: Student perceptions of differences between being male and being female.* Denver: Institute of Equality in Education, 1983.

Beck, A., & Kovacs, M. A new, fast therapy for depression. *Psychology Today,* January 1977, pp. 94–101.

Beck, S. B., Ward-Hull, C. I., & McLear, P. M. Variables related to women's somatic preferences of the male and female body. *Journal of Personality and Social Psychology,* 1976, *34,* 1200–1210.

Bell, D. H. *Being a man: The paradox of masculinity.* Lexington, Mass.: Lewis, 1982.

Belsky, J., & Steinberg, L. D. The effects of day care: A critical review. *Child Development,* 1978, *49,* 929–949.

Belzer, E. H. Orgasmic expulsions of women: A review and heuristic inquiry. *Journal of Sex Research,* 1981, *17,* 1–12.

Bem, S. L. Sex-role adaptability: One consequence of psychological androgyny. *Journal of Personality and Social Psychology,* 1974, *42,* 155–162.

Bem, S. L. The short Bem sex-role inventory. Palo Alto, Calif.: Consulting Psychologists Press, 1978.

Bem, S. L. Gender schema theory and its implications for child development: Raising gender-aschematic children in a gender-schematic society. *Signs,* Summer 1983, *8,* 598–616.

Benbow, C. P., & Stanley, J. C. Sex differences in mathematical ability: Fact or artifact? *Science,* 1980, *210,* 1262–1264.

Benson, H. *The relaxation response.* New York: Avon, 1975.

Benson, P. L., Karabenick, S. A., & Lerner, R. M. Pretty pleases: The effects of physical attractiveness, race, and sex on receiving help. *Journal of Experimental Social Psychology,* 1976, *12,* 409–415.

Bentler, P. M., & Peeler, W. H. Models of female orgasm. *Archives of Sexual Behavior,* 1979, *8,* 405–423.

Bergin, A. E. A self-regulation technique for impulse control disorders. *Psychotherapy: Theory, Research, and Practice,* 1969, *6,* 113–118.

Bernard, J. *The future of marriage.* New York: Bantam Books, 1973.

Berscheid, E., Walster, E., & Bohrnstedt, G. Body image. *Psychology Today,* November 1973, pp. 119–131.

Berscheid, E., Walster, E., & Campbell, R. Grow old along with me. Unpublished manuscript, University of Minnesota, 1972.

Berscheid, E., & Graziano, W. The initiation of social relationships and interpersonal attraction. In R. L. Burgess & T. L. Huston (Eds.), *Social exchange in developing relationships.* New York: Academic Press, 1979, pp. 31–58.

Berscheid, E. D., Stephan, W., & Walster, E. Sexual arousal and heterosexual perception. *Journal of Personality and Social Psychology,* 1971, *20,* 93–101.

Berscheid, E., & Walster, E. Physical attractiveness. In L. Berkowitz (Ed.), *Advances in experimental social psychology.* New York: Academic Press, 1974, pp. 158–215.

Berscheid, E., & Walster, E. *Interpersonal attraction.* Reading, Mass.: Addison-Wesley, 1978.

Betz, E. L. Two tests of Maslow's theory of need fulfillment. *Journal of Vocational Behavior,* 1984, *24,* 204–220.

Birdwhistle, R. L. *Kinesics and context.* Philadelphia: University of Pennsylvania Press, 1970.

Bissett, D. W. Self-disclosure and self-actualization as predictors of love. Unpublished doctoral dissertation, North Texas State University, 1983.

Blumberg, H. H. Communication of interpersonal evaluations. *Journal of Personality and Social Psychology,* 1972, *23,* 157–162.

Bower, G. H. *Psychology Today,* June 1981, pp. 60–69.

Boy, 12, accused of assaulting girl on pool table. *Dallas Times Herald.* Dallas: The Times Herald Printing Co., April 18, 1984, p. A-3.

Branden, N. *The psychology of romantic love.* Los Angeles: Tarcher, 1980.

Branden, N. Autonomy, self-growth defended. *APA Monitor.* Washington, D.C.: American Psychological Association, October 1984, p. 5.

Brehm, S. S., & Smith, T. W. The application of social psychology to clinical practice: A range of possibilities. In G. Weary & H. L. Mirels (Eds.), *Integrations of clinical and social psychology.* New York: Oxford University Press, 1982, pp. 9–24.

Brenner, C. *An elementary textbook of psychoanalysis.* New York: International Universities Press, 1973.

Bridges, C. F., Critelli, J. W., & Loos, V. E. Hypnotic susceptibility, inhibitory control, and orgasmic consistency. *Archives of Sexual Behavior,* 1985, *14,* 373–376.

Brody, J. E. *Jane Brody's* The New York Times *guide to personal health.* New York: Times Books, 1982.

Bronowski, J. *The common sense of science.* New York: Vintage Books, 1959.

Broverman, I. K., Broverman, D. M., Clarkson, F. E., Rosenkrantz, P., & Vogel, S. R. Sex-role stereotypes and clinical judgments of mental health. *Journal of Consulting Psychology,* 1970, *34,* 1–7.

Brownmiller, S. *Femininity.* New York: Linden, 1984.

Bullough, V. L. Technology and female sexuality and physiology: Some implications. *Journal of Sex Research,* 1980, *16,* 59–71.

Burns, D. D. The perfectionist's script for self-defeat. *Psychology Today,* November 1980, pp. 34–52.

Buscaglia, L. *Living, loving & learning.* New York: Holt, Rinehart and Winston, 1982.

Butler, C. A. New data about female sexual response. *Journal of Sex and Marital Therapy,* 1976, *2,* 40–46.

Byrne, C., London, O., & Reeves, K. The effects of physical attractiveness, sex, and attitude similarity on interpersonal attraction. *Journal of Personality,* 1968, *36,* 259–271.

Campbell, A., Converse, P. E., & Rodgers, W. L. *The quality of American life: Perceptions, evaluations, and satisfactions.* New York: Russell Sage Foundation, 1976.

Campbell, J. *The portable Jung.* New York: Viking, 1971.

Caplan, P. J., MacPherson, G. M., & Tobin, P. Do sex-related differences in spatial abilities exist? A multilevel critique with new data. *American Psychologist,* 1985, *40*(7), 786–799.

Carson, R. C. *Interaction concepts of personality.* Chicago: Aldine, 1969.

Casteñada, C. *The teachings of Don Juan: A yaquita way of knowledge.* Berkeley and Los Angeles: University of California Press, 1968, pp. 152–153.

Chance, P. The remedial thinker. *Psychology Today,* October 1981, pp. 63–73.

Charlip, R., cited in Pierpont, M., Body therapies and the modern dancer, *Dance-magazine,* August 1983, p. 12.

Cherlin, A., & Furstenberg, F. The American family in the year 2000. *The Futurist,* 1983, *17,* 7–14.

Cherulnik, P. D. Sex differences in the expression of emotion in a structured social encounter. *Sex Roles,* 1979, *5,* 413–424.

Cimbalo, R. S., Falling, V., & Mousaw, P. The course of love: A cross-sectional design. *Psychological Reports,* 1976, *38,* 1292–1294.

Clanton, G., & Smith, L. G. The self–inflicted pain of jealousy. *Psychology Today,* October 1977, pp. 44–47, 80–82.

Clark, C. C. *Enhancing wellness.* New York: Springer, 1981.

Clifford, M. M., & Walster, E. The effect of physical attractiveness on teacher expectation. *Sociology of Education,* 1973, *46,* 248–258.

Clore, G. L., & Byrne, D. A reinforcement-affect model of attraction. In T. L. Huston (Ed.), *Perspectives in interpersonal attraction.* New York: Academic Press, 1974.

Cohen, S. I., Miller L. G., & Ross, R. N. Stress: What can be done? *Bostonia,* December 1982, Boston University Alumni House Publications.

Coleman, J. C. *Contemporary psychology and effective behavior.* Glenview, Ill.: Scott, Foresman, 1980.

Coleman, J. C. *Intimate relationships, marriage, and family.* Indianapolis: Bobbs-Merrill, 1984.

Coleman, J. C., Butcher, J. N., & Carson, R. C. *Abnormal psychology and modern life.* Glenview, Ill.: Scott, Foresman, 1980.

Conniff, R. Living longer. *Next,* June 1981.

Constantinople, A. Masculinity-femininity: An exception to a famous dictum? *Psychological Bulletin,* 1973, *80,* 389–407.

Coombs, L. C. Preferences for sex of children among U.S. couples. *Family Planning Perspectives,* 1977, *9,* 259–265.

Coombs, R. H., & Kenkel, W. F. Sex differences in dating aspirations and satisfaction with computer-selected partners. *Journal of Marriage and the Family,* February 1966, pp. 62–66.

Cordes, S. M. Assessing health care needs: Elements and processes. *Family and Community Health,* 1978, *1,* 4.

Corliss, R. The new ideal of beauty. *Time,* August 30, 1982, pp. 72–77.

Cornish, E. The future of the family: Intimacy in an age of loneliness. *The Futurist,* February 1979, pp. 45–58.

Cozby, P. C. Self-disclosure: A literature review. *Psychological Bulletin,* 1973, *79,* 73–91.

Critelli, J. W. Sex differences in romantic attraction: A content analysis of love letters. Paper presented at the annual convention of the Southwestern Psychological Association, 1977.

Critelli, J. W. Placebo effects, common factors, and incremental effectiveness. *American Psychologist,* 1985, *40*(7), 850–851.

Critelli, J. W., & Loos, V. E. Double-binding messages and psychopathology. Unpublished manuscript, North Texas State University, 1984.

Critelli, J. W., Myers, E., & Loos, V. E. The components of love: Romantic attraction and sex-role orientation. *Journal of Personality,* 1986, *54,* 354–370.

Critelli, J. W., & Neumann, K. F. An interpersonal analysis of self-disclosure and feedback. *Social Behavior and Personality,* 1976, *6,* 173–177.

Critelli, J. W., & Neumann, K. F. The placebo: Conceptual analysis of a construct in transition. *American Psychologist,* 1985, *39,* 32–39.

Critelli, J. W., Tang, C., & Pickard, D. Dominance and laughter in heterosexual first meetings. Paper presented at the annual convention of the American Psychological Association, 1985, Los Angeles.

Critelli, J. W., & Waid, L. R. Physical attractiveness, romantic love, and equity restoration in dating relationships. *Journal of Personality Assessment,* 1980, *44,* 624–629.

Crouse, B. B., & Mehrabian, A. Affiliation of opposite-sexed strangers. *Journal of Research in Personality,* 1977, *11,* 38–47.

Curran, J. P., & Lippold, S. The effects of physical attraction and similarity on attraction in dating dyads. *Journal of Personality,* 1975, *43,* 528–539.

Dailey, J. Women's most versatile muscle: The PC. *Sexology Today,* July 1980.

Daniels, V., & Horowitz, L. J. *Being and caring.* Palo Alto, Calif.: Mayfield, 1984.

Davis, K. Wives and work: The sex role revolution and its consequences. *Population and Development Review,* 1984, *10,* 397–417.

Deaux, K. Ahhh, she was just lucky. *Psychology Today,* December 1976, pp. 70ff.

De Bruijn, G. From masturbation to orgasm with a partner: How some women bridge the gap—And why others don't. *Journal of Sex and Marital Therapy,* 1982, *8,* 151–167.

Dellas, M., & Gaier, E. L. Identification of creativity: The individual. *Psychological Bulletin,* 1970, *73,* 55–73.

Delora, J. S., Warren, C. A. B., & Ellison, C. R. *Understanding sexual interaction.* Boston: Houghton Mifflin, 1981.

Derlega, V. J., & Janda, S. H. *Personal adjustment.* Glenview, Ill.: Scott, Foresman, 1981.

Dermer, M., & Thiel, D. L. When beauty may fail. *Journal of Personality and Social Psychology,* 1975, *31,* 1168–1176.

Dion, K. K., Berscheid, E., & Walster, E. E. What is beautiful is good. *Journal of Personality and Social Psychology,* 1972, *24,* 285–290.

Dion, K. K., & Dion, K. L. Self-esteem and romantic love. *Journal of Personality,* 1975, *27,* 39–57.

DiPietro, J. A. Rough and tumble play: A function of gender. *Developmental Psychology,* 1981, *17,* 50–58.

Dodson, B. *Liberating masturbation: A meditation on self-love.* New York: Bodysex Designs, 1974.

Doherty, W. J. Locus of control differences and marital dissatisfaction. *Journal of Marriage and the Family,* May 1981, pp. 369–377.

Dohrenwend, B. S., & Dohrenwend, B. P. Overview and prospects for research on stressful life events. In B. S. Dohrenwend & B. P. Dohrenwend (Eds.), *Stressful life events.* New York: Wiley, 1974.

Driscoll, R., Davis, K. E., & Lipetz, M. E. Parental interference and romantic love: The Romeo and Juliet effect. *Journal of Personality and Social Psychology,* 1972, *24,* 1–10.

Droege, R. C. Sex differences in aptitude maturation during high school. *Journal of Counseling Psychology,* 1967, *14,* 407–411.

Duke, M., & Nowicki, S., Jr. *Abnormal psychology: Perspectives on being different.* Monterey, Calif.: Brooks/Cole, 1979.

Durlak, J. A. Relationship between individual attitudes toward life and death. *Journal of Consulting and Clinical Psychology,* 1972, *38,* 463.

Dush, D. M., Hirt, M. L., & Schroeder, H. Self-statement modification with adults: A meta-analysis. *Psychological Bulletin,* 1983, *94,* 408–422.

Eagly, A. H. Sex differences in influenceability. *Psychological Bulletin,* 1978, *85,* 86–116.

Ebel, R. L. Blind guessing on objective achievement tests. *Journal of Educational Measurement,* 1968, *5,* 321–325.

Eccles, J. Sex differences in math achievement and course enrollment. Paper presented at the annual meeting of the American Educational Research Association, New York, March 1982.

Edwards, C. P., & Whiting, B. Sex differences in children's social interaction. Unpublished report to Ford Foundation, 1977.

Efran, M. The effect of physical appearance on the judgment of guilt, interpersonal attraction, and severity of recommended punishment in a simulated jury task. *Journal of Research in Personality,* 1974, *8,* 45–54.

Ekman, P., & Friesen, W. V. *Unmasking the face.* Englewood Cliffs, N.J.: Prentice-Hall, 1975.

Elgin, S. H. *More on the gentle art of verbal self-defense.* Englewood Cliffs, N.J.: Prentice-Hall, 1983.

Ellington, J. E., March, L. A., & Critelli, J. W. Personality characteristics of women with masculine names. *Journal of Social Psychology,* 1980, *111,* 211–218.

Elliot, J. Feeling: The key to personal growth. *Personal Growth,* 1976, *25,* 9–16.

Ellis, A. *Reason and emotion in psychotherapy.* New York: Lyle Stuart, 1962.

Ellis, A. *Humanistic psychotherapy.* New York: McGraw-Hill, 1973.

Ellis, A. Adultery may be beneficial, psychologist maintains. *Behavior Today,* 1976, *7,* 6–7.

Erickson, M. H., & Kubie, L. S. Automatic drawing in the treatment of an obsessional depression. *Psychoanalytic Quarterly,* 1938, *7,* 443–466.

Erickson, M. H. Experimental demonstration of psychopathology of everyday life. *Psychoanalytic Quarterly,* 1939, *8,* 338–353.

Erikson, E. *Identity: Youth and crisis.* New York: Norton, 1968.

Escarpit, R. *The book revolution.* London: UNESCO, George G. Harrap, 1966, p. 83.

Etaugh, C. Effects of nonmaternal care on children: Research evidence and popular views. *American Psychologist,* 1980, *35,* 309–319.

Fabrikant, B. The psychotherapist and the female patient: Perceptions, misperceptions and change. In V. Franks and V. Burtle (Eds.), *Women in therapy.* New York: Bruner/Mazel, 1974, pp. 83–109.

Farberow, N. L. *Suicide.* Morristown, N.J.: General Learning Press, 1974.

Farberow, N. L., & Litman, R. E. A comprehensive suicide prevention program. Suicide Prevention Center of Los Angeles, 1958–1969. Los Angeles, 1970.

Feingold, A. Do taller men have prettier girlfriends? *Psychological Reports,* 1982, *50,* 810.

Feldenkrais, M. *Awareness through movement.* New York: Harper & Row, 1972.

Festinger, L. Architecture and group membership. *Journal of Social Issues,* 1951, *1,* 152–163.

Feuerstein, R. *Instrumental enrichment.* Baltimore: University Park Press, 1980.

Fingerette, H. *Self-deception.* New York: Humanities Press, 1969.

Fisher, S., & Cleveland, S. E. *Body image and personality.* Glencoe, Ill.: Free Press, 1968.

Fisher, S., & Greenberg, R. P. *The scientific credibility of Freud's theories and therapy.* New York: Basic Books, 1977.

Forisha, B. L. *Sex roles and personal awareness.* Morristown, N.J.: General Learning Press, 1978.

Francoeur, R. T. *Becoming a sexual person.* New York: Wiley, 1984.

Francoeur, R. T., & Francoeur, A. K. The pleasure bond: Reversing the antisex ethic. *The Futurist,* August 1976, pp. 176–180.

Frank, J. D. *Sanity and survival.* New York: Random House, 1967.

Frankl, V. E. *Man's search for meaning: An introduction to logotherapy.* New York: Washington Square Press, 1962.

Frankl, V. E. *The will to meaning.* New York: New American Library, 1969.

Franzoi, S. L., & Shields, S. A. The body esteem scale: Multidimensional structure and sex differences in a college population. *Journal of Personality Assessment,* 1984, *48,* 173–178.

Franzoi, S. L., & Herzog, M. E. The body esteem scale: A convergent and discriminant validity study. *Journal of Personality Assessment,* 1986, *50,* 24–31.

Freedman, J. L. *Happy people.* New York: Harcourt Brace Jovanovich, 1978.

Freud, S. *An outline of psychoanalysis.* New York: Norton, 1940/1952.

Friedman, M., & Rosenman, R. H. *Type A behavior and your heart.* New York: Knopf, 1974.

Frieze, I. H., Parsons, J. E., Johnson, P. B., Ruble, D. N., & Zellman, G. L. *Women and sex roles: A social psychological perspective.* New York: Norton, 1978.

Fromm, E. *The art of loving.* New York: Harper & Row, 1956.

Fuller, R. B., & McHale, J. *World design decade, 1965–1975.* Carbondale, Ill.: World Resources Inventory, Southern Illinois University, 1963.

Gardner, H. Human intelligence isn't what we think it is, *U.S. News & World Report,* March 19, 1984, pp. 75–78.

Garner, A. *Conversationally speaking.* New York: McGraw-Hill, 1981.

Garr, D. *The healing brain.* Escondido, Calif.: Omni Publications, 1981.

Gaylin, W. *Feelings: Our vital signs.* New York: Harper & Row, 1979.

Gebhard, P. H. Factors in marital orgasm. *Journal of Social Issues,* 1966, *22*(2), 88–95.

Geller, L. The failure of self-actualization theory: A critique of Carl Rogers and Abraham Maslow. *Journal of Humanistic Psychology,* 1982, *22,* 56–73.

Gelman, D. I can be open. *Newsweek,* January 16, 1978, p. 60.

Gershman, L., & Stedman, J. M. Oriental defense exercises as reciprocal inhibitors of anxiety. *Journal of Behavior Therapy and Experimental Psychiatry,* 1971, *2,* 117–119.

Gillen, B. Physical attractiveness: A determinant of two types of goodness. *Personality and Social Psychology Bulletin,* 1981, *7,* 277–281.

Gilligan, C. *In a different voice: Psychological theory and women's development.* Cambridge, Mass.: Harvard University Press, 1982.

Giovacchini, P. L. Psychoanalysis. In R. J. Corsini and A. J. Marsella (Eds.), *Personality theories, research, & assessment.* Itasca, Ill.: F. E. Peacock, 1983.

Gitter, A. C., & Black, H. Is self-disclosure self-revealing? *Journal of Counseling Psychology,* 1976, *23,* 327–332.

Gittleson, N. The fear that haunts our children. *McCalls,* May 1982, p. 77.

Glaister, G. A. *Encyclopedia of the book.* Cleveland: World Publishing, 1960.

Glass, D. C. Stress, competition and heart attacks. *Psychology Today,* December 1976, p. 55.

Glass, D. C. Behavior patterns, stress and coronary disease. Hillsdale, N.J.: Erlbaum, 1977.

Glenn, N. D. Children and marital happiness: A further specification of the relationship. *Journal of Marriage and the Family,* February 1982, pp. 63–72.

Glenn, N. D., & Weaver, C. N. The marital happiness of remarried divorced persons. *Journal of Marriage and the Family,* 1977, *39,* 331–337.

Glick, P. C. Remarriage. *Journal of Family Issues,* December 1980, pp. 455–478.

Goldberg, D. C., Whipple, B., Fishkin, R. E., Waxman, H., Fink, P. J., & Weisberg, M. The Grafenberg spot and female ejaculation: A review of initial hypotheses. *Journal of Sex and Marital Therapy,* 1983, *9,* 27–37.

Goldfried, M. R. The use of relaxation and cognitive relabelling as coping skills. In R. B. Stuart (Ed.), *Behavioral self-management: Strategies, techniques and outcomes.* New York: Brunner/Mazel, 1977, pp. 82–116.

Goldman, W., & Lewis, P. Beautiful is good: Evidence that the physically attractive are more socially skillful. *Journal of Experimental Social Psychology,* 1977, *13,* 125–130.

Goleman, D. Meditation helps break the stress spiral. *Psychology Today,* 1976, *9*(9), 82–86, 93.

Goleman, D. Special abilities of the sexes: Do they begin in the brain? *Psychology Today,* December 1978, pp. 53–63.

Gough, H. G. A creative personality scale for the adjective checklist. *Journal of Personality and Social Psychology,* 1979, *37,* 1398–1405.

Greenberg, E. F., & Nay, R. The intergenerational transmission of marital instability. *Journal of Marriage and the Family,* May 1982, pp. 335–347.

Greene, R. Column in *Chicago Tribune,* Tribune Company Syndicate, Inc. Copyright 1978 by Bob Greene. In Weiten, W. *Psychology applied to modern life.* Monterey, Calif.: Brooks/Cole, 1983.

Grossman, J. Inside the wellness movement. *Health,* November 1981, pp. 10–14.

Grossman, J. The wellness revolution: Will your town be next? *Health,* January 1982, pp. 44–46.

Guttentag, M., & Secord, P. *Too many women?* Beverly Hills, Calif.: Sage, 1983.

Hadamard, J. *The psychology of invention in the mathematical field.* Princeton, N.J.: Princeton University Press, 1945.

Haley, J. The art of one-upsmanship. In *The power tactics of Jesus Christ and other essays.* New York: Grossman, 1959, pp. 3–15.

Hall, C. S., & Lindzey, G. *Theories of personality.* New York: Wiley, 1978.

Hall, J. A. Gender effects in decoding nonverbal cues. *Psychological Bulletin,* 1978, *85,* 845–857.

Hall, R. My life measured out in abandoned words. In J. O. Stevens (Ed.), *Gestalt is.* Moab, Vt.: Real People Press, 1975.

Hamachek, D. E. *Encounters with the self.* New York: Holt, Rinehart and Winston, 1978.

Hamilton, S. B., & Waldman, D. A. Self-modification of depression via cognitive-behavioral intervention strategies: A time series analysis. *Cognitive Therapy and Research,* 1983, *7,* 99–106.

Hammen, C., & Mayol, A. Depression and cognitive characteristics of stressful life-event types. *Journal of Abnormal Psychology,* 1982, *91,* 165–174.

Hankins, N. E., McKinnie, W. T., & Bailey, R. C. Effects of height, physique and cranial hair on job-related attributes. *Psychological Reports,* 1979, *45,* 853–854.

Harari, H., & McDavid, J. W. Name stereotypes and teacher expectations. *Journal of Educational Psychology,* 1973, *65,* 222–225.

Hariton, E. B. The sexual fantasies of women. *Psychology Today,* 1973, *6*(10), 39–44.

Hariton, E. B., & Singer, J. L. Women's fantasies during sexual intercourse: Normative and theoretical implications. *Journal of Consulting and Clinical Psychology,* 1974, *42,* 313–322.

Harlow, H. F. Love in infant monkeys. *Scientific American,* June 1959, pp. 68–70.

Harris, M. Male supremacy is on the way out. A conversation by Carol Tavris. *Psychology Today,* January 1975, pp. 61–69.

Harrison, A. A., & Saeed, L. Let's make a deal: An analysis of revelations and stipulations in lonely hearts advertisements. *Journal of Personality and Social Psychology,* 1977, *35,* 257–264.

Heatherington, L., & Kirsch, I. The generality of negative self-reinforcement effects: Implications for the use of extrinsic rewards. *Cognitive Therapy and Research,* 1984, *8,* 67–76.

Heffernan, T., & Richards, C. S. Self-control of study behavior: Identification and evaluation of natural methods. *Journal of Counseling Psychology,* 1981, *28,* 361–364.

Heiby, E. M. A self-reinforcement questionnaire. *Behavior Research and Therapy,* 1982, *20,* 397–401.

Heiby, E. M. Toward the prediction of mood change. *Behavior Therapy,* 1983, *14,* 110–115.

Heilbrun, K. S. Silverman's subliminal psychodynamic activation: A failure to replicate. *Journal of Abnormal Psychology,* 1980, *89,* 560–566.

Helmreich, R. L., Spence, J. T., & Holahan, C. K. Psychological androgyny and sex role flexibility: A test of two hypotheses. *Journal of Personality and Social Psychology,* 1979, *37,* 1631–1644.

Henry, N., & Shaffer, R. Hinckley pursued actress for months. *Washington Post,* April 2, 1981, pp. 118, A8.

Herrnstein, R. J. IQ testing and the media. *Atlantic Monthly,* August 1982, pp. 68–74.

Hetherington, E. M., Cox, M., & Cox, R. Divorced fathers. *The Family Coordinator,* 1976, *25,* 417–428.

Hewson, M. How exercise can affect your period. *McCalls,* July 1979, p. 52.

Hill, C. T., Rubin, Z., & Peplau, L. A. Breakups before marriage: The end of 103 affairs. *Journal of Social Issues,* 1976, *32,* 147–168.

Hite, S. *The Hite report.* New York: Macmillan, 1976.

Hite, S. *The Hite report on male sexuality.* New York: Knopf, 1981.

Hoch, Z. The sensory arm of the female orgasmic reflex. *Journal of Sex Education and Therapy,* 1980, *6,* 4–7.

Hoffer, E. *The ordeal of change.* New York: Harper & Row, 1963.

Holland, J. L. Some exploration of theory of vocational choice. *Psychological Monographs: General and Applied,* 1962, *76,* 1–49.

Hollingshead, A. B. Class differences in family stability. In M. B. Sussman (Ed.), *Sourcebook in marriage and the family.* Boston: Houghton Mifflin, 1968.

Holmes, T. S. Adaptive behavior and health change. Medical thesis, University of Washington, Seattle, 1970.

Holmes, T. H., & Masuda, M. Life change and illness susceptibility. In B. S. Dohrenwend & B. P. Dohrenwend, *Stressful life events: Their nature and effects.* New York: Wiley, 1974.

Holmes, T. H., & Rahe, R. H. The social readjustment rating scale. *Journal of Psychosomatic Research,* 1967, *11,* 213–218.

Horvath, T. Physical attractiveness: The influence of selected torso parameters. *Archives of Sexual Behavior,* 1981, *10,* 21–24.

Houston, J. P. *The pursuit of happiness.* Glenview, Ill.: Scott, Foresman, 1981.

Hunt, M. *Sexual behavior in the 1970s.* Chicago: Playboy Press, 1974.

Hyde, J. S. *Human sexuality.* New York: McGraw-Hill, 1982.

Ickes, W., & Barnes, R. D. Boys and girls together—and alienated: On enacting stereotyped sex roles in mixed-sex dyads. *Journal of Personality and Social Psychology,* 1978, *36,* 669–683.

Inbar, M. The vulnerable age—when moving brings special problems. *Psychology Today,* March 1977, pp. 28–29.

Is he crazy about her? *Time,* 1981, *118,* 30.

Ismail, A. H., & Young, R. J. The effect of chronic exercise on the personality of middle-aged men by univariate and multivariate approaches. *Journal of Human Ergology,* 1973, *2,* 45–57.

Jacobson, E. *Progressive relaxation.* Chicago: University of Chicago Press, 1938.

James, W. *The varieties of religious experience.* New York: Longmans, Green, 1902.

Jaynes, J. *The origin of consciousness in the breakdown of the bicameral mind.* Boston: Houghton Mifflin, 1976.

Johnson, D. *The protean body: A Rolfer's view of human flexibility.* New York: Harper & Row, 1977.

Johnson, J. H., & Sarason, I. G. Life stress, depression and anxiety: Internal-external control as a moderator variable. *Journal of Psychosomatic Research,* 1978, *22,* 205–208.

Johnson, O. R., & Johnson, A. Male/female relations and the organization of work in a Machiguenga community. *American Ethnologist,* 1975, *2,* 634–648.

Johnson, R. Youth of 1980: Friends and peers more influential than parents. *Behavior Today,* February 1981, p. 2.

Jones, J. E., Rodnick, E., Goldstein, M., McPherson, S., & West, K. Parental transactional style deviance as a possible indicator of risk for schizophrenia. *Archives of General Psychiatry,* 1977, *34,* 71–74.

Jourard, S. Marriage is for life. *Journal of Marriage and Family Counseling,* July 1975.

Jourard, S. M., & Landsman, M. J. *Healthy personality.* New York: Macmillan, 1981.

Jung, C. G. The archetypes of the collective unconscious. In *The collected works of C. G. Jung,* Vol. 9i. Princeton, N.J.: Princeton University Press, 1936/1959.

Jung, C. G. *Memories, dreams, reflections.* New York: Vintage Books, 1965.

Kaats, G. R., & Davis, K. E. The dynamics of sexual behavior of college students. *Journal of Marriage and the Family,* 1970, *32,* 390–399.

Kaiser, R. B. The way of the journal. *Psychology Today,* March 1981, pp. 64–76.

Kaplan, H. S. *The new sex therapy.* New York: Brunner/Mazel, 1974.

Kaplan, K. J., & Firestone, I. J. Gradients of attraction as a function of the fit between social settings and stimulus person characteristics. *Journal of Experimental Social Psychology,* 1976, *12,* 539–551.

Kaplan, R. M. Is beauty talent? Sex interaction in the attractiveness halo effect. *Sex Roles,* 1978, *4,* 195–204.

Katz, J. L., Weiner, H., Gallagher, T. F., & Hellman, L. Stress, distress, and ego defenses. *Archives of General Psychiatry,* 1970, *23,* 131–142.

Kazdin, A. E. The separate and combined effects of covert and overt rehearsal in developing assertive behavior. *Behavior Research and Therapy,* 1982, *20,* 17–25.

Keen, E. *Three faces of being: Toward an existential psychology.* New York: Appleton-Century-Crofts, 1970.

Kegel, A. H. Sexual functions of the pubococcygeus muscle. *Western Journal of Surgery,* 1952, *60,* 521–524.

Kelley, H. H. The warm-cold variable in first impressions of persons. *Journal of Personality,* 1950, *18,* 431–439.

Kendler, H. H. Self-fulfillment: Psychological fact or moral prescription? *Academic Psychology Bulletin,* 1980, *2,* 287–295.

Kenrick, D. T., Gutierres, S. E., & Goldberg, L. Influence of popular erotica on interpersonal attraction judgments: The uglier side of pretty pictures. Unpublished manuscript, Arizona State University, 1984.

Kiesler, D. J. The 1982 interpersonal circle: A taxonomy for complementarity in human transactions. *Psychological Review,* 1983, *90,* 185–214.

Killian, L. M., & Bloomberg, S. The patient's narrative from rebirth in a therapeutic community: A case study. *Psychiatry,* 1975, *38*(1), 39–54.

Kinsey, A. C., Pomeroy, W. B., Martin, C. E., & Gebbhard, P. H. *Sexual behavior in the human female.* Philadelphia: Saunders, 1953.

Kipnis, D. The view from the top. *Psychology Today,* December 1984, pp. 30–36.

Kline, P. *Fact and fantasy in Freudian theory.* London: Methuen, 1972.

Kobassa, S. C. Stressful life events, personality, and health: An inquiry into hardiness. *Journal of Personality and Social Psychology,* 1979, *37,* 1–11.

Komarovsky, M. Cultural contradictions and sex roles: The masculine case. *American Journal of Sociology,* 1973, *18,* 1–26.

Konner, M. She & he. *Science 82,* September 1982.

Kurtz, R., & Prestera, H. *The body reveals.* New York: Harper & Row, 1976.

La Brecque, M. On making sounder judgments. *Psychology Today,* June 1980, pp. 33–40.

Laing, R. D. *The politics of experience.* New York: Ballantine Books, 1967.

Landy, D., & Sigall, H. Beauty is talent: Task evaluation as a function of the performer's physical attractiveness. *Journal of Personality and Social Psychology,* 1974, *29,* 299–304.

Lang, J. S. America's fitness binge. *U.S. News & World Report,* May 3, 1982, pp. 58–61.

Langer, E. J. Automated lives. *Psychology Today,* April 1982, pp. 60–75.

Lazarus, R. S. Positive denial: The case for not facing reality. *Psychology Today,* November 1979, pp. 44–60.

Leary, T. *Interpersonal diagnosis of personality.* New York: Ronald Press, 1957.

Lee, J. A. *The colours of love.* Toronto: New Press, 1973.

Lerner, R. M., Karabenick, S. A., Stuart, A., & Stuart, J. L. Relations among physical attractiveness, body attitudes, and self-concept in male and female college students. *Journal of Psychology,* 1973, *85,* 119–129.

Lester, G., & Lester, D. *Suicide: The gamble with death.* Englewood Cliffs, N.J.: Prentice–Hall, 1971.

Levad, K. Interfaith marriage. *Marriage and Family Living,* April 1982, pp. 10–11.

Levine, J., & Zigler, E. Denial and self-image in stroke, lung cancer, and heart disease patients. *Journal of Consulting and Clinical Psychology,* 1975, *43,* 751–757.

Levinger, G. Systematic distortion in spouses' reports of preferred and actual sexual behavior. *Sociometry,* 1966, *29,* 291–299.

Lewis, H. R., & Lewis, M. E. All about the clitoris. *Sexology,* January 1980.

Lewis, M. State as an infant-environment interaction: An analysis of mother–infant interaction as a function of sex. *Merrill-Palmer Quarterly,* 1972, *18,* 95–121.

Lewisohn, P. M., Mischel, W., Chaplain, W., & Barton, R. Social competence and depression: The role of illusory self-perceptions. *Journal of Abnormal Psychology,* 1980, *89,* 203–212.

Linde, S. *The whole health catalogue.* New York: Rawson, 1977.

Lindzey, G. Behavior and morphological variation. In J. N. Spuhler (Ed.), *Genetic diversity and human behavior.* Chicago: Aldine, 1967, pp. 227–240.

Locke, H. J. *Predicting adjustment in marriage: A comparison of a divorced and a happily married group.* New York: Holt, Rinehart and Winston, 1951.

Locksley, A. On the effects of wives' employment on marital adjustment and companionship. *Journal of Marriage and the Family,* 1980, *42,* 337–346.

Long Laws, J. The second x. New York: Elsevier, 1979.

Loos, V. E., Bridges, C. F., & Critelli, J. W. Weiner's attribution theory and female orgasmic consistency. *Journal of Sex Research,* in press, 1987.

Loos, V. E., Critelli, J. W., Stevenson, C. D., & Tang, C. S. K. Dysfunctional patterns of family interaction. Paper presented at the annual convention of the American Psychological Association, August 1984, Toronto.

LoPiccolo, J., & Lobitz, C. The role of masturbation in the treatment of sexual dysfunction. *Archives of Sexual Behavior,* 1972, *2,* 163–171.

Lowen, A. *Bioenergetics.* New York: Coward, McCann & Geoghegan, 1975.

Lowery, R. J. *A. H. Maslow: An intellectual portrait.* Monterey, Calif.: Brooks/Cole, 1973.

Lubinski, D., Tellegen, A., & Butcher, J. N. Masculinity, femininity, and androgyny viewed and assessed as distinct concepts. *Journal of Personality and Social Psychology,* 1983, *44,* 428–439.

Luthe, W. *Introduction to the methods of autogenic therapy: Manual for a workshop.* Denver: Biofeedback Society of America, 1977.

Lydon, S. The politics of orgasm. In M. Garskof (Ed.), *Roles women play: Readings toward women's liberation.* Monterey, Calif.: Brooks/Cole, 1971.

Maccoby, E. E. *Social development: Psychological growth and the parent–child relationship.* New York: Harcourt Brace Jovanovich, 1980.

Maccoby, E. E., & Jacklin, C. N. *The psychology of sex differences.* Stanford, Calif.: Stanford University Press, 1974.

MacKay, D. G., & Konishi, T. Pronouns, attitudes, personification, and sexism in language. Paper presented at the ninetieth meeting of the American Psychological Association, Washington, D.C., August 1982.

MacKinnon, D. W. Creativity: A multi-faceted phenomenon. In J. D. Roslansky (Ed.), *Creativity: A discussion at the Nobel conference.* Amsterdam: North-Holland, 1970.

Maddi, S. R. *Personality theories.* Homewood, Ill.: Dorsey, 1980.

Maddi, S. R., & Propst, B. Activation theory and personality. In S. R. Maddi (Ed.), *Perspectives on personality.* Boston: Little, Brown, 1971.

Mahoney, E. R. Body-cathexis and self-esteem: The importance of subjective importance. *Journal of Psychology,* 1974, *88,* 27–30.

Males and females and what you may not know about them. *Changing Times,* September 1981, pp. 35–40.

Marcus, M. G. The power of a name. *Psychology Today,* 1976, *10*(5), 76, 108.

Markman, H. J. Application of a behavioral model of marriage in predicting relationship satisfaction of couples planning marriage. *Journal of Consulting and Clinical Psychology,* 1979, *47,* 743–749.

Markman, H. J., & Floyd, F. Possibilities for the prevention of marital discord: A behavioral perspective. *American Journal of Family Therapy,* 1980, *8,* 29–48.

Marlatt, G. A., & Parks, G. A. Self-management of addictive disorders. In P. Karoly & F. H. Kanfer (Eds.), *Self-management and behavior change: From theory to practice.* Elmsford, N.Y.: Pergammon Press, 1982, pp. 443–488.

Marshall, W. L., Boutilier, J., & Minnes, P. The modification of phobic behavior by covert reinforcement. *Behavior Therapy,* 1974, *5,* 469–480.

Maslow, A. *Motivation and personality* (2nd ed.). New York: Harper & Row, 1954.

Maslow, A. Critique of self-actualization I: Some dangers of being-cognition. *Journal of Individual Psychology,* 1959, *15,* 24–32.

Maslow, A. *Toward a psychology of being* (2nd ed.). Princeton, N.J.: Van Nostrand, 1968.

Maslow, A. Comments on Dr. Frankl's paper. In A. J. Sutich & M. A. Vich (Eds.), *Readings in humanistic psychology.* New York: Free Press, 1969.

Maslow, A. H. *The farther reaches of human nature.* New York: Viking, 1971.

Masnick, G., & Bane, M. J. *The nation's families: 1960–1990.* Cambridge, Mass.: Joint Center for Urban Studies of M.I.T. and Harvard University, 1980.

Masters, W. H., & Johnson, V. E. *Human sexual response.* Boston: Little, Brown, 1966.

Masters, W. H., & Johnson, V. E. *Human sexual inadequacy.* Boston: Little, Brown, 1970.

Masters, W. H., & Johnson, V. E. *The pleasure bond.* Boston: Little, Brown, 1975.

Masters, W. H., Johnson, V. E., & Kolodny, R. C. *Human sexuality.* Boston: Little, Brown, 1985.

Mathes, E. W. Self-actualization, metavalues, and creativity. *Psychological Reports,* 1978, *43,* 215–222.

Matson, J. L. Social reinforcement by the spouse in weight control: A case study. *Journal of Behavior Therapy and Experimental Psychiatry,* 1977, *8,* 327–328.

Maw, W. H., & Maw, E. W. Nature of creativity in high- and low-curiosity boys. *Developmental Psychology,* 1970, *2,* 325–329.

May, R. *Love and will.* New York: Norton, 1969.

May, R. To be and not to be: Contributions of existential psychotherapy. In H-M Chiang & A. H. Maslow (Eds.), *The healthy personality: Readings.* New York: D. Van Nostrand, 1977.

McDavid, J. W., & Harari, M. Stereotyping of names in popularity of grade school children. *Child Development,* 1966, *37,* 453–459.

Mckean, K. In search of the unconscious mind. *Discover,* February 1985, pp. 12–18.

McKinnon, D. W. The nature and nurture of creative talent. *American Psychologist,* 1962, *17,* 484–495. (a)

McKinnon, D. W. The personality correlates of creativity: A study of American architects. In G. S. Nielsen (Ed.), *Proceedings of the XIV International Congress of Applied Psychology,* (Vol. Z). Copenhagen, 1961. Copenhagen: Munksgaard, 1962. (b)

Meador, B. D. Individual process in a basic encounter group. *Journal of Counseling Psychology,* 1971, *18,* 70–76.

Mehrabian, A. *Silent messages.* Belmont, Calif.: Wadsworth, 1971.

Michener, J. A. *The fires of spring.* New York: Random House, 1949.

Milholland, T. A., & Avery, A. W. Effects of marriage encounter on self-disclosure, trust, and marital satisfaction. *Journal of Marital and Family Therapy,* 1982, *3,* 67–89.

Mills, J., & Aronson, E. Opinion change as a function of the communicator's attractiveness and desire to influence. *Journal of Personality and Social Psychology,* 1965, *1,* 173–177.

Milner, M. A life of one's own. In H-M Chiang & A. H. Maslow (Eds.), *The healthy personality: Readings.* New York: D. Van Nostrand, 1977.

Minuchin, S. *Families and family therapy.* Cambridge, Mass.: Harvard University Press, 1974.

Mischel, W. Metacognition and the rules of delay. In J. H. Flavell & L. Ross (Eds.), *Social cognitive development: Frontiers and possible futures.* Cambridge, England: Cambridge University Press, 1981, pp. 240–271.

Mlott, S. R., & Lira, F. T. Dogmatism, locus of control, and life goals in stable and unstable marriages. *Journal of Clinical Psychology,* 1977, *33,* 142–146.

Monte, C. F. *Beneath the mask.* New York: Holt, Rinehart and Winston, 1980.

Morris, V. C. *Existentialism in education.* New York: Harper & Row, 1966.

Morse, S. J., Gruzen, J., & Reis, H. The "eye of the beholder": A neglected variable in the study of physical attractiveness? *Journal of Personality,* 1976, *44,* 209–225.

Murstein, B. I. *Love, sex, and marriage through the ages.* New York: Springer, 1974.

Murstein, B. I. Mate selection in the 1970s. *Journal of Marriage and the Family,* 1980, *42,* 777–792.

Murstein, B. I., & Christy, P. Physical attractiveness and marriage adjustment in middle-aged couples. *Journal of Personality and Social Psychology,* 1976, *34,* 537–542.

Myers, M. Body therapies and the modern dancer: Text. *Dancemagazine,* August 1983, *57*(8), 1–23.

Naisbitt, J. *Megatrends.* New York: Warner, 1982.

Neugarten, B. L., & Gutmann, D. L. Age-sex roles and personality in middle age: A thematic apperception study. *Psychological Monographs: General and Applied,* 1958, *17*(Whole No. 470).

Newlin, D. B. Modifying the type A behavior pattern. In C. J. Golden, S. S. Alcaparras, F. D. Strider, & B. Graber (Eds.), *Applied techniques in behavioral medicine.* New York: Grune & Stratton, 1981, pp. 169–190.

Nezu, A., & D'Zurilla, T. J. Effects of problem definition and formulation on the generation of alternatives in the social problem-solving process. *Cognitive Therapy and Research,* 1981, *5,* 265–271.

Nisbett, R., & Ross, L. *Human inference: Strategies and shortcomings of social judgment.* Englewood Cliffs, N.J.: Prentice–Hall, 1980.

Nisbett, R. E., & Wilson, T. D. The halo effect: Evidence for unconscious alteration of judgments. *Journal of Personality and Social Psychology,* 1977, *34,* 250–256.

Nuckolls, K. B., Cassel, J., & Kaplan, B. H. Psychosocial assets, life crisis and the prognosis of pregnancy. *American Journal of Epidemiology,* 1972, *95,* 431–441.

O'Connell, J. C. Children of working mothers: What the research tells us. *Young Children,* 1983, *38,* 62–70.

Offir, C. W. *Human sexuality.* New York: Harcourt Brace Jovanovich, 1982.

Otis, L. S. The facts on transcendental meditation. *Psychology Today,* 1974, 7(11), 41–46.

Parlee, H. B. Conversational politics. *Psychology Today,* May 1979, pp. 48–55.

Pease, A. *Signals.* New York: Bantam Books, 1984.

Pelletier, K. R. Mind as healer, mind as slayer. *Psychology Today,* February 1977, p. 35.

Perlman, D. The University of British Columbia, personal communication, Feb. 6, 1985.

Perry, J., & Whipple, B. Can women ejaculate? Yes! *Forum,* April 1981. (a)

Perry, J. D., & Whipple, B. Pelvic muscle strength of female ejaculators: Evidence in support of a new theory of orgasm. *Journal of Sex Research,* 1981, *17,* 22–39. (b)

Pew, T. W., Jr. Biofeedback seeks new medical uses for concept of yoga. *Smithsonian,* December 1979, pp. 106–117.

Piccard, D., Critelli, J. W., & Nite, L. Patterns of dominance and attraction in heterosexual first meetings. Paper presented at the annual convention of the American Psychological Association, 1984.

Pierpont, M. Body therapies and the modern dancer: Interviews. *Dancemagazine,* August 1983, *57*(8), 1–23.

Pines, M. Psychological hardiness. *Psychology Today,* December 1980, pp. 34–44.

Plutchik, R. A language for the emotions. *Psychology Today,* February 1980, pp. 68–78.

Pomeroy, W. The male orgasm: What every girl should know. *Cosmopolitan,* April 1976.

Pope, H., & Mueller, C. W. The intergenerational transmission of marital instability: Comparisons by rate and sex. In G. Levinger & O. C. Moles (Eds.), *Divorce and separation.* New York: Basic Books, 1979.

Powell, D. Building up your "hidden" sex muscle: The ultimate male orgasm. *Sexology Today,* November 1981.

Prentky, R. A. *Creativity and psychopathology.* New York: Praeger, 1980.

Prince, G. U. *The practice of creativity: A manual for dynamic group problem solving.* New York: Harper & Row, 1970.

Prochaska, J. O. Self-changers versus therapy changers versus Schachter. *American Psychologist,* 1983, *38,* 853–854.

Progoff, I. *The practice of process meditation.* New York: Dialogue House, 1980.

Raymond, M. J. Case of fetishism treated by aversion therapy. *British Medical Journal,* 1956, *2,* 854–857.

Reagan, R. Remarks to National Association of Evangelicals, Orlando, Fla., March 8, 1983. Weekly Compilation of Presidential Documents, 1983, *19,* 364–370.

Rees, L. Constitutional factors and abnormal behavior. In H. J. Eysenck (Ed.), *Handbook of abnormal psychology.* San Diego: Knapp, 1973, pp. 487–539.

Rehm, L. P. Self-management in depression. In P. Karoly & F. H. Kanfer (Eds.), *Self-management and behavior change: From theory to practice.* Elmsford, N.Y.: Pergammon Press, 1982, pp. 522–567.

Renne, K. S. Correlates of dissatisfaction in marriage. In M. E. Lasswell & T. E. Lasswell (Eds.), *Love, marriage, family.* Glenview, Ill.: Scott, Foresman, 1973.

Reps, P. *Zen flesh, Zen bones.* Rutland, Vt.: Charles Tuttle, 1958.

Rheingold, H. L., & Cook, K. B. The contents of boys' and girls' rooms as an index of parents' behavior. *Child Development,* 1975, *46,* 459–463.

Rice, B. How not to pick up a woman. *Psychology Today,* August 1981, p. 19.

Ringer, R. J. *Winning through intimidation.* New York: Fawcett, 1978.

Robbins, M. B., & Jenson, G. D. Multiple orgasm in males. In R. Gemme & C. C. Wheeler (Eds.), *Progress in Sexology.* New York: Plenum, 1977, pp. 323–334.

Roberts, E. J. Sex education versus sexual learning. In M. Kirkpatrick (Ed.),

Women's sexual development: Explorations of inner space. New York: Plenum, 1980, pp. 239–250.

Robinson, F. P. *Effective study.* New York: Harper & Row, 1970.

Rogers, C. R. *On becoming a person: A therapist's view of psychotherapy.* Boston: Houghton Mifflin, 1961.

Rogers, C. R. *A way of being.* Boston: Houghton Mifflin, 1980.

Rogers, C. R. What it means to become a person. From lectures delivered at Oberlin College, 1954. In *Personal growth and behavior 85/86.* Sluice Dock, Guilford, Conn.: Dushkin, 1985.

Rogers, C. R., & Skinner, B. F. Some issues concerning the control of human behavior: A symposium. *Science,* 1956, *124,* 1057–1066.

Rogers, C. R., & Wood, J. K. Client-centered theory: Carl R. Rogers. In A. Burton (Ed.), *Operational theories of personality.* New York: Brunner/Mazel, 1974.

Rosen, L. W. Self-control program in the treatment of obesity. *Journal of Behavior Therapy and Experimental Psychiatry,* 1981, *12,* 163–166.

Rosen, R., & Hall, E. *Sexuality.* New York: Random House, 1984.

Rosenberg, M. *Society and the adolescent self-image.* Princeton N.J.: Princeton University Press, 1965.

Rosenberg, M. *Conceiving the self.* New York: Basic Books, 1979.

Rosenman, R. H., Brand, R. J., Jenkins, C. D., Freidman, M., Straus, R., & Wurm, M. Coronary heart disease in the western collaborative group study: Final follow-up. *Journal of the American Medical Association,* 1975, *233,* 872–877.

Rothenberg, F. After a year in Cronkite's shadow, Dan Rather is developing his own style. *Dallas Morning News,* February 21, 1982, p. 30.

Rowley, G. L. Which examinees are most favoured by the use of multiple choice tests? *Journal of Educational Measurement,* 1974, *11,* 15–23.

Rubenstein, C. Wellness is all. *Psychology Today,* October 1982, pp. 28–37. (a)

Rubenstein, C. Real men don't earn less than their wives. *Psychology Today,* November 1982, pp. 36–41. (b)

Rubenstein, C. The modern art of courtly love. *Psychology Today,* July 1983, pp. 40–49.

Rubin, J., Provenzano, F., & Luria, Z. The eye of the beholder: Parents' views on sex of newborns. *American Journal of Orthopsychiatry,* 1974, *44,* 512–519.

Rubin, Z. Measurement of romantic love. *Journal of Personality and Social Psychology,* 1970, *16,* 265–273.

Rubin, Z. *Liking and loving.* New York: Holt, Rinehart and Winston, 1973.

Rubin, Z., Peplau, L. A., & Hill, C. T. Loving and leaving: Sex differences in romantic attachments. *Journal of Social Issues,* 1978, *34,* 7–27.

Russel, R. K, & Lent, R. W. Cue-controlled relaxation and systematic desensitization versus nonspecific factors in treating test anxiety. *Journal of Counseling Psychology,* 1982, *29,* 100–103.

Ryder, R. G. Longitudinal data relating marriage satisfaction and having a child. *Journal of Marriage and the Family,* 1973, *35,* 604–607.

Sackeim, H. A., & Gur, R. C. Self-deception, self-configuration and consciousness. In G. E. Schwartz & D. Shapiro (Eds.), *Consciousness and self-regulation: Advances in research.* Vol. 2. New York: Plenum, 1978, pp. 139–197.

Safan-Gerard, D. How to unblock. *Psychology Today,* January 1978, pp. 78–86.

Sandifer, B. A., & Buchanan, W. L. Relationship between adherence and weight loss in a behavioral weight reduction program. *Behavior Therapy,* 1983, *14,* 682–688.

Sarason, I. G., Johnson, J. H., & Siegel, J. M. Assessing the impact of life changes: Development of the life experiences survey. *Journal of Consulting and Clinical Psychology,* 1978, *46,* 932–946.

Sartre, J-P. *Existential psychoanalysis.* New York: Philosophical Library, 1953.

Satir, V. *Making contact.* Berkeley, Calif.: Celestial Arts, 1976.

Scanzoni, J., & Fox, G. L. Sex roles, family and society: The seventies and beyond. *Journal of Marriage and the Family,* 1980, *42,* 743–758.

Scarf, M. The more sorrowful sex. *Psychology Today,* April 1979, pp. 45–52, 89–90.

Scarf, M. Images that heal: A doubtful idea whose time has come. *Psychology Today,* September 1980, pp. 32–46.

Scarr, S., & Weinberg, R. A. Attitudes, interests, and IQ. *Human Nature,* April 1978, pp. 29–36.

Schachter, S. Recidivism and self-cure of smoking and obesity. *American Psychologist,* 1982, *37,* 436–444.

Schachter, S., & Singer, J. E. Cognitive, social and physiological determinants of emotional state. *Psychological Review,* 1962, *69,* 379–399.

Schachter, S. The interaction of cognitive and physiological determinants of emotional state. In L. Berkowitz (Ed.), *Advances in experimental social psychology.* Vol. 1. New York: Academic Press, 1964, pp. 49–80.

Scheer, R. With enough shovels. *Playboy,* December 1982, p. 118.

Schotte, D. E., & Clum, G. A. Suicide ideation in a college population: A test of a model. *Journal of Consulting and Clinical Psychology,* 1982, *50,* 690–696.

Seaman, B. *Free and female.* Greenwich, Conn.: Fawcett, 1972.

Sears, R. R. Relation of early socialization experiences to self-concepts and gender role in middle childhood. *Child Development,* 1970, *41,* 267–289.

Seliger, S. Stress can be good for you. *New York Times,* August 2, 1982.

Seligman, C., Fazio, R. H., & Zanna, M. P. Effects of salience of extrinsic rewards on liking and loving. *Journal of Personality and Social Psychology,* 1980, *38,* 453–460.

Selye, H. *The stress of life.* New York: McGraw-Hill, 1976.

Selye, H. On the real benefits of eustress. *Psychology Today,* March 1978, pp. 60–70.

Semans, J. Premature ejaculation: A new approach. *Southern Medical Journal,* 1956, *49,* 353–358.

Shaffer, J. B. P. *Humanistic psychology.* Englewood Cliffs, N.J.: Prentice-Hall, 1978.

Shames, R., & Sterin, C. *Healing with mind power.* Emmaus, Pa.: Rodale Press, 1978.

Shapiro, D. H., Jr. *Precision nirvana.* Englewood Cliffs, N.J.: Prentice–Hall, 1978.

Shaver, P., & Freedman, J. Your pursuit of happiness. *Psychology Today,* September 1976, pp. 26–29, 31–32, 75.

Sheldon, W. H. *Varieties of delinquent youth: An introduction to constitutional psychiatry.* New York: Harper & Row, 1949.

Shelton, J. L., Levy, R. L., and contributors. *Behavioral assignments and treatment compliance: A handbook of clinical strategies.* Champaign, Ill.: Research Press, 1981.

Shiels, M., Cook, W. J., Reese, M., Fraus, M., & Malamud, P. And man created the chip. *Newsweek,* June 30, 1980, pp. 50–56.

Shneidman, E. S., Farberow, N. L., & Litman, R. E. (Eds.). *The psychology of suicide.* New York: Science House, 1970.

Shostrum, E. L. *Actualizing therapy.* San Diego: EDITS Publishers, 1976.

Sigall, H., & Aronson, E. Liking for an evaluator as a function of her physical attractiveness and nature of the evaluations. *Journal of Experimental Social Psychology,* 1969, *5,* 93–100.

Sigall, H., & Michela, J. I'll bet you say that to all the girls: Physical attractiveness and reactions to praise. *Journal of Personality,* 1976, *44,* 611–626.

Silverman, I. Physical attractiveness and courtship. *Sexual Behavior,* September 1971, pp. 22–25.

Silverman, L. H. A comment on two subliminal psychodynamic activation studies. *Journal of Abnormal Psychology,* 1982, *91,* 126–130.

Silverman, L. H., Ross, D. L., Adler, J. M., & Lustig, S. A. Simple research paradigm for demonstrating subliminal psychodynamic activation: Effects of oedipal stimuli on dart-throwing accuracy in college males. *Journal of Abnormal Psychology,* 1978, *87,* 341–357.

Singer, I. *The goals of human sexuality.* New York: Schocken Books, 1973.

Singer, J., & Singer, I. Types of female orgasm. *The Journal of Sex Research,* 1972, *8,* 255–267.

Skinner, B. F. *Walden two.* New York: Macmillan, 1948.

Skinner, B. F. *About behaviorism.* New York: Knopf, 1974.

Slater, P. E. Sexual adequacy in America. *Intellectual Digest,* November 1973, pp. 17–20.

Smith, B. On self-actualization: A focal theme in Maslow's psychology. *Journal of Humanistic Psychology,* 1973, *13,* 17–33.

Smith, R. E., Johnson, J. H., & Sarason, I. G. Life change, the sensation seeking motive, and psychological distress. *Journal of Consulting and Clinical Psychology,* 1978, *46,* 348–349.

Snyder, D. K., & Berg, P. Determinants of sexual dissatisfaction in sexually distressed couples. *Archives of Sexual Behavior,* 1983, *12,* 237–245.

Snyder, M. Self-fulfilling stereotypes, *Psychology Today,* July 1982, pp. 60–68.

Spanier, G. B., & Glick, P. C. Marital instability in the United States: Some correlates and recent changes. *Family Relations,* 1981, *30,* 329–338.

Spanier, G., & Lewis, R. A. Marital quality: A review of the seventies. *Journal of Marriage and the Family,* 1980, *42,* 825–839.

Spence, J. T. Comment on Lubinski, Tellegen, and Butcher's "Masculinity, femininity, and androgyny viewed and assessed as distinct concepts." *Journal of Personality and Social Psychology,* 1983, *44,* 440–446.

Spitzer, R., & Wilson, P. Nosology and the official psychiatric nomenclature. In A. Freedman, H. Kaplan, & B. Sadock (Eds.), *Comprehensive textbook of psychiatry II* (3rd. ed.). Baltimore: Williams & Wilkins, 1980, pp. 581–592.

Spurr, J., & Stevens, V. J. Increasing study time and controlling student guilt: A case study in self-management. *Behavior Therapist,* 1980, *3,* 17–18.

Stein, M. I. Creativity. In E. F. Borgotta & W. W. Lambert (Eds.), *Handbook of personality theory and research.* Chicago: Rand McNally, 1968, pp. 900–942.

Stein, M. I. *Stimulating creativity.* Vol. 1. London: Academic Press, 1974.

Sterling, S. M., & Taylor, I. A. Creative self-perception, hemispheric laterality and sex differences. *Journal of Creative Behavior,* 1980, *14,* 274–275.

Sternberg, R. J., & Davidson, J. E. The mind of the puzzler. *Psychology Today,* June 1982, pp. 37–44.

Stewart, A. J., & Rubin, Z. The power motive in the dating couple. *Journal of Personality and Social Psychology,* 1974, *34,* 305–309.

Stewart, V. Social influences on sex differences in behavior. In M. S. Teitelbaum (Ed.), *Sex differences.* New York: Anchor Books, 1976.

Stoffer, G. R., Davis, K. E., & Brown, J. B., Jr. The consequences of changing initial answers on objective tests: A stable effect and stable misconception. *Journal of Educational Research,* 1977, *70,* 272–277.

Strassberg, D., Robak, H., D'Antonio, M., & Cabel, H. Self-disclosure. A critical and selective review of the clinical literature. *Comprehensive Psychiatry,* 1977, *18,* 31–40.

Sue, D. Erotic fantasies of college students during coitus. *Journal of Sex Research,* 1979, *15,* 299–305.

Suinn, R. M. Personal communication, cited in Watson, D. L., & Tharp, R. G. *Self-directed behavior.* Monterey, Calif.: Brooks/Cole, 1985, p. 152.

Suzuki, D. T. In Erich Fromm, (Ed.), *Psychoanalysis and Zen Buddhism.* London: Allen & Unwin, 1910, p. 7.

Swets, P. W. *The art of talking so that people will listen.* Englewood Cliffs, N.J.: Prentice-Hall, 1983.

Tageson, C. W. *Humanistic psychology: A synthesis.* Homewood, Ill.: Dorsey, 1982.

Tavris, C., & Jayaratne, T. How happy is your marriage? What 75,000 wives say about their most intimate relationship. *Redbook,* June 1976, pp. 90–92ff.

Tavris, C., & Wade, C. *The longest war.* New York: Harcourt Brace Jovanovich, 1984.

Taylor, C. B. Relaxation training and related techniques. In W. S. Agras (Ed.), *Behavior modification: Principles and clinical applications.* Boston: Little, Brown, 1978.

Taylor, M. C., & Hall, J. A. Psychological androgyny: Theories, methods, and conclusions. *Psychological Bulletin,* 1982, *92,* 347–366.

Taylor, S. E. Adjustment to threatening events: A theory of cognitive adaptation. *American Psychologist,* November 1983, pp. 1161–1172.

Tellegen, A., & Lubinski, D. Some methodological comments on labels, traits, interaction, and types in the study of "femininity" and "masculinity": Reply to Spence. *Journal of Personality and Social Psychology,* 1983, *44,* 447.

Tennov, D. *Love and limerence.* Briarcliff Manor, N.Y.: Stein & Day, 1979.

Terris, M., Wilson, F., & Nelson, J. H., Jr. Relation of circumcision to cancer of the cervix. *American Journal of Obstetrics and Gynecology,* 1973, *117,* 1056–1066.

Throll, D. A. Transcendental meditation and progressive relaxation: Their psychological effects. *Journal of Clinical Psychology,* 1981, *37,* 776–781.

Tiger, L., & Shepher, J. *Women in the kibbutz.* New York: Harcourt Brace Jovanovich, 1975.

Toffler, A. *Future shock.* New York: Morrow, 1972.

Toffler, A. *The third wave.* New York: Morrow, 1980.

Tomlinson, T. M. Three approaches to the study of psychotherapy: Process, outcome, and change. Unpublished doctoral dissertation, University of Wisconsin, 1962.

Umbarger, C., & Hare, R. A structural approach to patient and therapist disengagement from a schizophrenic family. *American Journal of Psychotherapy,* 1973, *27,* 274–284.

Usdansky, G., & Chapman, L. J. Schizophrenic-like responses in normal subjects under time pressure. *Journal of Abnormal and Social Psychology,* 1960, *60,* 143–146.

U.S. report fears most Americans will become scientific illiterates, *New York Times,* October 23, 1981.

Valins, S. Cognitive effects of false heart-rate feedback. *Journal of Personality and Social Psychology,* 1966, *4,* 400–408.

Veitch, R., & Griffitt, W. Good news, bad news: Affective and interpersonal effects. *Journal of Applied Social Psychology,* 1976, *6,* 69–75.

Vickery, D. *Life plan for your health.* Reading, Mass.: Addison-Wesley, 1978.

Vincent, L. M. *Competing with the sylph.* New York: Berkley, 1981.

Wagman, M. Sex differences in types of daydreams. *Journal of Personality and Social Psychology,* 1967, *3,* 329–332.

Wahba, M. A., & Bridwell, L. G., Maslow reconsidered: A review of research on the need hierarchy theory. *Organizational Behavior and Human Performance,* 1976, *15,* 212–240.

Waldron, H., & Routh, D. The effect of the first child on the marital relationship. *Journal of Marriage and the Family,* November 1981, pp. 785–788.

Wallace, R. K., & Benson, H. The physiology of meditation. *Scientific American,* 1972, *226,* 84–90.

Wallach, M. A., & Wallach, L. *Psychology's sanction for selfishness.* San Francisco: Freeman, 1983.

Wallach, M. A., & Wallach, L. Restraints may allow fulfillment. *APA Monitor.* Washington, D.C.: American Psychological Association, October 1984, p. 5.

Wallerstein, J. S., & Kelly, J. B. *Surviving the break-up: How children actually cope with divorce.* New York: Basic Books, 1980.

Wallis, C. Stress: Can we cope? *Time,* June 6, 1983, pp. 48–54.

Walster, E. The effect of self-esteem on romantic liking. *Journal of Experimental Social Psychology,* 1965, *1,* 184–197.

Walster, E., Aronson, V., Abrahams, D., & Rottmann, L. Importance of physical attractiveness in dating behavior. *Journal of Personality and Social Psychology,* 1966, *4,* 508–516.

Walster, E., & Berscheid, E. A little bit about love. A minor essay on a major topic. In T. L. Huston (Ed.), *Foundations of interpersonal attraction.* New York: Academic Press, 1974, pp. 355–381.

Walster, E., & Walster, G. W. *A new look at love.* Reading, Mass.: Addison-Wesley, 1978.

Walster, E., Walster, G. W., & Berscheid, E. *Equity: Theory and research.* Boston: Allyn & Bacon, 1978.

Wapner, S., Werner, H., & Comalli, P. E. Effect of enhancement of head boundary on head size and shape. *Perceptual and Motor Skills,* 1958, *8,* 319–325.

Watson, D. L., & Tharp, R. G. *Self-directed behavior.* Monterey, Calif.: Brooks/Cole, 1985.

Watts, A. *The wisdom of insecurity.* New York: Vintage Books/Random House, 1951.

Watts, A. *The spirit of Zen.* New York: Grove Press, 1958.

Weitzman, L. J., Eifler, D., Hokado, E., & Ross, C. Sex role socialization in picture books for pre-school children. *American Journal of Sociology,* 1972, *77,* 1125–1150.

Wesley, F., & Wesley, C. *Sex role psychology.* New York: Human Sciences Press, 1977.

West, U. The politics of courtship. *Working Woman,* March 1982, pp. 83–85.

Whimbey, A. E., & Whimbey, L. S. *Intelligence can be taught.* New York: Dutton, 1975.

White, G. L. Physical attractiveness and courtship progress. *Journal of Personality and Social Psychology,* 1980, *39,* 660–668.

White, G. L., Fishbein, S., & Rutstein, J. Passionate love and the misattribution of arousal. *Journal of Personality and Social Psychology,* 1981, *41,* 56–62.

Whiteside, M. Rare beasts in the sheepfold. *Journal of Creative Behavior,* 1981, *15,* 189–197.

Wiggins, J. S. Circumplex models of interpersonal behavior in clinical psychology. In P. C. Kendall & J. N. Butcher (Eds.), *Handbook of research methods in clinical psychology.* New York: Wiley, 1982.

Wiggins, J. S., Wiggins, N., & Conger, J. C. Correlates of heterosexual somatic preference. *Journal of Personality and Social Psychology,* 1968, *10,* 82–90.

Wild, C., Shapiro, D., & Goldenberg, I. Transactional communication disturbance in families of male schizophrenics. *Family Process,* 1975, *14,* 131–160.

Wilson, E. O. Sex role differences: Why? . . . And their future importance? *Science Digest,* February 1980, pp. 57–61.

Women on Words and Images. *Dick and Jane as victims: Sex stereotyping in children's readers.* (Expanded edition). Princeton, N.J.: Women on Words and Images, 1975.

Wood, P., & Schwartz, B. I mean *now. Psychology Today,* July 1977, pp. 110–116.

Wortman, C. B., Adesman, P., Herman, E., & Greenberg, P. Self-disclosure: An attributional perspective. *Journal of Personality and Social Psychology,* 1976, *33,* 184–191.

Wynne, L. C., Singer, M. T., Barko, J., & Toohey, M. Schizophrenics and their families: Recent research on parental communication. In J. M. Tanner (Ed.), *Psychiatric research: The widening perspective.* New York: International Universities Press, 1977.

Yankelovich, D. New rules in American life: Searching for self-fulfillment in a world turned upside down. *Psychology Today,* April 1981, pp. 35–91.

Youdin, R., & Hemmes, N. S. The urge to overeat: The initial link. *Journal of Behavior Therapy and Experimental Psychiatry,* 1978, *9,* 339–342.

Zimmerman, A. Femininity trap. *Dallas Times Herald,* February 15, 1984, p. E1.

Zuckerman, M. The search for high sensation. *Psychology Today,* February 1978, p. 38.

Zweigenhaft, R. L. The other side of unusual names. *Journal of Social Psychology,* 1977, *103,* 271–302.

Part One Opening: Jean-Claude Lejeune.

Chapter 1: *Page 4,* David S. Strickler/Monkmeyer; *page 7,* Michael Kagan/Monkmeyer; *page 8,* (left), Arthur Tress/Photo Researchers; (right), Douglas A. Land; *page 9,* from S. Heller (Ed.), *Feiffer: Jules Feiffer's America From Eisenhower To Reagan.* New York: Alfred A. Knopf, 1982. Reprinted by permission of the publisher; *page 15,* F. B. Gruneweig/Photo Researchers.

Chapter 2: *Page 26,* adapted from *Psychology Today: An Introduction,* third edition. Copyright © 1975 by Random House, Inc. Reprinted by permission of the publisher; *pages 30 and 47,* from S. Heller (Ed.), *Feiffer: Jules Feiffer's America From Eisenhower To Reagan.* New York: Alfred A. Knopf, Inc., 1982. Reprinted by permission of the publisher; *pages 35 and 36* (left), The Bettmann Archive; *page 36* (right), Ken Heyman; *page 37,* © 1961 United Feature Syndicate, Inc.

Chapter 3: *Page 61,* Hugh Rogers/Monkmeyer; *page 68,* Beryl Goldberg; *page 69,* Francis Cox/Omni; *page 71,* from S. Heller (Ed.), *Feiffer: Jules Feiffer's America From Eisenhower To Reagan.* New York: Alfred A. Knopf, Inc., 1982. Reprinted by permission of the publisher; *page 72,* Anderson/Monkmeyer; *page 74,* Museum of Modern Art/Film Still Archives, New York.

Part Two Opening: Charles Harbutt/Archive Pictures.

Chapter 4: *Page 91,* Tom McHugh/Photo Researchers; *page 92,* Joe Munroe/Photo Researchers; *page 98,* The Bettmann Archive; *page 102,* David M. Grossman/Photo Researchers; *page 104,* Mimi Forsyth/Monkmeyer; *page 106,* Shirley Zeiberg/Photo Researchers; *page 107,* Photo Researchers; *page 110* (top left), Alice S. Hall/Gamma-Liason; (top right), Mimi Forsyth/Monkmeyer; (bottom), Jean-Claude Lejeune.

Chapter 5: *Page 119* (top), Bettye Lane/Photo Researchers; (bottom), David Powers/Stock, Boston; *page 120* (top left, top right, and bottom left), Howard Frank Collection; (bottom right), Meylan/Sygma; *page 125,* Samuel Teicher; *page 127,* Beryl Goldberg; *page 130* (left), Victor Englebert/Photo Researchers; (right), Jean-Claude Lejeune; *page 137,* Rohn Engh/Photo Researchers.

Chapter 6: *Pages 153 and 154,* courtesy of Paul Ekman, Ph.D., Human Interaction Laboratory, University of California School of Medicine, San Francisco; *page 156,* The Bettman Archive; *page 157,* Mimi Cotter; *page 158,* © 1967 United Feature Syndicate, Inc.; *page 166,* © 1963 United Feature Syndicate, Inc.; *page 170,* Culver Pictures; *page 172,* Thoman W. Friedmann/Photo Researchers.

Chapter 7: *Page 180,* © 1961 United Feature Syndicate, Inc.; *page 184,* Michael Weisbrot; *page 185,* Samuel Teicher; *page 186,* Beryl Goldberg; *page 195,* Susan Woog Wagner/Photo Researchers; *page 198* (top left), Paul Sequeira/Photo Researchers; (top right), Thomas S. England/Photo Researchers; (bottom left), David Strickler/Monkmeyer; (bottom right), Bob Combs/Photo Researchers; *page 199,* Mimi Forsyth/Monkmeyer.

Part Three Opening: Lynn McLaren/Photo Researchers.

Chapter 8: *Page 217,* from S. Heller (Ed.), *Feiffer: Jules Feiffer's America From Eisenhower To Reagan.* New York: Alfred A. Knopf, Inc., 1982. Reprinted by permission of the publisher; *pages 220 and 225,* Beryl Goldberg; *page 229,* Mimi Forsyth/Monkmeyer; *page 233,* from Virginia Satir, *Peoplemaking.* Palo Alto, California: Science and Behavior Books, 1972. Reprinted by permission of the publisher; *page 235,* © 1964 United Feature Syndicate, Inc.; *page 239,* from A. Pease, *Signals.* New York: Bantam Books, 1984.

Chapter 9: *Pages 243, 250, 259, and 262,* from S. Heller (Ed.), *Feiffer: Jules Feiffer's America From Eisenhower To Reagan.* New York: Alfred A. Knopf, Inc., 1982. Reprinted by permission of the publisher; *page 248,* Bill Bachman/Photo Researchers; *page 254,* Culver Pictures; *page 255,* Michael Weisbrot; *page 256,* Howard Frank Collection; *page 261,* from W. H. Masters, V. E. Johnson, R. C. Kolodny, *Human Sexuality.* Boston: Little, Brown Company, 1982.

Chapter 10: *Page 273,* cartoon by John Caldwell, Schenectady, New York; *page 274,* adapted from Spencer A. Rathus, *Human Sexuality.* New York: CBS College Publishing, 1983; *page 276* (top), adapted from Herant A. Katchadourian, *Fundamentals of Human Sexuality,* fourth edition. New York: CBS College Publishing, 1985; (bottom), Scott F. Johnson/Masters and Johnson Institute, St. Louis, Missouri; *page 284,* from S. Heller (Ed.), *Feiffer: Jules Feiffer's America From Eisenhower To Reagan.* New York: Alfred A. Knopf, Inc., 1982. Reprinted by permission of the publisher; *page 290,* Peter Simon/Stock, Boston; *page 294,* Monique Manceau/Photo Researchers.

Chapter 11: *Page 299,* Jean-Claude Lejeune; *page 300,* F. Fonssagrives/Photo Researchers; *page 303,* from S. Heller (Ed.), *Feiffer: Jules Feiffer's America From Eisenhower To Reagan.* New York: Alfred A. Knopf, Inc., 1982. Reprinted by permission of the publisher; *page 305,* Beryl Goldberg; *page 315,* Richard Hutchings/Photo Researchers; *page 318,* Beryl Goldberg.

Part Four Opening: Arthur Tress/Photo Researchers.

Chapter 12: *Page 328,* Culver Pictures; *page 331,* Samuel Teicher; *page 334,* National Library of Medicine; *page 335,* Howard Frank Collection; *page 339,* adapted from Wiggins, Wiggins, and Conger, "Correlates of Heterosexual Somatic Preference," in *The Journal of Personality and Social Psychology.* Copyright 1968 by the American Psychological Association. Adaptation by permission of the author; *page 342* (left), Howard Frank Collection; (middle), S. Shapiro/Gamma-Liason; (right), Wide World; *page 351,* Gerry Cranham/Photo Researchers; *page 352,* from R. Kurtz and H. Prestera, *The Body Reveals.* New York: Harper & Row, Publishers, 1976.

Chapter 13: *Page 358,* Munch Museet, Nasjonal Galleriet, Oslo, Norway; *page 363* (top left), Marilu Paese/Monkmeyer; (top right), Peter Menzell/Stock, Boston; (bottom), Ken Heyman; *page 365,* Cheryl A. Traendly/Jeroboam, San Francisco; *page 371,* Harmit Singh/Rapho/Photo Researchers; *page 376,* Harvard University Archives; *page 377,* UPI/Bettmann Newsphotos; *page 379,* © 1963 United Feature Syndicate, Inc.

Chapter 14: *Page 387,* Mike Goldberg/Stock, Boston; *page 388,* courtesy of the Corporate Archives of the Leo Burnett Advertising Agency, Chicago, and the Stroh Beer Company, Detroit; *page 393,* © 1966 United Feature Syndicate, Inc.; *pages 394* and *404,* from S. Heller (Ed.), *Feiffer: Jules Feiffer's America From Eisenhower To Reagan.* New York: Alfred A. Knopf, 1982. Reprinted by permission of the publisher; *page 397,* Ed Lettau/Photo Researchers; *page 401,* Jan Kukas/Rapho/Photo Researchers; *page 406,* Munch Museet, Nasjonal Galleriet, Oslo, Norway.

ACKNOWLEDGMENTS

p. 79. From the Rosenberg New York State Self-Esteem Scale, in M. Rosenberg, *Conceiving the Self* (New York: Basic Books, 1979), p. 291.
Table 4–1. Reprinted by permission of Thomas H. Holmes, MD, and with permission from the *Journal of Psychosomatic Research 11,* 213–218, "The Social Readjustment Rating Scale" by T. H. Holmes and R. H. Rahe. Copyright 1967 Pergamon Press, Ltd.
pp. 159–160. Reprinted from *Humanistic Psychotherapy* by Albert Ellis, PhD. Copyright © 1973 by The Institute for Rational Living, Inc. Used by permission of The Julian Press, Inc.
p. 160. Perfectionism scale from D. D. Burns, "The Perfectionist's Script for Self-defeat, *Psychology Today* (November 1980), 44. Reprinted with permission. Copyright © 1980 American Psychological Association.

pp. 221, 230. From *The Art of Talking So That People Will Listen* by Paul W. Swets. Copyright © 1983 by Paul W. Swets. Reprinted by permission of the publisher, Prentice-Hall, Inc., Englewood Cliffs, NJ 07632.
Table 8–1 and Figure 8–2. Table adapted from text of A. Pease, *Signals: How to Use Body Language for Power, Success, and Love* (New York: Bantam Books, 1984); figure p. 154. Reprinted with permission of Bantam Books.
pp. 268–269. Adapted from *Living, Loving, and Learning* by Leo F. Buscaglia, copyright 1982. Thorofare, NJ: Charles B. Slack, Inc.
pp. 311–313. Case history from C. Umbarger and R. Hare, "A Structural Approach to Patient and Therapist Disengagement from a Schizophrenic Family," *American Journal of Psychotherapy 27* (1973), 276–278. Reprinted with permission of the author and the *American Journal of Psychotherapy.*
p. 309. From Carl R. Rogers, *A Way of Being* (Boston: Houghton Mifflin, 1980), pp. 208–210. Copyright © 1980 by Houghton Mifflin Company. Reprinted by permission.
pp. 341–342. Tables from S. L. Franzoi and S. A. Shields, "The Body Esteem Scale: Multidimensional Factor Structure and Sex Differences in a College Population," *Journal of Personality Assessment,* 1984, *48,* 173–178. Reprinted with the permission of the authors and the *Journal of Personality Assessment.*
pp. 389–390. Adapted from Daniel Yankelovich, "New Rules in American Life: Searching for Self-fulfillment in a World Turned Upside Down," *Psychology Today* (April 1981), 44–50. Used by permission of Dr. Yankelovich.

INDEXES

NAME INDEX

SUBJECT INDEX

Page numbers in boldface type indicate pages on which terms are defined.